CONNECT FEATURES

Tegrity

Make your classes available anytime, anywhere. With simple, one-click recording, students can search for a word or phrase and be taken to the exact place in your lecture that they need to review.

Connect Insight

The first and only analytics tool of its kind, Connect Insight is a series of visual data displays, each of which is framed by an intuitive question and provides at-a-glance information regarding how an instructor's class is performing. Connect Insight is available through Connect titles.

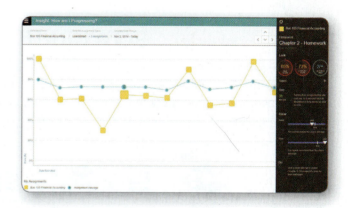

Graphing Tool

The graphing tool within Connect Economics provides opportunities for students to draw, interact with, manipulate, and analyze graphs in their online auto-graded assignments as they would with paper and pencil. The Connect graphs are identical in presentation to the graphs in the book, so students can easily relate their assignments to their reading material.

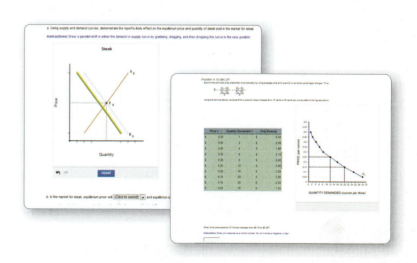

EASY TO USE

Learning Management System Integration

McGraw-Hill Campus is a one-stop teaching and learning experience available to use with any learning management system. McGraw-Hill Campus provides single sign-on to faculty and students for all McGraw-Hill material and technology from within the school website. McGraw-Hill Campus also allows instructors instant access to all supplements and teaching materials for all McGraw-Hill products.

Blackboard users also benefit from McGraw-Hill's industry-leading integration, providing single sign-on to access all Connect assignments and automatic feeding of assignment results to the Blackboard grade book.

The Best of Both Worlds

POWERFUL REPORTING

Connect generates comprehensive reports and graphs that provide instructors with an instant view of the performance of individual students, a specific section, or multiple sections. Since all content is mapped to learning objectives, Connect reporting is ideal for accreditation or other administrative documentation.

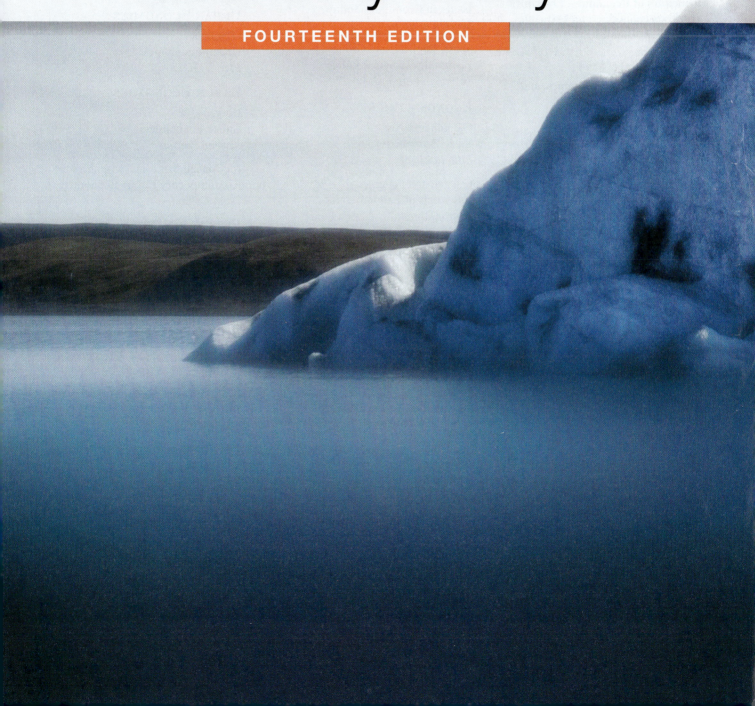

The **MACRO**
Economy Today

FOURTEENTH EDITION

The McGraw-Hill Series Economics

ESSENTIALS OF ECONOMICS

Brue, McConnell, and Flynn
Essentials of Economics
Third Edition

Mandel
Economics: The Basics
Second Edition

Schiller
Essentials of Economics
Ninth Edition

PRINCIPLES OF ECONOMICS

Asarta and Butters
Principles of Economics, Principles of Microeconomics, and Principles of Macroeconomics
First Edition

Colander
Economics, Microeconomics, and Macroeconomics
Ninth Edition

Frank, Bernanke, Antonovics, and Heffetz
Principles of Economics, Principles of Microeconomics, Principles of Macroeconomics
Sixth Edition

Frank and Bernanke
Brief Editions: Principles of Economics, Principles of Microeconomics, Principles of Macroeconomics
Second Edition

Karlan and Morduch
Economics, Microeconomics, and Macroeconomics
First Edition

McConnell, Brue, and Flynn
Economics, Microeconomics, and Macroeconomics
Twentieth Edition

McConnell, Brue, and Flynn
Brief Editions: Microeconomics and Macroeconomics
Second Edition

Miller
Principles of Microeconomics
First Edition

Samuelson and Nordhaus
Economics, Microeconomics, and Macroeconomics
Nineteenth Edition

Schiller
The Economy Today, The Micro Economy Today, and The Macro Economy Today
Fourteenth Edition

Slavin
Economics, Microeconomics, and Macroeconomics
Eleventh Edition

ECONOMICS OF SOCIAL ISSUES

Guell
Issues in Economics Today
Seventh Edition

Sharp, Register, and Grimes
Economics of Social Issues
Twentieth Edition

ECONOMETRICS

Gujarati and Porter
Basic Econometrics
Fifth Edition

Gujarati and Porter
Essentials of Econometrics
Fourth Edition

Hilmer and Hilmer
Practical Econometrics
First Edition

MANAGERIAL ECONOMICS

Baye and Prince
Managerial Economics and Business Strategy
Eighth Edition

Brickley, Smith, and Zimmerman
Managerial Economics and Organizational Architecture
Sixth Edition

Thomas and Maurice
Managerial Economics
Eleventh Edition

INTERMEDIATE ECONOMICS

Bernheim and Whinston
Microeconomics
Second Edition

Dornbusch, Fischer, and Startz
Macroeconomics
Twelfth Edition

Frank
Microeconomics and Behavior
Ninth Edition

ADVANCED ECONOMICS

Romer
Advanced Macroeconomics
Fourth Edition

MONEY AND BANKING

Cecchetti and Schoenholtz
Money, Banking, and Financial Markets
Fourth Edition

URBAN ECONOMICS

O'Sullivan
Urban Economics
Eighth Edition

LABOR ECONOMICS

Borjas
Labor Economics
Seventh Edition

McConnell, Brue, and Macpherson
Contemporary Labor Economics
Tenth Edition

PUBLIC FINANCE

Rosen and Gayer
Public Finance
Tenth Edition

Seidman
Public Finance
First Edition

ENVIRONMENTAL ECONOMICS

Field and Field
Environmental Economics: An Introduction
Sixth Edition

INTERNATIONAL ECONOMICS

Appleyard and Field
International Economics
Eighth Edition

King and King
International Economics, Globalization, and Policy: A Reader
Fifth Edition

Pugel
International Economics
Sixteenth Edition

The MACRO Economy Today

FOURTEENTH EDITION

Bradley R. Schiller

American University, emeritus

WITH KAREN GEBHARDT

Colorado State University

Mc
Graw
Hill
Education

THE MACRO ECONOMY TODAY, FOURTEENTH EDITION
Published by McGraw-Hill Education, 2 Penn Plaza, New York, NY 10121. Copyright © 2016 by McGraw-Hill Education. All rights reserved.
Printed in the United States of America. Previous editions © 2013, 2010, 2008, 2006, 2003, 2000, 1997, 1994, 1991, 1989, 1986, 1983, and 1980.

Some ancillaries, including electronic and print components, may not be available to customers outside the United States.

This book is printed on acid-free paper.

1 2 3 4 5 6 7 8 9 0 DOW/DOW 1 0 9 8 7 6 5

ISBN   978-1-259-29182-1
MHID   1-259-29182-0

Senior Vice President, Products & Markets: *Kurt L. Strand*
Vice President, General Manager, Products & Markets: *Marty Lange*
Vice President, Content Design & Delivery: *Kimberly Meriwether David*
Managing Director: *James Heine*
Brand Managers: *Scott Smith and Kathleen Hoenicke*
Director, Product Development: *Rose Koos*
Director of Digital Content Development: *Douglas Ruby*
Product Developer: *Sarah Otterness*
Digital Product Analyst: *Kevin Shanahan*
Director, Content Design & Delivery: *Linda Avenarius*
Program Manager: *Mark Christianson*
Content Project Managers: *Kathryn D. Wright and Kristin Bradley*
Buyer: *Laura Fuller*
Design: *Debra Kubiak*
Content Licensing Specialist: *Keri Johnson*
Cover Image: *© inhiu all rights reserved/Getty Images*
Compositor: *Aptara®, Inc.*
Printer: *R. R. Donnelley*

Library of Congress Cataloging-in-Publication Data

Schiller, Bradley R., 1943–
    The macro economy today / Bradley R. Schiller, American University with Karen Gebhardt, Colorado State University. — 14th edition.
        pages cm
    ISBN 978-1-259-29182-1 (alk. paper) — ISBN 1-259-29182-0 (alk. paper) 1. Macroeconomics. I. Gebhardt, Karen. II. Title.
    HB172.5.S3425 2016
    339—dc23

                                                                                                    2014045731

The Internet addresses listed in the text were accurate at the time of publication. The inclusion of a website does not indicate an endorsement by the
authors or McGraw-Hill Education, and McGraw-Hill Education does not guarantee the accuracy of the information presented at these sites.

www.mhhe.com

Bradley R. Schiller has more than four decades of experience teaching introductory economics at American University, the University of Nevada, the University of California (Berkeley and Santa Cruz), and the University of Maryland. He has given guest lectures at more than 300 colleges ranging from Fresno, California, to Istanbul, Turkey. Dr. Schiller's unique contribution to teaching is his ability to relate basic principles to current socioeconomic problems, institutions, and public policy decisions. This perspective is evident throughout *The Macro Economy Today.*

Dr. Schiller derives this policy focus from his extensive experience as a Washington consultant. He has been a consultant to most major federal agencies, many congressional committees, and political candidates. In addition, he has evaluated scores of government programs and helped design others. His studies of poverty, discrimination, training programs, tax reform, pensions, welfare, Social Security, and lifetime wage patterns have appeared in both professional journals and popular media. Dr. Schiller is also a frequent commentator on economic policy for television and radio, and his commentary has appeared in *The Wall Street Journal, The Washington Post, The New York Times,* and *Los Angeles Times,* among other major newspapers.

Dr. Schiller received his Ph.D. from Harvard and his B.A. degree, with great distinction, from the University of California (Berkeley). His current research focus is on Cuba—its post-revolution collapse and its post-Castro prospects. On his days off, Brad is on the tennis courts, the ski slopes, or the crystal-blue waters of Lake Tahoe.

Dr. Karen Gebhardt is a faculty member in the Department of Economics at Colorado State University (CSU). Dr. Gebhardt has a passion for teaching economics. She regularly instructs large, introductory courses in macro- and microeconomics; small honors sections of these core principles courses; and upper-division courses in pubic finance, microeconomics, and international trade, as well as a graduate course in teaching methods.

She is an early adopter of technology in the classroom and advocates strongly for it because she sees the difference it makes in student engagement and learning. Dr. Gebhardt has taught online consistently since 2005 and coordinates the online program within the Department of Economics at CSU. She also supervises and mentors the department's graduate teaching assistants and adjunct instructors.

Dr. Gebhardt was the recipient of the Water Pik Excellence in Education Award in 2006 and was nominated for Colorado State University Teacher of the Year in 2006, 2008, and 2013.

Her research interests, publications, and presentations involve the economics of human–wildlife interaction, economics education, and the economics of gender in the U.S. economy. Before joining CSU, she worked as an economist at the U.S. Department of Agriculture/Animal and Plant Health Inspection Service/Wildlife Services/National Wildlife Research Center, conducting research on the interactions of humans and wildlife, such as the economic effects of vampire bat–transmitted rabies in Mexico, the potential economic damage from introduction of invasive species to the Islands of Hawaii, bioeconomic modeling of the impacts of wildlife-transmitted disease, and others. In her free time, Dr. Gebhardt enjoys learning about new teaching methods that integrate technology and going rock climbing and camping in the Colorado Rockies and beyond.

The Great Recession of 2008–2009 lingered for far too long. But that devastating experience had at least one positive effect: it revitalized interest in economics. People wanted to know how a modern economy could stumble so badly—and why it took so long to recover. Public debates about economic theory became increasingly intense and partisan. Everything from Keynesian theory to environmental regulation became the subject of renewed scrutiny. These debates increased the demand for economic analysis and for principles instruction as well. Indeed, one could argue that the Great Recession proved that economics instruction is an inferior good: as the economy contracts, the demand for economics instruction increases.

While we might take offense at the thought of producing an inferior good, we should certainly rise to the occasion. This means bringing the real world into the classroom as never before: tying theoretical controversies about macro stability to both the ongoing business cycle and the intensely partisan policy debates about cause and effect; getting students to appreciate why and how economic issues are again the central focus of election campaigns.

The Macro Economy Today has always been a policy-driven introduction to economic principles. Indeed, that is one of its most distinctive features. This 14th edition continues that tradition with even more fervor. The 2014 midterm elections were largely a referendum on the economy. Were voters satisfied with the state of the economy? Why was unemployment still so high five years after the Great Recession ended? Had President Obama pursued the right policies? Republicans claimed they would have done things differently—and better. Democrats responded that the president (and their congressional majorities) had saved the economy from the brink of another depression and chalked up steady job and GDP gains.

Although voters tipped the balance in favor of Republicans in the 2014 midterm elections, the same issues were sure to enliven the 2016 presidential election campaigns. Those of us who teach economics should make every effort to inform students about the core economic principles that underlie these political debates. We can do this by explicitly highlighting contentious policy issues, then analyzing them in the context of core economic principles. That is the very heart and soul of this text. I use the real world of policy issues, public institutions, and private entities to enliven, illuminate, and apply the core concepts of economic theory. This is not a text full of fables; it's a text loaded with real-world applications. No other text comes close to this policy-driven, real-world-based approach. Students respond with greater interest, motivation, and even retention.

A section titled "The Economy Tomorrow" at the end of every chapter focuses on these kinds of front-page policy issues. But the real-world emphasis of this text is not confined to that feature. Every chapter has an array of In the News and World View boxes that offer real-world illustrations of basic economic principles. And the body of the text itself is permeated with actual companies, products, people, and policy issues that students will recognize. Israel's success with its "Iron Dome" antimissile defense in the latest Hamas–Israel flare-up is used as an example of what we economists call a "public good" (Chapter 4). The post-ISIS defense build-up here and in Europe highlights the age-old "guns vs. butter" dilemma (Chapter 1). The quest of bitcoins to replace government-sanctioned "money" is the subject of Chapter 13's Economy Tomorrow section. The impacts of the 2009 American Recovery and Reinvestment Act and the 2012 American Taxpayer Relief Act (which, ironically, brought higher tax rates, not relief!) get attention in Chapters 11 (fiscal policy) and 16 (supply-side policy). In the international sequence, I talk about new tariffs on Chinese solar panels, the Greek and Portuguese bailouts, and the impact of Russian aggression on the value of the Ukrainian hryvnia. You get the picture; this *is* the premier policy-driven, real-world-focused introduction to economic principles.

DIFFERENTIATING FEATURES

The policy-driven focus of *The Macro Economy Today* clearly differentiates it from other principles texts. Other texts may claim real-world content, but none comes close to the empirical perspectives of this text. Beyond this unique approach, *The Macro Economy Today* offers a combination of features that no other text matches, including the following.

Most principles texts moved away from the short-run business cycles to more emphasis on long-run macro dynamics about 10–15 years ago. Many even suggested the business cycle was dead. Now they know they missed the boat. And so do the students who have to read those texts and wonder why there is so little discussion of the macro events that have created so much economic and political turmoil. *The Macro Economy Today* is one of the few textbooks that still puts greater emphasis on short-run cyclicality than on long-run stability.

Macro Focus on Short-Run Cycles

Another pedagogical advantage of *The Macro Economy Today* is its use of a single framework for teaching all macro perspectives. Other principles texts continue to present both the Keynesian cross framework and the aggregate demand/supply (AD/AS) framework. This two-model approach is neither necessary nor efficient. All of the core ideas of Keynesian theory, including the multiplier, can be illustrated in the AD/AS framework. Keynes never drew the "Keynesian" cross and would not use it today, especially in view of the superiority of the AD/AS model in conveying his ideas. And we all know that the Keynesian cross is of no use in illustrating the short-run trade-off between inflation and full employment that bedevils policymakers and even defines our concept of full employment. Why overburden students with a two-model approach that confuses them and eats scarce instruction time? Instructors who adopt this text's one-model approach are invariably impressed with how much more efficient and effective it is.

One-Model Macro

We all know there is no such thing as a pure market-driven economy and that markets operate on the fringe even in the most centralized economics. So "markets versus government" is not an all-or-nothing proposition. It is still a central theme, however, in the real world. Should the government assume *more* responsibility for managing the economy—or will *less* intervention generate better macro outcomes? Public opinion is clear: as the accompanying News reveals, three out of four Americans have a negative view of federal intervention. The challenge for economics instructors is to enunciate principles that help define the boundaries of public and private sector activity. When do we expect **market failure** to

Markets versus Government Theme

market failure: An imperfection in the market mechanism that prevents optimal outcomes.

IN THE NEWS

Little Confidence in Government

Question: How confident are you in the ability of the federal government to make progress on the important problems and issues facing the country?

Answers:
- Not at all confident — 30%
- Not very confident — 40%
- Moderately confident — 23%
- Very confident — 3%
- Extremely confident — 1%

Source: Data gathered from AP-NORC opinion survey, December 12-16, 2013.

ANALYSIS: When people say they don't think the government can improve market outcomes, they are expecting "government failure."

government failure: Government intervention that fails to improve economic outcomes.

occur? How and why do we anticipate that government intervention might result in **government failure**? Can we get students to think critically about these central issues? *The Macro Economy Today* certainly tries, aided by scores of real-world illustrations.

Unique Topic Coverage

The staples of introductory economics are fully covered in *The Macro Economy Today*. Beyond the core chapters, however, there is always room for additional coverage. In fact, authors reveal their uniqueness in their choice of such chapters. Those choices tend to be more abstract in competing texts, offering "extra" chapters on public choice, behavioral economics, economics of information, uncertainty, and asymmetric information. All of these are interesting and important, but they entail opportunity costs that are particularly high at the principles level. The menu in *The Macro Economy Today* is more tailored to the dimensions and issues of the world around us. Chapter 2, for example, depicts the dimensions of the U.S. economy in a comparative global framework. Where else are students going to learn that China is *not* the world's largest economy, that U.S. workers are the most productive, or that income inequality is more severe in poor nations than rich ones?

The same empirical foundation is apparent in the chapters on unemployment (6) and inflation (7). We economists take for granted that these are central macroeconomic problems. But students have little personal experience with either problem and even less appreciation of their significance. Chapters 6 and 7 try to bridge this gap by discussing *why* unemployment and inflation are such central concerns—that is, the kinds of socioeconomic harm they inflict. The intent here is to help students understand and embrace our economic goals before we ask them to explore potential solutions.

Chapter 18 on "Theory versus Reality" offers yet another unique perspective on macroeconomics. It confronts the perennial question students ask: "If economic theory is so great, why is the economy so messed up?" Chapter 18 answers this question by reviewing the goal conflicts, measurement problems, design issues, and implementation obstacles that constrain even the best macro policies.

Global Perspective

"Global perspective," along with "real-world" content, is promised by just about every principles author. *The Macro Economy Today* actually delivers on that promise. This is manifestly evident in the titles of Chapter 2 (global comparisons) and Chapter 21 (global poverty). The global perspective is also easy to discern in the boxed World View features embedded in every chapter. More subtle, but at least as important, is the portrayal of an open economy from the get-go. While some texts start with a closed economy—or worse still, a closed, private economy—and then add international dimensions as an afterthought, *The Macro Economy Today* depicts an open economy from start to finish. These global linkages are a vital part of any coherent explanation of macro issues (e.g., cyclical instability, monetary control, and trade policy).

WHAT'S NEW AND UNIQUE IN THIS 14TH EDITION

Every edition of *The Macro Economy Today* introduces a wealth of new content and pedagogy. This is critical for a text that prides itself on currency of policy issues, institutions, and empirical perspectives. Every page, every example, and all the data have been reviewed for currency and updated where needed. Beyond this general upgrade, previous users of *The Macro Economy Today* will notice some specific revisions, including the following.

New "Economy Tomorrow" Topics

Each chapter ends with a feature called "The Economy Tomorrow" that challenges students to apply key concepts to current policy issues. Economy Tomorrow features range from "Harnessing the Sun" (the opportunity costs of solar energy) in Chapter 1 to "Policing World Trade" (international trade disputes) in Chapter 19. A new one in the Money and Banking chapter (13) examines the potential of bitcoins to replace government-sanctioned fiat money.

The boxed World Views in each chapter are designed to showcase the global reach of economic principles. There are nine new World Views in this 14th edition of *Macro,* including the oil-market response to the shoot-down of the Malaysian Airlines flight over Ukraine (Chapter 3), China's 2014 cut in its reserve requirements (Chapter 14), Venezuela's increasing socialism (Chapter 21), the U.S. 2014 imposition of tariffs on Chinese solar panels (Chapter 19), Heritage Foundation's 2015 global rankings on its Index of Economic Freedom (Chapter 1), and the World Bank's perspective on widening global inequality (Chapter 5). All of the World Views are annotated, are referred to in the body of the text, and often are the subject of end-of-chapter questions. These added dimensions help ensure that students will actually read the boxed material.

New "World Views"

The boxed In the News features highlight domestic applications of basic principles. There are 17 new In the News boxes in this edition of *Macro.* Among them are CBO estimates of the jobs impact of the 2011–2013 defense cuts (Chapter 11); the effect of tuition hikes on the inflation rate (Chapter 7); public opinion of the relative importance of the deficit problem (Chapter 12); recent changes in consumer confidence, spending, and wealth effects (Chapter 9); and CBO's assessment of the causes of the Great Recession of 2008–2009.

New "In the News" Content

At the end of every chapter there are both questions for discussion and a separate set of numerical and graphing problems. The problem set is designed so students can answer and submit manually if desired. The same problems are also embedded in the course management system *Connect* to facilitate online submissions, automatic grading, and course monitoring. Both the questions for discussion and problems utilize tables, graphs, and boxed material from the body of the chapter, requiring the students to read and process core content. As a result, the end-of-chapter material has to be updated along with the text itself. In this 14th edition of *Macro,* there are 130 new problems and 22 new questions for discussion.

New Problems and Questions for Discussion

We are pleased to welcome Karen Gebhardt (Colorado State University) to the author team. Karen has made important contributions to the 14th edition of *The Macro Economy Today* as a digital co-author, including helping create quality digital materials to accompany the textbook and ensuring that the Test Bank and end-of-chapter questions not only are accurate but contain effective and probing questions for students.

New Digital Coauthor and Enhanced Digital Content

CHAPTER-BY-CHAPTER CHANGES

The Macro Economy Today, 14th edition, features improved and expanded learning objectives, end-of-chapter content, and up-to-date material and data reflecting today's economy in every chapter. Changes include the following.

Chapter 1: Economics: The Core Issues introduces the core issues of What, How, and For Whom and the debate over market reliance or government regulation to resolve them. New global rankings on the extent of market reliance are highlighted. The 2011–2013 defense cutbacks and the post-ISIS call for a defense build-up highlight the guns vs. butter dilemma (opportunity cost), as does North Korea's continuing food shortages.

Chapter 2: The U.S. Economy: A Global View is intended to give students a sense of how the American economy stacks up to other nations in the world. The completely updated comparisons are organized around the core issues of What, How, and For Whom.

Chapter 3: Supply and Demand introduces the core elements of the market mechanism. Walmart's 2014 price cuts on the Galaxy S4 illustrate the law of demand. Ticket scalping at the NCAA finals illustrate disequilibrium pricing. Supply/demand shifts are illustrated with shrimp prices in the wake of the BP Gulf oil spill and oil prices in the wake of the Malaysian Airlines downing.

Chapter 4: The Role of Government focuses on the justifications for government intervention (market failures) and the growth of the public sector. Data on tax rates, public opinion about the role of government, state/local bond referenda, and government growth have all been updated. Israel's "Iron Dome" missile defense system is offered as a new example of a "public good."

Chapter 5: National Income Accounting emphasizes the linkage between aggregate output and income and the utility of their measurement. All the GDP data are updated, as well as the historical comparisons of real and nominal incomes. The World View on standard-of-living inequalities between rich and poor nations has been updated as well. So has the contrast between economic and social measure of well-being.

Chapter 6: Unemployment not only introduces the standard measures of unemployment but also emphasizes the socioeconomic costs of that macro failure. All of the unemployment, labor force participation, and social cost data have been updated.

Chapter 7: Inflation endeavors to explain not only how inflation is measured but also the kinds of socioeconomic costs it imposes. Recent changes in the prices of tuition and other specific goods help illustrate measurement issues. All price and wage series are updated.

Chapter 8: The Business Cycle offers a historical and analytical overview of the nature and origins of cyclical disturbances. The Great Recession of 2008–2009 and its agonizingly slow recovery provide lots of new context. Aggregate supply shifts due to a spate of recent global conflicts are also noted. The core AS/AD model is introduced as a framework for macro analysis.

Chapter 9: Aggregate Demand focuses on the nature and building blocks of the aggregate demand curve. There are six new In the News features, covering consumer confidence, the Leading Economic Index, cutbacks in private and public investment, and the wealth effect. All data on spending parameters are updated.

Chapter 10: Self-Adjustment or Instability? highlights the core concern of whether laissez-faire macro economies self-adjust or not. The multiplier is introduced and illustrated in the context of the AS/AD model. New information on the variability of consumption and investment spending is highlighted, as are new CBO perspectives on the causes of the Great Recession.

Chapter 11: Fiscal Policy examines the potential of tax, spending, and income-transfer policies to shift the aggregate-demand curve in desired directions. An explicit guide for computing the size of an optimal intervention in the context of both output and price variability is introduced (Table 11.3). A new graphic on potential unemployment/inflation trade-offs is included. The latest estimates of the job impacts of the American Recovery and Reinvestment Act of 2009 and the defense cutbacks of 2011–2013 are spotlighted.

Chapter 12: Deficits and Debt not only describes the size and history of U.S. debt, but also emphasizes the critical distinction between cyclical and structural (policy-induced) deficits and the real economic costs and consequences of both deficits and debt. Global comparisons of deficit ratios are provided, along with the latest information on debt ownership and public anxiety about debt and deficit levels. CBO estimates of the size of automatic stabilizers are illustrated.

Chapter 13: Money and Banks focuses on the nature and origins of what we call "money." M1 and M2 statistics are updated, and the nature of T-accounts is clarified. A new table on interest rates helps illustrate the opportunity costs of holding money. The Economy Tomorrow features the (unlikely) potential of bitcoins to replace government-sanctioned fiat money.

Chapter 14: The Federal Reserve System introduces Janet Yellen as the new chair of the Fed and assesses the policy tools at her disposal. The experience with three rounds of quantitative easing is reviewed, and the increasing constraints imposed by shadow banking institutions are noted. There is a new World View on China's 2014 cut in reserve requirements and updated depictions of the pile-up of excess reserves in U.S. banks.

Chapter 15: Monetary Policy explores both the theoretical potential and actual impact of Fed policy on macro outcomes. The Fed's adoption of employment targeting is highlighted, and the effects of quantitative easing are assessed.

Chapter 16: Supply-Side Policy: Short-Run Options emphasizes that demand-focused policies are not the only game in town—that the aggregate supply curve is important for macro outcomes as well. CBO's latest estimates of the tax elasticity of labor supply are included, along with stats on the increase in marginal tax rates imposed by the 2012 American Taxpayer Relief Act. The impacts of new trucking-safety regulations and health care reforms (the Affordable Care Act) are also discussed and illustrated.

Chapter 17: Growth and Productivity: Long-Run Possibilities explores the sources, prospects, and limits of economic growth. New global comparisons of productivity, savings, and economic growth are offered.

Chapter 18: Theory versus Reality is the macro capstone chapter that not only reviews macro problems and policy options but also examines the real-world obstacles that preclude perfect macro outcomes. Recent milestones in fiscal, monetary, and supply-side policy are depicted, along with a "report card" on our macroeconomic performance.

Chapter 19: International Trade not only examines the theory of comparative advantage, but also investigates the opposition to free trade and the impact of trade barriers that result. The latest data on trade flows and trade balances (both aggregate and bilateral) are injected. The new U.S. tariff on Chinese solar panels helps illustrate the winners and losers from trade barriers.

Chapter 20: International Finance explains how international exchange rates are determined and why they fluctuate. The depreciation of the Ukrainian hryvnia in the wake of Russia's invasion provides a new perspective on currency fluctuations. There is also a new World View depicting who gains and who loses from a strong (appreciating) dollar.

Chapter 21: Global Poverty is receding, but billions of people remain desperately poor around the world. This chapter describes the current dimensions of global poverty and the World Bank's new (2014) antipoverty goal. Emphasis is on the importance of productivity advance and the policies that accelerate or restrain that advance. A new World View on Venezuela's economic contraction provides a relevant illustration.

EFFECTIVE PEDAGOGY

Despite the abundance of real-world applications, this is at heart a *principles* text, not a compendium of issues. Good theory and interesting applications are not mutually exclusive. This is a text that wants to *teach economics,* not just increase awareness of policy issues. To that end, *The Macro Economy Today* provides a logically organized and uncluttered theoretical structure for macro, micro, and international theory. What distinguishes this text from others on the market is that it conveys theory in a lively, student-friendly manner.

Clean, Clear Theory

Student comprehension of core theory is facilitated with careful, consistent, and effective pedagogy. This distinctive pedagogy includes the following features:

Concept Reinforcement

Chapter Learning Objectives. Each chapter contains a set of chapter-level learning objectives. Students and professors can be confident that the organization of each chapter surrounds common themes outlined by three to five learning objectives listed on the first page of each chapter. End-of-chapter material, including the chapter summary, discussion questions, and student problem sets, is tagged to these learning objectives, as is the supplementary material, which includes the Test Bank and Instructor's Resource Manual.

Self-Explanatory Graphs and Tables. Graphs are *completely* labeled, colorful, and positioned on background grids. Because students often enter the principles course as graph-phobics, graphs are frequently accompanied by synchronized tabular data. Every table is also annotated. This shouldn't be a product-differentiating feature, but sadly, it is. Putting a table in a textbook without an annotation is akin to writing a cluster of numbers on the board, then leaving the classroom without any explanation.

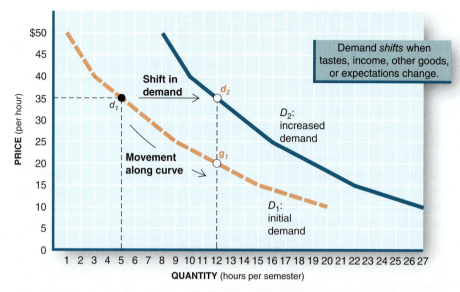

FIGURE 3.3
Shifts vs. Movements

A demand curve shows how a consumer responds to price changes. If the determinants of demand stay constant, the response is a *movement* along the curve to a new quantity demanded. In this case, the quantity demanded increases from 5 (point d_1), to 12 (point g_1), when price falls from $35 to $20 per hour.

If the determinants of demand *change*, the entire demand curve *shifts*. In this case, a rise in income increases demand. With more income, Tom is willing to buy 12 hours at the initial price of $35 (point d_2), not just the 5 hours he demanded before the lottery win.

		Quantity Demanded (Hours per Semester)	
	Price (per Hour)	Initial Demand	After Increase in Income
A	$50	1	8
B	45	2	9
C	40	3	10
D	35	5	12
E	30	7	14
F	25	9	16
G	20	12	19
H	15	15	22
I	10	20	27

Reinforced Key Concepts. Key terms are defined in the margin when they first appear and, unlike in other texts, redefined in the margin as necessary in subsequent chapters. Website references are directly tied to the book's content, not hung on like ornaments. End-of-chapter discussion questions use tables, graphs, and boxed news stories from the text, reinforcing key concepts, and are linked to the chapter's learning objectives.

Boxed and Annotated Applications. In addition to the real-world applications that run through the body of the text, *The Macro Economy Today* intersperses boxed domestic (In the News) and global (World View) case studies intertextually for further understanding and reference. Although nearly every text on the market now offers boxed applications, *The Macro Economy Today*'s presentation is distinctive. First, the sheer number of In the News (51) and World View (41) boxes is unique. Second, and more important, *every* boxed application is referenced in the body of the text. Third, *every* News and World View comes with a brief, self-contained explanation, as the accompanying example illustrates. Fourth, the News and World View boxes are the explicit subject of the end-of-chapter discussion questions and student problem set exercises. In combination, these distinctive features assure that students will actually *read* the boxed applications and discern their economic content. The Test Bank provides subsets of questions tied to the News and World View boxes so that instructors can confirm student use of this feature.

IN THE NEWS

Seafood Prices Rise after BP Oil Spill

Oily shrimp? No thank you! The National Oceanic and Atmospheric Administration (NOAA) has closed a third of the Gulf of Mexico in response to the BP oil spill. The explosion of BP's Deepwater Horizon oil rig has spilled nearly 5 million barrels of oil into the Gulf. Whatever their taste, oily fish and shrimp may be a health hazard.

Closure of the Gulf has caused seafood prices to soar. The price of top-quality white shrimp has jumped from $3.50 a pound to $7.50 a pound. Restaurants are jacking up their prices or taking shrimp off the menu.

Source: News reports, June 2010.

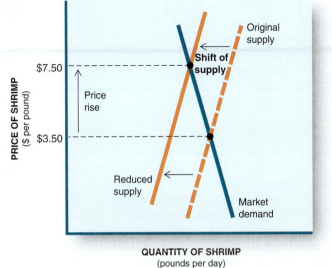

ANALYSIS: When factor costs or availability worsen, the supply curve *shifts* to the left. Such leftward supply-curve shifts push prices up the market demand curve.

Photos and Cartoons. The text presentation is also enlivened with occasional photos and cartoons that reflect basic concepts. The photos on page 36 are much more vivid testimony to the extremes of inequality than the data in Figure 2.3 (p. 39). Every photo and cartoon is annotated and referenced in the body of the text. These visual features are an integral part of the presentation, not diversions.

Analysis: An abundance of capital equipment and advanced technology make American farmers and workers far more productive than workers in poor nations.

Readability

The one adjective invariably used to describe *The Macro Economy Today* is "readable." Professors often express a bit of shock when they realize that students actually enjoy reading the book. (Well, not as much as a Stephen King novel, but a whole lot better than most textbooks they've had to plow through.) The writing style is lively and issue-focused. Unlike any other textbook on the market, every boxed feature, every graph, every table, and every cartoon is explained and analyzed. Every feature is also referenced in the text, so students actually learn the material rather than skipping over it. Because readability is ultimately in the eye of the beholder, you might ask a couple of students to read and compare a parallel chapter in *The Macro Economy Today* and in another text. This is a test *The Macro Economy Today* usually wins.

Student Problem Set

I firmly believe that students must *work* with key concepts in order to really learn them. Weekly homework assignments are *de rigueur* in my own classes. To facilitate homework assignments, I have prepared the student problem set, which includes built-in numerical and graphing problems that build on the tables, graphs, and boxed material that align with each chapter's learning objectives. Grids for drawing graphs are also provided. Students cannot complete all the problems without referring to material in the chapter. This increases the odds of students actually *reading* the chapter, the tables, and the boxed applications.

The student problem set at the end of each chapter is reproduced in the online student tutorial software (*Connect® Economics,* discussed in the following pages). This really helps students transition between the written material and online supplements. It also means that the online assignments are totally book-specific.

NEW AND IMPROVED SUPPLEMENTS

The following ancillaries are available for quick download and convenient access via the Instructor Resource material available through McGraw-Hill *Connect®*.

Instructor Aids

Test Bank. The Test Bank has been rigorously revised for this 14th edition of *The Macro Economy Today*. Digital co-author Karen Gebhardt enlisted the help of her grad students to carefully assess *every* problem in the Test Bank, assigning each problem a letter grade and identifying errors and opportunities for improvement. This in-depth and critical assessment and revision has ensured a high level of quality and consistency of the test questions and the greatest possible correlation with the content of the text. All questions are coded according to chapter learning objectives, AACSB Assurance of Learning, and Bloom's Taxonomy guidelines. The computerized Test Bank is available in EZ Test, a flexible and easy-to-use electronic testing program that accommodates a wide range of question types, including user-created questions. Tests created in EZ Test can be exported for use with course management systems such as WebCT, BlackBoard, or PageOut. The program is available for Windows, Macintosh, and Linux environments. Additionally, you can access the test bank through McGraw-Hill *Connect*.

PowerPoint Presentations. Mike Cohick of Collin College, with the help of Karen Gebhardt, revised presentation slides for the 14th edition. Developed using Microsoft PowerPoint software, these slides are a step-by-step review of the key points in each of the book's 21 chapters. They are equally useful to the student in the classroom as lecture aids or for personal review at home or the computer lab. The slides use animation to show students how graphs build and shift.

Digital Image Library. All of the text's tables and graphs have been reproduced as full-color images on the website for instructor access.

Solutions Manual. Prepared by Karen Gebhardt, this manual provides detailed answers to the end-of-chapter questions.

News Flashes. As up-to-date as *The Macro Economy Today* is, it can't foretell the future. As the future becomes the present, however, I write two-page News Flashes describing major economic events and relating them to specific text references. These News Flashes provide good lecture material and can be copied for student use. Adopters of *The Macro Economy Today* have the option of receiving News Flashes via fax or mail. They are also available via the Instructor Resource Material in *Connect*. Four to six News Flashes are sent to adopters each year. (Contact your local McGraw-Hill Education sales representative to get on the mailing list.)

Student Aids

Built-in Student Problem Set. The built-in student problem set is found at the end of every chapter of *The Macro Economy Today*. Each chapter has 8 to 10 numerical and graphing problems tied to the content of the text. Graphing grids are provided. The answer blanks are formatted to facilitate grading.

A mini website directory is provided in each chapter's marginal Web Click boxes, created and updated by Mark Wilson of West Virginia University Institute of Technology. These URLs aren't random picks; they were selected because they let students extend and update adjacent in-text discussions.

Web Click Boxes

McGraw-Hill is proud to offer a new mobile study app for students learning economics from Schiller's *The Macro Economy Today,* 14th edition. The features of the Study Econ app include flashcards for all key terms, a basic math review, customizable self-quizzes, common mistakes, and games. For additional information, please refer to the back inside cover of this book. Visit your mobile app store and download a trial version of the Schiller Study Econ app today!

Study Econ Mobile App

DIGITAL SOLUTIONS

Less Managing. More Teaching. Greater Learning.

 McGraw-Hill's *Connect® Economics* is an online assessment solution that connects students with the tools and resources they'll need to achieve success.

McGraw-Hill *Connect®* Economics

Connect Economics offers a number of powerful tools and features to make managing assignments easier, so faculty can spend more time teaching. With *Connect Economics,* students can engage with their coursework anytime and anywhere, making the learning process more accessible and efficient. *Connect Economics* offers the features as described here.

McGraw-Hill's *Connect Economics* Features

Simple Assignment Management. With *Connect Economics,* creating assignments is easier than ever, so you can spend more time teaching and less time managing. The assignment management function enables you to

- Create and deliver assignments easily with selectable end-of-chapter questions and test bank items.
- Streamline lesson planning, student progress reporting, and assignment grading to make classroom management more efficient than ever.
- Go paperless with the eBook and online submission and grading of student assignments.

Smart Grading. *Connect Economics* helps students learn more efficiently by providing feedback and practice material when they need it, where they need it. The grading function enables you to

- Have assignments scored automatically, giving students immediate feedback on their work and side-by-side comparisons with correct answers.
- Access and review each response, manually change grades, or leave comments for students to review.
- Reinforce classroom concepts with practice tests and instant quizzes.

Instructor Library. The *Connect Economics* Instructor Library is your repository for additional resources to improve student engagement in and out of class. You can select and use any asset that enhances your lecture. The *Connect Economics* Instructor Library includes all of the instructor supplements for this text.

Student Resources

Any supplemental resources that align with the text for student use will be available through *Connect*.

Student Progress Tracking. *Connect Economics* keeps instructors informed about how each student, section, and class is performing, allowing for more productive use of lecture and office hours. The progress-tracking function enables you to

- View scored work immediately and track individual or group performance with assignment and grade reports.
- Access an instant view of student or class performance relative to learning objectives.
- Collect data and generate reports required by many accreditation organizations, such as AACSB and AICPA.

Connect Insight. The first and only analytics tool of its kind, Connect Insight is a series of visual data displays that are each framed by an intuitive question and provide at-a-glance information that allows instructors to leverage aggregated information about their courses and students to provide a more personalized teaching and learning experience.

Lecture Capture. Increase the attention paid to lecture discussion by decreasing the attention paid to note taking. Lecture Capture offers new ways for students to focus on the in-class discussion, knowing they can revisit important topics later. Lecture Capture enables you to:

- Record and distribute your lecture with a click of a button.
- Record and index PowerPoint presentations and anything shown on your computer so they are easily searchable, frame by frame.
- Offer access to lectures anytime and anywhere by computer, iPod, or mobile device.
- Increase intent listening and class participation by easing students' concerns about note taking. Lecture Capture will make it more likely you will see students' faces, not the tops of their heads.

Diagnostic and Adaptive Learning of Concepts: LearnSmart

LEARNSMART® Students want to make the best use of their study time. The LearnSmart adaptive self-study technology within *Connect Economics* provides students with a seamless combination of practice, assessment, and remediation for every concept in the textbook. LearnSmart's intelligent software adapts to every student response and automatically delivers concepts that advance students' understanding while reducing time devoted to the concepts already mastered. The result for every student is the fastest path to mastery of the chapter concepts. LearnSmart

- Applies an intelligent concept engine to identify the relationships between concepts and to serve new concepts to each student only when he or she is ready.
- Adapts automatically to each student, so students spend less time on the topics they understand and practice more those they have yet to master.
- Provides continual reinforcement and remediation, but gives only as much guidance as students need.
- Integrates diagnostics as part of the learning experience.
- Enables you to assess which concepts students have efficiently learned on their own, thus freeing class time for more applications and discussion.

Smartbook

SMARTBOOK® Smartbook is an extension of LearnSmart—an adaptive eBook that helps students focus their study time more effectively. As students read, Smartbook assesses comprehension and dynamically highlights where they need to study more.

Student Progress Tracking *Connect Economics* keeps instructors informed about how each student, section, and class is performing, allowing for more productive use of lecture and office hours. The progress-tracking function enables you to

- View scored work immediately and track individual or group performance with assignment and grade reports.
- Access an instant view of student or class performance relative to learning objectives.
- Collect data and generate reports required by many accreditation organizations, such as AACSB.

For more information about *Connect*, go to **connect.mheducation.com**, or contact your local McGraw-Hill sales representative.

We understand that getting the most from your new technology can be challenging. That's why our services don't stop after you purchase our products. You can e-mail our Product Specialists 24 hours a day to get product-training online. Or you can search our knowledge bank of Frequently Asked Questions on our support website. For Customer Support, call **800-331-5094**, or visit **www.mhhe.com/support**.

McGraw-Hill's Customer Experience Group

Tegrity Campus is a fully automated lecture capture solution used in traditional, hybrid, "flipped classes," and online courses to record lessons, lectures, and skills. Its personalized learning features make study time incredibly efficient and its ability to affordably scale brings this benefit to every student on campus. Patented search technology and real-time LMS integrations make Tegrity the market-leading solution and service.

Tegrity Campus: Lectures 24/7

McGraw-Hill Create™ is a self-service website that allows you to create customized course materials using McGraw-Hill's comprehensive, cross-disciplinary content and digital products. You can even access third-party content such as readings, articles, cases, videos, and more. Arrange the content you've selected to match the scope and sequence of your course. Personalize your book with a cover design and choose the best format for your students—eBook, color print, or black-and-white print. And when you are done, you'll receive a PDF review copy in just minutes!

Create

Go paperless with eTextbooks from CourseSmart and move light years beyond traditional print textbooks. Read online or offline anytime, anywhere. Access your eTextbook on multiple devices with or without an Internet connection. CourseSmart eBooks include convenient, built-in tools that let you search topics quickly, add notes and highlights, copy/paste passages, and print any page.

CourseSmart

Many educational institutions today are focused on the notion of *assurance of learning*, an important element of some accreditation standards. *The Macro Economy Today* is designed specifically to support your assurance-of-learning initiatives with a simple yet powerful solution.

Each test bank question for *The Macro Economy Today* maps to a specific chapter learning outcome/objective listed in the text. You can use our test bank software, EZ Test, or *Connect® Economics* to easily query for learning outcomes/objectives that directly relate to the learning objectives for your course. You can then use the reporting features of EZ Test to aggregate student results in similar fashion, making the collection and presentation of assurance-of-learning data simple and easy.

Assurance-of-Learning Ready

McGraw-Hill Education is a proud corporate member of AACSB International. Understanding the importance and value of AACSB accreditation, *The Macro Economy Today*, 14th edition, recognizes the curricula guidelines detailed in the AACSB standards for business accreditation by connecting selected questions in the text and the test bank to the six general knowledge and skill guidelines in the AACSB standards.

The statements contained in *The Macro Economy Today*, 14th edition, are provided only as a guide for the users of this textbook. The AACSB leaves content coverage and assess-

AACSB Statement

ment within the purview of individual schools, the mission of the school, and the faculty. While *The Macro Economy Today,* 14th edition, and the teaching package make no claim of any specific AACSB qualification or evaluation, we have labeled within *The Macro Economy Today,* 14th edition, selected questions according to the six general knowledge and skills areas.

ACKNOWLEDGMENTS

This Fourteenth edition is unquestionably the finest edition of *The Macro Economy Today,* and I am deeply grateful to all those people who helped develop it. Sarah Otterness was my faithful, fastidious, and cheerful product developer, who checked every word and feature in the text, prompting scores of corrections. Kathryn Wright, the project manager, did an exceptional job in assuring that every page of the text was visually pleasing, properly formatted, error-free, and timely produced. Scott Smith and Katie Hoenicke served as brand managers, offering sage advice and savvy leadership. The design team, led by Debra Kubiak, created a vibrant palette of colors and features that enhanced *The Macro Economy Today*'s readability. My thanks to all of them and their supporting staff.

I also want to express my heartfelt thanks to the professors who have shared their reactions (both good and bad) with me. Direct feedback from users and reviewers has always been a great source of continuing improvements in *The Macro Economy Today:*

Reviewers

Cynthia E. Abadie
Southwest Tennessee Community College

Mark Abajian
San Diego Mesa College

Steve Abid
Grand Rapids Community College

Ercument G. Aksoy
Los Angeles Valley College

Mauro Cristian Amor
Northwood University

Catalina Amuedo-Dorantes
San Diego State University

Gerald Baumgardner
Penn College

Mack A. Bean
Franklin Pierce University

Adolfo Benavides
Texas A&M University–
Corpus Christi

Anoop Bhargava
Finger Lakes Community College

Joerg Bibow
Skidmore College

Eugenie Bietry
Pace University

John Bockino
Suffolk County Community College

Peter Boelman
Norco College

Walter Francis Boyle
Fayetteville Technical
Community College

Amber Brown
Grand Valley State University

Don Bumpass
Sam Houston State University

Suparna Chakraborty
Baruch College, CUNY

Stephen J. Conroy
University of San Diego

Sherry L. Creswell
Kent State University

Manabendra Dasgupta
University of Alabama–Birmingham

Antony Davies
Duquesne University

Diane de Freitas
Fresno City College

Diana Denison
Red Rocks Community College

Alexander Deshkovski
North Carolina Central University

John A. Doces
Bucknell University

Ishita Edwards
Oxnard College

Eric R. Eide
Brigham Young University

Yalcin Ertekin
Trine University

Kelley L. Fallon
Owensboro Community & Technical College

Frank Garland
Tri-County Technical College

Leroy Gill
The Ohio State University

Paul Graf
Indiana University

Barnali Gupta
Miami University

Sheila Amin Gutierrez de Pineres
University of Texas–Dallas

Jonatan Jelen
City College of New York

Hyojin Jeong
Lakeland Community College

Barbara Heroy John
University of Dayton

Tim Kochanski
Portland State University

David E. Laurel
South Texas College

Raymond Lawless
Quinsigamond Community College

Richard B. Le
Cosumnes River College

Jim Lee
Texas A&M University–Corpus Christi

Sang H. Lee
Southeastern Louisiana University

Minghua Li
Franklin Pierce University

Yan Li
University of Wisconsin–Eau Claire

Paul Lockard
Black Hawk College

Rotua Lumbantobing
North Carolina State University

Paula Manns
Atlantic Cape Community College

Jeanette Milius
Iowa Western Community College

Norman C. Miller
Miami University

Stanley Robert Mitchell
McLennan Community College

Stephen K. Nodine
Tri-County Technical College

Phacharaphot Nuntramas
San Diego State University

Seth Ari Roberts
Frederick Community College

Michael J. Ryan
Western Michigan University

Craig F. Santicola
Westmoreland County Community College

Rolando A. Santos
Lakeland Community College

Theodore P. Scheinman
Mt. Hood Community College

Marilyn K. Spencer
Texas A&M University–Corpus Christi

Irina Nikolayevna Strelnikova
Red Rocks Community College

Michael Swope
Wayne County Community College

Gary Lee Taylor
South Dakota State University

Deborah L. Thorsen
Palm Beach State College

Ngoc-Bich Tran
San Jacinto College

Markland Tuttle
Sam Houston State University

Kenneth Lewis Weimer
Kellogg Community College

Selin Yalcindag
Mercyhurst College

Erik Zemljic
Kent State University

Finally, I'd like to thank all the professors and students who are going to use *The Macro Economy Today* as an introduction to economics principles. I welcome any responses (even the bad ones) you'd like to pass on for future editions.

—**Bradley R. Schiller**

CONTENTS IN BRIEF

CONTENTS

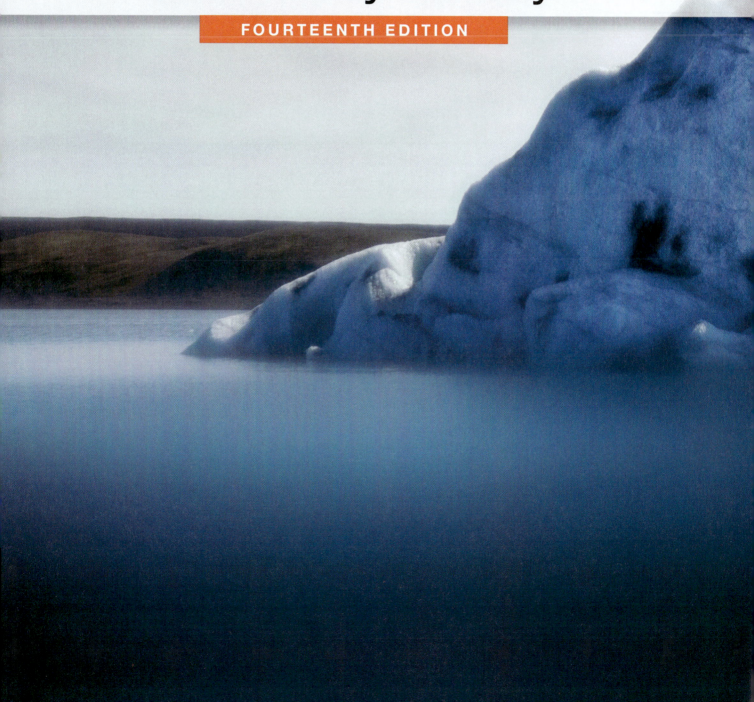

The MACRO Economy Today

FOURTEENTH EDITION

The Economic Challenge

People around the world want a better life. Whether rich or poor, everyone strives for a higher standard of living. Ultimately, the performance of the economy determines who attains that goal.

These first few chapters examine how the *limits* to output are determined and how the interplay of market forces and government intervention utilize and even expand those limits.

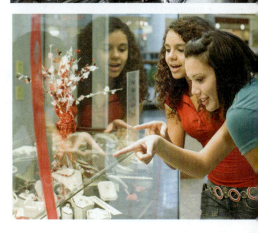

Economics:
The Core Issues

After reading this chapter, you should know

LO1-1 How scarcity creates opportunity costs.

LO1-2 What the production possibilities curve represents.

LO1-3 The three core economic questions that every society must answer.

LO1-4 How market and government approaches to economic problems differ.

"The Economist in Chief"

People understand that the president of the United States is the Commander in Chief of the armed forces. The president has the ultimate responsibility to decide when and how America's military forces will be deployed. He issues the orders that military officers must carry out. He is given credit for military successes and blame for military failures. He can't "pass the buck" down the line of command.

Less recognized is the president's role as "Economist in Chief." The president is held responsible not just for the *military* security of the United States, but for its *economic* security as well. Although he doesn't have the command powers in the economic arena that he has in the military arena, people expect him to take charge of the economy. They expect the Economist in Chief to keep the economy growing, to create jobs for everyone who wants one, and to prevent prices from rising too fast. Along the way, they expect the Economist in Chief to protect the environment, assure economic justice for all, and protect America's position in the global economy.

That is a tall order, especially in view of the president's limited constitutional powers to make economic policy decisions and the array of forces that shape economic outcomes. But no matter. Voters will hold the Economist in Chief responsible for economic misfortunes, whether or not he is able to single-handedly prevent them.

What everyone ultimately wants is a prosperous and growing economy: an economy in which people can find good jobs, enjoy rising living standards and wealth, pursue the education they desire, and enjoy the creature comforts of a prosperous economy. And we want to enjoy all these material comforts while protecting the environment, caring for the poor, and pursuing world peace.

We may know what we want, but how do we get it? Is "the economy" some sort of perpetual motion machine that will keep churning out more goods and services every year? Clearly not. During the Great Recession of 2008–2009 the economy churned out less output, eliminated jobs, and reduced living standards and wealth. A lot of college graduates had to move back home when they couldn't find jobs. What went wrong?

Even after the Great Recession ended in June 2009, economic pain persisted. The growth of the economy was agonizingly slow, and unemployment remained high for another 6 years. Was that much distress really necessary? Couldn't the Economist in Chief have fixed these problems? Or are private markets simply unresponsive to government policies? These questions are being debated again in the run-up to the 2016 presidential elections.

Just raising these questions begs the fundamental issue of what makes an economy tick. How are prices, wages, employment, and other economic outcomes actually determined?

Does Wall Street run the system? How about selfish, greedy capitalists? The banks? Or maybe foreign nations? Are incompetent bureaucrats and self-serving politicians the root of our occasional woes? Who, in fact, calls the shots?

The goal of this course is to understand how the economy works. To that end, we want to determine how *markets*—the free-wheeling exchange of goods and services—shape economic outcomes—everything from the price of this textbook to the national unemployment rate. Then we want to examine the role that government can and does play in (re)shaping economic performance. Once we've established this foundation, we'll be in a better position to evaluate what the Economist in Chief *can* do—and what he *should* do. We'll also better understand how we can make better economic decisions for ourselves.

We'll start our inquiry with some harsh realities. In a world of unlimited resources, we could have all the goods we desired. We'd have time to do everything we wanted and enough money to buy everything we desired. We could produce enough to make everyone rich while protecting the environment and exploring the universe. The Economist in Chief could deliver everything voters asked for. Unfortunately, we don't live in that utopia: **we live in a world of limited resources.** Those limits are the root of our economic problems. They force us to make difficult decisions about how *best* to use our time, our money, and our resources. The Economist in Chief has to decide how *best* to use the nation's limited resources. These are *economic* decisions.

In this first chapter we'll examine how the problem of limited resources arises and the kinds of choices it forces us to make. As we'll see, **three core choices confront every nation:**

- **WHAT to produce with our limited resources.**
- **HOW to produce the goods and services we select.**
- **FOR WHOM goods and services are produced—that is, who should get them.**

We also have to decide who should answer these questions. Should people take care of their own health and retirement, or should the government provide a safety net of health care and pensions? Should the government regulate airfares or let the airlines set prices? Should Microsoft decide what features get included in a computer's operating system, or should the government make that decision? Should Facebook decide what personal information is protected, or should the government make that decision? Should interest rates be set by private banks alone, or should the government try to control interest rates? The battle over *who* should answer the core questions is often as contentious as the questions themselves.

THE ECONOMY IS US

To learn how the economy works, let's start with a simple truth: *the economy is us.* "The economy" is simply an abstraction referring to the grand sum of all our production and consumption activities. What we collectively produce is what the economy produces; what we collectively consume is what the economy consumes. In this sense, the concept of "the economy" is no more difficult than the concept of "the family." If someone tells you that the Jones family has an annual income of $42,000, you know that the reference is to the collective earnings of all the Joneses. Likewise, when someone reports that the nation's income is $18 trillion per year—as it now is—we should recognize that the reference is to the grand total of everyone's income. If we work fewer hours or get paid less, both family income *and* national income decline. The "meaningless statistics" (see the cartoon on the next page) often cited in the news are just a summary of our collective market behavior.

The same relationship between individual behavior and aggregate behavior applies to specific outputs. If we as individuals insist on driving cars rather than taking public transportation, the economy will produce millions of cars each year and consume vast quantities of oil.

"Meaningless statistics were up one-point-five per cent this month over last month."

Analysis: Many people think of economics as dull statistics. But economics is really about human behavior—how people decide to use scarce resources and how those decisions affect market outcomes.

In a slightly different way, the economy produces billions of dollars of military hardware to satisfy our desire for national defense. In each case, the output of the economy reflects the collective behavior of the 320 million individuals who participate in the U.S. economy.

We may not always be happy with the output of the economy. But we can't ignore the link between individual action and collective outcomes. If the highways are clogged and the air is polluted, we can't blame someone else for the transportation choices we made. If we're disturbed by the size of our military arsenal, we must still accept responsibility for our choices (or nonchoices, if we failed to vote). In either case, we continue to have the option of reallocating our resources. We can create a different outcome tomorrow, next month, or next year.

SCARCITY: THE CORE PROBLEM

Although we can change economic outcomes, we can't have everything we want. If you go to the mall with $20 in your pocket, you can buy only so much. The money in your pocket sets a *limit* to your spending.

The output of the entire economy is also limited. The limits in this case are set not by the amount of money in people's pockets, but by the resources available for producing goods and services. Everyone wants more housing, new schools, better transit systems, and a new car. We also want to explore space and bring safe water to the world's poor. But even a country as rich as the United States can't produce everything people want. So, like every other nation, we have to grapple with the core problem of **scarcity**—the fact that **there aren't enough resources available to satisfy all our desires.**

Factors of Production

The resources used to produce goods and services are called **factors of production.** *The four basic factors of production are*

- *Land.*
- *Labor.*
- *Capital.*
- *Entrepreneurship.*

These are the *inputs* needed to produce desired *outputs*. To produce this textbook, for example, we needed paper, printing presses, a building, and lots of labor. We also needed

scarcity: Lack of enough resources to satisfy all desired uses of those resources.

factors of production: Resource inputs used to produce goods and services, such as land, labor, capital, and entrepreneurship.

people with good ideas who could put it together. To produce the education you're getting in this class, we need not only a textbook but a classroom, a teacher, a blackboard, and maybe a computer as well. Without factors of production, we simply can't produce anything.

Land. The first factor of production, land, refers not just to the ground but to all natural resources. Crude oil, water, air, and minerals are all included in our concept of "land."

Labor. Labor too has several dimensions. It's not simply a question of how many bodies there are. When we speak of labor as a factor of production, we refer to the skills and abilities to produce goods and services. Hence both the quantity and the quality of human resources are included in the "labor" factor.

Capital. The third factor of production is capital. In economics the term **capital** refers to final goods produced for use in further production. The residents of fishing villages in southern Thailand, for example, braid huge fishing nets. The sole purpose of these nets is to catch more fish. The nets themselves become a factor of production in obtaining the final goods (fish) that people desire. Thus they're regarded as *capital*. Blast furnaces used to make steel and desks used to equip offices are also capital inputs.

capital: Final goods produced for use in the production of other goods, such as equipment and structures.

Entrepreneurship. The more land, labor, and capital available, the greater the amount of potential output. A farmer with 10,000 acres, 12 employees, and six tractors can grow more crops than a farmer with half those resources. But there's no guarantee that he will. The farmer with fewer resources may have better ideas about what to plant, when to irrigate, or how to harvest the crops. *It's not just a matter of what resources you have but also of how well you use them.* This is where the fourth factor of production—**entrepreneurship**—comes in. The entrepreneur is the person who sees the opportunity for new or better products and brings together the resources needed for producing them. If it weren't for entrepreneurs, Thai fishers would still be using sticks to catch fish. Without entrepreneurship, farmers would still be milking their cows by hand. If someone hadn't thought of a way to miniaturize electronic circuits, you wouldn't be able to text your friends.

entrepreneurship: The assembling of resources to produce new or improved products and technologies.

The role of entrepreneurs in economic progress is a key issue in the market versus government debate. The British economist John Maynard Keynes argued that free markets unleash the "animal spirits" of entrepreneurs, propelling innovation, technology, and growth. Critics of government regulation argue that government interference in the marketplace, however well intentioned, tends to stifle those very same animal spirits.

Limits to Output

No matter how an economy is organized, there's a limit to how much it can produce. The most evident limit is the amount of resources available for producing goods and services. One reason the United States can produce so much is that it has nearly 4 million square miles of land. Tonga, with less than 300 square miles of land, will never produce as much. The United States also has a population of more than 320 million people. That's a lot less than China (1.4 billion) but far larger than 200 other nations (Tonga has a population of less than 125,000). So an abundance of raw resources gives us the potential to produce a lot of output. But that greater production capacity isn't enough to satisfy all our desires. We're constantly scrambling for additional resources to build more houses, make better movies, and provide more health care. That imbalance between available resources and our wish list is one of the things that makes the job of Economist in Chief so difficult.

The science of **economics** helps us frame these choices. In a nutshell, economics is the study of how people use scarce resources. How do you decide how much time to spend studying? How does Google decide how many workers to hire? How does Ford decide

economics: The study of how best to allocate scarce resources among competing uses.

whether to use its factories to produce sport utility vehicles or sedans? What share of a nation's resources should be devoted to space exploration, the delivery of health care services, or pollution control? In every instance, alternative ways of using scarce labor, land, and capital resources are available, and we have to choose one use over another.

OPPORTUNITY COSTS

Scientists have long sought to explore every dimension of space. President Kennedy initiated a lunar exploration program that successfully landed men on the moon on July 20, 1969. That only whetted the appetite for further space exploration. President George W. Bush initiated a program to land people on Mars, using the moon as a way station. Scientists believe that the biological, geophysical, and technical knowledge gained from the exploration of Mars will improve life here on Earth. But should we do it? In a world of unlimited resources the answer would be an easy "yes." But we don't live in that world.

Every time we use scarce resources in one way, we give up the opportunity to use them in other ways. If we use more resources to explore space, we have fewer resources available for producing earthly goods. The forgone earthly goods represent the **opportunity costs** of a Mars expedition. *Opportunity cost is what is given up to get something else.* Even a so-called free lunch has an opportunity cost (see the below cartoon). The resources used to produce the lunch could have been used to produce something else. A trip to Mars has a much higher opportunity cost. President Obama decided those opportunity costs were too high: he scaled back the Mars programs to make more resources available for Earthly uses (like highway construction and energy development).

Your economics class also has an opportunity cost. The building space used for your economics class can't be used to show movies at the same time. Your professor can't lecture (produce education) and repair motorcycles simultaneously. The decision to use these scarce resources (capital, labor) for an economics class implies producing less of other goods.

Even reading this book is costly. That cost is not measured in dollars and cents. The true (economic) cost is, instead, measured in terms of some alternative activity. What would you like to be doing right now? The more time you spend reading this book, the less time you have available for other uses of your time. The opportunity cost of reading this text is the best alternative use of your scarce time. If you are missing your favorite TV show, we'd say that show is the opportunity cost of reading this book. It is what you gave up to do this assignment. Hopefully, the benefits you get from studying will outweigh that cost. Otherwise this wouldn't be the best way to use your scarce time.

opportunity cost: The most desired goods or services that are forgone to obtain something else.

"There's no such thing as a free lunch."

© Dana Fradon/The New Yorker Collection/ www.cartoonbank.com.

Analysis: All goods and services have an opportunity cost. Even the resources used to produce a "free lunch" could have been used to produce something else.

Guns vs. Butter

One of the most difficult choices nations must make about resource use entails defense spending. After the September 11, 2001, terrorist attacks on the World Trade Center and Pentagon, American citizens overwhelmingly favored an increase in military spending. Even the unpopularity of the wars in Iraq and Afghanistan didn't quell the desire for more national defense. But national defense, like Mars exploration, requires the use of scarce resources; Americans wanted to feel *safe*. But there is a *cost* to assuring safety: the 1.4 million men and women who serve in the armed forces aren't available to build schools, program computers, or teach economics. Similarly, the land, labor, capital, and entrepreneurship devoted to producing military hardware aren't available for producing civilian goods. An *increase* in national defense implies more sacrifices of civilian goods and services. How many schools, hospitals, or cars are we willing to sacrifice in order to "produce" more national security? This is the "guns versus butter" dilemma that all nations confront.

PRODUCTION POSSIBILITIES

The opportunity costs implied by our every choice can be illustrated easily. Suppose a nation can produce only two goods, trucks and tanks. To keep things simple, assume that labor (workers) is the only factor of production needed to produce either good. Although other factors of production (land, machinery) are also needed in actual production, ignoring them for the moment does no harm. Let us assume further that we have a total of only 10 workers available per day to produce either trucks or tanks. Our initial problem is to determine the *limits* of output. How many trucks or tanks *can* be produced in a day with available resources?

Before going any further, notice how opportunity costs will affect the answer. If we use all 10 workers to produce trucks, no labor will be available to assemble tanks. In this case, forgone tanks would become the *opportunity cost* of a decision to employ all our resources in truck production.

We still don't know how many trucks could be produced with 10 workers or exactly how many tanks would be forgone by such a decision. To get these answers, we need more details about the production processes involved—specifically, how many workers are required to manufacture either good.

The Production Possibilities Curve

Table 1.1 summarizes the hypothetical choices, or **production possibilities,** that we confront in this case. Suppose we wanted to produce only trucks (i.e., no tanks). Row *A* of the table shows the *maximum* number of trucks we could produce. With 10 workers available and a labor requirement of 2 workers per truck, we can manufacture a maximum of five trucks per day.

Producing five trucks per day leaves no workers available to produce tanks. Our 10 available workers are all being used to produce trucks. On row *A* of Table 1.1 we've got "butter"

production possibilities: The alternative combinations of final goods and services that could be produced in a given time period with all available resources and technology.

TABLE 1.1

A Production Possibilities Schedule

As long as resources are limited, their use entails an opportunity cost. In this case, resources (labor) used to produce trucks can't be used for tank assembly at the same time. Hence the forgone tanks are the opportunity cost of additional trucks. If all our resources were used to produce trucks (row *A*), no tanks could be assembled. To produce tanks, we have to reduce truck production.

	Production Options	
	Output of Trucks per Day	Output of Tanks per Day
A	5	0
B	4	2.0
C	3	3.0
D	2	3.8
E	1	4.5
F	0	5.0

(trucks) but no "guns" (tanks). If we want tanks, we have to cut back on truck production. The remainder of Table 1.1 illustrates the trade-offs we confront in this simple case. By cutting truck production from five to four trucks per day (row *B*), we reduce labor use in truck production from 10 workers to 8. That leaves 2 workers available for other uses, including the production of tanks.

If we employ these remaining 2 workers to assemble tanks, we can build two tanks a day. We would then end up on row *B* of the table with four trucks and two tanks per day. What's the opportunity cost of these two tanks? It's the one additional truck (the fifth truck) that we could have produced but didn't.

As we proceed down the rows of Table 1.1, the nature of opportunity costs becomes apparent. Each additional tank built implies the loss (opportunity cost) of truck output. Likewise, every truck produced implies the loss of some tank output.

These trade-offs between truck and tank production are illustrated in the production possibilities curve of Figure 1.1. ***Each point on the production possibilities curve depicts an alternative mix of output* that could be produced.** In this case, each point represents a different combination of trucks and tanks that we could produce in a single day using all available resources (10 workers in this case).

Notice in particular how points *A* through *F* in Figure 1.1 represent the choices described in each row of Table 1.1. At point *A*, we're producing five trucks per day and no tanks. As we move down the curve from point *A* we're producing fewer trucks and more tanks. At point *B*, truck production has dropped from five to four vehicles per day while tank assembly has increased from zero to two. In other words, we've given up one truck to get two tanks assembled. The opportunity cost of those tanks is the one truck that is given up. A production possibilities curve, then, is simply a graphic summary of production possibilities, as described in Table 1.1. As such, ***the production possibilities curve illustrates two essential principles:***

- ***Scarce resources.*** There's a limit to the amount of output we can produce in a given time period with available resources and technology.
- ***Opportunity costs.*** We can obtain additional quantities of any particular good only by reducing the potential production of another good.

FIGURE 1.1

A Production Possibilities Curve

A production possibilities curve (PPC) describes the various output combinations that could be produced in a given time period with available resources and technology. It represents a menu of output choices an economy confronts.

Point *B* indicates that we could produce a *combination* of four trucks and two tanks per day. By producing one less truck, we could assemble a third tank and thus move to point *C*.

Points *A, D, E,* and *F* illustrate still other output combinations that could be produced. This curve is a graphic illustration of the production possibilities schedule in Table 1.1.

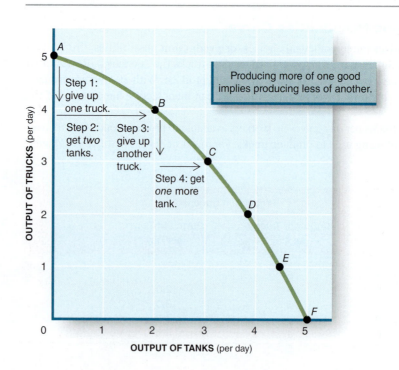

Increasing Opportunity Costs

The shape of the production possibilities curve reflects another limitation on our choices. Notice how opportunity costs increase as we move along the production possibilities curve. When we cut truck output from five to four (step 1, Figure 1.1), we get two tanks (step 2). When we cut truck production further, however (step 3), we get only one tank per truck given up (step 4). The opportunity cost of tank production is increasing. This process of increasing opportunity cost continues. By the time we give up the last truck (row *F*), tank output increases by only 0.5: we get only half a tank for the last truck given up. These increases in opportunity cost are reflected in the outward bend of the production possibilities curve.

Why do opportunity costs increase? Mostly because it's difficult to move resources from one industry to another. It's easy to transform trucks to tanks on a blackboard. In the real world, however, resources don't adapt so easily. Workers who assemble trucks may not have the right skills for tank assembly. As we continue to transfer labor from one industry to the other, we start getting fewer tanks for every truck we give up.

The difficulties entailed in transferring labor skills, capital, and entrepreneurship from one industry to another are so universal that we often speak of the *law* of *increasing opportunity cost*. This law says that we must give up ever-increasing quantities of other goods and services in order to get more of a particular good. The law isn't based solely on the limited versatility of individual workers. The *mix* of factor inputs makes a difference as well. Truck assembly requires less capital than tank assembly. In a pinch, wheels can be mounted on a truck almost completely by hand, whereas tank treads require more sophisticated machinery. As we move labor from truck assembly to tank assembly, available capital may restrict our output capabilities.

The Cost of North Korea's Military

The production possibilities curve illustrates why the core economic decision about WHAT to produce is so difficult. Consider, for example, North Korea's decision to maintain a large military. North Korea is a relatively small country: its population of 25 million ranks fiftieth in the world. Yet North Korea maintains the fifth-largest army in the world and continues to develop a nuclear weapons capability. To do so, it must allocate 16 percent of all its resources to feeding, clothing, and equipping its military forces. As a consequence, there aren't enough resources available to produce food. Without adequate machinery, seeds, fertilizer, or irrigation, Korea's farmers can't produce enough food to feed the population (see the World View on the next page). As Figure 1.2 illustrates, the opportunity cost of "guns" in Korea is a lot of needed "butter."

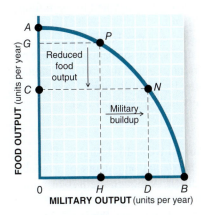

FIGURE 1.2
The Cost of War

North Korea devotes 16 percent of its output to the military. The opportunity cost of this decision is reduced output of food. As the military expands from 0H to 0D, food output drops from 0G to 0C.

WORLD VIEW

Chronic Food Shortage Shows Despite Efforts by North Korea to Hide It

NAMPO, North Korea—Along the sides of the road, people comb through the grass looking for edible weeds. In the center of town, a boy about 9 years old wears a tattered army jacket hanging below his knees. He has no shoes.

Sprawled on the lawn outside a bath house, poorly dressed people lie on the grass, either with no place better to go or no energy to do so at 10 a.m. on a weekday.

Despite efforts to keep North Korea's extreme poverty out of view, a glance around the countryside shows a population in distress. At the heart of the problem is a chronic food shortage. . . .

The UN World Food Program reached similar conclusions. In a recent survey of 375 North Korean households, more than 70 percent of North Koreans were found to be supplementing their diet with weeds and grasses foraged from the countryside. Such wild foods are difficult to digest, especially for children and the elderly.

The survey also determined that most adults had started skipping lunch, reducing their diet to two meals a day to cope with the food shortage.

These are some of the same signs that augured the mid-1990s famine that killed as many as 2 million people, 10 percent of the population.

—Barbara Demick

Source: "Hunger gnaws at N. Korea's facade," *Los Angeles Times,* November 2, 2008. Used with permission.

Rocket Launch Cost Enough to End Famine in North Korea for a Year

SEOUL—The rocket launched by North Korea on Sunday is believed to be an upgraded version of the country's Taepodong-2 missile, which was used in a failed missile test in 2006, according to a report by the South Korean military. . . .

A researcher at the National Intelligence Service estimated the cost of developing the missile at 300–500 million dollars, based on a previous statement by North Korean leader Kim Jong Il that the Taepodong-1 missile launched in 1998 cost 200–300 million dollars.

Insiders close to South Korean President Lee Myung-bak say the launch itself cost around 300 million dollars, enough to break the famine sweeping much of the nation for a year.

Source: *The Mainichi Daily News,* April 6, 2009. Used with permission.

ANALYSIS: North Korea's inability to feed itself is partly due to maintaining its large army: resources used for the military aren't available for producing food.

What is the opportunity cost of North Korea's army?

During World War II, the United States confronted a similar trade-off. In 1944 nearly 40 percent of all U.S. output was devoted to the military. Civilian goods were so scarce that they had to be rationed. Staples like butter, sugar, and gasoline were doled out in small quantities. Even golf balls were rationed. In North Korea, golf balls would be a luxury even without a military buildup. As the share of North Korea's output devoted to the military increased, even basic food production became more difficult.

Figure 1.3 illustrates how other nations divide available resources between military and civilian production. The $700 billion the United States now spends on national defense absorbs only 4 percent of total output. This made the opportunity costs of the post-9/11 military buildup and the wars in Iraq and Afghanistan less painful. By contrast, North Korea's commitment to military spending (16.3 percent) implies a very high opportunity cost.

Efficiency

efficiency: Maximum output of a good from the resources used in production.

Not all of the choices on the production possibilities curve are equally desirable. They are, however, all *efficient*. **Efficiency** means squeezing *maximum* output out of available resources. Every point of the PPC satisfies this condition. Although the *mix* of output changes as we move around the production possibilities curve (Figures 1.1 and 1.2), at every point we are getting as much *total* output as physically possible. Since efficiency in

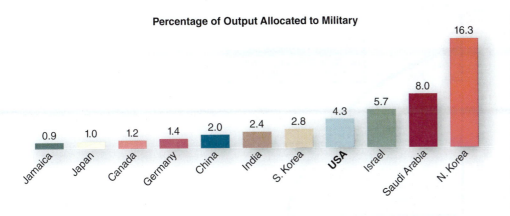

Percentage of Output Allocated to Military

Jamaica 0.9 · Japan 1.0 · Canada 1.2 · Germany 1.4 · China 2.0 · India 2.4 · S. Korea 2.8 · USA 4.3 · Israel 5.7 · Saudi Arabia 8.0 · N. Korea 16.3

FIGURE 1.3
The Military Share of Output

The share of total output allocated to the military indicates the opportunity cost of maintaining an army. North Korea has the highest cost, using 16.3 percent of its resources for military purposes. Although China and the United States have much larger armies, their military *share* of output is much smaller.

Source: U.S. Central Intelligence Agency (*WorldFactbook*, 2014).

production means simply getting the most from what you've got, **every point on the production possibilities curve is efficient.** At every point on the curve we are using all available resources in the best way we know how.

Inefficiency

There's no guarantee, of course, that we'll always use resources so efficiently. *A production possibilities curve shows* potential *output, not* actual *output.* If we're inefficient, actual output will be less than that potential. This happens. In the real world, workers sometimes loaf on the job. Or they call in sick and go to a baseball game instead of working. Managers don't always give the clearest directions or stay in touch with advancing technology. Even students sometimes fail to put forth their best effort on homework assignments. This kind of slippage can prevent us from achieving maximum production. When that happens, we end up *inside* the PPC rather than *on* it.

Point *Y* in Figure 1.4 illustrates the consequences of inefficient production. At point *Y*, we're producing only three trucks and two tanks. This is less than our potential. We could assemble a third tank without cutting back truck production (point *C*). Or we could get an extra truck without sacrificing any tank output (point *B*). Instead we're producing *inside* the production possibilities curve at point *Y*. **Whenever we're producing inside the production possibilities curve, we are forgoing the opportunity of producing (and consuming) additional output.**

Unemployment

We can end up inside the production possibilities curve by utilizing resources inefficiently or simply by not using all available resources. This happened repeatedly in the Great Recession of 2008–2009. In October 2009, more than 15 million Americans were unemployed (see the News below). These men and women were ready, willing, and available to work,

web click

To see how the share of U.S. output allocated to national defense has changed over time, visit the Government Printing Office website (**www.gpoaccess.gov/eop/tables11.html**) and scroll down to "Government Finance" data.

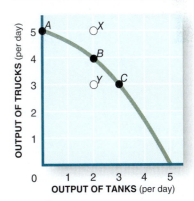

FIGURE 1.4
Points Inside and Outside the PPC Curve

Points outside the production possibilities curve (point *X*) are unattainable with available resources and technology. Points inside the PPC (point *Y*) represent the incomplete use of available resources. Only points on the PPC (*A, B, C*) represent maximum use of our production capabilities.

FIGURE 1.5

Growth: Increasing Production Possibilities

A production possibilities curve is based on *available* resources and technology. If more resources or better technology becomes available, production possibilities will increase. This economic growth is illustrated by the shift from PP_1 to PP_2.

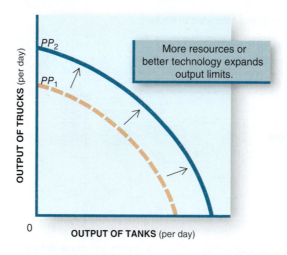

More resources or better technology expands output limits.

economic growth: An increase in output (real GDP); an expansion of production possibilities.

but no one hired them. As a result, we were stuck *inside* the PPC, producing less output than we could have. The goal of U.S. economic policy is to create more jobs and keep the United States on its production possibilities curve.

Economic Growth

The challenge of getting to the production possibilities curve increases with each passing day. People are born every day. As they age, they enter the labor force as new workers. Technology, too, keeps advancing each year. These increases in available labor and technology keep pushing the producing possibilities curve outward. This **economic growth** is a good thing in the sense that it allows us to produce more goods and raise living standards. But it also means that we have to keep creating more jobs every year just to stay on the PPC.

Figures 1.4 and 1.5 illustrate how economic growth raises our living standards. Point *X* in Figure 1.4 lies outside the PPC. It is an enticing point because it suggests we could get more trucks (five) without sacrificing any tanks (two). Unfortunately, point *X* is only a mirage. *All output combinations that lie outside the PPC are unattainable in the short run.*

In the long run, however, resources and technology increase, shifting the PPC outward, as in Figure 1.5. Before the appearance of new resources or better technology, our production possibilities were limited by the curve PP_1. *With more resources or better technology, our production possibilities increase.* This greater capacity to produce is represented by curve PP_2. This outward shift of the production possibilities curve is the essence of economic growth. With economic growth, countries can have more guns *and* more butter. Without economic growth, living standards decline as the population grows. This is the problem that plagues some of the world's poorest nations, where population increases every year but output often doesn't (see Table 2.1).

THREE BASIC DECISIONS

Production possibilities define the output choices that a nation confronts. From these choices every nation must make some basic decisions. As we noted at the beginning of this chapter, the three core economic questions are

- *WHAT to produce.*
- *HOW to produce.*
- *FOR WHOM to produce.*

WHAT

There are millions of points along a production possibilities curve, and each one represents a different mix of output. We can choose only *one* of these points at any time. The point we choose determines what mix of output gets produced. That choice determines how many guns are produced, and how much butter—or how many space expeditions and how many sewage treatment facilities.

The production possibilities curve doesn't tell us which mix of output is best; it just lays out a menu of available choices. It's up to us to pick out the one and only mix of output that will be produced at a given time. This WHAT decision is a basic decision every nation must make.

HOW

Decisions must also be made about HOW to produce. Should we generate electricity by burning coal, smashing atoms, or harnessing solar power? Should we harvest ancient forests even if that destroys endangered owls or other animal species? Should we dump municipal and industrial waste into nearby rivers, or should we dispose of it in some other way? Should we use children to harvest crops and stitch clothes, or should we use only adult labor? There are lots of different ways of producing goods and services, and someone has to make a decision about which production methods to use. The HOW decision is a question not just of efficiency but of social values as well.

FOR WHOM

After we've decided what to produce and how, we must address a third basic question: FOR WHOM? Who is going to get the output produced? Should everyone get an equal share? Should everyone wear the same clothes and drive identical cars? Should some people get to enjoy seven-course banquets while others forage in garbage cans for food scraps? How should the goods and services an economy produces be distributed? Are we satisfied with the way output is now distributed?

THE MECHANISMS OF CHOICE

Answers to the questions of WHAT, HOW, and FOR WHOM largely define an economy. But who formulates the answers? Who actually decides which goods are produced, what technologies are used, or how incomes are distributed?

The Invisible Hand of a Market Economy

Adam Smith had an answer back in 1776. In his classic work *The Wealth of Nations,* the Scottish economist Smith said the "invisible hand" determines what gets produced, how, and for whom. The invisible hand he referred to wasn't a creature from a science fiction movie but, instead, a characterization of the way markets work.

Consider the decision about how many cars to produce in the United States. Who makes that decision? There's no "auto czar" who dictates how many vehicles will be produced this year. Not even General Motors can make such a decision. Instead the *market* decides how many cars to produce. Millions of consumers signal their desire to have a car by browsing the Internet, visiting showrooms, and buying cars. Their purchases flash a green light to producers, who see the potential to earn more profits. To do so, they'll increase auto output. If consumers stop buying cars, profits will disappear. Producers will respond by reducing output, laying off workers, and even closing factories as they did during the recession of 2008–2009.

Notice how the invisible hand moves us along the production possibilities curve. If consumers demand more cars, the mix of output will include more cars and fewer

market mechanism: The use of market prices and sales to signal desired outputs (or resource allocations).

laissez faire: The doctrine of "leave it alone," of nonintervention by government in the market mechanism.

of other goods. If auto production is scaled back, the displaced autoworkers will end up producing other goods and services, changing the mix of output in the opposite direction.

Adam Smith's invisible hand is now called the **market mechanism.** Notice that it doesn't require any direct contact between consumers and producers. Communication is indirect, transmitted by market prices and sales. Indeed, *the essential feature of the market mechanism is the price signal.* If you want something and have sufficient income, you can buy it. If enough people do the same thing, the total sales of that product will rise, and perhaps its price will as well. Producers, seeing sales and prices rise, will want to exploit this profit potential. To do so, they'll attempt to acquire a larger share of available resources and use it to produce the goods we desire. That's how the "invisible hand" works.

The market mechanism can also answer the HOW question. To maximize their profits, producers seek the lowest-cost method of producing a good. By observing prices in the marketplace, they can identify the cheapest method and adopt it.

The market mechanism can also resolve the FOR WHOM question. A market distributes goods to the highest bidder. Individuals who are willing and able to pay the most for a product tend to get it in a pure market economy. That's why someone else—not you—is driving the new Maserati Quattroporte.

Adam Smith was so impressed with the ability of the market mechanism to answer the basic WHAT, HOW, and FOR WHOM questions that he urged government to "leave it alone" **(laissez faire). Adam Smith believed the price signals and responses of the marketplace were likely to do a better job of allocating resources than any government could.**

Government Intervention

The laissez-faire policy Adam Smith favored has always had its share of critics. The German economist Karl Marx emphasized how free markets tend to concentrate wealth and power in the hands of the few at the expense of the many. As he saw it, unfettered markets permit the capitalists (those who own the machinery and factories) to enrich themselves while the proletariat (the workers) toil long hours for subsistence wages. **Marx argued that the government not only had to intervene but had to *own* all the means of production**—the factories, the machinery, the land—in order to avoid savage inequalities. In *Das Kapital* (1867) and the revolutionary *Communist Manifesto* (1848), he laid the foundation for a communist state in which the government would be the master of economic outcomes.

The British economist John Maynard Keynes offered a less drastic solution. The market, he conceded, was pretty efficient in organizing production and building better mousetraps. However, individual producers and workers had no control over the broader economy. The cumulative actions of so many economic agents could easily tip the economy in the wrong direction. A completely unregulated market might veer off in one direction and then another as producers all rushed to increase output at the same time or throttled back production in a herdlike manner. The government, Keynes reasoned, could act like a pressure gauge, letting off excess steam or building it up as the economy needed. With the government maintaining overall balance in the economy, the market could live up to its performance expectations. While assuring a stable, full-employment environment, the government might also be able to redress excessive inequalities. **In Keynes's view, government should play an active but not all-inclusive role in managing the economy.**

Continuing Debates

These historical views shed perspective on today's political debates. The core of most debates is some variation of the WHAT, HOW, or FOR WHOM questions. Much of the debate is how these questions should be answered. Conservatives favor Adam Smith's

WORLD VIEW

Market Reliance vs. Government Reliance?

A public opinion poll conducted in countries from around the world found a striking global consensus that the free market economic system is best. In all but one country polled, a majority or plurality agreed with the statement that "the free enterprise system and free market economy is the best system on which to base the future of the world."

Source: GlobeScan Toronto—London—San Francisco 2010.

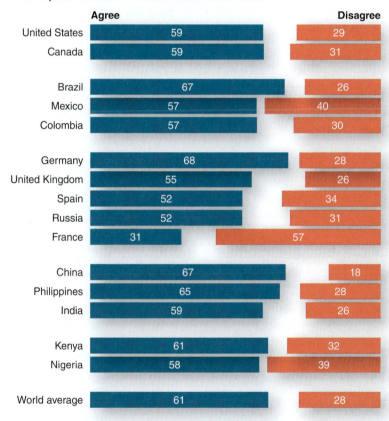

The free enterprise system and free market economy is the best system on which to base the future of the world.

Country	Agree	Disagree
United States	59	29
Canada	59	31
Brazil	67	26
Mexico	57	40
Colombia	57	30
Germany	68	28
United Kingdom	55	26
Spain	52	34
Russia	52	31
France	31	57
China	67	18
Philippines	65	28
India	59	26
Kenya	61	32
Nigeria	58	39
World average	61	28

ANALYSIS: People around the world believe that markets do a good job of answering the core questions of WHAT, HOW, and FOR WHOM.

web click

Comparative data on the percentage of goods and services the various national governments provide are available from the Penn World Tables at **www.pwt.econ.upenn.edu.**

laissez-faire approach, with minimal government interference in the markets. Liberals, by contrast, think government intervention is needed to improve market outcomes. Conservatives resist workplace regulation, price controls, and minimum wages because such interventions might impair market efficiency. Liberals argue that such interventions temper the excesses of the market and promote both equity and efficiency.

World Opinion. The debate over how best to manage the economy is not unique to the United States. **Countries around the world confront the same choice between reliance on the market and reliance on the government.** Public opinion clearly favors the market system, as the above World View documents. Yet few countries have ever relied exclusively on either the markets or the government to manage their economy.

web click

To learn how the Heritage Foundation defines economic freedom, visit its website at **www.heritage.org/index.**

WORLD VIEW

Index of Economic Freedom

Hong Kong ranks number one among the world's nations in economic freedom. It achieves that status with low tax rates, free-trade policies, minimal government regulation, and secure property rights. These and other economic indicators place Hong Kong at the top of the Heritage Foundation's 2014 country rankings by the degree of "economic freedom." The "most free" and the "least free" (repressed) economies on the list of 186 countries are listed here:

Greatest Economic Freedom	Least Economic Freedom
Hong Kong	North Korea
Singapore	Cuba
Australia	Zimbabwe
Switzerland	Venezuela
New Zealand	Eritrea
Canada	Iran
Chile	Congo
Mauritius	Turkmenistan

Source: Heritage Foundation, *2014 Index of Economic Freedom,* Washington, DC, 2014. Used with permission. **www.heritage.org**.

ANALYSIS: Nations differ in how much they rely on market signals or government intervention to shape economic outcomes. Nations that rely the least on government intervention score highest ("most free") on this Index of Economic Freedom.

Degrees of Market Reliance. The World View above categorizes nations by the extent of their actual market reliance. Hong Kong scores high on this "Index of Economic Freedom" because its tax rates are relatively low, the public sector is comparatively small, and there are few restrictions on private investment or trade. By contrast, North Korea scores extremely low because the government owns all property, directly allocates resources, sets wages, and limits trade. In other words, Hong Kong is the most market-reliant; North Korea is the most government-reliant.

The Heritage rankings simply *describe* differences in the extent of market/government reliance across different nations. By themselves, they don't tell us which mix of market and government reliance is best. Moreover, the individual rankings change over time. In 1989 Russia began a massive transformation from a state-controlled economy to a more market-oriented economy. Some of the former republics (e.g., Estonia) became relatively free, while others (e.g., Turkmenistan) still rely on extensive government control of the economy. China has greatly expanded the role of private markets in the last 20 years, and Cuba is grudgingly moving in the same direction in fits and starts. Venezuela has moved in the opposite direction, with sharply increased government control of production and prices.

Notice that the United States is not on the World View list. Although the United States relies heavily on private markets to make WHAT, HOW, and FOR WHOM decisions, it lags behind Hong Kong, Canada, and other nations on the Heritage Index. In 2014, the United States came in 12th, down a few notches from earlier years. That modest decline was due to the increased regulation, higher taxes, and increased government spending that the Obama administration adopted in response to the Great Recession. The tug-of-war between more government regulation and more market reliance continues—in both public opinion and the U.S. Congress.

A Mixed Economy

No one advocates *complete* dependence on markets, nor *total* government control of economic resources. Neither Adam Smith's invisible hand nor the governments' very visible hand always works perfectly. As a result, ***the United States, like most nations, uses a combination of market signals and government directives to direct economic outcomes.*** The resulting compromises are called **mixed economies.**

The reluctance of countries around the world to rely exclusively on either market signals or government directives is due to the recognition that both mechanisms can and do fail on occasion. As we've seen, market signals are capable of answering the three core questions of WHAT, HOW, and FOR WHOM. But the answers may not be the best possible ones.

mixed economy: An economy that uses both market signals and government directives to allocate goods and resources.

Market Failure

When market signals don't give the best possible answers to the WHAT, HOW, and FOR WHOM questions, we say that the market mechanism has *failed.* Specifically, **market failure** means that the invisible hand has failed to achieve the best possible outcomes. If the market fails, we end up with the wrong (*sub*optimal) mix of output, too much unemployment, polluted air, or an inequitable distribution of income.

market failure: An imperfection in the market mechanism that prevents optimal outcomes.

In a market-driven economy, for example, producers will select production methods based on cost. Cost-driven production decisions, however, may encourage a factory to spew pollution into the environment rather than to use cleaner but more expensive methods of production. The resulting pollution may be so bad that society ends up worse off as a result of the extra production. In such a case we may need government intervention to force better answers to the WHAT and HOW questions.

We could also let the market decide who gets to consume cigarettes. Anyone who had enough money to buy a pack of cigarettes would then be entitled to smoke. What if, however, children aren't experienced enough to balance the risks of smoking against the pleasures? What if nonsmokers are harmed by secondhand smoke? In this case as well, the market's answer to the FOR WHOM question might not be optimal.

Government Failure

Government intervention may move us closer to our economic goals. If so, the resulting mix of market signals and government directives would be an improvement over a purely market-driven economy. But government intervention may fail as well. **Government failure** occurs when government intervention fails to improve market outcomes or actually makes them worse.

government failure: Government intervention that fails to improve economic outcomes.

Government failure often occurs in unintended ways. For example, the government may intervene to force an industry to clean up its pollution. The government's directives may impose such high costs that the industry closes factories and lays off workers. Some cutbacks in output might be appropriate, but they could also prove excessive. The government might also mandate pollution control technologies that are too expensive or even obsolete. None of this has to happen, but it might. If it does, government failure will have worsened economic outcomes.

The government might also fail if it interferes with the market's answer to the FOR WHOM question. For 50 years, communist China distributed goods by government directive, not market performance. Incomes were more equal, but uniformly low. To increase output and living standards, China turned to market incentives. As entrepreneurs responded to these incentives, living standards rose dramatically—even while inequality increased. That surge in living standards made the vast majority of Chinese believers in the power of free markets (see the World View on page 15).

Excessive taxes and transfer payments can also worsen economic outcomes. If the government raises taxes on the rich to pay welfare benefits for the poor, neither the rich nor the poor may see much purpose in working. In that case, the attempt to give everybody a "fair" share of the pie might end up shrinking the size of the pie. If that happened, society could end up worse off.

Seeking Balance

None of these failures has to occur. But they might. ***The challenge for any society is to minimize economic failures by selecting the appropriate balance of market signals and*** *government directives.* This isn't an easy task. It requires that we know how markets work and why they sometimes fail. We also need to know what policy options the government has and how and when they might work.

WHAT ECONOMICS IS ALL ABOUT

Understanding how economies function is the basic purpose of studying economics. We seek to know how an economy is organized, how it behaves, and how successfully it achieves its basic objectives. Then, if we're lucky, we can discover better ways of attaining those same objectives.

Ends vs. Means

Economists don't formulate an economy's objectives. Instead they focus on the *means* available for achieving given *goals*. In 1978, for example, the U.S. Congress identified "full employment" as a major economic goal. Congress then directed future presidents (and their economic advisers) to formulate policies that would enable us to achieve full employment. The economist's job is to help design policies that will best achieve this and other economic goals.

Normative vs. Positive Analysis

The distinction between ends and means is mirrored in the difference between *normative* analysis and *positive* analysis. Normative analysis incorporates subjective judgments about what *ought* to be done. Positive analysis focuses on how things might be done without subjective judgments of what is "best." The Heritage Index of Economic Freedom (World View, page 16), for example, constitutes a *positive* analysis to the extent that it objectively describes global differences in the extent of market reliance. That effort entails collecting, sorting, and ranking mountains of data. Heritage slides into *normative* analysis when it suggests that market reliance is tantamount to "economic freedom" and inherently superior to more government intervention—that markets are good and governments are bad.

Debates over the core FOR WHOM question likewise reflect both positive and normative analysis. A positive analysis would observe that the U.S. incomes are very "unequal," with the richest 20 percent of the population getting half of all income (see Table 2.3). That's an observable fact—that is, positive analysis. To characterize that same distribution as "inequitable" or "unfair" is to transform (positive) fact into (normative) judgment. Economists are free, of course, to offer their judgments but must be careful to distinguish positive and normative perspectives.

Macro vs. Micro

The study of economics is typically divided into two parts: macroeconomics and microeconomics. **Macroeconomics** focuses on the behavior of an entire economy—the "big picture." In macroeconomics we worry about such national goals as full employment, control of inflation, and economic growth, without worrying about the well-being or behavior of specific individuals or groups. The essential concern of macroeconomics is to understand and improve the performance of the economy as a whole.

Microeconomics is concerned with the details of this big picture. In microeconomics we focus on the individuals, firms, and government agencies that actually compose the larger economy. Our interest here is in the behavior of individual economic actors. What are their goals? How can they best achieve these goals with their limited resources? How will they respond to various incentives and opportunities?

A primary concern of *macro*economics, for example, is to determine how much money, *in total,* consumers will spend on goods and services. In *micro*economics, the focus is much narrower. In micro, attention is paid to purchases of *specific* goods and services rather than just aggregated totals. Macro likewise concerns itself with the level of *total*

---

macroeconomics: The study of aggregate economic behavior, of the economy as a whole.

---

microeconomics: The study of individual behavior in the economy, of the components of the larger economy.

---

business investment, while micro examines how *individual* businesses make their investment decisions.

Although they operate at different levels of abstraction, macro and micro are intrinsically related. Macro (aggregate) outcomes depend on micro behavior, and micro (individual) behavior is affected by macro outcomes. One can't fully understand how an economy works until one understands how all the individual participants behave. But just as you can drive a car without knowing how its engine is constructed, you can observe how an economy runs without completely disassembling it. In macroeconomics we observe that the car goes faster when the accelerator is depressed and that it slows when the brake is applied. That's all we need to know in most situations. At times, however, the car breaks down. When it does, we have to know something more about how the pedals work. This leads us into micro studies. How does each part work? Which ones can or should be fixed?

Our interest in microeconomics is motivated by more than our need to understand how the larger economy works. The "parts" of the economic engine are people. To the extent that we care about the well-being of individuals, we have a fundamental interest in microeconomic behavior and outcomes. In this regard, we examine how individual consumers and business firms seek to achieve specific goals in the marketplace. The goals aren't always related to output. Gary Becker won the 1992 Nobel Prize in Economics for demonstrating how economic principles also affect decisions to marry, to have children, to engage in criminal activities—or even to complete homework assignments in an economics class.

Theory vs. Reality

The distinction between macroeconomics and microeconomics is one of many simplifications we make in studying economic behavior. The economy is much too vast and complex to describe and explain in one course (or one lifetime). Accordingly, we focus on basic relationships, ignoring annoying detail. In so doing, we isolate basic principles of economic behavior and then use those principles to predict economic events and develop economic policies. This means that we formulate theories, or *models,* of economic behavior and then use those theories to evaluate and design economic policy.

Our model of consumer behavior assumes, for example, that people buy less of a good when its price rises. In reality, however, people *may* buy *more* of a good at increased prices, especially if those high prices create a certain snob appeal or if prices are expected to increase still further. In predicting consumer responses to price increases, we typically ignore such possibilities by *assuming* that the price of the good in question is the *only* thing that changes. This assumption of "other things remaining equal" (unchanged) (in Latin, *ceteris paribus*) allows us to make straightforward predictions. If instead we described consumer responses to increased prices in any and all circumstances (allowing everything to change at once), every prediction would be accompanied by a book full of exceptions and qualifications. We'd look more like lawyers than economists.

ceteris paribus: The assumption of nothing else changing.

Although the assumption of *ceteris paribus* makes it easier to formulate economic theory and policy, it also increases the risk of error. If other things do change in significant ways, our predictions (and policies) may fail. But like weather forecasters, we continue to make predictions, knowing that occasional failure is inevitable. In so doing, we're motivated by the conviction that it's better to be approximately right than to be dead wrong.

Imperfect Knowledge. One last word of warning before you read further. Economics claims to be a science in pursuit of basic truths. We want to understand and explain how the economy works without getting tangled up in subjective value judgments. This may be an impossible task. First, it's not clear where the truth lies. For more than 200 years economists have been arguing about what makes the economy tick. None of the competing theories has performed spectacularly well. Indeed, few economists have successfully predicted major economic events with any consistency. Even annual forecasts of inflation, unemployment, and output are regularly in error. Worse still, never-ending arguments about what caused a major economic event continue long after it occurs. In fact, economists are still arguing over the primary causes of the Great Depression of the 1930s!

In view of all these debates and uncertainties, don't expect to learn everything there is to know about the economy today in this text or course. Our goals are more modest. We want to develop a reasonable perspective on economic behavior, an understanding of basic principles. With this foundation, you should acquire a better view of how the economy works. Daily news reports on economic events should make more sense. Congressional debates on tax and budget policies should take on more meaning. You may even develop some insights that you can apply toward running a business, planning a career, or simply managing your scarce time and money more efficiently.

THE ECONOMY TOMORROW

HARNESSING THE SUN

Powering our homes with solar power is an exciting prospect. Today, more than 50 percent of our electricity is generated from the burning of oil and coal. These fossil fuels pollute the air, damage the land, and, as we saw in the 2010 BP oil spill, damage marine life as well. By contrast, we don't have to burn anything to generate solar power. We just need to harness that power by absorbing it in solar panels that convert solar radiation into electricity. The U.S. Department of the Interior says solar stations built in the deserts of the southwestern states could deliver 2,300 gigawatts of energy, more than double America's entire electricity consumption. The substitution of solar power for fossil fuels would also reduce America's dependence on imported oil.

Solar power could also be used to fuel our cars. When automakers peer into the future, they see fleets of electric cars. Those fleets will have to be continuously charged with electricity. Why not solar-powered recharging stations? Just think how much that gasoline-to-solar conversion would help clean up the air we breathe!

Opportunity Costs

It's easy to get excited about a solar-powered future. But before we jump on the solar bandwagon, we have to at least consider the costs involved. Sure, the sun's rays are free. But you need a lot of capital investment to harness that solar power. Solar panels on the roof don't come free. Nor do solar-powered electrical charging stations, solar power plants, or the electrical grids that distribute electricity to users. President Obama set aside $300 million in the 2011 budget as a mere down payment on the development of solar power. The full-scale development of solar power infrastructure would cost *trillions* of dollars.

Remember, economists think in terms of real resources, not money. Paper money doesn't build solar panels; it takes real factors of production—land, labor, capital, and entrepreneurship. Those resources—worth trillions of dollars—could be used to produce something else. If we invested that many resources in medical technology, we might cure cancer, find an antidote for the AIDS virus, and maybe even eradicate the flu. Investing that many resources in education might make college not only more enjoyable but a lot more productive as well. To invest all those resources in solar development implies that solar development trumps all other social goals. In deciding whether and how intensively to develop solar power, we have to assess opportunity costs—what goods and services we implicitly forsake in order to harness the sun.

web click

The largest solar thermal power station in the United States is located in the Mojave Desert of California. For more information, see the National Renewable Energy Laboratory (NREL) at **www.nrel.gov,** then click the "Science and Technology" tab.

SUMMARY

- Scarcity is a basic fact of economic life. Factors of production (land, labor, capital, entrepreneurship) are scarce in relation to our desires for goods and services.   **LO1-1**
- All economic activity entails opportunity costs. Factors of production (resources) used to produce one output cannot simultaneously be used to produce something else. When

we choose to produce one thing, we forsake the opportunity to produce some other good or service.   **LO1-1**
- A production possibilities curve (PPC) illustrates the limits to production—the various combinations of goods and services that could be produced in a given period if all available resources and technology are used efficiently.

The PPC also illustrates opportunity costs—what is given up to get more of something else.   **LO1-2**
- The bent shape of the PPC reflects the law of increasing opportunity costs: Increasing quantities of any good can be obtained only by sacrificing ever-increasing quantities of other goods.   **LO1-2**
- Inefficient or incomplete use of resources will fail to attain production possibilities. Additional resources or better technologies will expand them. This is the essence of economic growth.   **LO1-2**
- Every country must decide WHAT to produce, HOW to produce, and FOR WHOM to produce with its limited resources.   **LO1-3**
- The WHAT, HOW, and FOR WHOM choices can be made by the market mechanism or by government directives.

Most nations are mixed economies, using a combination of these two choice mechanisms.   **LO1-4**
- Market failure exists when market signals generate suboptimal outcomes. Government failure occurs when government intervention worsens economic outcomes. The challenge for economic theory and policy is to find the mix of market signals and government directives that best fulfills our social and economic goals.   **LO1-4**
- The study of economics focuses on the broad question of resource allocation. Macroeconomics is concerned with allocating the resources of an entire economy to achieve aggregate economic goals (e.g., full employment). Microeconomics focuses on the behavior and goals of individual market participants.   **LO1-3**

Key Terms

scarcity	production possibilities	market failure
factors of production	efficiency	government failure
capital	economic growth	macroeconomics
entrepreneurship	market mechanism	microeconomics
economics	laissez faire	*ceteris paribus*
opportunity cost	mixed economy	

Questions for Discussion

1. What opportunity costs did you incur in reading this chapter? If you read another chapter today, would your opportunity cost (per chapter) increase? Explain.   **LO1-1**
2. How much time could you spend on homework in a day? How much do you spend? How do you decide?   **LO1-1**
3. What's the real cost of the food in the "free lunch" cartoon on page 6?   **LO1-1**
4. How might a nation's production possibilities be affected by the following?   **LO1-2**
   a. New solar technology.
   b. An increase in immigration.
   c. An increase in military spending.
   d. An increase in college attendance.
5. What are the opportunity costs of developing wind farms to generate "clean" electricity? Should we make the investment?   **LO1-1**

6. Who would go to college in a completely private (market) college system? How does government intervention change this FOR WHOM outcome?   **LO1-3**
7. Why do people around the world have so much faith in free markets (World View, p. 15)?   **LO1-4**
8. How many resources should we allocate to space exploration? How will we make this decision?   **LO1-4**
9. What is the connection between North Korea's missile program and its hunger problem? (World View, p. 10)   **LO1-1**
10. Why might more reliance on markets rather than government be desirable? When and how might it be undesirable?   **LO1-4**

    mobile app Visit your mobile app store and download the Schiller: Study Econ app *today*!

APPENDIX

USING GRAPHS

Economists like to draw graphs. In fact, we didn't even make it through the first chapter without a few graphs. This appendix looks more closely at the way graphs are drawn and used. The basic purpose of a graph is to illustrate a relationship between two *variables*. Consider, for example, the relationship between grades and studying. In general, we expect that additional hours of study time will lead to higher grades. Hence we should be able to see a distinct relationship between hours of study time and grade point average.

Suppose that we actually surveyed all the students taking this course with regard to their study time and grade point averages. The resulting information can be compiled in a table such as Table A.1.

According to the table, students who don't study at all can expect an F in this course. To get a C, the average student apparently spends 8 hours a week studying. All those who study 16 hours a week end up with an A in the course.

These relationships between grades and studying can also be illustrated on a graph. Indeed, the whole purpose of a graph is to summarize numerical relationships.

We begin to construct a graph by drawing horizontal and vertical boundaries, as in Figure A.1. These boundaries are called the *axes* of the graph. On the vertical axis (often called the *y*-axis) we measure one of the variables; the other variable is measured on the horizontal axis (the *x*-axis).

In this case, we shall measure the grade point average on the vertical axis. We start at the *origin* (the intersection of the two axes) and count upward, letting the distance between horizontal lines represent half (0.5) a grade point. Each horizontal line is numbered, up to the maximum grade point average of 4.0.

TABLE A.1

Hypothetical Relationship of Grades to Study Time

Study Time (Hours per Week)	Grade Point Average
16	4.0 (A)
14	3.5 (B+)
12	3.0 (B)
10	2.5 (C+)
8	2.0 (C)
6	1.5 (D+)
4	1.0 (D)
2	0.5 (F+)
0	0.0 (F)

web click

For online practice with graphs, visit **http://cls.syr.edu/mathtuneup/pretest/**.

FIGURE A.1

The Relationship of Grades to Study Time

The upward (positive) slope of the curve indicates that additional studying is associated with higher grades. The average student (2.0, or C grade) studies 8 hours per week. This is indicated by point *M* on the graph.

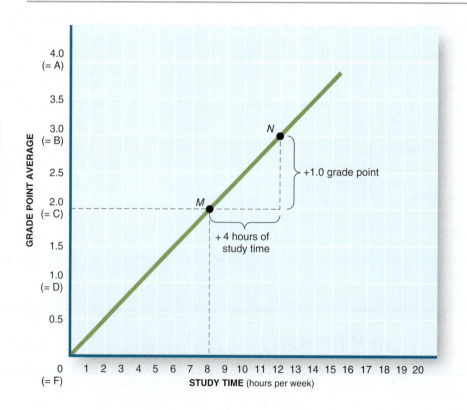

The number of hours each week spent doing homework is measured on the horizontal axis. We begin at the origin again and count to the right. The *scale* (numbering) proceeds in increments of 1 hour, up to 20 hours per week.

When both axes have been labeled and measured, we can begin illustrating the relationship between study time and grades. Consider the typical student who does 8 hours of homework per week and has a 2.0 (C) grade point average. We illustrate this relationship by first locating 8 hours on the horizontal axis. We then move up from that point a distance of 2.0 grade points, to point *M*. Point *M* tells us that 8 hours of study time per week are typically associated with a 2.0 grade point average.

The rest of the information in Table A.1 is drawn (or *plotted*) on the graph the same way. To illustrate the average grade for people who study 12 hours per week, we move upward from the number 12 on the horizontal axis until we reach the height of 3.0 on the vertical axis. At that intersection, we draw another point (point *N*).

Once we've plotted the various points describing the relationship of study time to grades, we may connect them with a line or curve. This line (curve) is our summary. In this case, the line slopes upward to the right—that is, it has a *positive* slope. This slope indicates that more hours of study time are associated with *higher* grades. Were higher grades associated with *less* study time, the curve in Figure A.1 would have a *negative* slope (downward from left to right).

Slopes

The upward slope of Figure A.1 tells us that higher grades are associated with increased amounts of study time. That same curve also tells us *by how much* grades tend to rise with study time. According to point *M* in Figure A.1, the average student studies 8 hours per week and earns a C (2.0 grade point average). To earn a B (3.0 average), students apparently need to study an average of 12 hours per week (point *N*). Hence an increase of 4 hours of study time per week is associated with a 1-point increase in grade point average. This relationship between *changes* in study time and *changes* in grade point average is expressed by the steepness, or *slope,* of the graph.

The slope of any graph is calculated as

$$\text{Slope} = \frac{\textbf{Vertical distance between two points}}{\textbf{Horizontal distance between two points}}$$

In our example, the vertical distance between *M* and *N* represents a change in grade point average. The horizontal distance between these two points represents the change in study time. Hence the slope of the graph between points *M* and *N* is equal to

$$\text{Slope} = \frac{\textbf{3.0 grade} - \textbf{2.0 grade}}{\textbf{12 hours} - \textbf{8 hours}} = \frac{\textbf{1 grade point}}{\textbf{4 hours}}$$

In other words, a 4-hour increase in study time (from 8 to 12 hours) is associated with a 1-point increase in grade point average (see Figure A.1).

Shifts

The relationship between grades and studying illustrated in Figure A.1 isn't inevitable. It's simply a graphical illustration of student experiences, as revealed in our hypothetical survey. The relationship between study time and grades could be quite different.

Suppose that the university decided to raise grading standards, making it more difficult to achieve higher grades. To achieve a C, a student now would need to study 12 hours per week, not just 8 (as in Figure A.1). Whereas students could previously get a B by studying 12 hours per week, now they'd have to study 16 hours to get that grade.

Figure A.2 illustrates the new grading standards. Notice that the new curve lies to the right of the earlier curve. We say that the curve has *shifted* to reflect a change in the

FIGURE A.2

A Shift

When a relationship between two variables changes, the entire curve *shifts*. In this case a tougher grading policy alters the relationship between study time and grades. To get a C, one must now study 12 hours per week (point R), not just 8 hours (point M).

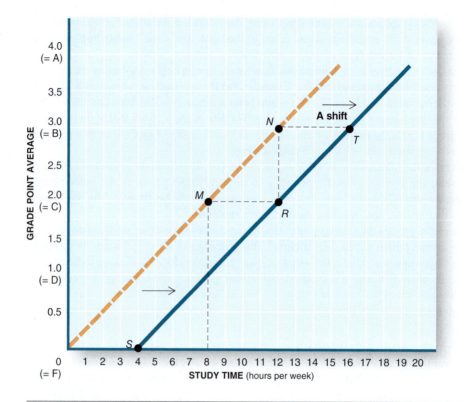

relationship between study time and grades. Point *R* indicates that 12 hours of study time now "produce" a C, not a B (point *N* on the old curve). Students who now study only 4 hours per week (point *S*) will fail. Under the old grading policy, they could have at least gotten a D. **When a curve shifts, the underlying relationship between the two variables has changed.**

A shift may also change the slope of the curve. In Figure A.2, the new grading curve is parallel to the old one; it therefore has the same slope. Under either the new grading policy or the old one, a 4-hour increase in study time leads to a 1-point increase in grades. Therefore, the slope of both curves in Figure A.2 is

$$\text{Slope} = \frac{\text{Vertical change}}{\text{Horizontal change}} = \frac{1}{4}$$

This too may change, however. Figure A.3 illustrates such a possibility. In this case, zero study time still results in an F. But now the payoff for additional studying is reduced. Now it takes 6 hours of study time to get a D (1.0 grade point), not 4 hours as before. Likewise, another 4 hours of study time (to a total of 10) raise the grade by only two-thirds of a point. It takes 6 hours to raise the grade a full point. The slope of the new line is therefore

$$\text{Slope} = \frac{\text{Vertical change}}{\text{Horizontal change}} = \frac{1}{6}$$

The new curve in Figure A.3 has a smaller slope than the original curve and so lies below it. What all this means is that it now takes a greater effort to improve your grade.

Linear vs. Nonlinear Curves

In Figures A.1–A.3 the relationship between grades and studying is represented by a straight line—that is, a *linear curve*. A distinguishing feature of linear curves is that they have the same (constant) slope throughout. In Figure A.1 it appears that *every* 4-hour increase in study time is associated with a 1-point increase in average grades. In Figure A.3

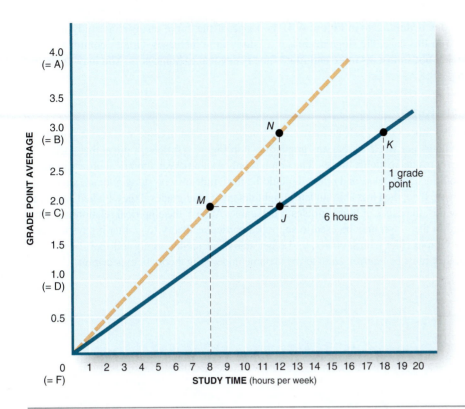

FIGURE A.3

A Change in Slope

When a curve shifts, it may change its slope as well. In this case a new grading policy makes each higher grade more difficult to reach. To raise a C to a B, for example, one must study 6 additional hours (compare points *J* and *K*). Earlier it took only 4 hours to move the grade scale up a full point. The slope of the line has declined from 0.25 (= 1 ÷ 4) to 0.17 (= 1 ÷ 6).

it appears that every 6-hour increase in study time leads to a 1-point increase in grades. But the relationship between studying and grades may not be linear. Higher grades may be more difficult to attain. You may be able to raise a C to a B by studying 4 hours more per week. But it may be harder to raise a B to an A. According to Figure A.4, it takes an additional 8 hours of studying to raise a B to an A. Thus the relationship between study time

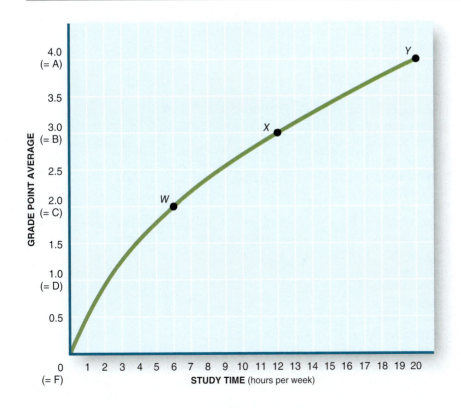

FIGURE A.4

A Nonlinear Relationship

Straight lines have a constant slope, implying a constant relationship between the two variables. But the relationship (and slope) may vary. In this case, it takes 6 extra hours of study to raise a C (point *W*) to a B (point *X*) but 8 extra hours to raise a B to an A (point *Y*). Th e slope decreases as we move up the curve.

and grades is *nonlinear* in Figure A.4; the slope of the curve changes as study time increases. In this case, the slope decreases as study time increases. Grades continue to improve, but not so fast, as more and more time is devoted to homework. You may know the feeling.

Causation

Figure A.4 doesn't by itself guarantee that your grade point average will rise if you study 4 more hours per week. In fact, the graph drawn in Figure A.4 doesn't prove that additional study ever results in higher grades. The graph is only a summary of empirical observations. It says nothing about cause and effect. It could be that students who study a lot are smarter to begin with. If so, then less able students might not get higher grades if they studied harder. In other words, the *cause* of higher grades is debatable. At best, the empirical relationship summarized in the graph may be used to support a particular theory (e.g., that it pays to study more). Graphs, like tables, charts, and other statistical media, rarely tell their own story; rather, they must be *interpreted* in terms of some underlying theory or expectation.

PROBLEMS FOR CHAPTER 1   Name: _____

LO1-1 1. According to Table 1.1 (or Figure 1.1), what is the opportunity cost of the first truck produced?   _____

LO1-2 2. (*a*) Compute the opportunity cost in forgone tanks for each additional truck produced:

Truck output	0	1	2	3	4	5
Tank output	5	4.5	3.8	3.0	2.0	0
Opportunity cost		___	___	<u>0.8</u>	___	___

  (*b*) As truck output increases, are opportunity costs (A) increasing, (B) decreasing, or (C) remaining constant?   _____

LO1-2 3. According to Figure 1.2 (p. 9), how much food production is sacrificed when North Korea moves from point *P* to point *N*?   _____

LO1-1 4. (*a*) What is the cost of the North Korean 2009 missile launch, according to South Korea (p. 10)?   _____
  (*b*) How many people could have been fed for an entire year at the World Bank standard of $2 per day with that money?   _____

LO1-1 5. What is the opportunity cost (in civilian output) of a defense buildup that raises military spending from 4.0 to 4.3 percent of an $18 trillion economy?   _____

LO1-3 6. What are the three core economic questions societies must answer?

  _____   _____   _____

LO1-2 7. According to Figure 1.4 (reproduced below),
  (*a*) At which point(s) is this society producing some of each type of output but still producing inefficiently?   _____
  (*b*) At which point(s) is this society producing the most output possible with the available resources and technology?   _____
  (*c*) At which point(s) is the output combination currently unattainable with current available resources and technology?   _____
  (*d*) Show the change that would occur if the resources of this society doubled. Label this curve PPC2.
  (*e*) Show the change that would occur with a huge natural disaster that destroyed 40 percent of production capacity. Label this curve PPC3.

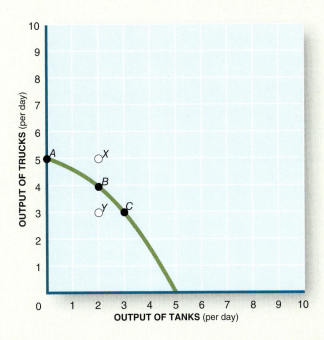

LO1-2   8. Suppose either computers or televisions can be assembled with the following labor inputs:

Units produced	1	2	3	4	5	6	7	8	9	10
Total labor used	3	7	12	15	25	33	42	54	70	90

(a) Draw the production possibilities curve for an economy with 42 units of labor. Label it P42.

(b) What is the opportunity cost of the sixth computer?   _____

(c) Suppose immigration brings in 28 more workers. Redraw the production possibilities curve to reflect this added labor. Label the new curve P70.

(d) Suppose advancing technology (e.g., the miniaturization of electronic circuits) increases the productivity of the 70-laborer workforce by 10 percent. Draw a third production possibilities curve (PT) to illustrate this change.

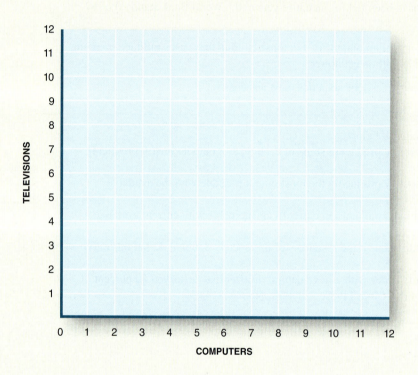

LO1-4   9. According to the World View on page 15, which nation has

(a) The highest level of faith in the market system?   _____

(b) The lowest level of faith in the market system?   _____

LO1-1 10. If a person literally had "nothing else to do,"

(a) What would be the opportunity cost of doing this homework?   _____

(b) What is the likelihood of that?   _____

LO1-2 11. Suppose there's a relationship of the following sort between study time and grades:

	(a)	(b)	(c)	(d)	(e)
Study time (hours per week)	0	2	6	12	20
Grade point average	0	1.0	2.0	3.0	4.0

If you have only 20 hours per week to use for either study time or fun time,

(*a*) Draw the (linear) production possibilities curve on the graph below that represents the alternative uses of your time.

(*b*) Indicate on the graph the point *C* that would get you a 2.0 grade average.

(*c*) What is the cost, in lost fun time, of raising your grade point average from 2.0 to 3.0? Illustrate this effort on the graph (point *C* to point *D*). _____

(*d*) What is the opportunity cost of increasing your grade point average from 3.0 to 4.0? Illustrate as point *D* to point *E*. _____

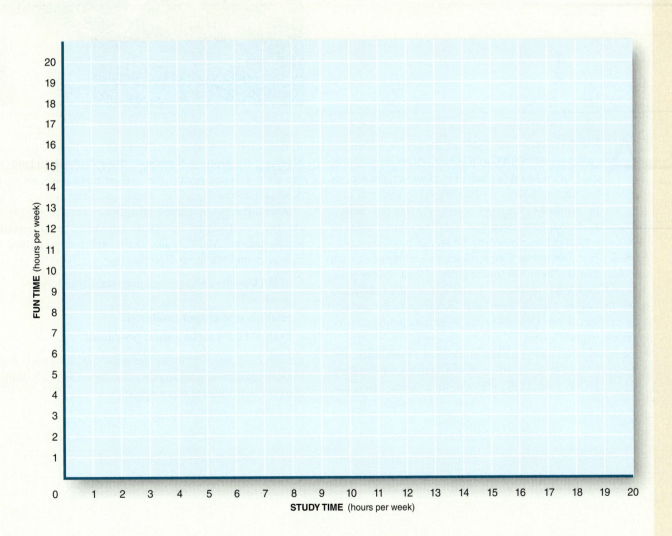

The U.S. Economy:
A Global View

CHAPTER
2

LEARNING OBJECTIVES

After reading this chapter, you should know

LO2-1 The relative size of the U.S. economy.

LO2-2 How the U.S. output mix has changed over time.

LO2-3 How the United States is able to produce so much output.

LO2-4 How incomes are distributed in the United States and elsewhere.

All nations must confront the central economic questions of WHAT to produce, HOW to produce, and FOR WHOM to produce it. However, the nations of the world approach these issues with vastly different production possibilities. China, Canada, the United States, Russia, and Brazil have more than *3 million* square miles of land each. All that land gives them far greater production possibilities than Dominica, Tonga, Malta, or Lichtenstein, each of which has less than 300 square miles of land. The population of China totals more than 1.4 billion people, nearly five times that of the United States, and 25,000 times the population of Greenland. Obviously these nations confront very different output choices.

In addition to vastly uneven production possibilities, the nations of the world use different mechanisms for deciding WHAT, HOW, and FOR WHOM to produce. Belarus,

Romania, North Korea, and Cuba still rely heavily on central planning. By contrast, Singapore, New Zealand, Ireland, and the United States permit the market mechanism to play a dominant role in shaping economic outcomes.

With different production possibilities and mechanisms of choice, you'd expect economic outcomes to vary greatly across nations. And they do. This chapter assesses how the U.S. economy stacks up. Specifically,

- **WHAT goods and services does the United States produce?**
- **HOW is that output produced?**
- **FOR WHOM is the output produced?**

In each case, we want to see not only how the United States has answered these questions but also how America's answers compare with those of other nations.

WHAT AMERICA PRODUCES

The United States has less than 5 percent of the world's population and only 12 percent of the world's arable land, yet it produces 20 percent of the world's output.

GDP Comparisons

The World View below shows how total U.S. production compares with that of other nations. Every country produces a different mix of output. So, it's nearly impossible to compare output in purely *physical* terms (e.g., so many cars, so many fish, etc.). But we can make comparisons based on the *value* of output. We do this by computing the total market value of all the goods and services a nation produces in a year—what we call **gross domestic product (GDP)**. In effect, GDP is the "pie" of output we bake each year.

In 2013 the U.S. economy baked a huge pie—one containing more than $16 trillion worth of goods and services. That was far more output than any other nation produced. The second-largest economy, China, produced only two-thirds that much. Japan came in third, with about a third of U.S. output. Cuba, by contrast, produced less than $2 *billion* of output, less than the state of South Dakota. Russia, which was once regarded as a superpower, produced only $2.1 trillion. The entire 28-member European Union produces less output than the United States.

gross domestic product (GDP): The total market value of all final goods and services produced within a nation's borders in a given time period.

WORLD VIEW

Comparative Output (GDP)

The United States is by far the world's largest economy. Its annual output of goods and services is one and a half times that of China's, three times Japan's, and more than all of the European Union's. The output of Third World countries is only a tiny fraction of U.S. output.

Source: *The World Bank*, **www.worldbank.org** (Atlas method).

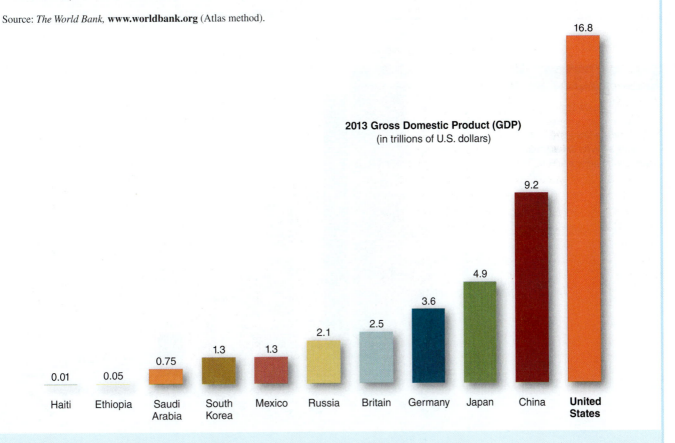

2013 Gross Domestic Product (GDP)
(in trillions of U.S. dollars)

Country	GDP
Haiti	0.01
Ethiopia	0.05
Saudi Arabia	0.75
South Korea	1.3
Mexico	1.3
Russia	2.1
Britain	2.5
Germany	3.6
Japan	4.9
China	9.2
United States	16.8

ANALYSIS: The market value of output (GDP) is a basic measure of an economy's size. The U.S. economy is far larger than any other and accounts for more than one-fifth of the entire world's output of goods and services.

Per Capita GDP. What makes the U.S. share of world output so remarkable is that we do it with so few people. The U.S. population of 320 million amounts to less than 5 percent of the world's total (7.3 billion). Yet we produce more than 20 percent of the world's output. That means we're producing a lot of output *per person*. China, by contrast, has the opposite ratios: 20 percent of the world's population producing less than 13 percent of the world's output. So China is producing a lot of output but relatively less *per person*.

per capita GDP: The dollar value of GDP divided by total population; average GDP.

This people-based measure of economic performance is called **per capita GDP.** Per capita GDP is simply a nation's total output divided by its total population. It doesn't tell us how much any specific person gets. ***Per capita GDP is an indicator of how much output the average person would get if all output were divided evenly among the population.*** In effect, GDP per capita tells us how large a slice of the GDP pie the average citizen gets.

In 2013 per capita GDP in the United States was roughly $54,000. That means the average U.S. citizen could have consumed $54,000 worth of goods and services. That's a staggering amount by global standards—five times the average for the rest of the world. The following World View provides a global perspective on just how "rich" America is.

WORLD VIEW

GDP per Capita around the World

The American standard of living is nearly five times higher than the average for the rest of the world. People in the poorest nations of the world (e.g., Haiti, Ethiopia) barely survive on per capita incomes that are a tiny fraction of U.S. standards.

Source: *The World Bank,* **www.worldbank.org.**

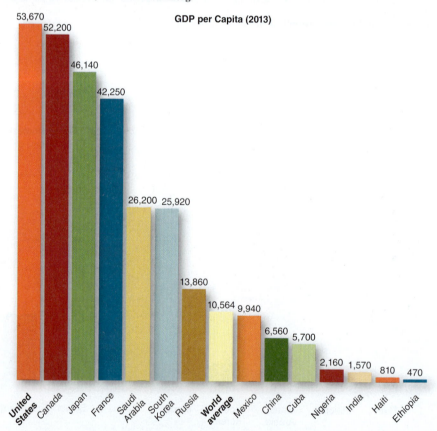

GDP per Capita (2013)

United States 53,670 · Canada 52,200 · Japan 46,140 · France 42,250 · Saudi Arabia 26,200 · South Korea 25,920 · Russia 13,860 · World average 10,564 · Mexico 9,940 · China 6,560 · Cuba 5,700 · Nigeria 2,160 · India 1,570 · Haiti 810 · Ethiopia 470

ANALYSIS: Per capita GDP is a measure of output that reflects average living standards. America's exceptionally high GDP per capita implies access to far more goods and services than people in other nations have.

web click

To find the latest data on national economic output, access the International Monetary Fund's website at **www.imf.org,** and visit the "Country Info" tab.

Some of the country-specific comparisons are startling. China, which produces the world's second-largest GDP, has such a low *per capita* income that most of its citizens would be considered "poor" by official American standards. Yet people in other nations (e.g., Haiti, Ethiopia) don't even come close to that low standard. According to the World Bank, one-third of the people on Earth subsist on incomes of less than $2 a day—a level completely unimaginable to the average American. *Homeless* people in the United States enjoy a higher living standard than billions of poor people in other nations (see chapter titled "Global Poverty"). In this context, it's easy to understand why the rest of the world envies (and sometimes resents) America's prosperity.

GDP Growth. What's even more startling about global comparisons is that the GDP gap between the United States and the world's poor nations keeps growing. The reason for that is **economic growth.** With few exceptions, U.S. output increases nearly every year: the pie keeps getting larger. ***On average, U.S. output has grown by roughly 3 percent a year, nearly three times faster than population growth (1 percent).*** So the U.S. pie is growing faster than the number of people coming to the table. Hence not only does *total* output keep rising, but *per capita* output keeps rising as well (see Figure 2.1). Even the Great Recession of 2008–2009 hardly made a dent in this pattern of ever-rising incomes.

economic growth: An increase in output (real GDP); an expansion of production possibilities.

Poor Nations. People in the world's poorest countries aren't so fortunate. China's economy has grown exceptionally fast in the last 20 years, propelling it to second place in the global GDP rankings. But in many other nations total output has actually *declined* year after year, further depressing living standards. Notice in Table 2.1, for example, what's been happening in Zimbabwe. From 2000 to 2009, Zimbabwe's output of goods and services (GDP) *declined* by an average of 7.5 percent a year. As a result, total Zimbabwean output in 2009 was 90 percent *smaller* than in 2000. During those same years, the Zimbabwean population kept growing—by 0.9 percent a year. So the Zimbabwean pie was shrinking every year even as the number of people coming to the table was increasing. As a result, Zimbabwe's per capita GDP fell below $400 a year. That low level of per capita GDP left two-thirds of Zimbabwe's population undernourished.

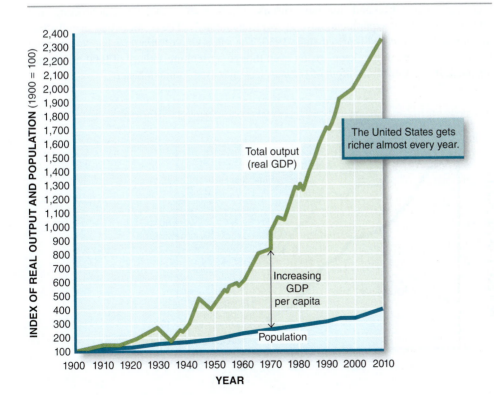

FIGURE 2.1

U.S. Output and Population Growth since 1900

Over time, the growth of output in the United States has greatly exceeded population growth. As a consequence, GDP per capita has grown tremendously. GDP per capita was five times higher in 2000 than in 1900.

Source: U.S. Department of Labor.

TABLE 2.1

GDP Growth vs. Population Growth

The relationship between GDP growth and population growth is very different in rich and poor countries. The populations of rich countries are growing very slowly, and gains in per capita GDP are easily achieved. In the poorest countries, population is still increasing rapidly, making it difficult to raise living standards. Notice how per capita incomes are *declining* in many poor countries (such as Zimbabwe, Haiti, and Gaza).

	Average Growth Rate (2000–2009) of		
	GDP	**Population**	**Per Capita GDP**
High-income countries			
United States	2.0	1.1	0.9
Canada	2.1	1.0	1.1
Japan	1.1	0.2	0.9
France	1.5	0.5	1.0
Low-income countries			
China	10.9	0.8	10.1
India	7.9	1.6	6.3
Ethiopia	7.5	2.8	4.7
Burundi	2.7	2.0	0.7
Haiti	0.7	1.8	−1.1
West Bank/Gaza	−0.9	3.8	−4.7
Zimbabwe	−7.5	0.9	−8.4

Source: *The World Bank, WDR2011 Data Set,* **data.worldbank.org.**

The Mix of Output

Regardless of how much output a nation produces, the *mix* of output always includes both *goods* (such as cars, big-screen TVs, and potatoes) and *services* (like this economics course, visits to a doctor, or a professional baseball game). A century ago, about two-thirds of U.S. output consisted of farm goods (37 percent), manufactured goods (22 percent), and mining (9 percent). Since then, more than 25 *million* people have left the farms and taken jobs in other sectors. As a result, today's mix of output is completely reversed: ***Eighty percent of U.S. output now consists of services, not goods*** (see Figure 2.2).

The *relative* decline in goods production (manufacturing, farming) doesn't mean that we're producing *fewer* goods today than in earlier decades. Quite the contrary. While some industries such as iron and steel have shrunk, others, such as chemicals, publishing, and telecommunications equipment, have grown tremendously. The result is that manufacturing output has increased fourfold since 1950. The same kind of thing has happened in the farm sector, where output keeps rising even though agriculture's *share* of total output has declined. It's just that our output of *services* has increased so much faster.

web click

Data on the mix of output in different nations are available at the World Bank's website **www.worldbank.org.** Click the "Data" tab.

FIGURE 2.2

The Changing Mix of Output

Two hundred years ago, almost all U.S. output came from farms. Today 80 percent of output consists of services, not farm or manufactured goods.

Source: U.S. Department of Commerce.

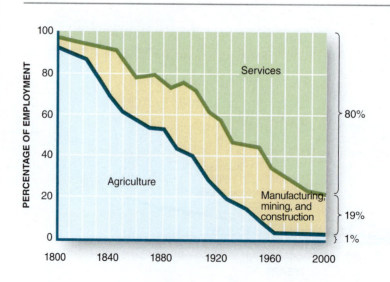

Development Patterns. The transformation of the United States into a service economy is a reflection of our high incomes. In Ethiopia, where the most urgent concern is to keep people from starving, more than 50 percent of output still comes from the farm sector. Poor people don't have enough income to buy dental services, vacations, or even an education, **so the mix of output in poor countries is weighted toward goods, not services.**

HOW AMERICA PRODUCES

Regardless of how much output a nation produces, every nation ultimately depends on its resources—its **factors of production**—to produce goods and services. So *differences* in GDP must be explained in part by HOW those resources are used.

Human Capital

We've already observed that America's premier position in global GDP rankings isn't due to the number of humans within our borders. We have far fewer bodies than China or India, yet produce far more output than either of those nations. What counts for production purposes is not just the *number* of workers a nation has, but the *skills* of those workers—what we call **human capital.**

Over time, the United States has invested heavily in human capital. In 1940 only 1 out of 20 young Americans graduated from college; today more than 30 percent of young people are college graduates. High school graduation rates have jumped from 38 percent to more than 85 percent in the same period. In the poorest countries, only 1 out of 3 youth ever *attend* high school, much less graduate (see the World View below). As a consequence, the United Nations estimates that 1.2 billion people—a fifth of humanity—are unable to read a book or even write their own names. Without even functional literacy, such workers are

factors of production: Resource inputs used to produce goods and services, such as land, labor, capital, entrepreneurship.

human capital: The knowledge and skills possessed by the workforce.

WORLD VIEW

The Education Gap between Rich and Poor Nations

Virtually all Americans attend high school and roughly 85 percent graduate. In poor countries, relatively few workers attend high school and even fewer graduate. Half the workers in the world's poorest nations are illiterate.

Source: *The World Bank, WDI2014 Data Set,* **data.worldbank.org.**

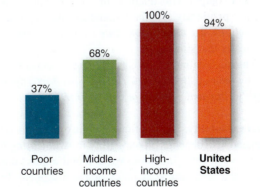

Enrollment in Secondary Schools (percentage of school-age youth attending secondary schools)

Poor countries 37% — Middle-income countries 68% — High-income countries 100% — United States 94%

web click

The Central Intelligence Agency provides cross-country data on educational attainment. Visit **www.cia.gov** and click on "World Factbook" to view this information.

ANALYSIS: The high productivity of the American economy is explained in part by the quality of its labor resources. Workers in poorer, less developed countries get much less education and training.

Analysis: An abundance of capital equipment and advanced technology make American farmers and workers far more productive than workers in poor nations.

doomed to low-productivity jobs. Despite low wages, they are not likely to "steal" many jobs from America's highly educated and trained workforce.

Capital Stock

America has also accumulated a massive stock of capital—more than $60 *trillion* worth of machinery, factories, and buildings. As a result of all this prior investment, U.S. production tends to be very **capital-intensive.** The contrast with *labor-intensive* production in poorer countries is striking. A farmer in India still works mostly with his hands and crude implements, whereas a U.S. farmer works with computers, automated irrigation systems, and mechanized equipment (see the photos above). Russian business managers don't have the computer networks or telecommunications systems that make U.S. business so efficient. In Haiti and Ethiopia, even telephones, indoor plumbing, and dependable sources of power are scarce.

capital-intensive: Production processes that use a high ratio of capital to labor inputs.

High Productivity

When you put educated workers together with sophisticated capital equipment, you tend to get more output. This relationship largely explains why the United States has such a lead in worker **productivity**—the amount of output produced by the average worker. *American households are able to consume so much because American workers produce so much.* It's really that simple.

productivity: Output per unit of input—for example, output per labor-hour.

   The huge output of the United States is thus explained not only by a wealth of resources but by their quality as well. *The high productivity of the U.S. economy results from using highly educated workers in capital-intensive production processes.*

Factor Mobility. Our continuing ability to produce the goods and services that consumers demand also depends on our agility in *reallocating* resources from one industry to another. Every year, some industries expand and others contract. Thousands of new firms start up each year, and almost as many others disappear. In the process, land, labor, capital, and entrepreneurship move from one industry to another in response to changing demands and technology. In 1975 Federal Express, Dell Computer, Staples, Oracle, and Amgen didn't exist. Walmart was still a small retailer. Starbucks was selling coffee on Seattle street corners, and the founders of Google and YouTube weren't even born. Today these companies employ millions of people. These workers came from other firms and industries that weren't growing as fast.

Technological Advance. One of the forces that keeps shifting resources from one industry to another is continuing advances in technology. Advances in technology can be as sophisticated as microscopic miniaturization of electronic circuits or as simple as the reorganization of production processes. Either phenomenon increases the productivity of the workforce and potential output. *Whenever technology advances, an economy can produce more output with existing resources;* its **production possibilities** curve shifts outward (see Figure 1.5, page 12).

Outsourcing and Trade. The same technological advances that fuel economic growth also facilitate *global* resource use. Telecommunications has become so sophisticated and inexpensive that phone workers in India or Grenada can answer calls directed to U.S. companies. Likewise, programmers in India can work online to write computer code, develop software, or perform accounting chores for U.S. corporations. Although such "outsourcing" is often viewed as a threat to U.S. jobs, it is really another source of increased U.S. output. By outsourcing routine tasks to foreign workers, U.S. workers are able to focus on higher-value jobs. U.S. computer engineers do less routine programming and more systems design. U.S. accountants do less cost tabulation and more cost analysis. By utilizing foreign resources in the production process, U.S. workers are able to pursue their *comparative advantage* in high-skill, capital-intensive jobs. In this way, both productivity and total output increase. Although some U.S. workers suffer temporary job losses in this process, the overall economy gains.

Role of Government

In assessing HOW goods are produced and economies grow, we must also take heed of the role the government plays. As we noted in Chapter 1, the amount of economic freedom varies greatly among the 200-plus nations of the world. Moreover, the Heritage Foundation has documented a positive relationship between the degree of economic freedom and economic growth. Quite simply, when entrepreneurs are unfettered by regulation or high taxes, they are more likely to design and produce better mousetraps. When the government owns the factors of production, imposes high taxes, or tightly regulates output, there is little opportunity or incentive to design better products or pursue new technology. This is one reason why more market-reliant economies grow faster than others.

Recognizing the importance of market incentives doesn't force us to reject all government intervention. No one really advocates the complete abolition of government. On the contrary, the government plays a critical role in establishing a framework in which private businesses can operate. Among its many roles are these:

- *Providing a legal framework.* One of the most basic functions of government is to establish and enforce the rules of the game. In some bygone era maybe a person's word was sufficient to guarantee delivery or payment. Businesses today, however, rely more on written contracts. The government gives legitimacy to contracts by establishing the rules for such pacts and by enforcing their provisions. In the absence of contractual rights, few companies would be willing to ship goods without prepayment (in cash). Even the incentive to write textbooks would disappear if government copyright laws didn't forbid unauthorized photocopying. By establishing ownership rights, contract rights, and other rules of the game, the government lays the foundation for market transactions.
- *Protecting the environment.* The government also intervenes in the market to protect the environment. The legal contract system is designed to protect the interests of a buyer and a seller who wish to do business. What if, however, the business they contract for harms third parties? How are the interests of persons who *aren't* party to the contract to be protected?

  Numerous examples abound of how unregulated production may harm third parties. Earlier in the century, the steel mills around Pittsburgh blocked out the sun with clouds

production possibilities: The alternative combinations of final goods and services that could be produced in a given period with all available resources and technology.

externalities: Costs (or benefits) of a market activity borne by a third party.

monopoly: A firm that produces the entire market supply of a particular good or service.

of sulfurous gases that spewed out of their furnaces. Local residents were harmed every time they inhaled. In the absence of government intervention, such side effects would be common. Decisions on how to produce would be based on costs alone, not on how the environment is affected. However, such **externalities**—spillover costs imposed on the broader community—affect our collective well-being. To reduce the external costs of production, the government limits air, water, and noise pollution and regulates environmental use.

- *Protecting consumers.* The government also uses its power to protect the interests of consumers. One way to do this is to prevent individual business firms from becoming too powerful. In the extreme case, a single firm might have a **monopoly** on the production of a specific good. As the sole producer of that good, a monopolist could dictate the price, the quality, and the quantity of the product. In such a situation, consumers would likely end up paying too much for too little.

  To protect consumers from monopoly exploitation, the government tries to prevent individual firms from dominating specific markets. Antitrust laws prohibit mergers or acquisitions that would threaten competition. The U.S. Department of Justice and the Federal Trade Commission also regulate pricing practices, advertising claims, and other behavior that might put consumers at an unfair disadvantage in product markets.

  Government also regulates the safety of many products. Consumers don't have enough expertise to assess the safety of various medicines, for example. If they rely on trial and error to determine drug safety, they might not get a second chance. To avoid this calamity, the government requires rigorous testing of new drugs, food additives, and other products.

- *Protecting labor.* The government also regulates how labor resources are used in the production process. In most poor nations, children are forced to start working at very early ages, often for minuscule wages. They often don't get the chance to go to school or to stay healthy. In Africa, 40 percent of children under age 14 work to survive or to help support their families. In the United States, child labor laws and compulsory schooling prevent minor children from being exploited. Government regulations also set standards for workplace safety, minimum wages, fringe benefits, and overtime provisions.

Striking a Balance

All these and other government interventions are designed to change the way resources are used. Such interventions reflect the conviction that the market alone might not always select the best possible way of producing goods and services. There's no guarantee, however, that government regulation of HOW goods are produced always makes us better off. Excessive regulation may inhibit production, raise product prices, and limit consumer choices. As noted in Chapter 1, *government* failure might replace *market* failure, leaving us no better off—possibly even worse off. This possibility underscores the importance of striking the right balance between market reliance and government regulation.

FOR WHOM AMERICA PRODUCES

As we've seen, America produces a huge quantity of output, using high-quality labor and capital resources. That leaves one basic question unanswered: FOR WHOM is all this output produced?

How many goods and services one gets largely depends on how much income one has to spend. The U.S. economy uses the market mechanism to distribute most goods and services. Those who receive the most income get the most goods. This goes a long way toward

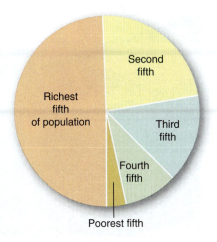

FIGURE 2.3
The U.S. Distribution of Income

The richest fifth of U.S. households gets half of all the income—a huge slice of the income pie. By contrast, the poorest fifth gets only a sliver.

Second fifth

Richest fifth of population

Third fifth

Fourth fifth

Poorest fifth

Income Quintile	2013 Income	Average Income	Share of Total Income (%)
Highest fifth	Above $106,000	$185,000	51.0
Second fifth	$65,000–106,000	$ 84,000	23.0
Third fifth	$40,000–65,000	$ 52,000	14.4
Fourth fifth	$21,000–40,000	$ 31,000	8.4
Lowest fifth	$0–21,000	$ 12,000	3.2

Source: U.S. Department of Commerce, Bureau of the Census (averages rounded to thousands of dollars; 2013 data).

web click

Past and present data on the U.S. income distribution are available at **www.census.gov**. In the "People and Households" category, click on the "Income" link.

explaining why millionaires live in mansions and homeless people seek shelter in abandoned cars. This is the kind of stark inequality that fueled Karl Marx's denunciation of capitalism. Even today, people wonder how some Americans can be so rich while others are so poor.

U.S. Income Distribution

Figure 2.3 illustrates the actual distribution of income in the United States. For this illustration the entire population is sorted into five groups of equal size, ranked by income. In this depiction, all the rich people are in the top **income quintile;** the poor are in the lowest quintile. To be in the top quintile in 2013, a household needed at least $106,000 of income. All the households in the lowest quintile had incomes under $21,000.

The most striking feature of Figure 2.3 is how large a slice of the income pie rich people get: *The top 20 percent (quintile) of U.S. households get half of all U.S. income.* By contrast, the poorest 20 percent (quintile) of U.S. households get only a sliver of the income pie—less than 4 percent. Those grossly unequal slices explain why nearly half of all Americans believe the nation is divided into "haves" and "have nots."

income quintile: One-fifth of the population, rank-ordered by income (e.g., top fifth).

Global Inequality

As unequal as U.S. incomes are, income disparities are actually greater in many other countries. Ironically, income inequalities are often greatest in the poorest countries. The richest *tenth* of U.S. families gets 30 percent of America's income pie. The richest tenth of South Africa's families gets 45 percent of that nation's income (see the World View on the next page). Given the small size of South Africa's pie, the *bottom* tenth of South African families is left with mere crumbs. As we'll see in the chapter titled "Global Poverty," 40 percent of

Analysis: The market distributes income (and, in turn, goods and services) according to the resources an individual owns and how well they are used. If the resulting inequalities are too great, some redistribution via government intervention may be desired.

South Africa's population lives in "severe poverty," defined by the World Bank as an income of less than $2 a day.

Comparisons across countries would manifest even greater inequality. As we saw earlier, third world GDP per capita is far below U.S. levels. As a consequence, even **poor** *people in the United States receive far more goods and services than the* **average** *household in most low-income countries.*

WORLD VIEW

Income Share of the Rich

Inequality tends to diminish as a country develops. In poor, developing nations, the richest tenth of the population typically gets 40 to 50 percent of all income. In developed countries, the richest tenth gets 20 to 30 percent of total income.

Source: *The World Bank, WDI2014 Data Set,* **data.worldbank.org.**

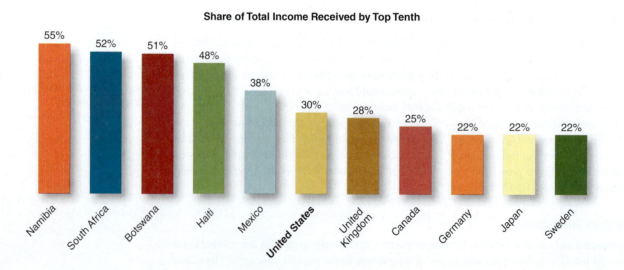

Share of Total Income Received by Top Tenth

Country	Percent
Namibia	55%
South Africa	52%
Botswana	51%
Haiti	48%
Mexico	38%
United States	30%
United Kingdom	28%
Canada	25%
Germany	22%
Japan	22%
Sweden	22%

ANALYSIS: The FOR WHOM question is reflected in the distribution of income. Although the U.S. distribution of income is very unequal, inequalities are even more severe in most poor nations.

THE ECONOMY TOMORROW

ENDING GLOBAL POVERTY

Global answers to the basic questions of WHAT, HOW, and FOR WHOM have been shaped by market forces and government intervention. Obviously the answers aren't yet fully satisfactory.

Millions of Americans still struggle to make ends meet. Worse yet, nearly 3 *billion* people around the world live in abject poverty—with incomes of less than $2 a day. More than a fourth of the world's population is illiterate, nearly half has no access to sanitation facilities, and a fifth is chronically malnourished.

The World Bank thinks we can do a lot better. In fact, it has set ambitious goals for the economy tomorrow. In the Millennium Declaration of October 2000, the 180 nation-members of the World Bank set specific goals for world development. By 2015, they agreed to

- Reduce extreme poverty and hunger by at least half.
- Achieve universal primary education.
- Reduce child and maternal mortality by two-thirds.
- Reduce by half the number of people without access to potable water.

Achieving these goals would obviously help billions of people. But it's obvious we did not achieve the World Bank's goal. What went wrong?

The rich nations of the world have enough resources to wipe out global poverty. But they're not willing to give them up. People in rich nations also have aspirations: they want higher living standards in the economy tomorrow. They already enjoy more comforts than people in poor nations even dream of. But that doesn't stop them from wanting more consumer goods, better schools, improved health care, a cleaner environment, and greater economic security. So the needs of the world's poor typically get lower priority.

How about the poor nations themselves? Couldn't they do a better job of mobilizing and employing their own resources to accelerate economic growth? Governments in many poor nations are notoriously self-serving and corrupt. Private property is often at risk of confiscation and contracts hard to enforce. This discourages the kind of investment poor nations desperately need. The unwillingness of rich nations to open their markets to the exports of poor nations also puts a lid on income growth. In reality, an array of domestic and international policies has perpetuated global poverty. Developing a better mix of market-based and government-directed policies is the prerequisite for ending global poverty in the economy. The chapter titled "Global Poverty" explores some of the possibilities.

SUMMARY

- Answers to the core WHAT, HOW, and FOR WHOM questions vary greatly across nations. These differences reflect varying production possibilities, choice mechanisms, and values.   **LO2-1, LO2-3, LO2-4**
- Gross domestic product (GDP) is the basic measure of how much an economy produces. The United States produces roughly $18 trillion of output per year, more than one-fifth of the world's total.   **LO2-1**
- Per capita GDP is a nation's total output divided by its population. It indicates the average standard of living. The U.S. GDP per capita is five times the world average.   **LO2-1**

- The high level of U.S. per capita GDP reflects the high productivity of U.S. workers. Abundant capital, education, technology, training, and management all contribute to high productivity. The relatively high degree of U.S. economic freedom (market reliance) is also an important cause of superior economic growth.   **LO2-3**
- More than 80 percent of U.S. output consists of services, including government services. This is a reversal of historical ratios and reflects the relatively high incomes in the United States. Poor nations produce much higher proportions of food and manufactured goods.   **LO2-2**

- U.S. incomes are distributed very unequally, with households in the highest income class (quintile) receiving more than 10 times more income than low-income households. Incomes are even less equally distributed in most poor nations. **LO2-4**

- The mix of output, production methods, and the income distribution continue to change. The WHAT, HOW, and FOR WHOM answers in tomorrow's economy will depend on the continuing interplay of (changing) market signals and (changing) government policy. **LO2-2, LO2-3, LO2-4**

Key Terms

gross domestic product (GDP)
per capita GDP
economic growth
factors of production

human capital
capital-intensive
productivity
production possibilities

externalities
monopoly
income quintile

Questions for Discussion

1. Americans already enjoy living standards that far exceed world averages. Do we have enough? Should we even try to produce more? **LO2-1**
2. Why is per capita GDP so much higher in the United States than in Mexico? **LO2-3**
3. Can we continue to produce more output every year? Is there a limit? **LO2-3**
4. The U.S. farm population has shrunk by more than 25 million people since 1900. Where did all the people go? Why did they move? **LO2-2**
5. Is the relative decline in U.S. farming and manufacturing (Figure 2.2) a good thing or a bad thing? **LO2-2**
6. How many people are employed by your local or state government? What do they produce? What is the opportunity cost of that output? **LO2-1**
7. Where do growing companies like Google and Facebook get their employees? What were those workers doing before? **LO2-2**
8. Should the government try to equalize incomes more by raising taxes on the rich and giving more money to the poor? How might such redistribution affect total output and growth? **LO2-4**
9. Why are incomes so much more unequal in poor nations than in rich ones? **LO2-4**
10. How might free markets help reduce global poverty? How might they impede that goal? **LO2-3**

 mobile app Visit your mobile app store and download the Schiller: Study Econ app *today!*

LO2-1 1. In 2013 the world's total output (real GDP) was roughly $73 trillion. What percent of this total was produced
    (*a*) By the three largest economies (World View, p. 31)?   _____ %
    (*b*) By the three smallest economies in that World View?   _____ %
    (*c*) How much larger is the U.S. economy than the Ethiopian economy?   _____
                                                                               (times larger)

LO2-1 2. According to the World View on page 32, how does per capita GDP in the following countries stack up against America's (in percentage terms)
                                                        (*a*) Russia?   _____ %
                                                        (*b*) China?   _____ %
                                                        (*c*) Cuba?   _____ %

LO2-4 3. In 1950, America's GDP per capita was approximately $15,000 (in today's dollars). How much higher in percentage terms is
    (*a*) America's GDP per capita in 2013?   _____ %
    (*b*) America's 1950 GDP per capita compared to
      (*i*) Cuba's in 2013?   _____ %
      (*ii*) China's in 2013?   _____ %

LO2-3 4. (*a*) How much more output does the $18 trillion U.S. economy produce when GDP increases by 1.0 percent? $_____
    (*b*) By how much does this increase the average (per capita) income if the population is 320 million? $_____

LO2-1 5. According to Table 2.1 (p. 34), how fast does total output (GDP) have to grow in order to raise per capita GDP in
                                                       (*a*) China?   _____
                                                      (*b*) Ethiopia?   _____

LO2-3 6. (*a*) If Haiti's per capita GDP of roughly $1,150 were to DOUBLE every decade (an annual growth rate of 7.2 percent), what would Haiti's per capita GDP be in 50 years? $_____
    (*b*) What was U.S. per capita GDP in 2013 (World View, p. 32)? $_____

LO2-2 7. U.S. real gross domestic product increased from $10 trillion in 2000 to $15 trillion in 2010. During that same decade the share of manufactured goods (e.g., cars, appliances) fell from 16 percent to 12 percent. What was the dollar value of manufactured output
    (*a*) In 2000? $_____
    (*b*) In 2010? $_____
    (*c*) By how much did manufacturing output change?   _____ %

LO2-4 8. Using the data in Figure 2.3,
    (*a*) Compute the average income of U.S. households. $_____
    (*b*) If all incomes were equalized by government taxes and transfer payments, how much would the average household in each income quintile gain (via transfers) or lose (via taxes)?
                                                       (*i*) Highest fifth $_____
                                                  (*ii*) Second fifth $_____
                                                  (*iii*) Third fifth $_____
                                                  (*iv*) Fourth fifth $_____
                                                  (*v*) Lowest fifth $_____
    (*c*) What is the implied tax rate (i.e., tax ÷ average income) on the highest quintile?   _____ %

LO2-3 9. If 150 million workers produced America's GDP in 2013 (World View, p. 31), how much output did the average worker produce? $_____

PROBLEMS FOR CHAPTER 2 (cont'd)

Name: _____

LO2-4 10. How much more output (income) per year will have to be produced in the world just to provide the 2.7 billion "severely" poor population with $1 more output per day? $ _____

LO2-1 11. Using data from Table 2.1 (p. 34), illustrate on the following graphs real GDP and population growth since 2000 (in the manner of Figure 2.1) for the nations indicated.

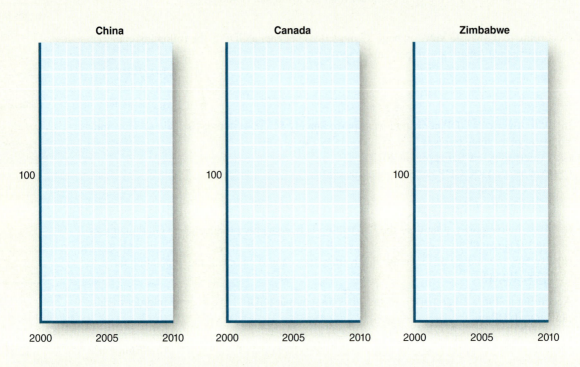

LO2-1 12. Using data from the endpapers, illustrate on the graph below
    (a) The federal government's share of the total output.
    (b) The state/local government's share of the total output.

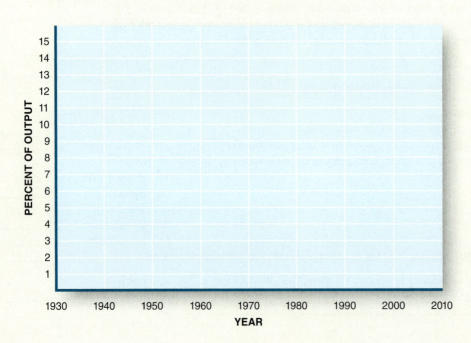

Supply and Demand

Gasoline prices surged in early 2008, rising from $2.99 a gallon in January to $4.05 in July. Consumers were angry every time they filled up their tanks. Popular opinion blamed the "Big Oil" companies and "speculators" for the sky-high prices. They demanded that the government intervene and force prices back down. Congressional hearings were conducted, government investigations were initiated, and "excess profits" taxes on oil companies were proposed.

By the end of 2008, gasoline prices had receded. In early 2009, pump prices were back to less than $2 a gallon. No oil executives or speculators had been arrested. No congressional reports had been completed. No government indictments had been issued. Economists explained this turn of events with "supply and demand." Surging demand and limited supply had caused the price spike; slowing demand and increased supply had pushed pump prices back down. Motorists weren't entirely convinced but were happy. They filled their tanks and drove off to other economic concerns. Anxiety over high gasoline prices subsided until 2011, when pump prices surged again.

The goal of this chapter is to explain how supply and demand really work. How do *markets* establish the price of gasoline and other products? Why do prices change so often? More broadly, how does the market mechanism decide WHAT to produce, HOW to produce, and FOR WHOM to produce? Specifically,

- **What determines the price of a good or service?**
- **How does the price of a product affect its production and consumption?**
- **Why do prices and production levels often change?**

Once we've seen how unregulated markets work, we'll observe how government intervention may alter market outcomes—for better or worse.

MARKET PARTICIPANTS

A good way to start figuring out how markets work is to see who participates in them. The answer is simple: just about every person and institution on the planet. Domestically, more than 320 million consumers, about 25 million business firms, and tens of thousands of government agencies participate directly in the U.S. economy. Millions of international buyers and sellers also participate in U.S. markets.

Maximizing Behavior

All these market participants enter the marketplace to pursue specific goals. Consumers, for example, come with a limited amount of income to spend. Their objective is to buy the most desirable goods and services that their limited budgets will permit. We can't afford *everything* we want, so we must make *choices* about how to spend our scarce dollars. Our goal is to *maximize* the utility (satisfaction) we get from our available incomes.

Businesses also try to maximize in the marketplace. In their case, the quest is for maximum *profits*. Business profits are the difference between sales receipts and total costs. To maximize profits, business firms try to use resources efficiently in producing products that consumers desire.

The public sector also has maximizing goals. The economic purpose of government is to use available resources to serve public needs. The resources available for this purpose are limited too. Hence local, state, and federal governments must use scarce resources carefully, striving to maximize the general welfare of society. International consumers and producers pursue these same goals when participating in our markets.

Market participants sometimes lose sight of their respective goals. Consumers sometimes buy impulsively and later wish they'd used their income more wisely. Likewise, a producer may take a two-hour lunch, even at the sacrifice of maximum profits. And elected officials sometimes put their personal interests ahead of the public's interest. In all sectors of the economy, however, ***the basic goals of utility maximization, profit maximization, and welfare maximization explain most market activity.***

Specialization and Exchange

We are driven to buy and sell goods and services in the market by two simple facts. First, most of us are incapable of producing everything we want to consume. Second, even if we *could* produce all our own goods and services, it would still make sense to *specialize,* producing only one product and *trading* it for other desired goods and services.

Suppose you were capable of growing your own food, stitching your own clothes, building your own shelter, and even writing your own economics text. Even in this little utopia, it would still make sense to decide how *best* to expend your limited time and energy, relying on others to fill in the gaps. If you were *most* proficient at growing food, you would be best off spending your time farming. You could then *exchange* some of your food output for the clothes, shelter, and books you wanted. In the end, you'd be able to consume *more* goods than if you'd tried to make everything yourself.

Our economic interactions with others are thus necessitated by two constraints:

1. Our absolute inability as individuals to produce all the things we need or desire.
2. The limited amount of time, energy, and resources we have for producing those things we could make for ourselves.

Together these constraints lead us to specialize and interact. Most of the interactions that result take place in the market.

International Trade. The same motivations lead us to engage in international trade. The United States is *capable* of producing just about everything. But we've learned that it's cheaper to import bananas from Ecuador than to grow them in hothouses in Idaho. So we *specialize* in production, exporting tractors to Ecuador in exchange for imported bananas. Both nations end up consuming more products than they could if they had to produce everything themselves. That's why *global* markets are so vital to economic prosperity.

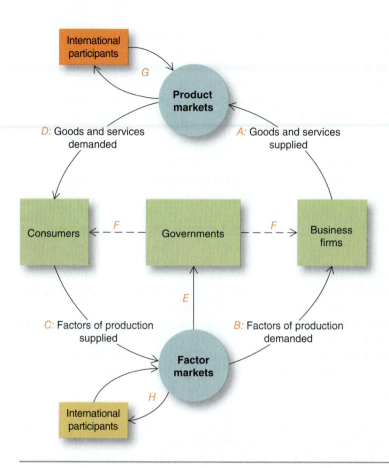

FIGURE 3.1

The Circular Flow

Business firms supply goods and services to product markets (point *A*) and purchase factors of production in factor markets (*B*). Individual consumers supply factors of production such as their own labor (*C*) and purchase final goods and services (*D*). Federal, state, and local governments acquire resources in factor markets (*E*) and provide services to both consumers and business (*F*). International participants also take part by supplying imports, purchasing exports (*G*), and buying and selling factors of production (*H*).

THE CIRCULAR FLOW

Figure 3.1 summarizes the kinds of interactions that occur among market participants. Note first that the figure identifies four separate groups of participants. Domestically, the rectangle labeled "Consumers" includes all 320 million consumers in the United States. In the "Business firms" box are grouped all the domestic business enterprises that buy and sell goods and services. The third participant, "Governments," includes the many separate agencies of the federal government, as well as state and local governments. Figure 3.1 also illustrates the role of global actors.

The Two Markets

The easiest way to keep track of all this activity is to distinguish two basic markets. Figure 3.1 makes this distinction by portraying separate circles for product markets and factor markets. In **factor markets,** factors of production are exchanged. Market participants buy or sell land, labor, or capital that can be used in the production process. When you go looking for work, for example, you're making a factor of production—your labor—available to producers. The producers will hire you—purchase your services in the factor market—if you're offering the skills they need at a price they're willing to pay.

Interactions within factor markets are only half the story. At the end of a hard day's work, consumers go to the grocery store (or to a virtual store online) to buy desired goods and services—that is, to buy *products*. In this context, consumers again interact with business firms, this time purchasing goods and services those firms have produced. These interactions occur in **product markets.** Foreigners also participate in the product market by supplying goods and services (imports) to the United States and buying some of our output (exports).

factor market: Any place where factors of production (e.g., land, labor, capital) are bought and sold.

product market: Any place where finished goods and services (products) are bought and sold.

The government sector also supplies services (e.g., education, national defense, highways). Most government services aren't explicitly sold in product markets, however. Typically, they're delivered "free," without an explicit price (e.g., public elementary schools, highways). This doesn't mean government services are truly free, though. There's still an **opportunity cost** associated with every service the government provides. Consumers and businesses pay that cost indirectly through taxes rather than directly through market prices.

In Figure 3.1, the arrow connecting product markets to consumers (D) emphasizes the fact that consumers, by definition, don't supply products. When individuals produce goods and services, they do so within the government or business sector. For instance, a doctor, a dentist, or an economic consultant functions in two sectors. When selling services in the market, this person is regarded as a "business"; when away from the office, he or she is regarded as a "consumer." This distinction is helpful in emphasizing that *the consumer is the final recipient of all goods and services produced.*

Locating Markets. Although we refer repeatedly to two kinds of markets in this book, it would be a little foolish to go off in search of the product and factor markets. Neither market is a single, identifiable structure. The term *market* simply refers to a place or situation where an economic exchange occurs—where a buyer and seller interact. The exchange may take place on the street, in a taxicab, over the phone, by mail, or in cyberspace. In some cases, the market used may in fact be quite distinguishable, as in the case of a retail store, the Chicago Commodity Exchange, or a state employment office. But whatever it looks like, *a market exists wherever and whenever an exchange takes place.*

Dollars and Exchange

Figure 3.1 neglects one critical element of market interactions: dollars. Each arrow in the figure actually has two dimensions. Consider again the arrow (D) linking consumers to product markets: it's drawn in only one direction because consumers, by definition, don't provide goods and services directly to product markets. But they do provide something: dollars. If you want to obtain something from a product market, you must offer to pay for it (typically with cash, check, debit or credit card). Consumers exchange dollars for goods and services in product markets.

The same kinds of exchange occur in factor markets. When you go to work, you exchange a factor of production (your labor) for income, typically a paycheck. Here again, the path connecting consumers to factor markets (C) really goes in two directions: one of real resources, the other of dollars. Consumers receive wages, rent, and interest for the labor, land, and capital they bring to the factor markets. Indeed, nearly *every market transaction involves an exchange of dollars for goods (in product markets) or resources (in factor markets).* Money is thus critical in facilitating market exchanges and the specialization the exchanges permit.

Supply and Demand

In every market transaction there must be a buyer and a seller. The seller is on the **supply** side of the market; the buyer is on the **demand** side. As noted earlier, we *supply* resources to the market when we look for a job—that is, when we offer our labor in exchange for income. We *demand* goods when we shop in a supermarket—that is, when we're prepared to offer dollars in exchange for something to eat. Business firms may *supply* goods and services in product markets at the same time they're *demanding* factors of production in factor markets. Whether one is on the supply side or the demand side of any particular market transaction depends on the nature of the exchange, not on the people or institutions involved.

DEMAND

To get a sense of how the demand side of market transactions works, we'll focus first on a single consumer. Then we'll aggregate to illustrate *market* demand.

---

opportunity cost: The most desired goods or services that are forgone in order to obtain something else.

supply: The ability and willingness to sell (produce) specific quantities of a good at alternative prices in a given time period, *ceteris paribus*.

demand: The ability and willingness to buy specific quantities of a good at alternative prices in a given time period, *ceteris paribus*.

Individual Demand

We can begin to understand how market forces work by looking more closely at the behavior of a single market participant. Let us start with Tom, a senior at Clearview College. Tom has majored in everything from art history to government in his five years at Clearview. He didn't connect to any of those fields and is on the brink of academic dismissal. To make matters worse, his parents have threatened to cut him off financially unless he gets serious about his course work. By that, they mean he should enroll in courses that will lead to a job after graduation. Tom thinks he has found the perfect solution: web design. Everything associated with the Internet pays big bucks. Plus, the girls seem to think webbies are "cool." Or at least so Tom thinks. And his parents would definitely approve. So Tom has enrolled in web design courses.

Unfortunately for Tom, he never developed computer skills. Until he got to Clearview College, he thought mastering Sony's latest alien-attack video game was the pinnacle of electronic wizardry. Tom didn't have a clue about "streaming," "interfacing," "animation," or the other concepts the web design instructor outlined in the first lecture.

Given his circumstances, Tom was desperate to find someone who could tutor him in web design. But desperation is not enough to secure the services of a web architect. In a market-based economy, you must also be willing to *pay* for the things you want. Specifically, *a demand exists only if someone is willing and able to pay for the good*—that is, exchange dollars for a good or service in the marketplace. Is Tom willing and able to *pay* for the web design tutoring he so obviously needs?

Let us assume that Tom has some income and is willing to spend some of it to get a tutor. Under these assumptions, we can claim that Tom is a participant in the *market* for web design services; he is a potential consumer.

But how much is Tom willing to pay? Surely Tom is not prepared to exchange *all* his income for help in mastering web design. After all, Tom could use his income to buy more desirable goods and services. If he spent all his income on a web tutor, that help would have an extremely high *opportunity cost*. He would be giving up the opportunity to spend that income on things he really likes. He'd pass his web design class but have little else. It doesn't sound like a good idea.

It seems more likely that there are *limits* to the amount Tom is willing to pay for web design tutoring. These limits will be determined by how much income Tom has to spend and how many other goods and services he must forsake to pay for a tutor.

Tom also knows that his grade in web design will depend in part on how much tutoring service he buys. He can pass the course with only a few hours of design help. If he wants a better grade, however, the cost is going to escalate quickly.

Naturally, Tom wants it all: an A in web design and a ticket to higher-paying jobs. But here again the distinction between *desire* and *demand* is relevant. He may *desire* to master web design, but his actual proficiency will depend on how many hours of tutoring he is willing to *pay* for.

The Demand Schedule

We assume, then, that when Tom starts looking for a web design tutor he has in mind some sort of **demand schedule,** like that described in Figure 3.2. According to row *A* of this schedule, Tom is willing and able to buy only 1 hour of tutoring service per semester if he must pay $50 an hour. At such an outrageous price he will learn minimal skills and just pass the course.

At lower prices, Tom would behave differently. According to Figure 3.2, Tom would purchase more tutoring services if the price per hour were less. Indeed, we see from row *I* of the demand schedule that Tom is willing to purchase 20 hours per semester—the whole bag of design tricks—if the price of tutoring got as low as $10 per hour.

Notice that the demand schedule doesn't tell us anything about *why* this consumer is willing to pay specific prices for various amounts of tutoring. Tom's expressed willingness to pay for web design tutoring may reflect a desperate need to finish a web design course, a lot

demand schedule: A table showing the quantities of a good a consumer is willing and able to buy at alternative prices in a given time period, *ceteris paribus.*

else. Software programs like PhotoShop, Flash, and Fireworks have made web design easier and more creative. And the cloud and Wi-Fi access have made the job more convenient. But teaching someone else to design web pages is still work. So why does anyone do it? Easy answer: for the money. People offer (supply) tutoring services to earn income that they, in turn, can spend on the goods and services *they* desire.

How much money must be offered to induce web designers to do a little tutoring depends on a variety of things. The ***determinants of market supply include***

- *Technology.*
- *Factor costs.*
- *Other goods.*

- *Taxes and subsidies.*
- *Expectations.*
- *Number of sellers.*

The technology of web design, for example, is always getting easier and more creative. With a program like PageOut, for example, it's very easy to create a bread-and-butter web page. A continuous stream of new software programs (e.g., Fireworks, DreamWeaver) keeps stretching the possibilities for graphics, animation, interactivity, and content. These technological advances mean that web design services can be supplied more quickly and cheaply. They also make *teaching* web design easier. As a result, they induce people to supply more tutoring services at every price.

How much web design service is offered at any given price also depends on the cost of factors of production. If the software programs needed to create web pages are cheap (or, better yet, free), web designers can afford to charge lower prices. If the required software inputs are expensive, however, they will have to charge more for their services.

Other goods can also affect the willingness to supply web design services. If you can make more income waiting tables than you can tutoring lazy students, why would you even boot up the computer? As the prices paid for other goods and services change, they will influence people's decision about whether to offer web services.

In the real world, the decision to supply goods and services is also influenced by the long arm of Uncle Sam. Federal, state, and local governments impose taxes on income earned in the marketplace. When tax rates are high, people get to keep less of the income they earn. Once taxes start biting into paychecks, some people may conclude that tutoring is no longer worth the hassle and withdraw from the market.

Expectations are also important on the supply side of the market. If web designers expect higher prices, lower costs, or reduced taxes, they may be more willing to learn new software programs. On the other hand, if they have poor expectations about the future, they may just find something else to do.

Finally, we note that the number of potential tutors will affect the quantity of service offered for sale at various prices. If there are lots of willing tutors on campus, a lot of tutorial service will be available at reasonable prices.

All these considerations—factor costs, technology, taxes, expectations—affect the decision to offer web services at various prices. In general, we assume that web architects will be willing to provide more tutoring if the per-hour price is high and less if the price is low. In other words, there is a **law of supply** that parallels the law of demand. ***The law of supply says that larger quantities will be offered for sale at higher prices.*** Here again, the laws rest on the *ceteris paribus* assumption: the quantity supplied increases at higher prices *if* the determinants of supply are constant. ***Supply curves are upward-sloping to the right,*** as shown in Figure 3.5. Note how the *quantity supplied* jumps from 39 hours (point *d*) to 130 hours (point *h*) when the price of web service doubles (from $20 to $40 per hour).

law of supply: The quantity of a good supplied in a given time period increases as its price increases, *ceteris paribus.*

Market Supply

Figure 3.5 also illustrates how *market* supply is constructed from the supply decisions of individual sellers. In this case, only three web masters are available. Ann is willing to provide a lot of tutoring at low prices, whereas Bob requires at least $20 an hour. Carlos won't talk to students for less than $30 an hour.

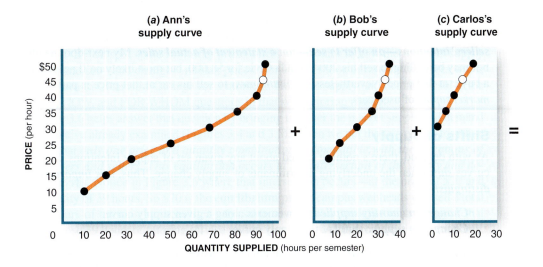

(a) Ann's supply curve   +   **(b) Bob's supply curve**   +   **(c) Carlos's supply curve**   =

QUANTITY SUPPLIED (hours per semester)

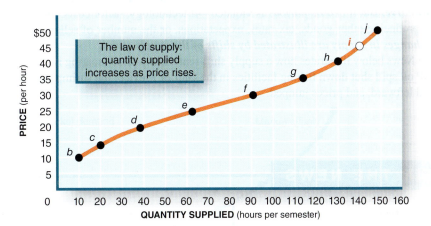

The law of supply: quantity supplied increases as price rises.

QUANTITY SUPPLIED (hours per semester)

FIGURE 3.5

Market Supply

The market supply curve indicates the *combined* sales intentions of all market participants—that is, the total quantities they are willing and able to sell at various prices. If the price of tutoring were $45 per hour (point *i*), the *total* quantity of services supplied would be 140 hours per semester. This quantity is determined by adding the supply decisions of all individual producers. In this case, Ann supplies 93 hours, Bob supplies 33, and Carlos supplies the rest.

	Price per Hour	Ann	+	Bob	+	Carlos	=	Market
				Quantity of Tutoring Supplied by				
j	$50	94		35		19		148
i	45	93		33		14		140
h	40	90		30		10		130
g	35	81		27		6		114
f	30	68		20		2		90
e	25	50		12		0		62
d	20	32		7		0		39
c	15	20		0		0		20
b	10	10		0		0		10

By adding the quantity each webhead is willing to offer at every price, we can construct the market supply curve. Notice in Figure 3.5 how the quantity supplied to the market at $45 (point *i*) comes from the individual efforts of Ann (93 hours), Bob (33 hours), and Carlos (14 hours). *The market supply curve is just a summary of the supply intentions of all producers.*

HOW

The market mechanism also determines HOW goods are produced. Profit-seeking producers will strive to produce web designs and automobiles in the most efficient way. They'll use market prices to decide not only WHAT to produce but also what resources to use in the production process. If new software simplifies web design—and is priced low enough—webheads will use it. Likewise, auto manufacturers will use robots rather than humans on the assembly line if robots reduce costs and increase profits.

FOR WHOM

Finally, the invisible hand of the market will determine who gets the goods produced. At Clearview College, who got web tutoring? Only those students who were willing and able to pay $20 per hour for that service. FOR WHOM are all those automobiles produced each year? The answer is the same: those consumers who are willing and able to pay the market price for a new car.

Optimal, Not Perfect

Not everyone is happy with these answers, of course. Tom would like to pay only $10 an hour for a tutor. And some of the Clearview students don't have enough income to buy any tutoring. They think it's unfair that they have to design their own web pages while rich students can have someone else do their design work for them. Students who can't afford cars are even less happy with the market's answer to the FOR WHOM question.

Although the outcomes of the marketplace aren't perfect, they're often optimal. Optimal outcomes are the best possible given our incomes and scarce resources. Sure, we'd like everyone to have access to tutoring and to drive a new car. But there aren't enough resources available to create such a utopia. So we have to ration available tutors and cars. The market mechanism performs this rationing function. People who want to supply tutoring or build cars are free to make that choice. And consumers are free to decide how they want to spend their income. In the process, we expect market participants to make decisions that maximize their own welfare. If they do, then we conclude that everyone is doing as well as possible, given their available resources.

THE ECONOMY TOMORROW

DEADLY SHORTAGES: THE ORGAN TRANSPLANT MARKET

As you were reading this chapter, dozens of Americans were dying from failed organs. More than 100,000 Americans are waiting for life-saving kidneys, livers, lungs, and other vital organs. They can't wait long, however. Every day at least 20 of these organ-diseased patients die. The clock is always ticking.

Modern technology can save most of these patients. Vital organs can be transplanted, extending the life of diseased patients. How many people are saved, however, depends on how well the organ "market" works.

The Supply of Organs. The only cure for liver disease and some other organ failures is a replacement organ. More than 50 years ago, doctors discovered that they could transplant an organ from one individual to another. Since then, medical technology has advanced to the point where organ transplants are exceptionally safe and successful. The constraint on this life-saving technique is the *supply* of transplantable organs.

Although more than 2 million Americans die each year, most deaths do not create transplantable organs. Only 20,000 or so people die in circumstances—such as brain death after a car crash—that make them suitable donors for life-saving transplants. Additional kidneys can be "harvested" from live donors (we have two kidneys but can function with only one; this is not true for liver, heart, or pancreas).

You don't have to die to supply an organ. Instead you become a donor by agreeing to release your organs after death. The agreement is typically certified on a driver's license and sometimes on a bracelet or "dog tag." This allows emergency doctors to identify potential organ supplies.

People become donors for many reasons. Moral principles, religious convictions, and humanitarianism all play a role in the donation decision. It's the same with blood donations: people give blood (while alive!) because they want to help save other individuals.

Market Incentives. Monetary incentives could also play a role. When blood donations are inadequate, hospitals and medical schools *buy* blood in the marketplace. People who might not donate blood come forth to *sell* blood when a price is offered. In principle, the same incentive might increase the number of *organ* donors. If offered cash now for a postmortem organ, would the willingness to donate increase? The law of supply suggests it would. Offer $1,000 in cash for signing up, and potential donors will start lining up. Offer more, and the quantity supplied will increase further.

Zero Price Ceiling. The government doesn't permit this to happen. In 1984 Congress forbade the purchase or sale of human organs in the United States (the National Organ Transplantation Act). In part, the prohibition was rooted in moral and religious convictions. It was also motivated by equity concerns—the FOR WHOM question. If organs could be bought and sold, then the rich would have a distinct advantage in living.

The prohibition on market sales is effectively a **price ceiling** set at zero. As a consequence, the only available organs are those supplied by altruistic donors—people who are willing to supply organs at a zero price. The quantity supplied can't be increased with (illegal) price incentives. In general, *price ceilings have three predictable effects: they*

price ceiling: An upper limit imposed on the price of a good.

- *Increase the quantity demanded*.
- *Decrease the quantity supplied.*
- *Create a market shortage.*

The Deadly Shortage. Figure 3.8 illustrates the consequences of this price ceiling. At a price of zero, only the quantity q_a of "altruistic" organs is available (roughly one-third of the potential supply). But the quantity q_d is demanded by all the organ-diseased individuals. The market shortage $q_d - q_a$ tells us how many patients will die.

Economists contend that many of these deaths are unnecessary. A University of Pennsylvania study showed that the quantity of organs supplied *doubled* when payment was offered. Without the government-set price ceiling, more organ-diseased patients would live. Figure 3.8 shows that q_E people would get transplants in a market-driven system. In the government-regulated system, only the quantity of q_a of transplants can occur.

Why does the government impose price controls that condemn more people to die? Because it feels the market unfairly distributes available organs. Only people who can afford

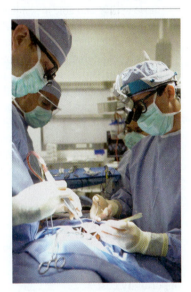

web click

The United Network for Organ Sharing (**www.unos.org**) maintains data on organ waiting lists and transplants.

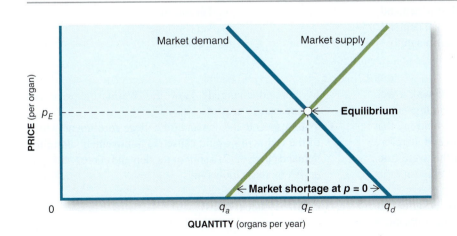

FIGURE 3.8

Organ Transplant Market

A market in human organs would deliver the quantity q_E at a price of p_E. The government-set price ceiling ($p = 0$) reduces the quantity supplied to q_a.

the price p_E end up living in the market-based system—a feature regulators say is unfair. In the absence of the market mechanism, however, the government must set other rules for who gets the even smaller quantity of organs supplied. That rationing system may be unfair as well.

SUMMARY

- People participate in the marketplace by offering to buy or sell goods and services, or factors of production. Participation is motivated by the desire to maximize utility (consumers), profits (business firms), or the general welfare (government agencies) from the limited resources each participant has. **LO3-1, LO3-2**
- All market transactions involve the exchange of either factors of production or finished products. Although the actual exchanges can occur anywhere, they take place in product markets or factor markets, depending on what is being exchanged. **LO3-1, LO3-2**
- People willing and able to buy a particular good at some price are part of the market demand for that product. All those willing and able to sell that good at some price are part of the market supply. Total market demand or supply is the sum of individual demands or supplies. **LO3-1, LO3-2**
- Supply and demand curves illustrate how the quantity demanded or supplied changes in response to a change in the price of that good, if nothing else changes (*ceteris paribus*). Demand curves slope downward; supply curves slope upward. **LO3-1, LO3-2**
- Determinants of market demand include the number of potential buyers and their respective tastes (desires), incomes, other goods, and expectations. If any of these determinants changes, the demand curve shifts. Movements along a demand curve are induced only by a change in the price of that good. **LO3-4**
- Determinants of market supply include factor costs, technology, profitability of other goods, expectations, tax rates, and number of sellers. Supply shifts when these underlying determinants change. **LO3-4**
- The quantity of goods or resources actually exchanged in each market depends on the behavior of all buyers and sellers, as summarized in market supply and demand curves. At the point where the two curves intersect, an equilibrium price—the price at which the quantity demanded equals the quantity supplied—is established. **LO3-3**
- A distinctive feature of the market equilibrium is that it's the only price-quantity combination acceptable to buyers and sellers alike. At higher prices, sellers supply more than buyers are willing to purchase (a market surplus); at lower prices, the amount demanded exceeds the quantity supplied (a market shortage). Only the equilibrium price clears the market. **LO3-3**
- Price ceilings are disequilibrium prices imposed on the marketplace. Such price controls create an imbalance between quantities demanded and supplied, resulting in market shortages. **LO3-5**

Key Terms

factor market	law of demand	law of supply
product market	substitute goods	equilibrium price
opportunity cost	complementary goods	market mechanism
supply	*ceteris paribus*	price floor
demand	shift in demand	market surplus
demand schedule	market demand	market shortage
demand curve	market supply	price ceiling

Questions for Discussion

1. In our story of Tom, the student confronted with a web design assignment, we emphasized the great urgency of his desire for web tutoring. Many people would say that Tom had an "absolute need" for web help and therefore was ready to "pay anything" to get it. If this were true, what shape would his demand curve have? Why isn't this realistic? **LO3-1**
2. How did Samsung's unveiling of the Galaxy S5 affect the demand for the S4 (News, p. 51)? What determinant(s) of demand changed? How did Walmart's price cut compensate? **LO3-1**
3. With respect to the demand for college enrollment, which of the following would cause (1) a movement along the demand curve or (2) a shift of the demand curve? **LO3-4**
   a. An increase in incomes.
   b. Lower tuition.
   c. More student loans.
   d. An increase in textbook prices.

4. What would have happened to shrimp prices and consumption if the government had prohibited price increases after the BP oil spill (see News, p. 58)? **LO3-5**

5. Why are scalpers able to resell tickets to the Final Four basketball games at such high prices (News, p. 61)? **LO3-2**

6. In Figure 3.8, why is the organ demand curve downward-sloping rather than vertical? **LO3-1**

7. The shortage in the organ market (Figure 3.8) requires a nonmarket rationing scheme. Who should get the available (q_a) organs? Is this fairer than the market-driven distribution? **LO3-5**

8. What would happen in the apple market if the government set a *minimum* price of $5.00 per apple? What might motivate such a policy? **LO3-5**

9. The World View on page 63 explains why gasoline prices rose in 2014. What will bring prices down? **LO3-4**

10. Is there a shortage of on-campus parking at your school? How might the shortage be resolved? **LO3-3**

mobile app Visit your mobile app store and download the Schiller: Study Econ app *today*!

PROBLEMS FOR CHAPTER 3

Name: _____

LO3-1 1. According to Figure 3.3, at what price would Tom buy 12 hours of web tutoring?
                 (a) Without a lottery win. _____
                 (b) With a lottery win. _____

LO3-3 2. According to Figures 3.5 and 3.6, what would the new equilibrium price of tutoring services be if Carlos decided to stop tutoring? _____

LO3-3 3. According to the News on page 61
       (a) What was the initial price of a ticket to the NCAA finals? _____
       (b) At that price was there (A) an equilibrium, (B) a shortage, or (C) a surplus? _____

LO3-3 4. Given the following data on gasoline supply and demand,
       (a) What is the equilibrium price? _____
       (b) How large a market shortage would exist if government set a price ceiling of $1 per gallon? _____

Price per gallon	$5.00	$4.00	$3.00	$2.00	$1.00			$5.00	$4.00	$3.00	$2.00	$1.00
Quantity demanded (gallons per day)							Quantity supplied (gallons per day)					
Al	1	2	3	4	5	Firm A		3	3	2	2	1
Betsy	0	1	1	1	2	Firm B		7	5	3	3	2
Casey	2	2	3	3	4	Firm C		6	4	3	3	1
Daisy	1	3	4	4	6	Firm D		6	5	3	2	0
Eddie	<u>1</u>	<u>2</u>	<u>2</u>	<u>3</u>	<u>5</u>	Firm E		<u>4</u>	<u>2</u>	<u>2</u>	<u>2</u>	<u>1</u>
Market total	__	__	__	__	__	Market total		__	__	__	__	__

LO3-2 5. As a result of the BP oil spill (News, p. 58), which of the following changed in the shrimp market (answer yes or no):
                 (a) Demand? _____
                 (b) Supply? _____
                 (c) Price? _____

LO3-4 6. Illustrate what's happening to oil prices in the World View on page 63.

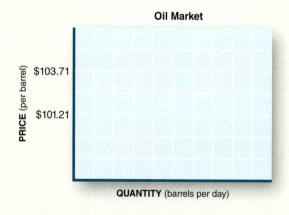

Oil Market

       (a) Which curve shifted? _____
       (b) Which direction did that curve shift (left or right)? _____
       (c) Did price (A) increase or (B) decrease? _____

LO3-5 7. According to Figure 3.8,
       (a) How many organs are supplied at a zero price? _____
       (b) How many people die in the government-regulated economy? _____
       (c) How many people die in the market-driven economy? _____

LO3-1 8. The goal of the price cut described in the News on page 51, was to (select one—enter letter)
       (A) Increase supply.   (C) Increase demand.
       (B) Increase quantity supplied.   (D) Increase quantity demanded. _____

LO3-5 9. In Figure 3.8, when a price ceiling of zero is imposed on the organ market, by how much does
    (*a*) The quantity of organs demanded increase?   _____
    (*b*) The demand increase?   _____
    (*c*) The quantity of organs supplied decrease?   _____
    (*d*) The supply decrease?   _____

LO3-5 10. Use the following data to draw supply and demand curves on the accompanying graph.

Price	$ 8	7	6	5	4	3	2	1
Quantity demanded	2	3	4	5	6	7	8	9
Quantity supplied	10	9	8	7	6	5	4	3

    (*a*) What is the equilibrium price?   _____
    (*b*) If a *minimum* price (price floor) of $6 is set,
        (*i*) What kind of disequilibrium situation results?   _____
        (*ii*) How large is it?   _____
    (*c*) If a *maximum* price (price ceiling) of $3 is set,
        (*i*) What disequilibrium situation results?   _____
        (*ii*) How large is it?   _____

Illustrate these answers.

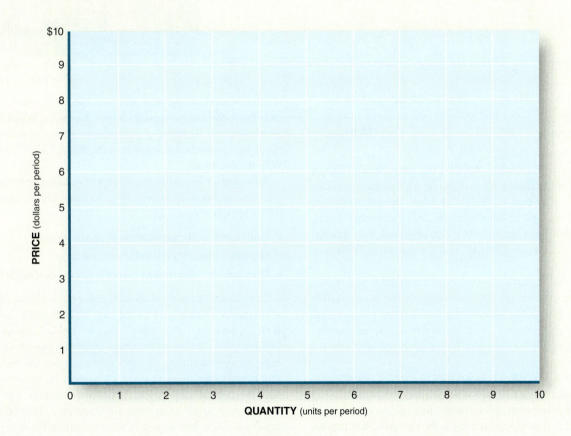

The Role of Government

After reading this chapter, you should know

LO4-1 The nature and causes of market failure.

LO4-2 How the public sector has grown.

LO4-3 Which taxes finance state, local, and federal governments.

LO4-4 The meaning of government failure.

The market has a keen ear for private wants, but a deaf ear for public needs.

—Robert Heilbroner

Markets do work: the interaction of supply and demand in product markets *does* generate goods and services. Likewise, the interaction of supply and demand in labor markets *does* yield jobs, wages, and a distribution of income. As we've observed, the market is capable of determining WHAT goods to produce, HOW, and FOR WHOM.

But are the market's answers good enough? Is the mix of output produced by unregulated markets the best possible mix? Will producers choose the production process that protects the environment? Will the market-generated distribution of income be fair enough? Will there be enough jobs for everyone who wants one?

In reality, markets don't always give us the best possible outcomes. Markets dominated by a few powerful corporations may charge excessive prices, limit output, provide poor service, or even retard technological advance. In the quest for profits, producers may sacrifice the environment for cost savings. In unfettered markets, some people may not get life-saving health care, basic education, or even adequate nutrition. When markets generate such outcomes, government intervention may be needed to ensure better answers to the WHAT, HOW, and FOR WHOM questions.

This chapter identifies the circumstances under which government intervention is desirable. To this end, we answer the following questions:

- **Under what circumstances do markets fail?**
- **How can government intervention help?**
- **How much government intervention is desirable?**

As we'll see, there's substantial agreement about how and when markets fail to give us the best WHAT, HOW, and FOR WHOM answers. But there's much less agreement about whether government intervention improves the situation. Indeed, an overwhelming majority of Americans are ambivalent about government intervention. They want the government to "fix" the mix of output, protect the environment, and ensure an adequate level of income for everyone. But voters are equally quick to blame government meddling for many of our economic woes.

MARKET FAILURE

We can visualize the potential for government intervention by focusing on the WHAT question. Our goal here is to produce the best possible mix of output with existing resources. We illustrated this goal earlier with production possibilities curves. Figure 4.1 assumes that of all the possible combinations of output we could produce, the unique combination at point *X* represents the most desirable one. In other words, it's the **optimal mix of output,** the one that maximizes our collective social utility. We haven't yet figured out how to pinpoint that optimal mix; we're simply using the arbitrary point *X* in Figure 4.1 to represent that best possible outcome.

Ideally, the **market mechanism** would lead us to point *X*. Price signals in the marketplace are supposed to move factors of production from one industry to another in response to consumer demands. If we demand more health care—offer to buy more at a given price—more resources (labor) will be allocated to health care services. Similarly, a fall in demand will encourage health care practitioners (doctors, nurses, and the like) to find jobs in another industry. *Changes in market prices direct resources from one industry to another, moving us along the perimeter of the production possibilities curve.*

Where will the market mechanism take us? Will it move resources around until we end up at the optimal point *X*? Or will it leave us at another point on the production possibilities curve with a *sub*optimal mix of output? (If point *X* is the *optimal,* or best possible, mix, all other output mixes must be *sub*optimal.)

We use the term **market failure** to refer to situations where the market generates imperfect (suboptimal) outcomes. If the invisible hand of the marketplace produces a mix of output that's different from the one society most desires, then it has failed. *Market failure implies that the forces of supply and demand haven't led us to the best point on the production possibilities curve.* Such a failure is illustrated by point *M* in Figure 4.1. Point *M* is assumed to be the mix of output generated by market forces. Notice that the market mix (*M*) doesn't represent the optimal mix, which is assumed to be at point *X*. We get less health care and more of other goods than are optimal. The market in this case *fails;* we get the wrong answer to the WHAT question.

Market failure opens the door for government intervention. If the market can't do the job, we need some form of *nonmarket* force to get the right answers. In terms of Figure 4.1, we need something to change the mix of output—to move us from point *M* (the market mix of output) to point *X* (the optimal mix of output). Accordingly, *market failure establishes a basis for government intervention.* We look to the government to push market outcomes closer to the ideal.

Causes of Market Failure. Because market failure is the justification for government intervention, we need to know how and when market failure occurs. *The four specific sources of market failure are*

- *Public goods.*
- *Externalities.*
- *Market power.*
- *Inequity.*

We will first examine the nature of these problems, then see why government intervention is called for in each case.

optimal mix of output: The most desirable combination of output attainable with existing resources, technology, and social values.

market mechanism: The use of market prices and sales to signal desired outputs (or resource allocations).

market failure: An imperfection in the market mechanism that prevents optimal outcomes.

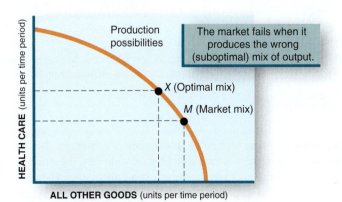

FIGURE 4.1
Market Failure

We can produce any mix of output on the production possibilities curve. Our goal is to produce the optimal (best possible) mix of output, as represented by point *X*. Market forces, however, might produce another combination, like point *M*. In that case, the market fails—it produces a *sub*optimal mix of output.

Public Goods

The market mechanism has the unique capability to signal consumer demands for various goods and services. By offering to pay for goods, we express our preferences about WHAT to produce. However, this mode of communication works efficiently only if the benefits of consuming a particular good are available only to the individuals who purchase that product.

Consider doughnuts, for example. When you eat a doughnut, you alone get the satisfaction from its sweet, greasy taste—that is, you derive a private benefit. No one else benefits from your consumption of a doughnut: The doughnut you purchase in the market is yours alone to consume; it's a **private good.** Accordingly, your decision to purchase the doughnut will be determined only by your anticipated satisfaction, your income, and your opportunity costs.

private good: A good or service whose consumption by one person excludes consumption by others.

No Exclusion. Most of the goods and services produced in the public sector are different from doughnuts—and not just because doughnuts look, taste, and smell different from "star wars" missile shields. When you buy a doughnut, you exclude others from consumption of that product. If Dunkin' Donuts sells you a particular pastry, it can't supply the same pastry to someone else. If you devour it, no one else can. In this sense, the transaction and product are completely private.

The same exclusiveness is not characteristic of national defense. If you buy a missile defense system to thwart enemy attacks, there's no way you can exclude your neighbors from the protection your system provides. Either the missile shield deters would-be attackers—like Israel's "Iron Dome" (see the accompanying World View)—or it doesn't. In the former case, both you and your neighbors survive happily ever after; in the latter case, we're all blown away together. In that sense, you and your neighbors consume the benefits of a missile shield *jointly*. National defense isn't a divisible service. There's no such thing as exclusive consumption here. The consumption of nuclear defenses is a communal feat, no matter who pays for them. Accordingly, national defense is regarded as a **public good** in the sense that *consumption of a public good by one person doesn't preclude consumption of the same good by another person.* By contrast, a doughnut is a private good because if I eat it, no one else can consume it.

public good: A good or service whose consumption by one person does not exclude consumption by others.

WORLD VIEW

Israel's "Iron Dome" Frustrates Hamas

The fragile peace between Israel and its Arab neighbors has broken down again. This time, though, Israel has a strategic advantage: its "Iron Dome" air defense system. The Iron Dome intercepts and destroys incoming missiles and mortars. So the hail of missiles Hamas is firing from Gaza into Israel rarely find their targets—they are destroyed in mid-air. The Israeli defense minister claims the Iron Dome is 90 percent effective in shielding population centers. Hamas has no such defense against artillery, bombs, and even ground forces dispatched by Israel into Gaza.

Source: News reports, July 20–28, 2014.

ANALYSIS: An air-defense system is a *public good,* as consumption of its services by one individual does not preclude consumption by others. Nonpayers cannot be excluded from its protection.

free rider: An individual who reaps direct benefits from someone else's purchase (consumption) of a public good.

The Free-Rider Dilemma. The communal nature of public goods creates a dilemma. If you and I will *both* benefit from nuclear defenses, which one of us should buy the missile shield? I'd prefer that *you* buy it, thereby giving me protection at no direct cost. Hence I may profess no desire for a missile shield, secretly hoping to take a **free ride** on your market purchase. Unfortunately, you too have an incentive to conceal your desire for national defenses. As a consequence, neither one of us may step forward to demand a missile shield in the marketplace. We'll both end up defenseless.

Flood control is also a public good. No one in the valley wants to be flooded out. But each landowner knows that a flood control dam will protect *all* the landowners, regardless of who pays. Either the entire valley is protected or no one is. Accordingly, individual farmers and landowners may say they don't want a dam and aren't willing to pay for it. Everyone is waiting and hoping that someone else will pay for flood control. In other words, everyone wants a *free ride*. Thus, if we leave it to market forces, no one will *demand* flood control, and all the property in the valley will be washed away.

The difference between public goods and private goods rests on *technical considerations,* not political philosophy. The central question is whether we have the technical capability to exclude nonpayers. In the case of national defense or flood control, we simply don't have that capability. Even city streets have the characteristics of public goods. Although theoretically we could restrict the use of streets to those who paid to use them, a tollgate on every corner would be exceedingly expensive and impractical. Here again, joint or public consumption appears to be the only feasible alternative. As the following News on local firefighting emphasizes, the technical capability to exclude nonpayers is the key factor in identifying "public goods."

Flood control is a public good.

IN THE NEWS

Firefighters Watch as Home Burns to the Ground

OBION COUNTY, Tenn.—Imagine your home catches fire, but the local fire department won't respond, then watches it burn. That's exactly what happened to a local family tonight.

A local neighborhood is furious after firefighters watched as an Obion County, Tennessee, home burned to the ground.

The homeowner, Gene Cranick, said he offered to pay whatever it would take for firefighters to put out the flames but was told it was too late. They wouldn't do anything to stop his house from burning.

Each year, Obion County residents must pay $75 if they want fire protection from the city of South Fulton. But the Cranicks did not pay.

The mayor said if homeowners don't pay, they're out of luck.

This fire went on for hours because garden hoses just wouldn't put it out.

It was only when a neighbor's field caught fire, a neighbor who had paid the county fire service fee, that the department responded. Gene Cranick asked the fire chief to make an exception and save his home; the chief wouldn't.

—Jason Hibbs

Source: WPSD Local 6, Paducah, KY, September 30, 2010. Used with permission.

ANALYSIS: A product is a "public good" only if nonpayers *cannot* be excluded from its consumption. Firefighters in Tennessee proved that fire protection is not inherently a public good: they let the nonpaying homeowner's house burn down!

web click

For examples of public goods in addition to those considered in the accompanying pages, visit **www.econlib.org** and search "public goods."

To the list of public goods we could add snow removal, the administration of justice (including prisons), the regulation of commerce, the conduct of foreign relations, airport security, and even Fourth of July fireworks. These services—which cost tens of *billions* of dollars and employ thousands of workers—provide benefits to everyone, no matter who

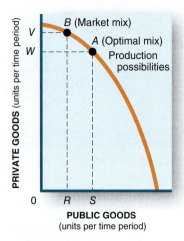

FIGURE 4.2

Underproduction of Public Goods

Suppose point A represents the optimal mix of output—that is, the mix of private and public goods that maximizes society's welfare. Because consumers won't demand purely public goods in the marketplace, the price mechanism won't allocate so many resources to their production. Instead the market will tend to produce a mix of output like point B, which includes fewer public goods (OR) than are optimal (OS).

pays for them. In each instance it's technically impossible or prohibitively expensive to exclude nonpayers from the services provided.

Underproduction of Public Goods. The free riders associated with public goods upset the customary practice of paying for what you get. If I can get all the national defense, flood control, and laws I want without paying for them, I'm not about to complain. I'm perfectly happy to let you pay for the services while we all consume them. Of course, you may feel the same way. Why should you pay for these services if you can consume just as much of them when your neighbors foot the whole bill? It might seem selfish not to pay your share of the cost of providing public goods. But you'd be better off in a material sense if you spent your income on doughnuts, letting others pick up the tab for public services.

Because the familiar link between paying and consuming is broken, public goods can't be peddled in the supermarket. People are reluctant to buy what they can get free. Hence, *if public goods were marketed like private goods, everyone would wait for someone else to pay.* The end result might be a total lack of public services. This is the kind of dilemma Robert Heilbroner had in mind when he spoke of the market's "deaf ear" (see the quote at the beginning of this chapter).

The production possibilities curve in Figure 4.2 illustrates the dilemma created by public goods. Suppose that point A represents the optimal mix of private and public goods. It's the mix of goods and services we'd select if everyone's preferences were known and reflected in production decisions. The market mechanism won't lead us to point A, however, because the *demand* for public goods will be hidden. If we rely on the market, nearly everyone will withhold demand for public goods, waiting for a free ride to point A. As a result, we'll get a smaller quantity of public goods than we really want. The market mechanism will leave us at point B, with few, if any, public goods. Since point A is assumed to be optimal, point B must be *suboptimal* (inferior to point A). The market fails: we can't rely on the market mechanism to allocate enough resources to the production of public goods, no matter how much they might be desired.

Note that we're using the term "public good" in a peculiar way. To most people, "public good" refers to any good or service the government produces. In economics, however, the meaning is much more restrictive. The term "public good" refers only to those nonexcludable goods and services that must be consumed jointly, both by those who pay for them and by those who don't. Public goods can be produced by either the government or the private sector. Private goods can be produced in either sector as well. The problem is that *the market tends to underproduce public goods and overproduce private goods.* If we want more public goods, we need a *nonmarket* force—government intervention—to get them. The government will have to force people to pay taxes, then use the tax revenues to pay for the production of national defense, flood control, snow removal, and other public goods.

Externalities

The free-rider problem associated with public goods is one justification for government intervention. It's not the only justification, however. Further grounds for intervention arise from the tendency of costs or benefits of some market activities to "spill over" onto third parties.

Consider the case of cigarettes. The price someone is willing to pay for a pack of cigarettes reflects the amount of satisfaction a smoker anticipates from its consumption. If that price is high enough, tobacco companies will produce the cigarettes demanded. That is how market-based price signals are supposed to work. In this case, however, the price paid isn't a satisfactory signal of the product's desirability. The smoker's pleasure is offset in part by nonsmokers' *dis*pleasure. In this case, smoke literally spills over onto other consumers, causing them discomfort, ill health, and even death (see the World View below). Yet their loss isn't reflected in the market price: the harm caused to nonsmokers is *external* to the market price of cigarettes.

WORLD VIEW

Secondhand Smoke Kills 600,000 People a Year

Secondhand smoke globally kills more than 600,000 people each year, accounting for 1 percent of all deaths worldwide.

Researchers estimate that annually secondhand smoke causes about 379,000 deaths from heart disease, 165,000 deaths from lower respiratory disease, 36,900 deaths from asthma, and 21,400 deaths from lung cancer.

Children account for about 165,000 of the deaths. Forty percent of children and 30 percent of adults regularly breathe in secondhand smoke.

Source: World Health Organization.

ANALYSIS: The health risks imposed on nonsmokers via passive smoke represent an external cost. The market price of cigarettes doesn't reflect these costs borne by third parties.

The term **externalities** refers to all costs or benefits of a market activity borne by a third party—that is, by someone other than the immediate producer or consumer. *Whenever externalities are present, market prices aren't a valid measure of a good's value to society.* As a consequence, the market will fail to produce the right mix of output. Specifically, *the market will underproduce goods that yield external benefits and overproduce those that generate external costs.*

externalities: Costs (or benefits) of a market activity borne by a third party; the difference between the social and private costs (benefits) of a market activity.

External Costs. Figure 4.3 shows how external costs cause the market to overproduce cigarettes. The market demand curve includes only the wishes of smokers—that is, people who are willing and able to purchase cigarettes. The forces of market demand and supply result in an equilibrium at E_M in which q_M cigarettes are produced and consumed. The market price P_M reflects the value of those cigarettes to smokers.

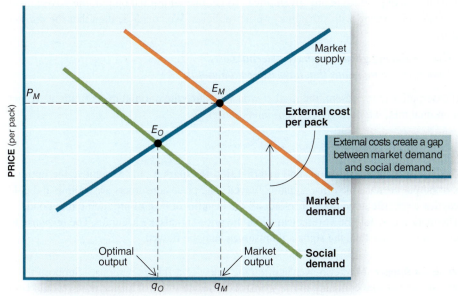

External costs create a gap between market demand and social demand.

FIGURE 4.3

Externalities

The market responds to consumer demands, not externalities. Smokers demand q_M cigarettes at the equilibrium price P_M. But external costs on nonsmokers imply that the *social* demand for cigarettes is less than (below) *market* demand. The socially optimal level of output is q_O, less than the market output q_M.

The well-being of *non*smokers isn't reflected in the market equilibrium. To take the *non*-smokers' interests into account, we must subtract the external costs imposed on *them* from the value that *smokers* put on cigarettes. In general,

Social demand = Market demand ± Externalities

In this case, the externality is a *cost,* so we must *subtract* the external cost from market demand to get a full accounting of social demand. The "social demand" curve in Figure 4.3 reflects this computation. To find this curve, we subtract the amount of external cost from every price on the market demand curve. Hence the social demand curve lies below the market demand curve in this case. What the social demand curve tells us is how much society would be willing and able to pay for cigarettes if the preferences of *both* smokers and nonsmokers were taken into account.

The social demand curve in Figure 4.3 creates a social equilibrium at E_O. At this juncture, we see that the socially *optimal* quantity of cigarettes is q_O, not the larger market-generated level at q_M. In this sense, the market produces too many cigarettes.

Externalities also exist in production. A power plant that burns high-sulfur coal damages the surrounding environment. Yet the damage inflicted on neighboring people, vegetation, and buildings is external to the cost calculations of the firm. Because the cost of such pollution is not reflected in the price of electricity, the firm will tend to produce more electricity (and pollution) than is socially desirable. To reduce this imbalance, the government has to step in and change market outcomes.

External Benefits. Externalities can also be beneficial. A product may generate external *benefits* rather than external *costs.* Your college is an example. The students who attend your school benefit directly from the education they receive. That's why they (and you) are willing to pay for tuition, books, and other services. The students in attendance aren't the only beneficiaries of this educational service, however. The research that a university conducts may yield benefits for a much broader community. The values and knowledge students acquire may also be shared with family, friends, and coworkers. These benefits would all be *external* to the market transaction between a paying student and the school. Positive externalities also arise from immunizations against infectious diseases: the person getting immunized benefits, as do all the people with whom that person comes into contact.

If a product yields external benefits, the social demand is greater than the market demand. In this case, the social value of the good *exceeds* the market price (by the amount of external benefit). Accordingly, society wants *more* of the product than the market mechanism alone will produce at any given price. To get that additional output, the government may have to intervene with subsidies or other policies. We conclude then that *the market fails by*

* *Overproducing goods that have external costs.*
* *Underproducing goods that have external benefits.*

If externalities are present, the market won't produce the optimal mix of output. To get that optimal mix, we need government intervention.

Market Power

In the case of both public goods and externalities, the market fails to achieve the optimal mix of output because the price signal is flawed. The price consumers are willing and able to pay for a specific good doesn't reflect all the benefits or cost of producing that good.

The market may fail, however, even when the price signals are accurate. The *response* to price signals, rather than the signals themselves, may be flawed.

monopoly: A firm that produces the entire market supply of a particular good or service.

Restricted Supply. Market power is often the cause of a flawed response. Suppose there were only one airline company in the world. This single seller of airline travel would be a **monopoly**—that is, the only producer in that industry. As a monopolist, the airline could charge extremely high prices without worrying that travelers would flock to a competing airline. At the same time, the high prices paid by consumers would express the importance of that service to society. Ideally, such prices would act as a signal to producers to build and fly more planes—to change the mix of output. But a monopolist doesn't have to cater to every consumer's whim. It can limit airline travel and obstruct our efforts to achieve an optimal mix of output.

Monopoly is the most severe form of **market power.** More generally, market power refers to any situation in which a single producer or consumer has the ability to alter the market price of a specific product. If the publisher (McGraw-Hill) charges a high price for this book, you'll have to pay the tab. McGraw-Hill has market power because there are relatively few economics textbooks and your professor has required you to use this one. You don't have power in the textbook market because your decision to buy or not won't alter the market price of this text. You're only one of the million students who are taking an introductory economics course this year.

market power: The ability to alter the market price of a good or a service.

The market power McGraw-Hill possesses is derived from the copyright on this text. No matter how profitable textbook sales might be, no one else is permitted to produce or sell this particular book. Patents are another common source of market power because they also preclude others from making or selling a specific product. Market power may also result from control of resources, restrictive production agreements, or efficiencies of large-scale production.

Whatever the source of market power, the direct consequence is that one or more producers attain discretionary power over the market's response to price signals. They may use that discretion to enrich themselves rather than to move the economy toward the optimal mix of output. In this case, the market will again fail to deliver the most desired goods and services.

The mandate for government intervention in this case is to prevent or dismantle concentrations of market power. That's the basic purpose of **antitrust** policy. Another option is to *regulate* market behavior. This was one of the goals of the antitrust case against Microsoft. The government was less interested in breaking Microsoft's near monopoly on operating systems than in changing the way Microsoft behaved.

antitrust: Government intervention to alter market structure or prevent abuse of market power.

In some cases, it may be economically efficient to have one large firm supply an entire market. Such a situation arises in **natural monopoly,** where a single firm can achieve economies of scale over the entire range of market output. Utility companies, local telephone service, subway systems, and cable all exhibit such scale (size) efficiencies. In these cases, a monopoly *structure* may be economically desirable. The government may have to regulate the *behavior* of a natural monopoly, however, to ensure that consumers get the benefits of that greater efficiency.

natural monopoly: An industry in which one firm can achieve economies of scale over the entire range of market supply.

Inequity

Public goods, externalities, and market power all cause resource misallocations. Where these phenomena exist, the market mechanism will fail to produce the optimal mix of output in the best possible way.

Beyond the questions of WHAT and HOW to produce, we're also concerned about FOR WHOM output is produced. The market answers this question by distributing a larger share of total output to those with the most income. Although this result may be efficient, it's not necessarily equitable. As we saw in Chapter 2, the market mechanism may enrich some people while leaving others to seek shelter in abandoned cars. If such outcomes violate our vision of equity, we may want the government to change the market-generated distribution of income.

Taxes and Transfers. The tax-and-transfer system is the principal mechanism for redistributing incomes. The idea here is to take some of the income away from those who have "too much" and give it to those whom the market has left with "too little." Taxes are levied to take back some of the income received from the market. Those tax revenues are then redistributed

transfer payments: Payments to individuals for which no current goods or services are exchanged, like Social Security, welfare, and unemployment benefits.

merit good: A good or service society deems everyone is entitled to some minimal quantity of.

via transfer payments to those deemed needy, such as the poor, the aged, and the unemployed. **Transfer payments** are income payments for which no goods or services are exchanged. They're used to bolster the incomes of those for whom the market itself provides too little.

Merit Goods. Often our vision of what is "too little" is defined in terms of specific goods and services. There is a widespread consensus in the United States that everyone is entitled to some minimum levels of shelter, food, and health care. These are regarded as **merit goods,** in the sense that everyone merits at least some minimum provision of such goods. When the market does not distribute that minimum provision, the government is called on to fill the gaps. In this case, the income transfers take the form of *in-kind* transfers (e.g., food stamps, housing vouchers, Medicaid) rather than *cash* transfers (e.g., welfare checks, Social Security benefits).

Some people argue that we don't need the government to help the poor—that private charity alone will suffice. Unfortunately, private charity alone has never been adequate. One reason private charity doesn't suffice is the "free-rider" problem. If I contribute heavily to the poor, you benefit from safer streets (fewer muggers), a better environment (fewer slums and homeless people), and a clearer conscience (knowing that fewer people are starving). In this sense, the relief of misery is a *public* good. Were I the only taxpayer to benefit substantially from the reduction of poverty, then charity would be a private affair. As long as income support substantially benefits the public at large, then income redistribution is a *public* good, for which public funding is appropriate. This is the *economic* rationale for public income redistribution activities. To this rationale one can add such moral arguments as seem appropriate.

Macro Instability

The micro failures of the marketplace imply that we're at the wrong point on the production possibilities curve or inequitably distributing the output produced. There's another basic question we've swept under the rug, however. How do we get to the production possibilities curve in the first place? To reach the curve, we must utilize all available resources and technology. Can we be confident that the invisible hand of the marketplace will use all available resources? That confidence was shattered in 2008–2009 when total output contracted and **unemployment** soared. Millions of people who were willing and able to work but unable to find jobs demanded that the government intervene to increase output and create more jobs. The market had failed.

And what about prices? Price signals are a critical feature of the market mechanism. But the validity of those signals depends on some stable measure of value. What good is a doubling of salary when the price of everything you buy doubles as well? Generally, rising prices will enrich people who own property and impoverish people who rent. That's why we strive to avoid **inflation**—a situation in which the *average* price level is increasing.

Historically, the marketplace has been wracked with bouts of both unemployment and inflation. These experiences have prompted calls for government intervention at the macro level. *The goal of macro intervention is to foster economic growth—to get us on the production possibilities curve (full employment), maintain a stable price level (price stability), and increase our capacity to produce (growth).*

unemployment: The inability of labor force participants to find jobs.

inflation: An increase in the average level of prices of goods and services.

GROWTH OF GOVERNMENT

The potential micro and macro failures of the marketplace provide specific justifications for government intervention. The question then turns to how well the activities of the public sector correspond to these implied mandates.

Federal Growth

Until the 1930s the federal government's role was largely limited to national defense (a public good), enforcement of a common legal system (also a public good), and provision of postal service (equity). The Great Depression of the 1930s spawned a new range of government activities, including welfare and Social Security programs (equity), minimum wage laws and workplace standards (regulation), and massive public works (public goods and externalities). In the 1950s the federal government also assumed a greater role in maintaining macroeconomic stability (macro failure), protecting the environment (externalities), and safeguarding the public's health (externalities and equity).

These increasing responsibilities have greatly increased the size of the public sector. In 1902 the federal government employed fewer than 350,000 people and spent a mere $650 *million.* Today the federal government employs nearly 4 million people and spends nearly $4 *trillion* a year.

Direct Expenditure. Figure 4.4 summarizes the growth of the public sector since 1930. World War II caused a massive increase in the size of the federal government. Federal purchases of goods and services for the war accounted for more than 40 percent of total output during the 1943–1944 period. The federal share of total U.S. output fell abruptly after World War II, rose again during the Korean War (1950–1953), and has declined slightly since then.

The decline in the federal share of total output is somewhat at odds with most people's perception of government growth. This discrepancy is explained by two phenomena. First, people see the *absolute* size of the government growing every year. But we're focusing here on the *relative* size of the public sector. From 1950 until 2008 the public sector grew a bit more slowly than the private sector, slightly reducing its relative size. The trend was broken in 2008–2011, when the private sector shrank and the federal government undertook massive stimulus spending.

Income Transfers. Figure 4.4 depicts only government spending on goods and services, not *all* public spending. Direct expenditure on goods and services absorbs real resources, but income transfers don't. Hence income transfers don't directly alter the mix of output. Their effect is primarily *distributional* (the FOR WHOM question), not *allocative* (the

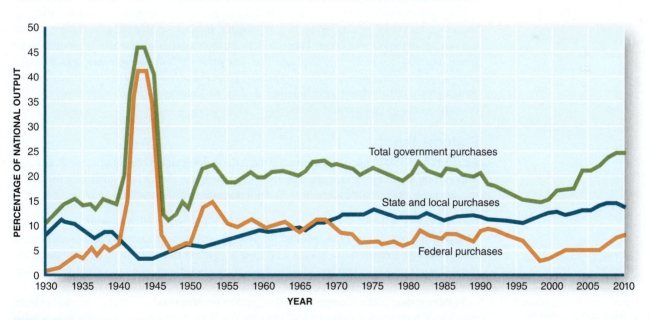

FIGURE 4.4
Government Growth

During World War II the public sector purchased nearly half of total U.S. output. Since the early 1950s the public sector share of total output has been closer to 20 percent. Within the public sector, however, there's been a major shift: state and local claims on

resources have grown, while the federal share has declined significantly.

Source: U.S. Bureau of Economic Analysis.

WHAT question). Were income transfers included, the relative size and growth of the federal government would be larger than Figure 4.4 depicts. This is because *most of the growth in federal spending has come from increased income transfers, not purchases of goods and services.* Income transfers now account for more than half of federal spending.

State and Local Growth

State and local spending on goods and services has followed a very different path from federal expenditure. Prior to World War II, state and local governments dominated public sector spending. During the war, however, the share of total output going to state and local governments fell, hitting a low of 3 percent in that period (Figure 4.4).

State and local spending caught up with federal spending in the mid-1960s and has exceeded it ever since. Today *more than 80,000 state and local government entities buy much more output than Uncle Sam and employ five times as many people.* Education is a huge expenditure at lower levels of government. Most direct state spending is on colleges; most local spending is for elementary and secondary education. The fastest-growing areas for state expenditure are prisons (public safety) and welfare. At the local level, sewage and trash services are claiming an increasing share of budgets.

TAXATION

Whatever we may think of any specific government expenditure, we must recognize one basic fact of life: we pay for government spending. We pay not just in terms of tax *dollars* but in the more fundamental form of a changed mix of output. Government expenditures on goods and services absorb factors of production that could be used to produce consumer goods. The mix of output changes toward *more* public services and *fewer* private goods and services. Resources used to produce missile shields, operate elementary schools, or journey to Mars aren't available to produce cars, houses, or restaurant meals. In real terms, *the cost of government spending is measured by the private sector output sacrificed when the government employs scarce factors of production.*

The **opportunity costs** of public spending aren't always apparent. We don't directly hand over factors of production to the government. Instead we give the government part of our income in the form of taxes. Those dollars are then used to buy factors of production or goods and services in the marketplace. Thus *the primary function of taxes is to transfer command over resources (purchasing power) from the private sector to the public sector.* Although the government also borrows dollars to finance its purchases, taxes are the primary source of government revenues.

Federal Taxes

As recently as 1902, much of the revenue the federal government collected came from taxes imposed on alcoholic beverages. The federal government didn't have authority to collect income taxes. As a consequence, *total* federal revenue in 1902 was only $653 million.

Income Taxes. All that changed, beginning in 1915. The Sixteenth Amendment to the U.S. Constitution, enacted in 1915, granted the federal government authority to collect *income* taxes. The government now collects well over $1 *trillion* in that form alone. Although the federal government still collects taxes on alcoholic beverages, the individual income tax has become the largest single source of government revenue (see Figure 4.5).

In theory, the federal income tax is designed to be **progressive**—that is, to take a larger *fraction* of high incomes than of low incomes. In 2014, for example, a single person with less than $9,000 of taxable income was taxed at 10 percent. People with incomes of $37,000–$89,000 confronted a 25 percent tax rate on their additional income. The marginal tax rate got as high as 39.6 percent for people earning more than $407,000 in income. Thus *people with high incomes not only pay more taxes but also pay a larger* **fraction** *of their income in taxes.*

web click

Information on government expenditures and national economic output for different countries can be found at **www.cia.gov.** Visit the "World Factbook" link.

opportunity costs: The most desired goods or services that are forgone in order to obtain something else.

progressive tax: A tax system in which tax rates rise as incomes rise.

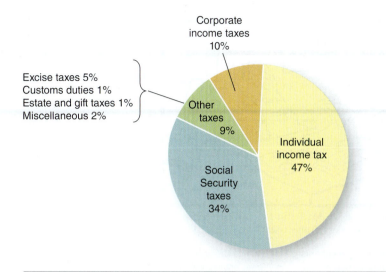

Corporate income taxes 10%

Excise taxes 5%
Customs duties 1%
Estate and gift taxes 1%
Miscellaneous 2%

Other taxes 9%

Individual income tax 47%

Social Security taxes 34%

FIGURE 4.5
Federal Taxes

Taxes transfer purchasing power from the private sector to the public sector. The largest federal tax is the individual income tax. The second-largest source of federal revenue is the Social Security payroll tax.

Source: Office of Management and Budget, FY2015 data.

web click

For the most recent budget information, visit the Office of Management and Budget website (**www.whitehouse.gov/omb),** and click on the tab labeled "The Budget."

Social Security Taxes. The second major source of federal revenue is the Social Security payroll tax. People working now transfer part of their earnings to retired workers by making "contributions" to Social Security. There's nothing voluntary about these "contributions"; they take the form of mandatory payroll deductions. In 2015, each worker paid 7.65 percent of his or her wages to Social Security, and employers contributed an equal amount. As a consequence, the government collected more than $1 trillion from this tax.

At first glance, the Social Security payroll tax looks like a **proportional tax**—that is, a tax that takes the *same* fraction of every taxpayer's income. But this isn't the case. The Social Security (FICA) tax isn't levied on every payroll dollar. Incomes above a certain ceiling ($118,500 in 2015) aren't taxed. As a result, workers with *really* high salaries turn over a smaller fraction of their incomes to Social Security than do low-wage workers. This makes the Social Security payroll tax a **regressive tax.**

proportional tax: A tax that levies the same rate on every dollar of income.

regressive tax: A tax system in which tax rates fall as incomes rise.

Corporate Taxes. The federal government taxes the profits of corporations as well as the incomes of consumers. But there are far fewer corporations (less than 4 million) than consumers (320 million), and their profits are small in comparison to total consumer income. In 2015, the federal government collected less than $350 billion in corporate income taxes, despite the fact that it imposed a top tax rate of 35 percent on corporate profits.

Excise Taxes. The last major source of federal revenue is excise taxes. Like the early taxes on whiskey, excise taxes are sales taxes imposed on specific goods and services. The federal government taxes not only liquor ($13.50 per gallon) but also gasoline (18.4 cents per gallon), cigarettes ($1.01 per pack), air fares (7.5 percent), firearms (10–11 percent), gambling (0.25 percent), and a variety of other goods and services. Such taxes not only discourage production and consumption of these goods by raising their price and thereby reducing the quantity demanded; they also raise a substantial amount of revenue.

web click

For charts and data on federal taxes and revenues, visit **crfb.org** (Committee for a Responsible Federal Budget).

State and Local Revenues

Taxes. State and local governments also levy taxes on consumers and businesses. In general, cities depend heavily on property taxes, and state governments rely heavily on sales taxes. Although nearly all states and many cities also impose income taxes, effective tax rates are so low (averaging less than 2 percent of personal income) that income tax revenues are much less than sales and property tax revenues.

Like the Social Security payroll tax, state and local taxes tend to be *regressive*—that is, they take a larger share of income from the poor than from the rich. Consider a 4 percent sales tax, for example. It might appear that a uniform tax rate like this would affect all

"I can't find anything wrong here, Mr. Truffle . . . you just seem to have too much left after taxes."

Analysis: Taxes are a financing mechanism that enables the government to purchase scarce resources. Higher taxes imply fewer private sector purchases.

consumers equally. But people with lower incomes tend to spend most of their income on goods and services. Thus most of their income is subject to sales taxes. By contrast, a person with a high income can afford to save part of his or her income and thereby shelter it from sales taxes. A family that earns $40,000 and spends $30,000 of it on taxable goods and services, for example, pays $1,200 in sales taxes when the tax rate is 4 percent. In effect, then, they are handing over 3 percent of their *income* ($1,200 ÷ $40,000) to the state. By contrast, the family that makes only $12,000 and spends $11,500 of it for food, clothing, and shelter pays $460 in sales taxes in the same state. Their total tax is smaller, but it represents a much larger *share* (3.8 versus 3.0 percent) of their income.

Local property taxes are also regressive because poor people devote a larger portion of their incomes to housing costs. Hence a larger share of a poor family's income is subject to property taxes. State lotteries are also regressive for the same reason (see the following News). Low-income players spend 1.4 percent of their incomes on lottery tickets while upper-income players devote only 0.1 percent of their income to lottery purchases.

IN THE NEWS

Perpetuating Poverty: Lotteries Prey on the Poor

A recently released Gallup survey confirms the fears of many who oppose government-promoted gambling: the poorest among us are contributing much more to lottery revenues than those with higher incomes. The poll found that people who played the lottery with an income of less than $20,000 annually spent an average of $46 per month on lottery tickets. That comes out to more than $550 per year, and it is nearly double the amount spent in any other income bracket.

The significance of this is magnified when we look deeper into the figures. Those with annual incomes ranging from $30,000 to $50,000 had the second-highest average—$24 per month, or $288 per year. A person making $20,000 spends three times as much on lottery tickets on average than does someone making $30,000. And keep in mind that these numbers represent average spending. For every one or two people who spend just a few bucks a year on lotteries, others spend thousands.

—Jordan Ballor

Source: Acton Institute, **www.acton.org**, March 3, 2004. Used with permission.

ANALYSIS: Poor people spend a larger percentage of their income on lottery tickets than do rich people. This makes lotteries a regressive source of government revenue.

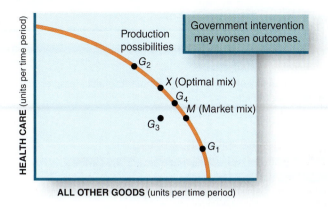

FIGURE 4.6
Government Failure

When the market produces a suboptimal mix of output like point *M*, the goal of government is to move output to the social optimum (point *X*). A move to G_4 would be an improvement in the mix of output. But government intervention *may* move the economy to points G_1, G_2, or G_3—all reflecting government failure.

GOVERNMENT FAILURE

Some government intervention in the marketplace is clearly desirable. The market mechanism can fail for a variety of reasons, leaving a laissez-faire economy short of its economic goals. But how much government intervention is desirable? Communist nations once thought that complete government control of production, consumption, and distribution decisions was the surest path to utopia. They learned the hard way that ***not only markets but governments as well can fail.*** In this context, **government failure** means that government intervention fails to move us closer to our economic goals.

In Figure 4.6, the goal of government intervention is to move the mix of output from point *M* (failed market outcome) to point *X* (the social optimum). But government intervention might unwittingly move us to point G_1, making matters worse. Or the government might overreact, sending us to point G_2. Red tape and onerous regulation might even force us to point G_3, *inside* the production possibilities curve (with less total output than at point *M*). All those possibilities (G_1, G_2, G_3) represent government failure. **Government intervention is desirable only to the extent that it *improves* market outcomes** (e.g., G_4). Government intervention in the FOR WHOM question is desirable only if the distribution of income gets better, not worse, as a result of taxes and transfers. Even when outcomes improve, government failure may occur if the costs of government intervention exceed the benefits of an improved output mix, cleaner production methods, or a fairer distribution of income.

government failure: Government intervention that fails to improve economic outcomes.

Perceptions of Government Failure

Taxpayers seem to have strong opinions about government failure. A 2013 poll asked people how confident they were that the federal government could successfully tackle important problems. As the accompanying News reveals, 70 percent of Americans don't have such confidence. In other words, they *expect* government failure.

Not surprisingly, people also feel that the federal government *wastes* their tax dollars. The average taxpayer now believes that state governments waste 42 cents out of each dollar, while the federal government wastes 51 cents out of each tax dollar!

Government "waste" implies that the public sector isn't producing as many services as it could with the resources at its disposal. Such inefficiency implies that we're producing somewhere *inside* our production possibilities curve rather than on it (e.g., point G_3 in Figure 4.6). If the government is wasting resources this way, we can't possibly be producing the optimal mix of output.

web click

For more public opinion on the role of government, visit the American National Election Studies website at **www.electionstudies.org.** Click on the "Tables and Graphs" tab.

Opportunity Cost

Even if the government wasn't wasting resources, it might still be guilty of government failure. Notice in Figure 4.6 that points G_1 and G_2 are on the production possibilities curve.

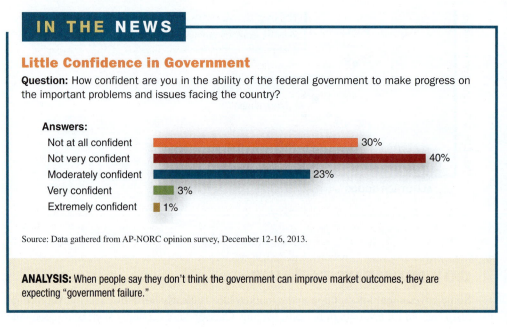

Little Confidence in Government

Question: How confident are you in the ability of the federal government to make progress on the important problems and issues facing the country?

Answers:

Not at all confident	30%
Not very confident	40%
Moderately confident	23%
Very confident	3%
Extremely confident	1%

Source: Data gathered from AP-NORC opinion survey, December 12-16, 2013.

ANALYSIS: When people say they don't think the government can improve market outcomes, they are expecting "government failure."

So resources aren't being "wasted." But those points still represent suboptimal outcomes. In reality, *the issue of government failure encompasses two distinct questions:*

- *Efficiency:* Are we getting as much service as we could from the resources we allocate to government?
- *Opportunity cost:* Are we giving up too many private sector goods in order to get those services?

When assessing government's role in the economy, *we must consider not only what governments do but also what we give up to allow them to do it.* The theory of public goods tells us only what activities are appropriate for government, not the proper *level* of such activity. National defense is clearly a proper function of the public sector. Not so clear, however, is how much the government should spend on tanks, aircraft carriers, and missile shields. The same is true of environmental protection or law enforcement.

The concept of opportunity costs puts a new perspective on the whole question of government size. *Everything the government does entails an opportunity cost.* Before we can decide how big is "too big," we must decide what we're willing to give up to support the public sector. A military force of 1.4 million men and women is "too big" from an economic perspective only if we value the forgone private production and consumption more highly than we value the added strength of our defenses. The government has gone "too far" if the highway it builds is less desired than the park and homes it replaced. In these and all cases, the assessment of bigness must come back to a comparison of what is given up with what is received. The assessment of government failure thus comes back to points on the production possibilities curve. Has the government moved us closer to the optimal mix of output (e.g., point G_4 in Figure 4.6) or not?

THE ECONOMY TOMORROW

"RIGHT"-SIZING GOVERNMENT

You don't have to be a genius to find the optimal mix of output in Figure 4.6—it's clearly marked. And Figure 4.2 clearly reveals the optimal size of the government as well. In both cases, the opportunity cost principle points to the right answer.

In practice, establishing the optimal size of the public sector isn't so easy. In fact, Gallup polls reveal that most Americans think the federal government is too big and too powerful—that we are at a point like G_2 rather than point X in Figure 4.6. Are they right?

In principle, we should be able to answer this question. We can say with theoretical confidence that *additional public sector activity is desirable only if the benefits from that activity exceed its opportunity costs.* In other words, we compare the benefits of a public project to the value of the private goods given up to produce it. By performing this calculation repeatedly along the perimeter of the production possibilities curve, we could locate the optimal mix of output—the point at which no further increase in public sector spending activity is desirable.

Valuation Problems

Although the principles of cost–benefit analysis are simple enough, they're deceptive. How are we to measure the potential benefits of improved police services, for example? Should we estimate the number of robberies and murders prevented, calculate the worth of each, and add up the benefits? And how are we supposed to calculate the worth of a saved life? By a person's earnings? Value of assets? Number of friends? And what about the increased sense of security people have when they know the police are patrolling their neighborhood? Should this be included in the benefit calculation? Some people will attach great value to this service; others will attach little. Whose values should be the standard? Should we consult liberals or conservatives on these questions?

When we're dealing with (private) market goods and services, we can gauge the benefits of a product by the amount of money consumers are willing to pay for it. This price signal isn't available for most public services, however, because of externalities and the nonexclusive nature of pure public goods (the free-rider problem). Hence *the value (benefits) of public services must be estimated because they don't have (reliable) market prices.* This opens the door to endless political squabbles about how beneficial any particular government activity is.

The same problems arise in evaluating the government's efforts to redistribute incomes. Government transfer payments now go to retired workers, disabled people, veterans, farmers, sick people, students, pregnant women, unemployed people, poor people, and a long list of other recipients. To pay for all these transfers, the government must raise tax revenues. With so many people paying taxes and receiving transfer payments, the net effects on the distribution of income aren't easy to figure out. Yet we can't determine whether this government intervention is worth it until we know how the FOR WHOM answer was changed and what the tax-and-transfer effort cost us.

Ballot Box Economics

In practice, we rely on political mechanisms, not cost–benefit calculations, to decide what to produce in the public sector and how to redistribute incomes. *Voting mechanisms substitute for the market mechanism in allocating resources to the public sector and deciding how to use them.* Some people have even suggested that the variety and volume of public goods are determined by the most votes, just as the variety and volume of private goods are determined by the most dollars. Thus governments choose the level and mix of output (and related taxation) that seem to command the most votes.

Sometimes the link between the ballot box and output decisions is very clear and direct. State and local governments, for example, are often compelled to get voter approval before building another highway, school, housing project, or sewage plant. *Bond referenda* are direct requests by a government unit for voter approval of specific public spending projects (e.g., roads, schools). In 2014, for example, governments sought voter approval for $20 billion of new borrowing to finance public expenditure; more than 70 percent of those requests were approved.

Bond referenda are more the exception than the rule. Bond referenda account for less than 1 percent of state and local expenditures (and no federal expenditures). As a consequence, voter control of public spending is typically much less direct. Although federal agencies must receive authorization from Congress for all expenditures, consumers get a chance to elect new representatives only every two years. Much the same is true at state and local levels. Voters may be in a position to dictate the general level and pattern of public expenditures but have little direct influence on everyday output decisions. In this sense, the ballot box is a poor substitute for the market mechanism.

Even if the link between the ballot box and allocation decisions were stronger, the resulting mix of output might not be optimal. A democratic vote, for example, might yield a 51 percent majority for approval of new local highways. Should the highways then be built? The answer isn't obvious. After all, a large minority (49 percent) of the voters have stated that they don't want resources used this way. If we proceed to build the highways, we'll make those people worse off. Their loss may be greater than what proponents gain. Hence the basic dilemma is really twofold. *We don't know what the real demand for public services is, and votes alone don't reflect the intensity of individual demands.* Moreover, real-world decision making involves so many choices that a stable consensus is impossible.

Public Choice Theory

In the midst of all this complexity and uncertainty, another factor may be decisive—namely self-interest. In principle, government officials are supposed to serve the people. It doesn't take long, however, before officials realize that the public is indecisive about what it wants and takes little interest in government's day-to-day activities. With such latitude, government officials can set their own agendas. Those agendas may give higher priority to personal advancement than to the needs of the public. Agency directors may foster new programs that enlarge their mandate, enhance their visibility, and increase their prestige or income. Members of Congress may likewise pursue legislative favors like tax breaks for supporters more diligently than they pursue the general public interest. In such cases, the probability of attaining the socially optimal mix of output declines.

public choice: Theory of public sector behavior emphasizing rational self-interest of decision makers and voters.

The theory of **public choice** emphasizes the role of self-interest in public decision making. Public choice theory essentially extends the analysis of market behavior to political behavior. Public officials are assumed to have specific personal goals (for example, power, recognition, wealth) that they'll pursue in office. *A central tenet of public choice theory is that bureaucrats are just as selfish (utility maximizing) as everyone else.*

Public choice theory provides a neat and simple explanation for public sector decision making. But critics argue that the theory provides a woefully narrow view of public servants. Some people do selflessly pursue larger, public goals, such critics argue, and ideas can overwhelm self-interest. Steven Kelman of Harvard, for example, argues that narrow self-interest can't explain the War on Poverty of the 1960s, the tax revolt of the 1970s, or the deregulation movement of the 1980s. These tidal changes in public policy reflect the power of ideas, not simple self-interest. Public choice theory tells us how many decisions about government are made; it doesn't tell us how they should be made. The "right" size of government in the economy tomorrow will depend less on self-interest and more on how much we trust *markets* to generate optimal outcomes or trust government intervention to *improve* on market failures.

SUMMARY

- Government intervention in the marketplace is justified by market failure—that is, suboptimal market outcomes. **LO4-1**
- The micro failures of the market originate in public goods, externalities, market power, and an inequitable distribution of income. These flaws deter the market from achieving the optimal mix of output or distribution of income. **LO4-1**
- Public goods are those that can't be consumed exclusively; they're jointly consumed regardless of who pays. Because everyone seeks a free ride, no one demands public goods in the marketplace. Hence, the market underproduces public goods. **LO4-1**

- Externalities are costs (or benefits) of a market transaction borne by a third party. Externalities create a divergence between social and private costs or benefits, causing suboptimal market outcomes. The market overproduces goods with external costs and underproduces goods with external benefits. **LO4-1**
- Market power enables a producer to thwart market signals and maintain a suboptimal mix of output. Antitrust policy seeks to prevent or restrict market power. The government may also regulate the behavior of powerful firms. **LO4-1**
- The market-generated distribution of income may be unfair. This inequity may prompt the government to

intervene with taxes and transfer payments that redistribute incomes. **LO4-1**
- The macro failures of the marketplace are reflected in unemployment and inflation. Government intervention is intended to achieve full employment and price stability. **LO4-1**
- The federal government expanded greatly after 1930. More recent growth has been in transfer payments and health programs. **LO4-2**
- State and local governments purchase more output (12 percent of GDP) than the federal government (8 percent) and employ five times as many workers. **LO4-2**

- Income and payroll taxes provide most federal revenues. States get most revenue from sales taxes; local governments rely on property taxes. **LO4-3**
- Government failure occurs when intervention doesn't move toward the optimal mix of output (or income). Failure may result from outright waste (operational inefficiency) or from a misallocation of resources. **LO4-4**
- All government activity must be evaluated in terms of its opportunity cost—that is, the *private* goods and services forgone to make resources available to the public sector. **LO4-4**

Key Terms

optimal mix of output	monopoly	inflation
market mechanism	market power	opportunity cost
market failure	antitrust	progressive tax
private good	natural monopoly	proportional tax
public good	transfer payments	regressive tax
free rider	merit good	government failure
externalities	unemployment	public choice

Questions for Discussion

1. Why should taxpayers subsidize public colleges and universities? What external benefits are generated by higher education? **LO4-1**
2. If Israel's "Iron Dome" (World View, p. 72) is so effective, why doesn't a private company produce it and sell its services directly to consumers? **LO4-1**
3. If everyone seeks a free ride, what mix of output will be produced in Figure 4.2? Why would anyone voluntarily contribute to the purchase of public goods like flood control or snow removal? **LO4-1**
4. Should the firefighters have saved the house in the News on page 73? What was the justification for their belated intervention? **LO4-1**
5. Why might Fourth of July fireworks be considered a public good? Who should pay for them? What about airport security? **LO4-1**
6. What is the specific market failure justification for government spending on (*a*) public universities, (*b*) health care, (*c*) trash pickup, (*d*) highways, (*e*) police, and

(*f*) solar energy? Would a purely private economy produce any of these services? **LO4-1**
7. If smoking generates external costs, should smoking simply be outlawed? How about cars that pollute? **LO4-1**
8. The government now spends more than $700 billion a year on Social Security benefits. Why don't we leave it to individuals to save for their own retirement? **LO4-1**
9. What government actions might cause failures like points G_1, G_2, and G_3 in Figure 4.6? Can you give examples? **LO4-4**
10. How does XM Satellite deter nonsubscribers from listening to its transmissions? Does this make radio programming a private good or a public good? **LO4-1**
11. Should the government be downsized? Which functions should be cut back? Which ones should be expanded? **LO4-2**
12. Which taxes hit the poor hardest—those of local, state, or federal governments? **LO4-3**

 mobile app Visit your mobile app store and download the Schiller: Study Econ app *today!*

National Income Accounting

After reading this chapter, you should know

LO5-1 What GDP measures—and what it doesn't.

LO5-2 The difference between real and nominal GDP.

LO5-3 Why aggregate income equals aggregate output.

LO5-4 The major submeasures of output and income.

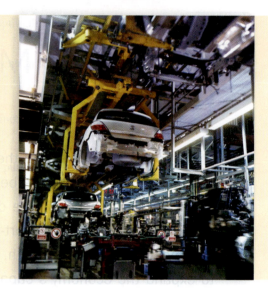

A **favorite cliché of policymakers** in Washington is that government likes to tackle only those problems it can measure. Politicians need visible results. They want to be able to brag to their constituents about the miles of new highways built, the number of students who graduated, the number of families that left welfare, and the number of unemployed workers who found jobs. To do this, they must be able to measure economic outcomes.

The Great Depression of the 1930s was a lesson in the need for better measures of economic performance. There were plenty of anecdotes about factories closing, farms failing, and people selling apples on the streets. But nobody knew the dimensions of the nation's economic meltdown until millions of workers had lost their jobs. The need for more timely information about the health of the national economy was evident. From that experience a commitment to **national income accounting**—the measurement of aggregate economic activity—emerged. During the 1930s the economist Simon Kuznets (who later received a Nobel Prize for his work) and the U.S. Department of Commerce developed an accounting system to gauge the economy's health. That national accounting system now churns out reams of data that track the economy's performance. They answer such questions as

- **How much output is being produced? What is it being used for?**
- **How much income is being generated in the marketplace?**
- **What's happening to prices and wages?**

It's tempting, of course, to ignore all these measurement questions, especially since they tend to be rather dull. But if we avoid measurement problems, we severely limit our ability to understand how well (or poorly) the economy is performing. We also limit our ability to design policies for improving economic performance.

National income accounting also provides a useful perspective on the way the economy works. It shows how factor markets relate to product markets, how output relates to income, and how consumer spending and business investment relate to production. It also shows how the flow of taxes and government spending affect economic outcomes.

MEASURES OF OUTPUT

The array of goods and services we produce is truly massive, including everything from professional baseball (a service) to guided-missile systems (a good). All these products are part of our total output; the first data challenge is to find a summary measure of all these diverse products.

Itemizing the amount of each good or service produced each year won't solve our measurement problem. The resulting list would be so long that it would be both unwieldy and meaningless. We couldn't even add it up because it would contain diverse goods measured in a variety of different units (e.g., miles, packages, pounds, quarts). Nor could we compare one year's output to another's. Suppose that last year we produced 2 billion oranges, 2 million bicycles, and 700 rock concerts, whereas this year we produced 3 billion oranges, 4 million bicycles, and 600 rock concerts. Which year's output was larger? With more of some goods, but less of others, the answer isn't obvious.

Gross Domestic Product

To facilitate our accounting chores, we need some mechanism for organizing annual output data into a more manageable summary. The mechanism we use is price. ***Each good and service produced and brought to market has a price. That price serves as a measure of value for calculating total output.*** Consider again the problem of determining how much output was produced this year and last. There's no obvious way to answer this question in physical terms alone. But once we know the price of each good, we can calculate the *value* of output produced. The total dollar value of final output produced each year is called the **gross domestic product (GDP).** GDP is simply the sum of all final goods and services produced for the market in a given time period, with each good or service valued at its market price.

Table 5.1 illustrates the use of prices to value total output in two hypothetical years. If oranges were 20 cents each last year and 2 billion oranges were produced, then the *value* of orange production last year was $400 million ($0.20 × 2 billion). In the same manner,

national income accounting: The measurement of aggregate economic activity, particularly national income and its components.

gross domestic product (GDP): The total market value of all final goods and services produced within a nation's borders in a given time period.

Output	Amount
a. Last Year's Output	
In physical terms:	
Oranges	2 billion
Bicycles	2 million
Rock concerts	700
Total	?
In monetary terms:	
2 billion oranges @ $0.20 each	$ 400 million
2 million bicycles @ $50 each	100 million
700 rock concerts @ $1 million each	700 million
Total	$1,200 million
b. This Year's Output	
In physical terms:	
Oranges	3 billion
Bicycles	4 million
Rock concerts	600
Total	?
In monetary terms:	
3 billion oranges @ $0.20 each	$ 600 million
4 million bicycles @ $50 each	200 million
600 rock concerts @ $1 million each	600 million
Total	$1,400 million

TABLE 5.1

The Measurement of Output

It's impossible to add up all output in *physical* terms. Accordingly, total output is measured in *monetary* terms, with each good or service valued at its market price. GDP refers to the total market value of all goods and services produced in a given time period. According to the numbers in this table, the total *value* of the oranges, bicycles, and rock concerts produced "last" year was $1.2 billion and $1.4 billion "this" year.

we can determine that the value of bicycle production was $100 million and the value of rock concerts was $700 million. By adding these figures, we can say that the value of last year's production—last year's GDP—was $1,200 million (Table 5.1*a*).

Now we're in a position to compare one year's output to another's. Table 5.1*b* shows that the use of prices enables us to say that the *value* of this year's output is $1,400 million. Hence *total output* has increased from one year to the next. ***The use of prices to value market output allows us to summarize output activity and to compare the output of one period with that of another.***

GDP vs. GNP. The concept of GDP is of relatively recent use in U.S. national income accounts. Prior to 1992, most U.S. statistics focused on gross *national* product or GNP. Gross *national* product refers to the output produced by American-owned factors of production regardless of where they're located. Gross *domestic* product refers to output produced within America's borders. Thus GNP would include some output from an Apple computer factory in Singapore but exclude some of the output produced by a Honda factory in Ohio. In an increasingly global economy, where factors of production and ownership move easily across international borders, the calculations of GNP became ever more complex. It also became a less dependable measure of the nation's economic health. ***GDP is geographically focused, including all output produced within a nation's borders regardless of whose factors of production are used to produce it.*** Apple's output in Singapore ends up in Singapore's GDP; the cars produced at Honda's Ohio plant are counted in America's GDP.

International Comparisons. The geographic focus of GDP facilitates international comparisons of economic activity. Is China's output as large as that of the United States? How could you tell? China produces a mix of output different from ours, making *quantity*-based comparisons difficult. We can compare the *value* of output produced in each country, however. The World View "Comparative Output" in Chapter 2 (page 31) shows that the value of America's GDP is much larger than China's.

GDP per Capita. International comparisons of total output are even more vivid in *per capita terms*. **GDP per capita** relates the total value of annual output to the number of people who share that output; it refers to the average GDP per person. In 2013, America's total GDP of $16 trillion was shared by 320 million citizens. Hence our average, or *per capita*, GDP was nearly $50,000. By contrast, the average GDP for the rest of the world's inhabitants was only $10,000. In these terms, America's position as the richest country in the world clearly stands out.

Statistical comparisons of GDP across nations are abstract and lifeless. They do, however, convey very real differences in the way people live. The following World View examines some everyday realities of living in a poor nation, compared with a rich nation. Disparities in per capita GDP mean that people in low-income countries have little access to telephones, televisions, paved roads, or schools. They also die a lot younger than do people in rich countries.

But even the World View fails to fully convey how tough life is for people at the *bottom* of the income distribution in both poor and rich nations. Per capita GDP isn't a measure of what every citizen is getting. In the United States, millions of individuals have access to far more goods and services than our *average* per capita GDP, while millions of others must get by with much less. Although per capita GDP in Kuwait is three times larger than that of Brazil's, we can't conclude that the typical citizen of Kuwait is three times as well off as the typical Brazilian. The only thing these figures tell us is that the average Kuwaiti *could have* almost three times as many goods and services each year as the average Brazilian *if* GDP were distributed in the same way in both countries. ***Measures of per capita GDP tell us nothing about the way GDP is actually distributed or used: they're only a statistical average.*** When countries are quite similar in structure, institutions, and income distribution, however—or when historical comparisons are made within a country—per capita GDP can be viewed as a rough-and-ready measure of relative living standards.

GDP per capita: Total GDP divided by total population; average GDP.

web click

Global data on per capita incomes and other social indicators are available from the World Bank at **www.worldbank.org.** Click the "Data" tab.

WORLD VIEW

Global Inequalities

The 900 million residents of the world's low-income nations have comparatively few goods and services. Their average income (per capita GDP) is only $1,800 a year, a mere 4 percent of the average income in high-income nations such as the United States, Japan, and Germany. It's not just a colossal *income* disparity; it's also a disparity in the quality and even the duration of life.
   Some examples:

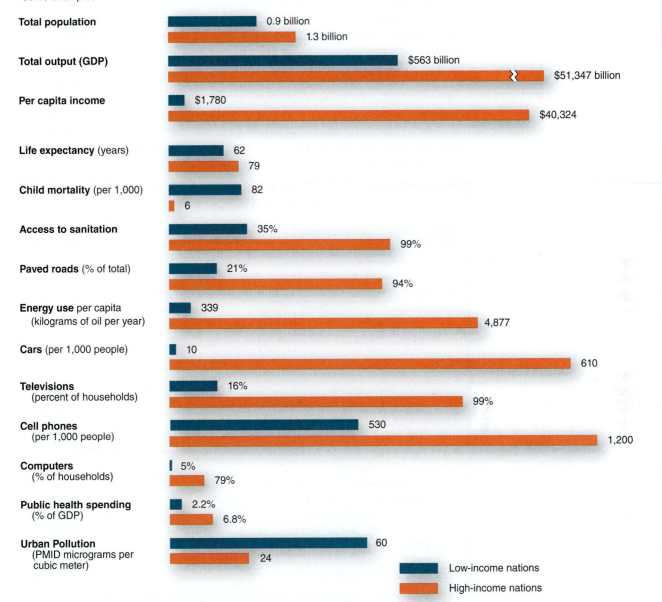

Source: *The World Bank,* 2014 World Development Indicators, **data.worldbank.org.**

ANALYSIS: Hidden behind dry statistical comparisons of per capita GDP lie very tangible and dramatic differences in the way people live. Low GDP per capita reflects a lot of deprivation.

Measurement Problems

Nonmarket Activities. Although the methods for calculating GDP and per capita GDP are straightforward, they do create a few problems. For one thing, *GDP measures exclude most goods and services that are* **produced** *but not* **sold** *in the market.* This may appear to be a trivial point, but it isn't. Vast quantities of output never reach the market. For example, the homemaker who cleans, washes, gardens, shops, and cooks definitely contributes to the output of goods and services. Because she's not paid a market wage for these services, however, her efforts are excluded from the calculation of GDP. At the same time, we do count the efforts of those workers who sell identical homemaking services in the marketplace. This seeming contradiction is explained by the fact that a homemaker's services aren't sold in the market and therefore carry no explicit, market-determined value.

The exclusion of homemakers' services from the GDP accounts is particularly troublesome when we want to compare living standards over time or between countries. In the United States, for example, most women now work outside the home. As a result households make greater use of *paid* domestic help (e.g., child care, housecleaning). Accordingly, a lot of housework and child care that were previously excluded from GDP statistics (because they were unpaid family help) are now included (because they're done by paid help). In this respect, our historical GDP figures may exaggerate improvements in our standard of living.

Homemaking services aren't the only output excluded. If a friend helps you with your homework, the services never get into the GDP accounts. But if you hire a tutor or engage the services of a term paper–writing agency, the transaction becomes part of GDP. Here again, the problem is simply that we have no way to determine how much output was produced until it enters the market and is purchased.[1]

Unreported Income. The GDP statistics also fail to capture market activities that aren't reported to tax or census authorities. Many people work "off the books," getting paid in

---

IN THE NEWS

A Lot Going On under the Table

- Percentage of households making untaxed or unmeasured "underground" purchases: 83.
- Estimated unreported income per person in 2000, excluding illegal activities: $4,300.
- Percentage of unreported income from wages and salaries: 18.
- Percentage of unreported income from capital gains: 13.
- Unreported income as a percentage of GDP: 12.
- Taxes lost from unreported income in 2006: $328 billion.

The underground economy—transactions that are untaxed or unaccounted for in GDP—involves a lot more than nannies and drug deals.

	Estimated Percentage of Services Supplied by the Underground Economy
Lawn maintenance	90
Domestic help	83
Child care	49
Home repair/improvements	34
Laundry/sewing services	25
Appliance repair	17
Car repairs	13
Haircuts/beauty service	8
Catering	8

Data from University of Michigan Institute for Social Research, U.S. Department of Labor.

Source: U.S. Internal Revenue Service, **www.irs.gov.**

ANALYSIS: GDP statistics include only the value of reported market transactions. Unreported transactions in the underground economy can't be counted and may therefore distort perceptions of economic activity.

---

[1]The U.S. Commerce Department does, however, *estimate* the value of some nonmarket activities (e.g., food grown by farmers for their own consumption, the rental value of home ownership) and includes such estimates in GDP calculations.

unreported cash. This so-called underground economy is motivated by both tax avoidance and the need to conceal illegal activities. Although illegal activities capture most of the headlines, tax evasion on income earned in otherwise legal pursuits accounts for most of the underground economy. The Internal Revenue Service estimates that more than two-thirds of underground income comes from legitimate wages, salaries, profits, interest, and pensions that simply aren't reported. As the previous News indicates, unreported income is particularly common in the service sector. People who mow lawns, clean houses, paint walls, or provide child care services are apt to get paid in cash that isn't reported. The volume of such mundane transactions greatly exceeds the underground income generated by drug dealers, prostitutes, or illegal gambling.

Value Added

Not every reported market transaction gets included at full value in GDP statistics. If it did, the same output would get counted over and over. The problem here is that the production of goods and services typically involves a series of distinct stages. Consider the production of a bagel, for example. For a bagel to reach Einstein's or some other bagel store, the farmer must grow some wheat, the miller must convert it to flour, and the baker must make bagels with it. Table 5.2 illustrates this chain of production.

What value is *added*?

Notice that each of the four stages of production depicted in Table 5.2 involves a separate market transaction. The farmer sells to the miller (stage 1), the miller to the baker (stage 2), the baker to the bagel store (stage 3), and, finally, the store to the consumer (stage 4). If we added up the separate value of each market transaction, we'd come to the conclusion that $1.75 of output had been produced. In fact, though, only one bagel has been produced, and it's worth only 75 cents. Hence we should increase GDP—the value of output—only by 75 cents.

To get an accurate measure of GDP we must distinguish between *intermediate* goods and *final* goods. **Intermediate goods** are goods purchased for use as input in further stages of production. Final goods are the goods produced at the end of the production sequence, for use by consumers (or other market participants).

intermediate goods: Goods or services purchased for use as input in the production of final goods or in services.

We can compute the value of *final* output in one of two ways. The easiest way would be to count only market transactions entailing final sales (stage 4 in Table 5.2). To do this, however, we'd have to know who purchased each good or service in order to know when we had reached the end of the process. Such a calculation would also exclude any output produced in stages 1, 2, and 3 in Table 5.2 but not yet reflected in stage 4.

Another way to calculate GDP is to count only the **value added** at each stage of production. Consider the miller, for example. He doesn't really contribute $0.28 worth of production to total output, but only $0.16. The other $0.12 reflected in the price of his flour represents the contribution of the farmer who grew the wheat. By the same token, the baker *adds* only $0.32 to the value of output, as part of his output was purchased from the miller. By considering only the value *added* at each stage of production, we eliminate double counting. We don't count twice the *intermediate* goods and services that producers buy from other producers, which are then used as inputs. As Table 5.2 confirms, we can determine that value of final output by summing up the value added at each stage of production. (Note that $0.75 is also the price of a bagel.)

value added: The increase in the market value of a product that takes place at each stage of the production process.

Stages of Production	Value of Transaction	Value Added
1. Farmer grows wheat, sells it to miller.	$0.12	$0.12
2. Miller converts wheat to flour, sells it to baker.	0.28	0.16
3. Baker bakes bagel, sells it to bagel store.	0.60	0.32
4. Bagel store sells bagel to consumer.	0.75	0.15
Total	$1.75	$0.75

TABLE 5.2

Value Added in Various Stages of Production

The value added at each stage of production represents a contribution to total output. Value added equals the market value of a product minus the cost of intermediate goods.

Real vs. Nominal GDP

Although prices are a convenient measure of market value, they can also distort perceptions of real output. Imagine what would happen to our calculations of GDP if all prices were to double from one year to the next. Suppose that the price of oranges, as shown in Table 5.1, rose from $0.20 to $0.40, the price of bicycles to $100, and the price of rock concerts to $2 million each. How would such price changes alter measured GDP? Obviously, the price increases would double the dollar *value* of final output. Measured GDP would rise from $1,400 million to $2,800 million.

Such a rise in GDP doesn't reflect an increase in the *quantity* of goods and services available to us. We're still producing the same quantities shown in Table 5.1; only the prices of those goods have changed. Hence **changes in GDP brought about by changes in the price level give us a distorted view of real economic activity.** Surely we wouldn't want to assert that our standard of living had improved just because price increases raised measured GDP from $1,400 million to $2,800 million.

To distinguish increases in the *quantity* of goods and services from increases in their *prices,* we must construct a measure of GDP that takes into account price level changes. We do so by distinguishing between *real* GDP and *nominal* GDP. **Nominal GDP** is the value of final output measured in *current* prices, whereas **real GDP** is the value of output measured in *constant* prices. **To calculate real GDP, we adjust the market value of goods and services for changing prices.**

Note, for example, that in Table 5.1 prices were unchanged from one year to the next. When prices in the marketplace are constant, interyear comparisons of output are simple. But if prices change, the comparison becomes more complicated. As we just saw, if all prices doubled from last year to this year, this year's nominal GDP would rise to $2,800 million. But these price increases wouldn't alter the quantity of goods produced. In other words, *real* GDP, valued at constant prices, would remain at $1,400 million. Thus **the distinction between nominal and real GDP is important whenever the price level changes.**

Because the price level does change every year, both real and nominal GDP are regularly reported. Nominal GDP is computed simply by adding the *current* dollar value of production. Real GDP is computed by making an adjustment for changes in prices from year to year.

Zero Growth. Consider the GDP statistics for 2007 and 2008, as displayed in Table 5.3. The first row shows *nominal* GDP in each year: Nominal GDP increased by $307 billion between 2007 and 2008 (row 2). At first blush, this 2.2 percent increase in GDP looks impressive; that works out to roughly $1,000 more output for every U.S. citizen.

But output didn't really grow that much. Row 3 indicates that *prices* increased by 2.2 percent from year to year. This wiped out the entire increase in the value of output. *Real* GDP actually decreased from 2007 to 2008!

Row 4 in Table 5.3 adjusts the GDP comparison for the change in prices. We represent the price increase as an index, with a base of 100. Thus, a price increase of 2.2 percent raises the base of 100 to 102.2. So the price level change can be expressed as 102.2/100.0, or 1.022.

To convert the *nominal* value of GDP in 2008 to its *real* value, we need only a little division. As row 4 of Table 5.3 shows, we divide the nominal GDP of $14,369 by the indexed

nominal GDP: The value of final output produced in a given period, measured in the prices of that period (current prices).

real GDP: The value of final output produced in a given period, adjusted for changing prices.

TABLE 5.3

Computing Real GDP

Real GDP is the inflation-adjusted value of nominal GDP. Between 2007 and 2008, *nominal* GDP increased by $307 billion (row 2). All of this gain was due to rising prices (row 3). After adjusting for inflation, *real* GDP actually decreased by $2 billion (row 5).

	2007	2008
1. Nominal GDP (in billions)	$14,062	$14,369
2. Change in nominal GDP		+$307
Inflation adjustment:		
3. Change in price level, 2007 to 2008		2.2%
4. Real GDP in 2007 dollars $\left(=\dfrac{\text{Nominal GDP}}{\text{Price index}}\right)$	$14,062	$14,060 $\left(=\dfrac{\$14,369}{1.022}\right)$
5. Change in real GDP		−$2

price change (1.022) and discover that *real* GDP in 2008 was only $14,060 billion. Hence *real* GDP actually decreased by $2 billion in 2008 (row 5).

Notice in Table 5.3 that in 2007 real and nominal GDP are identical because we're using that year as the basis of comparison. We're comparing performance in 2008 to that of the 2007 **base year.** Real GDP can be expressed in the prices of any particular year; whatever year is selected serves as the base for computing price level and output changes. In Table 5.3 we used 2007 as the base year for computing real GDP in subsequent years. The general formula for computing real GDP is

base year: The year used for comparative analysis; the basis for indexing price changes.

$$\text{Real GDP in year } t = \frac{\text{Nominal GDP in year } t}{\text{Price index}}$$

This is the formula we used in row 4 of Table 5.3 to compute real GDP in 2008, valued at 2007 base year prices.

The distinction between nominal and real GDP becomes critical when more distant years are compared. In the 70 years between 1933 and 2013, for example, prices rose by 1,300 percent. Table 5.4 shows how such price level changes can distort our views of how

Suppose we want to determine how much better off the average American was in 2013, as measured in terms of new goods and services, than people were during the Great Depression. To do this, we'd compare GDP per capita in 2013 with GDP per capita in 1933. The following data make that comparison.

	Nominal GDP	Population	Nominal per Capita GDP
1933	$ 57 billion	126 million	$ 452
2013	16,800 billion	310 million	54,194

In 1933 the nation's nominal GDP of $57 billion was shared by 126 million Americans, yielding a *per capita* GDP of $452. By contrast, nominal GDP in 2013 was more than 300 times larger, at $16,800 billion. This vastly larger GDP was shared by 310 million people, giving us a per capita GDP of $54,194. Hence it would appear that our standard of living in 2013 was 120 times higher than the standard of 1933.

But this increase in *nominal* GDP vastly exaggerates the gains in our material well-being. The average price of goods and services—the *price level*—increased by 1,300 percent between 1933 and 2013. The goods and services you might have bought for $1 in 1933 cost $14 in 2013. In other words, we needed a lot more dollars in 2013 to buy any given combination of real goods and services.

To compare our *real* GDP in 2013 with the real GDP of 1933, we have to adjust for this tremendous jump in prices (inflation). We do so by measuring both years' output in terms of *constant* prices. Since prices went up, on average, fourteenfold between 1933 and 2013, we simply divide the 2013 *nominal* output by 14. The calculation is

$$\begin{array}{c}\text{Real GDP}\\\text{in 2013}\\\text{(in 1933 prices)}\end{array} = \frac{\text{Nominal 2013 GDP}}{\text{Price index}}$$

By arbitrarily setting the level of prices in the base year 1933 at 100 and noting that prices have increased fourteenfold since then, we can calculate

$$\begin{array}{c}\text{Real GDP}\\\text{in 2013}\\\text{(1933 prices)}\end{array} = \frac{\$16,800}{14.0}$$

$$= \$1,200 \text{ billion}$$

With a population of 310 million, this left us with real GDP per capita of $3,870 in 2013—as measured in base year 1933 dollars. This was nearly nine times the *real* per capita GDP of the depression ($452), but not nearly so great an increase as comparisons of *nominal* GDP suggest.

TABLE 5.4

Real vs. Nominal GDP: A Historical View

Intangibles. All the economic measures discussed in this chapter are important indexes of individual and collective welfare; they tell us something about how well people are living. They don't, however, capture the completeness of the way in which we view the world or the totality of what makes our lives satisfying. A clear day, a sense of accomplishment, even a smile can do more for a person's sense of well-being than can favorable movements in the GDP accounts. Or as the economist John Kenneth Galbraith put it, "In a rational lifestyle, some people could find contentment working moderately and then sitting by the street—and talking, thinking, drawing, painting, scribbling, or making love in a suitably discreet way. None of these requires an expanding economy."[3]

The emphasis on economic outcomes arises not from ignorance of life's other meanings but from the visibility of the economic outcomes. We all realize that well-being arises from both material and intangible pleasures. But the intangibles tend to be elusive. It's not easy to gauge individual happiness, much less to ascertain the status of our collective satisfaction. We have to rely on measures we can see, touch, and count. As long as the material components of our environment bear some positive relation to our well-being, they at least serve a useful purpose.

In some situations, however, more physical output may actually worsen our collective welfare. If increased automobile production raises congestion and pollution levels, the rise in GDP occasioned by those additional cars is a misleading index of society's welfare. In such a case, the rise in GDP might actually mask a *decrease* in the well-being of the population. We might also wonder whether more casinos, more prisons, more telemarketing, more divorce litigation, and more Prozac—all of which contribute to GDP growth—are really valid measures of our well-being (see the below cartoon). Exclusive emphasis on measurable output would clearly be a mistake in many cases.

Index of Well-Being. Researchers at the Institute for Innovation in Social Policy at Vassar College have devised an alternative index of well-being. Their Index of Social Health includes a few economic parameters (such as unemployment and weekly earnings) but puts more emphasis on sociological behavior (such as child abuse, teen suicides, crime, poverty, and inequality). They claim that this broader view offers a more meaningful guidepost to everyday life than GDP measures of material wealth. According to their calculations, life has gotten *worse,* not better, as GDP has increased (see the News on the next page).

Analysis: GDP includes *everything* produced and sold in the product market, no matter how much each good or service contributes to our social well-being.

[3]Cited in Leonard Silk, *Nixonomics,* 2nd ed. (New York: Praeger, 1973), p. 163.

IN THE NEWS

Material Wealth vs. Social Health

National income accounts are regularly reported and widely quoted. They do not, however, adequately reflect the nation's *social* performance. To measure more accurately the country's social health, a Vassar College team of social scientists devised an Index of Social Health with 16 indicators, including infant mortality, drug abuse, health insurance coverage, and poverty among the aged. According to this index, America's social health increased only 6 percent from 1990 to 2011, despite a 34 percent increase in real GDP per capita.

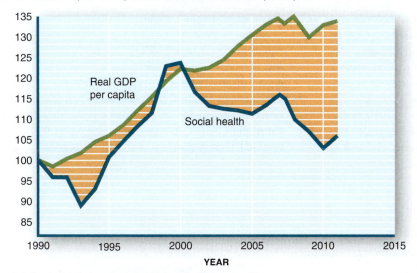

Source: Data from Institute for Innovation in Social Policy (**http://iisp.vassar.edu**).

ANALYSIS: The national income accounts emphasize material well-being. They are an important, but not a complete, gauge of our societal welfare.

web click

The United Nations has constructed a Human Development Index that offers a better view of social well-being than GDP alone. For details and country-by-country rankings, visit **www.undp.org** and click "Human Development Reports."

Not everyone would accept the Institute's dour view of our collective social health. Their index, however, does underscore the fact that *social welfare* and *economic welfare* aren't always synonymous. The GDP accounts tell us whether our economic welfare has increased, as measured by the value of goods and services produced. They don't tell us how highly we value additional goods and services relative to nonmarket phenomena. Nor do they even tell us whether important social costs were incurred in the process of production. These judgments must be made outside the market; they're social decisions.

Finally, note that any given level of GDP can encompass many combinations of output. Choosing WHAT to produce is still a critical question, even after the goal of *maximum* production has been established. The quality of life in the economy tomorrow will depend on what specific mix of goods and services we include in GDP.

SUMMARY

- National income accounting measures annual output and income flows. The national income accounts provide a basis for assessing our economic performance, designing public policy, and understanding how all the parts of the economy interact. **LO5-1**
- The most comprehensive measure of output is gross domestic product (GDP), the total market value of all final goods and services produced within a nation's borders during a given period. **LO5-1**
- In calculating GDP, we include only the value added at each stage of production. This value-added procedure eliminates the double counting that results when business firms buy intermediate goods from other firms and include those costs in their selling price. **LO5-1**

- To distinguish physical changes in output from monetary changes in its value, we compute both nominal and real GDP. Nominal GDP is the value of output expressed in *current* prices. Real GDP is the value of output expressed in *constant* prices (the prices of some *base year*).   **LO5-2**
- Each year some of our capital equipment is worn out in the process of production. Hence GDP is larger than the amount of goods and services we could consume without reducing our production possibilities. The amount of capital used up each year is referred to as *depreciation*.   **LO5-4**
- By subtracting depreciation from GDP we derive net domestic product (NDP). The difference between NDP and GDP is also equal to the difference between *gross* investment—the sum of all our current plant and equipment expenditures—and *net* investment—the amount of investment over and above that required to replace worn-out capital.   **LO5-4**
- All the income generated in market sales (GDP) is received by someone. Therefore, the value of aggregate output must equal the value of aggregate income.   **LO5-3**

- The sequence of flows involved in this process is
  GDP
  less depreciation
  equals **NDP**
  plus net foreign factor income
  equals national income (**NI**)
  less indirect business taxes,
      corporate profits,
      interest payments, and
      Social Security taxes
  plus transfer payments and
      capital income
  equals personal income (**PI**)
  less personal income taxes
  equals disposable income (**DI**)   **LO5-3**
- The incomes received by households, business firms, and governments provide the purchasing power required to buy the nation's output. As that purchasing power is spent, further GDP is created and the circular flow continues.   **LO5-3**

Key Terms

national income accounting	inflation	imports
gross domestic product (GDP)	production possibilities	net exports
GDP per capita	depreciation	national income (NI)
intermediate goods	net domestic product (NDP)	personal income (PI)
value added	investment	disposable income (DI)
nominal GDP	gross investment	saving
real GDP	net investment	
base year	exports	

Questions for Discussion

1. The manuscript for this book was typed for free by a friend. Had I hired a secretary to do the same job, GDP would have been higher, even though the amount of output would have been identical. Why is this? Does this make sense?   **LO5-1**
2. GDP in 1981 was $2.96 trillion. It grew to $3.07 trillion in 1982, yet the quantity of output actually decreased. How is this possible?   **LO5-2**
3. If gross investment is not large enough to replace the capital that depreciates in a particular year, is net investment greater or less than zero? What happens to our production possibilities?   **LO5-4**
4. Can we increase consumption in a given year without cutting back on either investment or government services? Under what conditions?   **LO5-4**
5. Why is it important to know how much output is being produced? Who uses such information?   **LO5-1**
6. What jobs are likely part of the underground economy?   **LO5-1**
7. Clear-cutting a forest adds to GDP the value of the timber, but it also destroys the forest. How should we value that loss?   **LO5-1**
8. Is the Index of Social Health, discussed in the News on page 109, a better barometer of well-being than GDP? What are its relative advantages or disadvantages?   **LO5-1**
9. More than 4 million websites sell a combined $100 billion of pornography a year. Should these sales be included in (*a*) GDP and (*b*) an index of social welfare?   **LO5-1**
10. Are you better off today than a year ago? How do you measure the change?   **LO5-1**
11. Why must the value of total expenditure equal the value of total income.   **LO5-3**

mobile app Visit your mobile app store and download the Schiller: Study Econ app *today!*

PROBLEMS FOR CHAPTER 5

LO5-1 1. Suppose that furniture production encompasses the following stages:

Stage 1: Trees are sold to lumber company.	$ 6,000
Stage 2: Lumber is sold to furniture company.	$19,000
Stage 3: Furniture company sells furniture to retail store.	$24,000
Stage 4: Furniture store sells furniture to consumer.	$52,000

    (*a*) What is the value added at each stage?

Stage 1: _____
Stage 2: _____
Stage 3: _____
Stage 4: _____

    (*b*) How much does this output contribute to GDP? _____

    (*c*) How would answer (*b*) change if the lumber were imported from Canada? _____

LO5-2 2. If real GDP increases by 1 percent next year and the price level goes up by 3 percent, by how much will nominal GDP increase? _____

LO5-2 3. What was real per capita GDP in 1933 measured in 2013 prices? (Use the data in Table 5.4 to compute your answer.) _____

LO5-4 4. Based on the following figures,

Consumption	$200 billion
Depreciation	20
Retained earnings	12
Gross investment	40
Imports	70
Exports	50
Net foreign factor income	10
Government purchases	80

    (*a*) How much is GDP? _____

    (*b*) How much is net investment? _____

    (*c*) How much is national income? _____

    (*d*) If all prices were to double overnight, what would be the

        (*i*) Change in real GDP? _____

        (*ii*) Change in nominal GDP? _____

LO5-4 5. What share of U.S. total income in 2013 consisted of

    (*a*) Wages and salaries? _____

    (*b*) Corporate profits? _____

    (*Note:* See Table 5.5 for data.)

LO5-2 6. (*a*) Compute real GDP for 2013 using average prices of 2000 as the base year. (On the inside covers of this book you'll find data for GDP and the GDP "price deflator" used to measure inflation.) _____

    (*b*) By how much did real GDP increase between 2000 and 2013? _____

    (*c*) By how much did nominal GDP increase between 2000 and 2013? _____

LO5-2 7. Suppose all the dollar values in Problem 4 were in 2000 dollars. Use the Consumer Price Index shown on the end cover of this book to convert Problem 4's GDP to 2013 dollars. What is the value of that GDP in 2013 dollars? (You'll be converting the figures from their nominal to their real values, with 2013 as the base year; use the following formula: $CPI_2/CPI_1 = GDP_2/GDP_1$.) _____

LO5-2 8. According to the data in Table 5.3, what is

    (*a*) Real GDP in 2008, at prices of 2007? _____

    (*b*) Real GDP in 2007, at prices of 2008? _____

LO5-2 9. On the accompanying graph, illustrate *(A)* nominal per capita GDP and *(B)* real per capita GDP
for each year. (The necessary data appear on the endpapers of this book.)
- (*a*) By what percentage did *nominal* per capita GDP increase from 2000 to 2010? _____
- (*b*) By what percentage did *real* per capita GDP increase in the same period? _____
- (*c*) In how many years did nominal per capita GDP decline? _____
- (*d*) In how many years did real per capita GDP decline? _____

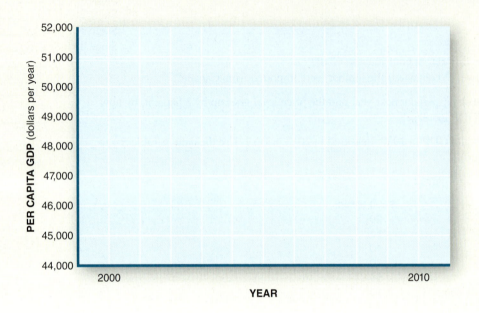

LO5-1 10. According to the News on page 109, do per capita GDP data (A) overstate or (B) understate the
rise in U.S. well-being since 1990? (Enter A or B.) _____

Unemployment

LEARNING OBJECTIVES

After reading this chapter, you should know

LO6-1 How unemployment is measured.

LO6-2 The socioeconomic costs of unemployment.

LO6-3 The major types of unemployment.

LO6-4 The meaning of "full employment."

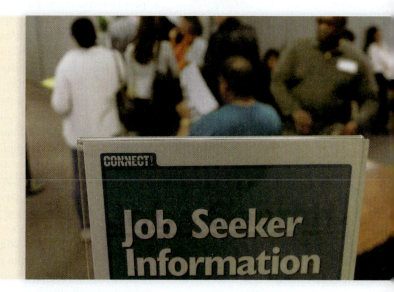

Geoge H. had worked at the General Electric lightbulb factory in Winchester, Virginia, for 18 years. Now he was 46 years old with a wife and three children. With his base salary of $48,200 and the performance bonus he received nearly every year, he was doing pretty well. He had his own home, two cars, company-paid health insurance for the family, and a growing nest egg in the company's pension plan. The H. family wasn't rich, but they were comfortable and secure.

Or so they thought. Overnight the H. family's comfort was shattered. On September 8, 2010, GE announced it was closing the plant permanently. George H., along with 300 fellow workers, was permanently laid off. The weekly paychecks stopped immediately; the pension nest egg was in doubt. Within a few weeks, George H. was on the street looking for a new job—an experience he hadn't had since high school. The unemployment benefits the state and union provided didn't come close to covering the mortgage payment, groceries, insurance, and other necessities. The H. family quickly used up its savings, including the $5,000 set aside for the children's college education.

George H. stayed unemployed for months. His wife found a part-time waitressing job, and his oldest son went to work rather than college. George himself ultimately found a warehousing job that paid only half as much as his previous job.

In the recession of 2008–2009 and its aftermath, more than *8 million* workers lost their jobs as companies "downsized," "restructured," or simply closed. Not all these displaced workers fared as badly as George H. and his family. But the job loss was a painful experience for every one of those displaced workers. That's the human side of an economic downturn.

The pain of joblessness is not confined to those who lose their jobs. In recessions, students discover that jobs are hard to find in the summer. No matter how good their grades are or how nice their résumés look, some graduates just don't get any job offers in a recession. Even people with jobs feel some economic pain: their paychecks shrink when hours or wages are scaled back.

In this chapter we take a closer look at the problem of unemployment, focusing on the following questions:

- **When is a person "unemployed"?**
- **What are the costs of unemployment?**
- **What's an appropriate policy goal for "full employment"?**

As we answer these questions, we'll develop a sense of why full employment is a major goal of macro policy and begin to see some of the obstacles we face in achieving it.

THE LABOR FORCE

To assess the dimensions of our unemployment problems, we first need to decide who wants a job. Millions of people are jobless, yet they're not part of our unemployment problem. Full-time students, young children playing with their toys, and older people living in retirement are all jobless. We don't expect them to be working, so we don't regard them as part of the unemployment problem. We're not trying to get *everybody* a job, just those people who are ready and willing to work.

To distinguish those people who want a job from those who don't, we separate the entire population into two distinct groups. One group consists of *labor force participants;* the other group encompasses all *nonparticipants.*

The **labor force** includes everyone age 16 and older who is actually working plus all those who aren't working but are actively seeking employment. Individuals are also counted as employed in a particular week if their failure to work is due to vacation, illness, labor dispute (strike), or bad weather. All such persons are regarded as "with a job but not at work." Also, unpaid family members working in a family enterprise (farming, for example) are counted as employed. ***Only those people who are either employed or actively seeking work are counted as part of the labor force.*** People who are neither employed *nor* actively looking for a job are referred to as *nonparticipants.* As Figure 6.1 shows, only half the U.S. population participates in the labor force.

Note that our definition of labor force participation excludes most household and volunteer activities. People who choose to devote their energies to household responsibilities or to unpaid charity work aren't counted as part of the labor force, no matter how hard they work. Because they are neither in paid employment nor seeking such employment in the marketplace, they are regarded as outside the labor market (nonparticipants). But if they decide to seek a paid job outside the home, we say that they are "entering the labor force." Students too are typically out of the labor force until they leave school. They *"enter"* the labor force when they go looking for a job, either during the summer or after graduation. People *"exit"* the labor force when they go back to school, return to household activities, go to prison, or retire. These entries and exits keep changing the size and composition of the labor force.

Since 1960, the U.S. labor force has more than doubled in size even though the U.S. population has grown by only 72 percent. The difference is explained by the rapid increase in the **labor force participation rate** of women. Notice in Figure 6.2 that only 1 out of 3 women participated in the labor force in 1950–1960, whereas 6 out of 10 now do so. The labor force participation of men actually declined during the same period, even though it remains higher than that of women.

labor force: All persons age 16 and over who are either working for pay or actively seeking paid employment.

labor force participation rate: The percentage of the working-age population working or seeking employment.

FIGURE 6.1

The Labor Force, 2010

Only half the total U.S. population participates in the civilian labor force. The rest of the population is too young, in school, at home, retired, or otherwise unavailable.

Unemployment statistics count only those participants who aren't currently working but are actively seeking paid employment. Nonparticipants are neither employed nor actively seeking employment.

Source: U.S. Bureau of Labor Statistics.

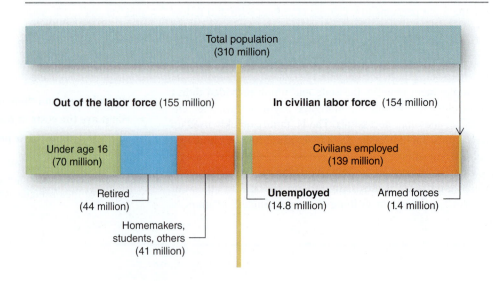

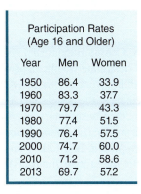

Participation Rates (Age 16 and Older)		
Year	Men	Women
1950	86.4	33.9
1960	83.3	37.7
1970	79.7	43.3
1980	77.4	51.5
1990	76.4	57.5
2000	74.7	60.0
2010	71.2	58.6
2013	69.7	57.2

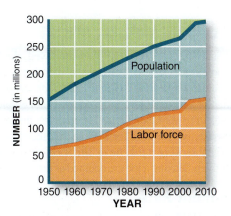

FIGURE 6.2

A Growing Labor Force

The labor force expands as births and immigration increase. A big increase in the participation rate of women after 1950 also added to labor force growth.

Source: *Economic Report of the President,* 2014.

Labor Force Growth

The labor force continues to grow each year along with population increases and continuing immigration. These sources add more than 2 million persons to the labor force every year. This is both good news and bad news. The good news is that labor force growth expands our **production possibilities,** enabling us to produce more output with each passing year. The bad news is that we've got to create at least 2 million *more* jobs every year to ensure that labor force participants can find a job. If we don't, we'll end up *inside* the production possibilities curve, as at point *F* in Figure 6.3.

Unemployment

If we end up inside the production possibilities curve, we are not producing at capacity. We're also not using all available resources, including labor force participants. This gives rise to the problem of **unemployment:** people who are willing and able to work aren't being hired. At point *F* in Figure 6.3 would-be workers are left unemployed; potential output isn't produced. Everybody suffers.

Okun's Law; Lost Output. Arthur Okun quantified the relationship between unemployment and the production possibilities curve. According to the original formulation of **Okun's law,** each additional 1 percent of unemployment translated into a loss of 3 percent in real output. More recent estimates of Okun's law put the ratio at about 1 to 2, largely due to the changing composition of both the labor force (more women and teenagers) and output (more services). Using that 1-to-2 ratio allows us to put a dollar value on the aggregate cost of unemployment. In 2010 the 14.8 milllion workers who couldn't find jobs (see Figure 6.1) could have produced more than $1 *trillion* worth of output. Hence their unemployment implied a loss of $3,000 of goods and services for every American. That's a high cost for macro failure.

production possibilities: The alternative combinations of final goods and services that could be produced in a given time period with all available resources and technology.

unemployment: The inability of labor force participants to find jobs.

Okun's law: 1 percent more unemployment results in 2 percent less output.

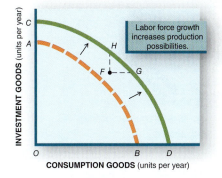

FIGURE 6.3

Labor Force Growth

The amount of labor available for work—the *labor force*—is a prime determinant of a nation's production possibilities. As the labor force grows, so does the capacity to produce. To produce at capacity, however, the labor force must be fully employed. At point *F,* resources are unemployed.

MEASURING UNEMPLOYMENT

To determine how many people are actually unemployed, the U.S. Census Bureau surveys about 60,000 households each month. The Census interviewers first determine whether a person is employed—that is, worked for pay in the previous week (or didn't work due to illness, vacation, bad weather, or a labor strike). If the person is not employed, he or she is classified as either *unemployed* or *out of the labor force.* To make that distinction, the Census interviewers ask whether the person actively looked for work in the preceding four weeks. ***If a person is not employed but is actively seeking a job, he or she is counted as unemployed.*** Individuals neither employed nor actively seeking a job are counted as outside the labor force (nonparticipants).

The Unemployment Rate

In 2013, an average of 11.5 million persons were counted as unemployed in any month. These unemployed individuals accounted for 7.4 percent of our total labor force in that year. Accordingly, the average **unemployment rate** in 2013 was 7.4 percent.

$$\text{Unemployment rate} = \frac{\text{Number of unemployed people}}{\text{Labor force}}$$

$$\text{in 2013} = \frac{11,460,000}{155,389,000} = 7.4\%$$

The Census surveys reveal not only the total amount of unemployment in the economy but also which groups are suffering the greatest unemployment. Typically, teenagers just entering the labor market have the greatest difficulty finding (or keeping) jobs. They have no job experience and relatively few marketable skills. Employers are reluctant to hire them, especially if they must pay the federal minimum wage. As a consequence, teenage unemployment rates are typically three times higher than adult unemployment rates (see Figure 6.4).

unemployment rate: The proportion of the labor force that is unemployed.

web click

Data on unemployment by race and gender from 1948 to the present are available from the Bureau of Labor Statistics at **www.bls.gov.** Click the "Subject Areas" tab for details.

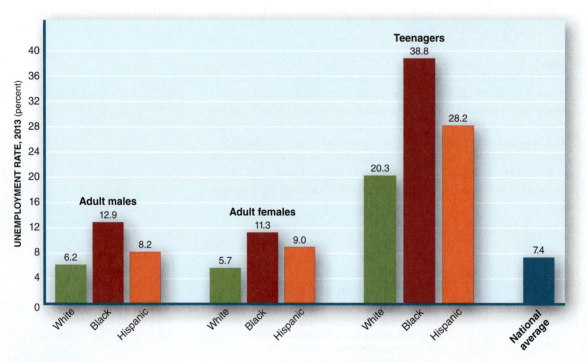

FIGURE 6.4

Unemployment Varies by Race and Sex

Minority groups, teenagers, and less-educated individuals experience higher rates of unemployment. Teenage unemployment rates are particularly high, especially for black and Hispanic youth.

Source: U.S. Department of Labor (2013 data).

Duration	Percentage of Unemployed
Less than 5 weeks	22.5%
5 to 14 weeks	24.1
15 to 26 weeks	15.8
27 weeks or more	37.6
Median duration	17.0 weeks

Source: U.S. Bureau of Labor Statistics (2013 data).

TABLE 6.1
Duration of Unemployment

The severity of unemployment depends on how long the spell of joblessness lasts. About one-third of unemployed workers return to work quickly, but many others remain unemployed for 6 months or longer.

Minority workers also experience above-average unemployment. Notice in Figure 6.4 that black and Hispanic unemployment rates are much higher than white workers' unemployment rates. In 2013 black teenagers had an extraordinary unemployment rate of 39 percent—five times the national average.

Education. Education also affects the chances of being unemployed. If you graduate from college, your chances of being unemployed drop sharply, regardless of gender or race. Advancing technology and a shift to services from manufacturing have put a premium on better-educated workers. Very few people with master's or doctoral degrees stand in unemployment lines.

The Duration of Unemployment

Although high school dropouts are three times more likely to be unemployed than college graduates, they don't *stay* unemployed. In fact, most people who become unemployed find jobs in 4.5 months. Even in the depressed labor market of 2013, the median spell of unemployment was 17 weeks (Table 6.1). Only one out of three unemployed individuals had been jobless for as long as 6 months (27 weeks or longer). People who lose their jobs do find new ones; how fast that happens depends on the state of the economy. ***When the economy is growing, both unemployment rates and the average duration of unemployment decline.*** Recessions have the opposite effect—raising both the rate and the duration of unemployment.

Reasons for Unemployment

The reason a person becomes unemployed also affects the length of time the person stays jobless. A person just entering the labor market might need more time to identify job openings and develop job contacts. By contrast, an autoworker laid off for a temporary plant closing can expect to return to work quickly. Figure 6.5 depicts these and other reasons for unemployment. In 2013 roughly 1 of every 2 unemployed persons was a job loser (laid off or fired), and only

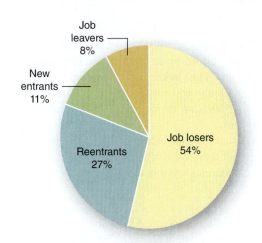

FIGURE 6.5
Reasons for Unemployment

People become unemployed for various reasons. Just over half of the unemployed in 2013 were job losers. About 40 percent of the unemployed were entering or reentering the labor market in search of a job. In recessions, the proportion of job losers shoots up.

Source: U.S. Labor Department.

"I've stopped looking for work, which, I believe, helps the economic numbers."

Analysis: People who stop searching for a job but want one aren't officially counted as "unemployed." They are called "discouraged workers."

1 in 12 was a job leaver (quit). The rest were new entrants (primarily teenagers) or reentrants (primarily mothers returning to the workforce). Like the duration of unemployment, the reasons for joblessness are very sensitive to economic conditions. In really bad years like 2008–2010, most of the unemployed are job losers, and they remain out of work a long time.

Discouraged Workers

Unemployment statistics don't tell the complete story about the human costs of a sluggish economy. When unemployment persists, job seekers become increasingly frustrated. After repeated rejections, job seekers often get so discouraged that they give up the search and turn to their families, friends, or public welfare for income support. When the Census Bureau interviewer asks whether they're actively seeking employment, such **discouraged workers** are apt to reply no. Yet they'd like to be working, and they'd probably be out looking for work if job prospects were better.

Discouraged workers aren't counted as part of our unemployment problem because they're technically out of the labor force (see the cartoon above). The Labor Department estimates that nearly 1 million individuals fell into this uncounted class of discouraged workers in 2013. That's on top of the 11.5 million officially counted as unemployed because they were still actively seeking jobs. In years of lower unemployment, this number declines sharply.

Underemployment

Some people can't afford to be discouraged. Many people who become jobless have family responsibilities and bills to pay: they simply can't afford to drop out of the labor force. Instead they're compelled to take some job—any job—just to keep body and soul together. The resultant job may be part-time or full-time and may pay very little. Nevertheless, any paid employment is sufficient to exclude the person from the count of the unemployed, though not from a condition of **underemployment.**

Underemployed workers represent labor resources that aren't being fully utilized. They're part of our unemployment problem, even if they're not officially counted as *unemployed*. In 2013, nearly 7 million workers were underemployed in the U.S. economy.

The Phantom Unemployed

Although discouraged and underemployed workers aren't counted in official unemployment statistics, some of the people who *are* counted probably shouldn't be. Many people

discouraged worker: An individual who isn't actively seeking employment but would look for or accept a job if one were available.

underemployment: People seeking full-time paid employment who work only part-time or are employed at jobs below their capability.

report that they're actively seeking a job even when they have little interest in finding employment. To some extent, public policy actually encourages such behavior. For example, welfare recipients are often required to look for a job, even though some welfare mothers would prefer to spend all their time raising their children. Their resultant job search is likely to be perfunctory at best. Similarly, most states require people receiving unemployment benefits (see the accompanying News) to provide evidence that they're looking for a job, even though some recipients may prefer a brief period of joblessness. Here again, reported unemployment may conceal labor force nonparticipation.

IN THE NEWS

Unemployment Benefits Not for Everyone

In 2013, more than 10 million people collected unemployment benefits averaging $335 per week. But don't rush to the state unemployment office yet—not all unemployed people are eligible. To qualify for weekly unemployment benefits you must have worked a substantial length of time and earned some minimum amount of wages, both determined by your state. Furthermore, you must have a "good" reason for having lost your last job. Most states will not provide benefits to students (or their professors!) during summer vacations, to professional athletes in the off-season, or to individuals who quit their last jobs.

If you qualify for benefits, the amount of benefits you receive each week will depend on your previous wages. In most states the benefits are equal to about one-half of the previous weekly wage, up to a state-determined maximum. The maximum benefit in 2013 ranged from $235 in Mississippi to a high of $653 in Massachusetts.

Unemployment benefits are financed by a tax on employers and can continue for as long as 26 weeks. During periods of high unemployment, eligibility may be extended another 13 weeks or more by the U.S. Congress. In 2010–2011, benefits were available for up to 99 weeks.

Source: U.S. Employment and Training Administration, **www.workforcesecurity.doleta.gov**

ANALYSIS: Some of the income lost due to unemployment is replaced by unemployment insurance benefits. Not all unemployed persons are eligible, however, and the duration of benefits is limited.

web click

For the latest information on unemployment benefit outlays by the federal government, visit the Department of Labor website **www.dol.gov.**

THE HUMAN COSTS

Our measures of unemployment are a valuable index to a serious macro problem. However, they don't adequately convey how devastating unemployment can be for individual workers and their families.

Lost Income. The most visible impact of unemployment on individuals is the loss of income. Even short spells of joblessness can force families to tighten their belts and fall behind on bills (see the News on the next page). For workers who've been unemployed for long periods, such losses can spell financial disaster. Typically, an unemployed person must rely on a combination of savings, income from other family members, and government unemployment benefits for financial support. After these sources of support are exhausted, public welfare is often the only legal support left.

Lost Confidence. Not all unemployed people experience such a financial disaster, of course. College students who fail to find summer employment are unlikely to end up on welfare the following semester. Similarly, teenagers and others looking for part-time employment won't suffer great economic losses from unemployment. Nevertheless, the experience of unemployment—of not being able to find a job when you want one—can be painful. This sensation isn't easily forgotten, even after one has finally found employment.

Social Stress. It is difficult to measure all the intangible effects of unemployment on individual workers. Studies have shown, however, that joblessness causes more crime, more health problems, more divorces, and other problems (see the next News). Such findings

web click

John Steinbeck's novel, *The Grapes of Wrath*, depicts the toll of the Great Depression upon unemployed farmers. Visit **video .nytimes.com** to learn more about this classic story and search "Grapes of Wrath."

underscore the notion that prolonged unemployment poses a real danger. Like George H., the worker discussed at the beginning of this chapter, many unemployed workers simply can't cope with the resulting stress. Thomas Cottle, a lecturer at Harvard Medical School, stated the case more bluntly: "I'm now convinced that unemployment is *the* killer disease in this country—responsible for wife beating, infertility, and even tooth decay."

Lost Lives. German psychiatrists have also observed that unemployment can be hazardous to your health. They estimate that the anxieties and other nervous disorders that accompany one year of unemployment can reduce life expectancy by as much as five years. In Japan, the suicide rate jumped by more than 50 percent when the economy plunged into recession. In New Zealand, suicide rates are twice as high for unemployed workers as they are for employed ones. A University of Oxford study estimated that the economic downturn of 2007–2010 triggered more than 10,000 suicides in the United States and Europe.

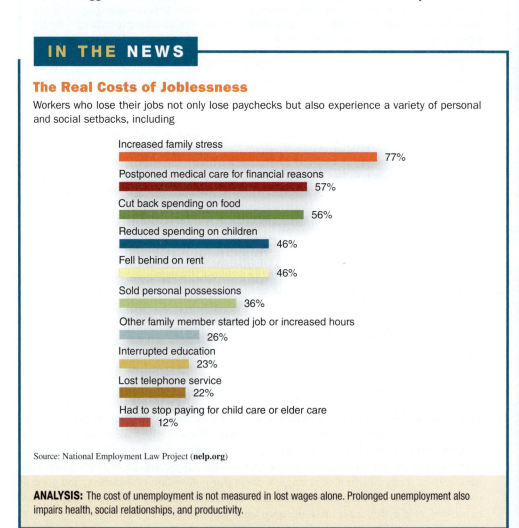

IN THE NEWS

The Real Costs of Joblessness

Workers who lose their jobs not only lose paychecks but also experience a variety of personal and social setbacks, including

Increased family stress — 77%
Postponed medical care for financial reasons — 57%
Cut back spending on food — 56%
Reduced spending on children — 46%
Fell behind on rent — 46%
Sold personal possessions — 36%
Other family member started job or increased hours — 26%
Interrupted education — 23%
Lost telephone service — 22%
Had to stop paying for child care or elder care — 12%

Source: National Employment Law Project (**nelp.org**)

ANALYSIS: The cost of unemployment is not measured in lost wages alone. Prolonged unemployment also impairs health, social relationships, and productivity.

DEFINING FULL EMPLOYMENT

In view of the economic and social losses associated with unemployment, it's not surprising that *full employment* is one of our basic macroeconomic goals. You may be surprised to learn, however, that ***"full" employment isn't the same thing as "zero" unemployment.*** There are in fact several reasons for regarding some degree of unemployment as inevitable and even desirable.

Seasonal Unemployment

Some joblessness is virtually inevitable as long as we continue to grow crops, build houses, or go skiing at certain seasons of the year. At the end of each such season, thousands of workers must go searching for new jobs, experiencing some **seasonal unemployment** in the process.

Seasonal fluctuations also arise on the supply side of the labor market. Teenage unemployment rates, for example, rise sharply in the summer as students look for temporary jobs. To avoid such unemployment completely, we'd either have to keep everyone in school or ensure that all students went immediately from the classroom to the workroom. Neither alternative is likely, much less desirable.[1]

seasonal unemployment:
Unemployment due to seasonal changes in employment or labor supply.

Frictional Unemployment

There are other reasons for expecting a certain amount of unemployment. Many workers have sound financial or personal reasons for leaving one job to look for another. In the process of moving from one job to another, a person may well miss a few days or even weeks of work without any serious personal or social consequences. On the contrary, people who spend more time looking for work may find *better* jobs.

The same is true of students first entering the labor market. It's not likely that you'll find a job the moment you leave school. Nor should you necessarily take the first job offered. If you spend some time looking for work, you're more likely to find a job you like. The job search period gives you an opportunity to find out what kinds of jobs are available, what skills they require, and what they pay. Accordingly, a brief period of job search may benefit labor market entrants and the larger economy. The unemployment associated with these kinds of job searches is referred to as **frictional unemployment.**

Three factors distinguish frictional unemployment from other kinds of unemployment. First, enough jobs exist for those who are frictionally unemployed—that is, there's adequate *demand* for labor. Second, individuals who are frictionally unemployed have the skills required for available jobs. Third, the period of job search will be relatively short. Under these conditions, frictional unemployment resembles an unconventional game of musical chairs. There are enough chairs of the right size for everyone, and people dance around them for only a brief period.

No one knows for sure just how much of our unemployment problem is frictional. Most economists agree, however, that friction alone is responsible for an unemployment rate of 2 to 3 percent. Accordingly, our definition of *"full employment"* should allow for at least this much unemployment.

frictional unemployment:
Brief periods of unemployment experienced by people moving between jobs or into the labor market.

Structural Unemployment

For many job seekers, the period between jobs may drag on for months or even years because they don't have the skills that employers require. Imagine, for example, the predicament of steelworkers. During the 1980s, the steel industry contracted as consumers demanded fewer and lighter-weight cars and as construction of highways, bridges, and buildings slowed. In the process, more than 300,000 steelworkers lost their jobs. Most of these workers had a decade or more of experience and substantial skill. But the skills they'd perfected were no longer in demand. They couldn't perform the jobs available in computer software, biotechnology, or other expanding industries. Although there were enough job vacancies in the labor market, the steelworkers couldn't fill them. These workers were victims of **structural unemployment.**

The same kind of structural displacement hit the construction industry from 2007 to 2010. The housing market collapsed, leaving millions of homes unsold and even unfinished. Tens of thousands of carpenters, electricians, and plumbers lost their jobs. These displaced

structural unemployment:
Unemployment caused by a mismatch between the skills (or location) of job seekers and the requirements (or location) of available jobs.

[1]Seasonal variations in employment and labor supply not only create some unemployment in the annual averages but also distort monthly comparisons. Unemployment rates are always higher in February (when farming and housing construction come to a virtual standstill) and June (when a mass of students goes looking for summer jobs). The Labor Department adjusts monthly unemployment rates according to this seasonal pattern and reports "seasonally adjusted" unemployment rates for each month. Seasonal adjustments don't alter *annual* averages, however.

workers soon discovered that their highly developed skills were no longer in demand. They couldn't fill job openings in the growing health care, financial, or Internet industries.

Teenagers from urban slums also suffer from structural unemployment. Most poor teenagers have an inadequate education, few job-related skills, and little work experience. For them, almost all decent jobs are "out of reach." As a consequence, they remain unemployed far longer than can be explained by frictional forces.

Structural unemployment violates the second condition for frictional unemployment: that the job seekers can perform the available jobs. Structural unemployment is analogous to a musical chairs game in which there are enough chairs for everyone, but some of them are too small to sit on. It's a more serious concern than frictional unemployment and incompatible with any notion of full employment.

Cyclical Unemployment

cyclical unemployment:
Unemployment attributable to a lack of job vacancies—that is, to an inadequate level of aggregate demand.

The fourth type of unemployment is **cyclical unemployment**—joblessness that occurs when there simply aren't enough jobs to go around. Cyclical unemployment exists when the number of workers demanded falls short of the number of persons supplied (in the labor force). This isn't a case of mobility between jobs (frictional unemployment) or even of job seekers' skills (structural unemployment). Rather, it's simply an inadequate level of demand for goods and services and thus for labor. Cyclical unemployment resembles the most familiar form of musical chairs, in which the number of chairs is always less than the number of players.

The Great Depression is the most striking example of cyclical unemployment. The dramatic increase in unemployment rates that began in 1930 (see Figure 6.6) wasn't due to any increase in friction or sudden decline in workers' skills. Instead the high rates of unemployment that persisted for a *decade* were caused by a sudden decline in the market demand for goods and services. How do we know? Just notice what happened to our unemployment rate when the demand for military goods and services increased in 1941!

Slow Growth. Cyclical unemployment can emerge even when the economy is expanding. Keep in mind that the labor force is always growing due to population growth and continuing immigration. If these additional labor force participants are to find jobs, the economy must grow. Specifically, ***the economy must grow at least as fast as the labor force to avoid cyclical unemployment.*** When economic growth slows below this threshold, unemployment rates start to rise.

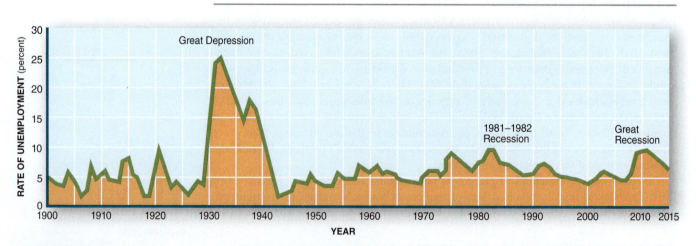

FIGURE 6.6
The Unemployment Record

Unemployment rates reached record heights (25 percent) during the Great Depression. In more recent decades, the unemployment rate has varied from 4 percent in full-employment years to 10 percent in the recession years of 1982 and 2009. Keeping the labor force fully employed is a primary macro policy goal.

Source: U.S. Department of Labor.

The Full-Employment Goal

In later chapters we examine the causes of cyclical unemployment and explore some potential policy responses. At this point, however, we just want to establish a macro policy goal. In the Employment Act of 1946, Congress committed the federal government to pursue a goal of "maximum" employment but didn't specify exactly what that rate was. Presumably, this meant avoiding as much cyclical and structural unemployment as possible while keeping frictional unemployment within reasonable bounds. As guidelines for public policy, these perspectives are a bit vague.

Inflationary Pressures. The first attempt to define *full employment* more precisely was undertaken in the early 1960s. At that time the Council of Economic Advisers (itself created by the Employment Act of 1946) decided that our proximity to full employment could be gauged by watching *prices*. As the economy approached its production possibilities, labor and other resources would become increasingly scarce. As market participants bid for these remaining resources, wages and prices would start to rise. Hence *rising prices are a signal that employment is nearing capacity.*

After examining the relationship between unemployment and inflation, the Council of Economic Advisers decided to peg full employment at 4 percent unemployment. The unemployment rate could fall below 4 percent. If it did, however, price levels would begin to rise at an accelerating rate. Hence this threshold came to be regarded as an **inflationary flashpoint:** a level of output that would trigger too much inflation. Thus 4 percent unemployment was seen as an acceptable compromise of our employment and price goals.

During the 1970s and early 1980s, this view of our full-employment potential was considered overly optimistic. Unemployment rates stayed far above 4 percent, even when the economy expanded. Moreover, inflation began to accelerate at higher levels of unemployment.

In view of these factors, the Council of Economic Advisers later raised the level of unemployment thought to be compatible with price stability. In 1983 the Reagan administration concluded that the "inflation-threshold" unemployment rate was between 6 and 7 percent (see the cartoon below).

inflationary flashpoint: The rate of output at which inflationary pressures intensify; the point on the AS curve where the slope increases sharply.

"I don't like six per-cent unemployment, either. But I can live with it."

© Lee Lorenz/The New Yorker Collection/www.cartoonbank.com.

Analysis: So-called full employment entails a compromise between employment and inflation goals. That compromise doesn't affect everyone equally.

Changed Labor Force. The quest for low unemployment got easier in the 1990s, largely due to changes in the labor force. The number of teenagers declined by 3 million between 1981 and 1993. The upsurge in women's participation in the labor force also leveled off. High school and college attendance and graduation rates increased. And welfare programs were reformed in ways that encouraged more work. All these structural changes made it easier to reduce unemployment rates without increasing inflation. In 1991 the first Bush administration concluded that **full employment** was equivalent to 5.5 percent unemployment. In 1999 the Clinton administration suggested the full-employment threshold might have dropped even further, to 5.3 percent. In reality, the national unemployment rate stayed below even that benchmark for four years (Figure 6.6) without any upsurge in inflation. In 2004 the Bush administration set the full-employment threshold at 5.1 percent. The Obama administration left that threshold intact. The consensus was that *full employment entails 4–6 percent unemployment*.

The "Natural" Rate of Unemployment

The ambiguity about which rate of unemployment might trigger an upsurge in inflation has convinced some analysts to abandon the inflation-based concept of full employment. They prefer to specify a "natural" rate of unemployment that doesn't depend on inflation trends. In this view, the natural rate of unemployment consists of frictional and structural components only. It's the rate of unemployment that will prevail in the long run. In the short run, both the unemployment rate and the inflation rate may go up and down. However, the economy will tend to gravitate toward the long-run **natural rate of unemployment.**

Although the natural rate concept avoids specifying a short-term inflation trigger, it too is subject to debate. As we've seen, the *structural* determinants of unemployment (e.g., age and composition of the labor force) change over time. When structural forces change, the level of natural unemployment presumably changes as well.

Congressional Targets

Although most economists agree that an unemployment rate of 4–6 percent is consistent with either natural or full employment, Congress has set tougher goals for macro policy. According to the Full Employment and Balanced Growth Act of 1978 (commonly called the Humphrey-Hawkins Act), our national goal is to attain a 4 percent rate of unemployment. The act also requires a goal of 3 percent inflation. There was an escape clause, however. In the event that both goals couldn't be met, the president could set higher, provisional definitions of full employment.

THE HISTORICAL RECORD

Our greatest failure to achieve full employment occurred during the Great Depression. As Figure 6.6 shows, as much as one-fourth of the labor force was unemployed in the 1930s.

Unemployment rates fell dramatically during World War II. In 1944 virtually anyone who was ready and willing to work quickly found a job; the civilian unemployment rate hit a rock-bottom 1.2 percent.

Since 1950 the unemployment rate has fluctuated from a low of 2.8 percent during the Korean War (1953) to a high of 10.8 percent during the 1981–1982 recession. From 1982 to 1989 the unemployment rate receded, but it shot up again in the 1990–1991 recession.

During the last half of the 1990s the unemployment rate fell steadily and hit the low end of the full-employment range in 2000. Slow GDP growth in 2000–2001 and the economic stall caused by the September 11, 2001, terrorist attacks pushed the unemployment rate sharply higher in late 2001. The subsequent recovery of the U.S. economy pushed the unemployment rate down into the "full-employment" range again in 2006–2007. But the Great Recession of 2008–2009 wiped out that gain, sending the unemployment rate to near-record heights once again (see the following News). The unemployment rate started declining as the economy recovered, but the return to full employment was agonizingly slow.

---

full employment: The lowest rate of unemployment compatible with price stability, variously estimated at between 4 percent and 6 percent unemployment.

natural rate of unemployment: The long-term rate of unemployment determined by structural forces in labor and product markets.

IN THE NEWS

Unemployment Rate Hits a 26-Year High

The nation's unemployment rate climbed to 10.2 percent in October, the highest rate since 1983. Nonfarm payrolls dropped another 190,000 last month, adding to 22 consecutive months of job losses. The biggest job losses were in manufacturing, construction, and retail employment.

Since the recession began over 7.3 million jobs have been lost. The unemployment rate has more than doubled from 4.9 percent in December 2007 to its current level of 10.2 percent.

In October, 35.6 percent of unemployed persons were jobless for 27 weeks or more, while 20 percent of the unemployed were jobless for 5 weeks or less

Among the major worker groups, the unemployment rates for adult men (10.7 percent) and whites (9.5 percent) rose in October. The jobless rates for adult women (8.1 percent), teenagers (27.6 percent), blacks (15.7 percent), and Hispanics (13.1 percent) were little changed over the month.

Source: U.S. Bureau of Labor Statistics, November 10, 2009.

ANALYSIS: When the economy contracts, millions of workers lose jobs, and the unemployment rate rises—sometimes sharply.

THE ECONOMY TOMORROW

OUTSOURCING JOBS

To keep unemployment rates low in the economy tomorrow, job growth in U.S. product markets must exceed labor force growth. As we've observed, this will require at least 2 million *new* jobs every year. Achieving that net job growth is made more difficult when U.S. firms shut down their U.S. operations and relocate production to Mexico, China, and other foreign nations.

Cheap Labor. Low wages are the primary motivation for all this **outsourcing**. Telephone operators and clerks in India are paid a tenth as much as are their U.S. counterparts. Indian accountants and paralegals get paid less than half the wages of their U.S. counterparts. Polish workers are even cheaper. With cheap, high-speed telecommunications, that offshore labor is an attractive substitute for U.S. workers. Over the next 10 years, more than 3 million U.S. jobs are expected to move offshore in response to such wage differentials.

outsourcing: The relocation of production to foreign countries.

Small Numbers. In the short run, outsourcing clearly worsens the U.S. employment outlook. But there's a lot more to the story. To begin with, the total number of outsourced jobs averages less than 300,000 per year. That amounts to only 0.002 percent of all U.S. jobs and only 3 percent of total U.S. *un*employment. So even in the worst case, outsourcing can't be a major explanation for U.S. unemployment.

Insourcing. We also have to recognize that outsourcing of U.S. jobs has a counterpart in the "insourcing" of foreign production. The German Mercedes Benz company builds cars in Alabama to reduce production and distribution costs. In the process German autoworkers lose some jobs to U.S. autoworkers. In addition to this direct investment, foreign nations and firms hire U.S. workers to design, build, and deliver a wide variety of products. In other words, *trade in both products and labor resources is a two-way street.* Looking at the flow of jobs in only one direction distorts the jobs picture.

web click

To get a sense of how global commerce is changing, see the *2011 Economic Report of the President* at **www.gpoaccess.gov/eop**. Of special relevance is Chapter 4, "The World Economy."

Productivity and Growth. Even the gross flow of outsourced jobs is not all bad. The cost savings realized by U.S. firms due to outsourcing increase U.S. profits. Those profits may finance new investment or consumption in U.S. product markets, thereby creating new jobs. The accompanying News suggests more jobs are gained than lost as a result. Outsourcing routine tasks to foreign workers also raises the productivity of U.S. workers by allowing U.S. workers to focus on more complex and high-value tasks. In other words, outsourcing promotes specialization and higher productivity both here and abroad. *Production possibilities expand, not contract, with outsourcing.*

IN THE NEWS

Outsourcing May Create U.S. Jobs

Estimated New U.S. Jobs Created from Outsourcing Abroad

	2003	2008
Natural resources and mining	1,046	1,182
Construction	19,815	75,757
Manufacturing	3,078	25,010
Wholesale trade	20,456	43,359
Retail trade	12,552	30,931
Transportation and utilities	18,895	63,513
Publishing, software, and communications	−24,860	−50,043
Financial services	5,604	32,066
Professional and business services	14,667	31,623
Education and health services	18,015	47,260
Leisure, hospitality, and other services	4,389	12,506
Government	−3,393	4,203
Total employment	**90,264**	**317,367**

Source: IHS Global Insight; North American Industry Classification System.

ANALYSIS: Outsourcing increases U.S. productivity and profits while reducing U.S. production costs and prices. These outcomes may increase demand for U.S. jobs by more than the immediate job loss.

Creating Jobs. Greater efficiency and expanded production possibilities don't guarantee jobs in the economy tomorrow. The challenge is still to *use* that expanded capacity to the fullest. To do so, we have to use macroeconomic tools to keep output growing faster than the labor force. Stopping the outsourcing of jobs won't achieve that goal—and may even worsen income and job prospects in the economy tomorrow.

SUMMARY

- To understand unemployment, we must distinguish the labor force from the larger population. Only people who are working (employed) or spend some time looking for a job (unemployed) are participants in the labor force. People neither working nor looking for work are outside the labor force.   **LO6-1**
- The labor force grows every year due to population growth and immigration. This growth increases production possibilities but also necessitates continued job creation.   **LO6-1**

- The economy (output) must grow at least as fast as the labor force to keep the unemployment rate from rising. Unemployment implies that we're producing inside the production possibilities curve rather than on it.   **LO6-1**
- The macroeconomic loss imposed by unemployment is reduced output of goods and services. Okun's Law suggests that 1 percentage point in unemployment is equivalent to a 2 percentage point decline in output.   **LO6-2**

- The human cost of unemployment includes not only financial losses but social, physical, and psychological costs as well. **LO6-2**
- Unemployment is distributed unevenly: minorities, teenagers, and the less educated have much higher rates of unemployment. Also hurt are discouraged workers—those who've stopped looking for work—and those working at part-time or menial jobs because they can't find full-time jobs equal to their training or potential. **LO6-1**
- There are four types of unemployment: seasonal, frictional, structural, and cyclical. **LO6-3**
- Because some seasonal and frictional unemployment is inevitable and even desirable, full employment is not defined as zero unemployment. These considerations, plus fear of inflationary consequences, result in full employment being defined as an unemployment rate of 4–6 percent. **LO6-4**
- The natural rate of unemployment is based on frictional and structural forces, without reference to short-term price (inflation) pressures. **LO6-4**
- Unemployment rates got as high as 25 percent in the 1930s. Since 1960 the unemployment rate has ranged from 3.4 to 10.8 percent. **LO6-1**
- Outsourcing of U.S. production directly reduces domestic employment. But the indirect effects of higher U.S. productivity, profits, and global competitiveness may create even more jobs. **LO6-3**

Key Terms

labor force
labor force participation rate
production possibilities
unemployment
Okun's Law
unemployment rate

discouraged worker
underemployment
seasonal unemployment
frictional unemployment
structural unemployment

cyclical unemployment
inflationary flashpoint
full employment
natural rate of unemployment
outsourcing

Questions for Discussion

1. Is it possible for unemployment rates to increase at the same time that the number of employed persons is increasing? How? **LO6-1**
2. If more teenagers stay in school longer, what happens to (a) production possibilities? (b) unemployment rates? **LO6-1**
3. When the housing industry implodes, what do construction workers do? **LO6-3**
4. Why might job market (re)entrants have a harder time finding a job than job losers? **LO6-3**
5. Should the government replace the wages of anyone who is unemployed? How might this affect output and unemployment? **LO6-3**
6. When the GE lightbulb plant in Virginia closed (p. 113), how was the local economy affected? **LO6-2**
7. Why is frictional unemployment deemed desirable? **LO6-3**
8. Why do people expect inflation to heat up when the unemployment rate approaches 4 percent? **LO6-4**
9. Identify (a) two jobs at your school that could be outsourced and (b) two jobs that would be hard to outsource. **LO6-4**
10. How can the outsourcing of U.S. computer jobs generate new U.S. jobs in construction or retail trade? (See News, p. 126.) **LO6-4**

 mobile app Visit your mobile app store and download the Schiller: Study Econ app *today!*

LO6-1   1. According to Figure 6.1 (p. 114),
    (*a*) What percentage of the civilian labor force was employed?   _____%
    (*b*) What percentage of the civilian labor force was unemployed?   _____%
    (*c*) What percentage of the *population* was employed in civilian jobs?   _____%

LO6-1   2. If the unemployment rate in 2013 had been 5 percent instead of 7.4 percent,
    (*a*) How many more workers would have been employed?   _____
    (*b*) How many fewer would have been unemployed?   _____

LO6-1   3. Between 2000 and 2013, by how much did
    (*a*) The labor force increase?   _____
    (*b*) Total employment increase?   _____
    (*c*) Total unemployment increase?   _____
    (*d*) Total output (real GDP) increase?   _____
    (*Note:* Data on inside covers of the text.)

LO6-1   4. If the labor force of 155 million people is growing by 1.2 percent per year, how many new jobs
    have to be created each *month* to keep unemployment from increasing?   _____

LO6-1   5. Between 1990 and 2000, by how much did the labor force participation rate (Figure 6.2) of
    (*a*) Men fall?   _____%
    (*b*) Women rise?   _____%

LO6-2   6. According to Okun's law, how much output (real GDP) was lost in 2009 when the
    nation's unemployment rate increased from 5.8 percent to 9.3 percent?   _____%

LO6-1   7. Suppose the following data describe a nation's population:

	Year 1	Year 2
Population	300 million	310 million
Labor force	140 million	150 million
Unemployment rate	6 percent	6 percent

    (*a*) How many people are unemployed in each year?   Year 1: _____
                                             Year 2: _____

    (*b*) How many people are employed in each year?   Year 1: _____
                                             Year 2: _____

    (*c*) Compute the employment rate (i.e., Number employed ÷ Population) in each year.   Year 1: _____
                                             Year 2: _____

LO6-1   8. Based on the data in the previous problem, what happens ("up" or "down") to each of the
    following numbers in Year 2 when 1 million jobseekers become "discouraged workers"?
    (*a*) Number of unemployed persons.   _____
    (*b*) Unemployment rate.   _____
    (*c*) Employment rate.   _____

LO6-1   9. According to the News on page 125, in October 2009
    (*a*) How many people were in the labor force?   _____
    (*b*) How many people were employed?   _____

LO6-1   10. In 2013, how many of the 800,000 black teenagers who participated in the labor market
    (*a*) Were unemployed?   _____
    (*b*) Were employed?   _____
    (*c*) Would have been employed if they had the same unemployment rate as
        white teenagers?   _____
    (See Figure 6.4 for needed info.)

PROBLEMS FOR CHAPTER 6 (cont'd)

Name: _____

LO6-4 11. On the accompanying graph, illustrate both the unemployment rate and the real GDP growth rate for each year. (The data required for this exercise are on the inside cover of this book.)

(a) In how many years was "full employment" achieved? (Use the current benchmark.)   _____

(b) Unemployment and growth rates tend to move in opposite directions. Which appears to change direction first?   _____

(c) In how many years does the unemployment rate increase even when output is expanding?   _____

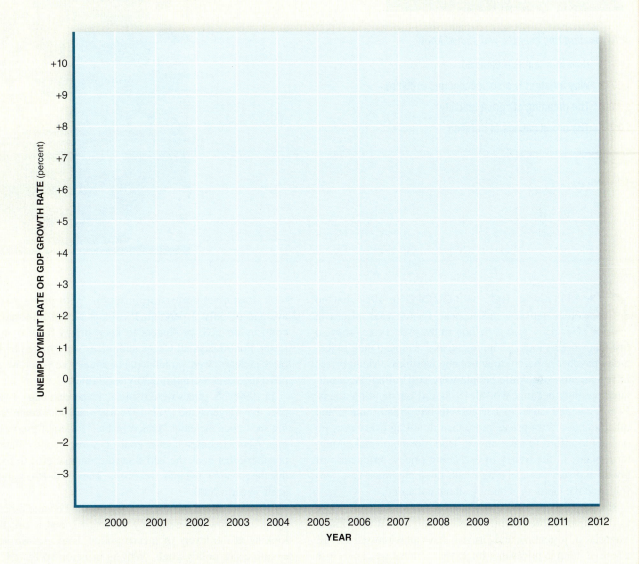

LO6-3 12. For each situation described here, determine the type of unemployment:

(a) Steelworkers losing their jobs due to decreased demand for steel.   _____

(b) A college graduate waiting to accept a job that allows her to utilize her level of education.   _____

(c) The Great Recession of 2008–2009.   _____

(d) A homemaker entering the labor force.   _____

LO6-4 13. (a) What was the unemployment rate in 2013?   _____

(b) How many more jobs were needed to bring the unemployment rate down to the 5 percent full-employment threshold?   _____

(c) Using Okun's law, how much more would total output (GDP) have had to grow to create that many jobs?   _____

CHAPTER 7

Inflation

Germany set a record in 1923 that no other nation wants to beat. In that year, prices in Germany rose a *trillion* times over. Prices rose so fast that workers took "shopping breaks" to spend their twice-a-day paychecks before they became worthless. Menu prices in restaurants rose while people were still eating! Accumulated savings became worthless, as did outstanding loans. People needed sacks of currency to buy bread, butter, and other staples. With prices more than doubling every *day,* no one could afford to save, invest, lend money, or make long-term plans. In the frenzy of escalating prices, production of goods and services came to a halt, unemployment rose tenfold, and the German economy all but collapsed.

Hungary had a similar episode of runaway inflation in 1946, as did Japan. More recently, Russia, Bulgaria, Brazil, Zaire, Yugoslavia, Argentina, and Uruguay have all witnessed at least a tenfold jump in prices in a single year. Zimbabwe came close to breaking Germany's record in 2008, with an inflation rate of *231 million* percent (see the World View on page 136).

The United States has never experienced such a price frenzy. During the Revolutionary War, prices did double in one year, but that was a singular event. In the last decade, U.S. prices have risen just 1 to 4 percent a year. Despite this enviable record, Americans still worry a lot about inflation. In response to this anxiety, every president since Franklin Roosevelt has expressed a determination to keep prices from rising. In 1971 the Nixon administration took drastic action to stop inflation. With prices rising an average of only 3 percent, President Nixon imposed price controls on U.S. producers to keep prices from rising any faster. For 90 days all wages and prices were frozen by law—price increases were prohibited. For three more years, wage and price increases were limited by legal rules.

In 1990 U.S. prices were rising at a 6 percent clip—twice the pace that triggered the 1971–1974 wage and price controls. Calling such price increases "unacceptable," Federal Reserve Chairman Alan Greenspan set a goal of *zero* percent inflation. In pursuit of that goal, the Fed slowed economic growth so much that the economy fell into a recession. The Fed did the same thing again in early 2000.

In later chapters we'll examine how the Fed and other policymakers slow the economy down or speed it up. Before looking at the levers of macro policy, however, we need to examine our policy goals. Why is inflation so feared? How much inflation is unacceptable? To get a handle on this basic issue, we'll ask and answer the following questions:

- **What kind of price increases are referred to as *inflation*?**
- **Who is hurt (or helped) by inflation?**
- **What is an appropriate goal for *price stability*?**

As we'll discover, inflation is a serious problem, but not for the reasons most people cite. We'll also see why deflation—falling prices—isn't so welcome either.

WHAT IS INFLATION?

Most people associate **inflation** with price increases for specific goods and services. The economy isn't necessarily experiencing inflation, however, every time the price of a cup of coffee goes up. We must distinguish the phenomenon of inflation from price increases for specific goods. *Inflation is an increase in the average level of prices, not a change in any specific price.*

inflation: An increase in the average level of prices of goods and services.

The Average Price

Suppose you wanted to know the average price of fruit in the supermarket. Surely you wouldn't have much success in seeking out an average fruit—nobody would be quite sure what you had in mind. You might have some success, however, if you sought out the prices of apples, oranges, cherries, and peaches. Knowing the price of each kind of fruit, you could then compute the average price of fruit. The resultant figure wouldn't refer to any particular product but would convey a sense of how much a typical basket of fruit might cost. By repeating these calculations every day, you could then determine whether fruit prices, *on average,* were changing. On occasion, you might even notice that apple prices rose while orange prices fell, leaving the *average* price of fruit unchanged.

The same kinds of calculations are made to measure inflation in the entire economy. We first determine the average price of all output—the average price level—and then look for changes in that average. A rise in the average price level is referred to as inflation.

The average price level may fall as well as rise. A decline in average prices—**deflation**—occurs when price decreases on some goods and services outweigh price increases on all others. This happened in Japan in 1995 and again in 2003. Such deflations are rare, however: The United States has not experienced any general deflation since 1940.

deflation: A decrease in the average level of prices of goods and services.

Relative Prices vs. the Price Level

Because inflation and deflation are measured in terms of average price levels, it's possible for individual prices to rise or fall continuously without changing the average price level. We already noted, for example, that the price of apples can rise without increasing the average price of fruit, so long as the price of some other fruit, such as oranges, falls. In such circumstances, **relative prices** are changing, but not *average* prices. An increase in the *relative* price of apples simply means that apples have become more expensive in comparison with other fruits (or any other goods or services).

relative price: The price of one good in comparison with the price of other goods.

Changes in relative prices may occur in a period of stable average prices, or in periods of inflation or deflation. In fact, in an economy as vast as ours—in which literally millions of goods and services are exchanged in the factor and product markets—*relative prices are always changing.* Indeed, relative price changes are an essential ingredient of the market mechanism. Recall from Chapter 3 what happens when the market price of web design services rises relative to other goods and services. This (relative) price rise alerts web architects (producers) to increase their output, cutting back on other production or leisure activities.

A general inflation—an increase in the *average* price level—doesn't perform this same market function. If all prices rise at the same rate, price increases for specific goods are of little value as market signals. In less extreme cases, when most but not all prices are rising, changes in relative prices do occur but aren't so immediately apparent. Table 7.1 reminds us that some prices fall even during periods of general inflation.

REDISTRIBUTIVE EFFECTS OF INFLATION

The distinction between relative and average prices helps us determine who's hurt by inflation—and who's helped. Popular opinion notwithstanding, it's simply not true that everyone is worse off when prices rise. *Although inflation makes some people worse off, it makes other people better off.* Some people even get rich when prices rise! The micro consequences

TABLE 7.1

Prices That Have Fallen

Inflation refers to an increase in the *average* price level. It doesn't mean that *all* prices are rising. In fact, many prices fall, even during periods of general inflation.

Item	Early Price	2010 Price
Long-distance telephone call (per minute)	$ 6.90 (1915)	$ 0.03
Pocket electronic calculator	200.00 (1972)	1.99
Digital watch	2,000.00 (1972)	1.99
Pantyhose	2.16 (1967)	1.29
Ballpoint pen	0.89 (1965)	0.29
DVD player	800.00 (1997)	49.00
Laptop computer	3,500.00 (1986)	199.00
Airfare (New York–Paris)	490.00 (1958)	358.00
Microwave oven	400.00 (1972)	49.00
Contact lenses	275.00 (1972)	39.00
Television (19-inch, color)	469.00 (1980)	139.00
Compact disk player	1,000.00 (1985)	29.00
Digital camera	748.00 (1994)	69.00
Digital music player (MP3)	399.00 (2001)	8.00
Cell phone	3,595.00 (1983)	19.99
Smartphone	400.00 (1999)	48.99
E-reader	398.00 (2007)	99.00

of inflation are reflected in redistributions of income and wealth, not general declines in either measure of our economic welfare. These redistributions occur because people buy different combinations of goods and services, own different assets, and sell distinct goods or services (including labor). The impact of inflation on individuals therefore depends on how prices change for the goods and services each person actually buys or sells.

Price Effects

Price changes are the most visible consequence of inflation. If you've been paying tuition, you know how painful a price hike can be. Fifteen years ago the average tuition at public colleges and universities was $1,000 per year. Today the average tuition exceeds $9,000 for in-state residents. At private universities, tuition has increased eightfold in the past 10 years, to more than $30,000 (see the News below). You don't need a whole course in economics to figure out the implications of these tuition hikes. To stay in college, you (or your parents) must forgo increasing amounts of other goods and services. You end up being worse off since you can't buy as many goods and services as you could before tuition went up.

IN THE NEWS

College Tuition Up Again

College gets more expensive—again. Tuition at public four-year colleges rose 2.9 percent this year, to an average of $8,893 per year. Out-of-state students pay an average of $22,203 to attend.

Private four-year colleges also saw tuition increases of 2.9 percent—to an average of $30,094. These tuition hikes come on the heels of a 4.5 percent jump in 2012–2013 and 8.5 percent in 2011–2012. Tuition prices have been outpacing general inflation rates for many years.

Source: The College Board

ANALYSIS: Tuition increases reduce the real income of students. How much you suffer from inflation depends on what happens to the prices of the products you purchase.

The effect of tuition increases on your economic welfare is reflected in the distinction between nominal income and real income. **Nominal income** is the amount of money you receive in a particular time period; it's measured in current dollars. **Real income,** by contrast, is the purchasing power of that money, as measured by the quantity of goods and services your dollars will buy. If the number of dollars you receive every year is always the same, your *nominal income* doesn't change—but your *real income* will rise or fall with price changes.

Suppose your parents agree to give you $6,000 a year while you're in school. Out of that $6,000 you must pay for your tuition, room and board, books, and everything else. The budget for your first year at school might look like this:

FIRST YEAR'S BUDGET

Nominal income	$6,000
Consumption	
Tuition	$3,000
Room and board	2,000
Books	300
Everything else	700
Total	$6,000

After paying for all your essential expenses, you have $700 to spend on clothes, entertainment, or anything else you want. That's not exactly living high, but it's not poverty.

Now suppose tuition increases to $3,500 in your second year, while all other prices remain the same. What will happen to your nominal income? Nothing. Unless your parents take pity on you, you'll still be getting $6,000 a year. Your nominal income is unchanged. Your *real* income, however, will suffer. This is evident in the second year's budget:

SECOND YEAR'S BUDGET

Nominal income	$6,000
Consumption	
Tuition	$3,500
Room and board	2,000
Books	300
Everything else	200
Total	$6,000

You now have to use more of your income to pay tuition. This means you have less income to spend on other things. Since room and board and books still cost $2,300 per year, there's only one place to cut: the category of "everything else." After tuition increases, you can spend only $200 per year on movies, clothes, pizzas, and dates—not $700 as in the "good old days." This $500 reduction in purchasing power represents a *real* income loss. Even though your *nominal* income is still $6,000, you have $500 less of "everything else" in your second year than you had in the first.

Although tuition hikes reduce the real income of students, nonstudents aren't hurt by such price increases. In fact, if tuition *doubled,* nonstudents really wouldn't care. They could continue to buy the same bundle of goods and services they'd been buying all along. Tuition increases reduce the real incomes only of people who go to college.

Two basic lessons about inflation are to be learned from this sad story:

- *Not all prices rise at the same rate during an inflation.* In our example, tuition increased substantially while other prices remained steady. Hence the "average" price increase wasn't representative of any particular good or service. Typically some prices rise rapidly, others rise only modestly, and some actually fall.
- *Not everyone suffers equally from inflation.* This follows from our first observation. Those people who consume the goods and services that are rising faster in price bear a greater burden of inflation; their real incomes fall further. Other consumers bear a lesser burden, or even none at all, depending on how fast the prices rise for the goods they enjoy.

nominal income: The amount of money income received in a given time period, measured in current dollars.

real income: Income in constant dollars; nominal income adjusted for inflation.

TABLE 7.2

Price Changes in 2013

The average rate of inflation conceals substantial differences in the price changes of specific products. The impact of inflation on individuals depends in part on which goods and services are consumed. People who buy goods whose prices are rising fastest lose more real income. In 2013 college students and smokers were particularly hard-hit by inflation.

Prices That Rose (%)		Prices That Fell (%)	
Oranges	+9.1%	Televisions	−13.5%
Bacon	+7.7	Lettuce	−11.7
Eggs	+6.1	Coffee	−7.6
Donuts	+3.6	Peanut butter	−7.5
College tuition	+3.5	Apples	−6.9
Cigarettes	+3.4	Air fares	−4.8
Text books	+2.8	Ice cream	−1.5
Average inflation rate: +1.6%			

Source: U.S. Bureau of Labor Statistics.

web click

To see how much college tuition, gasoline, or any other price has changed over time, use the CPI Calculator provided by the Federal Reserve Bank of Minneapolis at **www.minneapolisfed.org.**

Table 7.2 illustrates some of the price changes that occurred in 2013. The average rate of inflation was only 1.6 percent. This was little solace to college students, however, who confronted tuition increases of 3.5 percent and 2.8 percent price hikes on textbooks (sorry!). On the other hand, price reductions on televisions, coffee, and peanut butter spared consumers of these products from the pain of the *average* inflation rate.

Income Effects

Even if all prices rose at the *same* rate, inflation would still redistribute income. The redistributive effects of inflation originate in not only *expenditure* patterns but also *income* patterns. Some people have fixed incomes that *don't* go up with inflation. Fixed-income groups include retired people who depend primarily on private pensions and workers with multiyear contracts that fix wage rates at preinflation levels. Lenders (like banks) that have lent funds at fixed interest rates also suffer real income losses when price levels rise. They continue to receive interest payments fixed in *nominal* dollars that have increasingly less *real* value. All these market participants experience a declining share of real income (and output) in inflationary periods.

Not all market participants suffer a real income decline when prices rise. Some people's nominal income rises *faster* than average prices, thereby boosting their *real* incomes. Keep in mind that there are two sides to every market transaction. **What looks like a price to a buyer looks like an income to a seller.** Orange growers profited from the 9.1 percent rise in orange prices in 2013. When students pay 3.5 percent higher tuition, the university takes in more income. It is able to buy *more* goods and services (including faculty, buildings, and library books) after a period of inflation than it could before. When the price of this textbook goes up, my *nominal* income goes up. If the text price rises faster than other prices, my *real* income increases as well. In either case, you lose (sorry!).

Once we recognize that nominal incomes and prices don't all increase at the same rate, it makes no sense to say that "inflation hurts everybody." **If prices are rising, incomes must be rising too.** In fact, on *average,* incomes rise just as fast as prices. Notice in Figure 7.1 that inflation increased *prices* by 81 percent from 1990 to 2014. However, *wages* more than kept pace—at least on average. That fact is of little comfort, however, to those whose wages didn't keep pace; they end up losing real income in the inflation game.

Wealth Effects

Still more winners and losers of the inflation game are selected on the basis of the assets they hold. Suppose you deposit $100 in a savings account on January 1, where it earns 5 percent interest. At the end of the year you'll have more nominal wealth ($105) than you started with ($100). But what if all prices have doubled in the meantime? In that case, your $105 will buy you no more at the end of the year than $52.50 would have bought you at the beginning. Inflation in this case reduces the *real* value of your savings, and you end up worse off than those individuals who spent all their income earlier in the year!

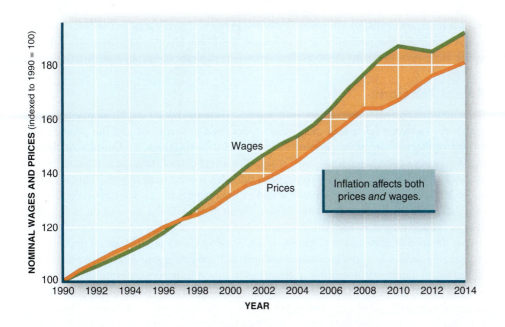

FIGURE 7.1

Nominal Wages and Prices

Inflation implies not only higher prices but higher incomes as well. Hence inflation can't make *everyone* worse off. In fact, average wages increase along with average prices. They rise even faster than prices when productivity increases. Wages rise slower than prices when fringe benefits or payroll taxes are increasing.

Source: U.S. Bureau of Labor Statistics.

Table 7.3 shows how the value of various assets has changed. Between 1991 and 2001, the average price level increased 32 percent. The average value of stocks, diamonds, and homes rose much faster than the price level, increasing the *real* value of those assets. Farmland prices rose too, but just a bit more than average prices. People who owned bonds, silver, and gold weren't so lucky; their *real* wealth declined.

Redistributions

By altering relative prices, incomes, and the real value of wealth, inflation turns out to be a mechanism for redistributing incomes and wealth. ***The redistributive mechanics of inflation include***

- ***Price effects.*** People who buy products that are increasing in price the fastest end up worse off.
- ***Income effects.*** People whose nominal incomes rise more slowly than the rate of inflation end up worse off.
- ***Wealth effects.*** People who own assets that are declining in real value end up worse off.

On the other hand, people whose nominal incomes increase faster than inflation end up with larger shares of total output. The same thing is true of those who enjoy goods that are rising slowest in price or who hold assets whose real value is increasing. In this sense, ***inflation acts***

Asset	Change in Value (%), 1991–2001
Stocks	+250%
Diamonds	+71
Oil	+66
Housing	+56
U.S. farmland	+49
Average price level	**+32**
Silver	+22
Bonds	+20
Stamps	−9
Gold	−29

TABLE 7.3

The Real Story of Wealth

Households hold their wealth in many different forms. As the value of various assets changes, so does a person's wealth. Between 1991 and 2001, inflation was very good to people who held stocks. By contrast, the real value of bonds, gold, and silver fell.

just like a tax, taking income or wealth from one group and giving it to another. But we have no assurance that this particular tax will behave like Robin Hood, taking from the rich and giving to the poor. In reality, inflation often redistributes income in the opposite direction.

Social Tensions

Because of its redistributive effects, inflation also increases social and economic tensions. Tensions—between labor and management, between government and the people, and among consumers—may overwhelm a society and its institutions. As Gardner Ackley of the University of Michigan observed, "A significant real cost of inflation is what it does to morale, to social coherence, and to people's attitudes toward each other." "This society," added Arthur Okun, "is built on implicit and explicit contracts. . . . They are linked to the idea that the dollar means something. If you cannot depend on the value of the dollar, this system is undermined. People will constantly feel they've been fooled and cheated."[1] This is how the middle class felt in Germany in 1923 and in China in 1948, when the value of their savings was wiped out by sudden and unanticipated inflation. A surge in prices also stirred social and political tensions in Russia as it moved from a price-controlled economy to a market-driven economy in the 1990s. The same kind of sociopolitical tension arose in Zimbabwe in 2008–2009 when prices skyrocketed (see the World View below). On a more personal level, psychotherapists report that "inflation stress" leads to more frequent marital spats, pessimism, diminished self-confidence, and even sexual insecurity. Some people turn to crime as a way of solving the problem.

WORLD VIEW

Zimbabwe's Trillion-Dollar Currency

Imagine the price of coffee *doubling* every day. Or the price of a textbook soaring from $100 to $12,800 in a single week! Sounds unbelievable. But that was the day-to-day reality in Zimbabwe in 2008–2009, when the inflation rate reached an astronomical 231 *million* percent.

The Zimbabwean currency lost so much value that people needed a sackful to buy a loaf of bread. To facilitate commerce, the Zimbabwe central bank printed the world's first $100 *trillion* banknote. Within a week, that $100 trillion note was worth about 33 U.S. dollars—enough to buy six loaves of bread.

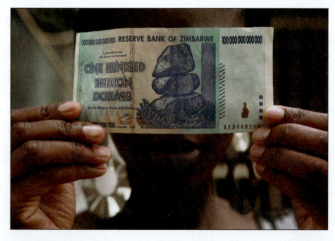

Source: News reports, January 2009.

ANALYSIS: Hyperinflation renders a currency useless for market transactions. The economy contracts, and social tensions rise.

[1]Quoted in *BusinessWeek,* May 22, 1978, p. 118.

Money Illusion

Even people whose nominal incomes keep up with inflation often feel oppressed by rising prices. People feel that they *deserve* any increases in wages they receive. When they later discover that their higher (nominal) wages don't buy any additional goods, they feel cheated. They feel worse off, even though they haven't suffered any actual loss of real income. This phenomenon is called **money illusion.** People suffering from money illusion are forever reminding us that they used to pay only $5 to see a movie or $20 for a textbook. What they forget is that nominal *incomes* were also a lot lower in the "good old days" than they are today.

money illusion: The use of nominal dollars rather than real dollars to gauge changes in one's income or wealth.

MACRO CONSEQUENCES

Although microeconomic redistributions of income and wealth are the primary consequences of inflation, inflation has *macroeconomic* effects as well.

Uncertainty

One of the most immediate consequences of inflation is uncertainty. When the average price level is changing significantly in either direction, economic decisions become more difficult. As the accompanying cartoon suggests, even something as simple as ordering a restaurant meal is more difficult if menu prices are changing (as they did during Germany's 1923 runaway inflation). In Zimbabwe, postponing bread purchases cost a *billion* Zimbabwean dollars a day (see the previous World View). The $100 trillion banknote issued in January 2009 was worthless two months later.

Inflation makes longer-term decisions even more difficult. Should you commit yourself to four years of college, for example, if you aren't certain that you or your parents will be able to afford the full costs? In a period of stable prices you can be fairly certain of what a college education will cost. But if prices are rising, you can't be sure how large the bill will be. Under such circumstances, some individuals may decide not to enter college rather than risk the possibility of being driven out later by rising costs.

Price uncertainties affect production decisions as well. Imagine a firm that wants to build a new factory. Typically the construction of a factory takes two years or more, including planning, site selection, and actual construction. If construction costs change rapidly, the firm may find that it's unable to complete the factory or to operate it profitably. Confronted with this added uncertainty, the firm may decide not to build a new plant. This deprives the economy of new investment and expanded production possibilities.

From The Wall Street Journal, permission Cartoon Features Syndicate.

"Do I have your assurance that prices will not be increased before we are served?"

Analysis: The uncertainty caused by rising prices causes stress and may alter consumption and investment decisions.

Quality Changes

The second argument for setting our price stability goal above zero inflation relates to our measurement capabilities. The Consumer Price Index isn't a perfect measure of inflation. In essence, the CPI simply monitors the price of specific goods over time. Over time, however, the goods themselves change, too. Old products become better as a result of *quality improvements*. A flat-screen TV set costs more today than a TV did in 1955, but today's television also delivers a bigger, clearer picture, in digital sound and color, and with a host of on-screen programming options. Hence increases in the price of TV sets tend to exaggerate the true rate of inflation: Most of the higher price represents more product.

The same is true of automobiles. The best-selling car in 1958 (a Chevrolet Bel Air) had a list price of only $2,618. That makes a 2015 Ford Focus look awfully expensive at $20,230. The quality of today's cars is much better, however. Improvements since 1958 include seat belts, air bags, variable-speed windshield wipers, electronic ignitions, rear-window defrosters, radial tires, antilock brakes, emergency flashers, remote-control mirrors, crash-resistant bodies, a doubling of fuel mileage, a 100-fold decrease in exhaust pollutants, and global positioning systems. As a result, today's higher car prices also buy cars that are safer, cleaner, and more comfortable.

The U.S. Bureau of Labor Statistics does adjust the CPI for quality changes. Such adjustments inevitably entail subjective judgments, however. Critics are quick to complain that the CPI overstates inflation because quality improvements are undervalued.

New Products

The problem of measuring quality improvements is even more difficult in the case of new products. The computers and word processors used today didn't exist when the Census Bureau conducted its 1972–1973 survey of consumer expenditure. The 1982–1984 expenditure survey included those products but not still newer ones such as the cellular phone. As the News below explains, the omission of cellular phones caused the CPI to overstate the rate of inflation. The consumer expenditure survey of 1993–1995 included cell phones but not digital cameras, DVD players, flat-screen TVs, or MP3 players—all of which have had declining prices. As a result, there's a significant (though unmeasured) element of error in the CPI insofar as it's intended to gauge changes in the average prices paid by consumers. The goal of 3 percent inflation allows for such errors.

IN THE NEWS

Ignoring Cell Phones Biases CPI Upward

Cellular telephones have been in commercial operation in the United States for 13 years. Beginning in Chicago in late 1983, and then at the Los Angeles Olympic Games in 1984, cellular telephone usage spread first to the top 30 metropolitan statistical areas (MSAs), then to the other 300 or so MSAs, and finally to rural areas. At year-end 1996, there were more than 40 million cellular subscribers in the United States. . . .

Yet the cellular telephone will not be included in the calculation of the Consumer Price Index (CPI) until 1998 or 1999. "This neglect of new goods leads to an upward bias in the CPI," NBER Research Associate Jerry Hausman concludes.

The CPI estimates that since 1988, telecommunications prices have increased by 8.5 percent, or 1.02 percent per year. A corrected index that includes cellular service decreased 1.28 percent per year since 1988, Hausman figures. "Thus, the bias in the BLS [Bureau of Labor Statistics] telecommunications services CPI equals approximately 2.3 percentage points per year."

Source: National Bureau of Economic Research, *NBER Digest*, June 1997, **www.nber.org/digest.**

ANALYSIS: Because the CPI tracks prices for a fixed basket of goods, it misses the effects of falling prices on new goods that appear between survey periods.

Year	CPI	Year	CPI	Year	CPI	Year	CPI
1800	17.0	1915	10.1	1950	24.1	1982–1984	100.0
1825	11.3	1920	20.0	1960	29.6	1990	130.5
1850	8.3	1930	16.7	1970	38.8	2000	172.8
1875	11.0	1940	14.0	1980	82.4	2010	220.3
1900	8.3						

Note: Data from 1915 forward reflect the official all-items Consumer Price Index, which used the pre-1983 measure of shelter costs. Estimated indexes for 1800 through 1900 are drawn from several sources.
Source: U.S. Bureau of Labor Statistics.

TABLE 7.5

Two Centuries of Price Changes

Before World War II, the average level of prices rose in some years and fell in others. Since 1945, prices have risen continuously. The Consumer Price Index has more than doubled since 1982–1984. It stood at 238.7 in July 2014.

THE HISTORICAL RECORD

In the long view of history, the United States has done a good job of maintaining price stability. On closer inspection, however, our inflation performance is very uneven. Table 7.5 summarizes the long view, with data going back to 1800. The base period for pricing the market basket of goods is again 1982–1984. Notice that the same market basket cost only $17 in 1800. Consumer prices increased 500 percent in 183 years. But also observe how frequently the price level *fell* in the 1800s and again in the 1930s. These recurrent deflations held down the long-run inflation rate. Because of these periodic deflations, average prices in 1945 were at the same level as in 1800! Since then, however, prices have risen almost every year.

Figure 7.3 provides a closer view of our more recent experience with inflation. In this figure we transform annual changes in the CPI into percentage rates of inflation. The CPI increased from 72.6 to 82.4 during 1980. This 9.8-point jump in the CPI translates into a 13.5 percent rate

web click

At the U.S. Bureau of Labor Statistics, **www.bls.gov,** you can find the CPI for the most recent month and the same month last year. You can find monthly data all the way back to 1913.

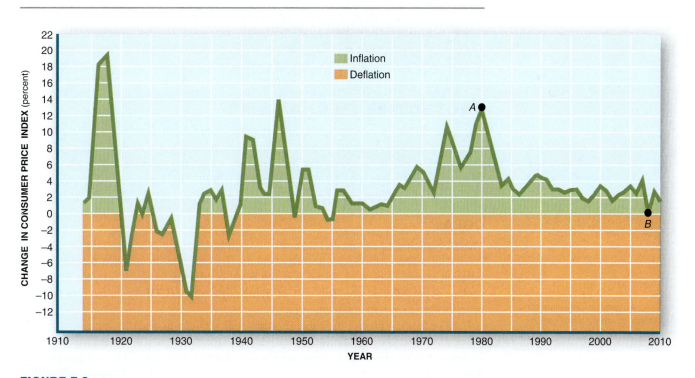

FIGURE 7.3

Annual Inflation Rates

During the 1920s and 1930s, consumer prices fell significantly, causing a general deflation. Since the Great Depression, however, average prices have risen almost every year. But the annual rate of price increases has varied widely: The highest rate of inflation was 13.5 percent in 1980 (point A); the lowest rate (0.1 percent) occurred in 2008 (point B).

Source: U.S. Bureau of Labor Statistics.

of inflation (9.8 ÷ 72.6 = 0.135). This inflation rate, represented by point *A* in Figure 7.3, was the highest in a generation. Since then, prices have continued to increase, but at much slower rates. These low rates of inflation in the United States are far below the pace in most nations.

CAUSES OF INFLATION

The evident variation in year-to-year inflation rates requires explanation. So do the horrifying bouts of hyperinflation that have erupted in other nations at various times. What causes price levels to rise or fall?

In the most general terms, this is an easy question to answer. Recall that all market transactions entail two converging forces, namely *demand* and *supply*. Accordingly, any explanation of changing price levels must be rooted in one of these two market forces.

Demand-Pull Inflation

Excessive pressure on the demand side of the economy is often the cause of inflation. Suppose the economy was already producing at capacity but that consumers were willing and able to buy even more goods. With accumulated savings or easy access to credit, consumers could end up trying to buy more output than the economy was producing. This would be a classic case of "too much money chasing too few goods." As consumers sought to acquire more goods, store shelves (inventory) would begin to empty. Seeing this, producers would begin raising prices. The end result would be a demand-driven rise in average prices, or demand-pull inflation.

Cost-Push Inflation

The pressure on prices could also originate on the supply side. When Hurricanes Katrina and Rita destroyed oil-producing facilities in the Gulf (August 2005), oil prices increased abruptly, raising transportation and production costs in a broad array of industries. To cover these higher costs, producers raised output prices. When a tsunami devastated Sri Lanka in December 2004, it destroyed a huge portion of that country's production capacity, including its vital fishing industry. As market participants scurried for the remaining output, prices rose across the board. The same thing happened in Haiti in January 2010, when an earthquake destroyed production facilities and transportation routes, making goods scarce and increasingly more expensive.

PROTECTIVE MECHANISMS

Whatever the *causes* of inflation, market participants don't want to suffer the consequences. Even at a relatively low rate of inflation, the real value of money declines over time. If prices rise by an average of just 4 percent a year, the real value of $1,000 drops to $822 in 5 years and to only $676 in 10 years (see Table 7.6). *Low rates of inflation don't have the drama of hyperinflation, but they still redistribute real wealth and income.*

COLAs

Market participants can protect themselves from inflation by *indexing* their nominal incomes, as is done with Social Security benefits, for example. In any year that the rate of inflation exceeds 3 percent, Social Security benefits go up *automatically* by the same percentage as the inflation rate. This **cost-of-living adjustment (COLA)** ensures that nominal benefits keep pace with the rising prices.

Landlords often protect their real incomes with COLAs as well, by including in their leases provisions that automatically increase rents by the rate of inflation. COLAs are also common in labor union agreements, government transfer programs (like food stamps), and many other contracts. In every such case, *a COLA protects real income from inflation.*

cost-of-living adjustment (COLA): Automatic adjustments of nominal income to the rate of inflation.

ARMs

Cost-of-living adjustments have also become more common in loan agreements. As we observed earlier, debtors win and creditors lose when the price level rises. Suppose a loan

Year	Annual Inflation Rate				
	2%	4%	6%	8%	10%
2015	$1,000	$1,000	$1,000	$1,000	$1,000
2016	980	962	943	926	909
2017	961	925	890	857	826
2018	942	889	840	794	751
2019	924	855	792	735	683
2020	906	822	747	681	621
2021	888	790	705	630	564
2022	871	760	665	584	513
2023	853	731	627	540	467
2024	837	703	592	500	424
2025	820	676	558	463	386

TABLE 7.6

Inflation's Impact, 2015–2025

In the past 20 years, the U.S. rate of inflation ranged from a low of 0.1 percent to a high of 13.5 percent. Does a range of 13 percentage points really make much difference? One way to find out is to see how a specific sum of money will shrink in real value in a decade.

Here's what would happen to the real value of $1,000 from January 1, 2015, to January 1, 2025, at different inflation rates. At 2 percent inflation, $1,000 held for 10 years would be worth $820. At 10 percent inflation that same $1,000 would buy only $386 worth of goods in the year 2025.

web click

The U.S. Treasury offers a bond that protects one's principal from inflation. For information on the Treasury Inflation Protected Securities called "TIPS," visit **www.savingsbonds.gov.**

requires interest payments equal to 5 percent of the amount (principal) borrowed. If the rate of inflation jumps to 7 percent, prices will be rising faster than interest is accumulating. Hence the **real interest rate**—the inflation-adjusted rate of interest—will actually be negative. The interest payments made in future years will buy fewer goods than can be bought today.

The real rate of interest is calculated as

Real interest rate = Nominal interest rate − Anticipated rate of inflation

In this case, the nominal interest rate is 5 percent and inflation is 7 percent. Hence the *real* rate of interest is *minus* 2 percent.

The distinction between real and nominal interest rates isn't too important if you're lending or borrowing money for just a couple of days. But the distinction is critical for long-term loans like home mortgages. Mortgage loans typically span a period of 25 to 30 years. If the inflation rate stays higher than the nominal interest rate during this period, the lender will end up with less *real* wealth than was initially lent.

To protect against such losses, the banking industry offers home loans with adjustable interest rates. An **adjustable-rate mortgage (ARM)** stipulates an interest rate that changes during the term of the loan. A mortgage paying 5 percent interest in a stable (3 percent inflation) price environment may later require 9 percent interest if the inflation rate jumps to 7 percent. Such an adjustment would keep the real rate of interest at 2 percent. These and other inflation-indexing mechanisms underscore the importance of measuring price changes accurately.

real interest rate: The nominal interest rate minus the anticipated inflation rate.

adjustable-rate mortgage (ARM): A mortgage (home loan) that adjusts the nominal interest rate to changing rates of inflation.

THE ECONOMY TOMORROW

THE VIRTUES OF INFLATION

Despite evidence to the contrary, most people still believe that "inflation hurts everybody." In fact, the distaste for inflation is so strong that sizable majorities say they prefer low inflation and high unemployment to the combination of high inflation and low unemployment. A study by Yale economist Robert Shiller confirmed that *money illusion* contributes to this sentiment: People feel worse off when they have to pay higher prices, even if their nominal incomes are keeping pace with (or exceeding) the rate of inflation. Politically, this implies a policy bias toward keeping inflation under control, even at the sacrifice of high unemployment and slower economic growth.

There are times, however, when a little inflation might be a good thing. In the wake of the Great Recession of 2008–2009, the rate of inflation fell to zero. Investors and home purchasers could borrow money at unprecedented low rates. Yet market participants were still reluctant to borrow and spend. So the economy was frustratingly slow to recover.

What if, however, people thought prices were going to rise? If prospective home buyers expected housing prices to go up, they'd be more willing to purchase a new home. If investors thought prices were going up, they'd want to get in the game while prices were still low. In other words, *expectations of rising prices can encourage more spending.* A little inflation might actually be a virtue in such circumstances.

The challenge for the economy tomorrow is to find the optimal rate of inflation—the one that's just high enough to encourage more spending, but not so high as to raise the specter of an **inflationary flashpoint.** No one wants to experience a Zimbabwean-type hyperinflation or even a less drastic bout of accelerating inflation. The risk of using a little inflation to motivate buyers is that inflationary expectations may quickly get out of hand. This was a major concern for the British government in early 2011 and an increasing concern in the United States as well in 2015.

inflationary flashpoint: The rate of output at which inflationary pressures intensify; the point on the AS curve where slope increases sharply.

SUMMARY

- Inflation is an increase in the average price level. Typically it's measured by changes in a price index such as the Consumer Price Index (CPI). **LO7-1**
- At the micro level, inflation redistributes income by altering relative prices, income, and wealth. Because not all prices rise at the same rate and because not all people buy (and sell) the same goods or hold the same assets, inflation doesn't affect everyone equally. Some individuals actually gain from inflation, whereas others suffer a loss of real income or wealth. **LO7-2**
- At the macro level, inflation threatens to reduce total output because it increases uncertainties about the future and thereby inhibits consumption and production decisions. Fear of rising prices can also stimulate spending, forcing the government to take restraining action that threatens full employment. Rising prices also encourage speculation and hoarding, which detract from productive activity. **LO7-2**
- Fully anticipated inflation reduces the anxieties and real losses associated with rising prices. However, few people can foresee actual price patterns or make all the necessary adjustments in their market activity. **LO7-2**
- The U.S. goal of price stability is defined as an inflation rate of less than 3 percent per year. This goal recognizes potential conflicts between zero inflation and full employment as well as the difficulties of measuring quality improvements and new products. **LO7-3**
- From 1800 to 1945, prices both rose and fell, leaving the average price level unchanged. Since then, prices have risen nearly every year but at widely different rates. **LO7-3**
- Inflation is caused by either excessive demand (demand-pull inflation) or structural changes in supply (cost-push inflation). **LO7-4**
- Cost-of-living adjustments (COLAs) and adjustable-rate mortgages (ARMs) help protect real incomes from inflation. Universal indexing, however, wouldn't eliminate inflationary redistributions of income and wealth. **LO7-2**

Key Terms

inflation	bracket creep	nominal GDP
deflation	Consumer Price Index (CPI)	real GDP
relative price	inflation rate	price stability
nominal income	base year	cost-of-living adjustment (COLA)
real income	item weight	real interest rate
money illusion	core inflation rate	adjustable-rate mortgage (ARM)
hyperinflation	GDP deflator	inflationary flashpoint

Questions for Discussion

1. Why would farmers rather store their output than sell it during periods of hyperinflation? How does this behavior affect prices? **LO7-2**
2. How might rapid inflation affect college enrollments? **LO7-2**
3. Who gains and who loses from rising house prices? **LO7-2**
4. Who gained and who lost from the price changes in Table 7.2? What happened to the price of breakfast? **LO7-2**
5. Whose real wealth (see Table 7.3) declined in the 1990s? Who else might have lost real income or wealth? Who gained as a result of inflation? **LO7-2**
6. If *all* prices increased at the same rate (i.e., no *relative* price changes), would inflation have any redistributive effects? **LO7-2**
7. Would it be advantageous to borrow money if you expected prices to rise? Would you want a fixed-rate loan or one with an adjustable interest rate? **LO7-2**
8. Are people worse off when the price level rises as fast as their income? Why do people often feel worse off in such circumstances? **LO7-2**
9. Identify two groups that benefit from deflation and two that lose. **LO7-2**
10. Could demand-pull inflation occur before an economy was producing at capacity? How? **LO7-4**
11. How much do higher gasoline prices contribute to inflation? **LO7-1**

 mobile app Visit your mobile app store and download the Schiller: Study Econ app *today!*

PROBLEMS FOR CHAPTER 7

Name: _____

connect | ECONOMICS

LO7-1   1. According to the World View on page 136, what was the price of a loaf of bread in Zimbabwe, measured in
     (*a*) U.S. dollars?   _____
     (*b*) Zimbabwe dollars?   _____

LO7-1   2. By how much did the pace of tuition hikes (News, p. 132) exceed the 2013 rate of inflation (Table 7.2)?   _____

LO7-1   3. If tuition was $10,000 in 2010–2011, how much was it in
     (*a*) 2011–2012?   _____
     (*b*) 2012–2013?   _____
     (*c*) 2013–2014?   _____
     (See News, p. 132.)

LO7-2   4. If tuition keeps increasing at the same rate as in 2013–2014 (see News, p. 132), how much will it cost to complete a degree at a private college in four years?   _____

LO7-1   5. Suppose you'll have an annual nominal income of $30,000 for each of the next three years, and the inflation rate is 5 percent per year.
     (*a*) Find the real value of your $30,000 salary for each of the next three years.

                                                     Year 1: _____
                                                     Year 2: _____
                                                     Year 3: _____

     (*b*) If you have a COLA in your contract, and the inflation rate is 5 percent, what is the real value of your salary for each year?

                                                     Year 1: _____
                                                     Year 2: _____
                                                     Year 3: _____

LO7-2   6. Suppose you borrow $100 of principal that must be repaid at the end of two years, along with interest of 4 percent a year. If the annual inflation rate turns out to be 8 percent,
     (*a*) What is the real rate of interest on the loan?   _____
     (*b*) What is the real value of the principal repayment?   _____
     (*c*) Who loses, (A) the debtor or (B) the creditor? (Enter A or B.)   _____

LO7-1   7. If apples and oranges have identical weights in the "fruit price index," by how much did fruit prices rise in 2013? (See Table 7.2.)   _____

LO7-1   8. Assuming that the following table describes a typical consumer's complete budget, compute the item weights for each product.

Item	Quantity	Unit Price	Item Weight
Coffee	20 pounds	$ 6	_____
Tuition	1 year	4,000	_____
Pizza	150 pizzas	10	_____
Cable TV	12 months	30	_____
Vacation	1 week	250	_____
		Total:	_____

LO7-1   9. Suppose the prices listed in the table for Problem 8 changed from one year to the next, as shown here. Use the rest of the table to compute the average inflation rate.

Item	Unit Price Last Year	Unit Price This Year	Percentage Change in Price	×	Item Weight	=	Inflation Impact
Coffee	$ 6	$ 8	_____		_____		_____
Tuition	4,000	5,000	_____		_____		_____
Pizza	10	12	_____		_____		_____
Cable TV	30	36	_____		_____		_____
Vacation	250	300	_____		_____		_____
					Average inflation:		_____

LO7-1 10. Use the item weights in Figure 7.2 to determine the percentage change in the CPI that would result from a
   (a) 20 percent increase in entertainment prices.   _____
   (b) 8 percent decrease in transportation costs.   _____
   (c) Doubling of clothing prices.   _____
   (*Note:* Review Table 7.4 for assistance.)

LO7-1 11. Use the GDP deflator data on the inside cover of this book to compute real GDP in 2000 at 2013 prices.   _____

LO7-1 12. According to Table 7.3 (p. 135), what happened during the period shown to the
   (a) Nominal price of gold?   _____
   (b) Real price of gold?   _____

LO7-3 13. On the accompanying graph, illustrate for each year (A) the nominal interest rate (use the prime rate of interest), (B) the CPI inflation rate, and (C) the real interest rate (adjusted for same-year CPI inflation). The required data appear on the inside cover of this book.
   (a) In what years was the official goal of price stability met?   _____
   (b) In what years was the inflation rate lowest?   _____
   (c) What was the range of rates during this period for
        (i) Nominal interest rates?   _____
        (ii) Real interest rates?   _____
   (d) On a year-to-year basis, which varies more—nominal or real interest rates? _____

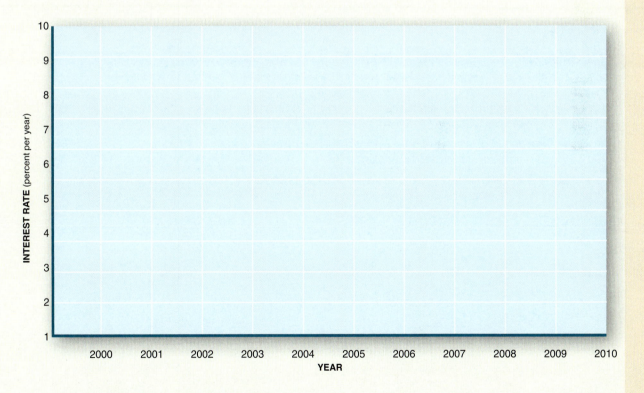

LO7-4 14. If a basic input like oil goes up in price by 20 percent and accounts for 3 percent of total costs in the economy, how much cost-push inflation results?   _____

Cyclical Instability

One of the central concerns of macroeconomics is the short-run business cycle—recurrent episodes of expansion and contraction of the nation's output. These cycles affect jobs, prices, economic growth, and international trade and financial balances. Chapters 8 through 10 focus on the nature of the business cycle and the underlying market forces that can cause both macroeconomic gain and macroeconomic pain.

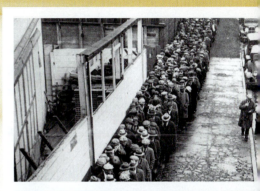

The Business Cycle

LEARNING OBJECTIVES

After reading this chapter, you should know

LO8-1 The major macro outcomes and their determinants.

LO8-2 Why the debate over macro stability is important.

LO8-3 The nature of aggregate demand (AD) and aggregate supply (AS).

LO8-4 How changes in AD and AS affect macro outcomes.

In 1929 it looked as though the sun would never set on the U.S. economy. For eight years in a row, the U.S. economy had been expanding rapidly. During the Roaring Twenties, the typical American family drove its first car, bought its first radio, and went to the movies for the first time. With factories running at capacity, virtually anyone who wanted to work found a job readily.

Everyone was optimistic. In his Acceptance Address in November 1928, President-elect Herbert Hoover echoed this optimism by declaring, "We in America today are nearer to the final triumph over poverty than ever before in the history of any land. . . . We shall soon with the help of God be in sight of the day when poverty will be banished from this nation."

The booming stock market seemed to confirm this optimistic outlook. Between 1921 and 1927 the stock market's value more than doubled, adding billions of dollars to the wealth of U.S. households and businesses. The stock market boom accelerated in 1927, causing stock prices to double again in less than two years. The roaring stock market made it look easy to get rich in America.

The party ended abruptly on October 24, 1929. On what came to be known as Black Thursday, the stock market crashed. In a few short hours, the market value of U.S. corporations tumbled in the most frenzied selloff ever seen (see the News on the next page). The next day President Hoover tried to assure America's stockholders that the economy was "on a sound and prosperous basis." But despite his assurances, the stock market continued to plummet. The following Tuesday (October 29) the pace of selling quickened. By the end of the year, more than $40 billion of wealth had vanished in the Great Crash. Rich men became paupers overnight; ordinary families lost their savings, their homes, and even their lives.

The devastation was not confined to Wall Street. The financial flames engulfed farms, banks, and industry. Between 1930 and 1935, millions of rural families lost their farms. Automobile production fell from 4.5 million cars in 1929 to only 1.1 million in 1932. So many banks were forced to close that newly elected President Roosevelt had to declare a "bank holiday" in March 1933: he closed all of the nation's banks for five days to curtail the outflow of cash to anxious depositors.

Throughout these years, the ranks of the unemployed continued to swell. In October 1929, only 3 percent of the workforce was unemployed. A year later the total was more than 9 percent. Still things got worse. By 1933, more than one-fourth of the labor force was unable to find work. People slept in the streets, scavenged for food, and sold apples on Wall Street.

The Great Depression seemed to last forever. In 1933 President Roosevelt lamented that one-third of the nation was ill-clothed, ill-housed, and ill-fed. Thousands of unemployed workers marched to the Capitol to demand jobs and aid. In 1938, nine years after Black Thursday, nearly 20 percent of the workforce was still idle.

Market in Panic as Stocks Are Dumped in 12,894,600-Share Day; Bankers Halt It

Effect Is Felt on the Curb and throughout Nation—Financial District Goes Wild

The stock markets of the country tottered on the brink of panic yesterday as a prosperous people, gone suddenly hysterical with fear, attempted simultaneously to sell a record-breaking volume of securities for whatever they would bring.

The result was a financial nightmare, comparable to nothing ever before experienced in Wall Street. It rocked the financial district to its foundations, hopelessly overwhelmed its mechanical facilities, chilled its blood with terror.

In a society built largely on confidence, with real wealth expressed more or less inaccurately by pieces of paper, the entire fabric of economic stability threatened to come toppling down.

Into the frantic hands of a thousand brokers on the floor of the New York Stock Exchange poured the selling orders of the world. It was sell, sell, sell—hour after desperate hour until 1:30 p.m.

—Laurence Stern

Source: *The World,* October 25, 1929.

ANALYSIS: Stock markets are a barometer of confidence in the economy. If people have doubts about the economy, they're less willing to hold stocks. The crash of 1929 mirrored and worsened consumer confidence.

The Great Depression shook not only the foundations of the world economy but also the self-confidence of the economics profession. No one had predicted the Depression, and few could explain it. The ensuing search for explanations focused on three central questions:

- **How stable is a market-driven economy?**
- **What forces cause instability?**
- **What, if anything, can the government do to promote steady economic growth?**

The basic purpose of **macroeconomics** is to answer these questions—to *explain* how and why economies grow and what causes the recurrent ups and downs of the economy that characterize the **business cycle.** In this chapter we introduce the theoretical model economists use to describe and explain the short-run business cycle. We'll also preview some of the policy options the government might use to dampen those cycles, including the slew of actions taken in 2008–2009 to reverse another macro downturn: the Great Recession of 2008–2009.

macroeconomics: The study of aggregate economic behavior, of the economy as a whole.

business cycle: Alternating periods of economic growth and contraction.

....

STABLE OR UNSTABLE?

Prior to the 1930s, macro economists thought there could never be a Great Depression. The economic thinkers of the time asserted that a market-driven economy was inherently stable. There was no need for government intervention.

Classical Theory

This **laissez-faire** view of macroeconomics seemed reasonable at the time. During the 19th century and the first 30 years of the 20th, the U.S. economy experienced some bad years in which the nation's output declined and unemployment increased. But most of these episodes were relatively short-lived. The dominant feature of the Industrial Era was *growth:* an expanding economy with more output, more jobs, and higher incomes nearly every year.

laissez faire: The doctrine of "leave it alone," of nonintervention by government in the market mechanism.

A Self-Regulating Economy. In this environment, classical economists, as they later became known, propounded an optimistic view of the macro economy. *According to the classical view, the economy "self-adjusts" to deviations from its long-term growth trend.*

Producers might occasionally reduce their output and throw people out of work, but these dislocations would cause little damage. If output declined and people lost their jobs, the internal forces of the marketplace would quickly restore prosperity. **Economic downturns were viewed as temporary setbacks, not permanent problems.**

The cornerstones of classical optimism were flexible prices and flexible wages. If producers couldn't sell all their output at current prices, they had two choices. Either they could (1) reduce the rate of output and throw some people out of work or they could (2) reduce the price of their output, thereby stimulating an increase in the quantity demanded. Classical economists liked the second option. According to the **law of demand**, price reductions cause an increase in unit sales. If prices fall far enough, everything can be sold. Thus flexible prices—prices that would drop when consumer demand slowed—virtually guaranteed that all output could be sold. No one would have to lose a job because of weak consumer demand.

Flexible prices had their counterpart in factor markets. If some workers were temporarily out of work, they'd compete for jobs by offering their services at lower wages. As wage rates declined, producers would find it profitable to hire more workers. Ultimately, flexible wages would ensure that everyone who wanted a job would have a job.

These optimistic views of the macro economy were summarized in Say's law. **Say's law**—named after the 19th-century economist Jean-Baptiste Say—decreed that "supply creates its own demand." Whatever was produced would be sold. All workers who sought employment would be hired. *Unsold goods and unemployed labor could emerge in this classical system, but both would disappear as soon as people had time to adjust prices and wages.* There could be no Great Depression—no protracted macro failure—in this classical view of the world.

Macro Failure. The Great Depression was a stunning blow to classical economists. At the onset of the Depression, classical economists assured everyone that the setbacks in production and employment were temporary and would soon vanish. Andrew Mellon, Secretary of the U.S. Treasury, expressed this optimistic view in January 1930, just a few months after the stock market crash. Assessing the prospects for the year ahead, he said, "I see nothing . . . in the present situation that is either menacing or warrants pessimism. . . . I have every confidence that there will be a revival of activity in the spring and that during the coming year the country will make steady progress."[1] Merrill Lynch, one of the nation's largest brokerage houses, was urging that people should buy stocks. But the Depression deepened. Indeed, unemployment grew and persisted *despite* falling prices and wages (see Figure 8.1). The classical self-adjustment mechanism simply didn't work.

The Keynesian Revolution

The Great Depression effectively destroyed the credibility of classical economic theory. As the British economist John Maynard Keynes pointed out in 1935, classical economists

> were apparently unmoved by the lack of correspondence between the results of their theory and the facts of observation:—a discrepancy which the ordinary man has not failed to observe. . . .
> The celebrated optimism of [classical] economic theory . . . is . . . to be traced, I think, to their having neglected to take account of the drag on prosperity which can be exercised by an insufficiency of effective demand. For there would obviously be a natural tendency towards the optimum employment of resources in a Society which was functioning after the manner of the classical postulates. It may well be that the classical theory represents the way in which we should like our Economy to behave. But to assume that it actually does so is to assume our difficulties away.[2]

Inherent Instability. Keynes went on to develop an alternative view of how the macro economy works. Whereas the classical economists viewed the economy as inherently stable,

law of demand: The quantity of a good demanded in a given time period increases as its price falls, *ceteris paribus.*

Say's law: Supply creates its own demand.

[1]David A. Shannon, *The Great Depression* (Englewood Cliffs, NJ: Prentice Hall, 1960), p. 4.
[2]John Maynard Keynes, *The General Theory of Employment, Interest and Money* (London: Macmillan, 1936), pp. 33–34.

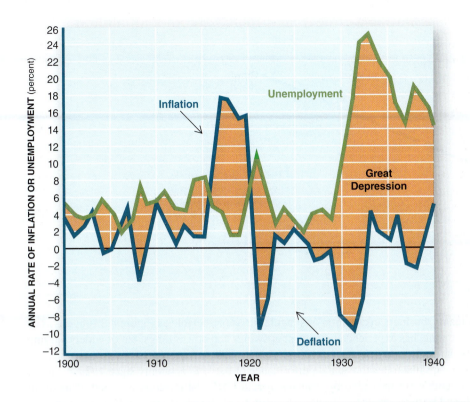

FIGURE 8.1

Inflation and Unemployment, 1900–1940

In the early 1900s, falling price levels (deflation) appeared to limit increases in unemployment. Periods of high unemployment also tended to be brief. These experiences bolstered the confidence of classical economists in the stability of the macro economy. Say's law seemed to work.

In the 1930s, unemployment rates rose to unprecedented heights and stayed high for a decade. Falling wages and prices (deflation) did not restore full employment. This macro failure prompted calls for new theories and policies to control the business cycle.

Source: U.S. Bureau of the Census, *The Statistics of the United States,* 1957.

Keynes asserted that a market-driven economy is inherently unstable. Small disturbances in output, prices, or unemployment were likely to be magnified, not muted, by the invisible hand of the marketplace. The Great Depression was not a unique event, Keynes argued, but a calamity that would recur if we relied on the market mechanism to self-adjust.

Government Intervention. In Keynes's view, the inherent instability of the marketplace required government intervention. When the economy falters, we can't afford to wait for some assumed self-adjustment mechanism but must instead intervene to protect jobs and income. The government can do this by "priming the pump": buying more output, employing more people, providing more income transfers, and making more money available. When the economy overheats, the government must cool it down with higher taxes, spending reductions, and less money.

Keynes's denunciation of classical theory didn't end the macroeconomic debate. On the contrary, economists continue to wage fierce debates about the inherent stability of the economy. Those debates—which became intense again in 2008–2014—fill the pages of the next few chapters. But before examining them, let's first take a quick look at the economy's actual performance since the Great Depression.

HISTORICAL CYCLES

The upswings and downturns of the business cycle are gauged in terms of changes in total output. An economic upswing, or expansion, refers to an increase in the volume of goods and services produced. An economic downturn, or contraction, occurs when the total volume of production declines.

Figure 8.2 depicts the stylized features of a business cycle. Over the long run, the output of the economy grows at roughly 3 percent per year. There's a lot of year-to-year variation around this growth trend, however. The short-run cycle looks like a roller coaster, climbing steeply, then dropping from its peak. Once the trough is reached, the upswing starts again.

FIGURE 8.2

The Business Cycle

The model business cycle resembles a roller coaster. Output first climbs to a peak, then decreases. After hitting a trough, the economy recovers, with real GDP again increasing.

A central concern of macroeconomic theory is to determine whether a recurring business cycle exists and, if so, what forces cause it.

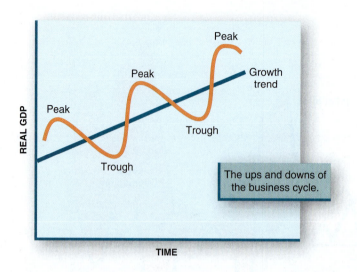

real GDP: The value of final output produced in a given period, adjusted for changing prices.

In reality, business cycles aren't as regular or as predictable as Figure 8.2 suggests. The U.S. economy has experienced recurrent upswings and downswings, but of widely varying length, intensity, and frequency.

Figure 8.3 illustrates the actual performance of the U.S. economy since 1929. Changes in total output are measured by changes in **real GDP,** the inflation-adjusted value of all goods and services produced. From a long-run view, the growth of real GDP has been impressive: real GDP today is 15 times larger than it was in 1929. Americans now consume a vastly greater variety of goods and services, and in greater quantities, than earlier generations ever dreamed possible.

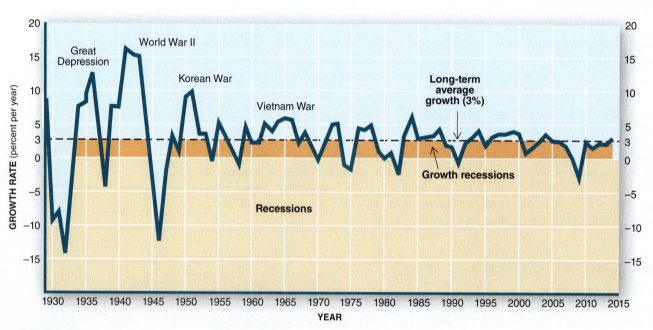

FIGURE 8.3

The Business Cycle in U.S. History

From 1929 to 2014, real GDP increased at an average rate of 3 percent a year. But annual growth rates have departed widely from that average. Years of above-average growth seem to alternate with years of sluggish growth (*growth recessions*) and actual decreases in total output (*recessions*).

Source: U.S. Department of Commerce.

Our long-term success in raising living standards is clouded, however, by a spate of short-term macro setbacks. On closer inspection, *the growth path of the U.S. economy isn't a smooth, rising trend but a series of steps, stumbles, and setbacks.* This short-run instability is evident in Figure 8.3. The dashed horizontal line across the middle of the chart represents the long-term *average* growth rate of the U.S. economy. From 1929 through 2014, the U.S. economy expanded at an average rate of 3 percent per year. But Figure 8.3 clearly shows that we didn't grow so nicely every year. There were lots of years when real GDP grew by less than 3 percent. Worse still, there were many years of *negative* growth, with real GDP *declining* from one year to the next. These successive short-run contractions and expansions are the essence of the business cycle.

The Great Depression

The most prolonged departure from our long-term growth path occurred during the Great Depression. Between 1929 and 1933, total U.S. output steadily declined. Notice in Figure 8.3 how the growth rate is negative in each of these years. During these four years of negative growth, real GDP contracted a total of nearly 30 percent. Investments in new plant and equipment virtually ceased. Economies around the world came to a grinding halt (see the World View below).

WORLD VIEW

Global Depression

The Great Depression wasn't confined to the U.S. economy. Most other countries suffered substantial losses of output and employment over a period of many years. Between 1929 and 1932, industrial production around the world fell 37 percent. The United States and Germany suffered the largest losses, while Spain and the Scandinavian countries lost only modest amounts of output.

Some countries escaped the ravages of the Great Depression altogether. The Soviet Union, largely insulated from Western economic structures, was in the midst of Stalin's forced industrialization drive during the 1930s. China and Japan were also relatively isolated from world trade and finance and so suffered less damage from the Depression.

Country	Decline in Industrial Output
Chile	−22%
France	−31
Germany	−47
Great Britain	−17
Japan	−2
Norway	−7
Spain	−12
United States	−46

ANALYSIS: International trade and financial flows tie nations together. When the U.S. economy tumbled in the 1930s, other nations lost export sales. Such interactions made the Great Depression a worldwide calamity.

web click

The *Concise Encyclopedia of Economics* provides a thorough account of the Great Depression at **www.econlib.org/library.** Search for "Great Depression."

The U.S. economy rebounded in April 1933 and continued to expand for three years (see the positive growth rates in Figure 8.3). By 1937, however, the rate of output was still below that of 1929. Then things got worse again. During 1938 and 1939 output again contracted and more people lost their jobs. **At the end of the 1930s, GDP per capita was lower than it had been in 1929.**

FIGURE 8.5

Aggregate Demand

Aggregate demand refers to the total output (real GDP) demanded at alternative price levels, *ceteris paribus.* The vertical axis measures the average level of all prices rather than the price of a single good. Likewise, the horizontal axis refers to the real quantity of all goods and services, not the quantity of only one product.

The downward slope of the aggregate demand curve is due to the real balances, foreign trade, and interest rate effects.

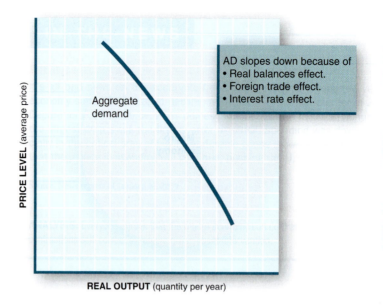

aggregate demand: The total quantity of output (real GDP) demanded at alternative price levels in a given time period, *ceteris paribus.*

By conceptualizing the inner workings of the macro economy in supply and demand terms, economists have developed a remarkably simple model of how the economy works.

Aggregate Demand

Economists use the term *aggregate demand* to refer to the collective behavior of all buyers in the marketplace. Specifically, **aggregate demand** refers to the various quantities of output (real GDP) that all people, taken together, are willing and able to buy at alternative price levels in a given period. Our view here encompasses the collective demand for *all* goods and services rather than the demand for any single good.

To understand the concept of aggregate demand better, imagine that everyone is paid on the same day. With their incomes in hand, people then enter the product market. The question becomes, how much output will people buy?

To answer this question, we have to know something about prices. If goods and services are cheap, people will be able to buy more with their available income. On the other hand, high prices will limit both the ability and willingness to purchase goods and services. Note that we're talking here about the *average* price level, not the price of any single good.

Figure 8.5 illustrates this simple relationship between average prices and real spending. The horizontal axis depicts the various quantities of (real) output that might be purchased. The vertical axis shows various price levels that might exist.

The aggregate demand curve illustrates how the real value of purchases varies with the average level of prices. The downward slope of the aggregate demand curve suggests that with a given (constant) level of income, people will buy more goods and services at lower price levels. Why would this be the case? *Three separate reasons explain the downward slope of the aggregate demand curve:*

- *The real balances effect.*
- *The foreign trade effect.*
- *The interest rate effect.*

Real Balances Effect. The most obvious explanation for the downward slope of the aggregate demand curve is that cheaper prices make dollars more valuable. Suppose you had $1,000 in your savings account. How much output could you buy with that savings balance? That depends on the price level. At current prices, you could buy $1,000 worth of output. But what if the price level rose? Then your $1,000 wouldn't stretch as far. *The* *real value of money is measured by how many goods and services each dollar will buy.* When the *real* value of your savings declines, your ability to purchase goods and services declines as well.

Suppose inflation pushes the price level up by 25 percent in a year. What will happen to the real value of your savings balance? At the end of the year, you'll have

$$\begin{array}{l} \text{Real value of savings} \\ \text{at year-end} \end{array} = \dfrac{\text{Savings balance}}{\dfrac{\text{Price level at year-end}}{\text{Price level at year-start}}}$$

$$= \dfrac{\$1,000}{\dfrac{125}{100}} = \dfrac{\$1,000}{1.25}$$

$$= \$800$$

In effect, inflation has wiped out a chunk of your purchasing power. At year's end, you can't buy as many goods and services as you could have at the beginning of the year. The *quantity* of output you demand will decrease. In Figure 8.5 this would be illustrated by a movement up the aggregate demand curve.

A declining price level (deflation) has the opposite effect. Specifically, lower price levels make you "richer": *the cash balances you hold in your pocket, in your bank account, or under your pillow are worth more when the price level falls.* As a result, you can buy *more* goods, even though your *nominal income* hasn't changed.

Lower price levels increase the purchasing power of other dollar-denominated assets as well. Bonds, for example, rise in value when the price level falls. This may tempt consumers to sell some bonds and buy more goods and services. With greater real wealth, consumers might also decide to save less and spend more of their current income. In either case, the quantity of goods and services demanded at any given income level will increase. These real balances effects create an inverse relationship between the price level and the real value of output demanded—that is, a downward-sloping aggregate demand curve.

Foreign Trade Effect. The downward slope of the aggregate demand curve is reinforced by changes in imports and exports. Consumers have the option of buying either domestic or foreign goods. A decisive factor in choosing between them is their relative price. If the average price of U.S.-produced goods is rising, Americans may buy more imported goods and fewer domestically produced products. Conversely, falling price levels in the United States may convince consumers to buy more "made in the USA" output and fewer imports.

International consumers are also swayed by relative price levels. When U.S. price levels decline, overseas tourists flock to Disney World. Global consumers also buy more U.S. wheat, airplanes, and computers when our price levels decline. Conversely, a rise in the relative price of U.S. products deters foreign buyers. These changes in import and export flows contribute to the downward slope of the aggregate demand curve.

Interest Rate Effect. Changes in the price level also affect the amount of money people need to borrow. At lower price levels, consumer borrowing needs are smaller. As the demand for loans diminishes, interest rates tend to decline as well. This "cheaper" money stimulates more borrowing and loan-financed purchases. These interest rate effects reinforce the downward slope of the aggregate demand curve, as illustrated in Figure 8.5.

Aggregate Supply

Although lower price levels tend to increase the volume of output demanded, they have the opposite effect on the aggregate quantity *supplied.* As we observed, our production possibilities are defined by available resources and technology. Within those limits, however, producers must decide how much output they're *willing* to supply. Their supply decisions are influenced by changes in the price level.

FIGURE 8.6
Aggregate Supply
Aggregate supply is the real value of output (real GDP) producers are willing and able to bring to the market at alternative price levels, *ceteris paribus.* The upward slope of the aggregate supply curve reflects both profit effects (the lure of widening profit margins) and cost effects (increasing cost pressures).

web click

The steepness of the aggregate supply curve depends in part on what producers pay for their inputs. Find out about producer prices at **www.bls.gov/ppi.**

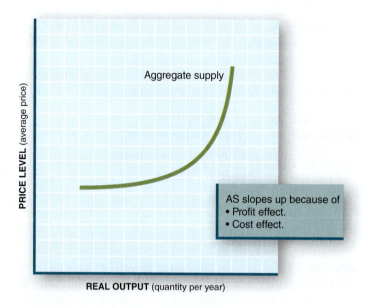

aggregate supply: The total quantity of output (real GDP) producers are willing and able to supply at alternative price levels in a given time period, *ceteris paribus.*

Profit Effect. The primary motivation for supplying goods and services is the chance to earn a profit. Producers can earn a profit so long as the prices they receive for their output exceed the costs they pay in production. Hence *changing price levels will affect the profitability of supplying goods.*

If the price level declines, profits tend to drop. In the short run, producers are saddled with some relatively constant costs like rent, interest payments, negotiated wages, and inputs already contracted for. If output prices fall, producers will be hard-pressed to pay these fixed costs, much less earn a profit. Their response will be to reduce the rate of output.

Higher output prices have the opposite effect. Because many costs are relatively constant in the short run, higher prices for goods and services tend to widen profit margins. As profit margins widen, producers will want to produce and sell more goods. Thus *we expect the rate of output to increase when the price level rises.* This expectation is reflected in the upward slope of the aggregate supply curve in Figure 8.6. **Aggregate supply** reflects the various quantities of real output that firms are willing and able to produce at alternative price levels in a given time period.

Cost Effect. The upward slope of the aggregate supply curve is also explained by rising costs. The profit effect depends on some costs remaining constant when the average price level rises. Not all costs will remain constant, however. Producers may have to pay overtime wages, for example, to increase output, even if *base* wages are constant. Tight supplies of other inputs may also unleash cost increases. Such cost pressures tend to multiply as the rate of output increases. As time passes, even costs that initially stayed constant may start creeping upward.

All these cost pressures will make producing output more expensive. Producers will be willing to supply additional output only if prices rise at least as fast as costs.

The upward slope of the aggregate supply curve in Figure 8.6 illustrates this cost effect. Notice how the aggregate supply curve is practically horizontal at low rates of aggregate output and then gets increasingly steeper. At high output levels the aggregate supply curve almost turns straight up. This changing slope reflects the fact that *cost pressures are minimal at low rates of output but intense as the economy approaches capacity.*

Macro Equilibrium

When all is said and done, what we end up with here is two rather conventional-looking supply and demand curves. But these particular curves have special significance. Instead of

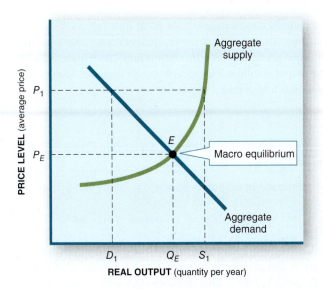

REAL OUTPUT (quantity per year)

FIGURE 8.7

Macro Equilibrium

The aggregate demand and supply curves intersect at only one point (*E*). At that point, the price level (P_E) and output (Q_E) combination is compatible with both buyers' and sellers' intentions. The economy will gravitate to those equilibrium price (P_E) and output (Q_E) levels. At any other price level (e.g., P_1), the behavior of buyers and sellers is incompatible.

describing the behavior of buyers and sellers in a single product market, ***aggregate supply and demand curves summarize the market activity of the whole (macro) economy.*** These curves tell us what *total* amount of goods and services will be supplied or demanded at various price levels.

These graphic summaries of buyer and seller behavior provide some important clues about the economy's performance. The most important clue is point *E* in Figure 8.7, where the aggregate demand and supply curves intersect. This is the only point at which the behavior of buyers and sellers is compatible. We know from the aggregate demand curve that people are willing and able to buy the quantity Q_E when the price level is at P_E. From the aggregate supply curve we know that businesses are prepared to sell quantity Q_E at the price level P_E. Hence buyers and sellers are willing to trade exactly the same quantity (Q_E) at that price level. We call this situation **macro equilibrium**—the unique combination of prices and output compatible with *both* buyers' and sellers' intentions.

Disequilibrium. To appreciate the significance of macro equilibrium, suppose that another price or output level existed. Imagine, for example, that prices were higher, at the level P_1 in Figure 8.7. How much output would people want to buy at that price level? How much would business want to produce and sell?

The aggregate demand curve tells us that people would want to buy only the quantity D_1 at the higher price level P_1. In contrast, business firms would want to sell a larger quantity, S_1. This is a *dis*equilibrium situation in which the intentions of buyers and sellers are incompatible. The aggregate *quantity supplied* (S_1) exceeds the aggregate *quantity demanded* (D_1). Accordingly, a lot of goods will remain unsold at price level P_1.

To sell these goods, producers will have to reduce their prices. As prices drop, producers will decrease the volume of goods sent to market. At the same time, the quantities that consumers seek to purchase will increase. This adjustment process will continue until point *E* is reached and the quantities demanded and supplied are equal. At that point, the lower price level P_E will prevail.

The same kind of adjustment process would occur if a lower price level first existed. At lower prices, the aggregate quantity demanded would exceed the aggregate quantity supplied. The resulting shortages would permit sellers to raise their prices. As they did so, the aggregate quantity demanded would decrease, and the aggregate quantity supplied would increase. Eventually we would return to point *E*, where the aggregate quantities demanded and supplied are equal.

Equilibrium is unique; it's the only price level–output combination that is mutually compatible with aggregate supply and demand. In terms of graphs, it's the only place

equilibrium (macro): The combination of price level and real output that is compatible with both aggregate demand and aggregate supply.

where the aggregate supply and demand curves intersect. At point *E* there's no reason for the level of output or prices to change. The behavior of buyers and sellers is compatible. By contrast, any other level of output or prices creates a *dis*equilibrium that requires market adjustments. All other price and output combinations, therefore, are unstable. They won't last. Eventually the economy will return to point *E*.

Macro Failures

There are two potential problems with the macro equilibrium depicted in Figure 8.7. The *two potential problems with macro equilibrium are*

- *Undesirability:* The equilibrium price or output level may not satisfy our macroeconomic goals.
- *Instability:* Even if the designated macro equilibrium is optimal, it may not last long.

Undesirability. The macro equilibrium depicted in Figure 8.7 is simply the intersection of two curves. All we know for sure is that people want to buy the same quantity of output that businesses want to sell at the price level P_E. This quantity (Q_E) may be more or less than our full-employment capacity. This contingency is illustrated in Figure 8.8. The output level Q_F represents our **full-employment GDP** potential. It is the rate of output that would be produced if we were fully employed. In Figure 8.8, however, we are producing only the smaller quantity Q_E. In this case, the equilibrium rate of output (Q_E) falls far short of capacity production Q_F. We've failed to achieve our goal of full employment.

Similar problems may arise from the equilibrium price level. Suppose that P^* represents the most desired price level. In Figure 8.8, we see that the equilibrium price level P_E exceeds P^*. If market behavior determines prices, the price level will rise above the desired level. The resulting increase in the average level of prices is what we call **inflation.**

It could be argued, of course, that our apparent macro failures are simply an artifact. We could have drawn the aggregate supply and demand curves to intersect at point *F* in Figure 8.8. At that intersection we'd have both price stability and full employment. Why didn't we draw them there, instead of intersecting at point *E*?

On the graph we can draw curves anywhere we want. In the real world, however, *only one set of aggregate supply and demand curves will correctly express buyers' and sellers' behavior.* We must emphasize here that these real-world curves may *not* intersect at point *F*, thus denying us price stability or full employment, or both. That is the kind of economic outcome illustrated in Figure 8.8.

Instability. Figure 8.8 is only the beginning of our macro worries. Suppose that the real-world AS and AD curves actually intersected in the perfect spot (point *F*). That is, imagine that macro equilibrium yielded the optimal levels of both employment and prices. If this happened, could we stop fretting about the state of the economy?

full-employment GDP: The total market value of final goods and services that could be produced in a given time period at full employment; potential GDP.

inflation: An increase in the average level of prices of goods and services.

FIGURE 8.8

An Undesired Equilibrium

Equilibrium establishes only the level of prices and output compatible with both buyers' and sellers' intentions. These outcomes may not satisfy our policy goals. In this case, the equilibrium price level (P_E) is too high (above P^*), and the equilibrium output rate (Q_E) falls short of full employment (Q_F).

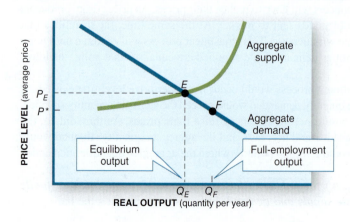

Unhappily, even a "perfect" macro equilibrium doesn't ensure a happy ending. Real-world AS and AD curves aren't permanently locked into their respective positions. They can *shift*—and they will whenever the behavior of buyers and sellers changes.

AS Shifts. Suppose another conflict erupts in oil-producing regions of the Middle East or North Africa, as happened in 2014. The price of oil quickly rises. These oil price hikes directly increased the cost of production in a wide range of U.S. industries, making producers less willing and able to supply goods at prevailing prices. Thus the aggregate supply curve *shifted to the left,* as in Figure 8.9a.

The September 11, 2001, terrorist strikes against the World Trade Center and Pentagon also caused a leftward shift of aggregate supply. Physical destruction and fear of further terrorism kept some producers out of the market. Intensified security of transportation systems and buildings also increased the costs of supplying goods and services to the market.

The impact of a leftward AS shift on the economy is evident in Figure 8.9. Whereas macro equilibrium was originally located at the optimal point *F,* the new equilibrium is located at point *G.* At point *G,* less output is produced and prices are higher. Full employment and price stability have vanished before our eyes. This is the kind of shift that contributed to the 2001 recession (Table 8.1).

AD Shifts. A shift of the aggregate demand curve could do similar damage. In the fall of 2008, the stock and credit markets took a real beating. Home prices were also falling rapidly. Consumers were seeing some of their wealth vanish before their eyes. As they became increasingly anxious about their future, they cut back on their spending. They were willing to buy *less* output at any given price level; the AD curve shifted to the left, as in Figure 8.9b. This AD shift led to lower output and falling prices. The Great Recession of 2008–2009 picked up downward speed (see the News on page 160).

Multiple Shifts. The situation gets even crazier when the aggregate supply and demand curves shift repeatedly in different directions. A leftward shift of the AD curve can cause a

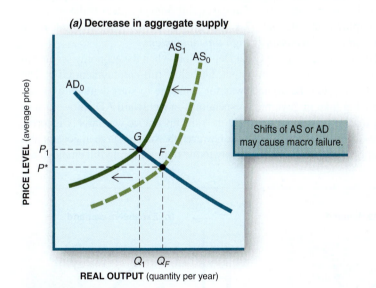

(a) Decrease in aggregate supply

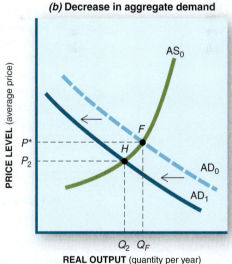

(b) Decrease in aggregate demand

Shifts of AS or AD may cause macro failure.

FIGURE 8.9
Macro Disturbances

(a) **Aggregate supply shifts** A decrease (leftward shift) of the aggregate supply curve tends to reduce real GDP and raise average prices. When supply shifts from AS_0 to AS_1, the equilibrium moves from *F* to *G.* At *G,* output is lower and prices are higher than at *F.* Such a supply shift may result from higher import prices, natural disasters, changes in tax policy, or other events.

(b) **Aggregate demand shifts** A decrease (leftward shift) in aggregate demand reduces output and price levels. When demand shifts from AD_0 to AD_1, both real output and the price level decline. A fall in demand may be caused by decreased export demand, changes in expectations, higher taxes, or other events.

recession, as the rate of output falls. A later rightward shift of the AD curve can cause a recovery, with real GDP (and employment) again increasing. Shifts of the aggregate supply curve can cause similar upswings and downswings. Thus *business cycles are likely to result from recurrent shifts of the aggregate supply and demand curves.*

COMPETING THEORIES OF SHORT-RUN INSTABILITY

Figures 8.8 and 8.9 hardly inspire optimism about the macro economy. Figure 8.8 suggests that the odds of the market generating an equilibrium at full employment and price stability are about the same as finding a needle in a haystack. Figure 8.9 suggests that if we're lucky enough to find the needle, we'll probably drop it again.

The classical economists had no such worries. As we saw earlier, they believed that the economy would gravitate toward full employment. Keynes, on the other hand, worried that the macro equilibrium might start out badly and get worse in the absence of government intervention.

The AS/AD model doesn't really settle this controversy. It does, however, provide a convenient framework for comparing these and other theories about how the economy works. Essentially, *macro controversies focus on the shape of aggregate supply and demand curves and the potential to shift them.* With the right shape—or the correct shift—any desired equilibrium could be attained. As we'll see, there are differing views as to whether and how this happy outcome might come about. These differing views can be classified as demand-side explanations, supply-side explanations, or some combination of the two.

Demand-Side Theories

Keynesian Theory. Keynesian theory is the most prominent of the demand-side theories. Keynes argued that a deficiency of spending would tend to depress an economy. This deficiency might originate in consumer saving, inadequate business investment, or insufficient government spending. Whatever its origins, the lack of spending would leave goods unsold and production capacity unused. This contingency is illustrated in the News on page 160 and here by point E_1 in Figure 8.10a. Notice that the equilibrium at E_1 leaves the economy at Q_1, below its full-employment potential (Q_F). Thus *Keynes concluded that inadequate aggregate demand would cause persistently high unemployment.*

Keynes developed his theory during the Great Depression, when the economy seemed to be stuck at a very low level of equilibrium output, far below full-employment GDP. The only way to end the Depression, he argued, was for someone to start demanding more goods. He advocated a big hike in government spending—a rightward AD shift—to start the economy moving toward full employment. At the time his advice was largely ignored. When the United States mobilized for World War II, however, the sudden surge in government spending shifted the aggregate demand curve sharply to the right, restoring full employment

FIGURE 8.10

Demand-Side Theories

Inadequate demand may cause unemployment. In part (*a*), the demand AD_1 creates an equilibrium at E_1. The resulting output Q_1 falls short of full employment Q_F.

In part (*b*), excessive aggregate demand causes inflation. The price level rises from P_0 to P_2 when aggregate demand expands to AD_2. Demand-side theories emphasize how inadequate or excessive AD can cause macro failures.

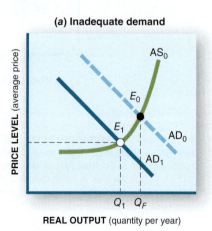

(a) Inadequate demand

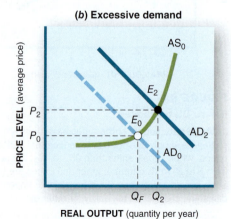

(b) Excessive demand

(e.g., a reverse shift from AD_1 to AD_0 in Figure 8.10*a*). In times of peace, Keynes also advocated changing government taxes and spending to shift the aggregate demand curve in whatever direction is desired.

Monetary Theories. Another demand-side theory emphasizes the role of money in financing aggregate demand. Money and credit affect the ability and willingness of people to buy goods and services. If credit isn't available or is too expensive, consumers won't be able to buy as many cars, homes, or other expensive products. "Tight" money might also curtail business investment. In these circumstances, aggregate demand might prove to be inadequate, as illustrated in Figure 8.10*a*. In this case, an increase in the money supply and/or lower interest rates might help shift the AD curve into the desired position.

Both the Keynesian and monetarist theories also regard aggregate demand as a prime suspect for inflationary problems. In Figure 8.10*b*, the curve AD_2 leads to an equilibrium at E_2. At first blush, that equilibrium looks desirable, as it offers more output (Q_2) than the full-employment threshold (Q_F). Notice, however, what's happening to prices: the price level rises from P_0 to P_2. Hence *excessive aggregate demand may cause inflation.*

The more extreme monetary theories attribute all our macro successes and failures to management of the money supply. According to these *monetarist* theories, the economy will tend to stabilize at something like full-employment GDP. Thus only the price level will be affected by changes in the money supply and resulting shifts of aggregate demand. We'll examine the basis for this view in a moment. At this juncture we simply note that *both Keynesian and monetarist theories emphasize the potential of aggregate-demand shifts to alter macro outcomes.*

Supply-Side Theories

Figure 8.11 illustrates an entirely different explanation of the business cycle. Notice that the aggregate *supply* curve is on the move in Figure 8.11. The initial equilibrium is again at point E_0. This time, however, aggregate demand remains stationary, while aggregate supply shifts. The resulting decline of aggregate supply causes output and employment to decline (to Q_3 from Q_F).

Figure 8.11 tells us that aggregate supply may be responsible for downturns as well. Our failure to achieve full employment may result from the unwillingness of producers to provide more goods at existing prices. That unwillingness may originate in simple greed, in rising costs, in resource shortages, or in government taxes and regulation. Inadequate investment in infrastructure (e.g., roads, sewer systems) or skill training may also limit supply potential. Whatever the cause, if the aggregate supply curve is AS_1 rather than AS_0, full employment will not be achieved with the demand AD_0.

The inadequate supply illustrated in Figure 8.11 causes not only unemployment but inflation as well. At the equilibrium E_3, the price level has risen from P_0 to P_3. Hence a decrease in aggregate supply can cause multiple macro problems. On the other hand, an increase—a

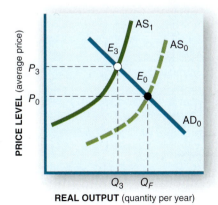

FIGURE 8.11

Supply-Side Theories

Inadequate supply can keep the economy below its full-employment potential and cause prices to rise as well. AS_1 leads to equilibrium output Q_3 and increases the price level from P_0 to P_3. Supply-side theories emphasize how AS shifts can worsen or improve macro outcomes.

web click

The U.S. Bureau of Economic Analysis compiles data on gross domestic product. Using data from its website **www.bea.gov**, calculate the U.S. GDP growth rate for each of the last six quarters. What supply or demand shifts might explain recent quarterly fluctuations in real GDP?

rightward shift—in aggregate supply can move us closer to both our price-stability and full-employment goals. Chapter 16 examines the many ways of inducing such a shift.

Eclectic Explanations

Not everyone blames either the demand side or the supply side exclusively. *The various macro theories tell us that either AS or AD can cause us to achieve or miss our policy goals.* These theories also demonstrate how various shifts of the aggregate supply and demand curves can achieve any specific output or price level. One could also shift *both* the AS and AD curves to explain unemployment, inflation, or recurring business cycles. Such eclectic explanations of macro failure draw from both sides of the market.

LONG-RUN SELF-ADJUSTMENT

Some economists argue that these various theories of short-run instability aren't only confusing but also pointless. As they see it, what really matters is the *long*-run trend of the economy, not *short*-run fluctuations around those trends. In their view, month-to-month or quarter-to-quarter fluctuations in real output or prices are just statistical noise. The *long*-term path of output and prices is determined by more fundamental factors.

This emphasis on long-term outcomes is reminiscent of the classical theory: the view that the economy will self-adjust. A decrease in aggregate demand is only a *temporary* problem. Once producers and workers make the required price and wage adjustments, the economy will return to its long-run equilibrium growth path.

The monetarist theory we encountered a moment ago has a similar view of long-run stability. According to the monetarist theory, the supply of goods and services is determined by institutional factors such as the size of the labor force and technology. These factors determine a "natural" rate of output that's relatively immune to short-run fluctuations in aggregate demand. If this argument is valid, the long-run aggregate supply curve is vertical, not sloped.

Figure 8.12 illustrates the classical/monetarist view of long-run stability. The vertical long-run AS curve is anchored at the natural rate of output Q_N. The natural rate Q_N is itself determined by demographics, technology, market structure, and the institutional infrastructure of the economy.

If the long-run AS curve is really vertical, as the classical and monetarist theories assert, some startling conclusions follow. The most startling implication is that *shifts of the aggregate demand curve affect prices but not output in the long run.* Notice in Figure 8.12 how the shift from AD_1 to AD_2 raises the price level (from P_1 to P_2) but leaves output anchored at Q_N.

What has happened here? Didn't we suggest earlier that an increase in aggregate demand would spur producers to increase output? And aren't rising prices an extra incentive for doing so?

FIGURE 8.12

The "Natural" Rate of Output

Monetarists and neoclassical theorists assert that the level of output is fixed at the natural rate Q_N by the size of the labor force, technology, and other institutional factors. As a result, fluctuations in aggregate demand affect the price level but not real output.

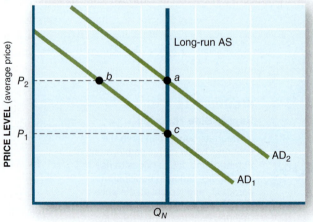

Monetarists concede that *short-run* price increases tend to widen profit margins. This profit effect is an incentive to increase the rate of output. In the *long run,* however, costs are likely to catch up with rising prices. Workers will demand higher wages, landlords will increase rents, and banks will charge higher interest rates as the price level rises. Hence a rising price level has only a *temporary* profit effect on supply behavior. In the *long run,* cost effects will dominate. In the *long run,* a rising price level will be accompanied by rising costs, giving producers no special incentive to supply more output. Accordingly, output will revert to its natural rate Q_N.

Classical economists use the vertical AS curve to explain also how the economy self-adjusts to temporary setbacks. If AD declines from AD_2 to AD_1 in Figure 8.12, the economy may move from point *a* to point *b*, leaving a lot of unsold output. As producers respond with price cuts, however, the volume of output demanded increases as the economy moves from point *b* to point *c*. At point *c*, full employment is restored. Thus flexible prices (and wages) enable the economy to maintain the natural rate of output Q_N.

Short- vs. Long-Run Perspectives

All this may well be true. But as Keynes pointed out, it's also true that "in the long run we are all dead." How long are we willing to wait for the promised "self-adjustment"? In the Great Depression, people waited for 10 years—and still saw no self-adjustment.

Whatever the long run may hold, it's in the short run that we must consume, invest, and find a job. However stable and predictable the long run might be, short-run variations in macro outcomes will determine how well we fare in any year. Moreover, ***the short-run aggregate supply curve is likely to be upward-sloping,*** as shown in our earlier graphs. This implies that both aggregate supply and aggregate demand influence short-run macro outcomes.

By distinguishing between short-run and long-run aggregate supply curves, competing economic theories achieve a standoff. Theories that highlight the necessity of policy intervention emphasize the importance of short-run macro outcomes. People *care* about short-run changes in job prospects and prices. If inflation or unemployment is too high, voters insist that "Washington" fix the problem—now.

Theories that emphasize the "natural" stability of the market point to the predictability of long-run outcomes. They prefer to let the economy self-adjust rather than risk government intervention that might worsen macro outcomes. Even if these theories are true, however, the duration of acceptable "short-" and "long-" run periods remains controversial.

THE ECONOMY TOMORROW

COPING WITH RECESSION: 2008–2014

The AS/AD model is a convenient summary of how the macro economy works. A market-driven economy will gravitate to an equilibrium that is compatible with the behavior of both buyers (AD) and sellers (AS). As we've observed, however, that short-run macro equilibrium may not be consistent with our economic goals. That was certainly the case in the Great Recession of 2008–2009, when the equilibrium rate of output was less than full-employment output. People expected newly elected President Obama—the new Economist in Chief—to do something about it. What *could* he do?

Policy Strategies. The beauty of the AS/AD model is that it highlights the strategic options for coping with a recession. In the AS/AD framework, there are really only ***three strategy options for macro policy:***

- ***Shift the aggregate demand curve to the right.*** Find and use policy tools that will stimulate total spending.
- ***Shift the aggregate supply curve to the right.*** Find and implement policy levers that reduce the cost of production or otherwise stimulate more output at every price level.
- ***Laissez faire.*** Don't interfere with the market; let markets self-adjust.

The first two strategies assume some form of government intervention is needed to end a recession. The third strategy places more faith in the market's ability to self-adjust.

Policy Tools. There are a host of different policy tools available for implementing any given AS/AD strategy, as President Obama discovered.

- *Classical Laissez Faire.* The laissez-faire strategy advocated by classical economists requires no tools, of course. Classical economists count on the self-adjustment mechanisms of the market—flexible prices and wages—to bring a quick end to recessions. Falling home prices would ultimately spur more sales; declining wages would encourage more hiring. In this view, AS and AD curves "naturally" shift back into an optimal position, where full employment (Q_F) prevails.

- *Fiscal Policy.* Keynes rejected this hands-off approach. He advocated using the federal budget as a policy tool. The government can shift the AD curve to the right by spending more money. Or it can cut taxes, leaving consumers with more income to spend. These budgetary tools are the hallmark of fiscal policy. Specifically, **fiscal policy** is the use of government tax and spending powers to alter economic outcomes.

- *Monetary Policy.* The budget isn't the only tool in the interventionist toolbox. Interest rates and the money supply can also shift the AD curve. Lower interest rates encourage consumers to buy more big-ticket items like cars, homes, and appliances—purchases typically financed with loans. Businesses also take advantage of lower interest rates to buy more loan-financed plant and equipment. **Monetary policy** refers to the use of money and credit controls to alter economic outcomes.

- *Supply-Side Policy.* Fiscal and monetary tools are used to fix the AD side of the macro economy. **Supply-side policy** pursues a different strategy: it uses tools that shift the aggregate supply curve. Tax incentives that encourage more work, saving, or investment are in the supply-side toolbox. So are deregulation actions that make it easier or cheaper to supply products.

- *Trade Policy.* International trade and money flows offer yet another option for shifting aggregate supply and demand. A reduction in trade barriers makes imports cheaper and more available. This shifts the aggregate supply to the right, reducing price pressures at every output level. Reducing the international value (exchange rate) of the dollar lowers the relative price of U.S.-made goods, thereby encouraging foreigners to buy more U.S. exports. Hence trade policy is another tool in the macroeconomic toolbox.

Taking Action. President Obama never really considered following the do-nothing-and-wait classical approach. He had been elected in November 2008 on the promise of change for the better. In his view, that meant using the available array of activist policy tools to get the economy moving again. His first major intervention was a massive fiscal policy package of increased government spending and tax cuts—the kind of policy Keynes advocated. Over the next five years, President Obama, Congress, and the Federal Reserve used additional policy tools to push the economy out of the Great Recession. Some worked; some didn't. In subsequent chapters we'll examine which tools worked, which didn't, and why.

fiscal policy: The use of government taxes and spending to alter macroeconomic outcomes.

monetary policy: The use of money and credit controls to influence macroeconomic outcomes.

supply-side policy: The use of tax incentives, (de)regulation, and other mechanisms to increase the ability and willingness to produce goods and services.

SUMMARY

- The long-term growth rate of the U.S. economy is approximately 3 percent a year. But output doesn't increase 3 percent every year. In some years real GDP grows much faster; in other years growth is slower. Sometimes GDP actually declines (recession). **LO8-1**

- These short-run variations in GDP growth are a central focus of macroeconomics. Macro theory tries to explain the alternating periods of growth and contraction that

characterize the business cycle; macro policy attempts to control the cycle. **LO8-1**

- The primary outcomes of the macro economy are output, prices, jobs, and international balances. The outcomes result from the interplay of internal market forces, external shocks, and policy levers. **LO8-1**

- All the influences on macro outcomes are transmitted through aggregate supply or aggregate demand. Aggregate demand refers to the rates of output people are willing to purchase at various price levels. Aggregate supply is the rate of output producers are willing to supply at various price levels.   **LO8-3**

- Aggregate supply and demand determine the equilibrium rate of output and prices. The economy will gravitate to that unique combination of output and price levels.   **LO8-3**
- The market-driven macro equilibrium may not satisfy our employment or price goals. Macro failure occurs when the economy's equilibrium isn't optimal.   **LO8-2**
- Macro equilibrium may be disturbed by changes in aggregate supply (AS) or aggregate demand (AD). Such changes are illustrated by shifts of the AS and AD curves, and they lead to a new equilibrium.   **LO8-4**

- Competing economic theories try to explain the shape and shifts of the aggregate supply and demand curves, thereby explaining the business cycle. Specific theories tend to emphasize demand or supply influences.   **LO8-2**
- In the long run the AS curve tends to be vertical, implying that changes in aggregate demand affect prices but not output. In the short run, however, the AS curve is sloped, making macro outcomes sensitive to both supply and demand.   **LO8-3**
- Macro policy options range from laissez faire (the classical approach) to various strategies for shifting either the aggregate demand curve or the aggregate supply curve.   **LO8-3**

Key Terms

macroeconomics	recession	full-employment GDP
business cycle	growth recession	inflation
laissez faire	aggregate demand	fiscal policy
law of demand	aggregate supply	monetary policy
Say's law	equilibrium (macro)	supply-side policy
real GDP		

Questions for Discussion

1. If business cycles were really inevitable, what purpose would macro policy serve?   **LO8-2**
2. What events might prompt consumers to demand fewer goods at current prices?   **LO8-3**
3. If equilibrium is compatible with both buyers' and sellers' intentions, how can it be undesirable?   **LO8-3**
4. How did the decline in U.S. home prices in 2006–2008 affect aggregate demand?   **LO8-3**
5. What exactly did Say mean when he said that "supply creates its own demand"?   **LO8-1**
6. What's wrong with the classical theory of self-adjustment? Why didn't sales and employment increase in 1929–1933 in response to declining prices and wages (see Figure 8.1)?   **LO8-3**
7. What might have caused real GDP to decline so dramatically in (a) 1929 and (b) 1946 (see Figure 8.3)? What caused output to increase again in each case?   **LO8-4**
8. How would a sudden jump in U.S. prices affect (a) imports from Mexico, (b) exports to Mexico, and (c) U.S. aggregate demand?   **LO8-4**
9. Why might rising prices stimulate short-run production but have no effect on long-run production?   **LO8-4**
10. Recovery from the 2008–2009 recession was agonizingly slow. What factors might have constrained faster growth?   **LO8-2**

mobile app Visit your mobile app store and download the Schiller: Study Econ app *today!*

LO8-3 1. (a) How much output is unsold at the price level P_1 in Figure 8.7?   _____
        (b) At what price level is all output produced sold?   _____

LO8-2
LO8-3 2. In Figure 8.8, what price level will induce people to buy all the output produced at full
     employment?   _____

LO8-1 3. Suppose you have $5,000 in savings when the price level index is at 100.
        (a) If inflation pushes the price level up by 10 percent, what will be the real value of your
           savings?   _____
        (b) What is the real value of your savings if the price level *declines* by 10 percent?   _____

LO8-3 4. Use the following information to draw aggregate demand (AD) and aggregate supply (AS) curves
     on the following graph. Both curves are assumed to be straight lines.

Price Level	Output Demanded	Output Supplied
800	0	$800
100	$700	100

        (a) At what rate of real output does equilibrium occur?   _____
        (b) What curve (AD or AS) would have shifted if a new equilibrium were to occur at an
           output level of 600 and a price level of $600?   _____
        (c) What curve would have shifted if a new equilibrium were to occur at an output level
           of 600 and a price level of $200?   _____

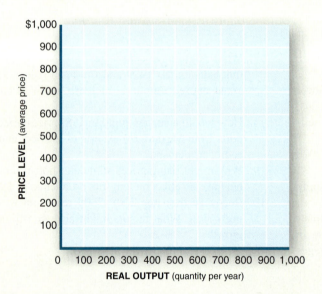

LO8-1 5. According to the News on page 160,
        (a) By what percentage did GDP decline in the fourth quarter of 2008?   _____%
        (b) At that rate, how much output would have been lost in the $14 trillion economy of 2008? $ _____
        (c) How much income did this represent for each of the 300 million U.S. citizens? $ _____

LO8-1 6. According to Table 8.1
        (a) What was the largest percentage GDP decline in a post–World War II U.S. recession?   _____%
        (b) What was
           (i) The longest post–World War II recession?   _____
           (ii) The shortest post–World War II recession?   _____

PROBLEMS FOR CHAPTER 8 (cont'd)   Name: _____

LO8-3 7. If the AS curve shifts to the right, what happens (A = increases or B = decreases) to
   (a) The equilibrium rate of output?   _____
   (b) The equilibrium price level?   _____

LO8-4 8. If the AD curve shifts to the right, what happens (A = increases or B = decreases) to
   (a) The equilibrium rate of output?   _____
   (b) The equilibrium price level?   _____

LO8-4 9. Assume that the accompanying graph depicts aggregate supply and demand conditions in
      an economy. Full employment occurs when $5 trillion of real output is produced.
   (a) What is the equilibrium rate of output?   _____
   (b) How far short of full employment is the equilibrium rate of output? _____
   (c) Illustrate a shift of aggregate demand that would change the equilibrium rate of output
        to $5 trillion. Label the new curve AD_2.
   (d) What is the price level at this full-employment equilibrium?   _____
   (e) Illustrate a shift of aggregate supply (AS_2) that would, when combined with AD_1,
        move equilibrium output to $5 trillion.
   (f) What is the price level at this new equilibrium?   _____

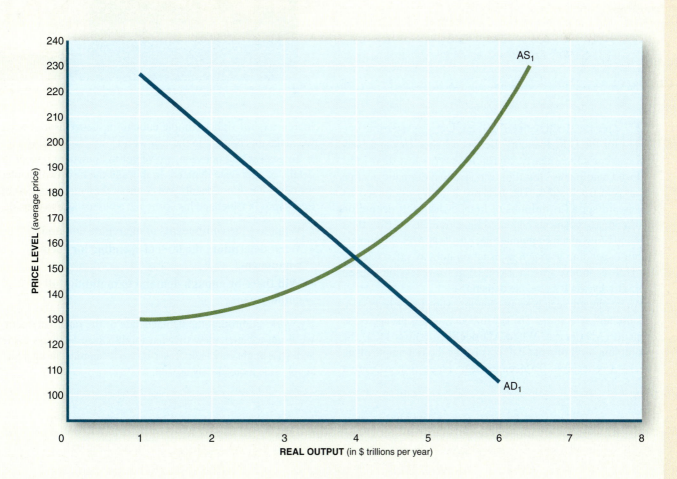

175

Aggregate Demand

The last quarter of 2008 was a terrible one for the U.S. economy. Between Labor Day and New Year's Eve, nearly *2 million* workers lost their jobs. A dozen auto plants closed in response to a dramatic decline in car and truck sales. The housing industry continued its downward spiral as millions of homeowners fell behind on their mortgage payments and faced foreclosure. Even Christmas failed to bring much economic cheer in 2008; U.S. consumers weren't spending as much as usual on holiday gifts. Clearly the U.S. economy was in a recession—a recession caused primarily by weak aggregate demand.

We've already seen how an economy slips into a recession, and also how it recovers. The key to both events is the aggregate demand (AD) curve. When AD declines (shifts left), the equilibrium level of real GDP falls below the full-employment level—a recession. To escape from recession, AD must increase (shift right). Simple enough in theory. But how can we make this happen in the real world?

To answer that question, we've got to know more about the details of aggregate demand. In this and the next two chapters we delve into those details. We confront the same questions the Economist in Chief and his economic advisers have to consider:

- **What are the components of aggregate demand?**
- **What determines the level of spending for each component?**
- **Will there be enough demand to maintain full employment?**

By working through the demand side of the macro economy, we'll get a better view of what might cause business cycles and what might cure them. Later on we'll examine the aggregate supply side more closely as well.

MACRO EQUILIBRIUM

In Chapter 8 we got a bird's-eye view of how macro equilibrium is established. Producers have some notion of how much output they're willing and able to produce at various price levels. Likewise, consumers, businesses, governments, and foreign buyers have some notion of how much output they're willing and able to buy at different price levels. These forces of **aggregate demand** and **aggregate supply** confront each other in the marketplace. Eventually, buyers and sellers discover that only one price level and output combination is acceptable to *both* sides. This is the price–output combination we designate as **(macro) equilibrium.** At equilibrium, the rate of output equals the rate of spending. Producers have no reason to change production levels. In the absence of macro disturbances, the economy will gravitate toward that equilibrium.

The Desired Adjustment

Figure 9.1 illustrates again this general view of macro equilibrium. In the figure, aggregate supply (AS) and demand (AD_1) establish an equilibrium at E_1. At this particular equilibrium, the value of real output is Q_E, significantly short of the economy's full-employment potential at Q_F. Accordingly, the economy depicted in Figure 9.1 is producing below capacity and thus is saddled with excessive unemployment. This is the kind of situation the U.S. economy confronted in 2008–2009.

All economists recognize that such a *short-run* macro failure is possible. We also realize that the unemployment problem depicted in Figure 9.1 would disappear if either the AD or AS curve shifted rightward. A central macro debate is over whether the curves *will* shift on their own (self-adjust). If not, the government might have to step in and do some heavy shifting.

Components of Aggregate Demand

To assess the possibilities for self-adjustment, we need to examine the nature of aggregate demand more closely. Who's buying the output of the economy? What factors influence their purchase decisions? Why aren't people buying more output?

We can best understand the nature of aggregate demand by breaking it down into its various components. ***The four components of aggregate demand are***

- *Consumption (C).*
- *Investment (I).*
- *Government spending (G).*
- *Net exports (X – M).*

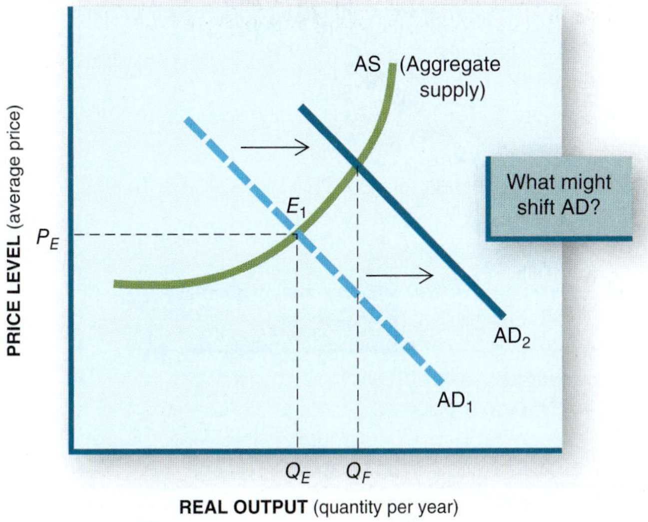

aggregate demand: The total quantity of output demanded at alternative price levels in a given time period, *ceteris paribus.*

aggregate supply: The total quantity of output producers are willing and able to supply at alternative price levels in a given time period, *ceteris paribus.*

equilibrium (macro): The combination of price level and real output that is compatible with both aggregate demand and aggregate supply.

FIGURE 9.1

Escaping a Recession

Aggregate demand (AD) might be insufficient to ensure full employment (Q_F), as illustrated by the intersection of AD_1 and the aggregate supply curve. The question is whether and how AD will increase—that is, *shift* rightward—say, to AD_2. To answer these questions, we must examine the components of aggregate demand.

Each of these components represents a stream of spending that contributes to aggregate demand. What we want to determine is how these various spending decisions are made. We also want to know what factors might *change* the level of spending, thereby *shifting* aggregate demand.

CONSUMPTION

consumption: Expenditure by consumers on final goods and services.

Consider first the largest component of aggregate demand, namely, **consumption.** Consumption refers to expenditures by households (consumers) on final goods and services. As we observed in Chapter 5, *consumer expenditures account for more than two-thirds of total spending.* Hence whatever factors alter consumer behavior are sure to have an impact on aggregate demand.

Income and Consumption

The aggregate demand curve tells us that consumers will buy more output at lower price levels with a *given* amount of income. But what if *incomes* themselves were to change? If incomes were to increase, consumers would have more money to spend at any given price level. This could cause a rightward *shift* of the AD curve, exactly the kind of move a recessionary economy (e.g., Figure 9.1) needs.

As far as the British economist John Maynard Keynes was concerned, this was a no-brainer. Experience shows that *consumers tend to spend most of whatever income they have.* This is apparent in Figure 9.2: year after year, consumer spending has risen in tandem with income. Hence, with more income, we expect more spending at any given price level.

disposable income: After-tax income of consumers; personal income less personal taxes.

Disposable income is the key concept here. As noted in Chapter 5, **disposable income** is the amount of income consumers actually take home after all taxes have been paid, transfers (e.g., Social Security benefits) have been received, and depreciation charges and retained earnings have been subtracted (see Table 5.6).

What will consumers do with their disposable income? There are only two choices: they can either spend their disposable income on consumption, or they can save (not spend) it. At

FIGURE 9.2

U.S. Consumption and Income

The points on the graph indicate the actual rates of U.S. disposable income and consumption for the years 1980–2000. By connecting these dots, we can approximate the long-term consumption function. Clearly, consumption rises with income. Indeed, consumers spend almost every extra dollar they receive.

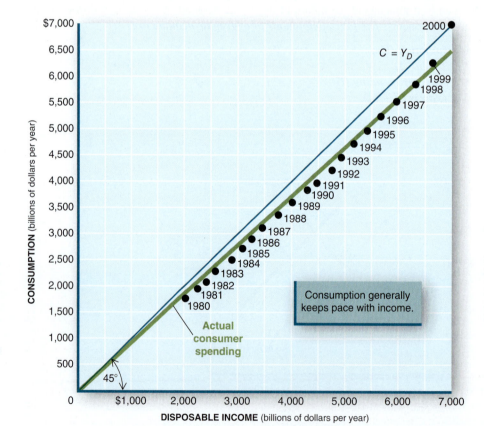

this point we don't care what form household **saving** might take (e.g., cash under the mattress, bank deposits, stock purchases); all we want to do is distinguish that share of disposable income spent on consumer goods and services from the remainder that is *not* spent. By definition, then, ***all disposable income is either consumed (spent) or saved (not spent); that is,***

$$\text{Disposable income} = \text{Consumption} + \text{Saving}$$
$$(Y_D) \qquad\qquad (C) \qquad\qquad (S)$$

saving: That part of disposable income not spent on current consumption; disposable income less consumption.

Consumption vs. Saving

To figure out how much consumer spending will actually occur, we need to know what fraction of disposable income will be consumed and how much will be saved. There are two ways of looking at this decision: first in terms of *averages,* and then in terms of *marginal* decisions.

APC. The proportion of *total* disposable income spent on consumer goods and services is referred to as the **average propensity to consume (APC).** To determine the APC, we simply observe how much consumers spend in a given time period out of that period's disposable income. In 2013, for example, the disposable income of U.S. households amounted to more than $12 trillion. Out of this amount, consumers spent nearly every available dollar, saving a measly $608 billion. Accordingly, we may calculate the average propensity to consume as

average propensity to consume (APC): Total consumption in a given period divided by total disposable income.

$$\text{APC} = \frac{\textbf{Total consumption}}{\textbf{Total disposable income}} = \frac{C}{Y_D}$$

For 2013 this works out to

$$\text{APC} = \frac{\$11{,}897 \text{ billion}}{\$12{,}505 \text{ billion}} = 0.951$$

In other words, U.S. consumers spent just about every nickel they received in 2013. Specifically, consumers spent, on average, 95.1 cents out of every dollar of income. Less than 5 cents out of every disposable dollar was saved. (How much do *you* save?)

The relatively high APC in the United States distinguishes our consumer-oriented economy. In recent years, the U.S. APC has even *exceeded* 1.0 on occasion, forcing U.S. households to finance some of their consumption with credit or past savings. Prior to 9/11, a lot of U.S. households were doing exactly that, as the accompanying News reports. The APC can exceed 1.0 when consumers finance their purchases with both current income and credit.

IN THE NEWS

Overspending

Four out of ten Americans admit to overspending—spending more money than they earn. Young adults are particularly prone to overspending. Seniors are a bit more cautious with their wallets.

Source: Lutheran Brotherhood/Yankelovich Partners Survey of 1,010 Adults in January 2001.

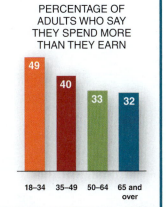

PERCENTAGE OF ADULTS WHO SAY THEY SPEND MORE THAN THEY EARN

ANALYSIS: When consumer spending exceeds disposable income, consumer saving is negative; households are *dissaving.* Dissaving is financed with credit or prior savings.

web click

The Federal Reserve Board has a repayment calculator that allows debtors to find the time it takes to repay a credit card. See **www.federalreserve.gov/creditcardcalculator.**

The Marginal Propensity to Consume

If consumers *always* spent 95 cents out of every income dollar, predicting consumer spending would be an easy task. But life is never that simple; consumer behavior changes from time to time. This led Keynes to develop a second measure of consumption behavior called the *marginal* propensity to consume. The **marginal propensity to consume (MPC)** tells us how much consumer expenditure will *change* in response to *changes* in disposable income. With the delta symbol, Δ, representing "change in," MPC can be written as

$$\text{MPC} = \frac{\textbf{Change in consumption}}{\textbf{Change in disposable income}} = \frac{\Delta C}{\Delta Y_D}$$

marginal propensity to consume (MPC): The fraction of each additional (marginal) dollar of disposable income spent on consumption; the change in consumption divided by the change in disposable income.

To calculate the marginal propensity to consume, we could ask how consumer spending in 2013 was affected by the *last* dollar of disposable income. That is, how did consumer spending change when disposable income increased from $12,504,999,999 to $12,505,000,000? Suppose consumer spending increased by only 80 cents when this last $1.00 was received. In that case, we'd calculate the *marginal* propensity to consume as

$$\text{MPC} = \frac{\Delta C}{\Delta Y_D} = \frac{\$0.80}{\$1.00} = 0.8$$

Notice that the MPC in this particular case (0.8) is lower than the APC (0.951). Suppose we had incorrectly assumed that consumers would always spend $0.951 of every dollar's income. Then we'd have expected the rate of consumer spending to rise by 95.1 cents as the last dollar was received. In fact, however, the rate of spending increased by only 80 cents. In other words, consumers responded to an *increase* in their income differently than past averages implied.

No one would be upset if our failure to distinguish the APC from the MPC led to an error of only 15.1 cents in forecasts of consumer spending. After all, the rate of consumer spending in the U.S. economy now exceeds $12 *trillion* per year! But those same trillion-dollar dimensions make the accuracy of the MPC that much more important. Annual *changes* in disposable income entail hundreds of billions of dollars. When we start playing with those sums—the actual focus of economic policymakers—the distinction between APC and MPC is significant.

The Marginal Propensity to Save

Once we know how much of their income consumers will spend, we also know how much they'll save. Remember that all *disposable income is, by definition, either consumed (spent on consumption) or saved.* Saving is just whatever income is left over after consumption expenditures. Accordingly, if the MPC is 0.80, then 20 cents of each additional dollar are being saved and 80 cents are being spent (see Figure 9.3). The **marginal propensity to save (MPS)**—the fraction of each additional dollar saved (that is, *not* spent)—is simply

marginal propensity to save (MPS): The fraction of each additional (marginal) dollar of disposable income not spent on consumption; 1 − MPC.

$$\text{MPS} = 1 - \text{MPC}$$

FIGURE 9.3
MPC and MPS

The marginal propensity to consume (MPC) tells us what portion of an extra dollar of income will be spent. The remaining portion is, by definition, "saved." The MPC and MPS help us predict consumer behavior.

MPS = 0.20   MPC = 0.80

TABLE 9.1

Average and Marginal
Propensities to Consume

MPC. The marginal propensity to consume (MPC) is the *change* in consumption that accompanies a *change* in disposable income; that is,

$$MPC = \frac{\Delta C}{\Delta Y_D}$$

MPS. The marginal propensity to save (MPS) is the fraction of each additional (marginal) dollar of disposable income *not* spent—that is, saved. This is summarized as

$$MPS = \frac{\Delta S}{\Delta Y_D}$$

MPS equals 1 − MPC since every additional dollar is either spent (consumed) or not spent (saved).

APC. The average propensity to consume is the proportion of *total* disposable income that's spent on consumption. It is computed as

$$APC = \frac{C}{Y_D}$$

APS. The average propensity to save is $\frac{S}{Y_D}$ and must equal 1 − APC.

web click

Go to the U.S. Bureau of Economic Analysis (BEA) website at **www.bea.gov,** and click "Consumer Spending." Determine the rate of disposable income and consumer spending in the two most recent calendar quarters. What was the APC in the most recent quarter? What was the MPC between the two most recent quarters?

As Table 9.1 illustrates, if we know how much of their income consumers spend, we also know how much of it they save.

THE CONSUMPTION FUNCTION

The MPC, MPS, APC, and APS are simply statistical measures of observed consumer behavior. What we really want to know is what drives these measures. If we know, then we'll be in a position to *predict* rather than just *observe* consumer behavior. This ability would be of immense value in anticipating and controlling short-run business cycles. President Obama certainly could have used that information from 2009 to 2014.

Autonomous Consumption

Keynes had several ideas about the determinants of consumption. Although he observed that consumer spending and income were highly correlated (Figure 9.2), he knew consumption wasn't *completely* determined by current income. In extreme cases, this is evident. People who have no income in a given period continue to consume goods and services. They finance their purchases by dipping into their savings accounts (past income) or using credit (future income) instead of spending current income. We also observe that people's spending sometimes changes even when income doesn't, suggesting that income isn't the only determinant of consumption. Other, *non*income determinants of consumption include

- *Expectations:* People who anticipate a pay raise, a tax refund, or a birthday check often start spending that money even before they get it. Conversely, workers who anticipate being laid off tend to save more and spend less than usual. Hence expectations may alter consumer spending before income itself changes.
- *Wealth effects:* The amount of wealth an individual owns also affects a person's ability and willingness to consume. A homeowner may take out a home equity loan to buy a flat-screen TV, a vacation, or a new car. In this case, consumer spending is being financed by wealth, not current income. Changes in wealth will also change consumer behavior. When the stock market rises, stockholders respond by saving less and spending more of their current income. This **wealth effect** was particularly evident in the late 1990s, when a persistent rise in the stock market helped fuel a consumption spree (and a negative savings rate). When the stock market plunged by 50 percent in 2008–2009, consumers cut back their spending sharply.

wealth effect: A change in consumer spending caused by a change in the value of owned assets.

Changes in housing prices have a similar effect. A five-year surge in housing prices made consumers feel rich in 2002–2006. Many homeowners tapped into those higher prices by borrowing money with home-equity loans. They used those loans to increase their consumption. When housing prices started declining in 2007, this source of consumer finance dried up. As we've already noted, this negative wealth effect contributed to the 2008–2009 recession.

- **Credit:** The availability of credit allows people to spend more than their current income. Here again, changes in credit availability or cost (interest rates) may alter consumer behavior. When banks curtailed credit in 2008, consumers had to stop buying cars and homes. When interest rates later fell, auto sales rose again.
- **Taxes:** Taxes are the wedge between total income and disposable income. The tax cuts enacted in 2001–2003 put more income into consumer hands immediately (via tax rebates) and left them with more income from future paychecks (via tax rate cuts). Tax rebates in early 2008 had the same effect: These tax reductions stimulated more aggregate demand at existing price levels. Were income taxes to go up, disposable incomes and consumer spending would decline.

Income-Dependent Consumption

In recognition of these many determinants of consumption, Keynes distinguished between two kinds of consumer spending: (1) spending *not* influenced by current income and (2) spending that *is* determined by current income. This simple categorization is summarized as

$$\text{Total consumption} = \frac{\text{Autonomous consumption}}{} + \text{Income-dependent consumption}$$

autonomous consumption: Consumer spending not dependent on current income.

where **autonomous consumption** refers to that portion of consumption spending that is independent of current income. The level of autonomous spending depends instead on expectations, wealth, credit, taxes, and other nonincome influences.

These various determinants of consumption are summarized in an equation called the **consumption function,** which is written as

$$C = a + bY_D$$

consumption function: A mathematical relationship indicating the rate of desired consumer spending at various income levels.

where C = current consumption
a = autonomous consumption
b = marginal propensity to consume
Y_D = disposable income

At first blush, the consumption function is just a mathematical summary of consumer behavior. It has important *predictive* power, however. ***The consumption function tells us***

- ***How much consumption will be included in aggregate demand at the prevailing price level.***
- ***How the consumption component of AD will change (shift) when incomes change.***

One Consumer's Behavior

To see how the consumption function works, consider the plight of Justin, a college freshman who has no income. How much will Justin spend? Obviously he must spend *something;* otherwise he'll starve. At a very low rate of income—in this case zero—consumer spending depends less on current income than on basic survival needs, past savings, and credit. The *a* in the consumption function expresses this autonomous consumption; let's assume it's $50 per week. Thus the weekly rate of consumption expenditure in this case is

$$C = \$50 + bY_D$$

Notice again that Justin has no income. So how is he able to spend $50 a week? Taking money out of his bank account (past savings), perhaps. Or using his credit card—hoping to be able to pay it off later.

Now suppose that Justin finds a job and begins earning $100 per week. Will his spending be affected? The $50 per week he'd been spending didn't buy much. Now that he's earning a little income, Justin will want to improve his lifestyle. That is, ***we expect*** *consumption to rise with income.* The marginal propensity to consume tells us how fast spending will rise.

Suppose Justin responds to the newfound income by increasing his consumption from $50 per week to $125. The change in his consumption is therefore $75. Dividing this change in his consumption ($75) by the change in income ($100) reveals that his marginal propensity to consume is 0.75.

Predictive Power. Once we know the level of autonomous consumption ($50 per week) and the marginal propensity to consume (0.75), we can predict consumer behavior with uncanny accuracy. In this case, Justin's consumption function is

$$C = \$50 + 0.75Y_D$$

With these numerical values we can advance from simple observation (what he's spending now) to prediction (what he'll spend at different income levels). Figure 9.4 summarizes this predictive power.

We've already noted that Justin will spend $125 per week when his income is only $100. This observation is summarized in row *B* of the table in Figure 9.4 and by point *B* on the graph. Notice that his spending exceeds his income by $25 at this point. The other $25 is still being begged, borrowed, or withdrawn from savings. Without peering further into Justin's personal

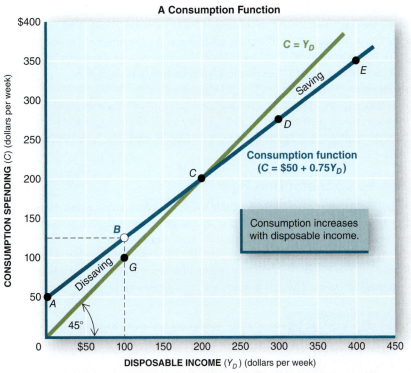

A Consumption Function

FIGURE 9.4

A Consumption Function

The rate of consumer spending (*C*) depends on autonomous consumption and disposable income (Y_D). The marginal propensity to consume indicates how much consumption will *increase* with each *added* dollar of income. In this case, when disposable income rises from $100 to $200, consumption increases by $75 (from point *B* to point *C*). The MPC = 0.75.

The consumption function can be expressed in an equation, a table, or a graph. Point *B* on the graph, for example, corresponds to row *B* in the table. Both indicate that this consumer desires to spend $125 per week when his income is $100 per week. The difference between income and consumption equals (dis)saving.

Consumption ($C = \$50 + 0.75 Y_D$)

	Disposable Income (Y_D)	Autonomous Consumption	+	Income-Dependent Consumption	=	Total Consumption
A	$ 0	$50		$ 0		$ 50
B	100	50		75		125
C	200	50		150		200
D	300	50		225		275
E	400	50		300		350
F	500	50		375		425

dissaving: Consumption expenditure in excess of disposable income; a negative saving flow.

finances, we simply say that he's **dissaving** $25 per week. *Dissaving occurs whenever current consumption exceeds current income.* As the News on page 179 revealed, dissaving is common in the United States, especially among younger people who are "livin' large."

If Justin's income continues to rise, he'll stop dissaving at some point. Perhaps he'll even start saving enough to pay back all the people who have sustained him through these difficult months. Figure 9.4 shows just how and when this will occur.

The 45-Degree Line. The green line in Figure 9.4, with a 45-degree angle, represents all points where consumption and income are exactly equal ($C = Y_D$). Recall that Justin currently has an income of $100 per week. By moving up from the horizontal axis at $Y_D = $100, we see all his consumption choices. Were he to spend exactly $100 on consumption, he'd end up on the 45-degree line at point G. But we already know he doesn't stop there. Instead he proceeds further to point B. At point B the consumption function lies *above* the 45-degree line, so Justin's spending exceeds his income; dissaving is occurring.

Observe, however, what happens when his disposable income rises to $200 per week (row C in the table in Figure 9.4). The upward slope of the consumption function (see graph) tells us that consumption spending will rise with income. In fact, *the slope of the consumption function equals the marginal propensity to consume.* In this case, we see that when income increases from $100 to $200, consumption rises from $125 (point B) to $200 (point C). Thus the change in consumption ($75) equals three-fourths of the change in income. The MPC is still 0.75.

Point C has further significance. At an income of $200 per week Justin is no longer dissaving. At point C his spending exactly equals his income. As a result, he is neither saving nor dissaving; he is breaking even. That is, disposable income equals consumption, so saving equals zero. Notice that point C lies *on* the 45-degree line, where current consumption equals current income.

What would happen to spending if income increased still further? According to Figure 9.4, Justin will start *saving* once income exceeds $200 per week. To the right of point C, the consumption function always lies below the 45-degree line. If spending is less than income, saving must be positive.

The Aggregate Consumption Function

Repeated studies of consumers suggest that there's nothing remarkable about Justin. The consumption function we've constructed for him can be used to depict all consumers simply by changing the numbers involved. Instead of dealing in hundreds of dollars per week, we now play with trillions of dollars per year. But the basic relationship is the same. As we observed earlier in Figure 9.2, we can predict consumer spending if we know how much income consumers have. That's why there are no surprises in the News below, which

IN THE NEWS

Disposable Income and Outlays: May 2014

Disposable income increased $55 billion, or 0.42 percent, in May, according to the Bureau of Economic Analysis. Personal spending increased $40 billion.

(in $ billions)	April 2014	May 2014
Disposable income	12,915	12,970
Personal outlays	12,242	12,282
Personal savings	673	688

Source: U.S. Bureau of Economic Analysis.

ANALYSIS: When household incomes increase, consumer spending increases as well. The marginal propensity to consume summarizes this relationship.

confirms that when disposable income increased in May 2014, people increased both their consumption spending and their saving. (What was the MPC? The MPS?)

Shifts of the Consumption Function

Although the consumption function is a handy device for predicting consumer behavior, it's not infallible. People change their behavior. Neither autonomous consumption (the a in the consumption function) nor the marginal propensity to consume (the b in $C = a + bY_D$) is set in stone. Whenever one of these parameters changes, the entire consumption function moves. *A change in "a"* shifts *the consumption function up or down; a change in "b" alters the* slope *of the function.*

Consider first the value for a. We noted earlier that autonomous consumption depends on wealth, credit, expectations, taxes, and price levels. If any of these nonincome determinants changes, the value of the a in the consumption function will change as well.

The plunge in consumer confidence that occurred in December 2008 illustrates how consumer behavior can change abruptly. The continued decline in home prices, mounting job losses, and a declining stock market all weighed heavily on consumer confidence. As the below News relates, one out of three consumers expected the economy to worsen further in 2009. With such dismal expectations, they became more cautious about spending their income. That caution caused autonomous consumption to decline from a_1 to a_2 in Figure 9.5, *shifting* the consumer function downward.

IN THE NEWS

Consumer Confidence Index at Record Low

The Conference Board reported yesterday that consumer confidence has plunged. The Board's closely watched Consumer Confidence Index fell to 38 in December—an all-time low. Just 16 months ago the Index stood at 111.

The deteriorating job market appeared to be the main culprit for the loss of confidence. Nearly 2 million jobs were lost this year, and unemployment is spreading. On top of that worry is the plunging stock market that is decimating household savings. Nearly one in three Americans expects business conditions to worsen further in 2009.

Source: News reports, December 2008.

ANALYSIS: When consumer confidence declines, autonomous spending drops and the consumption function shifts downward (as in Figure 9.5). This causes a leftward shift of the AD curve (as in Figure 9.6).

web click

For the latest U.S. Consumer Confidence Index value, visit **www.conference-board.org.**

Shifts of Aggregate Demand. Shifts of the consumption function are reflected in shifts of the aggregate demand curve. Consider again the December 2008 downward shift of the consumption function. A decrease in consumer spending at any given income level implies

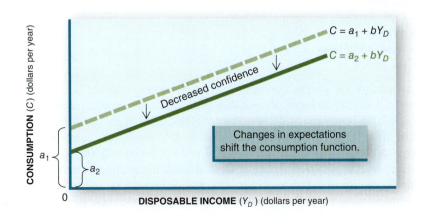

FIGURE 9.5

A Shift in the Consumption Function

Consumers' willingness to spend current income is affected by their confidence in the future. If consumers become more worried or pessimistic, autonomous consumption may decrease from a_1 to a_2. This change will shift the entire consumption function downward.

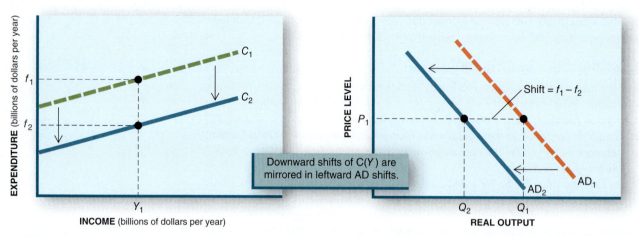

FIGURE 9.6

AD Effects of Consumption Shifts

A downward shift of the consumption function implies that households want to spend less of their income. Here consumption at the income level Y_1 decreases from f_1 to f_2. This decreased expenditure is reflected in a leftward shift of the aggregate demand curve. At the initial price level P_1 consumers demanded Q_1 output. At that same price level, consumers now demand less output, $Q_2 = [Q_1 - (f_1 - f_2)]$.

a decrease in aggregate demand as well. Recall that the aggregate demand curve depicts how much real output will be demanded at various price levels, *with income held constant.* When the consumption function shifts downward, households spend less of their income. Hence, less real output is demanded at any given price level. To summarize,

- *A downward shift of the consumption function implies a leftward shift of the aggregate demand curve.*
- *An upward shift of the consumption function implies an increase (a rightward shift) in aggregate demand.*

These relationships are illustrated in Figure 9.6.

AD Shift Factors

Keep in mind what we're doing here. Our goal is to predict consumer spending. We want to know how much consumer spending will contribute to AD at any given price level. We get that information from the consumption function. That information helps us position the AD curve correctly. Then we want to know what might cause the AD curve to *shift.* We now know that *the AD curve will shift if consumer incomes change, if autonomous consumption changes,* or if the MPC changes. Hence *the AD curve will shift in response to*

- *Changes in income.*
- *Changes in expectations* (consumer confidence).
- *Changes in wealth.*
- *Changes in credit conditions.*
- *Changes in tax policy.*

As we've seen, a recession can change incomes quickly. Consumer confidence can change even more abruptly. A decline in home prices can reduce household wealth enormously. Between 2006 and 2008 home equity declined by roughly 2 trillion dollars. The stock market decline of 2008 further eroded consumer wealth. All these forces combined to shift the AD curve to the left. The end result was the Great Recession of 2008–2009.

The wealth effect reversed in 2014. Rising home and stock-market prices greatly improved the financial situation of U.S. households. They responded with an *upward* shift of the consumption function and a *rightward* shift of the aggregate demand curve (see News).

IN THE NEWS

Wealth Effect Boosts Spending

Rising home prices are bringing smiles to America's retailers. Retail sales climbed 0.2 percent in July, marking the fourth consecutive month of increased sales, according to the U.S. Commerce Department. Analysts credit rising home prices and a surging stock market for the resurgent spending. Home prices are up 19.1 percent so far this year, and the Dow Jones Industrial Average is up 17.9 percent. As household wealth has risen, consumers have been more willing to open their wallets.

Source: U.S. Commerce Department, August 2014.

Shifts and Cycles

Clearly shifts of aggregate demand can be a cause of macro instability. As we first observed in Chapter 8, recurrent shifts of aggregate demand may cause real output to alternately expand and contract, thereby giving rise to short-run business cycles. What we've observed here is that those aggregate demand shifts may originate in consumer behavior. Changes in consumer confidence, in wealth, or in credit conditions alter the rate of consumer spending. If consumer spending increases abruptly, demand-pull inflation may follow. If consumer spending slows abruptly, a recession may occur.

Knowing that consumer behavior *might* cause macro problems is a bit worrisome. But it's also a source of policy power. What if we *want* AD to increase in order to achieve full employment? Our knowledge of consumer-based AD shift factors gives us huge clues about which macro policy tools to look for.

INVESTMENT

Consumption is only one of four AD components. To determine where AD is and whether it might shift, we need to examine the other components of spending as well.

Determinants of Investment

As we observed in Chapter 5, investment spending accounts for roughly 15 percent of total output. That spending includes not only expenditures on new plant, equipment, and business software (all referred to as *fixed investment*) but also spending on inventories (called *inventory investment*). Residential construction is also counted in investment statistics because houses and apartment buildings continue to produce housing services for decades. All these forms of **investment** represent a demand for output; they are part of aggregate demand.

Expectations. Expectations play a critical role in investment decisions. No firm wants to purchase a new plant and equipment unless it is convinced people will later buy the output produced by that plant and that equipment. Nor do producers want to accumulate inventories of goods unless they expect consumers to eventually buy them. Thus *favorable expectations of future sales are a necessary condition for investment spending.*

Interest Rates. A second determinant of investment spending is the rate of interest. Business firms typically borrow money to purchase plants and equipment. The higher the rate of interest, the costlier it is to invest. Accordingly, *we anticipate a lower rate of investment spending when interest rates are high, and more investment at lower rates,* ceteris paribus.

Technology and Innovation. A third determinant of investment is changes in technology and innovation. When scientists learned how to miniaturize electronic circuitry, an entire new industry of electronic calculators, watches, and other goods sprang to life. In this case, the demand for investment goods shifted to the right as a result of improved miniaturized circuits and imaginative innovation (the use of the new technology in pocket calculators). More recently, technological advances and cost reductions have stimulated an investment

investment: Expenditures on (production of) new plants, equipment, and structures (capital) in a given time period, plus changes in business inventories.

FIGURE 9.7

Investment Demand

The rate of desired investment depends on expectations, the rate of interest, and innovation. A *change* in expectations will *shift* the investment demand curve. With given expectations, a change in the rate of interest will lead to *movements* along the existing investment demand curve. In this case, an increase in investment beyond $150 billion per year (point *A*) may be caused by lower interest rates (point *B*) or improved expectations (point *C*).

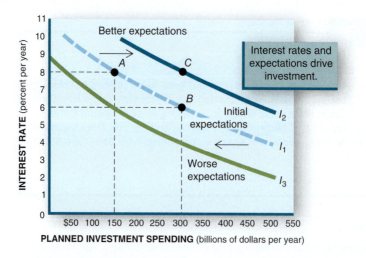

Interest rates and expectations drive investment.

spree in digital music players, laptop computers, smartphones, videoconferencing, fiber optic networks, and just about anything associated with the Internet.

The Investment Function. The curve I_1 in Figure 9.7 depicts the general shape of the investment function. To find the rate of investment spending in this figure, we first have to know the rate of interest. At an interest rate of 8 percent, for example, we expect to see $150 billion of investment (point *A* in Figure 9.7). At 6 percent interest, we'd expect $300 billion of investment (point *B*).

Shifts of Investment

As was the case with consumer spending, predicting investment spending isn't quite as easy as it first appears. Any specific investment function (like I_2 in Figure 9.7) is based on a specific set of investor expectations about future sales and profits. Those expectations can change, however.

Altered Expectations. Business expectations are essentially a question of confidence in future sales. An upsurge in current consumer spending could raise investor expectations for future sales, shifting the investment function rightward (to I_2). New business software might induce a similar response. New business tax breaks might have the same effect. If any of these things happened, businesses would be more eager to invest. They'd borrow more money at any given interest rate (e.g., point *C* in Figure 9.7) and use it to buy more plants, equipment, and inventory.

Business expectations could worsen as well. Imagine you were the CEO of a company contemplating a major expansion. Then you read a story about plunging consumer confidence, as in the News on page 185. Would you rethink your plans? Probably. That's what Panasonic's president did in January 2009 (see the World View on the next page). When *business* expectations worsen, investments get postponed or canceled. Suddenly there's less investment spending at any given interest rate. This investment shift is illustrated by the curve I_3 in Figure 9.7.

AD Shifts. As was the case with consumer behavior, we are looking at investor behavior to help us understand aggregate demand. From Figure 9.7 we see that knowledge of investor expectations and interest rates will tell us how much investment will be included in aggregate demand at the current price level. We also see that a change in expectations will alter investment behavior and thereby *shift* the AD curve. **When investment spending declines, the aggregate demand curve shifts to the left.**

Empirical Instability. Figure 9.8 shows that unstable investment is more than just a theoretical threat to macro stability. What is depicted here are the quarter-to-quarter changes in

Panasonic Cuts Spending

Panasonic Corporation yesterday announced it is slashing planned investment in two Japanese factories that make flat-screen TVs. With consumer spending declining in all its major markets, Panasonic decided to cut its investment by 23 percent over the next three years. The company now plans to invest only 445 billion yen, down from its earlier target of 580 billion yen—a cut of about $1.5 billion.

Source: News reports, January 8–10, 2009.

ANALYSIS: Business investment is based more on expected future sales than on current sales and income. When expectations for future sales growth diminish, investment spending on plants, equipment, and inventory drops.

web click

To view the volatility of investment expenditures from quarter to quarter, visit **http://research.stlouisfed.org** and search "gross private domestic investment."

both consumer spending and investor spending for the years 2000–2008. Quarterly changes in *consumer* spending never exceeded 6.5 percent and only became negative twice. By contrast, *investment* spending plummeted by 13.3 percent in the post-9/11 quarter and jumped by more than 14 percent in three other quarters. Those abrupt changes in investment (and related AD shifts) were a major cause of the 2001 recession as well as the Great Recession of 2008–2009.

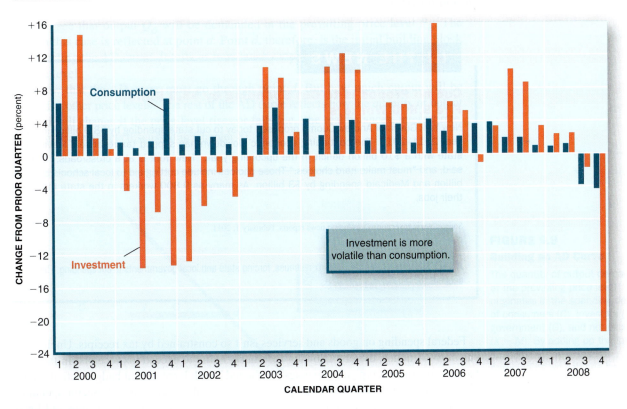

FIGURE 9.8
Volatile Investment Spending

Investment spending fluctuates more than consumption. Shown here are the quarter-to-quarter changes in the real rate of spending for fixed investment (excluding residential construction and inventory changes) and total consumption. Notice the sharp drops in investment spending just prior to the March 2001

recession and the plunge in investment that occurred in 2008. Consumption spending is far less volatile.

Source: *U.S. Bureau of Economic Analysis* (quarterly data seasonally adjusted).

MACRO FAILURE

In principle, the construction of the AD curve is simple. In practice, it requires an enormous amount of information about the intentions and behavior of market participants. Let's assume for the moment, however, that we have all that information and can therefore accurately depict the AD curve. What then?

Once we know the shape and position of the AD curve, we can put it together with the AS curve and locate macro equilibrium. Here's where our macro problems may emerge. As we noted earlier, ***there are two chief concerns about macro equilibrium:***

1. ***The market's macro equilibrium might not give us full employment or price stability.***
2. ***Even if the market's macro equilibrium were perfectly positioned (i.e., with full employment and price stability), it might not last.***

Undesired Equilibrium

Figure 9.10a depicts the perfect macro equilibrium that everyone hopes for. Aggregate demand and aggregate supply intersect at E_1. At that macro equilibrium we get both full employment (Q_F) and price stability (P^*)—an ideal situation.

Keynes didn't think such a perfect outcome was likely. Why should aggregate demand intersect with aggregate supply exactly at point E_1? As we've observed, consumers, investors, government, and foreigners make independent spending decisions, based on many influences. Why should all these decisions add up to just the right amount of aggregate demand? Keynes didn't think they would. ***Because market participants make independent spending decisions, there's no reason to expect that the sum of their expenditures will generate exactly the right amount of aggregate demand.*** Instead, there's a high likelihood that we'll confront an imbalance between desired spending and full-employment output levels—that is, too much or too little aggregate demand.

full-employment GDP: The value of total output (real GDP) produced at full employment.

Recessionary GDP Gap. Figure 9.10b illustrates one of the undesired equilibriums that Keynes worried about. **Full-employment GDP** is still at Q_F and stable prices are at the level P^*. In this case, however, the rate of output demanded at price level P^* is only Q_2, far short of full-employment GDP (Q_F). How could this happen? Quite simple: the spending

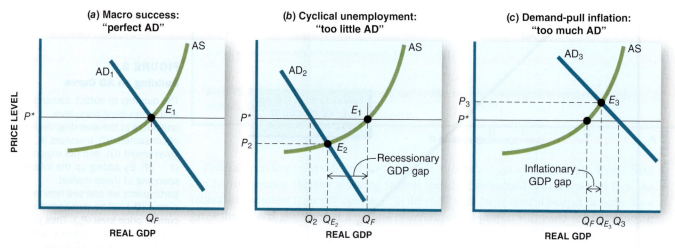

FIGURE 9.10

Macro Failures

Keynesian theory emphasizes that the combined spending decisions of consumers, investors, governments, and net exporters may not be compatible with the desired full employment (Q_F)–price stability (P^*) equilibrium (as they are in Figure a).

Aggregate demand may be too small (Figure b) or too great (Figure c), causing cyclical unemployment (b) or demand-pull inflation (c). Worse yet, even a desirable macro equilibrium (a) may be upset by abrupt shifts of aggregate demand.

plans of consumers, investors, government, and export buyers don't generate enough aggregate demand at current (P^*) prices.

The economy depicted in Figure 9.10b is in trouble. At full employment, a lot more output would be produced than market participants would be willing to buy. As unsold inventories rose, production would get cut back, workers would get laid off, and prices would decline. Eventually, the economy would settle at E_2, where AD$_2$ and AS intersect. **Equilibrium GDP** would be equal to Q_{E_2} and the equilibrium price level would be at P_2.

E_2 is clearly not a happy equilibrium. What particularly concerned Keynes was the **recessionary GDP gap,** the amount by which equilibrium GDP falls short of full-employment GDP. In Figure 9.10b, the recessionary GDP gap equals Q_F minus Q_{E_2}. This gap represents unused productive capacity: lost GDP and unemployed workers. It is the breeding ground of **cyclical unemployment,** the kind of situation President Obama confronted in 2009.

Figure 9.11 illustrates this dilemma with more numerical details on aggregate demand. The table depicts the demand for GDP at different price levels by consumers, investors, government, and net export buyers. Full-employment GDP is set at $10 trillion and the price level at 100. Producers are hoping to sell all the output produced, as indicated by

equilibrium GDP: The value of total output (real GDP) produced at macro equilibrium (AS = AD).

recessionary GDP gap: The amount by which equilibrium GDP falls short of full-employment GDP.

cyclical unemployment: Unemployment attributable to a lack of job vacancies—that is, to inadequate aggregate demand.

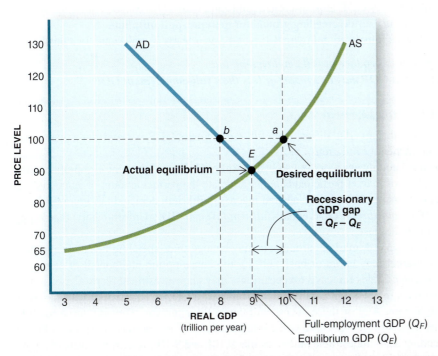

FIGURE 9.11

A Recessionary GDP Gap

The level of aggregate demand depends on the spending behavior of market participants. In this case, the level of GDP demanded at current (P = 100) prices ($8 trillion) is less than full-employment GDP ($10 trillion). More output is being produced (point a) than purchased (point b) at prevailing prices. This results in a lower *equilibrium* GDP ($9 trillion) and a recessionary GDP gap ($1 trillion). The price level also declines from 100 to 90.

	Real GDP Demanded (in $ trillions) by:					
Price Level	Consumers +	Investors +	Government +	Net Exports =	Aggregate Demand	Aggregate Supply
130	3.0	0.25	1.5	0.25	5.0	12.0
120	3.5	0.50	1.5	0.50	6.0	11.5
110	4.0	0.75	1.5	0.75	7.0	11.0
100	4.5	1.0	1.5	1.0	8.0	10.0
90	5.0	1.25	1.5	1.25	9.0	9.0
80	5.5	1.50	1.5	1.50	10.0	7.0
70	6.0	1.75	1.5	1.75	11.0	5.0
60	6.5	2.0	1.5	2.0	12.0	3.0

point *a* on the graph. As is evident, however, the quantity of output demanded at that price level is only $8 trillion (point *b* in Figure 9.11). This shortfall of aggregate demand will lead to output and price reductions, pushing the economy downward to the equilibrium GDP at point *E*. At that AS = AD intersection, the *equilibrium* GDP is at $9 trillion, with a price level of 90. The recessionary GDP gap is therefore $1 trillion $(Q_F - Q_E)$. The economy's output is $1 trillion less than its full-employment potential. This recessionary gap spells job losses and economic misery.

Inflationary GDP Gap. Aggregate demand won't always fall short of potential output. But Keynes saw it as a distinct possibility. He also realized that aggregate demand might even *exceed* the economy's full-employment/price stability capacity. This contingency is illustrated in Figure 9.10*c*.

In Figure 9.10*c*, the AD_3 curve represents the combined spending plans of all market participants. According to this aggregate demand curve, market participants demand more output (Q_3) at current prices than the economy can produce (Q_F). To meet this excessive demand, producers will use overtime shifts and strain capacity. This will push prices up. The economy will end up at the macro equilibrium E_3. At E_3 the price level is higher (inflation) and short-run output exceeds sustainable levels.

What we end up with in Figure 9.10*c* is another undesirable equilibrium. In this case we have an **inflationary GDP gap,** wherein equilibrium GDP (Q_{E_3}) exceeds full-employment GDP (Q_F). This is a fertile breeding ground for **demand-pull inflation.**

The GDP gaps illustrated in Figure 9.10*b* and *c* are clearly troublesome. In a nutshell,

- *The goal is to produce at full employment, but*
- *Equilibrium GDP may be greater or less than full-employment GDP.*

Unstable Equilibrium

Whenever equilibrium GDP differs from full-employment GDP, we confront a macro failure (unemployment or inflation).

Things need not always work out so badly. Although Keynes thought it improbable, the spending plans of market participants *might* generate the perfect amount of aggregate demand, leaving the economy at the desired macro equilibrium depicted in Figure 9.10*a*. In Figure 9.10*a*, *equilibrium* GDP equals *full-employment* GDP. Unfortunately, that happy outcome might not last.

As we've observed, market participants may change their spending behavior abruptly. The stock market may boom or bust, shifting the consumption component of aggregate demand. Changed sales forecasts (expectations) may alter investment plans. Crises in foreign economies may disrupt export sales. A terrorist attack or outbreak of war may rock everybody's boat. Any of these events will cause the aggregate demand curve to shift. When this happens, the AD curve will get knocked out of its "perfect" position in Figure 9.10*a*, sending us to undesirable outcomes like 9.10*b* and 9.10*c*. Recurrent shifts of aggregate demand could even cause a **business cycle.**

Macro Failures

Economies can get into macro trouble from the supply side of the market place as well, as we'll see later (Chapter 16). Keynes's emphasis on demand-side inadequacies serves as an early warning of potential macro failure, however. *If aggregate demand is too little, too great, or too unstable, the economy will not reach and maintain the goals of full employment and price stability.*

Self-Adjustment?

As we noted earlier, not everyone is as pessimistic as Keynes was about the prospects for macro bliss. The critical question is not whether undesirable outcomes might *occur* but whether they'll *persist*. In other words, the seriousness of any short-run macro failure

inflationary GDP gap: The amount by which equilibrium GDP exceeds full-employment GDP.

demand-pull inflation: An increase in the price level initiated by excessive aggregate demand.

business cycle: Alternating periods of economic growth and contraction.

depends on how markets *respond* to GDP gaps. If markets self-adjust, as classical economists asserted, then macro failures would be temporary.

How might markets self-adjust? If investors stepped up *their* spending whenever consumer spending faltered, the right amount of aggregate demand could be maintained. Such self-adjustment requires that some components of aggregate demand shift in the right direction at just the right time. In other words, *macro self-adjustment requires that any shortfalls in one component of aggregate demand be offset by spending in another component*. If such offsetting shifts occurred, then the desired macro equilibrium in Figure 9.10*a* could be maintained. Keynes didn't think that likely, however, for reasons we'll explore in the next chapter.

THE ECONOMY TOMORROW

ANTICIPATING AD SHIFTS

The Index of Leading Indicators. Keynes's theory of macro failure gave economic policymakers a lot to worry about. If Keynes was right, abrupt changes in aggregate demand could ruin even the best of economic times. Even if he was wrong about the ability of the economy to self-adjust, sudden shifts of aggregate demand could cause a lot of temporary pain. To minimize such pain, **policymakers need some way of peering into the future— to foresee shifts of aggregate demand.** With such a crystal ball, they might be able to take defensive actions and keep the economy on track.

Market participants have developed all kinds of crystal balls for anticipating AD shifts. The Foundation for the Study of Cycles has identified 4,000 different crystal balls people use to foretell changes in spending. They include the ratio of used car to new car sales (it rises in economic downturns); the number of divorce petitions (it rises in bad times); animal population cycles (they peak just before economic downturns); and even the optimism/ pessimism content of popular music (a reflection of consumer confidence).

One of the more conventional crystal balls is the Leading Economic Index (LEI). The index includes 10 gauges that are supposed to indicate in what direction the economy is moving. What's appealing about the LEI is the plausible connection between its components and future spending. Equipment orders, for example, are one of the leading indicators (number 5 in Table 9.2). This seems reasonable since businesses don't order equipment

Indicator	Expected Impact
1. Average workweek	Hours worked per week typically increase when greater output and sales are expected.
2. Unemployment claims	Initial claims for unemployment benefits reflect changes in industry layoffs.
3. New orders	New orders for consumer goods trigger increases in production and employment.
4. Delivery times	The longer it takes to deliver ordered goods, the greater the ratio of demand to supply.
5. Equipment orders	Orders for new equipment imply increased production capacity and higher anticipated sales.
6. Building permits	A permit represents the first step in housing construction.
7. Stock prices	Higher stock prices reflect expectations of greater sales and profits.
8. Money supply	Faster growth of the money supply implies a pickup in aggregate demand.
9. Interest rates	Larger differences between long- and short-term rates indicate faster growth.
10. Consumer confidence	Optimism spurs more consumer spending.

TABLE 9.2

The Leading Economic Indicators

Everyone wants a crystal ball to foresee economic events. In reality, forecasters must reckon with very crude predictors of the future. One of the most widely used predictors is the Leading Economic Index, which includes 10 factors believed to predict economic activity 3 to 6 months in advance. Changes in the leading indicators are used to forecast changes in GDP.

The leading indicators rarely move in the same direction at the same time. They're weighted together to create the index. Up-and-down movements of the index are reported each month by the nonprofit Conference Board.

unless they later plan to buy it. The same is true of building permits (indicator 6); people obtain permits only if they plan to build something. Hence both indicators appear to be dependable signs of future investment. That's why an uptick in the LEI is viewed as good news for the economy (see the accompanying News).

Unfortunately, the leading indicators aren't a perfect crystal ball. Equipment orders are often canceled. Building plans get delayed or abandoned. Hence shifts of aggregate demand still occur without warning. No crystal ball could predict a terrorist strike or the timing and magnitude of a natural disaster. Compared to other crystal balls, however, the LEI has a pretty good track record—and a very big audience. It helps investors and policymakers foresee what aggregate demand in the economy tomorrow might look like.

IN THE NEWS

U.S. Leading Indicators Signal Continuing Recovery

The Conference Board Leading Economic Index® (LEI) for the United States increased 0.3 percent in June to 102.2 (2004 = 100), following a 0.7 percent increase in May and a 0.3 percent increase in April.

"Broad-based increases in the LEI over the last six months signal an economy that is expanding in the near term and may even somewhat accelerate in the second half," said Ataman Ozyildirim, economist at The Conference Board. "Housing permits, the weakest indicator during this period, reflects some risk to this improving outlook. But favorable financial conditions, generally positive trends in the labor markets and the outlook for new orders in manufacturing have offset the housing market weakness over the past six months."

Source: Conference Board, **www.conference-board.org**, July 18, 2014.

ANALYSIS: Market participants try to predict the economic outlook with measurable indicators like new orders and building permits.

web click

See **www.conference-board.org** for details and updates on the LEI.

SUMMARY

- Macro failure occurs when the economy fails to achieve full employment and price stability. **LO9-5**
- Too much or too little aggregate demand can cause macro failure. Too little aggregate demand causes cyclical unemployment; too much aggregate demand causes demand-pull inflation. **LO9-5**
- Aggregate demand reflects the spending plans of consumers (C), investors (I), government (G), and foreign buyers (net exports = $X - M$). **LO9-1**
- Consumer spending is affected by nonincome (autonomous) factors and current income, as summarized in the consumption function: $C = a + bY_D$. **LO9-2**
- Autonomous consumption (a) depends on wealth, expectations, taxes, credit, and price levels. Income-dependent consumption depends on the marginal propensity to consume (MPC), the b in the consumption function. **LO9-2**
- Consumer saving is the difference between disposable income and consumption (that is, $S = Y_D - C$). All disposable income is either spent (C) or saved (S). **LO9-1**

- The consumption function shifts up or down when autonomous influences such as wealth and expectations change. **LO9-2**
- The AD curve shifts left or right whenever the consumption function shifts up or down. **LO9-4**
- Investment spending depends on interest rates, expectations for future sales, and innovation. *Changes in investment spending will also shift the AD curve.* **LO9-3**
- Government spending and net exports are influenced by a variety of cyclical and noncyclical factors and may also change abruptly. **LO9-1**
- Even a "perfect" macro equilibrium may be upset by abrupt shifts of spending behavior. Recurrent shifts of the AD curve may cause a business cycle. **LO9-5**

Key Terms

aggregate demand	marginal propensity to consume (MPC)	full-employment GDP
aggregate supply	marginal propensity to save (MPS)	equilibrium GDP
equilibrium (macro)	wealth effect	recessionary GDP gap
consumption	autonomous consumption	cyclical unemployment
disposable income	consumption function	inflationary GDP gap
saving	dissaving	demand-pull inflation
average propensity to consume (APC)	investment	business cycle

Questions for Discussion

1. What percentage of last month's income did you spend? How much more would you spend if you won a $1,000 lottery prize? Why might your average and marginal propensities to consume differ?   **LO9-2**

2. Why do rich people have a higher marginal propensity to save than poor people?   **LO9-2**

3. How do households dissave? Where do they get the money to finance their extra consumption? Can everyone dissave at the same time?   **LO9-2**

4. Why would an *employed* consumer cut spending when other workers were being laid off (see News, p. 185)?   **LO9-2**

5. According to the World View on page 189, why did Panasonic cut investment spending in 2009? Was this a rational response?   **LO9-3**

6. Why did New York Governor Cuomo cut state spending in 2011–2012? How did that affect AD? (See News, p. 190.)   **LO9-4**

7. Why are declining housing permits considered a negative leading indicator? (See News, p. 196.)   **LO9-5**

8. Why wouldn't market participants always want to buy all the output produced?   **LO9-5**

9. If an inflationary GDP gap exists, what will happen to business inventories. How will producers respond?   **LO9-5**

10. How might a "perfect" macro equilibrium (Figure 9.10*a*) be affected by (a) a stock market crash, (b) rising home prices, (c) a recession in Canada, and (d) a spike in oil prices?   **LO9-1, LO9-5**

 mobile app Visit your mobile app store and download the Schiller: Study Econ app *today*!

APPENDIX

THE KEYNESIAN CROSS

The Keynesian view of the macro economy emphasizes the potential instability of the private sector and the undependability of a market-driven self-adjustment. We have illustrated this theory with shifts of the AD curve and resulting real GDP gaps. The advantage of the AS/AD model is that it illustrates how both real output and the price level are simultaneously affected by AD shifts. At the time Keynes developed his theory of instability, however, inflation was not a threat. In the Great Depression prices were *falling*. With unemployment rates reaching as high as 25 percent, no one worried that increased aggregate demand would push price levels up. The only concern was to get back to full employment.

Because inflation was not seen as an immediate threat, early depictions of Keynesian theory didn't use the AS/AD model. Instead they used a different graph called the "Keynesian cross." *The Keynesian cross focuses on the relationship of total spending to the value of total output, without an explicit distinction between price levels and real output.* As we'll see, the Keynesian cross doesn't change any conclusions we've come to about macro instability. It simply offers an alternative, and historically important, framework for explaining macro outcomes.

Focus on Aggregate Expenditure

Keynes said that in a really depressed economy we could focus exclusively on the rate of *spending* in the economy without distinguishing between real output and price levels. All he worried about was whether **aggregate expenditure**—the sum of consumer, investor, government, and net export buyers' spending plans—would be compatible with the dollar value of full-employment output.

aggregate expenditure: The rate of total expenditure desired at alternative levels of income, *ceteris paribus.*

For Keynes, the critical question was how much each group of market participants would spend at different levels of nominal *income.* As we saw earlier, Keynes showed that consumer spending directly varies with the level of income. That's why the consumption function in Figure 9.4 had *spending* on the vertical axis and nominal *income* on the horizontal axis.

Figure 9A.1 puts the consumption function into the larger context of the macro economy. In this figure, the focus is exclusively on *nominal* incomes and spending. Y_F indicates the dollar value of full-employment output at current prices. In this figure, $3,000 billion is assumed to be the value of Y_F. The 45-degree line shows all points where total spending equals total income.

The consumption function in Figure 9A.1 is the same one we used before, namely

$$C = \$100 + 0.75(Y_D)$$

Notice again that consumers *dissave* at lower income levels but *save* at higher income levels.

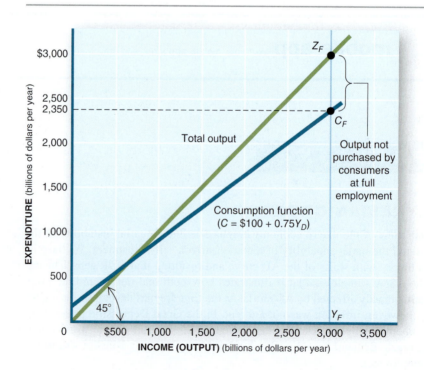

FIGURE 9A.1

The Consumption Shortfall

To determine how much output consumers will demand at full-employment output (Y_F), we refer to the consumption function. First locate full-employment output on the horizontal axis (at Y_F). Then move up until you reach the consumption function. In this case, the amount C_F (equal to $2,350 billion per year) will be demanded at full-employment output ($3,000 billion per year). This leaves $650 billion of output not purchased by consumers.

The Consumption Shortfall

What particularly worried Keynes was the level of intended consumption at full employment. At full employment, $3 trillion of income (output) is generated. But consumers plan to spend only

$$C = \$100 + 0.75(\$3{,}000 \text{ billion}) = \$2{,}350 \text{ billion}$$

and save the rest ($650 billion).[1] Were product market sales totally dependent on consumers, this economy would be in trouble: Consumer spending falls short of full-employment output. In Figure 9A.1, this consumption shortfall is the vertical difference between points Z_F and C_F.

Nonconsumer Spending

The evident shortfall in consumer spending need not doom the economy to macro failure. There are other market participants, and their spending will add to aggregate expenditure. Keynes, however, emphasized that the spending decisions of investors, governments, and net export buyers are made independently. They *might* add up to just the right amount—or they might not.

To determine how much other market participants might spend, we'd have to examine their behavior. Suppose we did so and ended up with the information in Figure 9A.2. The data in that figure reveal how many dollars will be spent at various income levels. By vertically stacking these expenditure components, we can draw an *aggregate* (total) expenditure curve as in Figure 9A.2. The aggregate expenditure curve shows how *total* spending varies with income.

A Recessionary Gap

Keynes used the aggregate expenditure curve to assess the potential for macro failure. He was particularly interested in determining how much market participants would spend if the economy were producing at full-employment capacity.

With the information in Figure 9A.2, it is easy to answer that question. At full employment (Y_F), total income is $3,000 billion. From the table, we see that total spending at that income level is

Consumer spending at	$Y_F = \$100 + 0.75(\$3{,}000) =$	$2,350
Investment spending at	Y_F =	150
Government spending at	Y_F =	200
Net export spending at	Y_F =	50
Aggregate spending at	Y_F =	$2,750

In this case, we end up with less aggregate expenditure in product markets ($2,750 billion) than the value of full-employment output ($3,000 billion). This is illustrated in Figure 9A.2 by point *f* on the graph and row *f* in the table.

The economy illustrated in Figure 9A.2 is in trouble. If full employment were achieved, it wouldn't last. At full employment, $3,000 billion of output would be produced. But only $2,750 of output would be sold. There isn't enough aggregate

---

[1] In principle, we first have to determine how much *disposable* income is generated by any given level of *total* income, then use the consumption function to determine how much consumption occurs. If Y_D is a constant percentage of Y, this two-step computation boils down to

$$Y_D = dY$$

where d = the share of total income received as disposable income, and

$$C = a + b(dY)$$
$$= a + (b \times d)Y$$

The term ($b \times d$) is the marginal propensity to consume out of *total* income.

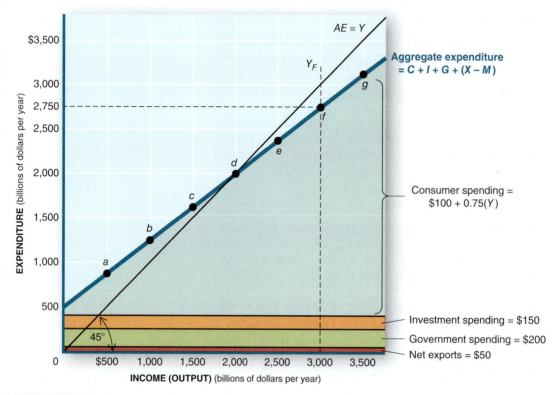

FIGURE 9A.2

Aggregate Expenditure

The aggregate expenditure curve depicts the desired spending of market participants at various income (output) levels. In this case, *I, G,* and (*X* − *M*) don't vary with income, but *C* does. Adding these four components gives us total desired spending. If total income were $1,000 billion, desired spending would total $1,250 billion, as shown in row *b* in the table and by point *b* in the graph.

	At Income (Output) of	Consumers Desire to Spend	+	Investors Desire to Spend	+	Governments Desire to Spend	+	Net Export Spending	=	Aggregate Expenditure
a	$ 500	$ 475		$150		$200		$50		$ 875
b	1,000	850		150		200		50		1,250
c	1,500	1,225		150		200		50		1,625
d	2,000	1,600		150		200		50		2,000
e	2,500	1,975		150		200		50		2,375
f	3,000	2,350		150		200		50		2,750
g	3,500	2,725		150		200		50		3,125

recessionary gap: The amount by which aggregate spending at full employment falls short of full-employment output.

expenditure at current price levels to sustain full employment. As a result, $250 billion of unsold output piles up in warehouses and on store shelves. That unwanted inventory is a harbinger of trouble.

The difference between full-employment output and desired spending at full employment is called a **recessionary gap.** Not enough output is willingly purchased at full employment to sustain the economy. Producers may react to the spending shortfall by cutting back on production and laying off workers.

A Single Equilibrium. You might wonder whether the planned spending of market participants would ever be exactly equal to the value of output. It will, but not necessarily at the rate of output we seek.

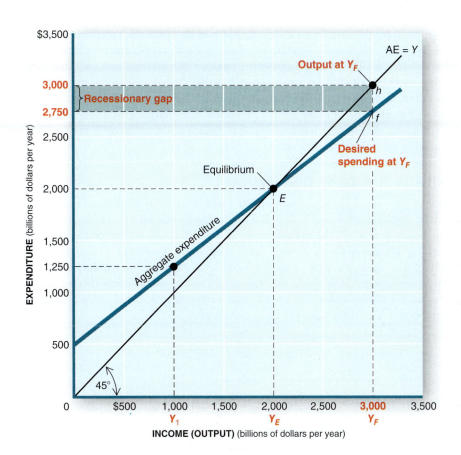

FIGURE 9A.3

Expenditure Equilibrium

There's only one rate of output at which desired expenditure equals the value of output. This expenditure equilibrium occurs at point *E,* where the aggregate expenditure and 45-degree lines intersect. At this equilibrium, $2,000 billion of output is produced and willingly purchased.

At full-employment output (Y_F = $3,000), aggregate expenditure is only $2,750 billion. This spending shortfall leaves $250 billion of output unsold. The difference between full-employment output (point *h*) and desired spending at full employment (point *f*) is called the recessionary gap.

Figure 9A.3 illustrates where this **expenditure equilibrium** exists. Recall the significance of the 45-degree line in that figure. The 45-degree line represents all points where expenditure *equals* income. At any point on this line there would be no difference between total spending and the value of output.

The juxtaposition of the aggregate expenditure function with the 45-degree line is called the Keynesian cross. *The Keynesian cross relates aggregate expenditure to total income (output) without explicit consideration of (changing) price levels.* As is evident in Figure 9A.3, the aggregate expenditure curve crosses the 45-degree line only once, at point *E.* At that point, therefore, desired spending is *exactly* equal to the value of output. In Figure 9A.3 this equilibrium occurs at an output rate of $2,000 billion. Notice in the accompanying table how much market participants desire to spend at that rate of output. We have

Consumer spending at	Y_E = $100 + 0.75($2,000) =	$1,600
Investment spending at	Y_E =	150
Government spending at	Y_E =	200
Net export spending at	Y_E =	50
Aggregate spending at	Y_E =	$2,000

At Y_E we have spending behavior that's completely compatible with the rate of production. At this equilibrium rate of output, no goods remain unsold. At that one rate of output where desired spending and the value of output are exactly equal, an expenditure equilibrium exists. *At macro equilibrium producers have no incentive to change the rate of output because they're selling everything they produce.*

Macro Failure

Unfortunately, the equilibrium depicted in Figure 9A.3 isn't the one we hoped to achieve. At Y_E the economy is well short of its full-employment goal (Y_F).

expenditure equilibrium: The rate of output at which desired spending equals the value of output.

inflationary gap: The amount by which aggregate spending at full employment exceeds full-employment output.

The expenditure equilibrium won't always fall short of the economy's productive capacity. Indeed, market participants' spending desires could also *exceed* the economy's full-employment potential. This might happen if investors, the government, or foreigners wanted to buy more output or if the consumption function shifted upward. In such circumstances an **inflationary gap** would exist. An inflationary gap arises when market participants want to buy more output than can be produced at full employment. The resulting scramble for goods may start a bidding war that pushes price levels even higher. This would be another symptom of macro failure.

Two Paths to the Same Conclusion

The Keynesian analysis of aggregate *expenditure* looks remarkably similar to the Keynesian analysis of aggregate *demand*. In fact, it is: both approaches lead to the same conclusions about macro instability. The key difference between the "old" (expenditure) analysis and the "new" (AD) analysis is the level of detail about macro outcomes. In the old aggregate expenditure analysis, the focus was simply on total spending, the product of output and prices. ***In the newer AD analysis, the separate effects of macro instability on prices and real output are distinguished.***[2] In a world where changes in both real output and price levels are important, the AD/AS framework is more useful.

Key Terms

aggregate expenditure   expenditure equilibrium   inflationary gap
recessionary gap

---

[2]This distinction is reflected in the differing definitions for the traditional *recessionary gap* (the *spending* shortfall at full-employment income) and the newer *recessionary real GDP gap* (the real output gap between full-employment GDP and equilibrium GDP).

LO9-2 1. From the information on pages 179–81, in 2013 what was
    (*a*) The APC?   _____
    (*b*) The APS?   _____
    (*c*) The MPC?   _____
    (*d*) The MPS?   _____

LO9-2 2. According to the News on page 184, by how much did
    (*a*) Disposable income increase?   _____
    (*b*) Consumption increase?   _____
    (*c*) Savings increase?   _____
    (*d*) What was the MPC?   _____
    (*e*) What was the MPS?   _____
    (*f*) What was the APC?   _____

LO9-2
LO9-4 3. On the accompanying graph, draw the consumption function $C = \$300 + 0.50Y_D$.
    (*a*) At what level of income do households begin to save?
        Designate that point on the graph with the letter *A*.   _____
    (*b*) By how much does consumption increase when income rises $100 beyond point *A*?
        Designate this new level of consumption with point *B*.   _____
    (*c*) Illustrate the impact on consumption of the change in consumer confidence described in the
        News on page 185.

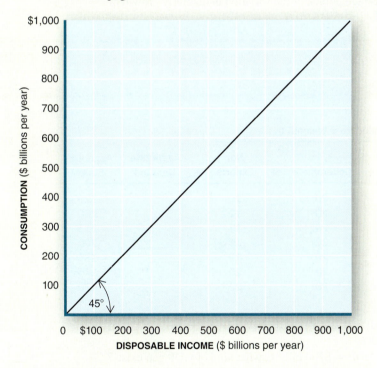

LO9-4 4. Illustrate on the following two graphs the impact of increased consumer confidence.

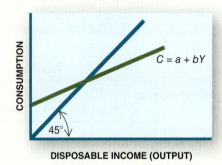

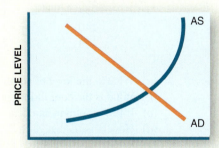

What direction did
(*a*) The consumption function shift?   _____
(*b*) AD shift?   _____

LO9-4 5. If every $1,000 increase in the real price of homes adds 7 cents to annual consumer spending (the "wealth effect"), by how much did consumption *decline* when home prices fell by $2 trillion in 2006–2008?

_____

LO9-3 6. Illustrate on the following graphs the impact of Panasonic's changed investment plans (World View, p. 189).

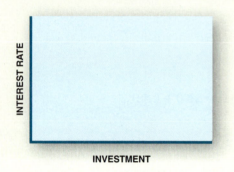

INVESTMENT

REAL OUTPUT

LO9-4 7. What was the range, in absolute percentage points, of the variation in quarterly growth rates between 2005 and 2008 of
(*a*) Consumer spending?

_____

(*b*) Investment spending?

_____

(*Note:* See Figure 9.8 for data.)

LO9-5 8. Complete the following table:

Price Level	Real Output Demanded (in $ billions) by				Aggregate Demand	Aggregate Supply
	Consumers +	Investors +	Government +	Net Exports +		
120	80	15	20	10	___	320
110	92	16	20	12	___	260
100	104	17	20	14	___	215
90	116	18	20	16	___	200
80	128	19	20	18	___	185
70	140	20	20	20	___	175
60	154	21	20	22	___	170

(*a*) What is the level of equilibrium GDP?

_____

(*b*) What is the equilibrium price level?

_____

(*c*) If full employment occurs at real GDP = $200 billion, what kind of GDP gap exists?

_____

(*d*) How large is that gap?

_____

(*e*) Which macro problem exists here (unemployment or inflation)?

_____

LO9-1
LO9-5

9. On the following graph, draw the AD and AS curves with these data: _____

Price level	140	130	120	110	100	90	80	70	60	50
Real output										
Demanded	600	700	800	900	1,000	1,100	1,200	1,300	1,400	1,500
Supplied	1,200	1,150	1,100	1,050	1,000	950	900	800	600	400

(a) What is the equilibrium
    (i) Real output level?
    (ii) Price level?   _____
                                                         _____

Suppose net exports decline by $100 at all price levels, but all other components of aggregate demand remain constant.

(b) Draw the new AD curve.
(c) What is the new equilibrium
    (i) Output level?
    (ii) Price level?   _____
                                                            _____

(d) What macro problem has arisen in this economy: (A) unemployment or (B) inflation?   _____

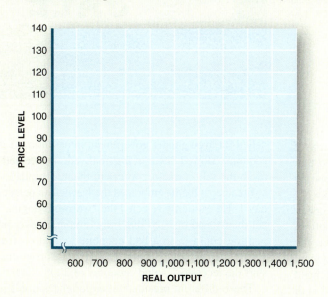

Self-Adjustment or Instability?

After reading this chapter, you should know

LO10-1 The sources of circular flow leakages and injections.

LO10-2 What the multiplier is and how it works.

LO10-3 How recessionary and inflationary GDP gaps arise.

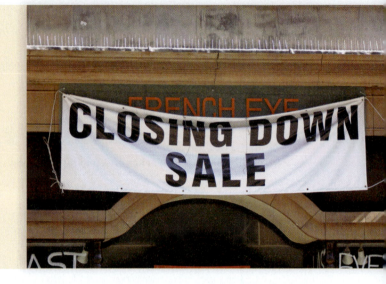

John Maynard Keynes took a dim view of a market-driven macro economy. He emphasized that (1) macro failure is likely to occur in such an economy and, worse yet, (2) macro failure isn't likely to go away. As noted earlier, the first prediction wasn't all that controversial. The classical economists had conceded the possibility of occasional recession or inflation. In their view, however, the economy would quickly self-adjust, restoring full employment and price stability. Keynes's second proposition challenged this view. The most distinctive, and frightening, proposition of Keynes's theory was that there would be no automatic self-adjustment; the economy could stagnate in *persistent* unemployment or be subjected to *continuing* inflation.

President Herbert Hoover was a believer in the market's ability to self-adjust. So was President George H. Bush. As Hoover and Bush Sr. waited for the economy to self-adjust, however, they both lost their reelection bids. President George W. Bush wasn't willing to take that chance. As soon as he was elected, he pushed tax cuts through Congress that boosted consumer disposable incomes and helped bolster a sagging economy. After the terrorist attacks of September 11, 2001, he

called for even greater government intervention. Yet when the economy slowed down in his final year, he seemed willing to await the self-correcting forces of the marketplace.

President Obama embraced the Keynesian perspective from day 1. He explicitly rejected the "worn-out dogma" of classical theory and insisted that only dramatic government intervention could keep a bad economic situation from getting worse. He advocated massive spending programs to jump-start the recession-bound economy of 2008–2009.

These different presidential experiences don't resolve the self-adjustment debate; rather, they emphasize how important the debate is. In this chapter we'll focus on the *adjustment process*—that is, how markets *respond* to an undesirable equilibrium. We're especially concerned with the following questions:

- **Why does anyone think the market might self-adjust (returning to a desired equilibrium)?**
- **Why might markets *not* self-adjust?**
- **Could market responses actually *worsen* macro outcomes?**

LEAKAGES AND INJECTIONS

Chapter 9 demonstrated how the economy could end up at the wrong macro equilibrium—with too much or too little aggregate demand. Such an undesirable outcome might result from an initial imbalance between **aggregate demand** at the current price level and full-employment GDP. Or the economy could fall into trouble from a *shift* in aggregate demand that pushes the economy out of a desirable full-employment–price-stability equilibrium. Whatever the sequence of events might be, the bottom line is the same: total spending doesn't match total output at the desired full-employment–price-stability level.

The Circular Flow. The circular flow of income illustrates how such an undesirable outcome comes about. Recall that all income originates in product markets, where goods and services are sold. If the economy were producing at **full-employment GDP,** then enough income would be available to buy everything a fully employed economy produces. As we've seen, however, aggregate demand isn't so certain. It could happen that market participants choose *not* to spend all their income, leaving some goods unsold. Alternatively, they might try to buy *more* than full-employment output, pushing prices up.

To see how such imbalances might arise, Keynes distinguished *leakages* from the circular flow and *injections* into that flow, as illustrated in Figure 10.1.

Consumer Saving

As we observed in Chapter 9, consumers typically don't spend *all* the income they earn in product markets; they *save* some fraction of it. This is the first leak in the circular flow. Some income earned in product markets isn't being instantly converted into spending. This circular flow **leakage** creates the potential for a spending shortfall.

Suppose the economy were producing at full employment, with $3,000 billion of output at the current price level, indexed at $P = 100$. This initial output rate is marked by point F

aggregate demand (AD): The total quantity of output demanded at alternative price levels in a given time period, *ceteris paribus.*

full-employment GDP: The value of total output (real GDP) produced at full employment.

leakage: Income not spent directly on domestic output but instead diverted from the circular flow—for example, saving, imports, taxes.

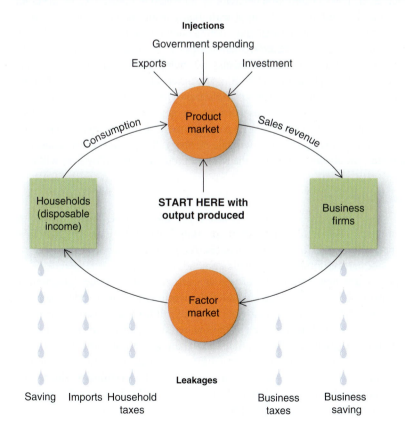

FIGURE 10.1
Leakages and Injections

The income generated in production doesn't return completely to product markets in the form of consumer spending. Consumer saving, imports, taxes, and business saving all leak from the circular flow, *reducing* potential aggregate demand. If this leakage isn't offset, some of the output produced will remain unsold.

Business investment, government purchases of goods and services, and exports inject spending into the circular flow, *adding* to aggregate demand. The focus of macro concern is whether injections will offset leakage at full employment.

FIGURE 10.2

Leakage and AD

The disposable income consumers receive is only about 70 percent of total income (GDP) due to taxes and income held by businesses. Consumers also tend to save some of their disposable income and buy imported products. As a result of these leakages, consumers will demand less output at the current price level ($P = 100$) than the economy produces at full-employment GDP (Q_F). In this case, $3,000 billion of output (income) is produced (point F), but consumers demand only $2,350 billion of output at the price level $P = 100$ (point C_F).

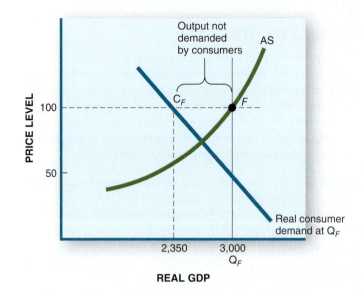

in Figure 10.2. Suppose further that *all* of the income generated in product markets went to consumers. In that case, would consumers *spend* enough to *maintain* full employment? We already observed in Chapter 9 that such an outcome is unlikely. Typically, consumers *save* a small fraction of their incomes.

If the consumption function were $C_F = \$100$ billion $+ 0.75Y$, consumers will spend only

$$C_F = \$100 \text{ billion} + 0.75(\$3,000 \text{ billion})$$
$$= \$2,350 \text{ billion}$$

at the current price level. This consumption behavior is illustrated in Figure 10.2 by the point C_F. Consumers would demand more real output with their current income if prices were to fall (due to the real balances, foreign trade, and interest rate effects, pages 162–64). Hence the consumption component of aggregate demand slopes downward from point C_F. Our immediate concern, however, focuses on how much (real) output consumers will purchase at the *current* price level. At the price level $P = 100$ consumers choose to save $650 billion, leaving consumption ($2,350 billion) far short of full-employment GDP ($3,000 billion).

The decision to save some fraction of household income isn't necessarily bad, but it does present a potential problem. Unless other market participants, such as business, government, and foreigners, buy this unsold output, goods will pile up on producers' shelves. As undesired inventory accumulates, producers will reduce the rate of output and unemployment will rise.

Imports and Taxes

Saving isn't the only source of leakage. ***Imports also represent leakage from the circular flow.*** When consumers buy imported goods, their spending leaves (that is, leaks out of) the domestic circular flow and goes to foreign producers. As a consequence, income spent on imported goods is not part of domestic aggregate demand.

In the real world, ***taxes are a form of leakage as well.*** A lot of revenue generated in market sales gets diverted into federal, state, and local government coffers. Sales taxes are taken out of the circular flow in product markets. Then payroll taxes and income taxes are taken out of paychecks. Households never get the chance to spend any of that income. They start with **disposable income,** which is much less than the total income generated in product markets. In 2013, disposable income was only $12.5 trillion while total income (GDP) was $16.8 trillion. Hence consumers couldn't have bought everything produced that year with their current incomes even if they had saved nothing. Their disposable income was $4.3 trillion less than the value of output produced.

disposable income: After-tax income of consumers; personal income less personal taxes.

Business Saving

The business sector keeps some of the income generated in product markets. Businesses set aside some of their revenue to cover the costs of maintaining, repairing, and replacing plants and equipment. The revenue held aside for these purposes is called a *depreciation allowance*. In addition, corporations keep some part of total profit (retained earnings) for continuing business uses rather than paying all profits out to stockholders in the form of dividends. The total value of depreciation allowances and retained earnings is called **gross business saving.** The income businesses hold back in these forms represents further leakage from the circular flow—income that consumers never see and that doesn't automatically flow directly back into product markets.

Although leakage from the circular flow is a potential source of unemployment problems, we shouldn't conclude that the economy will sink as soon as consumers start saving some of their income, buy a few imports, or pay their taxes. Consumers aren't the only source of aggregate demand; business firms and government agencies also contribute to total spending. So do international consumers who buy our exports. So before we run out into the streets and scream, "The circular flow is leaking!" we need to look at what other market participants are doing.

Injections into the Circular Flow

The top half of Figure 10.1 completes the picture of the circular flow by depicting **injections** of new spending. When businesses buy plants and equipment, they add to the dollar value of product market sales. Government purchases and exports also inject spending into the product market. These *injections of investment, government, and export spending help offset leakage from saving, imports, and taxes.* As a result, there may be enough aggregate demand to maintain full employment at the current price level, even if consumers aren't spending every dollar of income.

The critical issue for macro stability is whether spending injections will actually equal spending leakage at full employment. *Injections must equal leakages if all the output supplied is to equal the output demanded* (macro equilibrium). Ideally, the economy will satisfy this condition at full employment and we can stop worrying about short-run macro problems. If not, we've still got some work to do.

Self-Adjustment?

As we noted earlier, classical economists had no worries. They assumed that spending injections would always equal spending leakage. That was the foundation of their belief in the market's self-adjustment. The mechanism they counted on for equalizing leakages and injections was the interest rate.

Flexible Interest Rates. Ignore all other injections and leakages for the moment and focus on just consumer saving and business investment (Figure 10.3). If consumer saving (a leakage) exceeds business investment (an injection), unspent income must be piling up

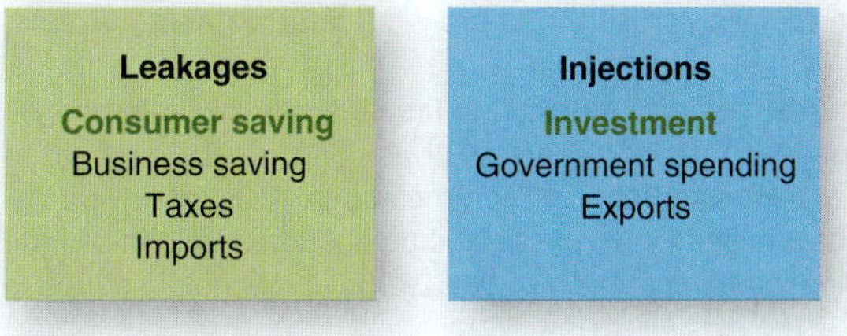

gross business saving:
Depreciation allowances and retained earnings.

injection: An addition of spending to the circular flow of income.

Leakages	Injections
Consumer saving	**Investment**
Business saving	Government spending
Taxes	Exports
Imports	

FIGURE 10.3
Leakages and Injections

Macro equilibrium is possible only if leakages equal injections. Of these, consumer saving and business investment are the primary sources of (im)balance in a wholly private and closed economy. Hence the relationship between saving and investment reveals whether a market-driven economy will self-adjust to a full-employment equilibrium.

somewhere (in bank accounts, for example). These unspent funds will be a tempting lure for business investors. Businesses are always looking for funds to finance expansion or modernization. So they aren't likely to leave a pile of consumer savings sitting idle. Moreover, the banks and other institutions that are holding consumer savings will be eager to lend more funds as consumer savings pile up. To make more loans, they can lower the interest rate. As we observed in Chapter 9 (Figure 9.7), lower interest rates prompt businesses to borrow and invest more. Hence *classical economists concluded that if interest rates fell far enough, business investment (injections) would equal consumer saving (leakage).*

From this classical perspective, any spending shortfall in the macro economy would soon be closed by this self-adjustment of leakage and injection flows. If saving leakage increased, interest rates would drop, prompting an offsetting rise in investment injections. Aggregate demand would be maintained at full-employment GDP because investment spending would soak up all consumer saving. The *content* of AD would change (less *C*, more *I*), but the *level* would remain at full-employment GDP.

Changing Expectations. Keynes argued that classical economists ignored the role of expectations. As Figure 9.7 illustrated, the level of investment *is* sensitive to interest rates. But the whole investment function *shifts* when business expectations change. Keynes thought it preposterous that investment spending would *increase* in response to *declining* consumer sales. A decline in investment is more likely, Keynes argued.

Flexible Prices. The classical economists said self-adjustment was possible even without flexible interest rates. Flexible *prices* would do the trick. Look at Figure 10.2 again. It says consumers will demand only $2,350 billion of output *at the current price level.* But what if prices *fell?* Then consumers would buy more output. In fact, if prices fell far enough, consumers might buy *all* the output produced at full employment. In Figure 10.2, the price level $P = 50$ elicits such a response. (Notice how much output is demanded at the $P = 50$ price level.)

Expectations (Again). Keynes again chided the classical economists for their naïveté. Sure, a nationwide sale might prompt consumers to buy more goods and services. But how would businesses react? They had planned on selling Q_F amount of output at the price level $P = 100$. If prices must be cut in half to move their merchandise, businesses are likely to rethink their production and investment plans. Keynes argued that declining (retail) prices would prompt businesses to invest *less,* not more. This was a real fear in 2008–2009, as the accompanying News suggests.

IN THE NEWS

Everything Is on Sale and That's Not Good

The Bureau of Labor Statistics reported that consumer prices fell in October at their fastest pace in more than 60 years. Prices were down across the board—for cars, clothes, gasoline, and electronics. Housing prices also continued to drop.

Consumers might like the short-term rewards of a nationwide fire sale. But declining prices can eventually hurt. Declining prices squeeze the profit margins of producers, causing them to cut back production and lay off workers. Retailers become more hesitant to restock inventory. A kind of downward spiral may emerge that pushes both prices and production down. This is the kind of deflationary spiral that made the Great Depression of the 1930s so painful.

Source: U.S. Bureau of Labor Statistics and news accounts of December 2008.

ANALYSIS: Deflation does make products cheaper for consumers. But declining prices also reduce business revenues, profits, and sales expectations.

THE MULTIPLIER PROCESS

Keynes not only rejected the classical notion of self-adjustment; he also argued that things were likely to get *worse,* not better, once a spending shortfall emerged. This was the scariest part of Keynes's theory.

To understand Keynes's fears, imagine that the economy is initially at the desired full-employment GDP equilibrium, as represented again by point *F* in Figure 10.4. Included in that full-employment equilibrium GDP is

Consumption	=	$2,350 billion
Investment	=	400 billion
Government	=	150 billion
Net exports	=	100 billion
Aggregate demand at current price level	=	$3,000 billion

Everything looks good in this macro economy. This is pretty much how the U.S. economy looked in 2006–2007: we had full employment and price stability.

The 2007:4 Investment Decline

In the fourth quarter of 2007, the U.S. economy took a turn for the worse. The problem began in the housing industry. Housing prices had risen dramatically from 1998 to 2006. This surge in home prices had increased household wealth by trillions of dollars and prompted home builders to construct more new homes every year. These injections of investment spending helped keep GDP growing for a decade. But the party ended in July 2006 when home prices stopped rising. That made home builders rethink their construction plans. When home prices actually began falling in 2007, many home builders called it quits. In the fourth quarter of 2007, residential investment (home construction) declined by a staggering 29 percent (see the News on the next page), dragging total U.S. investment down by more than $50 billion. The die was cast: a recession was sure to follow.

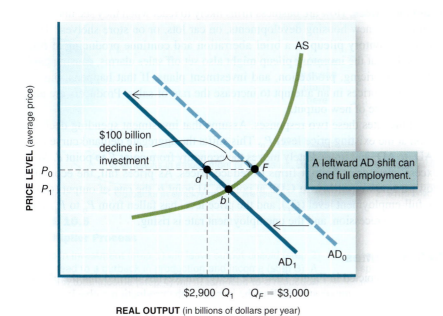

FIGURE 10.4

AD Shift

When investment spending drops, aggregate demand shifts to the left. In the short run, this causes output and the price level to fall. The initial full-employment equilibrium at *F* is pushed to a new and lower equilibrium at point *b*.

FIGURE 10.7
Recessionary GDP Gap

The real GDP gap is the difference between equilibrium GDP (Q_E) and full-employment GDP (Q_F). It represents the lost output due to a recession.

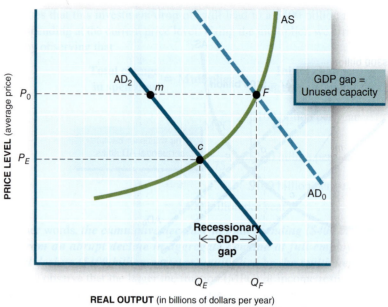

GDP gap = Unused capacity

Short-Run Inflation–Unemployment Trade-Offs

Figure 10.7 not only illustrates how much output declines when AD falls but also provides an important clue about the difficulty of restoring full employment. Suppose the recessionary GDP gap were $200 billion, as illustrated in Figure 10.8. How much more AD would we need to get back to full employment?

Upward-Sloping AS. Suppose aggregate demand at the equilibrium price level (P_E) were to increase by exactly $200 billion (including multiplier effects), as illustrated by the shift to AD_3. Would that get us back to full-employment output? Not according to Figure 10.8. *When AD increases, both output and prices go up.* Because the AS curve is upward-sloping, the $200 billion shift from AD_2 to AD_3 moves the new macro equilibrium to

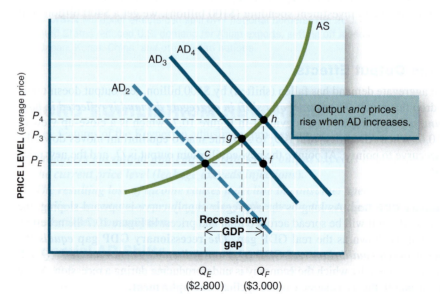

Output *and* prices rise when AD increases.

FIGURE 10.8
The Unemployment–Inflation Trade-Off

If the short-run AS curve is upward-sloping, an AD increase will raise output *and* prices. If AD increases by the amount of the recessionary GDP gap only (AD_2 to AD_3), full employment (Q_F) won't be reached. Macro equilibrium moves to point g, not point f.

point *g* rather than point *f*. We'd like to get to point *f* with full employment and price stability. But as demand picks up, producers are likely to raise prices. This leads us up the AS curve to point *g*. At point *g*, we're still short of full employment and have experienced a bit of inflation (an increased price level). *So long as the short-run AS is upward-sloping, there's a trade-off between unemployment and inflation.* We can get lower rates of unemployment (more real output) only if we accept some inflation.

"Full" vs. "Natural" Unemployment. The short-term trade-off between unemployment and inflation is the basis for the definition of "full" employment. We don't define full employment as *zero* unemployment; we define it as the rate of unemployment *consistent with price stability.* As noted in Chapter 6, **full employment** is typically defined as a 4 to 6 percent rate of unemployment. What the upward-sloping AS curve tells us is that *the closer the economy gets to capacity output, the greater the risk of inflation.* To get back to full employment in Figure 10.8, aggregate demand would have to increase to AD_4, with the price level rising to P_4.

full employment: The lowest rate of unemployment compatible with price stability, variously estimated at between 4 and 6 percent unemployment.

Not everyone accepts this notion of full employment. As we saw in Chapter 8, neoclassical and monetarist economists prefer to focus on *long*-run outcomes. In their view, the long-run AS curve is vertical (see Figure 8.12). In that long-run context, there's no unemployment–inflation trade-off: An AD shift doesn't change the "natural" (institutional) rate of unemployment but does alter the price level. We'll examine this argument in Chapters 16 and 17.

ADJUSTMENT TO AN INFLATIONARY GDP GAP

As we've observed, *a sudden shift in aggregate demand can have a cumulative effect on macro outcomes* that's larger than the initial imbalance. This multiplier process works both ways. Just as a *decrease* in investment (or any other AD component) can send the economy into a recessionary tailspin, an *increase* in investment might initiate an inflationary spiral.

Figure 10.9 illustrates the consequences of a sudden jump in investment spending. We start out again in the happy equilibrium (point *F*), where full employment (Q_F) and price stability (P_0) prevail. Initial spending consists of

$$C = \$2{,}350 \text{ billion} \qquad G = \$150 \text{ billion}$$
$$I = \$400 \text{ billion} \qquad X - M = \$100 \text{ billion}$$

Increased Investment

Then investors suddenly decide to step up the rate of investment. Perhaps their expectations for future sales have risen. Maybe new technology has become available that compels firms to modernize their facilities. Whatever the reason, investors decide to raise the level of investment from $400 billion to $500 billion at the current price level (P_0). This change in investment spending shifts the aggregate demand curve from AD_0 to AD_5 (a horizontal shift of $100 billion).

Inventory Depletion. One of the first things you'll notice when AD shifts like this is that available inventories shrink. Investors can step up their *spending* more quickly than firms can increase their *production.* A lot of the increased investment demand will have to be satisfied from existing inventory. The decline in inventory is a signal to producers that it might be a good time to raise prices a bit. Thus *inventory depletion is a warning sign of potential inflation.* As the economy moves up from point *F* to point *r* in Figure 10.9, that inflation starts to become visible.

Household Incomes

Whether or not prices start rising quickly, household incomes will get a boost from the increased investment. Producers will step up the rate of output to rebuild inventories and

FIGURE 10.9
Demand-Pull Inflation

An increase in investment or other autonomous spending sets off multiplier effects shifting AD to the right. AD shifts to the right *twice,* first (AD_0 to AD_5) because of increased investment and then (AD_5 to AD_6) because of increased consumption. The increased AD moves the economy up the short-run AS curve, causing some inflation. How much inflation results depends on the slope of the AS curve.

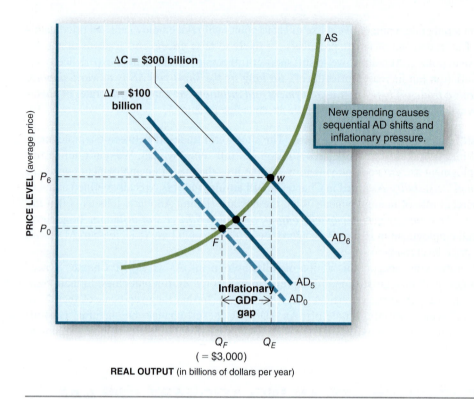

New spending causes sequential AD shifts and inflationary pressure.

REAL OUTPUT (in billions of dollars per year)

---

supply more investment goods (equipment and structures). To do so, they'll hire more workers or extend working hours. The end result for workers will be fatter paychecks.

Induced Consumption

What will households do with these heftier paychecks? By now, you know what the consumer response will be. The marginal propensity to consume prompts an increase in consumer spending. Eventually, consumer spending increases by a *multiple* of the income change. In this case, the consumption increase is $300 billion (see Table 10.1).

Figure 10.9 illustrates the results of the sequential AD shifts caused by multiplier-induced consumption. Notice how the AD curve shifts a second time, from AD_5 to AD_6.

A New Equilibrium

The ultimate impact of the investment surge is reflected in the new equilibrium at point *w.* As before, the shift of AD has affected both real output and prices. Real output does increase beyond the full-employment level, but it does so only at the expense of accelerating inflation. This is a classic case of **demand-pull inflation.** The initial increase in investment was enough to kindle a little inflation. The multiplier effect worsened the problem by forcing the economy further along the ever-steeper AS curve. The **inflationary GDP gap** ends up as $Q_E - Q_F$.

Booms and Busts

The Keynesian analysis of leakages, injections, and the multiplier paints a fairly grim picture of the prospects for macro stability. *The basic conclusion of the Keynesian analysis is that the economy is vulnerable to abrupt changes in spending behavior and won't self-adjust to a desired macro equilibrium.* A shift in aggregate demand can come from almost anywhere. The September 2001 terrorist attacks on the World Trade Center and Pentagon shook both

demand-pull inflation: An increase in the price level initiated by excessive aggregate demand.

inflationary GDP gap: The amount by which equilibrium GDP exceeds full-employment GDP.

consumer and investor confidence. Businesses started cutting back production even *before* inventories started piling up. Worsened *expectations* rather than rising inventories caused investment demand to shift, setting off the multiplier process. In 2008 declining home and stock prices curtailed both confidence and spending, setting off a negative multiplier process.

When the aggregate demand curve shifts, macro equilibrium will be upset. Moreover, *the responses of market participants to an abrupt AD shift are likely to worsen rather than improve market outcomes.* As a result, the economy may gravitate toward an equilibrium of stagnant recession (point *c* in Figure 10.6) or persistent inflation (point *w* in Figure 10.9).

As Keynes saw it, the combination of alternating AD shifts and multiplier effects also causes recurring business cycles. A drop in consumer or business spending can set off a recessionary spiral of declining GDP and prices. A later increase in either consumer or business spending can set the ball rolling in the other direction. This may result in a series of economic booms and busts.

THE ECONOMY TOMORROW

MAINTAINING CONSUMER CONFIDENCE

This chapter emphasized how a sudden change in investment might set off the multiplier process. Investors aren't the only potential culprits, however. A sudden change in government spending or exports could just as easily start the multiplier ball rolling. In fact, the whole process could originate with a change in *consumer* spending.

Consumer Confidence. Recall the two components of consumption: *autonomous* consumption and *induced* consumption. These two components may be expressed as

$$C = a + bY$$

We've seen that autonomous consumption (*a* in the equation) is influenced by *non*income factors, including consumer confidence. As we first observed in Chapter 8, *changes* in consumer confidence can therefore be an AD shift factor: a force that changes the value of autonomous consumption and thus shifts the AD curve to the right or left. A change in consumer confidence can change the marginal propensity to consume (*b* in the equation) as well, further shifting the AD curve.

These AD shifts can be substantial. According to the World Bank, every 1 percent change in consumer confidence alters autonomous consumption by $1.1 billion. That makes the 2007–2008 plunge in consumer confidence particularly scary. As Figure 10.10 illustrates, consumer confidence declined by more than 40 percent from the beginning of 2007 to the end of 2008. That loss of confidence caused consumer spending to drop even further than the cutbacks induced by falling incomes.

Ironically, when consumers try to cope with recession by cutting their spending and saving more of their incomes, they actually make matters worse (see the News on the next page). This "paradox of thrift" recognizes that what might make sense for an *individual* consumer doesn't necessarily make sense for *aggregate* demand.

The Official View: Always a Rosy Outlook. Because consumer spending vastly outweighs any other component of aggregate demand, the threat of abrupt changes in consumer behavior is serious. Recognizing this, public officials strive to maintain consumer confidence in the economy tomorrow, even when such confidence might not be warranted. That's why President Hoover, bank officials, and major brokerage houses tried to assure the public in 1929 that the outlook was still rosy. (Look back at the first few pages of Chapter 8.) The "rosy outlook" is still the official perspective on the economy tomorrow. The White House

web click

For data on consumer confidence, visit the Institute for Social Research (ISR) at **www.sca.isr.umich.edu**.

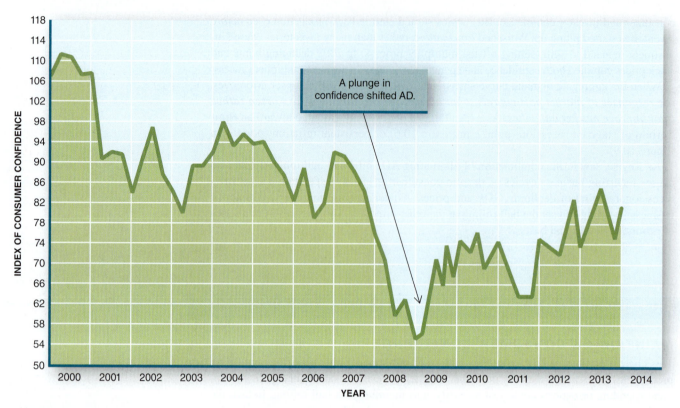

FIGURE 10.10

Consumer Confidence

Consumer confidence is affected by various financial, political, and international events. Changes in consumer confidence affect consumer behavior and thereby shift the AD curve right or left.

The steep loss of confidence in 2007–2009 deepened and lengthened the Great Recession.

Source: University of Michigan.

web click

To understand how the unemployment rate affects consumer confidence, visit **http://research.stlouisfed.org** and search "consumer confidence and unemployment."

IN THE NEWS

The Paradox of Thrift

With incomes falling and more job layoffs announced daily, American families are getting thrifty. They are cutting back on spending, reducing credit card debt, and even setting aside a little more money for the proverbial rainy day. This might be a sound financial strategy for individual households. But such thriftiness can drive the economy deeper into recession. It's what economists call the "paradox of thrift": saving more money in a recession pulls the reins on spending just when the economy needs it the most.

Source: News accounts, January 2009.

ANALYSIS: When consumers become more pessimistic about their economy, they start saving more and spending less. This shifts AD leftward and deepens a recession.

is always upbeat about prospects for the economy. If it weren't—if it were even to hint at the possibility of a recession—consumer and investor confidence might wilt. Then the economy might quickly turn ugly.

SUMMARY

- The circular flow of income has offsetting leakages (consumer saving, taxes, business saving, imports) and injections (autonomous consumption, investment, government spending, exports). **LO10-1**
- When desired injections equal leakage, the economy is in equilibrium (output demanded = output supplied at prevailing price level). **LO10-3**
- An imbalance of injections and leakages will cause the economy to expand or contract. An imbalance at full-employment GDP will cause cyclical unemployment or demand-pull inflation. How serious these problems become depends on how the market responds to the initial imbalance. **LO10-3**
- Classical economists believed (flexible) interest rates and price levels would equalize injections and leakages (especially consumer saving and investment), restoring full-employment equilibrium. **LO10-3**
- Keynes showed that spending imbalances might actually *worsen* if consumer and investor expectations changed. **LO10-2**

- An abrupt change in autonomous spending (injections) shifts the AD curve, setting off a sequential multiplier process (further AD shifts) that magnifies changes in equilibrium GDP. **LO10-2**
- The multiplier itself is equal to $1/(1 - MPC)$. It indicates the cumulative change (shift) in aggregate demand that follows an initial (autonomous) disruption of spending flows. **LO10-2**
- As long as the short-run aggregate supply curve slopes upward, AD shifts will affect both real output and prices. **LO10-2**
- The recessionary GDP gap measures the amount by which equilibrium GDP falls short of full-employment GDP. **LO10-3**
- Sudden changes in consumer confidence shift the AD curve right or left and may destabilize the economy. To avoid this, policymakers always maintain a rosy outlook. **LO10-3**

Key Terms

aggregate demand (AD)
full-employment GDP
leakage
disposable income
gross business saving

injection
equilibrium GDP
marginal propensity to consume (MPC)
multiplier
recessionary GDP gap

cyclical unemployment
full employment
demand-pull inflation
inflationary GDP gap

Questions for Discussion

1. How might declining prices affect a firm's decision to borrow and invest? (See News, p. 212.) **LO10-3**
2. Why wouldn't investment and saving flows at full employment always be equal? **LO10-1**
3. When unwanted inventories pile up in retail stores, how is production affected? What are the steps in this process? **LO10-3**
4. How can equilibrium output exceed full-employment output (as in Figure 10.9)? **LO10-3**
5. How might construction industry job losses affect incomes in the clothing and travel industries? **LO10-2**
6. What forces might turn an economic bust into an economic boom? What forces might put an end to the boom? **LO10-3**
7. How high did economists expect the unemployment rate to rise in 2009 (see News, p. 215)? How far did it rise (see Figure 6.6 or Table 8.1)? What explains the difference? **LO10-2**
8. Why might "belt-tightening" by consumers in a recession be unwelcome? (See News, p. 222.) **LO10-3**
9. What is the "ripple effect" in the News on page 215? **LO10-2**
10. Will the price level always rise when AD increases? Why or why not? **LO10-3**
11. What causes consumer confidence to change (Figure 10.10)? **LO10-3**

 mobile app Visit your mobile app store and download the Schiller: Study Econ app *today!*

LO10-3 1. From 1990 to 2013, in how many years did
    (a) Real consumption decline?   _____
    (b) Real investment decline?   _____
    (c) Real government spending increase at least $100 billion?   _____
       (See the data on pp. T-1–T-4.)

LO10-1 2. If the consumption function is $C = \$400$ billion $+ 0.8Y$,
    (a) What is the MPC?   _____
    (b) How large is autonomous C?   _____
    (c) How much do consumers spend with incomes of $4 trillion?   _____
    (d) How much do they save?   _____

LO10-2 3. If the marginal propensity to consume is 0.9,
    (a) What is the value of the multiplier?   _____
    (b) What is the marginal propensity to save?   _____

LO10-2 4. Suppose that investment demand increases by $300 billion in a closed and private economy (no government or foreign trade). Assume further that households have a marginal propensity to consume of 75 percent.
    (a) Compute four rounds of multiplier effects:

	Changes in This Cycle's Spending	Cumulative Change in Spending
First cycle	_____	_____
Second cycle	_____	_____
Third cycle	_____	_____
Fourth cycle	_____	_____

    (b) What will be the final cumulative impact on spending?   _____

LO10-3 5. Illustrate in the following graph the impact of a sudden decline in consumer confidence that reduces autonomous consumption by $100 billion at the price level P_F. Assume $MPC = 0.5$.
    (a) What is the new equilibrium level of real output? (Don't forget the multiplier.)   _____
    (b) How large is the real GDP gap?   _____
    (c) Did average prices (A) increase or (B) decrease?   _____

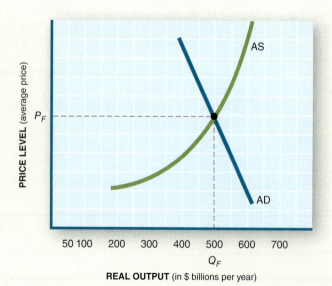

LO10-1 6. By how much did annualized consumption decline in November 2008 when GDP was
$14 trillion? (See News, p. 214.)   _____

LO10-2 7. If Korean exports to the United States decline by $15 billion (World View, p. 216) by how
much will cumulative Korean spending drop if their MPC is 0.75?   _____

LO10-3 8. According to World Bank estimates (see p. 222), by how much did consumer spending decline
as a result of the 40-point drop in the index of consumer confidence between 2007 and 2009
(Figure 10.10)?   _____

LO10-3 9. How large is the inflationary GDP gap in Figure 10.9?   _____

LO10-2 10. The accompanying graph depicts a macro equilibrium. Answer the questions based on the
LO10-3   information in the graph.
    (*a*) What is the equilibrium rate of GDP?   _____
    (*b*) If full-employment real GDP is $1,200, what problem does this economy have?   _____
    (*c*) How large is the real GDP gap?   _____
    (*d*) If the multiplier were equal to 4, how much additional investment would be needed to
         increase aggregate demand by the amount of the initial GDP gap?   _____
    (*e*) Illustrate the changes in autonomous investment and induced consumption that occur in (*d*).
    (*f*) What happens to prices when aggregate demand increases by the amount of the initial
         GDP gap?   _____
    (*g*) Is full employment restored by the AD shift?   _____

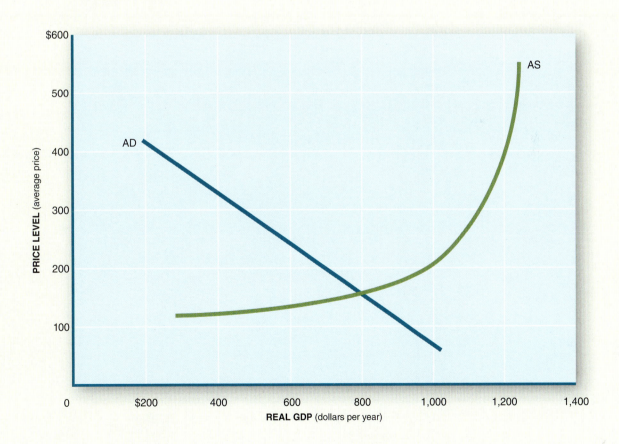

Fiscal Policy Tools

The government's tax and spending activities influence economic outcomes. Keynesian theory emphasizes the market's lack of self-adjustment, particularly in recessions. If the market doesn't self-adjust, the government may have to intervene. Specifically, the government may have to use its tax and spending power (fiscal policy) to stabilize the macro economy at its full-employment equilibrium. Chapters 11 and 12 look closely at the policy goals, strategies, and tools of fiscal policy.

Multiplier effects then increase consumption spending by \$600 billion more. This additional consumption shifts aggregate demand repeatedly, ultimately reaching AD_3. Thus **the impact of fiscal stimulus on aggregate demand includes both the new government spending and all subsequent increases in consumer spending triggered by multiplier effects.** In Figure 11.5, the shift from AD_1 to AD_3 includes

AD_1 to AD_2: Shift due to \$200 billion injection of new government spending.
AD_2 to AD_3: Shift due to multiplier-induced increases in consumption (\$600 billion).

As a result of these initial and multiplier-induced shifts, aggregate demand at the current price level (P_E) increases by \$800 billion. Thus

$$\text{Cumulative increase (horizontal shift) in AD} = \text{New spending injection (fiscal stimulus)} + \text{Induced increase in consumption}$$

$$= \text{Multiplier} \times \text{fiscal stimulus (new spending injection)}$$

The second equation is identical to the first but is expressed in the terminology of fiscal policy. The "fiscal stimulus" is the "new spending injection" that sets the multiplier process in motion. The multiplier carries the ball from there.

The Desired Stimulus. Multiplier effects make changes in government spending a powerful policy lever. The multiplier also increases the risk of error, however. Just as too little fiscal stimulus may leave the economy in a recession, too much can rapidly lead to excessive spending and inflation. This was the dilemma President Obama confronted in his first year. He wanted a fiscal stimulus package of at least \$850 billion. Critics worried, however, that too much fiscal stimulus might accelerate inflation. A compromise (\$787 billion) was struck in early 2009 (see the accompanying News).

IN THE NEWS

U.S. Congress Gives Final Approval to \$787 Billion Stimulus

Feb. 13 (Bloomberg)—The U.S. Congress gave final approval to President Barack Obama's \$787 billion economic stimulus package in hopes of wresting the economy out of recession through a mix of tax cuts and federal spending.

The Senate approved the package 60 to 38 with three Republicans joining Democrats in voting "yes." Earlier today, the House passed the measure 246 to 183 with no Republicans in favor and seven Democrats opposed. . .

The stimulus plan would provide a half-trillion dollars for jobless benefits, renewable energy projects, highway construction, food stamps, broadband, Pell college tuition grants, high-speed rail projects and scores of other programs. . . .

"After all the debate, this legislation can be summed up in one word: Jobs," said House Speaker Nancy Pelosi, a California Democrat, during today's floor debate. "The American people need action and they need action now."

—Brian Faler

Source: *BusinessWeek*, February 13, 2009. Used with permission of Bloomberg L.P. Copyright © 2015. All rights reserved.

ANALYSIS: President Obama's huge fiscal stimulus package included both increased government spending and tax cuts. The package was intended to shift the AD curve substantially to the right.

Policy decisions would be a lot easier if we knew the exact dimensions of aggregate demand, as in Figure 11.3. With such perfect information about AD, AS, and the AD shortfall, we could easily calculate the required increase in the rate of government spending. The general formula for computing the *desired* stimulus (such as an increase in government spending) is a simple rearrangement of the earlier formula:

$$\text{Desired fiscal stimulus} = \frac{\text{AD shortfall}}{\text{Multiplier}}$$

In the economy in Figure 11.3, we assumed the policy goal was to increase aggregate demand by the amount of the AD shortfall ($800 billion). Accordingly, we conclude that

$$\text{Desired fiscal stimulus} = \frac{\$800 \text{ billion}}{4}$$

$$= \$200 \text{ billion}$$

In other words, a $200 billion increase in government spending at the current price level would be enough fiscal stimulus to close the $800 billion AD shortfall and achieve full employment.

In practice, we rarely know the exact size of the shortfall in aggregate demand. The multiplier is also harder to calculate when taxes and imports enter the picture. Nevertheless, the foregoing formula does provide a useful rule of thumb for determining how much fiscal stimulus is needed to achieve any desired increase in aggregate demand.

Tax Cuts

There is no doubt that increased government spending can shift the AD curve to the right, helping to close a GDP gap. But increased government spending isn't the only way to get there. The increased demand required to raise output and employment levels from Q_E to Q_F could emerge from increases in autonomous consumption or investment as well as from increased government spending. An AD shift could also originate overseas, in the form of increased demand for our exports. In other words, any "big spender" would help, whether from the public sector or the private sector. Of course the reason we're initially at Q_E instead of Q_F in Figure 11.3 is that consumers, investors, and export buyers have chosen *not* to spend as much as required for full employment.

Consumer and investor decisions are subject to change. Moreover, fiscal policy can encourage such changes. Congress not only buys goods and services but also levies taxes. By lowering taxes, the government increases the **disposable income** of the private sector. This was the objective of the 2008 Bush tax cuts, which gave all taxpayers a rebate of $300–600 in the summer of 2008. By putting $168 billion more after-tax income into the hands of consumers, Congress hoped to stimulate (shift) the consumption component of aggregate demand. President Obama used the tax cut tool as part of his 2009 stimulus package and again in 2011.

disposable income: After-tax income of consumers; personal income less personal taxes.

Taxes and Consumption. A tax cut directly increases the disposable income of consumers. The question here, however, is how a tax cut affects *spending*. By how much will consumption increase for every dollar of tax cuts?

The answer lies in the marginal propensity to consume. Consumers won't spend every dollar of tax cuts; they'll *save* some of the cut and spend the rest. The MPC tells us how the tax cut dollar will be split between saving and spending. If the MPC is 0.75, consumers will spend $0.75 out of every tax cut $1.00. In other words,

Initial increase in consumption = MPC × Tax cut

If taxes were cut by $200 billion, the resulting shopping spree would amount to

$$\text{Initial increase in consumption} = 0.75 \times \$200 \text{ billion}$$

$$= \$150 \text{ billion}$$

Hence *the effect of a tax cut that increases disposable incomes is to stimulate consumer spending.* A tax cut therefore shifts the aggregate demand curve to the right.

Multiplier Effects. The initial shopping spree induced by a tax cut starts the multiplier process in motion. The new consumer spending creates additional income for producers and workers, who will then use the additional income to increase their own consumption. This will propel us along the multiplier path already depicted in Figure 11.5. The cumulative change in total spending will be

$$\text{Cumulative change in spending} = \text{Multiplier} \times \text{Initial change in consumption}$$

In this case, the cumulative change is

$$\text{Cumulative change in spending} = \frac{1}{1 - \text{MPC}} \times \$150 \text{ billion}$$

$$= 4 \times \$150 \text{ billion}$$

$$= \$600 \text{ billion}$$

Here again we see that the multiplier increases the impact on aggregate demand of a fiscal policy stimulus. There's an important difference here, though. When we increased government spending by \$200 billion, aggregate demand increased by \$800 billion. When we cut taxes by \$200 billion, however, aggregate demand increases by only \$600 billion. Hence *a tax cut contains less fiscal stimulus than an increase in government spending of the same size.*

The lesser stimulative power of tax cuts is explained by consumer saving. Only part of a tax cut gets spent. Consumers save the rest. This is evident in Figure 11.6, which illustrates the successive rounds of the multiplier process. Notice that the tax cut is used to increase both consumption and saving, according to the MPC. Only that part of the tax cut that's used for consumption enters the circular flow as a spending injection. Hence *the initial spending injection is less than the size of the tax cuts.* By contrast, every dollar of government purchases goes directly into the circular flow. Accordingly, tax cuts are less powerful than government purchases because the initial *spending* injection is smaller.

This doesn't mean we can't close the AD shortfall with a tax cut. It simply means that the desired tax cut must be larger than the required stimulus. It remains true that

$$\textbf{Desired fiscal stimulus} = \frac{\textbf{AD shortfall}}{\textbf{Multiplier}}$$

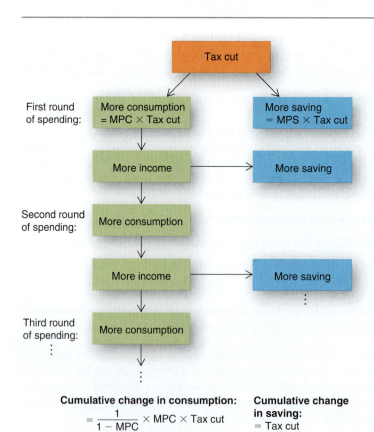

FIGURE 11.6

The Tax Cut Multiplier

Only part of a tax cut is used to increase consumption; the remainder is saved. Accordingly, the initial spending injection is less than the tax cut. This makes tax cuts less stimulative than government purchases of the same size. The multiplier still goes to work on that new consumer spending, however.

Cumulative change in consumption:

$$= \frac{1}{1 - \text{MPC}} \times \text{MPC} \times \text{Tax cut}$$

$$= \text{Multiplier} \times \text{MPC} \times \text{Tax cut}$$

Cumulative change in saving:

$$= \text{Tax cut}$$

But now we're using a consumption shift as the fiscal stimulus rather than increased government spending. Hence we have to allow for the fact that the initial surge in consumption (the fiscal stimulus) will be *less* than the tax cut. Specifically,

$$\textbf{Initial consumption injection} = \textbf{MPC} \times \textbf{Tax cut}$$

If we want to use a consumer tax cut to close a GDP gap, we have

$$\textbf{Desired tax cut} = \frac{\textbf{Desired fiscal stimulus}}{\textbf{MPC}}$$

In the economy in Figure 11.3, we assumed that the desired stimulus is $200 billion and the MPC equals 0.75. Hence the desired tax cut is

$$\text{Desired tax cut} = \frac{\$200 \text{ billion}}{0.75} = \$267 \text{ billion}$$

By cutting taxes $267 billion, we directly increase disposable income by the same amount. Consumers then increase their rate of spending by $200 billion (0.75 × $267 billion); they save the remaining $67 billion. As the added spending enters the circular flow, it starts the multiplier process, ultimately increasing aggregate demand by $800 billion per year.

This comparison of government purchases and tax cuts clearly reveals their respective power. What we've demonstrated is that *a dollar of tax cuts is less stimulative than a dollar of government purchases.* This doesn't mean that tax cuts are undesirable, just that they need to be larger than the desired injection of spending. The following News shows that the 2008 tax cut boosted consumer spending by 3.5 percent, thereby shifting AD to the right and accelerating real GDP growth.

IN THE NEWS

Just How Stimulating Are Those Checks?

To get an idea of how much those government rebate checks have spurred spending—and who's benefiting from the buying—business school professors Jonathan Parker (Northwestern) and Christian Broda (University of Chicago) analyzed the spending of 30,000 rebate-receiving households. Using data provided by AC-Nielsen's Homescan, whose participants scan the barcodes on their purchases into a database, the researchers found the rebates "clearly have increased household spending," Parker says. Lower-income households boosted consumption most—spending 6 percent more, compared with a 3.5 percent rise across all households.

—Tara Kalwarski

THE 2008 REBATE BOOST
Additional dollars spent due to stimulus checks*

Appliances, electronics, and furniture $91

Entertainment and personal services $87

Food, health, beauty, and household products $60

Clothing, shoes, and accessories $32

*Average per rebate-receiving household.

ANALYSIS: The 2008 tax cuts were a form of fiscal stimulus that boosted consumption (personal spending), increased real GDP growth, and reduced unemployment.

web click

For details on federal spending and tax collections over time, go to the Congressional Budget Office at **www.cbo.gov**. Click "Budget & Economy."

The different effects of tax cuts and increased government spending have an important implication for government budgets. Because some of the power of a tax cut "leaks" into saving, tax increases don't "offset" government spending of equal value. This unexpected result is described in Table 11.1.

GDP share (from 10 percent in 1930 to 19 percent today) to the big-government bias of Keynesian fiscal policy.

In principle, this big-government bias doesn't exist. Keynes never said government spending was the only lever of fiscal policy. Even in 1934 he advised President Roosevelt to pursue only *temporary* increases in government spending. As we've seen, tax policy can be used to alter consumer and investor spending as well. Hence fiscal policy can just as easily focus on changing the level of *private* sector spending as on changing *public* sector spending. In 1934, however, business confidence was so low that tax-induced increases in investment seemed unlikely. In less desperate times, the choice of which fiscal tool to use is a political decision, not a Keynesian mandate. President Clinton favored increased government spending to stimulate the economy, whereas President George W. Bush favored tax cuts to bolster private spending. President Obama reversed that course, with more emphasis on increased government spending, especially infrastructure and alternative energy development (see the News on page 234).

Output Mixes within Each Sector. In addition to choosing whether to increase public or private spending, fiscal policy must also consider the specific content of spending within each sector. Suppose we determine that stimulation of the private sector is preferable to additional government spending as a means of promoting full employment. We still have many choices. We could, for example, cut corporate taxes, cut individual taxes, reduce excise taxes, or increase Social Security benefits. Each alternative implies a different mix of consumption and investment and a different distribution of income.

The same choices exist when we decide to stimulate AD with more government spending. Do we increase highway construction, bridge repair, military procurement, cancer research, or space exploration? Here again, the content of spending has a profound effect on the shape of the economy tomorrow.

SUMMARY

- The economy's short-run macro equilibrium may not coincide with full employment and price stability. Keynes advocated government intervention to shift the AD curve to a more desirable equilibrium.   **LO11-1**
- Fiscal policy refers to the use of the government's tax and spending powers to achieve desired macro outcomes. The tools of fiscal stimulus include increasing government purchases, reducing taxes, and raising income transfers.   **LO11-2**
- Fiscal restraint may originate in reductions in government purchases, increases in taxes, or cuts in income transfers.   **LO11-3**
- Government purchases add directly to aggregate demand; taxes and transfers have an indirect effect by inducing changes in consumption and investment. This makes changes in government spending more powerful per dollar than changes in taxes or transfers.   **LO11-4**
- Fiscal policy initiatives have a multiplied impact on total spending and output. An increase in government spending, for example, will result in more disposable income, which will be used to finance further consumer spending.   **LO11-4**
- The objective of fiscal policy is to close GDP gaps. To do this, the aggregate demand curve must shift by *more* than the size of the GDP gap to compensate for changing price levels. The desired shift is equal to the AD shortfall (or AD excess).   **LO11-1**
- Because of multiplier effects, the desired fiscal stimulus or restraint is always less than the size of the AD shortfall or AD excess.   **LO11-3**
- Time lags in the design, authorization, and implementation of fiscal policy reduce its effectiveness.   **LO11-4**
- Changes in government spending and taxes alter the content of GDP and thus influence what to produce. Fiscal policy affects the relative size of the public and private sectors as well as the mix of output in each sector.   **LO11-4**

Key Terms

aggregate demand	fiscal stimulus	disposable income
income transfers	aggregate supply	fiscal restraint
fiscal policy	AD shortfall	inflationary GDP gap
equilibrium (macro)	multiplier	AD excess
recessionary GDP gap	marginal propensity to consume (MPC)	crowding out

Questions for Discussion

1. How can you tell if the economy is in equilibrium? How could you estimate the real GDP gap? **LO11-1**
2. How did consumers spend their 2008 tax cut (News, p. 237)? Does it matter what they spend it on? Explain. **LO11-4**
3. What happens to aggregate demand when transfer payments and the taxes to pay them both rise by the same amount? **LO11-4**
4. Why are the AD shortfall and AD excess larger than their respective GDP gaps? Are they ever the same size as the GDP gap? **LO11-3**
5. Will consumers always spend the same percentage of any tax cut? Why might they spend more or less than usual? **LO11-4**
6. How does the slope of the AS curve affect the size of the AD shortfall? If the AS curve were horizontal, how large would the AD shortfall be in Figure 11.3? **LO11-1**
7. In Figure 11.4, why did inflation accelerate when the economy was still so far short of full employment? **LO11-2**
8. How quickly should Congress act to remedy an AD excess or AD shortfall? What are the risks of quick fiscal policy responses? **LO11-4**
9. Why do critics charge that fiscal policy has a "big-government bias"? **LO11-2**
10. When Barack Obama was campaigning for president in 2008, he proposed more government spending paid for with higher taxes on "the rich." What impact would those options have on macro equilibrium? **LO11-4**
11. How did the 2009 fiscal stimulus create more jobs in 2013? (See Table 11.2.) **LO11-4**
12. If fiscal stimulus can close a GDP gap, why not do so immediately? **LO11-4**

---

 mobile app Visit your mobile app store and download the Schiller: Study Econ app *today!*

Deficits and Debt

After reading this chapter, you should know

LO12-1 The origins of cyclical and structural deficits.

LO12-2 How the national debt has accumulated.

LO12-3 How and when "crowding out" occurs.

LO12-4 What the real burden of the national debt is.

President Obama's massive 2009 stimulus package was designed to jump-start the recession-bound economy. Critics argued about both the content and size of that package. But the most controversial critique of Obama's fiscal stimulus was that it would ultimately do more harm than good. Those critics argued that the massive deficits generated by Obama's "American Recovery and Reinvestment Act" (see the News on the next page) would undermine America's financial stability. To pay those deficits off, the government would later be forced to *raise* taxes and *cut* spending, taking the wind out of the economy's sails. Whatever short-term boost the economy got from the fiscal stimulus would be reversed in later years.

How can this be? Didn't we just show how tax cuts shift aggregate demand rightward, propelling the economy toward full employment? Why would anyone have misgivings about such beneficial intervention?

The core critique of fiscal stimulus focuses on the *budget* consequences of government pump priming. Fiscal stimulus entails either tax cuts or increased government spending. Either option can increase the size of the government's budget deficit. Hence we need to understand how fiscal stimulus is *financed*. We start with these questions:

- **How do deficits arise?**
- **What harm, if any, do deficits cause?**
- **Who will pay off the accumulated national debt?**

As you'll see, the answers to these questions add an essential dimension to fiscal policy debates.

IN THE NEWS

Deficits to Swell with Obama Stimulus

According to the Congressional Budget Office (CBO) and the Joint Committee on Taxation, federal budget deficits will more than double over the next ten years. President Obama's ambitious plans to increase government spending, reduce taxes, reform the health care system, and strengthen the social safety net will add trillions to the nation's budget's deficits over the next ten years. The CBO says cumulative deficits over the next ten years will amount to $9.3 trillion, more than double the $4.4 trillion projected before the president's proposals were put forth. This will force the federal government to borrow trillions more in the nation's credit markets over the next decade. By 2019, the federal debt will climb to 82 percent of GDP, up from the earlier projection of 56 percent.

Source: Congressional Budget Office, *Preliminary Analysis of the President's 2010 Budget Proposals,* March 20, 2009.

ANALYSIS: Fiscal stimulus widens budget deficits. The Obama $787 billion stimulus package caused a spike in the federal budget deficit and accumulated national debt. Would this cause future problems?

BUDGET EFFECTS OF FISCAL POLICY

Keynesian theory highlights the potential of **fiscal policy** to solve our macro problems. The guidelines are simple. Use fiscal stimulus—stepped-up government spending, tax cuts, increased transfers—to eliminate unemployment. Use fiscal restraint—less spending, tax hikes, reduced transfers—to keep inflation under control. From this perspective, the federal budget is a key policy tool for controlling the economy.

fiscal policy: The use of government taxes and spending to alter macroeconomic outcomes.

Budget Surpluses and Deficits

Use of the budget to stabilize the economy implies that federal expenditures and receipts won't always be equal. In a recession, for example, the government has sound reasons both to cut taxes and to increase its own spending. By reducing tax revenues and increasing expenditures simultaneously, however, the federal government will throw its budget out of balance. This practice is called **deficit spending,** a situation in which the government borrows funds to pay for spending that exceeds tax revenues. The size of the resulting **budget deficit** is equal to the difference between expenditures and receipts:

deficit spending: The use of borrowed funds to finance government expenditures that exceed tax revenues.

$$\text{Budget deficit} = \text{Government spending} - \text{Tax revenues} > 0$$

As Table 12.1 shows, the federal government had a relatively small budget deficit ($161 billion) in 2007. But that deficit nearly *tripled* in 2008 and then almost *tripled*

budget deficit: The amount by which government spending exceeds government revenue in a given time period.

Budget Total (in Billions of Dollars)	2006	2007	2008	2009	2010	2011	2012	2013	2014
Revenues	2,407	2,568	2,524	2,105	2,162	2,304	2,450	2,775	3,032
Outlays	−2,655	−2,729	−2,983	−3,518	−3,456	−3,603	−3,537	−3,455	−3,523
Surplus (deficit)	(248)	(161)	(459)	(1,413)	(1,294)	(1,301)	(1,087)	(680)	(492)

Source: Congressional Budget Office.

TABLE 12.1

Budget Deficits and Surpluses

Budget deficits arise when government outlays (spending) exceed revenues (receipts). When revenues exceed outlays, a budget surplus exists.

FIGURE 12.1

A String of Deficits

Budget deficits are the rule, not the exception. A budget surplus was achieved in only four years (1998–2001) since 1970. Deficits result from both cyclical slowdowns and discretionary policies. Both forces contributed to the massive deficits of 2009–2011.

Source: Congressional Budget Office.

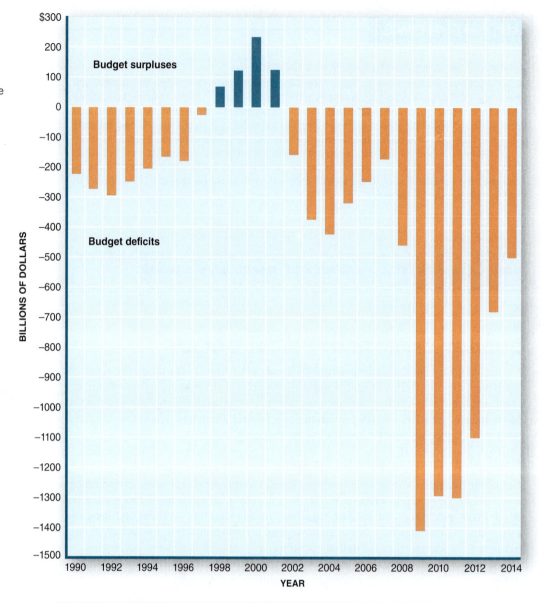

budget surplus: An excess of government revenues over government expenditures in a given time period.

again in 2009. As a result, the 2009 deficit was nearly 9 times larger than the 2007 deficit!

Figure 12.1 illustrates how far out of line with prior experience these deficits were. While budget deficits arise nearly every year, prior deficits were small fractions of the 2009–2012 deficits. There were even a few years (1998–2001) in which the federal government managed a **budget surplus**—that is, it brought in more tax revenue than it spent.

The surge in the size of the budget deficit in 2009–2011 caused a lot of anxiety. In early 2011 opinion polls revealed that these huge deficits were the number one economic worry of Americans. In 2014—after sizable drops in the deficit (Figure 12.1)—the federal deficit was still near the top of Americans' concerns (see the accompanying News).

Keynesian View. John Maynard Keynes wouldn't have been so worried. As far as he was concerned, budget deficits and surpluses are just a routine by-product of countercyclical fiscal policy. Deficits can easily arise when the government uses fiscal stimulus to increase aggregate demand, just as fiscal restraint (tax hikes, spending cuts) may cause a budget surplus. As Keynes saw it, *the goal of macro policy is not to balance the budget but to balance the economy (at full employment)*. If a budget deficit or surplus is needed to shift aggregate demand to the desired equilibrium, then so be it. In Keynes's view, a balanced

IN THE NEWS

America's Biggest Worries

When asked about the extent of their concern about various problems, Americans responded as follows:

Problem	Level of Concern		
	Great Deal	Fair Amount	A Little/Not at All
The economy	59%	29%	11%
Federal spending and deficits	58	22	20
Hunger and homelessness	43	33	23
Crime and violence	39	31	29
Illegal immigration	33	24	42
Quality of the environment	31	35	34
Climate change	24	25	51

Source: Gallup poll of March 6–9, 2014.

ANALYSIS: People worry about the federal government's persistent deficit spending. This makes budget deficits an important political, as well as economic, issue.

budget would be appropriate only if all other injections and leakages were in balance and the economy was in full-employment equilibrium. As the accompanying World View confirms, other nations evidently subscribe to that conclusion as well.

WORLD VIEW

Budget Imbalances Common

Although U.S. budget deficits receive the most attention, budget imbalances are a common feature of fiscal policy, as these figures reveal.

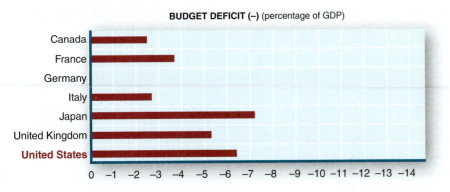

BUDGET DEFICIT (–) (percentage of GDP)

Source: International Monetary Fund, **www.imf.org** (2014).

ANALYSIS: To compare U.S. budget balances to those of other industrialized countries, we must adjust for differences in size by computing the *ratio* of deficits or surpluses to GDP. By this measure, U.S. budget imbalances were among the largest in recent years.

Discretionary vs. Automatic Spending

Theory aside, budget analysts tell us that Congress couldn't balance the federal budget every year even if it wanted to. Congress doesn't have as much control over spending and revenues as people assume. Hence neither deficits nor surpluses are necessarily the result of fiscal policy decisions. To understand the limits of budget management, we have to take a closer look at how budget outlays and receipts are actually determined.

At the beginning of each year, the president and Congress put together a budget blueprint for the next **fiscal year (FY).** They don't start from scratch, however. Most budget line items reflect commitments made in earlier years. In FY 2014, for example, the federal budget included $846 billion in Social Security benefits. The FY 2014 budget also provided for $85 billion in veterans benefits, $233 billion for interest payments on the national debt, and many billions more for completion of projects begun in previous years. Can Congress just reduce Social Security benefits being paid to retired workers or refuse to pay the interest due on the accumulated debt? Short of repudiating all prior commitments, there's little that Congress or the president can do to alter these expenditures in any given year. *To a large extent, current revenues and expenditures are the result of decisions made in prior years.* In this sense, much of each year's budget is considered "uncontrollable."

At present, uncontrollables account for roughly 80 percent of the federal budget. This leaves only 20 percent for **discretionary fiscal spending**—that is, spending decisions not "locked in" by prior legislative commitments. In recent years, rising interest payments and increasing entitlements (Social Security, Medicare, civil service pensions, etc.) have reduced the discretionary share of the budget even further. This doesn't mean that discretionary fiscal policy is no longer important; it simply means that the potential for *changing* budget outlays in any year is much smaller than it might first appear. Yet the ability to *change* tax or spending levels is the force behind Keynesian fiscal policy. Recall that deliberate changes in government spending or taxes are the essence of **fiscal restraint** and **fiscal stimulus.** If most of the budget is uncontrollable, those policy tools are less effective.

Automatic Stabilizers. Most of the uncontrollable line items in the federal budget have another characteristic that directly affects budget deficits: their value *changes* with economic conditions. Consider unemployment insurance benefits. The unemployment insurance program, established in 1935, provides that persons who lose their jobs will receive some income (an average of $300 per week) from the government. The law establishes the *entitlement* to unemployment benefits but not the amount to be spent in any year. Each year's expenditure depends on how many workers lose their jobs and qualify for benefits. In 2009, for example, outlays for unemployment benefits increased by $82 billion. That increase in federal spending was due to the 2008–2009 recession: the millions of workers who lost their jobs became eligible for unemployment benefits. The spending increase was *automatic*, not *discretionary*.

Welfare benefits also increased by $70 billion in 2009. This increase in spending also occurred automatically in response to worsened economic conditions. As more people lost jobs and used up their savings, they turned to welfare for help. They were *entitled* to food stamps, housing assistance, and cash welfare benefits according to eligibility rules already written; no new congressional or executive action was required to approve this increase in government spending.

Notice that ***outlays for unemployment compensation and welfare benefits increase when the economy goes into recession.*** This is exactly the kind of fiscal policy that Keynes advocated. The increase in **income transfers** helps offset the income losses due to recession. These increased transfers therefore act as **automatic stabilizers**—injecting new spending into the circular flow during economic contractions. Conversely, transfer payments *decline* when the economy is *expanding* and fewer people qualify for unemployment or welfare benefits. Hence no one has to pull the fiscal policy lever to inject more or less entitlement spending into the circular flow; much of it happens automatically.

Automatic stabilizers also exist on the revenue side of the federal budget. Income taxes are an important stabilizer because they move up and down with the value of spending and

---

fiscal year (FY): The 12-month period used for accounting purposes; begins October 1 for the federal government.

discretionary fiscal spending: Those elements of the federal budget not determined by past legislative or executive commitments.

fiscal restraint: Tax hikes or spending cuts intended to reduce (shift) aggregate demand.

fiscal stimulus: Tax cuts or spending hikes intended to increase (shift) aggregate demand.

income transfers: Payments to individuals for which no current goods or services are exchanged, such as Social Security, welfare, unemployment benefits.

automatic stabilizer: Federal expenditure or revenue item that automatically responds countercyclically to changes in national income, like unemployment benefits and income taxes.

- ***Changes in Real GDP Growth***
When the GDP growth rate decreases by one percentage point
    1. Government spending (*G*) automatically increases for
        Unemployment insurance benefits.
        Food stamps.
        Welfare benefits.
        Social Security benefits.
        Medicaid.
    2. Government tax revenues (*T*) automatically decline for
        Individual income taxes.
        Corporate income taxes.
        Social Security payroll taxes.
    3. **The deficit increases by $50 billion.**

- ***Changes in Inflation***
When the inflation rate increases by one percentage point
    1. Government spending (*G*) automatically increases for
        Indexed retirement and Social Security benefits.
        Higher interest payments.
    2. Government tax revenues (*T*) automatically increase for
        Corporate income taxes.
        Social Security payroll taxes.
    3. **The deficit increases by $53 billion.**

Source: Congressional Budget Office (first-year effects).

TABLE 12.2

The Budget Impact of Cyclical Forces (in 2015 dollars)

Changes in economic conditions alter federal revenue and spending. When GDP growth slows, tax revenues decline and income transfers increase. This widens the budget deficit.

Higher rates of inflation increase both outlays and revenues, but not equally.

The cyclical balance reflects the budget impacts of changing economic circumstances.

output. As we've observed, if household incomes increase, a jump in consumer spending is likely to follow. The resultant multiplier effects might create some demand-pull inflation. The tax code lessens this inflationary pressure. When you get more income, you have to pay more taxes. Hence income taxes siphon off some of the increased purchasing power that might have found its way to product markets. Progressive income taxes are particularly effective stabilizers because they siphon off increasing proportions of purchasing power when incomes are rising and decreasing proportions when aggregate demand and output are falling.

Cyclical Deficits

Automatic stabilizers imply that policymakers don't have total control of each year's budget. In reality, *the size of the federal deficit or surplus is sensitive to expansion and contraction of the macro economy.*

Effects of GDP Growth. Table 12.2 shows just how sensitive the budget is to cyclical forces. When the GDP growth rate slows, tax revenues decline. As the economy slows, people also turn to the government for additional income support: unemployment benefits and other transfer payments increase. As a consequence, the budget deficit increases. This is exactly what happened in FY 2009: the recession increased the budget deficit by $350 billion (see Table 12.3).

Effects of Inflation. Inflation also affects the budget. Because Social Security benefits are automatically adjusted to inflation, federal outlays increase as the price level rises. Interest rates also rise with inflation, forcing the government to pay more for debt services. Tax revenues also rise with inflation, but not as fast as expenditures.

web click

For more historical data on cyclical and structural deficits, visit the U.S. Congressional Budget Office website at **www.cbo.gov**. Click "Budget & Economy."

Fiscal Year	Budget Balance	=	Cyclical Component	+	Structural Component
2000	+236		+138		+98
2001	+128		+79		+49
2002	−158		−21		−137
2003	−378		−66		−311
2004	−413		−27		−386
2005	−318		+13		−331
2006	−248		+41		−289
2007	−161		+25		−185
2008	−459		−34		−424
2009	−1,413		−350		−1,063
2010	−1,293		−417		−876
2011	−1,300		−409		−891
2012	−1,089		−386		−703
2013	−845		−422		−423

Source: Congressional Budget Office (March 2014).

TABLE 12.3

Cyclical vs. Structural Budget Balances (in billions of dollars)

The budget balance includes both cyclical and structural components. Changes in the structural component result from policy changes; changes in the cyclical component result from changes in the economy. In 2006 the cyclical surplus increased by $28 billion (from +13 billion to +41 billion) due to faster GDP growth. In 2009 the opposite occurred: the recession widened the cyclical deficit by $316 billion (from −34 to −350 billion).

Table 12.2 shows that a one-point increase in the inflation rate *increases* the budget deficit by $53 billion.

The most important implication of Table 12.2 is that neither the president nor the Congress has complete control of the federal deficit. ***Actual budget deficits and surpluses may arise from economic conditions as well as policy.*** Perhaps no one learned this better than President Reagan. In 1980 he campaigned on a promise to balance the budget. The 1981–1982 recession, however, caused the actual deficit to soar. The president later had to admit that actual deficits aren't solely the product of big spenders in Washington.

President Clinton had more luck with the deficit. Although he increased discretionary spending in his first two years, the annual budget deficit *shrank* by more than $90 billion between 1993 and 1995. Most of the deficit reduction was due to automatic stabilizers that kicked in as GDP growth accelerated and the unemployment rate fell. As the economy continued to grow sharply, the unemployment rate fell to 4 percent. That surge in the economy increased tax revenues, reduced income transfers, and propelled the 1998 budget into surplus. It was primarily the economy, not the president or the Congress, that produced the first budget surplus in a generation.

President George W. Bush also benefited from GDP growth. From 2003–2007, economic growth raised both incomes and tax payments. Notice in Table 12.1 how tax revenue jumped from $2,407 billion in 2006 to $2,568 billion in 2007. Tax *rates* weren't increased during those years; people were simply earning more money. The *automatic* increase in revenues helped shrink the deficit from $248 billion in 2006 to $161 billion in 2007.

The recession of 2008–2009 reversed these favorable trends. Even before President Obama convinced Congress to cut taxes and increase government spending, the federal deficit was increasing. Tax receipts were declining as more and more workers lost paychecks. Federal spending was increasing as more workers sought unemployment benefits, welfare, and medical assistance.

That part of the federal deficit attributable to cyclical disturbances (unemployment and inflation) is referred to as the **cyclical deficit.** As we've observed,

cyclical deficit: That portion of the budget balance attributable to short-run changes in economic conditions.

- *The cyclical deficit widens when GDP growth slows or inflation increases.*
- *The cyclical deficit shrinks when GDP growth accelerates or inflation decreases.*

If observed budget balances don't necessarily reflect fiscal policy decisions, how are we to know whether fiscal policy is stimulative or restrictive? Clearly some other indicator is needed.

Structural Deficits

To isolate the effects of fiscal policy, economists break down the actual budget balance into *cyclical* and *structural* components:

$$\frac{\text{Total budget}}{\text{balance}} = \frac{\text{Cyclical}}{\text{balance}} + \frac{\text{Structural}}{\text{balance}}$$

The cyclical portion of the budget balance reflects the impact of the business cycle on federal tax revenues and spending. The **structural deficit** reflects fiscal policy decisions. Rather than comparing actual outlays to actual receipts, the structural deficit compares the outlays and receipts that would occur if the economy were at full employment.[1] This technique eliminates budget distortions caused by cyclical conditions. Any remaining changes in spending or outlays must be due to policy decisions. Hence, *part of the deficit arises from cyclical changes in the economy; the rest is the result of discretionary fiscal policy.*

structural deficit: Federal revenues at full employment minus expenditures at full employment under prevailing fiscal policy.

Table 12.3 shows how the total, cyclical, and structural balances have behaved in recent years. Consider what happened to the federal budget in 2000–2001. In 2000 the federal surplus was $236 billion. In 2001 the surplus shrank to $128 billion. The shrinking surplus suggests that the government was trying to stimulate economic activity with expansionary fiscal policies (tax cuts, spending hikes). But this wasn't the case. The primary reason for the smaller 2001 surplus was an abrupt halt in GDP growth. As the economy slipped into recession, the *cyclical* component shifted from a *surplus* of $138 billion in 2000 to only $79 billion in 2001. This $59 billion swing in the cyclical budget accounted for most of the decrease in the total budget surplus. By contrast, the *structural* surplus shrank by only $49 billion, reflecting the absence of significant *discretionary* fiscal stimulus.

The distinction between the structural and cyclical components of the budget allows us to figure out who's to "blame" for deficit increases. This was a hot topic when the deficit soared in 2009–2011. According to CBO (Table 12.3), the trillion-dollar *increase* in the 2009 budget deficit was due in part to the economic downturn ($316 billion, i.e., the *change* in the cyclical component from −34 to −350) and the rest to discretionary fiscal policy ($639 billion).

This CBO conclusion reflects the fact that both automatic stabilizers and policy initiatives affect the budget at the same time. To assess the impact of policy decisions alone, we must focus on changes in the *structural* deficit, not the *total* deficit. Specifically,

- *Fiscal stimulus is measured by an increase in the structural deficit* (or shrinkage in the structural surplus).
- *Fiscal restraint is gauged by a decrease in the structural deficit* (or increase in the structural surplus).

According to this measure, fiscal policy was actually restrictive during the Great Depression, when fiscal stimulus was desperately needed (see the News on the next page). Both Presidents Hoover and Roosevelt thought the government should rein in its spending when tax revenues declined so as to keep the federal budget balanced. It took years of economic devastation before the fiscal policy lever was reversed.

---

[1] The structural deficit is also referred to as the "full-employment," "high-employment," or "standardized" deficit.

IN THE NEWS

Fiscal Policy in the Great Depression

In 1931 President Herbert Hoover observed, "Business depressions have been recurrent in the life of our country and are but transitory." Rather than proposing fiscal stimulus, Hoover complained that expansion of public works programs had unbalanced the federal budget. In 1932 he proposed *cutbacks* in government spending and *higher* taxes. In his view, the "unquestioned balancing of the federal budget . . . is the first necessity of national stability and is the foundation of further recovery."

Franklin Roosevelt shared this view of fiscal policy. He criticized Hoover for not balancing the budget and in 1933 warned Congress that "all public works must be considered from the point of view of the ability of the government treasury to pay for them."

As the accompanying figure shows, the budget deficit persisted throughout the Great Depression. But these deficits were the result of a declining economy, not stimulative fiscal policy. The structural deficit actually *decreased* from 1931 to 1933 (see figure), when fiscal *restraint* was pursued. This restraint reduced aggregate spending at a time when producers were desperate for increasing sales. Only when the structural deficit was expanded tremendously by spending during World War II did fiscal policy have a decidedly positive effect. Federal defense expenditures jumped from $2.2 billion in 1940 to $87.4 billion in 1944!

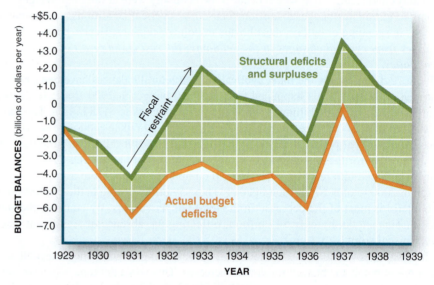

Source: Adapted from E. Cary Brown, "Fiscal Policy in the Thirties: A Reappraisal," *American Economic Review,* December 1956. Table 1. Used by permission of The American Economic Association.

ANALYSIS: From 1931 to 1933, the structural deficit decreased from $4.5 billion to a $2 billion *surplus.* This fiscal restraint reduced aggregate demand and deepened the Great Depression.

ECONOMIC EFFECTS OF DEFICITS

No matter what the origins of budget deficits, most people are alarmed by them. Should they be? What are the *consequences* of budget deficits?

Crowding Out

We've already encountered one potential consequence of deficit financing: *If the government borrows funds to finance deficits, the availability of funds for private sector spending may be reduced.* This is the **crowding-out** problem first noted in Chapter 11. If crowding out occurs, the increase in government expenditure will be at least partially offset by reductions in consumption and investment.

crowding out: A reduction in private sector borrowing (and spending) caused by increased government borrowing.

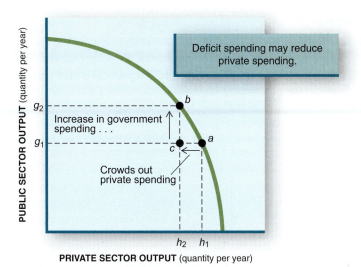

FIGURE 12.2
Crowding Out

If the economy is fully employed, an increase in public sector expenditure (output) will reduce private sector expenditure (output). In this case a deficit-financed increase in government expenditure moves the economy from point *a* to point *b*. In the process the quantity $h_1 - h_2$ of private sector output is crowded out to make room for the increase in public sector output (from g_1 to g_2). If the economy started at point *c*, however, with unemployed resources, crowding out need not occur.

If the economy were operating at full employment, crowding out would be inevitable. At full employment, we'd be on the production possibilities curve, using all available resources. As Figure 12.2 reminds us, additional government purchases can occur only if private sector purchases are reduced. In real terms, ***crowding out implies less private sector output.***

Crowding out is complete only if the economy is at full employment. If the economy is in recession, it's possible to get more public sector output (like highways, schools, defense) without cutbacks in private sector output. This possibility is illustrated by the move from point *c* to point *b* in Figure 12.2.

Tax cuts have crowding-out effects as well. The purpose of the 2001 tax cuts was to stimulate consumer spending. As the economy approaches full employment, however, how can more consumer output be produced? At the production possibilities limit, the added consumption will force cutbacks in either investment or government services.

What Figure 12.2 emphasizes is that ***the risk of crowding out is greater the closer the economy is to full employment.*** This implies that deficits are less appropriate at high levels of employment but more appropriate at low levels of employment.

Opportunity Cost

Even if crowding out does occur, that doesn't mean that deficits are necessarily too big. Crowding out simply reminds us that there's an **opportunity cost** to government spending. We still have to decide whether the private sector output crowded out by government expenditure is more or less desirable than the increased public sector output.

opportunity cost: The most desired goods or services that are forgone in order to obtain something else.

President Clinton defended government expenditure on education, training, and infrastructure as public "investment." He believed that any resulting crowding out of private sector expenditure wasn't necessarily an unwelcome trade-off. Public investments in education, health care, and transportation systems might even accelerate long-term economic growth.

President George W. Bush saw things differently. He preferred a mix of output that included less public sector output and more private sector output. Accordingly, he didn't regard any resulting crowding out of government spending as a real loss.

For his part, President Obama believes that government has to play a leading role in education, health care, infrastructure, and the development of alternative energy sources. He viewed a shift of resources from the private sector to the public sector as a necessity to promote both short-run stimulus and long-term growth. Crowding out, if it occurred, wasn't a bad thing from his perspective.

Interest Rate Movements

Although the production possibilities curve illustrates the inevitability of crowding out at full employment, it doesn't explain *how* the crowding out occurs. Typically, the mechanism that enforces crowding out is the rate of interest. When the government borrows more funds to finance larger deficits, it puts pressure on financial markets. That added pressure may cause interest rates to rise. If they do, households will be less eager to borrow more money to buy cars, houses, and other debt-financed products. Businesses, too, will be more hesitant to borrow and invest. Hence *rising interest rates are both a symptom and a cause of crowding out.*

Rising interests may also crowd out *government* spending in the wake of tax cuts. As interest rates rise, government borrowing costs rise as well. According to the Congressional Budget Office, a one-point rise in interest rates increases Uncle Sam's debt expenses by more than $100 billion over four years. These higher interest costs leave less room in government budgets for financing new projects.

How much interest rates rise again depends on how close the economy is to its productive capacity. If there is a lot of excess capacity, interest rate–induced crowding out isn't very likely. This was the case in early 2009. Interest rates stayed low despite a run-up in government spending and new tax cuts. There was enough excess capacity in the economy to accommodate fiscal stimulus without crowding out. As capacity is approached, however, interest rates and crowding out are both likely to increase.

ECONOMIC EFFECTS OF SURPLUSES

Although budget deficits are clearly the norm, we might at least ponder the economic effects of budget *surpluses*. Essentially, they are the mirror image of those for deficits.

Crowding In

When the government takes in more revenue than it spends, it adds to leakage in the circular flow. But Uncle Sam doesn't hide the surplus under a mattress. And the sums involved (such as $236 billion in FY 2000) are too large to put in a bank. Were the government to buy corporate stock with the budget surplus, it would effectively be nationalizing private enterprises. So where does the surplus go?

There are really only four potential uses for a budget surplus:

- *Spend it on goods and services.*
- *Cut taxes.*
- *Increase income transfers.*
- *Pay off old debt ("save it").*

The first three options effectively wipe out the surplus by changing budget outlays or receipts. There are important differences here, though. The first option—increased government spending—not only reduces the surplus but enlarges the public sector. Cutting taxes or increasing income transfers, by contrast, puts the money into the hands of consumers and enlarges the private sector.

The fourth budget option is to use the surplus to pay off some of the debt accumulated from earlier deficits. This has a similar but less direct **crowding-in** effect. If Uncle Sam pays off some of his accumulated debt, households that were holding that debt (government bonds) will end up with more money. If they use that money to buy goods and services, then private sector output will expand.

Even people who haven't lent any money to Uncle Sam will benefit from the debt reduction. When the government reduces its level of borrowing, it takes pressure off market interest rates. As interest rates drop, consumers will be more willing and able to purchase big-ticket items such as cars, appliances, and houses, thus changing the mix of output in favor of private sector production.

crowding in: An increase in private sector borrowing (and spending) caused by decreased government borrowing.

Cyclical Sensitivity

Like crowding out, the extent of crowding in depends on the state of the economy. In a recession, a surplus-induced decline in interest rates isn't likely to stimulate much spending. If consumer and investor confidence are low, even a surplus-financed tax cut might not lift private sector spending much.

THE ACCUMULATION OF DEBT

Because the U.S. government has had many more years of budget deficits than budget surpluses, Uncle Sam has accumulated a large **national debt.** In fact, the United States started out in debt. The Continental Congress needed to borrow money in 1777 to continue fighting the Revolutionary War. The Congress tried to raise tax revenues and even printed new money (the Continental dollar) to buy needed food, tents, guns, and ammunition. But by the winter of 1777, these mechanisms for financing the war were failing. To acquire needed supplies, the Continental Congress plunged the new nation into debt.

national debt: Accumulated debt of the federal government.

Debt Creation

As with today's deficits, the Continental Congress acknowledged its loans by issuing bonds. Today the U.S. Treasury is the fiscal agent of the U.S. government. The Treasury collects tax revenues, signs checks for federal spending, and—when necessary—borrows funds to cover budget deficits. When the Treasury borrows funds, it issues **Treasury bonds;** these are IOUs of the federal government. People buy bonds—lend money to the U.S. Treasury—because bonds pay interest and are a very safe haven for idle funds.

Treasury bonds: Promissory notes (IOUs) issued by the U.S. Treasury.

The total stock of all outstanding bonds represents the national debt. It's equal to the sum total of our accumulated deficits, less net repayments in those years when a budget surplus existed. In other words, *the national debt is a stock of IOUs created by annual deficit flows.* Whenever there's a budget deficit, the national debt increases. In years when a budget surplus exists, the national debt can be pared down.

Early History, 1776–1900

The United States began accumulating debt as soon as independence was declared. By 1783 the United States had borrowed more than $8 million from France and $250,000 from Spain. Most of these funds were secretly obtained to help finance the Revolutionary War.

During the period 1790–1812, the United States often incurred debt but typically repaid it quickly. The War of 1812, however, caused a massive increase in the national debt. With neither a standing army nor an adequate source of tax revenues to acquire one, the U.S. government had to borrow money to repel the British. By 1816 the national debt was more than $129 million. Although that figure seems tiny by today's standards, it amounted to 13 percent of national income in 1816.

1835–1836: Debt-Free! After the War of 1812, the U.S. government used recurrent budget surpluses to repay its debt. These surpluses were so frequent that the U.S. government was completely out of debt by 1835. In 1835 and again in 1836, the government had neither national debt nor a budget deficit. The dilemma in those years was how to use the budget *surplus!* Since there was no accumulated debt, the option of using the surplus to reduce the debt didn't exist. In the end, Congress decided simply to distribute the surplus funds to the states. That was the last time the U.S. government was completely out of debt.

The Mexican-American War (1846–1848) necessitated a sudden increase in federal spending. The deficits incurred to fight that war caused a fourfold increase in the debt. That debt was pared down the following decade. Then the Civil War (1861–1865) broke out, and both sides needed debt financing. By the end of the Civil War, the North owed more than $2.6 billion, or approximately half its national income. The South depended more heavily on newly printed Confederate currency to finance its side of the Civil War, relying on bond issues for only one-third of its financial needs. When the South lost, however, neither Confederate currency nor Confederate bonds had any value.[2]

Twentieth Century

The Spanish-American War (1898) also increased the national debt. But all prior debt was dwarfed by World War I, which increased the national debt from 3 percent of national income in 1917 to 41 percent at the war's end.

The national debt declined during the 1920s because the federal government was consistently spending less revenue than it took in. Budget surpluses disappeared quickly when the economy fell into the Great Depression, however, and the cyclical deficit widened (see the News on page 258).

World War II. The most explosive jump in the national debt occurred during World War II, when the government had to mobilize all available resources. Rather than raise taxes to the fullest, the U.S. government restricted the availability of consumer goods. With consumer goods rationed, consumers had little choice but to increase their saving. Uncle Sam encouraged people to lend their idle funds to the U.S. Treasury by buying U.S. war bonds. The resulting bond purchases raised the national debt from 45 percent of GDP in 1940 to more than 125 percent of GDP in 1946 (see Figure 12.3).

The 1980s. During the 1980s, the national debt jumped again—by nearly $2 *trillion*. This 10-year increase in the debt exceeded all the net debt accumulation since the country was founded. This time, however, the debt increase wasn't war-related. Instead the debt explosion of the 1980s originated in recessions (1980–1981 and 1981–1982), massive tax cuts (1981–1984), and increased defense spending. The recessions caused big jumps in the cyclical deficit while the Reagan tax cuts and military buildup caused the structural deficit to jump fourfold in only four years (1982–1986).

The 1990s. The early 1990s continued the same trend. Discretionary federal spending increased sharply in the first two years of the George H. Bush administration. The federal government was also forced to bail out hundreds of failed savings and loan associations. Although taxes were raised a bit and military spending was cut back, the structural deficit was little changed. Then the recession of 1990–1991 killed any chance of achieving smaller deficits. In only four years (1988–1992) the national debt increased by another $1 trillion.

In 1993 the Clinton administration persuaded Congress to raise taxes, thereby reducing the structural deficit. Continuing recovery from the 1990–1991 recession also reduced the cyclical deficit. Nevertheless, the budget deficits of 1993–1996 pushed the national debt to more than $5 trillion.

The 2000s. After a couple of years of budget surplus, the accumulated debt still exceeded $5.6 trillion in 2002. Then the Bush tax cuts and the defense buildup kicked in, increasing the structural deficit by nearly $300 billion in only three years (FY 2002–2004) (Table 12.4). As a consequence, the national debt surged again. By January 2009—*before* the Obama stimulus plan was enacted—the debt exceeded $10 trillion.

[2]In anticipation of this situation, European leaders had forced the South to guarantee most of its loans with cotton. When the South was unable to repay its debts, these creditors could sell the cotton they had held as collateral. But most holders of Confederate bonds or currency received nothing.

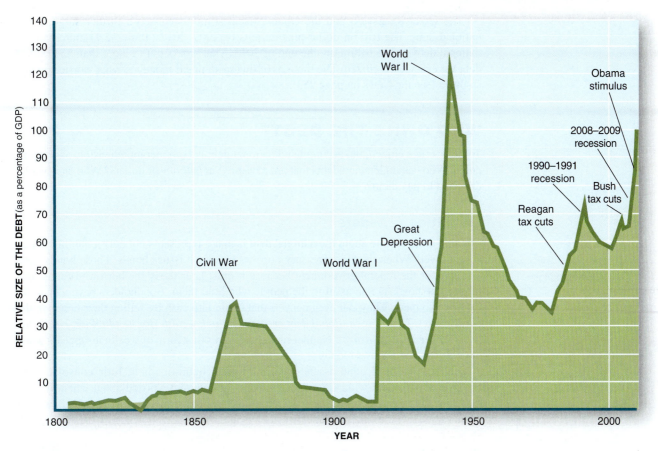

FIGURE 12.3

Historical View of the Debt/GDP Ratio

From 1790 to 1917, the national debt exceeded 10 percent of GDP during the Civil War years only. After 1917, however, the debt ratio grew sharply. World War I, the Great Depression, and World War II all caused major increases in the debt ratio. The tax cuts of 1981–1984 and 2001–2005 and the recessions of 1990–1991, 2001, and 2008–2009 caused further increases in the debt/GDP ratio. The Obama fiscal stimulus pushed the debt ratio still higher.

Source: Office of Management and Budget.

Year	Total Debt Outstanding (Millions of Dollars)	Year	Total Debt Outstanding (Millions of Dollars)
1791	75	1930	16,185
1800	83	1940	42,967
1810	53	1945	258,682
1816	127	1960	286,331
1820	91	1970	370,919
1835	0	1980	914,300
1850	63	1985	1,827,500
1865	2,678	1990	3,163,000
1900	1,263	2000	5,629,000
1915	1,191	2010	14,025,615
1920	24,299	2015	est. 18,000,000

Source: Office of Management and Budget.

web click

To see how much debt is owed by the U.S. government to the penny, visit **www.treasurydirect .gov.** Click "Find information on the public debt."

TABLE 12.4

The National Debt

It took nearly a century for the national debt to reach $1 trillion. The debt tripled in a mere decade (1980–1990) and then quintupled again in 20 years. The accumulated debt now totals more than $18 trillion.

The Great Recession and the Obama fiscal stimulus caused a further surge in the national debt. The trillion-dollar-plus deficits of 2009–2012 (Table 12.1) increased the national debt to $16 trillion by the end of 2013. That works out to more than $51,000 of debt for every U.S. citizen. The thought of owing so much money is what worries people so much (see the News on page 253).

WHO OWNS THE DEBT?

To the average citizen, the accumulated national debt is both incomprehensible and frightening. Who can understand debts that are measured in *trillions* of dollars? Who can ever be expected to pay them?

Liabilities = Assets

The first thing to note about the national debt is that it represents not only a liability but an asset as well. When the U.S. Treasury borrows money, it issues bonds. Those bonds are a **liability** for the federal government because it must later repay the borrowed funds. But those same bonds are an **asset** to the people who hold them. Bondholders have a claim to future repayment. They can even convert that claim into cash by selling their bonds in the bond market. Therefore, *national debt creates as much wealth (for bondholders) as liabilities (for the U.S. Treasury).* Neither money nor any other form of wealth disappears when the government borrows money.

The fact that total bond assets equal total bond liabilities is of little consolation to taxpayers confronted with $18 trillion of national debt and worried about when, if ever, they'll be able to repay it. The fear that either the U.S. government or its taxpayers will be "bankrupted" by the national debt always lurks in the shadows. How legitimate is that fear?

Ownership of the Debt

Figure 12.4 shows who owns the bonds the U.S. Treasury has issued. The largest bondholder is the U.S. government itself: *federal agencies hold more than 40 percent of all outstanding Treasury bonds.* The Federal Reserve System, an independent agency of the U.S. government, acquires Treasury bonds in its conduct of monetary policy (see Chapters 14 and 15). Other agencies of the U.S. government also purchase bonds. The Social Security Administration, for example, maintains a trust fund balance to cover any shortfall between monthly payroll tax receipts and retirement benefits. Most of that balance is held

liability: An obligation to make future payment; debt.

asset: Anything having exchange value in the marketplace; wealth.

web click

Would you like to own part of the national debt? You can, and it's easy. Go to **www.treasurydirect .gov** and click "Buy Electronic Savings Bonds through Payroll Savings."

FIGURE 12.4

Debt Ownership

The bonds that create the national debt represent wealth that's owned by bondholders. Almost half of that wealth is held by the U.S. government itself. The private sector in the United States holds only 21 percent of the debt, and foreigners own 33 percent.

Source: U.S. Treasury Department (2014 data).

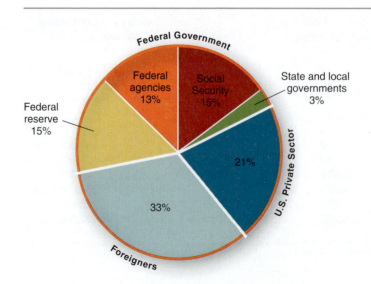

in the form of interest-bearing Treasury bonds. Thus one arm of the federal government (the U.S. Treasury) owes another arm (the U.S. Social Security Administration) a significant part of the national debt.

State and local governments hold another 3 percent of the national debt. This debt, too, arises when state and local governments use their own budget surpluses to purchase interest-bearing Treasury bonds.

The private sector in the United States owns about a fifth of the national debt. This private wealth is in the form of familiar U.S. savings bonds or other types of Treasury bonds. Much of this private wealth is held *indirectly* by banks, insurance companies, money market funds, corporations, and other institutions. All this wealth is ultimately owned by the people who have deposits at the bank or in money market funds, who own stock in corporations, or who are insured by companies that hold Treasury bonds. Thus **U.S. households hold about one-fifth of the national debt, either directly or indirectly.**

All the debt held by U.S. households, institutions, and government entities is referred to as **internal debt.** As Figure 12.4 illustrates, two-thirds of the national debt is internal. In other words, **we owe most of the national debt to ourselves.**

The remaining third of the national debt is held by foreign banks, corporations, households, and governments. U.S. Treasury bonds are attractive to global participants because of their relative security, the interest they pay, and the general acceptability of dollar-denominated assets in world trade. Bonds held by foreign households and institutions are referred to as **external debt.**

internal debt: U.S. government debt (Treasury bonds) held by U.S. households and institutions.

external debt: U.S. government debt (Treasury bonds) held by foreign households and institutions.

BURDEN OF THE DEBT

It may be comforting to know that most of our national debt is owned internally, and much of it by the government itself. Figure 12.4 won't still the fears of most taxpayers, however, especially those who don't hold any Treasury bonds. From their perspective, the total debt still looks frightening.

Refinancing

refinancing: The issuance of new debt in payment of debt issued earlier.

How much of a "burden" the debt really represents isn't so evident. For nearly 30 years (1970–1997), the federal government kept piling up more debt without apparent economic damage. The few years that the government had a budget surplus (1998–2001) weren't markedly different from the deficit years. As we saw earlier (Figure 12.3), deficits and debt stretched out over even longer periods in earlier decades without apparent economic damage.

How was the government able to pile debt upon debt? Quite simple: as debts have become due, the federal government has simply borrowed new funds to pay them off. New bonds have been issued to replace old bonds. This **refinancing** of the debt is a routine feature of the U.S. Treasury's debt management.

The ability of the U.S. Treasury to refinance its debt raises an intriguing question. What if the debt could be eternally refinanced? What if no one *ever* demanded to be paid off more than others were willing to lend Uncle Sam? Then the national debt would truly grow forever.

Two things are worrisome about this scenario. First, eternal refinancing seems like a chain letter that promises to make everyone rich. In this case, the chain requires that people hold ever-larger portions of their wealth in the form of Treasury bonds. People worry that the chain will be broken and that they'll be forced to repay all the outstanding debt. Parents worry that the scheme might break down in the next generation, unfairly burdening their own children or grandchildren (see the accompanying cartoon).

Aside from its seeming implausibility, the notion of eternal refinancing seems to defy a basic maxim of economics—namely that "there ain't no free lunch." Eternal refinancing makes it look as though government borrowing has no cost, as though federal spending financed by the national debt is really a free lunch.

"What's this I hear about you adults mortgaging my future?"

Analysis: The fear that present generations are passing the debt burden to future generations is exaggerated.

There are two flaws in this way of thinking. The first relates to the interest charges that accompany debt. The second, and more important, oversight relates to the real economic costs of government activity.

Debt Service

debt service: The interest required to be paid each year on outstanding debt.

With more than $18 trillion in accumulated debt, the U.S. government must make enormous interest payments every year. **Debt service** refers to these annual interest payments. In FY 2015, the U.S. Treasury paid more than $250 billion in interest charges. These interest payments force the government to reduce outlays for other purposes or to finance a larger budget each year. In this respect, *interest payments restrict the government's ability to balance the budget or fund other public sector activities.*

Although the debt servicing requirements may pinch Uncle Sam's spending purse, the real economic consequences of interest payments are less evident. Who gets the interest payments? What economic resources are absorbed by those payments?

As noted, most of the nation's outstanding debt is internal—that is, owned by domestic households and institutions. Therefore, most interest payments are made to people and institutions within the United States. *Most debt servicing is simply a redistribution of income from taxpayers to bondholders.* In many cases, the taxpayer and bondholder are the same person. In all cases, however, the income that leaks from the circular flow in the form of taxes to pay for debt servicing returns to the circular flow as interest payments. Total income is unchanged. Thus debt servicing may not have any direct effect on the level of aggregate demand.

Debt servicing also has little impact on the real resources of the economy. The collection of additional taxes and the processing of interest payments require the use of some land, labor, and capital. But the value of the resources used for the processing of debt service is trivial—a tiny fraction of the interest payments themselves. This means that *interest payments themselves have virtually no direct opportunity cost for the economy as a whole.* The amount of goods and services available for other purposes is virtually unchanged as a result of debt servicing.

Opportunity Costs

If debt servicing absorbs few economic resources, can we conclude that the national debt really does represent a free lunch? Unfortunately not. But the concept of opportunity cost provides a major clue about the true burden of the debt and who bears it.

Opportunity costs are incurred only when real resources (factors of production) are used. The amount of that cost is measured by the other goods and services that could have been produced with those resources, but weren't. As noted earlier, the *process* of debt servicing absorbs few resources and so has negligible opportunity cost. To understand the true burden of the national debt, we have to look at what that debt financed. *The true burden of the debt is the opportunity cost of the activities financed by the debt.* To assess that burden, we need to ask what the government did with the borrowed funds.

Government Purchases. Suppose Congress decides to upgrade our naval forces and borrows $10 billion for that purpose. What's the opportunity cost of that decision? The economic cost of the fleet upgrade is measured by the goods and services forgone in order to build more ships. The labor, land, and capital used to upgrade the fleet can't be used to produce something else. We give up the opportunity to produce another $10 billion worth of private goods and services when Congress upgrades the fleet.

The economic cost of the naval buildup is unaffected by the method of government finance. Whether the government borrows $10 billion or increases taxes by that amount, the forgone civilian output will still be $10 billion. *The opportunity cost of government purchases is the true burden of government activity, however financed.* The decision to finance such activity with debt rather than taxes doesn't materially alter that cost.

The Real Trade-Offs

Although the national debt poses no special burden to the economy, the transactions it finances have a substantial impact on the basic questions of WHAT, HOW, and FOR WHOM to produce. The mix of output is influenced by how much deficit spending the government undertakes. The funds obtained by borrowing allow the federal government to bid for scarce resources. Private investors and consumers will have less access to lendable funds and be less able to acquire incomes or goods. The larger the deficit, the more the private sector gets crowded out. Hence deficit financing allows the government to obtain more resources and change the mix of output. In general, *deficit financing changes the mix of output in the direction of more public sector goods.*

As noted earlier, the deficits of the 1980s helped finance a substantial military buildup. The same result could have been financed with higher taxes. Taxes are more visible and always unpopular, however. By borrowing rather than taxing, the federal government's claim on scarce resources is less apparent. Either financing method allows the public sector to expand at the expense of the private sector. This resource reallocation reveals the true burden of the debt: *the burden of the debt is really the opportunity cost (crowding out) of deficit-financed government activity.* How large that burden is depends on how many unemployed resources are available and the behavioral responses of consumers and investors to increased government activity.

Timing of Burden. Notice also *when* that cost is incurred. If the military is upgraded this year, then the opportunity cost is incurred this year. It's only while resources are actually being used by the military that we give up the opportunity to use them elsewhere. Opportunity costs are incurred at the time a government activity takes place, not when the resultant debt is paid. In other words, *the primary burden of the debt is incurred when the debt-financed activity takes place.*

If the entire military buildup is completed this year, what costs are borne next year? None. The land, labor, and capital available next year can be used for whatever purposes are then desired. Once the military buildup is completed, no further resources are allocated to that purpose. The real costs of government projects can't be postponed until a later year. In other words, the real burden of the debt can't be passed on to future generations. On the contrary, future generations will benefit from the sacrifices made today to build ships, parks, highways, dams, and other public sector projects. Future taxpayers will be able to *use* these projects without incurring the opportunity costs of their construction.

Economic Growth. Although future generations may benefit from current government spending, they may also be adversely affected by today's opportunity costs. Of particular concern is the possibility that government deficits might crowd out private investment. Investment is essential to enlarging our production possibilities and attaining higher living standards in the future. If federal deficits and debt-servicing requirements crowd our private investment, the rate of economic growth will slow, leaving future generations with less productive capacity than they would otherwise have. Thus *if debt-financed government spending crowds out private investment, future generations will bear some of the debt burden.* Their burden will take the form of smaller-than-anticipated productive capacity.

There's no certainty that such crowding out will occur. Also, any reduction in private investment may be offset by public works (such as highways, schools, defense systems) that benefit future generations. So future generations may not suffer a net loss in welfare even if the national debt slows private investment and economic growth. From this perspective, *the whole debate about the burden of the debt is really an argument over the optimal mix of output.* If we permit more deficit spending, we're promoting more public sector activity. On the other hand, limits on deficit financing curtail growth of the public sector. *Battles over deficits and debts are a proxy for the more fundamental issue of private versus public spending.*

optimal mix of output: The most desirable combination of output attainable with existing resources, technology, and social values.

Repayment. All this sounds a little too neat. Won't future generations have to pay interest on the debts we incur today? And might they even have to pay off some of the debt?

We've already observed that the collection of taxes and processing of interest payments absorb relatively few resources. Hence the mechanisms of repayment entail little burden.

Notice also who *receives* future interest payments. When we die, we leave behind not only the national debt but also the bonds that represent ownership of that debt. Hence future grandchildren will be both taxpayers *and* bondholders. If interest payments are made 30 years from today, only people who are alive and holding bonds at that time will receive interest payments. *Future interest payments entail a redistribution of income among taxpayers and bondholders living in the future.*

The same kind of redistribution occurs if and when our grandchildren decide to pay off the debt. Tax revenues will be used to pay off the debt. The debt payments will go to people then holding Treasury bonds. The entire redistribution will occur among people living in the future.

EXTERNAL DEBT

The nature of opportunity costs makes it difficult but not impossible to pass the debt burden on to future generations. The exception is the case of external debt.

No Crowding Out

When we borrow funds from abroad, we increase our ability to consume, invest, and finance government activity. In effect, other nations are lending us the income necessary to *import* more goods. If we can buy imports with borrowed funds (without offsetting exports), our real income will exceed our production possibilities. As Figure 12.5 illustrates, external borrowing allows us to enjoy a mix of output that lies *outside* our production possibilities curve. Specifically, *external financing allows us to get more public sector goods without cutting back on private sector production (or vice versa) in the short run.* When we use external debt to finance government spending, we move from point *a* to point *d* in Figure 12.5. Imported goods and services eliminate the need to cut back on private sector activity, a cutback that would otherwise force us to point *b*. External financing eliminates this opportunity cost. The move from point *a* to point *d* reflects the additional imports financed by external debt.

The imports needn't be public sector goods. A tax cut at point *b* might increase consumption and imports by $h_1 - h_2$, moving the economy to point *d*. At *d* we have *more* consumption and *no less* government activity.

FIGURE 12.5

External Financing

A closed economy must forsake some private sector output to increase public sector output (see Figure 12.2). External financing temporarily eliminates that opportunity cost. Instead of having to move from *a* to *b*, external borrowing allows us to move from *a* to *d*. At point *d* we have more public output and no less private output.

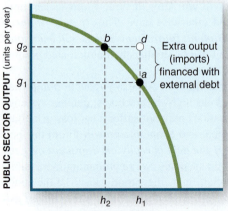

PRIVATE SECTOR OUTPUT (units per year)

External financing appears to offer the proverbial free lunch. It would be a free lunch if foreign lenders were willing to accumulate U.S. Treasury bonds forever. They would then own stacks of paper (Treasury bonds), and we'd consume some of their output (our imports) each year. *As long as outsiders are willing to hold U.S. bonds, external financing imposes no real cost.* No goods or services are given up to pay for the additional output received.

Repayment

Foreign investors may not be willing to hold U.S. bonds indefinitely. At some point they'll want to collect their bills. To do this, they'll cash in (sell) their bonds, then use the proceeds to buy U.S. goods and services. When this happens, the United States will be *exporting* goods and services to pay off its debts. Recall that the external debt was used to acquire imported goods and services. Hence *external debt must be repaid with exports of real goods and services.*

DEFICIT AND DEBT LIMITS

Although external and internal debts pose very different problems, most policy discussions overlook these distinctions. In policy debates, the aggregate size of the national debt is usually the only concern. The key policy questions are whether and how to limit or reduce the national debt.

Deficit Ceilings

The only way to stop the growth of the national debt is to eliminate the budget deficits that create debt. The first step in debt reduction, therefore, is a balanced annual budget. A balanced budget will at least stop the debt from growing further. **Deficit ceilings** are explicit limitations on the size of the annual budget deficit. A deficit ceiling of zero compels a balanced budget.

deficit ceiling: An explicit, legislated limitation on the size of the budget deficit.

The Balanced Budget and Emergency Deficit Control Act of 1985—popularly referred to as the Gramm-Rudman-Hollings Act—was the first explicit attempt to force the federal budget into balance. The essence of the Gramm-Rudman-Hollings Act was simple:

- First, it set a lower ceiling on each year's deficit until budget balance was achieved.
- Second, it called for automatic cutbacks in spending if Congress failed to keep the deficit below the ceiling.

The original Gramm-Rudman-Hollings law required Congress to pare the deficit from more than $200 billion in FY 1985 to zero (a balanced budget) by 1991. But Congress wasn't willing to cut spending and increase taxes enough to meet those targets. And the Supreme Court declared that the "automatic" mechanism for spending cuts was unconstitutional.

In 1990 President George H. Bush and the Congress developed a new set of rules for reducing the deficit. They first acknowledged that they lacked total control of the deficit. At best, Congress could close the *structural* deficit by limiting discretionary spending or raising taxes. The Budget Enforcement Act (BEA) of 1990 laid out a plan for doing exactly this. The BEA set separate limits on defense spending, discretionary domestic spending, and international spending. It also required that any new spending initiative be offset with increased taxes or cutbacks in other programs—a process called "pay as you go," or simply "paygo."

The Budget Enforcement Act was successful in reducing the structural deficit somewhat. But the political pain associated with spending cuts and higher taxes was too great for elected officials to bear. Since then, recurrent legislated deficit ceilings have proved to be more political ornaments than binding budget mandates.

debt ceiling: An explicit, legislated limit on the amount of outstanding national debt.

Debt Ceilings

Explicit **debt ceilings** are another mechanism for forcing Congress to adopt specific fiscal policies. A debt ceiling can be used either to stop the accumulation of debt or to force the federal government to start *reducing* the accumulated national debt. In effect, debt ceilings are a backdoor approach to deficit reduction. *Like deficit ceilings, debt ceilings are really just political mechanisms for forging compromises on how best to reduce budget deficits.* This was evident in August 2011 when the national debt was again approaching its legislated ceiling ($14.3 trillion). Republicans insisted on cutting federal spending without any tax increases. Democrats insisted that the pain of deficit reduction had to include higher taxes, especially on the wealthy. The prospect of a government shutdown that would accompany a prohibition on federal borrowing forced a budget compromise that included an *increase* in the debt ceiling.

THE ECONOMY TOMORROW

DIPPING INTO SOCIAL SECURITY

The Social Security Trust Fund has been a major source of funding for the federal government for more than 25 years. Since 1985 the Trust Fund has collected more payroll (FICA) taxes each year than it has paid out in retirement benefits. As we noted already, all of those surpluses have been "invested" in Treasury securities, making the Social Security Trust Fund the U.S. Treasury's largest creditor. The Trust Fund now holds $2.57 trillion of Treasury securities (Figure 12.4).

Aging Baby Boomers. The persistent surpluses in the Social Security Trust Fund have largely been the result of aging Baby Boomers. In the 15 years after World War II ended, birthrates soared. These Baby Boomers were in their peak earning years (45–60) between 1990 and 2010 and paying lots of payroll taxes. That kept the Social Security Trust Fund flush with cash.

As we peer into the economy tomorrow, however, the fiscal outlook is not so bright. The Baby Boomers are fast reaching retirement age. As they retire, the Baby Boomers throw the budget of the Social Security Trust Fund out of whack. Since 2010 Social Security benefit payments have exceeded payroll tax receipts. That has curbed the Trust Fund's ability to buy government bonds. By 2030 Social Security finances will be much worse as there will be only 2 workers for every retiree, down from today's 2.7 worker/retiree ratio (see Table 12.5). By then, a primary source of government financing will have completely disappeared.

Social Security Deficits. As the Trust Fund balance shifts from annual surpluses to annual deficits, Social Security will be able to pay promised benefits only if (1) the U.S. Treasury pays all interest due on bonds held by the Trust Fund and, ultimately, (2) the U.S. Treasury redeems the bonds the Trust Fund will then be holding. This is what scares aging Baby Boomers (and should worry you).

TABLE 12.5

Changing Worker/Retiree Ratios

Fifty years ago there were more than 16 taxpaying workers for every retiree. Today there are only 3, and the ratio slips further when the Baby Boomers start retiring. This demographic change will convert Social Security surpluses into deficits, causing future budget problems.

Year	Workers per Beneficiary	Year	Workers per Beneficiary
1950	16.5	2000	3.4
1960	5.1	2015	2.7
1970	3.7	2030	2.0

Source: U.S. Social Security Administration.

The Baby Boomers wonder where the Treasury is going to get the funds needed to repay the Social Security Trust Fund. There really aren't many options. ***To pay back Social Security loans, the Congress will have to raise future taxes significantly, make substantial cuts in other (non–Social Security) programs, or sharply increase budget deficits.*** None of these options is attractive. Worse yet, the budget squeeze created by the Social Security payback will severely limit the potential for discretionary fiscal policy.

When GDP growth slows in the economy tomorrow, it will be increasingly difficult to cut taxes or increase government spending while the U.S. Treasury is scurrying to repay Social Security Trust Fund loans. Aging Baby Boomers worry that Congress might instead cut their promised retirement benefits.

SUMMARY

- Budget deficits result from both discretionary fiscal policy (structural deficits) and cyclical changes in the economy (cyclical deficits). **LO12-1**
- Fiscal restraint is measured by the reduction in the structural deficit; fiscal stimulus occurs when the structural deficit increases. **LO12-1**
- Automatic stabilizers increase federal spending and reduce tax revenues during recessions. When the economy expands, they have the reverse effect, thereby shrinking the cyclical deficit. **LO12-1**
- Deficit financing of government expenditure may crowd out private investment and consumption. The risk of crowding out increases as the economy approaches full employment. If investment becomes the opportunity cost of increased government spending or consumer tax cuts, economic growth may slow. **LO12-3**
- Crowding in refers to the increase in private sector output made possible by a decline in government borrowing. **LO12-3**
- Each year's deficit adds to the national debt. The national debt grew sporadically until World War II and then skyrocketed. Tax cuts, recessions, and increased government spending have increased the national debt to more than $18 trillion. **LO12-2**

- Budget surpluses may be used to finance tax cuts or more government spending, or used to reduce accumulated national debt. **LO12-1**
- Every dollar of national debt represents a dollar of assets to the people who hold U.S. Treasury bonds. Most U.S. bonds are held by U.S. government agencies, U.S. households, and U.S. banks, insurance companies, and other institutions, and are thus "internal debt." **LO12-4**
- The real burden of the debt is the opportunity cost of the activities financed by the debt. That cost is borne at the time the deficit-financed activity takes place. The benefits of debt-financed activity may extend into the future. **LO12-4**
- External debt (bonds held by foreigners) permits the public sector to expand without reducing private sector output. External debt also makes it possible to shift some of the real debt burden on to future generations. **LO12-4**
- Deficit and debt ceilings are largely symbolic efforts to force consideration of real trade-offs, to restrain government spending, and to change the mix of output. **LO12-4**
- The retirement of the Baby Boomers (born 1946–1960) is transforming Social Security surpluses into deficits, imposing severe constraints on future fiscal policy. **LO12-1**

Key Terms

fiscal policy	automatic stabilizer	asset
deficit spending	cyclical deficit	internal debt
budget deficit	structural deficit	external debt
budget surplus	crowding out	refinancing
fiscal year (FY)	opportunity cost	debt service
discretionary fiscal spending	crowding in	optimal mix of output
fiscal restraint	national debt	deficit ceiling
fiscal stimulus	Treasury bonds	debt ceiling
income transfers	liability	

Questions for Discussion

1. Why are people worried more about federal budget deficits than climate change (News, p. 253)? **LO12-4**
2. Who paid for the Revolutionary War? Did the deficit financing initiated by the Continental Congress pass the cost of the war on to future generations? **LO12-4**
3. When are larger deficits desirable? **LO12-1**
4. Can you forecast next year's deficit without knowing how fast GDP will grow? **LO12-1**
5. In what ways do *future* generations benefit from this generation's deficit spending? Cite three examples. **LO12-2, LO12-4**
6. If deficit spending "crowds out" some private investment, could future generations be worse off? If external financing eliminates crowding out, are future generations thereby protected? **LO12-3**
7. A constitutional amendment has been proposed that would require Congress to balance the budget each year. Is it possible to balance the budget each year? Is it desirable? **LO12-1**
8. What did the surge in defense spending from 1940 to 1944 crowd out? **LO12-3**
9. How long would it take to pay off the national debt? How would the economy be affected? **LO12-4**
10. Which of the following options do you favor for resolving future Social Security deficits? What are the advantages and disadvantages of each option? (a) cutting Social Security benefits, (b) raising payroll taxes, (c) cutting non–Social Security programs, and (d) raising income taxes. **LO12-1**

 mobile app Visit your mobile app store and download the Schiller: Study Econ app *today!*

LO12-2 1. From 2008 to 2010 by how much did each of the following change?
   (*a*) Tax revenue.   _____
   (*b*) Government spending.   _____
   (*c*) Budget deficit.   _____
   (*Note:* See Table 12.1.)

LO12-2 2. Since 1980, in how many years has the federal budget had a surplus? (See Figure 12.1.)   _____

LO12-2 3. What country had the largest budget deficit (as a percentage of GDP) in 2013
   (World View, p. 253)?   _____

LO12-1 4. What would happen to the budget deficit if the
   (*a*) GDP growth rate jumped from 2 percent to 4 percent?   _____
   (*b*) Inflation rate increased by two percentage points?   _____
   (*Note:* See Table 12.2 for clues.)

LO12-1 5. Between 2000 and 2013, in how many years was fiscal restraint initiated? (See Table 12.3.)   _____

LO12-1 6. Use Table 12.3 to determine how much fiscal stimulus or restraint occurred between
                                       (*a*) 2007 and 2008.   _____
                                       (*b*) 2012 and 2013.   _____

LO12-1 7. According to Table 12.3, the federal deficit fell from $1,300 billion in 2011 to $845 billion in
   2013. How much of this $455 billion deficit reduction was due to
   (*a*) The growing economy?   _____
   (*b*) Fiscal restraint?   _____

LO12-4 8. Suppose a government has no debt and a balanced budget. Suddenly it decides to spend
   $4 trillion while raising only $3 trillion worth of taxes.
   (*a*) What will be the government's deficit?   _____
   (*b*) If the government finances the deficit by issuing bonds, what amount of bonds will it issue?   _____
   (*c*) At a 4 percent rate of interest, how much interest will the government pay each year?   _____
   (*d*) Add the interest payment to the government's $4 trillion expenditures for the next year, and
          assume that tax revenues remain at $3 trillion. In the second year, compute the
       (*i*)   Deficit.   _____
       (*ii*) Amount of new debt (bonds) issued.   _____
       (*iii*) Total debt at end of year.   _____
       (*iv*) Debt service requirement.   _____

LO12-1 9. (*a*) According to the News on page 258, how much fiscal restraint occurred between 1931 and
              1933?   _____
       (*b*) By how much did this policy reduce aggregate demand if the MPC was 0.80?   _____

LO12-3 10. In Figure 12.5, what is the opportunity cost of increasing government spending from g_1 to g_2 if
   (*a*) No external financing is available?   _____
   (*b*) Complete external financing is available?   _____

LO12-4 11. (*a*) What percentage of U.S. debt do foreigners hold? (See Figure 12.4.)   _____
       (*b*) If the interest rate on U.S. Treasury debt is 4 percent, how much interest do foreigners collect
              each year from the U.S. Treasury? (Assume a *total* debt of $18 trillion.)   _____

LO12-1 12. Use the accompanying graph to illustrate *changes* in the structural and total deficits for fiscal
years 2007–2013 (use the data in Table 12.3).

(*a*) In how many years do the two deficits change in *different* directions?   _____

(*b*) In how many years was the government pursuing fiscal restraint?   _____

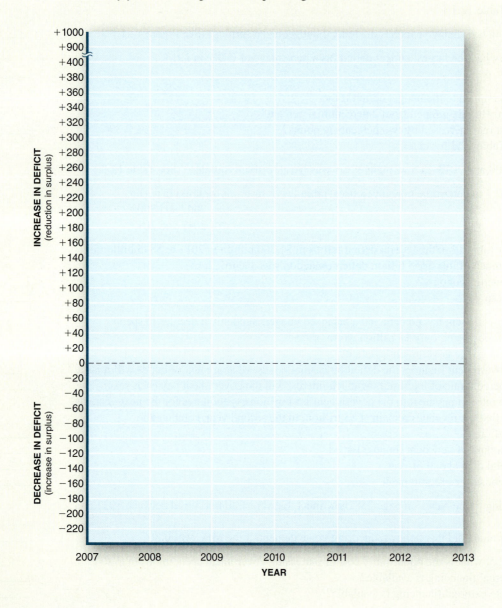

Monetary Policy Options

Monetary policy tries to alter macro outcomes by managing the amount of money available in the economy. By changing the money supply and/or interest rates, monetary policy seeks to shift the aggregate demand curve in the desired direction. Chapters 13 through 15 illustrate how this policy tool works.

Money and Banks

After reading this chapter, you should know

LO13-1 What money is.

LO13-2 What a bank's assets and liabilities are.

LO13-3 How banks create money.

LO13-4 How the money multiplier works.

Sophocles, the ancient Greek playwright, had strong opinions about the role of money. As he saw it, "Of evils upon earth, the worst is money. It is money that sacks cities, and drives men forth from hearth and home; warps and seduces native intelligence, and breeds a habit of dishonesty."

In modern times, people may still be seduced by the lure of money and fashion their lives around its pursuit. Nevertheless, it's hard to imagine an economy functioning without money. Money affects not only morals and ideals but also the way an economy works.

This and the following two chapters examine the role of money in the economy today. We begin with a simple question:

- **What is money?**

As we'll discover, money isn't exactly what you might think it is. There's a lot more money in the economy than there is cash. And there's a lot more income out there than money. So money is something quite different from either cash or income.

Once we've established the characteristics of money, we go on to ask,

- **How is money created?**
- **What role do banks play in the circular flow of income and spending?**

In Chapter 14 we look at how the Federal Reserve System controls the amount of money created. In Chapter 15 we look at the implications for monetary policy, another tool in our macro policy toolbox.

WHAT IS "MONEY"?

To appreciate the significance of money for a modern economy, imagine for a moment that there were no such thing as money. How would you get something for breakfast? If you wanted eggs for breakfast, you'd have to tend your own chickens or go see Farmer Brown. But how would you pay Farmer Brown for his eggs? Without money, you'd have to offer him some goods or services that he could use. In other words, you'd have to engage in primitive **barter**—the direct exchange of one good for another—to get eggs for breakfast. You'd get those eggs only if Farmer Brown happened to want the particular goods or services you had to offer.

The use of money greatly simplifies market transactions. It's a lot easier to exchange money for eggs at the supermarket than to go into the country and barter with farmers every time you crave an omelet. Our ability to use money in market transactions, however, depends on the grocer's willingness to accept money as a *medium of exchange.* The grocer sells eggs for money only because he can use the same money to pay his help and buy the goods he himself desires. He too can exchange money for goods and services.

Without money, the process of acquiring goods and services would be much more difficult and time-consuming. This was evident when the value of the Russian ruble plummeted. Trading goods for Farmer Brown's eggs seems simple compared to the complicated barter deals Russian factories had to negotiate when paper money was no longer accepted (see the World View below). And Russian workers certainly would have preferred to be paid in cash rather than in bras and coffins.

barter: The direct exchange of one good for another, without the use of money.

WORLD VIEW

The Cashless Society

Bartering Chokes Russian Economy

NARO-FOMINSK, RUSSIA—Natalya Karpova, a supervisor at a fabric factory here on the outskirts of Moscow, heard good news a couple of weeks ago. Three carloads of concrete utility poles had arrived at the train station.

This was a matter of utmost importance to Karpova because her factory was a year behind on its electric bill and had no cash on hand. The electric company agreed to accept utility poles instead, but how to pay for utility poles with no rubles?

Simple. First, her factory shipped fabric 200 miles to a sewing factory in Nizhny Novgorod. In exchange for the fabric, that factory sewed shirts for the security guards who work at a nearby automobile manufacturer. In exchange for the shirts, the auto factory shipped a car and truck to a concrete plant. In exchange for the vehicles, the concrete plant delivered the poles to the electric company.

Thus did the Narfomsholk fabric factory pay for the power to run its dye machines.

But only for a while. "Now they want a steam shovel," said Karpova, with a little sigh.

This is how Karpova's factory and much of Russia's industry survives these days: barter. By some estimates, it accounts for almost three-fourths of all transactions.

Barter is poisoning the development of capitalism in Russia because it consumes huge amounts of time that would be better spent producing goods.

Many workers have no expectation of a real paycheck. Unpaid wages now amount to an estimated $11 billion. Instead of money, the workers are stuck with whatever the factory or farm is handing out, usually what it produces. The practice is so common now that only the more bizarre substitutes for wages draw notice, such as bras or coffins.

—Sharon LaFraniere

Source: *The Washington Post,* © September 3, 1998. All rights reserved. Used with permission.

ANALYSIS: When the Russian ruble lost its value, people would no longer accept it in payment as a medium of exchange. Market transactions had to be bartered, a clumsy and inefficient process.

web click

Though bartering is inefficient, it is practiced at low levels even in countries with a stable currency. This is partly because bartering helps market participants lawfully avoid certain taxes. To see the tax rules on barter, go to **www.irs.gov** and search "barter."

THE MONEY SUPPLY

Although markets can't function well without money, they can get along without *dollars*.

Many Types of Money

In the early days of colonial America, there were no U.S. dollars; a lot of business was conducted with Spanish and Portuguese gold coins. Later people used Indian wampum, then tobacco, grain, fish, and furs as media of exchange. Throughout the colonies, gunpowder and bullets were frequently used for small change. These forms of money weren't as convenient as U.S. dollars, but they did the job.

This historical perspective on money highlights its essential characteristics. ***Anything that serves all the following purposes can be thought of as money:***

- ***Medium of exchange:*** is accepted as payment for goods and services (and debts).
- ***Store of value:*** can be held for future purchases.
- ***Standard of value:*** serves as a yardstick for measuring the prices of goods and services.

All the items used during the colonial days satisfied these conditions and were thus properly regarded as money.

After the colonies became an independent nation, the U.S. Constitution prohibited the federal government from issuing paper money. Money was instead issued by state-chartered banks. Between 1789 and 1865, more than 30,000 different paper bills were issued by 1,600 banks in 34 states. People often preferred to get paid in gold, silver, or other commodities rather than in one of these uncertain currencies.

The first paper money the federal government issued consisted of $10 million worth of "greenbacks," printed in 1861 to finance the Civil War. Soon thereafter, the National Banking Act of 1863 gave the federal government permanent authority to issue money.

Modern Concepts

The "greenbacks" we carry around today aren't the only form of "money" we use. Most people realize this when they offer to pay for goods with a check rather than cash. People do distinguish between "cash" and "money," and for good reason. The "money" you have in a checking account can be used to buy goods and services or to pay debts, or it can be retained for future use. In these respects, your checking account balance is as much a part of your "money" as are the coins and dollars in your pocket or purse. You can access your balance by writing a check or using an ATM or debit card. Checks are more convenient than cash because they eliminate trips to the bank. Checks are also safer: lost or stolen cash is gone forever; checkbooks and debit cards are easily replaced at little or no cost. We might use checks and debit cards even more frequently if everyone accepted them.

There's nothing unique about cash, then, insofar as the market is concerned. ***Checking accounts can and do perform the same market functions as cash.*** Accordingly, we must include checking account balances in our concept of **money.** The essence of money isn't its taste, color, or feel but, rather, its ability to purchase goods and services.

Credit cards are another popular medium of exchange. People use credit cards for about one-third of all purchases greater than $100. This use is not sufficient, however, to qualify credit cards as a form of "money." Credit card balances must be paid by check or cash—that is, with *money*. The same holds true for balances in online electronic credit accounts ("e-cash"). Electronic purchases on the Internet or online services are ultimately paid by withdrawals from a bank account (by check or computer). Online payment mechanisms and credit cards are a payment *service,* not a final form of payment (credit card companies charge fees and interest for this service). The cards themselves are not a store of value, in contrast to cash or bank account balances.

The Diversity of Bank Accounts. To determine how much money is available to purchase goods and services, we need to count not just our coins and currency, but also our bank account balances. This effort is complicated by the variety of bank accounts people have. In addition to

---

money: Anything generally accepted as a medium of exchange.

simple no-interest checking accounts at full-service banks, people have bank accounts that pay interest, offer automatic transfers, require minimum holding periods, offer overdraft protection, or limit the number of checks that can be written. People also have "bank" accounts in credit unions, brokerage houses, and other nontraditional financial institutions.

Although all bank account balances can be spent, they're not all used the same way. People use regular checking accounts all the time to pay bills or make purchases. But consumers can't write checks on most savings accounts. And few people want to cash in a certificate of deposit just to go to the movies. Hence *some bank accounts are better substitutes for cash than others.*

M1: Cash and Transactions Accounts

Several different measures of money have been developed to accommodate the diversity of bank accounts and other payment mechanisms. The narrowest definition of the **money supply** is designated **M1,** *which includes*

- *Currency in circulation.*
- *Transactions account balances.*
- *Traveler's checks.*

As Figure 13.1 indicates, people hold much more money in **transactions accounts**—bank accounts that are readily accessed by check—than they do in cash. Most people refer to these simply as "checking accounts." The term "transactions account" is broader, however, including NOW accounts, ATS accounts, credit union share drafts, and demand deposits at mutual savings banks. *The distinguishing feature of all transactions accounts is that they permit direct payment to a third party (by check or debit card)* without requiring a trip to the bank to make a special withdrawal. Because of this feature, transactions accounts are the readiest substitutes for cash in market transactions. Traveler's checks issued by nonbank firms such as American Express can also be used directly in market transactions, just like good old-fashioned cash. But few people use traveler's checks these days, as Figure 13.1 confirms.

money supply (M1): Currency held by the public, plus balances in transactions accounts.

transactions account: A bank account that permits direct payment to a third party—for example, with a check or debit card.

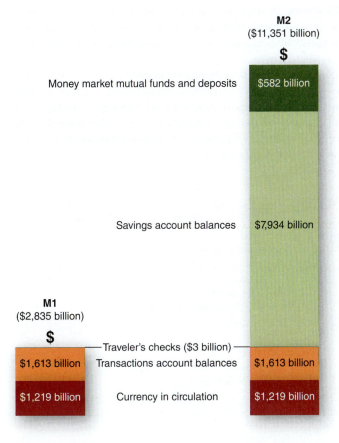

M2
($11,351 billion)

$

Money market mutual funds and deposits — $582 billion

Savings account balances — $7,934 billion

M1
($2,835 billion)

$

Traveler's checks ($3 billion)

Transactions account balances — $1,613 billion | $1,613 billion

Currency in circulation — $1,219 billion | $1,219 billion

What do you pay with? Which one is *not* "money"?

FIGURE 13.1
Composition of the Money Supply

Cash is only a part of the money supply. People also have easy access to transactions account balances by check or debit card. So M1 includes both cash and transactions accounts.

The much larger M2 includes savings accounts, CDs, and other less used bank balances.

Source: Federal Reserve (July 2014 data).

IN THE NEWS

CDs Not Paying Much

Stash your money away for five years and you won't reap much of a reward. The highest rate offered by major banks this week on 5-year certificates of deposit (CDs) is only 1.60 percent. While that's better than the interest paid on checking accounts (0.5 percent), it's not much compensation for five years of thriftiness. Deposit $1,000 in a CD today and you'll end up with a paltry $1,082.60 in five years. And if you bail out of your CD before the five years are up, you pay an "early withdrawal" penalty that wipes out the little bit of interest earned. Might as well hold onto the cash.

Source: News reports, August 4–8, 2014.

ANALYSIS: The interest rate paid on a CD account is higher if you promise to keep your money in the bank longer. Because people rarely use CD balances to buy things, CD balances are in M2, but not M1.

M2: M1 + Savings Accounts

Transactions accounts aren't the only substitute for cash. People can and do dip into savings accounts on occasion. People sometimes even cash in their certificates of deposit to buy something, despite the interest penalty associated with early withdrawal (see the News above). And banks have made it easy to transfer funds from one type of account to another. Savings accounts can be transformed into transactions accounts with a phone call or computer instruction. As a result, *savings account balances are almost as good a substitute for cash as transactions account balances.*

Another popular way of holding money is to buy shares of money market mutual funds. Deposits into money market mutual funds are pooled and used to purchase interest-bearing securities such as Treasury bills. The interest rates paid on these funds are typically higher than those paid by banks. Moreover, the deposits made into the funds can often be withdrawn immediately, just like those in transactions accounts. When interest rates are high, deposits move out of regular transactions accounts into money market mutual funds in order to earn a higher return.

Additional measures of the money supply have been constructed to account for the possibility of using savings account balances, money market mutual funds, and various other deposits to finance everyday spending. The most widely watched money measure is **M2,** which includes all of M1 *plus* balances in savings accounts, money market mutual funds, and some CDs ("time deposits"). As Figure 13.1 shows, M2 is four times larger than M1. Table 13.1 summarizes the content of these measures of money.

M2 money supply: M1 plus balances in most savings accounts and money market mutual funds.

TABLE 13.1

M1 versus M2

Measures of the money supply are intended to gauge the extent of purchasing power held by consumers. But the extent of purchasing power depends on how accessible assets are and how often people use them.

Measure	Components
M1	Currency in circulation outside bank vaults
	Demand deposits at commercial banks
	NOW and ATS accounts
	Credit union share drafts
	Demand deposits at mutual savings banks
	Traveler's checks (nonbank)
M2	M1 plus
	Savings accounts
	CDs of less than $100,000
	Money market mutual funds

Our concern about the specific nature of money stems from our broader interest in **aggregate demand.** What we want to know is how much purchasing power consumers have because this affects their ability to purchase goods and services. What we've observed, however, is that money isn't so easily defined. How much spending power people have depends not only on the number of coins in their pockets but also on their willingness to write checks, make trips to the bank, or convert other assets into cash.

In an increasingly complex financial system, the core concept of "money" isn't easy to pin down. Nevertheless, the official measures of the money supply (M1 and M2) are fairly reliable benchmarks for gauging how much purchasing power market participants have.

aggregate demand: The total quantity of output demanded at alternative price levels in a given time period, *ceteris paribus.*

CREATION OF MONEY

Once we've decided what money is, we still have to explain where it comes from. Part of the explanation is simple. Currency must be printed. Some nations use private printers for this purpose, but all U.S. currency is printed by the Bureau of Engraving and Printing in Washington, D.C., or Ft. Worth, Texas. Coins come from the U.S. mints located in Philadelphia and Denver. As we observed in Figure 13.1, however, currency is only a fraction of our total money supply. So we need to look elsewhere for the origins of most money. Specifically, where do all the transactions accounts come from? How do people acquire bank balances? How does the total amount of such deposits—and therefore the money supply of the economy—change?

Deposit Creation

Most people assume that all bank balances come from cash deposits. But this isn't the case. Direct deposits of paychecks, for example, are carried out by computer, not by the movement of cash (see the accompanying cartoon). Moreover, the employer who issues the paycheck probably didn't make any cash deposits. It's more likely that she covered those paychecks with customers' checks that she deposited or with loans granted by the bank itself.

The ability of banks to lend money opens up a whole new set of possibilities for creating money. ***When a bank lends someone money, it simply credits that individual's bank account.*** The money appears in an account just as it would with a cash deposit. And the owner of the account is free to spend that money as with any positive balance. Hence, ***in making a loan, a bank effectively creates money because transactions account balances are counted as part of the money supply.***

To understand the origins of our money supply, then, we must recognize two basic principles:

- Transactions account balances are a large portion of the money supply.
- Banks can create transactions account balances by making loans.

Analysis: People see very little of their money—most deposits and loans are computer entries in the banking system.

The following two sections examine this process of **deposit creation** more closely. We determine how banks actually create deposits and what forces might limit the process of deposit creation.

Bank Regulation. Banks' deposit creation activities are regulated by the government. The most important agency in this regard is the Federal Reserve System. "The Fed" puts limits on the amount of bank lending, thereby controlling the basic money supply. We'll discuss the structure and functions of the Fed in the next chapter; here we focus on the process of deposit creation itself.

A Monopoly Bank

There are thousands of banks, of various sorts, in the United States. To understand how banks create money, however, we'll make life simple. We'll assume for the moment that there's only one bank in town, University Bank. Imagine also that you've been saving some of your income by putting loose change into a piggy bank. Now, after months of saving, you break the bank and discover that your thrift has yielded $100. You immediately deposit this money in a new checking account at University Bank. How will this deposit affect the money supply?

Your initial deposit will have no immediate effect on the money supply. The coins in your piggy bank were already counted as part of the money supply (M1 and M2) because they represented cash held by the public. **When you deposit cash or coins in a bank, you're only changing the composition of the money supply, not its size.** The public (you) now holds $100 less of coins but $100 more of transactions deposits. Accordingly, no money is created by the demise of your piggy bank (the initial deposit). This transaction will be recorded on the books of the bank.

T-Accounts. The "books" the bank uses to record this transaction are called **"T-accounts."** On the left side of the T-account, the bank keeps track of all its assets: things of value in its possession. On the right side of the ledger the bank lists its liabilities: what it is obligated to pay to others. When you deposit your coins in the bank, the bank acquires an asset—your coins. It also acquires a liability—the promise to return your $100 when you so demand (your "demand deposit"). These two entries appear in the bank's T-account as shown here:

University Bank		Money Supply	
Assets	Liabilities	Cash held by the public	−$100
+$100 in coins	+$100 in deposits	Transactions deposits at bank	+$100
		Change in M	0

The total money supply is unaffected by your cash deposit because two components of the money supply change in opposite directions (i.e., $100 less cash, $100 more bank deposits). This initial deposit is just the beginning of the money creation process, however. Banks aren't in business for your convenience; they're in business to earn a profit. To earn a profit on your deposit, University Bank will have to put your money to work. This means using your deposit as the basis for making a loan to someone who's willing to pay the bank interest for use of money. If the function of banks was merely to store money, they wouldn't pay interest on their accounts or offer free checking services. Instead you'd have to pay them for these services. Banks pay you interest and offer free (or inexpensive) checking because **banks can use your money to make loans that earn interest.**

The Initial Loan. Typically a bank doesn't have much difficulty finding someone who wants to borrow money. Someone is always eager to borrow money. The question is, How much money can a bank lend? Can it lend your entire deposit? Or must University Bank keep some of your coins in reserve in case you want to withdraw them? The answer will surprise you.

Suppose University Bank decided to lend the entire $100 to Campus Radio. Campus Radio wants to buy a new antenna but doesn't have any money in its own checking account. To acquire the antenna, Campus Radio must take out a loan.

When University Bank agrees to lend Campus Radio $100, it does so by crediting the account of Campus Radio. Instead of giving Campus Radio $100 cash, University Bank simply adds an electronic $100 to Campus Radio's checking account balance. That is, the loan is made with a simple bookkeeping entry as follows:

University Bank		Money Supply	
Assets	Liabilities	Cash held by the public	No change
		Transactions deposits at bank	+$100
$100 in coins	$100 your account balance	Change in M	+$100
$100 in loans	$100 Campus Radio account		

Notice that the bank's assets have increased. It now has your $100 in coins *plus* an IOU worth $100 from Campus Radio. On the right side of the T-account, deposit liabilities now include $100 in your account and $100 in the Campus Radio account.

This simple bookkeeping procedure is the key to creating money. When University Bank lends $100 to the Campus Radio account, it "creates" money. Keep in mind that transactions deposits are counted as part of the money supply. Once the $100 loan is credited to its account, Campus Radio can use this new money to purchase its desired antenna, without worrying that its check will bounce.

Or can it? Once University Bank grants a loan to Campus Radio, both you and Campus Radio have $100 in your checking accounts to spend. But the bank is holding only $100 of **reserves** (your coins). In other words, the increased account balance obtained by Campus Radio doesn't limit *your* ability to write checks. There's been a net *increase* in the value of transactions deposits but no increase in bank reserves.

bank reserves: Assets held by a bank to fulfill its deposit obligations.

Secondary Deposits. What happens if Campus Radio actually spends the $100 on a new antenna? Won't this "use up all" the reserves held by the bank, endangering your check-writing privileges? The answer is no.

Consider what happens when Atlas Antenna receives the check from Campus Radio. What will Atlas do with the check? Atlas could go to University Bank and exchange the check for $100 of cash (your coins). But Atlas may prefer to deposit the check in its own checking account at University Bank (still the only bank in town). This way, Atlas not only avoids the necessity of going to the bank (it can deposit the check by mail or smartphone) but also keeps its money in a safe place. Should Atlas later want to spend the money, it can simply write a check. In the meantime, the bank continues to hold its entire reserves (your coins), and both you and Atlas have $100 to spend.

Fractional Reserves. Notice what's happened here. The money supply has increased by $100 as a result of deposit creation (the loan to Campus Radio). Moreover, the bank has been able to support $200 of transaction deposits (your account and either the Campus Radio or Atlas account) with only $100 of reserves (your coins). In other words, *bank reserves are only a fraction of total deposits.* In this case, University Bank's reserves (your $100 in coins) are only 50 percent of total deposits. Thus the bank's **reserve ratio** is 50 percent—that is,

reserve ratio: The ratio of a bank's reserves to its total transactions deposits.

$$\frac{\text{Reserve}}{\text{ratio}} = \frac{\text{Bank reserves}}{\text{Total deposits}}$$

The ability of University Bank to hold reserves that are only a fraction of total deposits results from two facts: (1) people use checks and debit cards for most transactions and (2) there's no other bank. Accordingly, reserves are rarely withdrawn from this monopoly bank. In fact, if people *never* withdrew their deposits and *all* transactions accounts were held at University Bank, University Bank wouldn't need *any* reserves. In this most unusual case, University Bank could make as many loans as it wanted. Every loan it made would increase the supply of money.

In reality, many banks are available, and people both withdraw cash from their accounts and write checks to people who have accounts in other banks. In addition, bank lending practices are regulated by the Federal Reserve System. *The Federal Reserve System requires banks to maintain some minimum reserve ratio.* This reserve requirement directly limits banks' ability to grant new loans.

Required Reserves. The potential impact of Federal Reserve requirements on bank lending can be readily seen. Suppose that the Federal Reserve imposed a minimum reserve requirement of 75 percent on University Bank. Such a requirement would prohibit University Bank from lending $100 to Campus Radio. That loan would result in $200 of deposits, supported by only $100 of reserves. The actual ratio of reserves to deposits would be 50 percent ($100 of reserves ÷ $200 of deposits), which would violate the Fed's assumed 75 percent reserve requirement. A 75 percent reserve requirement means that University Bank must hold **required reserves** equal to 75 percent of *total* deposits, including those created through loans.

The bank's dilemma is evident in the following equation:

$$\frac{\text{Required}}{\text{reserves}} = \frac{\text{Required reserve}}{\text{ratio}} \times \frac{\text{Total}}{\text{deposits}}$$

To support $200 of total deposits, University Bank would need to satisfy this equation:

$$\frac{\text{Required}}{\text{reserves}} = 0.75 \times \$200 = \$150$$

But the bank has only $100 of reserves (your coins) and so would violate the reserve requirement if it increased total deposits to $200 by lending $100 to Campus Radio.

University Bank can still issue a loan to Campus Radio. But the loan must be less than $100 to keep the bank within the limits of the required reserve formula. Thus *a minimum reserve requirement directly limits deposit creation (lending) possibilities.* It's still true, however, as we'll now illustrate, that the banking system, taken as a whole, can create multiple loans (money) from a single deposit.

A Multibank World

Table 13.2 illustrates the process of deposit creation in a multibank world with a required reserve ratio. In this case, we assume that legally required reserves must equal at least 20 percent of transactions deposits. Now when you deposit $100 in your checking account, University Bank must hold at least $20 as required reserves.[1]

Excess Reserves. The remaining $80 the bank obtains from your deposit is regarded as **excess reserves.** These reserves are "excess" because your bank is *required* to hold in reserve only $20 (equal to 20 percent of your initial $100 deposit):

$$\frac{\text{Excess}}{\text{reserves}} = \frac{\text{Total}}{\text{reserves}} - \frac{\text{Required}}{\text{reserves}}$$

The $80 of excess reserves aren't required and may be used to support additional loans. Hence the bank can now lend $80. In view of the fact that banks earn profits (interest) by making loans, we assume that University Bank will try to use these excess reserves as soon as possible.

To keep track of the changes in reserves, deposit balances, and loans that occur in a multibank world we'll have to do some more bookkeeping. For this purpose we'll again use the

required reserves: The minimum amount of reserves a bank is required to hold; equal to required reserve ratio times transactions deposits.

excess reserves: Bank reserves in excess of required reserves.

---

[1]The reserves themselves may be held in the form of cash in the bank's vault but are usually held as credits with one of the regional Federal Reserve banks.

Step 1: You deposit cash at University Bank. The deposit creates $100 of reserves, $20 of which are designated as required reserves. This leaves $80 of excess reserves.

University Bank

Assets		Liabilities	
Required reserves	$ 20	Your deposit	$100
Excess reserves	80		
Total	$100		100

Banking System

Change in Transactions Deposits	Change in M
+$100	$0

Step 2: The bank uses its excess reserves ($80) to make a loan to Campus Radio. Total deposits now equal $180. The money supply has increased.

University Bank

Assets		Liabilities	
Required reserves	$ 36	Your account	$100
Excess reserves	64	Campus Radio account	80
Loans	80		
Total	$180	Total	$180

Banking System

Δ Deposits	Δ M
+$80	+$80

Step 3: Campus Radio buys an antenna. This depletes Campus Radio's account but increases Atlas's balance. Eternal Savings gets $80 of reserves when the Campus Radio check clears.

University Bank

Assets		Liabilities	
Required reserves	$ 20	Your account	$100
Excess reserves	0	Campus Radio account	0
Loan	80		
Total	$100	Total	$100

Eternal Savings

Assets		Liabilities	
Required reserves	$16	Atlas Antenna account	$80
Excess reserves	64		
Total	$80	Total	$80

Banking System

Δ Deposits	Δ M
$0	$0

Step 4: Eternal Savings lends money to Herman's Hardware. Deposits, loans, and M all increase by $64.

University Bank

Assets		Liabilities	
Required reserves	$ 20	Your account	$100
Excess reserves	0	Campus Radio account	0
Loan	80		
Total	$100	Total	$100

Eternal Savings

Assets		Liabilities	
Required reserves	$28.80	Atlas Antenna account	$ 80
Excess reserves	51.20	Herman's Hardware account	64
Loans	64		
	$ 144		$144

Banking System

Change in Transaction Deposits	Change in M
+$64	+$64

nth step: Some bank lends $1.00

Banking System: +1 (Deposits), +1 (M)

Cumulative Change in Banking System

Bank Reserves	Transactions Deposits	Money Supply
+$100	+$500	+$400

TABLE 13.2

Deposit Creation

Excess reserves (step 1) are the basis of bank loans. When a bank uses its excess reserves to make a loan, it creates a deposit (step 2). When the loan is spent, a deposit will be made somewhere else (step 3). This new deposit creates additional excess reserves (step 3) that can be used for further loans (step 4, etc.). The process of deposit creation continues until the money supply has increased by a multiple of the initial deposit.

same balance sheet, or "T-account," that banks themselves use. Table 13.2 takes us down the accounting path.

Step 1: Cash Deposit Notice how the balance of University Bank looks immediately after it receives your initial deposit (step 1, Table 13.2). Your deposit of coins is entered on *both* sides of University's balance sheet. On the left side, your deposit is regarded as an asset because your piggy bank's coins have an immediate market value and can be used to pay off the bank's liabilities. The coins now appear as *reserves*. The reserves these coins represent are further divided into required reserves ($20, or 20 percent of your deposit) and excess reserves ($80).

On the right side of the balance sheet, the bank reminds itself that it has an obligation (liability) to return your deposit when you demand. Thus the bank's accounts balance, with assets and liabilities being equal. In fact, *a bank's books must always balance because all the bank's assets must belong to someone (its depositors or the bank's owners).*

Step 2: Bank Loan University Bank wants to do more than balance its books, however; it wants to earn profits. To do so, it will have to make loans—that is, put its excess reserves to work. Suppose that it lends $80 to Campus Radio.[2] As step 2 in Table 13.2 illustrates, this loan alters both sides of University Bank's balance sheet. On the right side, the bank creates a new transactions deposit for (credits the account of) Campus Radio; this item represents an additional liability (promise to pay). On the left side of the balance sheet, two things happen. First, the bank notes that Campus Radio owes it $80 ("loans"). Second, the bank recognizes that it's now required to hold $36 in *required* reserves, in accordance with its higher level of transactions deposits ($180). (Recall we're assuming that required reserves are 20 percent of total transactions deposits.) Since its total reserves are still $100, $64 is left as *excess* reserves. Note again that *excess reserves are reserves a bank isn't required to hold.*

Changes in the Money Supply. Before examining further changes in the balance sheet of University Bank, consider again what's happened to the economy's money supply during these first two steps. In the first step, you deposited $100 of cash in your checking account. This initial transaction didn't change the value of the money supply. Only the composition of the money supply (M1) was affected ($100 less cash held by the public, $100 more in transactions accounts).

Not until step 2—when the bank makes a loan—does all the excitement begin. In making a loan, the bank automatically increases the total money supply by $80. Why? Because someone (Campus Radio) now has more money (a transactions deposit) than it did before, *and no one else has any less.* And Campus Radio can use its money to buy goods and services, just like anybody else.

This second step is the heart of money creation. Money effectively appears out of thin air when a bank makes a loan. To understand how this works, you have to keep reminding yourself that money is more than the coins and currency we carry around. Transactions deposits are money too. Hence *the creation of transactions deposits via new loans is the same thing as creating money.*

Step 3: Spending the Loan Suppose again that Campus Radio actually uses its $80 loan to buy an antenna. The rest of Table 13.2 illustrates how this additional transaction leads to further changes in balance sheets and the money supply.

In step 3, we see that when Campus Radio buys the $80 antenna, the balance in its checking account at University Bank drops to zero because it has spent all its money. As University Bank's liabilities fall (from $180 to $100), so does the level of its required reserves (from $36 to $20). (Note that required reserves are still 20 percent of its remaining transactions deposits.) But University Bank's excess reserves have disappeared

web click

Find the most recent data on total bank reserves, borrowed reserves, excess reserves, and required reserves at **www .federalreserve.gov**. Search for "aggregate reserves of depository institutions and the monetary base."

---

[2]Because of the Fed's assumed minimum reserve requirement (20 percent), University Bank can now lend only $80 rather than $100, as before.

completely! This disappearance reflects the fact that Atlas Antenna keeps *its* transactions account at another bank (Eternal Savings). When Atlas deposits the check it received from Campus Radio, Eternal Savings does two things. First, it credits Atlas's account by $80. Second, it goes to University Bank to get the reserves that support the deposit.[3] The reserves later appear on the balance sheet of Eternal Savings as both required ($16) and excess ($64) reserves.

Observe that the money supply hasn't changed during step 3. The increase in the value of Atlas Antenna's transactions account balance exactly offsets the drop in the value of Campus Radio's transactions account. Ownership of the money supply is the only thing that has changed.

Step 4: More Deposit Creation In step 4, Eternal Savings takes advantage of its newly acquired excess reserves by making a loan to Herman's Hardware. As before, the loan itself has two primary effects. First, it creates a transactions deposit of $64 for Herman's Hardware and thereby increases the money supply by the same amount. Second, it increases the required level of reserves at Eternal Savings. (To how much? Why?)

THE MONEY MULTIPLIER

By now it's perhaps obvious that the process of deposit creation won't come to an end quickly. On the contrary, it can continue indefinitely, just like the income multiplier process in Chapter 10. Indeed, people often refer to deposit creation as the money multiplier process, with the **money multiplier** expressed as the reciprocal of the required reserve ratio. That is,

$$\text{Money multiplier} = \frac{1}{\text{Required reserve ratio}}$$

money multiplier: The number of deposit (loan) dollars that the banking system can create from $1 of excess reserves; equal to 1 ÷ required reserve ratio.

Figure 13.2 illustrates the money multiplier process. When a new deposit enters the banking system, it creates both excess and required reserves. The required reserves

[3]In actuality, banks rarely "go" anywhere; such interbank reserve movements are handled by bank clearinghouses and regional Federal Reserve banks. The effect is the same, however. The nature and use of bank reserves are discussed more fully in Chapter 14.

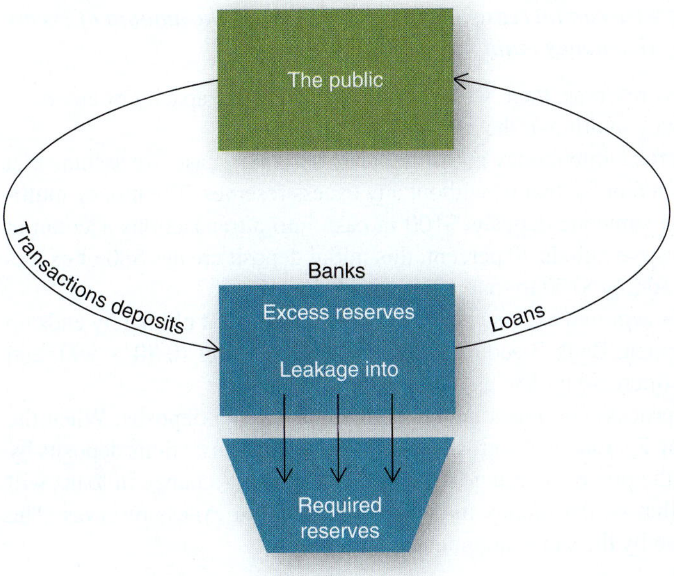

FIGURE 13.2
The Money Multiplier Process

Part of every new bank deposit leaks into required reserves. The rest—excess reserves—can be used to make loans. These loans, in turn, become deposits elsewhere. The process of money creation continues until all available reserves become required reserves.

represent leakage from the flow of money because they can't be used to create new loans. Excess reserves, on the other hand, can be used for new loans. Once those loans are made, they typically become transactions deposits elsewhere in the banking system. Then some additional leakage into required reserves occurs, and further loans are made. The process continues until all excess reserves have leaked into required reserves. Once excess reserves have completely disappeared, the total value of new loans will equal initial excess reserves multiplied by the money multiplier.

The potential of the money multiplier to create loans is summarized by the equation

$$\frac{\text{Excess}}{\text{reserves}} \atop \text{of banking} \atop \text{system} \times \frac{\text{Money}}{\text{multiplier}} = \frac{\text{Potential}}{\text{deposit creation}}$$

Notice how the money multiplier worked in our previous example. The value of the money multiplier was equal to 5 because we assumed that the required reserve ratio was 0.20. Moreover, the initial level of excess reserves was $80 as a consequence of your original deposit (step 1). According to the money multiplier, then, the deposit creation potential of the banking system was

$$\frac{\text{Excess reserves}}{(\$80)} \times \frac{\text{Money multiplier}}{(5)} = \frac{\text{Potential}}{\text{deposit}} \atop \text{creation} (\$400)$$

When all the banks fully utilized their excess reserves at each step of the money multiplier process, the ultimate increase in the money supply was in fact $400 (see the last row in Table 13.2).

Excess Reserves as Lending Power

While you're struggling through Table 13.2, notice the critical role that excess reserves play in the process of deposit creation. A bank can make additional loans only if it has excess reserves. Without excess reserves, all of a bank's reserves are required, and no further liabilities (transactions deposits) can be created with new loans. On the other hand, a bank with excess reserves can make additional loans. In fact,

- *Each bank may lend an amount equal to its excess reserves and no more.*

As such loans enter the circular flow and become deposits elsewhere, they create new excess reserves and further lending capacity. As a consequence,

- *The entire banking system can increase the volume of loans by the amount of excess reserves multiplied by the money multiplier.*

By keeping track of excess reserves, then, we can gauge the lending capacity of any bank or, with the aid of the money multiplier, the entire banking system.

Table 13.3 summarizes the entire money multiplier process. In this case, we assume that all banks are initially "loaned up"—that is, without any excess reserves. The money multiplier process begins when someone deposits $100 in cash into a transactions account at Bank A. If the required reserve ratio is 20 percent, this initial deposit creates $80 of excess reserves at Bank A while adding $100 to total transactions deposits.

If Bank A uses its newly acquired excess reserves to make a loan that ultimately ends up in Bank B, two things happen: Bank B acquires $64 in excess reserves (0.80 × $80) and total transactions deposits increase by $80 as well.

The money multiplier process continues with a series of loans and deposits. When the 26th loan is made (by Bank Z), total loans grow by only $0.30 and transactions deposits by an equal amount. Should the process continue further, the *cumulative* change in loans will ultimately equal $400—that is, the money multiplier times initial excess reserves. The money supply will increase by the same amount.

Required reserves = 0.20	Change in Transactions Deposits	Change in Total Reserves	Change in Required Reserves	Change in Excess Reserves	Change in Lending Capacity
If $100 in cash is deposited in Bank A, Bank A acquires	$100.00	$100.00	$20.00	$80.00	$80.00
If loan made and deposited elsewhere, Bank B acquires	80.00	80.00	16.00	64.00	64.00
If loan made and deposited elsewhere, Bank C acquires	64.00	64.00	12.80	51.20	51.20
If loan made and deposited elsewhere, Bank D acquires	51.20	51.20	10.24	40.96	40.96
If loan made and deposited elsewhere, Bank E acquires	40.96	40.96	8.19	32.77	32.77
If loan made and deposited elsewhere, Bank F acquires	32.77	32.77	6.55	26.22	26.22
If loan made and deposited elsewhere, Bank G acquires	26.22	26.22	5.24	20.98	20.98
. . .					
If loan made and deposited elsewhere, Bank Z acquires	0.38	0.38	0.08	0.30	0.30
Cumulative, through Bank Z	$498.80	$100.00	$99.76	$0.24	$398.80
. . .					
And if the process continues indefinitely	$500.00	$100.00	$100.00	$0.00	$400.00

Note: A $100 cash deposit creates $400 of new lending capacity when the required reserve ratio is 0.20. Initial excess reserves are $80 (= $100 deposit − $20 required reserves). The money multiplier is 5 (= 1 ÷ 0.20). New lending potential equals $400 (= $80 excess reserves × 5).

TABLE 13.3

The Money Multiplier at Work

The process of deposit creation continues as money passes through different banks in the form of multiple deposits and loans. At each step, excess reserves and new loans are created. The lending capacity of this system equals the money multiplier times excess reserves. In this case, initial excess reserves of $80 create the possibility of $400 of new loans when the reserve ratio is 0.20 (20 percent).

BANKS AND THE CIRCULAR FLOW

The bookkeeping details of bank deposits and loans are rarely exciting and often confusing. But they demonstrate convincingly that banks can create money. In that capacity, *banks perform two essential functions for the macro economy:*

- *Banks transfer money from savers to spenders by lending funds (reserves) held on deposit.*
- *The banking system creates additional money by making loans in excess of total reserves.*

In performing these two functions, banks change the size of the money supply—that is, the amount of purchasing power available for buying goods and services. Changes in the money supply may in turn alter *spending* behavior and thereby shift the aggregate demand curve.

Figure 13.3 is a simplified perspective on the role of banks in the circular flow. As before, income flows from product markets through business firms to factor markets and

FIGURE 13.3

Banks in the Circular Flow

Banks help transfer income from savers to spenders by using their deposits to make loans to business firms and consumers who want to spend more money than they have. By lending money, banks help maintain any desired rate of aggregate demand.

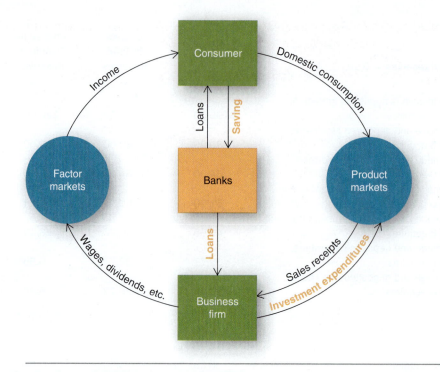

returns to consumers in the form of disposable income. Consumers spend most of their income but also save (don't spend) some of it.

Financing Injections

The leakage represented by consumer saving is a potential source of stabilization problems, particularly unemployment. If additional spending by business firms, foreigners, or governments doesn't compensate for consumer saving at full employment, a recessionary GDP gap will emerge, creating unemployment (see Chapters 9 and 10). Our interest here is in the role the banking system can play in encouraging such additional spending.

Suppose for the moment that *all* consumer saving was deposited in piggy banks rather than depository institutions (banks) and that no one used checks. Under these circumstances, banks couldn't transfer money from savers to spenders by holding deposits and making loans.

In reality, a substantial portion of consumer saving *is* deposited in banks. These and other bank deposits can be used as the basis of loans, thereby returning purchasing power to the circular flow. In fact, **the primary economic function of banks isn't to store money but to transfer purchasing power from savers to spenders.** They do so by lending money to businesses for new plants and equipment, to consumers for new homes or cars, and to government entities to build sports stadiums and toll roads. Moreover, because the banking system can make *multiple* loans from available reserves, banks don't have to receive all consumer saving to carry out their function. On the contrary, *the banking system can create any desired level of money supply if allowed to expand or reduce loan activity at will.*

Constraints on Deposit Creation

There are four major constraints on the deposit creation of the banking system.

Deposits. The first constraint is the willingness of consumers and businesses to continue using and accepting checks or debit cards rather than cash in the marketplace. If people preferred to hold cash rather than bank balances, banks wouldn't be able to acquire or maintain the reserves that are the foundation of bank lending activity.

Willingness to Lend. Once banks are holding sufficient reserves, they must be willing to make new loans. In 2009–2010, this condition was violated. Banks had accumulated huge losses on previous mortgage loans. In addition, the economy was sliding into a deepening recession. So banks were reluctant to make new loans that might not get repaid. This put a serious crimp on aggregate demand.

Willingness to Borrow. The third constraint on deposit creation is the willingness of consumers, businesses, and governments to borrow the money that banks make available. The chain of events we've observed in deposit creation depends on the willingness of Campus Radio to borrow $80, of Herman's Hardware to borrow $64, and so on. If no one wanted to borrow any money, deposit creation would never begin. By the same reasoning, if all excess reserves aren't borrowed (lent), deposit creation won't live up to its theoretical potential.

Regulation. The fourth major constraint on deposit creation is the Federal Reserve System. As we've observed, the Fed may limit deposit creation by imposing reserve requirements. These and other tools of monetary policy are discussed in Chapter 14.

THE ECONOMY TOMORROW

ARE BITCOINS TOMORROW'S MONEY?

People worry about the origins and nature of money. As we have seen, banks create money with electronic entries into borrowers' bank accounts. There is no physical limit to the number of such dollars created. Confidence in the value of the dollar is an act of faith—faith in the stability of banks and the government (Federal Reserve) that regulates their deposit creation.

Many people want a more secure and objective limit on the amount of money created. Bitcoins appear to offer such a limit. Created in 2009, bitcoins are also electronic blips. But they have no physical counterparts (like dollar bills and coins). In addition, their supply is allegedly limited by a computer protocol that creates more bitcoins each year until 2140, when 21 million bitcoins would exist. People acquire ("mine") some of each year's new bitcoins by solving increasingly complex mathematical problems. Geeks love the idea.

Every bitcoin has a unique electronic identifier, similar to the physical serial number on a dollar bill. If you own a bitcoin, you have a unique "private key" (like a password) that allows you access to that specific bitcoin. You can transfer bitcoins by giving your "private key" information to someone else. Such electronic transfers enable you to buy and sell goods, making bitcoins an effective medium of exchange.

What distinguishes bitcoin transfers from dollar transfers is their anonymity. Dollar transfers go through banks and other financial institutions. Bitcoin transfers can be made directly without any third-party intermediary, so there is no public record of the transaction. This anonymity made bitcoins an early favorite of drug traffickers, gamblers, and other black marketers. Ordinary citizens also liked the speed and negligible cost of bitcoin transactions.

Bitcoins quickly became a speculative sensation. When first introduced in 2009, a bitcoin was worth 30 cents. In 2011, that value rose to $1. Then the value of bitcoins soared, hitting a peak of $1,147.25 on December 4, 2013. Bitcoins looked more like Zimbabwean dollars or penny stocks than a stable currency. In 2014, the market value of bitcoins tumbled to $400.

Will bitcoins be "money" in the economy tomorrow? Not likely. The wild fluctuations in their value make bitcoins a dubious store of value. Those fluctuations and their exclusive electronic nature also constrain their ability to serve as a medium of exchange. As of 2014, only a handful of merchants were accepting bitcoins in payment for real goods and services. The collapse of the major bitcoin exchange (Tokyo-based Mt. Gox) in early 2014—together with the electronic disappearance of millions of bitcoins—further undermined their acceptability. The electronic "bank" ("blockchain") that stores bitcoin

web click

For more information on bitcoins, visit **bitcoin.org**.

identifiers is vulnerable to hackers, as are the "private keys" that denote bitcoin ownership. Last but not least, the Internal Revenue Service ruled in 2014 that bitcoins were deemed *property,* not money. This requires bitcoin users to keep track of the price they pay for bitcoins and the value they get in subsequent transactions. The bitcoin user is then subject to a capital-gains tax on any increase in the value of the bitcoins. This ruling negates the anonymity of bitcoin transactions—or subjects the user to the risk of tax evasion prosecution. Bitcoins aren't going to replace dollars in our concept of money in the economy tomorrow.

SUMMARY

- In a market economy, money serves a critical function in *facilitating exchanges* and specialization, thus permitting increased output. **LO13-1**
- *Money* refers to any medium that's generally accepted in exchange, serves as a store of value, and acts as a standard of value. **LO13-1**
- Because people use bank account balances to buy goods and services (with checks or debit cards), such balances are also regarded as money. The money supply M1 includes cash plus transactions account (checkable) deposits. M2 adds savings account balances and other deposits to form a broader measure of the money supply. **LO13-1**
- The assets a bank holds must always equal its liabilities. **LO13-2**
- Banks have the power to create money by making loans. In making loans, banks create new transactions deposits, which become part of the money supply. **LO13-3**
- A bank's ability to make loans—create money—depends on its reserves. Only if a bank has excess reserves—

  reserves greater than those required by federal regulation—can it make new loans. **LO13-3**
- As loans are spent, they create deposits elsewhere, making it possible for other banks to make additional loans. The money multiplier (1 ÷ required reserve ratio) indicates the total value of deposits that can be created by the banking system from excess reserves. **LO13-4**
- The role of banks in creating money includes the transfer of money from savers to spenders as well as deposit creation in excess of deposit balances. Taken together, these two functions give banks direct control over the amount of purchasing power available in the marketplace. **LO13-3**
- The deposit creation potential of the banking system is limited by government regulation. It's also limited by the willingness of market participants to hold deposits or borrow money. **LO13-4**
- When banks fail, the federal government (FDIC) guarantees to pay deposits. In extreme cases the government may also lend banks more reserves, purchase depressed assets, or even acquire an ownership stake. **LO13-3**

Key Terms

barter	aggregate demand	reserve ratio
money	deposit creation	required reserves
money supply (M1, M2)	T-accounts	excess reserves
transactions account	bank reserves	money multiplier

Questions for Discussion

1. Why are checking account balances, but not credit cards, regarded as "money"? **LO13-1**
2. In what respects are modern forms of money superior to the colonial use of wampum as money? **LO13-1**
3. How are an economy's production possibilities affected when workers are paid in goods rather than in cash? (See World View, p. 277, about bartering in Russia.) **LO13-1**
4. What percentage of your monthly bills do you pay with (a) cash, (b) check, (c) credit card, and (d) automatic transfers? How do you pay off the credit card balance? How does your use of cash compare with the composition of the money supply (Figure 13.1)? **LO13-1**
5. Why must a bank's assets always equal its liabilities? **LO13-2**

6. Does the fact that your bank keeps only a fraction of your account balance in reserve make you uncomfortable? Why don't people rush to the bank and retrieve their money? What would happen if they did?   **LO13-3**

7. If people never withdrew cash from banks, how much money could the banking system potentially create? Could this really happen? What might limit deposit creation in this case?   **LO13-4**

8. If all banks heeded Shakespeare's admonition "Neither a borrower nor a lender be," what would happen to the circular flow?   **LO13-3**

9. What makes bitcoins an unlikely form of money?   **LO13-1**

mobile app Visit your mobile app store and download the Schiller: Study Econ app *today!*

		Required Reserve Ratio	
		20 Percent	25 Percent
1.	Total deposits	$100 billion	$100 billion
2.	Total reserves	30 billion	30 billion
3.	Required reserves	20 billion	25 billion
4.	Excess reserves	10 billion	5 billion
5.	Money multiplier	5	4
6.	Unused lending capacity	$ 50 billion	$ 20 billion

respectively. What the increased reserve requirement does affect is the way those reserves can be used. Before the increase, only $20 billion in reserves were *required,* leaving $10 billion of *excess* reserves. Now, however, banks are required to hold $25 billion ($0.25 \times \$100$ billion) in reserves, leaving them with only $5 billion in excess reserves. Thus an increase in the reserve requirement immediately reduces excess reserves, as illustrated in row 4, Table 14.1.

There's also a second effect. Notice what happens to the money multiplier ($1 \div$ reserve ratio). Previously it was 5 (= $1 \div 0.20$); now it's only 4 (= $1 \div 0.25$). Consequently, a higher reserve requirement not only reduces excess reserves but diminishes their lending power as well.

A change in the reserve requirement, therefore, hits banks with a triple whammy. *A change in the reserve requirement causes a change in*

- *Excess reserves.*
- *The money multiplier.*
- *The lending capacity of the banking system.*

These changes sharply reduce bank lending power. Whereas the banking system initially had the power to increase the volume of loans by $50 billion ($10 billion of excess reserves $\times$ 5), it now has only $20 billion ($5 million $\times$ 4) of unused lending capacity, as noted in the last row in Table 14.1.

Changes in reserve requirements are a powerful tool for altering the lending capacity of the banking system. The Fed uses this tool sparingly so as not to cause abrupt changes in the money supply and severe disruptions of banking activity. From 1970 to 1980, for example, reserve requirements were changed only twice, and then by only half a percentage point each time (for example, from 12.0 to 12.5 percent). The Fed last cut the reserve requirement from 12 to 10 percent in 1992 to increase bank profits and encourage more lending. In 2014, China did the same thing, hoping to accelerate economic growth (see the World View).

WORLD VIEW

China Cuts Reserve Requirements

With its vast economy showing signs of slower growth, China has opted to encourage more bank lending. China's central bank, the People's Bank of China, said it is trimming the required reserve ratio for its banks by half a percentage point—to 19.5 percent, down from 20 percent. The lower reserve requirement enables banks to lend more of their reserves. The move is expected to free up about $16 billion in bank reserves.

Source: News reports, June 8–10, 2014.

ANALYSIS: A reduction in the reserve requirement transforms some of the banking system's required reserves into excess reserves, thus increasing potential lending activity and profits. It also increases the size of the money multiplier.

The Discount Rate

Banks have a tremendous incentive to maintain their reserves at or close to the minimum established by the Fed. Bank reserves held at the Fed earn lower rates of interest than banks could get from making loans or holding bonds. Hence a profit-maximizing bank seeks to keep its excess reserves as low as possible, preferring to put its reserves to better, more profitable work. In fact, banks have demonstrated an uncanny ability to keep their reserves close to the minimum federal requirement. As Figure 14.2 illustrates, the few times banks held huge excess reserves were in the Great Depression of the 1930s and during the 2009–2014 recession. The banks didn't want to make any more loans and were

web click

To learn more about the discount rate, see **www.frbdiscountwindow.org.** You'll find historical rates by clicking the "Discount Rates" tab.

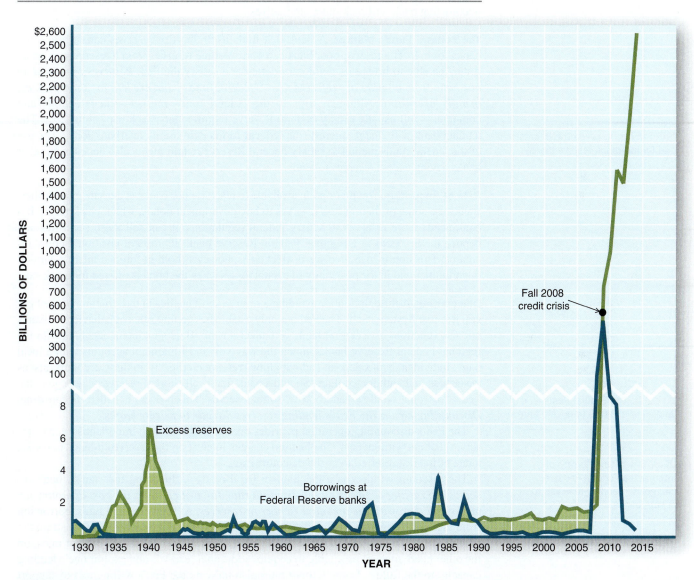

FIGURE 14.2
Excess Reserves and Borrowings

Excess reserves represent unused lending capacity. Hence banks strive to keep excess reserves at a minimum. One exception to this practice occurred during the Great Depression, when banks were hesitant to make any loans. It happened even more dramatically during the Great Recession of 2008–2009, when bank assets lost value and new loans looked risky. By 2014 banks had stockpiled more than $2 trillion in excess reserves.

In more normal circumstances, banks try to minimize excess reserves, occasionally falling short of required reserves in the process. At such times they may borrow from other banks (the federal funds market), or they may borrow reserves from the Fed. Borrowing from the Fed is called "discounting."

fearful of loan defaults and panicky customers withdrawing their deposits. Notice in Figure 14.2 the enormous jump in excess reserves in 2009–2014 when banks decided to curtail new lending activity.

Because banks continually seek to keep excess reserves at a minimum, they run the risk of falling below reserve requirements. A large borrower may be a little slow in repaying a loan, or the rate of deposit withdrawals and transfers may exceed expectations, or as we saw in the 2008 credit crisis (Chapter 13), defaults and price declines may reduce the value of assets held by the bank. At such times, a bank may find that it doesn't have enough reserves to satisfy Fed requirements.

Banks could ensure continual compliance with reserve requirements by maintaining large amounts of excess reserves. But that's an unprofitable procedure, and a profit-maximizing bank will seek other alternatives.

The Federal Funds Market. A bank that finds itself short of reserves can turn to other banks for help. If a reserve-poor bank can borrow some reserves from a reserve-rich bank, it may be able to bridge its temporary deficit and satisfy the Fed. ***Reserves borrowed by one bank from another are referred to as "federal funds" and are lent for short periods, usually overnight.*** Although trips to the federal funds market—via telephone and computer—will usually satisfy Federal Reserve requirements, such trips aren't free. The lending bank will charge interest (the **federal funds rate**) on its interbank loan.[1] The use of the federal funds market to satisfy Federal Reserve requirements also depends on other banks having excess reserves to lend.

Sale of Securities. Another option available to reserve-poor banks is the sale of securities. Banks use some of their excess reserves to buy government bonds, which pay interest. If a bank needs more reserves to satisfy federal regulations, it can sell these securities and deposit the proceeds at a regional Federal Reserve bank. Its reserve position thereby increases. This option also involves distinct costs, however, both in forgone interest-earning opportunities and in the possibility of capital losses when the bond is offered for quick sale.

Discounting. A third option for avoiding a reserve shortage lies in the structure of the Federal Reserve System itself. The Fed not only establishes certain rules of behavior for banks but also functions as a central bank, or banker's bank. Banks maintain accounts with the regional Federal Reserve banks, much the way you and I maintain accounts with a local bank. Individual banks deposit and withdraw "reserve credits" from these accounts, just as we deposit and withdraw dollars. Should a bank find itself short of reserves, it can go to the Fed's "discount window" and borrow some reserves. This process is called **discounting.** ***Discounting means the Fed is lending reserves directly to private banks.***[2]

The Fed's discounting operation provides private banks with an important source of reserves, but not without cost. The Fed too charges interest on the reserves it lends to banks, a rate of interest referred to as the **discount rate.**

The discount window is a mechanism for directly influencing the size of bank reserves. ***By raising or lowering the discount rate, the Fed changes the cost of money for banks and therewith the incentive to borrow reserves.*** At high discount rates, borrowing from the Fed is expensive. High discount rates also signal the Fed's desire to restrain the money supply and an accompanying reluctance to lend reserves. Low discount rates, on the other hand, make it profitable to acquire additional reserves and exploit one's lending capacity to the fullest. Low discount rates also indicate the Fed's willingness to support credit expansion.

federal funds rate: The interest rate for interbank reserve loans.

discounting: Federal Reserve lending of reserves to private banks.

discount rate: The rate of interest the Federal Reserve charges for lending reserves to private banks.

---

[1] An overnight loan of $1 million at 6 percent interest (per year) costs $165 in interest charges plus any service fees that might be added. Banks make multimillion-dollar loans in the federal funds market.

[2] In the past banks had to present loan notes to the Fed in order to borrow reserves. The Fed "discounted" the notes by lending an amount equal to only a fraction of their face value. Although banks no longer have to present loans as collateral, the term "discounting" endures.

In the wake of the 2008 credit crisis, the Fed not only reduced the discount rate but urged banks to borrow more reserves. Notice in Figure 14.2 the spectacular increase in Fed-loaned reserves ("borrowings") in late 2008. The Fed wanted to reassure market participants that the banks had enough reserves to weather the economic storm.

Open Market Operations

Reserve requirements and discount window operations are important tools of monetary policy. But they don't come close to open market operations in day-to-day impact on the money supply. *Open market operations are the principal mechanism for directly altering the reserves of the banking system.* Because reserves are the lifeblood of the banking system, open market operations are of immediate and critical interest to private banks and the larger economy.

Portfolio Decisions. To appreciate the impact of open market operations, you have to think about the alternative uses for idle funds. All of us have some idle funds, even if they amount to just a few dollars in our pocket or a minimal balance in our checking account. Other consumers and corporations have great amounts of idle funds, even millions of dollars at any time. Here we're concerned with what people decide to do with such funds.

People (and corporations) don't hold all their idle funds in transactions accounts or cash. Idle funds are also used to purchase stocks, build up savings account balances, and purchase bonds. These alternative uses of idle funds are attractive because they promise some additional income in the form of interest, dividends, or capital appreciation, such as higher stock prices. Deciding where to place idle funds is referred to as the **portfolio decision.**

portfolio decision: The choice of how (where) to hold idle funds.

Hold Money or Bonds? The Fed's *open market operations focus on one of the portfolio choices people make: whether to deposit idle funds in bank accounts or purchase government bonds.* The Fed attempts to influence this choice by making bonds more or less attractive, as circumstances warrant. The Fed's goal is to encourage people to move funds from banks to bond markets or vice versa. In the process, reserves either enter or leave the banking system, thereby altering the lending capacity of banks.

Figure 14.3 depicts the general nature of the Fed's open market operations. As we first observed in Chapter 13 (Figure 13.2), the process of deposit creation begins when people deposit money in the banking system. But people may also hold their assets in the form of

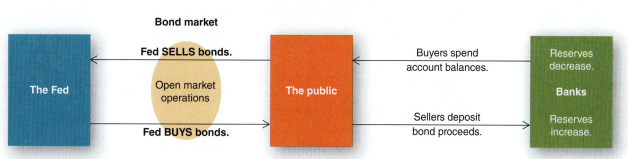

FIGURE 14.3

Open Market Operations

People may hold assets in the form of bank deposits (money) or bonds. When the Fed buys bonds from the public, it increases the flow of deposits (and reserves) to the banks. When the Fed sells bonds, it diminishes the flow of deposits and therewith the banks' capacity to lend (create money).

bonds. The fed's objective is to alter this portfolio decision by buying or selling bonds. *When the Fed buys bonds from the public, it increases the flow of deposits (reserves) to the banking system. Bond sales by the Fed reduce the inflow.*

The Bond Market. To understand how open market operations work, let's look more closely at the bond market. Not all of us buy and sell bonds, but a lot of consumers and corporations do: daily volume in bond markets exceeds $1 *trillion.* What's being exchanged in this market, and what factors influence decisions to buy or sell?

In our discussion thus far, we've portrayed banks as intermediaries between savers and spenders. Banks aren't the only mechanism available for transferring purchasing power from nonspenders to spenders. Funds are lent and borrowed in bond markets as well. In this case, a corporation may borrow money directly from consumers or other institutions. When it does so, it issues a bond as proof of its promise to repay the loan. A **bond** is simply a piece of paper certifying that someone has borrowed money and promises to pay it back at some future date. In other words, *a bond is nothing more than an IOU.* In the case of bond markets, however, the IOU is typically signed by a giant corporation or a government agency rather than a friend. It's therefore more widely accepted by lenders.

bond: A certificate acknowledging a debt and the amount of interest to be paid each year until repayment; an IOU.

Because most corporations and government agencies that borrow money in the bond market are well known and able to repay their debts, their bonds are actively traded. If I lend $1,000 to General Motors on a 10-year bond, for example, I don't have to wait 10 years to get my money back; I can resell the bond to someone else at any time. If I do, that person will collect the face value of the bond (plus interest) from GM when it's due. The actual purchase and sale of bonds take place in the bond market. Although a good deal of the action occurs on Wall Street in New York, the bond market has no unique location. Like other markets we've discussed, the bond market exists whenever and however (electronically) bond buyers and sellers get together.

Bond Yields. People buy bonds because bonds pay interest. If you buy a General Motors bond, GM is obliged to pay you interest during the period of the loan. For example, an 8 percent 2025 GM bond in the amount of $1,000 states that GM will pay the bondholder $80 interest annually (8 percent of $1,000) until 2025. At that point GM will repay the initial $1,000 loan (the "principal").

yield: The rate of return on a bond; the annual interest payment divided by the bond's price.

The current **yield** paid on a bond depends on the promised interest rate (8 percent in this case) and the actual purchase price of the bond. Specifically,

$$\text{Yield} = \frac{\textbf{Annual interest payment}}{\textbf{Price paid for bond}}$$

If you pay $1,000 for the bond, then the current yield is

$$\text{Yield} = \frac{\$80}{\$1,000} = 0.08, \text{ or } 8\%$$

which is the same as the interest rate printed on the face of the bond. But what if you pay only $900 for the bond? In this case, the interest rate paid by GM remains at 8 percent ($80 per year), but the *yield* jumps to

$$\text{Yield} = \frac{\$80}{\$900} = 0.089, \text{ or } 8.9\%$$

Buying a $1,000 bond for only $900 might seem like too good a bargain to be true. But bonds are often bought and sold at prices other than their face value (see the accompanying News). In fact, *a principal objective of Federal Reserve open market activity is to alter the price of bonds, and therewith their yields.* By doing so, the Fed makes bonds a more or less attractive alternative to holding money.

IN THE NEWS

Treasury Prices Fall with Improved Economic Outlook

Better-than-expected economic data pushed Treasury prices down. The 10-year note was down 21/32 point, or $6.5625 per $1,000 face value. The yield climbed to 2.914 percent, up from yesterday's 2.842 percent. The closing price stood at 107 2/32.

The 30-year bond was also down, closing at 114 24/32, down 30/32 point. The yield rose to 3.673 from yesterday's 3.626 percent.

Source: News reports, February 5, 2009.

ANALYSIS: Bond prices and yields move in opposite directions. If the Fed sells bonds, bond prices fall and yields (interest rates) rise.

Open Market Activity. The basic premise of open market activity is that participants in the bond market will respond to changes in bond prices and yields. As we've observed, *the less you pay for a bond, the higher its yield.* Accordingly, the Fed can induce people to *buy* bonds by offering to sell them at a lower price (e.g., a $1,000, 8 percent bond for only $900). Similarly, the Fed can induce people to *sell* bonds by offering to buy them at higher prices. In either case, the Fed hopes to move reserves into or out of the banking system. In other words, **open market operations** entail the purchase and sale of government securities (bonds) for the purpose of altering the flow of reserves into and out of the banking system.

open market operations: Federal Reserve purchases and sales of government bonds for the purpose of altering bank reserves.

Open Market Purchases. Suppose the Fed's goal is to increase the money supply. Its strategy is to provide the banking system with additional reserves. To do so, it must persuade people to deposit a larger share of their financial assets in banks and hold less in other forms, particularly government bonds. The tool for doing this is bond prices. *If the Fed offers to pay a higher price for bonds ("bids up bonds"), it will effectively lower bond yields and market interest rates.* The higher prices and lower yields will reduce the attractiveness of holding bonds. If the price offered by the Fed is high enough, people will sell some of their bonds to the Fed. What will they do with the proceeds of those bond sales? Deposit them in their bank accounts, of course. This influx of deposits into bank accounts will directly increase both the money supply and bank reserves—goal achieved.

Figure 14.4 illustrates the dynamics of open market operations in more detail. When the Fed buys a bond from the public, it pays with a check written on itself (step 1 in Figure 14.4). What will the bond seller do with the check? There really aren't any options. If the seller wants to use the proceeds of the bond sale, he or she will have to deposit the Fed check at a bank (step 2 in the figure). The bank, in turn, deposits the check at a regional Federal Reserve bank in exchange for a reserve credit (step 3). The bank's reserves are directly increased by the amount of the check. Thus, *by buying bonds, the Fed increases bank reserves.* These reserves can be used to expand the money supply still further as banks put their newly acquired reserves to work making loans.

Quantitative Easing. Federal Reserve open-market purchases were pursued so aggressively in 2009–2011 that they acquired a new name—"quantitative easing," or "QE." The Fed's QE program entailed two important changes in its traditional open market operations. First, it expanded the scope of Fed purchases beyond short-term government bonds to longer-term bonds and other securities (e.g., mortgage-backed securities). Second, the QE program allowed the Fed to purchase bonds directly from commercial banks rather than

FIGURE 14.4

An Open Market Purchase

The Fed can increase bank reserves by buying bonds from the public. The Fed check used to buy bonds (step 1) gets deposited in a private bank (step 2). The bank returns the check to the Fed (step 3), thereby obtaining additional reserves. To decrease bank reserves, the Fed would sell bonds, thus reversing the flow of reserves.

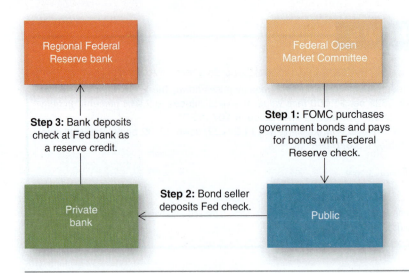

exclusively through the bond market. This gave the Fed more direct control of bank assets, reserves, and solvency. The Fed used its broadened powers to inject more reserves directly into the banking system and shore up confidence in bank solvency.

The first round of quantitative easing (QE1) began in November 2008 and continued through June 2010. During that period, the Fed purchased $1.5 trillion of securities, boosting bank reserves by the same amount (note the spike in excess reserves in Figure 14.2). When economic growth failed to accelerate as hoped, the Fed began a second round of asset purchases in November 2010 that continued to June 2011. A third round (QE3) was initiated in September 2012, with scheduled Fed purchases of $85 billion per month. As excess reserves continued to rise and interest rates fall, the Fed started to reduce its monthly purchases. This "tapering" schedule continued until late in 2014. By the end of the QE programs, the Fed had accumulated more than $2 trillion in bonds and other securities, and bank reserves had risen by a similar amount. These huge bond purchases helped to keep interest rates at historic lows.

Open Market Sales. Should the Fed desire to slow the growth in the money supply, it can reverse the whole process. Instead of offering to *buy* bonds, the Fed in this case will try to *sell* bonds. If the Fed "bids bonds down" (offers to sell them at low prices), bond yields will rise. In response, individuals, corporations, and government agencies will convert some of their transactions deposits into bonds. When they do so, they write a check, paying the Fed for the bonds.[3] The Fed then returns the check to the depositor's bank, taking payment through a reduction in the bank's reserve account. The reserves of the banking system are thereby diminished, as is the capacity to make loans. Thus, *by selling bonds, the Fed reduces bank reserves.*

The Fed Funds Rate

A market signal of these changing reserve flows is provided by the federal funds rate. Recall that "fed funds" are excess reserves traded among banks. If the Fed pumps more reserves into the banking system (by buying bonds), the interest rate charged for overnight reserve loans—the federal funds rate—will decline. Conversely, if the Fed is reducing bank reserves (by selling bonds), the federal funds rate will increase. Hence *the federal funds rate is a highly visible signal of Federal Reserve open market operations.* When Alan Greenspan reduced the federal funds rate *11 times* in 2001, the Fed was underscoring

---

[3]In actuality, the Fed deals directly with only 36 "primary" bond dealers. These intermediaries then trade with each other, "secondary" dealers, financial institutions, and individuals. These additional steps don't significantly alter the flow of funds depicted here. Using electronic transactions rather than paper checks doesn't alter the flow of funds either.

the urgency of monetary stimulus to combat the recession and the aftereffects of the September 11 terrorist attacks.

Beginning in June 2004 the Fed used this same tool to *reduce* lending activity. In fact, the Fed completely reversed course and raised the fed funds rate *17 times* between June 2004 and June 2006.

The Fed changed course yet again in 2007. Between September 2007 and December 2008 the Fed lowered the federal funds rate *10 times* (see the News below). The Fed's goal this time was to push bond yields so low that people would prefer to hold their idle funds in banks rather than buy bonds. The result was a massive increase in excess reserves, as we saw in Figure 14.2. The lower interest rates that accompanied the Fed bond purchases were intended to encourage people to borrow and spend these increased excess reserves. The Fed kept interest rates low and excess reserves high in 2010–2014 through successive waves of open market purchases (quantitative easing).

IN THE NEWS

U.S. Federal Reserve Cuts Interest Rates to Historic Low

U.S. Central Bank Decision Aimed at Reassuring Market, Stimulating Economy

Washington—The U.S. central bank on December 16 cut interest rates to an all-time low, a move aimed at reassuring financial markets and stimulating banks to lend money.

The Federal Reserve Board lowered the target federal funds rate to a range of 0 percent to 0.25 percent, the lowest level in the history of modern monetary policy. The federal funds rate is the rate at which banks lend to one another. The rate, historically, has an effect on the rates consumers are charged for home mortgage loans and other types of credit. . . .

A cut in the Fed's target rate lowers the interest rates consumers and businesses pay, making it more appealing for them to borrow money. When they spend that lent cash, it boosts the economy by increasing the demand for goods, services, and labor.

—Katherine Lewis

Source: **www.America.gov,** December 16, 2008.

ANALYSIS: The Fed uses open market operations to change short-term interest rates. In this case the Fed intended to cut interest rates to nearly zero by aggressively buying Treasury bonds.

web click

Has the federal funds rate changed recently? What does it signal about Federal Reserve policy? For information about the fed funds rate, visit the Fed's website at **www.federalreserve .gov.** Click the "Monetary Policy" tab and read the "FOMC statement."

When the Fed announces a change in the federal funds rate, it always refers to the "target" rate. The Fed doesn't actually *set* the fed funds rate. It only establishes a desired "target" rate. When the Fed lowers the target rate, it seeks to hit it by buying more bonds in the market.

Volume of Activity. To appreciate the significance of open market operations, you need a sense of the magnitudes involved. As we noted earlier, the volume of trading in U.S. bond markets exceeds $1 *trillion* a day. The Fed alone owned more than $2 trillion worth of government securities at the beginning of 2015 and bought or sold enormous sums daily. Thus open market operations involve tremendous amounts of money and, by implication, potential bank reserves. Each $1 of reserves represents something like $10 of potential lending capacity (via the money multiplier). Thus open market operations can have a profound impact on the money supply.

INCREASING THE MONEY SUPPLY

The three major tools of monetary policy are reserve requirements, discount rates, and open market operations. The Fed can use these tools individually or in combination to change the money supply. This section illustrates the use of each tool to attain a specific policy goal.

TABLE 14.2

How to Increase the Money Supply

The accompanying data depict a banking system that has $340 billion of money (M1) and no further lending capacity (excess reserves = 0). To enlarge M1 to $400 billion, the Fed can (1) lower the required reserve ratio, (2) reduce the discount rate, or (3) buy bonds held by the public.

Item	Amount
1. Cash held by public	$100 billion
2. Transactions deposits	240 billion
3. Total money supply (M1)	$340 billion
4. Required reserves	$ 60 billion
5. Excess reserves	0
6. Total reserves of banks	$ 60 billion
7. U.S. bonds held by public	$460 billion
8. Discount rate	5%

web click

For an inside view of how the Fed uses its policy tools, visit **www.federalreserveeducation.org.**

Suppose the policy goal is to increase the money supply from an assumed level of $340 billion to $400 billion. In surveying the nation's banks, the Fed discovers the facts shown in Table 14.2. On the basis of the facts presented in Table 14.2, it's evident that

- The banking system is "loaned up." Because excess reserves are zero (see row 5 in Table 14.2), there's no additional lending capacity.
- The required reserve ratio must be equal to 25 percent because this is the current ratio of required reserves ($60 billion) to total deposits ($240 billion).

Accordingly, if the Fed wants to increase the money supply, it will have to pump additional reserves into the banking system or lower the reserve requirement. *To increase the money supply, the Fed can*

- *Lower reserve requirements.*
- *Reduce the discount rate.*
- *Buy bonds.*

Lowering Reserve Requirements

Lowering the reserve requirements is an expedient way of increasing the lending capacity of the banking system. But by how much should the reserve requirement be reduced?

Recall that the Fed's goal is to increase the money supply from $340 billion to $400 billion, an increase of $60 billion. If the public isn't willing to hold any additional cash, this entire increase in money supply will have to take the form of added transactions deposits. In other words, total deposits will have to increase from $240 billion to $300 billion. These additional deposits will have to be *created* by the banks in the form of new loans to consumers or business firms.

If the banking system is going to support $300 billion in transactions deposits with its *existing* reserves, the reserve requirement will have to be reduced from 25 percent. We can compute the desired reserve requirement as follows:

$$\frac{\text{Total reserves}}{\text{Desired level of deposits}} = \frac{\$60 \text{ billion}}{\$300 \text{ billion}} = 0.20$$

So the next move is to lower the reserve requirement from 0.25 to 0.20. At the moment the Fed lowers the minimum reserve ratio to 0.20, *total* reserves won't change. The bank's potential lending power will change, however. Required reserves will drop to $48 billion ($0.20 \times \$240$ billion), and excess reserves will jump from zero to $12 billion. These new excess reserves imply an additional lending capacity:

$$\underset{(\$12 \text{ billion})}{\textbf{Excess reserves}} \times \underset{(5)}{\textbf{Money multiplier}} = \underset{(\$60 \text{ billion})}{\textbf{Unused lending capacity}}$$

If the banks succeed in putting all this new lending power to work—actually make $60 billion in new loans—the Fed's objective of increasing the money supply will be attained.

Lowering the Discount Rate

The second monetary tool available to the Fed is the discount rate. We assumed it was 5 percent initially (see row 8 in Table 14.2). If the Fed lowers this rate, it will become cheaper for banks to borrow reserves from the Fed. The banks will be more willing to borrow (cheaper) reserves so long as they can make additional loans to their own customers at higher interest rates. The profitability of discounting depends on the *difference* between the discount rate and the interest rate the bank charges its loan customers. The Fed increases this difference when it lowers the discount rate.

There's no way to calculate the appropriate discount rate without more detailed knowledge of the banking system's willingness to borrow reserves from the Fed. Nevertheless, we can determine how much reserves the banks *must* borrow if the Fed's money supply target is to be attained. The Fed's objective is to increase transactions deposits by $60 billion. If these deposits are to be created by the banks—and the reserve requirement is unchanged at 0.25—the banks will have to borrow an additional $15 billion of reserves ($60 billion divided by 4, the money multiplier).

Buying Bonds

The Fed can also get additional reserves into the banking system by buying U.S. bonds in the open market. As row 7 in Table 14.2 indicates, the public holds $460 billion in U.S. bonds, none of which are counted as part of the money supply. If the Fed can persuade people to sell some of these bonds, bank reserves will surely rise.

To achieve its money supply target, the Fed will offer to buy $15 billion of U.S. bonds. It will pay for these bonds with checks written on its own account at the Fed. The people who sell the bonds will deposit these checks in their own transactions accounts. As they do so, they'll directly increase bank deposits and reserves by $15 billion.

Is $15 billion of open market purchases enough? Yes. The $15 billion is a direct addition to transactions deposits, and therefore to the money supply. The additional deposits bring in $15 billion of reserves, only $3.75 billion of which is required (0.25 × $15 billion). Hence the new deposits bring in $11.25 billion of *excess* reserves. These new excess reserves themselves create additional lending capacity:

$$\underset{\text{(\$11.25 billion)}}{\textbf{Excess reserves}} \times \underset{\text{(4)}}{\textbf{Money multiplier}} = \underset{\text{(\$45 billion)}}{\textbf{Unused lending capacity}}$$

Thus the $15 billion of open market purchases will eventually lead to a $60 billion increase in M1 as a consequence of both direct deposits ($15 billion) and subsequent loan activity ($45 billion).

Federal Funds Rate. When the Fed starts bidding up bonds, bond yields and market interest rates will start falling. So will the federal funds rate. This will give individual banks an incentive to borrow any excess reserves available, thereby accelerating deposit (loan) creation.

DECREASING THE MONEY SUPPLY

All the tools used to increase the money supply can also be used in reverse. *To reduce the money supply, the Fed can*

- *Raise reserve requirements.*
- *Increase the discount rate.*
- *Sell bonds.*

On a week-to-week basis the Fed does occasionally seek to reduce the total amount of cash and transactions deposits held by the public. These are minor adjustments, however, to broader policies. A growing economy needs a steadily increasing supply of money to finance market exchanges. Hence the Fed rarely seeks an outright reduction in the size of the money supply. What it does is regulate the *rate of growth* in the money supply. When the Fed wants to slow the rate of consumer and investor spending, it restrains the *growth* of money and credit. Although many people talk about "reducing" the money supply, they're really talking about slowing its rate of growth. More immediately, they expect to see *rising* interest rates. To slow economic growth (and potential price inflation), China pursued this sort of monetary restraint in 2011.

IS THE FED LOSING CONTROL?

The policy tools at the Fed's disposal imply tight control of the nation's money supply. By altering reserve requirements, discount rates, or open market purchases, the Fed apparently has the ability to increase or decrease the money supply at will. But the Fed's control is far from complete. The nature of "money," as well as our notion of what a "bank" is, keeps changing. As a result, the Fed has to run pretty fast just to stay in place.

Monetary Control Act. Before 1980, the Fed's control of the money supply wasn't only incomplete but actually weakening. The Fed didn't have authority over all banks. Only one-third of all commercial banks were members of the Federal Reserve System and subject to its regulations. All savings and loan associations and other savings banks remained outside the Federal Reserve System. These banks were subject to regulations of state banking commissions and other federal agencies but not to Federal Reserve requirements. As a consequence, a substantial quantity of money and near-money lay beyond the control of the Fed.

To increase the Fed's control of the money supply, Congress passed the Depository Institutions Deregulation and Monetary Control Act of 1980. Commonly referred to simply as the Monetary Control Act, that legislation subjected *all* commercial banks, S&Ls, savings banks, and most credit unions to Fed regulation. All depository institutions now have to satisfy Fed reserve requirements. All depository institutions also enjoy access to the Fed's discount window. These reforms (phased in over a period of seven years) obliterated the distinction between member and nonmember banks and greatly strengthened the Fed's control of the banking system.

Shadow Banking. Ironically, *as the Fed's control of the banks was increasing, the banks themselves were declining in importance.* Banks are part of a larger financial services industry that provides deposit, credit, and payment services. Traditional banks take in insured deposits and make loans. But other financial institutions also make loans. These "shadow banks" have grown in importance while traditional banks have declined in number and importance.

Money market mutual funds (MMMFs), for example, hold a lot of assets. MMMFs typically pay higher interest rates than traditional bank accounts and also permit limited check-writing privileges. They thus serve as a potential substitute for traditional banks. Many brokerage houses also offer to hold idle cash in interest-earning accounts for their stock and bond customers.

Shadow banks also compete with traditional banks for loan business; 30 percent of all consumer loans are now made through credit cards. Banks themselves were once the primary source of credit cards. Now corporate giants like AT&T, GM, Sears, and American Airlines offer nonbank credit cards. Large corporations also offer loans to consumers who want to buy their products and even extend loans to unaffiliated businesses.

Insurance companies and pension funds also use their vast financial resources to make loans. The Teachers Insurance and Annuity Association (TIAA)—the pension fund for college professors—has lent more than $10 billion directly to corporations. Many insurance companies provide long-term loans for commercial real estate.

Global Finance. Foreign banks, corporations, and pension funds may also extend credit to American businesses. They may also hold deposits of U.S. dollars abroad (for example, Eurodollars). Also, the Fed estimates that at least 25 percent of U.S. currency circulates outside the United States. So the Fed can't totally control the money supply.

All this credit and deposit activity by global and nonbank institutions competes with traditional banks. And the nonbanks are winning the competition. In the past 20 years, the share of all financial institution assets held by banks has dropped from 37 percent to 27 percent, which means that banks are less important than they once were. This has made control of the money supply increasingly difficult.

Focus on Fed Funds Rate, Not Money Supply. Because of the difficulties in managing an increasingly globalized and electronic flow of funds, the Fed has shifted away from money supply targets to interest rate targets. Although changes in the money supply and in interest rates are intrinsically related, interest rates are easier and faster to track. The Fed also has the financial power to change short-term interest rates through its massive open market operations. Last, but not least, the Fed recognizes that interest rates, not more obscure data on the money supply or bank reserves, are the immediate concern in investment and big-ticket consumption decisions. As a result, the Fed will continue to use the federal funds rate as its primary barometer of monetary policy in the economy tomorrow.

SUMMARY

- The Federal Reserve System controls the nation's money supply by regulating the loan activity (deposit creation) of private banks (depository institutions). **LO14-2**
- The core of the Federal Reserve System is the 12 regional Federal Reserve banks, which provide check clearance, reserve deposit, and loan ("discounting") services to individual banks. Private banks are required to maintain minimum reserves on deposit at the regional Federal Reserve banks. **LO14-1**
- The general policies of the Fed are set by its Board of Governors. The Board's chair is selected by the U.S. president and confirmed by the Senate. The chair serves as the chief spokesperson for monetary policy. The Fed's policy strategy is implemented by the Federal Open Market Committee (FOMC), which directs open market sales and purchase of U.S. bonds. **LO14-1**
- The Fed has three basic tools for changing the money supply. By altering the reserve requirement, the Fed can immediately change both the quantity of excess reserves

in the banking system and the money multiplier, which limits banks' lending capacity. By altering discount rates (the rate of interest charged by the Fed for reserve borrowing), the Fed can also influence the amount of reserves maintained by banks. Finally, and most important, the Fed can increase or decrease the reserves of the banking system by buying or selling government bonds—that is, by engaging in open market operations. **LO14-2**
- When the Fed buys bonds, it causes an increase in bank reserves (and lending capacity). When the Fed sells bonds, it induces a reduction in reserves (and lending capacity). **LO14-3**
- The federal funds (interest) rate is a market signal of Fed open market activity and intentions. **LO14-2**
- In the 1980s, the Fed gained greater control of the banking system. Global and nonbank institutions such as pension funds, insurance companies, and nonbank credit services have grown in importance, however, making control of the money supply more difficult. **LO14-2**

Key Terms

monetary policy	money multiplier	portfolio decision
money supply (M1, M2)	federal funds rate	bond
required reserves	discounting	yield
excess reserves	discount rate	open market operations

Questions for Discussion

1. Why do banks want to maintain as little excess reserves as possible? Under what circumstances might banks want to hold excess reserves? (*Hint:* See Figure 14.2.) **LO14-2**

2. Why do people hold bonds rather than larger savings account or checking account balances? Under what circumstances might they change their portfolios, moving their funds out of bonds and into bank accounts? **LO14-3**

3. What are the current price and yield of 10-year U.S. Treasury bonds? Of General Motors bonds? (Check the financial section of your daily newspaper.) What accounts for the difference? **LO14-3**

4. Why did China reduce reserve requirements in 2014? How did they expect consumers and businesses to respond? (See World View, p. 300.) **LO14-2**

5. Why might the Fed want to decrease the money supply? **LO14-1**

6. Why did bond prices decline at the February 2009 auction? (See News, p. 305.) **LO14-3**

7. In early 2009, short-term bond yields in the United States fell to less than 0.5 percent. Yet relatively few people moved their assets out of bonds into banks. How might this failure of open market operations be explained? **LO14-3**

8. In 2008 the Fed reduced both the discount and federal fund rates dramatically. But bank loan volume didn't increase. What considerations might have constrained the market's response to Fed policy? **LO14-2**

9. If bondholders expect the Fed to raise interest rates, what action might they take? How would this affect the Fed's goal? **LO14-3**

10. What are the economic risks of aggressive Fed open market purchases? **LO14-3**

 mobile app Visit your mobile app store and download the Schiller: Study Econ app *today!*

LO14-1 1. What is the money multiplier when the reserve requirement is

　　　　　(*a*) 0.05　　　　　　　　　　　　　　　_____
　　　　　(*b*) 0.10　　　　　　　　　　　　　　　_____
　　　　　(*c*) 0.125?　　　　　　　　　　　　　　_____
　　　　　(*d*) 0.111?　　　　　　　　　　　　　　_____

LO14-2 2. In Table 14.1, what would the following values be if the required reserve ratio fell from 0.20 to 0.10?

　　　　　(*a*) Total deposits　　　　　　　　　　_____
　　　　　(*b*) Total reserves　　　　　　　　　　_____
　　　　　(*c*) Required reserves　　　　　　　　　_____
　　　　　(*d*) Excess reserves　　　　　　　　　　_____
　　　　　(*e*) Money multiplier　　　　　　　　　_____
　　　　　(*f*) Unused lending capacity　　　　　　_____

LO14-2 3. Assume that the following data describe the condition of the banking system:

Total reserves	$100 billion
Transactions deposits	$800 billion
Cash held by public	$400 billion
Reserve requirement	0.10

　　　　　(*a*) How large is the money supply (M1)?　　　　　　　　　　　_____
　　　　　(*b*) How large are *required* reserves?　　　　　　　　　　　_____
　　　　　(*c*) How large are *excess* reserves?　　　　　　　　　　　　_____
　　　　　(*d*) What is the money multiplier?　　　　　　　　　　　　　_____
　　　　　(*e*) By how much could the banks increase their lending activity?　_____

LO14-2 4. In Problem 3, suppose the Fed wanted to stop further lending activity. To do this, what reserve requirement should the Fed impose?　　_____

LO14-2 5. According to the World View on page 300, what was the money multiplier in China

　　　　　(*a*) Before the rate cut?　　　　　　_____
　　　　　(*b*) After the rate cut?　　　　　　　_____

LO14-2 6. By how much did the following increase when China cut the reserve requirement (see World View, p. 300):

　　　　　(*a*) Excess reserves?　　　　　　　　　　　　　　　_____
　　　　　(*b*) The lending capacity of the banking system?　　_____

LO14-2 7. Assume the banking system contains the following amounts:

Total reserves	$ 90 billion
Transactions deposits	$900 billion
Cash held by public	$100 billion
Reserve requirement	0.10

　　　　　(*a*) Are the banks fully utilizing their lending capacity?　　　　　　　　　　_____
　　　　　(*b*) What would happen to the money supply *initially* if the public deposited another $20 billion of cash in transactions accounts?　　_____
　　　　　(*c*) What would the lending capacity of the banking system be after such a portfolio switch?　　_____
　　　　　(*d*) How large would the money supply be if the banks fully utilized their lending capacity?　　_____
　　　　　(*e*) What three steps could the Fed take to offset that potential growth in M1?　　_____
　　　　　　　　_____
　　　　　　　　_____

PROBLEMS FOR CHAPTER 14 (cont'd)   Name: _____

LO14-3 8. Assume that a $1,000 bond issued in 2015 pays $100 in interest each year. What is the current yield on the bond if it can be purchased for

(a) $1,200?   _____

(b) $1,000?   _____

(c) $800?   _____

LO14-3 9. Suppose a $1,000 bond pays $60 per year in interest.

(a) What is the contractual interest rate ("coupon rate") on the bond?   _____

(b) If market interest rates rise to 7 percent, what price will the bond sell for?   _____

LO14-3 10. What was the Fed's target for the fed funds rate in December 2008 (News, p. 307)?   _____

LO14-3 11. If the GM bond described on page 304 was resold for $1,200, what would its yield be?   _____

LO14-3 12. Suppose a banking system with the following balance sheet has no excess reserves. Assume that banks will make loans in the full amount of any excess reserves that they acquire and will immediately be able to eliminate loans from their portfolio to cover inadequate reserves.

Assets (in Billions)		Liabilities (in Billions)	
Total reserves	$ 30	Transactions accounts	$400
Securities	190		
Loans	180		
Total	$400	Total	$400

(a) What is the reserve requirement?   _____

(b) Suppose the reserve requirement is changed to 5 percent. Reconstruct the balance sheet of the total banking system after all banks have fully utilized their lending capacity.

Assets (in Billions)		Liabilities (in Billions)	
Total reserves	_____	Transactions accounts	_____
Securities	_____		
Loans	_____		
Total	_____	Total	_____

(c) By how much has the money supply changed as a result of the lower reserve requirement (step b)?   _____

(d) Suppose the Fed now buys $10 billion of securities directly from the banks. What will the banks' books look like after this purchase?

Assets (in Billions)		Liabilities (in Billions)	
Total reserves	_____	Transactions accounts	_____
Securities	_____		
Loans	_____		
Total	_____	Total	_____

(e) How much excess reserves do the banks have now?   _____

(f) By how much can the money supply now increase?   _____

Monetary Policy

After reading this chapter, you should know

LO15-1 How interest rates are set in the money market.

LO15-2 How monetary policy affects macro outcomes.

LO15-3 The constraints on monetary policy impact.

LO15-4 The differences between Keynesian and monetarist monetary theories.

So what if the Federal Reserve System controls the nation's money supply? Why is this significant? Does it matter how much money is available?

Vladimir Lenin thought so. The first communist leader of the Soviet Union once remarked that the best way to destroy a society is to destroy its money. If a society's money became valueless, it would no longer be accepted in exchange for goods and services in product markets. People would have to resort to barter, and the economy's efficiency would be severely impaired. Adolf Hitler tried unsuccessfully to use this weapon against Great Britain during World War II. His plan was to counterfeit British currency, then drop it from planes flying over England. He believed that the sudden increase in the quantity of money, together with its suspect origins, would render the British pound valueless.

Even in peacetime, the quantity of money in circulation influences its value in the marketplace. Moreover, interest rates and access to credit (bank loans) are basic determinants of spending behavior. As we witnessed in 2008, when credit becomes unavailable, the economy can grind to a halt. Consequently, control over the money supply is a critical policy tool for altering macroeconomic outcomes.

But how much influence does the money supply have on macro performance? Specifically,

- **What's the relationship between the money supply, interest rates, and aggregate demand?**
- **How can the Fed use its control of the money supply or interest rates to alter macro outcomes?**
- **How effective is monetary policy, compared to fiscal policy?**

Economists offer very different answers to these questions. Some argue that changes in the money supply directly affect macro outcomes; others argue that the effects of such changes are indirect and less certain.

Paralleling these arguments about *how* **monetary policy** works are debates over the relative effectiveness of monetary and fiscal policy. Some economists argue that monetary policy is more effective than fiscal policy; others contend the reverse is true. This chapter examines these different views of money and assesses their implications for macro policy.

monetary policy: The use of money and credit controls to influence macroeconomic outcomes.

interest rate: The price paid for the use of money.

money supply (M1): Currency held by the public, plus balances in transactions accounts.

money supply (M2): M1 plus balances in most savings accounts and money market mutual funds.

demand for money: The quantities of money people are willing and able to hold at alternative interest rates, *ceteris paribus.*

portfolio decision: The choice of how (where) to hold idle funds.

THE MONEY MARKET

The best place to learn how monetary policy works is the money *market*. You must abandon any mystical notions you may harbor about money and view it like any other commodity that's traded in the marketplace. Like other goods, there's a supply of money and a demand for money. Together they determine the "price" of money, or the **interest rate.**

At first glance, it may appear strange to call interest rates the price of money. But when you borrow money, the "price" you pay is measured by the interest rate you're charged. When interest rates are high, money is "expensive." When interest rates are low, money is "cheap."

Money Balances

Even people who don't borrow must contend with the price of money. People hold cash and maintain positive bank balances as part of the **money supply (M1, M2).** There's an opportunity cost associated with such money balances, however. Money held in transactions accounts earns little or no interest. Money held in savings accounts and money market mutual funds does earn interest but usually at relatively low rates. By contrast, money used to buy bonds or stocks or to make loans is likely to earn a higher rate of return, as Table 15.1 illustrates.

The Price of Money. The nature of the "price" of money should be apparent: People who hold *cash* are forgoing an opportunity to earn interest. So are people who hold money in checking accounts that pay no interest. In either case, *forgone interest is the opportunity cost (price) of money people choose to hold.* How high is that price? It's equal to the market rate of interest.

Money held in interest-paying bank accounts does earn some interest. In this case, the opportunity cost of holding money is the *difference* between the prevailing rate of interest and the rate paid on deposit balances. In Table 15.1 the opportunity cost of holding cash rather than Treasury bonds is 2.55 percent per year.

The Demand for Money

Once we recognize that money does have a price, we can formulate a *demand* for money. When we talk about the "demand" for money, we're not referring to your ceaseless craving for more income. Instead, the **demand for money** refers to the ability and willingness to *hold* money in the form of cash or bank balances. As is the case with all goods, the demand for money is a schedule (or curve) showing the quantity of money demanded at alternative prices (interest rates).

So why would anyone want to "hold" money? The decision to hold (demand) money balances is the kind of **portfolio decision** we examined in Chapter 14. While at first glance it might seem irrational to hold money balances that pay little or no interest, there are many good reasons for doing so.

Transactions Demand. Even people who have mastered the principles of economics hold money. They do so because they want to buy goods and services. To transact business in product or factor markets, we need money in the form of either cash or a positive bank account

TABLE 15.1
Portfolio Choices

Idle funds can be held in many forms. Holding funds in cash or checking accounts pays little or no interest. The "price" of holding money is the interest forgone from alternative portfolio choices. When that price is high, people hold (demand) less money.

Option	Interest Rate
Cash	0.00%
Checking accounts	0.50
6-month CD	0.70
10-year Treasury bond	2.55
Corporate bond (Aaa)	4.19

Source: Federal Reserve (July 2014 rates).

balance. Debit cards and ATM cards don't work unless there's money in the bank. Payment by e-cash also requires a supporting bank balance. Even when we use credit cards, we're only postponing the date of payment by a few weeks or so. Some merchants won't even accept credit cards, especially for small purchases. Accordingly, we recognize the existence of a basic **transactions demand for money**—that is, money held for everyday purchases.

Precautionary Demand. Another reason people hold money is their fear of the proverbial rainy day. A sudden emergency may require money purchases over and above normal transactions needs. Such needs may arise when the banks are closed or when one is in a community where one's checks aren't accepted. Also, future income is uncertain and may diminish unexpectedly. Therefore, people hold a bit more money (cash or bank account balances) than they anticipate spending. This **precautionary demand for money** is the extra money being held as a safeguard against the unexpected.

Speculative Demand. People also hold money for speculative purposes. Suppose you were interested in buying stocks or bonds but hadn't yet picked the right ones or regarded their present prices as too high. In such circumstances, you might want to hold some money so that you could later buy a "hot" stock or bond at a price you think attractive. Thus you'd be holding money in the hope that a better financial opportunity would later appear. In this sense, you'd be *speculating* with your money balances, forgoing present opportunities to earn interest in the hope of hitting a real jackpot later. These money balances represent a **speculative demand for money.**

The Market Demand Curve. These three motivations for holding money combine to create a *market demand* for money. What shape does this demand curve take? Does the quantity of money demanded decrease sharply as the rate of interest rises? Or do people tend to hold the same amount of money, regardless of its price?

People do cut down on their money balances when interest rates rise. At such times, the opportunity cost of holding money is simply too high. This explains why so many people move their money out of transactions deposits (M1) and into money market mutual funds (M2) when interest rates are extraordinarily high (for example, in 1980–1982). Corporations are even more careful about managing their money when interest rates rise. Better money management requires watching checking account balances more closely and even making more frequent trips to the bank, but the opportunity costs are worth it.

Figure 15.1 illustrates the total market demand for money. Like nearly all demand curves, the market demand curve for money slopes downward. The downward slope indicates that *the quantity of money people are willing and able to hold (demand) increases as interest rates fall* (*ceteris paribus*).

The Money Supply. The money supply curve is assumed to be a vertical line. As we saw in Chapter 13, the Federal Reserve has the power to regulate the money supply through its

transactions demand for money: Money held for the purpose of making everyday market purchases.

precautionary demand for money: Money held for unexpected market transactions or for emergencies.

speculative demand for money: Money held for speculative purposes, for later financial opportunities.

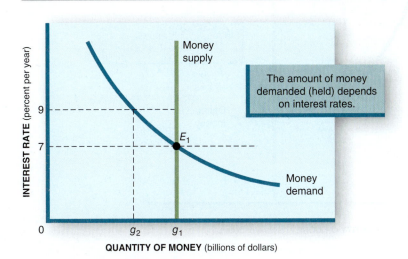

QUANTITY OF MONEY (billions of dollars)

FIGURE 15.1
Money Market Equilibrium

All points on the money demand curve represent the quantity of money people are willing to hold at a specific interest rate. The equilibrium interest rate occurs at the intersection (E_1) of the money supply and money demand curves. At that rate of interest, people are willing to hold as much money as is available. At any other interest rate (for example, 9 percent), the quantity of money people are *willing* to hold won't equal the quantity available, and people will adjust their portfolios.

reserve requirements, discount window, and open market operations. By using these policy tools, the Fed can target a specific quantity for the money supply (M1 or M2).

Equilibrium

Once a money demand curve and a money supply curve are available, the action in money markets is easy to follow. Figure 15.1 summarizes this action. The money demand curve in Figure 15.1 reflects existing demands for holding money. The money supply curve is drawn at an arbitrary level of g_1. In practice, its position depends on Federal Reserve policy (Chapter 14), the lending behavior of private banks, and the willingness of consumers and investors to borrow money.

equilibrium rate of interest:
The interest rate at which the quantity of money demanded in a given time period equals the quantity of money supplied.

The intersection of the money demand and money supply curves (E_1) establishes an **equilibrium rate of interest.** Only at this interest rate is the quantity of money supplied equal to the quantity demanded. In this case, we observe that an interest rate of 7 percent equates the desires of suppliers and demanders.

At any rate of interest other than 7 percent, the quantity of money demanded wouldn't equal the quantity supplied. Look at the imbalance that exists in Figure 15.1, for example, when the interest rate is 9 percent. At that rate, the quantity of money supplied (g_1 in Figure 15.1) exceeds the quantity demanded (g_2). All the money (g_1) must be held by someone, of course. But the demand curve indicates that people aren't *willing* to hold so much money at that interest rate (9 percent). People will adjust their portfolios by moving money out of cash and bank accounts into bonds or other assets that offer higher returns. This will tend to lower interest rates (recall that buying bonds tends to lower their yields). As interest rates drop, people are willing to hold more money. Ultimately we get to E_1, where the quantity of money demanded equals the quantity supplied. At that equilibrium, people are content with their portfolio choices.

Changing Interest Rates

The equilibrium rate of interest is subject to change. As we saw in Chapter 14, the Federal Reserve System can alter the money supply through changes in reserve requirements, changes in the discount rate, or open market operations. By implication, then, *the Fed can alter the equilibrium rate of interest.*

Figure 15.2 illustrates the potential impact of monetary policy on the equilibrium rate of interest. Assume that the money supply is initially at g_1 and the equilibrium interest rate is 7 percent, as indicated by point E_1. The Fed then increases the money supply to g_3 by lowering the reserve requirement, reducing the discount rate, or, most likely, purchasing additional bonds in the open market. This expansionary monetary policy brings about a new equilibrium at E_3. At this new intersection, the market rate of interest is only 6 percent. Hence *by increasing the money supply, the Fed tends to lower the equilibrium rate of interest.* To put the matter differently, people are *willing* to hold larger money balances only at lower interest rates.

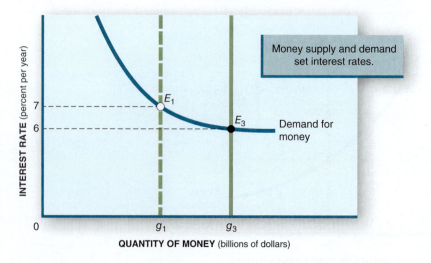

FIGURE 15.2

Changing the Rate of Interest

Changes in the money supply alter the equilibrium rate of interest. In this case, an increase in the money supply (from g_1 to g_3) lowers the equilibrium rate of interest (from 7 percent to 6 percent).

Interest Rate	Type of Loan	Rate
Federal funds rate	Interbank reserves, overnight	0.09%
Discount rate	Reserves lent to banks by Fed	0.75
Prime rate	Bank loans to blue-chip corporations	3.25
Mortgage rate	Loans for house purchases; up to 30 years	4.13
Auto loan	Financing of auto purchases	6.72
Consumer installment credit	Loans for general purposes	11.10
Credit cards	Financing of unpaid credit card purchases	13.50

Source: Federal Reserve (July 2014 rates).

TABLE 15.2
The Hierarchy of Interest Rates

Interest rates reflect the risks and duration of loans. Because risks and loan terms vary greatly, dozens of different interest rates are available. Here are a few of the more common rates as of July 2014.

web click

Compare the interest rates in Table 15.2 with today's rates. Fed loan rates can be found at **www.federalreserve.gov** by searching for "H.15." Consumer loan rates can be found at **www.bankrate.com.**

federal funds rate: The interest rate for interbank reserve loans.

Were the Fed to reverse its policy and *reduce* the money supply, interest rates would rise. You can see this result in Figure 15.2 by observing the change in the rate of interest that occurs when the money supply *shrinks* from g_3 to g_1.

Federal Funds Rate. As we noted in Chapter 14, the most visible market signal of the Fed's activity is the **federal funds rate.** When the Fed injects or withdraws reserves from the banking system (via open market operations), the interest rate on interbank loans is most directly affected. Any change in the federal funds rate, moreover, is likely to affect a whole hierarchy of interest rates (see Table 15.2). ***The federal funds rate reflects the cost of funds for banks.*** When that cost decreases, banks respond by lowering the interest rates *they* charge to businesses (the prime rate), home buyers (the mortgage rate), and consumers (e.g., auto loans, installment credit, and credit cards), as the accompanying News explains.

IN THE NEWS

Fed Cut Means Lower Rates for Consumers

The Federal Reserve took extraordinary actions Tuesday to revive the feeble U.S. economy. USA TODAY *reporters Sue Kirchhoff and John Waggoner answer questions about the Fed's moves:*

Q: What's the good news in the Fed's actions?

A: The Fed's decision to nudge its key fed funds rate to a range of zero to 0.25 percent—along with its plans to buy securities that are backed by mortgages—should mean lower consumer interest rates, particularly mortgage rates. Low mortgage rates mean that more people can afford to buy houses, which will help revive the moribund housing market. A drop in mortgage rates will also allow home owners to refinance their loans at lower rates, easing some of the burdens of their debts.

Low rates also make it cheaper for companies to borrow and expand. That, in turn, is a powerful economic stimulus. Most major banks, including Bank of America and Wachovia, lowered their prime lending rate to 3.25 percent from 4 percent Tuesday.

Q: What is the Fed trying to do?

A: The Fed is pulling out all the stops to revive business and consumer lending and get the economy moving. The central bank is particularly focused on the wide difference, or spread, on interest rates between supersafe Treasury bills, for example, and market-based loans for autos, homes, and other purchases.

Fed officials think the wide spreads are due to a lack of liquidity as lenders pull back. They hope that by flooding markets with cash, using such strategies as buying mortgage-backed bonds, they can bring interest rates down and relieve such pressures.

Source: *USA TODAY*, December 17, 2008, p. 3B. Reprinted with permission.

ANALYSIS: The ultimate goal of monetary stimulus is to increase aggregate demand. By reducing the cost of money for banks, the Fed expects banks to reduce interest rates for consumers.

INTEREST RATES AND SPENDING

A change in the interest rate isn't the end of this story. The ultimate goal of monetary policy is to alter macroeconomic outcomes: prices, output, employment. This requires a change in aggregate demand. Hence the next question is

- **How do changes in interest rates affect consumer, investor, government, and net export spending?**

Monetary Stimulus

Consider first a policy of monetary stimulus. The strategy of monetary stimulus is to increase **aggregate demand.** A tactic for doing so is to lower interest rates.

Investment. Will lower interest rates encourage spending? In Chapter 9 we observed that investment decisions are sensitive to the rate of interest. Specifically, we demonstrated that lower rates of interest reduce the cost of buying plants and equipment, making capital investment more profitable. Lower interest rates also reduce the opportunity cost of holding inventories. Accordingly, a lower rate of interest should result in a higher rate of desired investment spending, as shown by the movement down the investment demand curve in step 2 of Figure 15.3.

Aggregate Demand. The increased investment brought about by lower interest rates represents an injection of new spending into the circular flow. That jump in spending will kick off multiplier effects and result in an even larger increase in aggregate demand. Step 3 in Figure 15.3 illustrates this increase by the rightward *shift* of the AD curve. Market participants, encouraged by lower interest rates, are now willing to buy more output at the prevailing price level.

Consumers too may change their behavior when interest rates fall. As interest rates fall, mortgage payments decline. Monthly payments on home equity and credit card balances may also decline. These lower interest changes free up billions of consumer dollars. This increased net cash flow and lower interest rates may encourage consumers to buy new cars, appliances, or other big-ticket items. State and local governments may also conclude that

aggregate demand: The total quantity of output demanded at alternative price levels in a given time period, *ceteris paribus.*

Step 1: An increase in the money supply lowers the rate of interest.

Step 2: Lower interest rates stimulate investment.

Step 3: More investment increases aggregate demand (including multiplier effects).

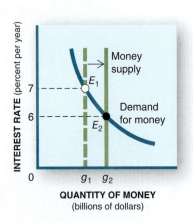
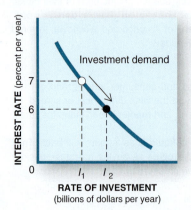
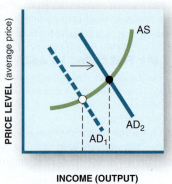

FIGURE 15.3

Monetary Stimulus

An increase in the money supply may reduce interest rates (step 1) and encourage more investment (step 2). The increase in investment will shift AD to the right and trigger multiplier effects that increase aggregate demand by an even larger amount (step 3).

Fed to Expand Bond-Purchase Program

Information received since the Federal Open Market Committee met in January indicates that the economy continues to contract. Job losses, declining equity and housing wealth, and tight credit conditions have weighed on consumer sentiment and spending. Weaker sales prospects and difficulties in obtaining credit have led businesses to cut back on inventories and fixed investment.

In these circumstances, the Federal Reserve will employ all available tools to promote economic recovery and to preserve price stability. . . . To provide greater support to mortgage lending and housing markets, the Committee decided today to increase the size of the Federal Reserve's balance sheet further by purchasing up to an additional $750 billion of agency mortgage-backed securities, bringing its total purchases of these securities to up to $1.25 trillion this year.

Source: **www.federalreserve.gov,** March 18, 2009.

ANALYSIS: Lower interest rates encourage market participants to borrow and spend more money. This shifts the AD curve rightward, setting off multiplier effects.

lower interest rates increase the desirability of bond-financed public works. All such responses add to aggregate demand.

From this perspective, *the Fed's goal of stimulating the economy is achieved in three distinct steps:*

- *An increase in the money supply.*
- *A reduction in interest rates.*
- *An increase in aggregate demand.*

This was the intent of the Fed's aggressive open market purchases in 2009 (see the above News).

Quantitative Impact. Just how much stimulus can monetary policy create? According to former Fed Chairman Ben Bernanke, the impact of monetary policy can be impressive:

$$\text{Bernanke's policy guide:} \quad \frac{\frac{1}{4} \text{ point reduction in long-term interest rate}}{} = \frac{\$50 \text{ billion}}{\text{fiscal stimulus}}$$

By this rule of thumb, a full-point reduction in long-term interest rates would increase aggregate demand just as much as a $200 billion injection of new government spending.

Monetary Restraint

Like fiscal policy, monetary policy is a two-edged sword, at times seeking to increase aggregate demand and at other times trying to restrain it. When inflation threatens, the goal of monetary policy is to reduce the rate of total spending, which puts the Fed in the position of "leaning against the wind." If successful, the resulting reduction in spending will keep aggregate demand from increasing inflationary pressures.

Higher Interest Rates. The mechanics of monetary policy designed to combat inflation are similar to those used to fight unemployment; only the direction is reversed. In this case, we seek to discourage spending by increasing the rate of interest. The Fed can push interest rates up by selling bonds, *increasing* the discount rate, or increasing the reserve requirement. All these actions reduce the money supply and help establish a new and higher equilibrium rate of interest (e.g., g_3 to g_1 in Figure 15.2).

web click

For an official explanation of monetary policy, with links to relevant data and videos, visit the "Monetary Policy" tab at **www.federalreserve.gov.**

The ultimate objective of a restrictive monetary policy is to reduce aggregate demand. For monetary restraint to succeed, spending behavior must be responsive to interest rates.

Reduced Aggregate Demand. Figure 15.3 showed the impact of reduced interest rates on investment and aggregate demand. The same figure can be used in reverse. If the interest rate rises from 6 to 7 percent, investment declines from I_2 to I_1 and the AD curve shifts *leftward.* At higher rates of interest, many marginal investments will no longer be profitable. Likewise, many consumers will decide that they can't afford the higher monthly payments associated with increased interest rates; purchases of homes, cars, and household appliances will be postponed. State and local governments may also decide to cancel or postpone bond-financed projects. Thus *monetary restraint is achieved with*

- *A decrease in the money supply.*
- *An increase in interest rates.*
- *A decrease in aggregate demand.*

The resulting leftward shift of the AD curve lessens inflationary pressures.

POLICY CONSTRAINTS

The mechanics of monetary policy are simple enough. They won't always work as well as we might hope, however. Several constraints can limit the Fed's ability to alter the money supply, interest rates, or aggregate demand.

Constraints on Monetary Stimulus

Short- vs. Long-Term Rates. One of the most visible constraints on monetary policy is the distinction between short-term interest rates and long-term interest rates. Bernanke's policy guide (on the previous page) focuses on changes in *long-term* rates like mortgages and installment loans. Yet the Fed's open market operations have the most direct effect on *short-term* rates (e.g., the overnight federal funds rate). As a consequence, *the success of Fed intervention depends in part on how well changes in long-term interest rates mirror changes in short-term interest rates.*

In 2001 the Fed reduced the federal funds rate by three full percentage points between January and September, the biggest reduction in short-term rates since 1994. Long-term rates fell much less, however. The interest rate on 30-year mortgages, for example, fell less than half a percentage point in the first few months of monetary stimulus.

The same thing happened when the Fed reversed direction in 2004–2006. The *short*-run fed funds rate was ratcheted up from 1.0 to 5.25 percent during that period—a huge increase. But *long*-term rates (e.g., 10-year Treasury bonds and home mortgages) rose only modestly. Fed Chairman Alan Greenspan characterized these disparate trends as a "conundrum."

The same "conundrum" frustrated Fed Chairman Bernanke in 2008. The Fed was successful in pushing the short-term federal funds rate down from 4.25 percent at the start of 2008 to near zero at year's end, but long-term mortgage and bond rates didn't drop nearly as much. Hence the aggregate demand stimulus was less than hoped for. That was why the Fed started buying longer-term securities through several rounds of "quantitative easing" (see pages 305–306).

Reluctant Lenders. There are several reasons why long-term rates might not closely mirror cuts in short-term rates. The first potential constraint is the willingness of private banks to increase their lending activity. The Fed can reduce the cost of funds to the banking system; the Fed can even reduce reserve requirements. But *the money supply won't increase unless banks lend more money.*

If the banks instead choose to accumulate excess reserves, the money supply won't increase as much as intended. We saw this happen in the Great Depression (Figure 14.2). This happened again in 2008–2014, when the Fed was trying to stimulate the economy. Despite three rounds of quantitative easing (QE1, QE2, and QE3)—massive open market purchases—banks were reluctant to increase their loan activity (see the accompanying News). Banks were trying to shore up their own equity and were wary of making any new loans that might not get repaid in a weak economy. In such cases, long-term rates stay relatively high even when short-term rates are falling. They were also worried about new banking regulations that could change both the appropriateness and the profitability of new loans. Rather than making new loans, the banks simply stockpiled their excess reserves (see Figure 14.2). At the beginning of 2015, banks held more than $2 trillion of excess reserves—more than at any other time in history.

IN THE NEWS

Prices Are Low! Mortgages Cheap! But You Can't Get One

NEW YORK (CNNMoney)—Yep, mortgage interest rates are low, but there's a catch: It doesn't matter how cheap rates are if you can't get a loan.

And these days, only highly qualified borrowers can get financing—let alone the best rates.

. . . Lenders now require much more up-front cash. The median down payment for purchase is about 15 percent. During the housing boom, it approached zero.

On most loans, banks want 20 percent down. On $200,000 purchases, that's $40,000, an insurmountable obstacle for many young house hunters. Or, in New York City, where the median home price is $800,000, buyers need $160,000 up front.

Industry insiders say all these factors have reduced the pool of buyers, lowering demand for homes and hurting prices.

—Les Christie

Source: CNNMoney.com, April 6, 2011. © 2011 Time Inc. Used under license.

ANALYSIS: If banks are reluctant to make new loans in a depressed economy, new bank reserves created by the Fed won't bolster more spending.

Liquidity Trap. There are circumstances in which even *short-term* rates may not fall when the Fed wants them to. The possibility that interest rates may not respond to changes in the money supply is illustrated by the "liquidity trap." When interest rates are low, the opportunity cost of holding money is cheap. At such times people may decide to hold all the money they can get, waiting for income-earning opportunities to improve. Bond prices, for example, may be high and their yields low. Buying bonds at such times entails the risk of capital losses (when bond prices fall) and little reward (since yields are low). Accordingly, market participants may decide just to hold any additional money the Fed supplies. At this juncture—a phenomenon Keynes called the **liquidity trap**—further expansion of the money supply has no effect on the rate of interest. The horizontal section of the money demand curve in Figure 15.4a portrays this situation.

What happens to interest rates when the initial equilibrium falls into this trap? Nothing at all. Notice that the equilibrium rate of interest doesn't fall when the money supply is increased from g_1 to g_2 (Figure 15.4a). People are willing to hold all that additional money without a reduction in the rate of interest.

liquidity trap: The portion of the money demand curve that is horizontal; people are willing to hold unlimited amounts of money at some (low) interest rate.

Low Expectations. Even if both short- and long-term interest rates do fall, we have no assurance that aggregate demand will increase as expected. Keynes put great emphasis on *expectations*. Recall that **investment decisions are motivated not only by interest rates but by expectations as well.** During a recession—when unemployment is high and the rate of spending is low—corporations have little incentive to expand production capacity. With little expectation of future profit, investors are likely to be unimpressed by "cheap money" (low interest rates) and may decline to use the lending capacity that banks make available.

Investment demand that's slow to respond to the lure of cheap money is said to be *inelastic* because it won't expand. Consumers too are reluctant to borrow when current and

(a) A liquidity trap can stop interest rates from falling.

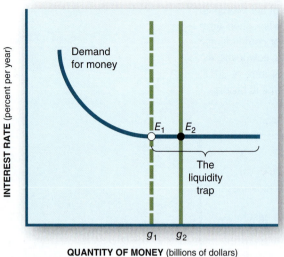

(b) Inelastic investment demand can also impede monetary policy.

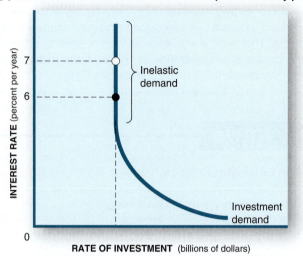

FIGURE 15.4
Constraints on Monetary Stimulus

(a) Liquidity Trap   If people are willing to hold unlimited amounts of money (cash and bank balances) at the prevailing interest rate, increases in the money supply won't push interest rates lower. A liquidity trap—the horizontal segment of the money demand curve—prevents interest rates from falling (step 1 in Figure 15.3).

(b) Inelastic Demand   A lower interest rate won't always stimulate investment. If investors have unfavorable expectations for future sales, small reductions in interest rates may not alter their investment decisions. Here the rate of investment remains constant when the interest rate drops from 7 to 6 percent. This kind of situation blocks the second step in the Keynesian approach to monetary policy (step 2 in Figure 15.3).

future income prospects are uncertain or distinctly unfavorable. Accordingly, even if the Fed is successful in lowering interest rates, there's no assurance that lower interest rates will stimulate borrowing and spending. Such a reluctance to spend was evident in 2008–2014. Although the Fed managed to push interest rates down to historic lows, investors and consumers preferred to pay off old debts rather than incur new ones (see the News below). Expectations, not interest rates, dominated spending decisions.

IN THE NEWS

Consumer Borrowing Dips More Than Expected in February

WASHINGTON (AP)—Consumer borrowing plunged more than expected in February as Americans cut back their use of credit cards by a record amount.

The Federal Reserve said Tuesday that consumer borrowing dropped at an annual rate of $7.48 billion in February, or 3.5 percent, from January. . . .

"Consumers don't want to borrow as much; they want to build up their savings," said Zach Pandl, an economist at Nomura Securities International. "People are adjusting to new spending habits." . . .

Consumer spending accounts for about 70 percent of U.S. economic activity. It fell by 4.3 percent in the final quarter of 2008, the largest drop in more than 28 years. That decline contributed to the economy's steep 6.3 percent contraction during that period.

—Christopher S. Rugaber

ANALYSIS: Interest rate cuts are supposed to stimulate investment and consumption. But gloomy expectations may deter people from borrowing and spending.

The vertical portion of the investment demand curve in Figure 15.4*b* illustrates the possibility that investment spending may not respond to changes in the rate of interest. Notice that a reduction in the rate of interest from 7 percent to 6 percent doesn't increase investment spending. In this case, businesses are simply unwilling to invest any more funds. As a consequence, aggregate spending doesn't rise. The Fed's policy objective remains unfulfilled, even though the Fed has successfully lowered the rate of interest. Recall that the investment demand curve may also *shift* if expectations change. If expectations worsened, the investment demand curve would shift to the left and might result in even *less* investment at 6 percent interest (see Figure 15.4*b*).

Time Lags. Even when expectations are good, businesses won't respond *instantly* to changes in interest rates. Lower interest rates make investments more profitable. But it still takes time to develop and implement new investments. Hence *there is always a time lag between interest rate changes and investment responses.*

The same is true for consumers. Consumers don't rush out the door to refinance their homes or buy new ones the day the Fed reduces interest rates. They might start *thinking* about new financing, but they aren't likely to *do* anything for a while. It may take 6–12 months before market behavior responds to monetary policy. It took at least that long before investors and consumers responded to the monetary stimulus of 2001–2002 and 2008–2014.

Limits on Monetary Restraint

Expectations. Time lags and expectations could also limit the effectiveness of monetary restraint. In pursuit of "tight" money, the Fed could drain bank reserves and force interest rates higher. Yet market participants might continue to borrow and spend if high expectations for rising sales and profits overwhelm high interest rates in investment decisions. Consumers too might believe that future incomes will be sufficient to cover larger debts and higher interest charges. Both groups might foresee accelerating inflation that would make even high interest rates look cheap in the future. This was apparently the case in Britain in 2004, as the World View below documents.

WORLD VIEW

Rising Rates Haven't Thwarted Consumers

The Bank of England continued its tightening of monetary policy on June 10. And with the British economy still expanding at a decent clip, more hikes are on the way.

As expected by most economists, the BOE raised its lending rate by a quarter point, to 4.5 percent. It was the fourth bump up since November 2003. In explaining the move, the BOE's statement pointed to above-trend output growth, strong household, business, and public spending, as well as a labor market that "has tightened further." . . .

The BOE is the first of the world's major central banks to raise rates, but the moves have done little to curb borrowing, especially by consumers. Home buying remains robust. . . .

The easy access to credit and the strong labor markets are boosting consumer spending.

—James C. Cooper and Kathleen Madigan

Source: *BusinessWeek*, June 28, 2004, p. 14. Used with permission of Bloomberg L.P. Copyright © 2015. All rights reserved.

ANALYSIS: Strong expectations and rising incomes may fuel continued spending even when interest rates are rising.

web click

For a global view of how interest rates and inflation move together, visit the central bank of Australia at **www.rba.gov.au**.

Global Money. Market participants might also tap global sources of money. If money gets too tight in domestic markets, business may borrow funds from foreign banks or institutions. GM, Disney, ExxonMobil, and other multinational corporations can borrow funds from foreign subsidiaries, banks, and even bond markets. As we saw in Chapter 14, market participants can also secure funds from nonbank sources in the United States. These nonbank and global lenders make it harder for the Fed to restrain aggregate demand.

How Effective? In view of all these constraints on monetary policies, some observers have concluded that monetary policy is an undependable policy lever. Keynes, for example, emphasized that monetary policy wouldn't be very effective in ending a deep recession. He believed that the combination of reluctant bankers, the liquidity trap, and low expectations would render monetary stimulus ineffective. Using monetary policy to stimulate the economy in such circumstances would be akin to "pushing on a string." Alan Greenspan came to much the same conclusion in September 1992 when he said that further Fed stimulus would be ineffective in accelerating a recovery from the 1990–1991 recession. He believed, however, that earlier cuts in interest rates would help stimulate spending once banks, investors, and consumers gained confidence in the economic outlook. The same kind of problem existed in 2001: the Fed's actions to reduce interest rates (11 times in as many months!) weren't enough to propel the economy forward in 2001–2002. Market participants had to recover their confidence in the future before they would start spending "cheap" money. The same lack of confidence limited the effectiveness of monetary stimulus in 2008–2014.

The limitations on monetary restraint aren't considered as serious. The Fed has the power to reduce the money supply. If the money supply shrinks far enough, the rate of spending will have to slow down.

THE MONETARIST PERSPECTIVE

The Keynesian view of money emphasizes the role of interest rates in fulfilling the goals of monetary policy. *In the Keynesian model, changes in the money supply affect macro outcomes primarily through changes in interest rates.* The three-step sequence of (1) money supply change, (2) interest rate movement, and (3) aggregate demand shift makes monetary policy subject to several potential uncertainties. As we've seen, the economy doesn't always respond as expected to Fed policy.

An alternative view of monetary policy seizes on those occasional failures to offer a different explanation of how the money supply affects macro outcomes. The so-called *monetarist* school dismisses changes in short-term interest rates (e.g., the federal funds rate) as unpredictable and ineffective. They don't think real output levels are affected by monetary stimulus. As they see it, only the price level is affected by Fed policy, and then only by changes in the money supply. *Monetarists assert that monetary policy isn't an effective tool for fighting short-run business cycles, but it is a powerful tool for managing inflation.*

The Equation of Exchange

Monetarists emphasize that the potential of monetary policy can be expressed in a simple equation called the **equation of exchange,** written as

$$MV = PQ$$

where M refers to the quantity of money in circulation and V to its **velocity** of circulation. Total spending in the economy is equal to the average price (P) of goods times the quantity (Q) of goods sold in a period. This spending is financed by the supply of money (M) times the velocity of its circulation (V).

Suppose, for example, that only two participants are in the market and that the money supply consists of one crisp $20 bill. What's the limit to total spending in this case? If you answer "$20," you haven't yet grasped the nature of the circular flow.

Suppose I begin the circular flow by spending $20 on eggs, bacon, and a gallon of milk. The money I spend ends up in Farmer Brown's pocket because he is the only other market participant. Once in possession of the money, Farmer Brown may decide to satisfy his

equation of exchange: Money supply (M) times velocity of circulation (V) equals level of aggregate spending ($P \times Q$).

velocity of money (V): The number of times per year, on average, a dollar is used to purchase final goods and services; $PQ \div M$.

long-smoldering desire to learn something about economics and buy one of my books. If he acts on that decision, the $20 will return to me. At that point, both Farmer Brown and I have sold $20 worth of goods. Hence $40 of total spending has been financed with one $20 bill.

As long as we keep using this $20 bill to buy goods and services from each other, we can continue to do business. Moreover, the faster we pass the money from hand to hand during any period of time, the greater the value of sales each of us can register. If the money is passed from hand to hand eight times, then I'll be able to sell $80 worth of textbooks and Farmer Brown will be able to sell $80 worth of produce during that period, for a total nominal output of $160. *The quantity of money in circulation and the velocity with which it travels (changes hands) in product markets will always be equal to the value of total spending and income (nominal GDP).* This relationship is summarized as

$$M \times V = P \times Q$$

In this case, the *equation of exchange* confirms that

$$\$20 \times 8 = \$160$$

The value of total sales for the year is $160.

Monetarists use the equation of exchange to simplify the explanation of how monetary policy works. There's no need, they argue, to follow the effects of changes in M through the money markets to interest rates and further to changes in total spending. The basic consequences of monetary policy are evident in the equation of exchange. The two sides of the equation of exchange must always be in balance. Hence we can be absolutely certain that *if M increases, prices (P) or output (Q) must rise, or V must fall.*

The equation of exchange is an incontestable statement of how the money supply is related to macro outcomes. The equation itself, however, says nothing about *which* variables will respond to a change in the money supply. The *goal* of monetary policy is to change the macro outcomes on the right side of the equation. It's *possible,* however, that a change in M might be offset with a reverse change in V, leaving P and Q unaffected. Or it could happen that the *wrong* macro outcome is affected. Prices (P) might rise, for example, when we're trying to increase real output (Q).

Stable Velocity

Monetarists add some important assumptions to transform the equation of exchange from a simple identity to a behavioral *model* of macro performance. The first assumption is that the velocity of money (V) is stable. How fast people use their money balances depends on the institutional structure of money markets and people's habits. Neither the structure of money markets nor people's habits are likely to change in the short run. Accordingly, a short-run increase in M won't be offset by a reduction in V. Instead the impact of an increased money supply will be transmitted to the right side of the equation of exchange, which means that *total spending must rise if the money supply (M) grows and V is stable.*

Money Supply Focus

From a monetarist perspective, there's no need to trace the impacts of monetary policy through interest rate movements. The focus on interest rates is a uniquely Keynesian perspective. Monetarists claim that interest rate movements are secondary to the major thrust of monetary policy. *As monetarists see it, changes in the money supply must alter total spending, regardless of how interest rates move.*

A monetarist perspective leads to a whole different strategy for the Fed. Because interest rates aren't part of the monetarist explanation of how monetary policy works, the Fed shouldn't try to manipulate interest rates; instead it should focus on the money supply itself. Monetarists also argue that the Fed can't really control interest rates well because they depend on both the supply of and the demand for money. What the Fed *can* control is the supply of money, and the equation of exchange clearly shows that money matters.

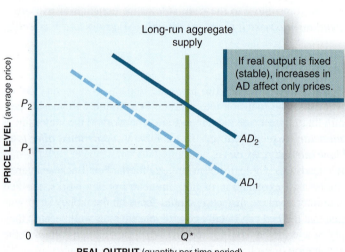

Analysis: If the money supply shrinks (or its growth rate slows), price levels will rise less quickly.

"Natural" Rate of Unemployment

Some monetarists add yet another perspective to the equation of exchange. They assert that not only V but Q as well is stable. If this is true, then changes in the money supply (M) would affect only prices (P).

What does it mean for Q to be stable? The argument here is that the quantity of goods produced is primarily dependent on production capacity, labor market efficiency, and other "structural" forces. These structural forces establish a **"natural" rate of unemployment** that's fairly immune to short-run policy intervention. This is the *long-run* aggregate supply curve we first encountered in Chapter 8. From this perspective, there's no reason for producers to depart from this "natural" rate of output when the money supply increases. Producers are smart enough to know that both prices and costs will rise when spending increases. Hence rising prices won't create any new profit incentives for increasing output. Firms will just continue producing at the "natural" rate with higher (nominal) prices and costs. As a result, increases in aggregate spending—whether financed by more M or faster V—aren't likely to alter real output levels. Q will stay constant.

If the quantity of real output is in fact stable, then P is the only thing that can change. Thus *the most extreme monetarist perspective concludes that changes in the money supply affect prices only.* As the "simple economics" in the above cartoon suggests, a decrease in M should directly reduce the price level. When M increases, total spending rises, but the higher nominal value of spending is completely absorbed by higher prices. In this view, monetary policy affects only the rate of inflation. This is the kind of money-driven inflation that bedeviled George Washington's army (see the News on the next page).

Figure 15.5 illustrates the extreme monetarist argument in the context of aggregate supply and demand. The assertion that real output is fixed at the natural rate of unemployment

natural rate of unemployment: Long-term rate of unemployment determined by structural forces in labor and product markets.

FIGURE 15.5

The Monetarist View

Monetarists argue that the rate of real output is set by structural factors. Furthermore, firms aren't likely to be fooled into producing more just because prices are rising because costs are likely to rise just as much. Hence long-run aggregate supply remains at the "natural" level Q^*. Any monetary-induced increases in aggregate demand, therefore, raise the price level (inflation) but not output.

"Not Worth a Continental": The U.S. Experience with Hyperinflation

The government of the United States had no means to pay for the Revolutionary War. Specifically, the federal government had no power to levy taxes that might transfer resources from the private sector to the public sector. Instead, it could only request the states to levy taxes of their own and contribute them to the war effort. The states were not very responsive, however: state contributions accounted for only 6 percent of federal revenues during the war years.

To pay for needed weapons and soldiers, the federal government had only two other options: either (1) borrow money or (2) create new money. When loans proved to be inadequate, the Continental Congress started issuing new paper money—the "Continental" dollar—in 1775. By the end of 1779, Congress had authorized issuance of more than $250 million in Continental dollars.

At first the paper money enabled George Washington's troops to acquire needed supplies, ammunition, and volunteers. But soon the flood of paper money inundated product markets. Wholesale prices of key commodities skyrocketed. Commodity prices *doubled* in 1776, in 1777, and again in 1778. Then prices increased *tenfold* in the next two years.

Many farmers and storekeepers refused to sell goods to the army in exchange for Continental dollars. Rapid inflation had taught them that the paper money George Washington's troops offered was nearly worthless. The expression "not worth a Continental" became a popular reference to things of little value.

The states tried price controls and even empowered themselves to seize needed war supplies. But nothing could stop the inflation fueled by the explosive increase in the money supply. Fortunately, the war ended before the economy collapsed. After the war, the U.S. Congress established a new form of money, and in 1787 it empowered the federal government to levy taxes and mint gold and silver coins.

—Sidney Ratner, James H. Soltow, and Richard Sylla

Source: *The Evolution of the American Economy,* 2nd ed. (1993). © 1979 Sidney Ratner Estate. Reprinted by permission of the authors.

ANALYSIS: Rapid expansion of the money supply will push the price level up. As inflation accelerates, money becomes less valuable.

web click

For essays on bouts of hyperinflation in various countries in the world, search "hyperinflation" at **www.pbs.org**.

is reflected in the vertical, long-run aggregate supply curve. With real output stuck at Q^*, any increase in aggregate demand directly raises the price level.

Monetarist Policies

At first glance, the monetarist argument looks pretty slick. Keynesians worry about how the money supply affects interest rates, how interest rates affect spending, and how spending affects output. By contrast, monetarists point to a simple equation ($MV = PQ$) that produces straightforward responses to monetary policy.

There are fundamental differences between the two schools here, not only about how the economy works but also about how successful macro policy might be. To appreciate those differences, consider monetarist responses to inflationary and recessionary gaps.

Fighting Inflation. Consider again the options for fighting inflation. The policy goal is to reduce aggregate demand. From a Keynesian perspective, the way to achieve this reduction is to shrink the money supply and drive up interest rates. But monetarists argue that nominal interest rates are already likely to be high. Furthermore, if an effective anti-inflation policy is adopted, interest rates will come *down,* not go up. Yes, interest rates will come *down,* not go up, when the money supply is tightened, according to monetarists.

Real vs. Nominal Interest. To understand this monetarist conclusion, we have to distinguish between *nominal* interest rates and *real* ones. Nominal interest rates are the ones we actually see and pay. When a bank pays 5½ percent interest on your bank account, it's quoting (and paying) a nominal rate.

Real interest rates are never actually seen and rarely quoted. These are "inflation-adjusted" rates. Specifically, the **real interest rate** equals the nominal rate *minus* the anticipated rate of inflation; that is,

real interest rate: The nominal rate of interest minus the anticipated inflation rate.

$$\begin{array}{c} \text{Real} \\ \text{interest} \\ \text{rate} \end{array} = \begin{array}{c} \text{Nominal} \\ \text{interest} \\ \text{rate} \end{array} - \begin{array}{c} \text{Anticipated} \\ \text{inflation} \\ \text{rate} \end{array}$$

Recall what inflation does to the purchasing power of the dollar: As inflation continues, each dollar purchases fewer goods and services. As a consequence, dollars borrowed today are of less real value when they're paid back later. The real rate of interest reflects this inflation adjustment.

Suppose you lend someone $100 at the beginning of the year, at 8 percent interest. You expect to get more back at the end of the year than you start with. That "more" you expect refers to *real* goods and services, not just dollar bills. Specifically, you anticipate that when the loan is repaid with interest at the end of the year, you'll be able to buy more goods and services than you could at the beginning. This expectation of a *real* gain is at least part of the reason for making a loan.

Your expected gain won't materialize, however, if all prices rise by 8 percent during the year. If the inflation rate is 8 percent, you'll discover that $108 buys you no more at the end of the year than $100 would have bought you at the beginning. Hence you'd have given up the use of your money for an entire year without any real compensation. In such circumstances, the *real* rate of interest turns out to be zero; that is,

$$\begin{array}{c} \text{Real} \\ \text{interest} \\ \text{rate} \end{array} = \begin{array}{c} 8\% \text{ nominal} \\ \text{interest} \\ \text{rate} \end{array} - \begin{array}{c} 8\% \text{ inflation} \\ \text{rate} \end{array}$$
$$= 0$$

The nominal rate of interest, then, really has two components: (1) the real rate of interest and (2) an inflation adjustment. This is evident when we rearrange the previous formula as follows:

$$\begin{array}{c} \text{Nominal} \\ \text{interest rate} \end{array} = \begin{array}{c} \text{Real} \\ \text{interest rate} \end{array} + \begin{array}{c} \text{Anticipated rate} \\ \text{of inflation} \end{array}$$

If the real rate of interest was 4 percent and an inflation rate of 9 percent was expected, the nominal rate of interest would be 13 percent. If inflationary expectations *declined*, the *nominal* interest rate would *fall*. If the real interest rate is 4 percent and anticipated inflation falls from 9 to 6 percent, the nominal interest rate would decline from 13 to 10 percent.

A central assumption of the monetarist perspective is that the real rate of interest is fairly stable. This is a critical point. ***If the real rate of interest is stable, then changes in the nominal interest rate reflect only changes in anticipated inflation.*** From this perspective, high nominal rates of interest are a symptom of inflation, not a cure. Indeed, high nominal rates may even look cheap if inflationary expectations are worsening faster than interest rates are rising. This was the case in Zimbabwe in 2008, when the nominal interest rate rose above 400 percent (see the World View on page 136).

Consider the implications of all this for monetary policy. Suppose we want to close an inflationary GDP gap. Monetarists and Keynesians agree that a reduced money supply (*M*) will deflate total spending. But Keynesians rely on a "quick fix" of *higher* interest rates to slow consumption and investment spending. Monetarists, by contrast, assert that nominal interest rates will *fall* if the Fed tightens the money supply. Once market participants are convinced that the Fed is going to reduce money supply growth, inflationary expectations diminish. When inflationary expectations diminish, nominal interest rates will begin to fall.

Short- vs. Long-Term Rates (Again). The monetarist argument helps resolve the "conundrum" that puzzled former Fed Chairman Alan Greenspan and bedeviled his successor, Ben Bernanke—that is, the contradictory movements of short-term and long-term interest rates. As we observed earlier, short-run rates (like the federal funds rate) are very responsive to Fed intervention. But long-term rates are much slower to respond. This suggests that banks and borrowers look beyond current economic conditions in making long-term financial commitments.

If the Fed is reducing money supply growth, short-term rates may rise quickly. But long-term rates won't increase unless market participants expect inflation to worsen. Given the pivotal role of long-term rates in investment decisions, the Fed may have to stall GDP growth—even spark a recession—to restrain aggregate demand enough to stop prices from rising. Rather than take such risks, ***monetarists advocate steady and predictable changes in the money supply.*** Such a policy, they believe, would reduce uncertainties and thus stabilize both long-term interest rates and GDP growth.

Fighting Unemployment. The link between anticipated inflation and nominal interest rates also constrains monetary stimulus. The Keynesian cure for a recession is to expand M and lower interest rates. But monetarists fear that an increase in M will lead—via the equation of exchange—to higher P. If everyone believed this would happen, then an unexpectedly large increase in M would immediately raise people's inflationary expectations. Even if short-term interest rates fell, long-term interest rates might actually rise. This would defeat the purpose of monetary stimulus.

From a monetarist perspective, expansionary monetary policies aren't likely to lead us out of a recession. On the contrary, such policies might heap inflation problems on top of our unemployment woes. All monetary policy should do, say the monetarists, is ensure a stable and predictable rate of growth in the money supply. Then people could concentrate on real production decisions without worrying so much about fluctuating prices.

THE CONCERN FOR CONTENT

Monetary policy, like fiscal policy, can affect more than just the *level* of total spending. We must give some consideration to the impact of Federal Reserve actions on the *content* of the GDP if we're going to be responsive to the "second crisis" of economic theory.[1]

The Mix of Output

Both Keynesians and monetarists agree that monetary policy will affect nominal interest rates. When interest rates change, not all spending decisions will be affected equally. High interest rates don't deter consumers from buying pizzas, but they do deter purchases of homes, cars, and other big-ticket items typically financed with loans. Hence the housing and auto industries bear a disproportionate burden of restrictive monetary policy. Accordingly, when the Fed pursues a policy of tight money—high interest rates and limited lending capacity—it not only restrains total spending but reduces the share of housing and autos in that spending. Utility industries, public works projects, and state and local finances are also disproportionately impacted by monetary policy.

In addition to altering the content of output, monetary policy affects the competitive structure of the market. When money is tight, banks must ration available credit among loan applicants. Large and powerful corporations aren't likely to run out of credit because banks will be hesitant to incur their displeasure and lose their business. Thus General Motors and Google stand a much better chance of obtaining tight money than does the corner grocery store. Moreover, if bank lending capacity becomes too small, GM and Google can always resort to the bond market and borrow money directly from the public. Small businesses seldom have such an alternative.

[1]See the quotation from Joan Robinson in Chapter 11, calling attention to the exclusive focus of economists on the *level* of economic activity (the "first crisis"), to the neglect of content (the "second crisis").

Income Redistribution

Monetary policy also affects the distribution of income. When interest rates fall, borrowers pay smaller interest charges. On the other hand, lenders get smaller interest payments. Hence a lower interest rate redistributes income from lenders to borrowers. When interest rates declined sharply in 2008–2009, home owners refinanced their mortgages and saved billions of dollars in interest payments. The decline in interest rates, however, *reduced* the income of retired persons, who depend heavily on interest payments from certificates of deposit, bonds, and other assets. Money supply increases also push up stock and bond prices, disproportionately benefiting higher-income households.

THE ECONOMY TOMORROW

WHICH LEVER TO PULL?

Our success in managing the macro economy of tomorrow depends on pulling the right policy levers at the right time. But which levers should be pulled? Keynesians and monetarists offer very different prescriptions for treating an ailing economy. Can we distill some usable policy guidelines from this discussion for policy decisions in the economy tomorrow?

The Policy Tools. The equation of exchange is a convenient summary of the differences between the Keynesian and monetarist perspectives. There's no disagreement about the equation itself: aggregate spending ($M \times V$) *must* equal the value of total sales ($P \times Q$). *What Keynesians and monetarists argue about is which of the policy tools—M or V—is likely to be effective in altering aggregate spending.*

- *Monetarists* point to changes in the money supply (M) as the principal lever of macroeconomic policy. They assume V is reasonably stable.
- *Keynesian* fiscal policy *must* rely on changes in the velocity of money (V) because tax and expenditure policies have no direct impact on the money supply.

Crowding Out. The extreme monetarist position that *only* money matters is based on the assumption that the velocity of money (V) is constant. *If V is constant, changes in total spending can come about only through changes in the money supply.* There are no other policy tools on the left side of the equation of exchange.

Think about an increase in government spending designed to stimulate the economy. How does the government pay for this fiscal policy stimulus? Monetarists argue that there are only two ways to pay for this increased expenditure (G): the government must either raise additional taxes or borrow more money. If the government raises taxes, the disposable income of consumers will be reduced, and private spending will fall. On the other hand, if the government *borrows* more money to pay for its expenditures, there will be less money available for loans to private consumers and investors. In either case, more government spending (G) implies less private spending (C or I). Thus *increased G* effectively **"crowds out"** some C or I, leaving total spending unchanged. From this viewpoint, fiscal policy is ineffective; it can't even shift the aggregate demand curve. At best, fiscal policy can change the composition of demand and thus the mix of output. Only changes in M (monetary policy) can shift the aggregate demand curve.

Milton Friedman, formerly of the University of Chicago, championed the monetarist view with this argument:

> I believe that the state of the government budget matters; matters a great deal—for some things. The state of the government budget determines what fraction of the nation's income is spent through the government and what fraction is spent by individuals privately. The state of the government budget determines what the level of our taxes is, how much of our income we turn over to the government. The state of the government budget has a considerable effect on interest rates. If the federal government runs a large deficit, that means the government has to borrow in the market, which raises the demand for loanable funds and so tends to raise interest rates.

crowding out: A reduction in private sector borrowing (and spending) caused by increased government borrowing.

If the government budget shifts to a surplus, that adds to the supply of loanable funds, which tends to lower interest rates. It was no surprise to those of us who stress money that enactment of the surtax was followed by a decline in interest rates. That's precisely what we had predicted and what our analysis leads us to predict. But—and I come to the main point—in my opinion, the state of the budget by itself has no significant effect on the course of nominal income, on inflation, on deflation, or on cyclical fluctuations.[2]

Keynesians reply that the alleged constant velocity of money is a monetarist's pipe dream. Some even argue that the velocity of money is so volatile that changes in V can completely offset changes in M, leaving us with the proposition that money doesn't matter.

The liquidity trap illustrates the potential for V to change. Keynes argued that people tend to accumulate money balances—slow their rate of spending—during recessions. *A slowdown in spending implies a reduction in the velocity of money.* Indeed, in the extreme case of the liquidity trap, the velocity of money falls toward zero. Under these circumstances, changes in M (monetary policy) won't influence total spending. The velocity of money falls as rapidly as M increases. On the other hand, increased government spending (fiscal policy) can stimulate aggregate spending by putting idle money balances to work (thereby increasing V). Changes in fiscal policy will also influence consumer and investor expectations, and thereby further alter the rate of aggregate spending.

How Fiscal Policy Works: Two Views. Tables 15.3 and 15.4 summarize these different perspectives on fiscal and monetary policy. The first table evaluates fiscal policy from both Keynesian and monetarist viewpoints. The central issue is whether and how a change in government spending (G) or taxes (T) will alter macroeconomic outcomes. Keynesians

Do Changes in G or T Affect	Monetarist View	Keynesian View
1. Aggregate demand?	No (stable V causes crowding out)	Yes (V changes)
2. Prices?	No (aggregate demand not affected)	Maybe (if at capacity)
3. Real output?	No (aggregate demand not affected)	Yes (output responds to demand)
4. Nominal interest rates?	Yes (crowding out)	Maybe (may alter demand for money)
5. Real interest rates?	No (determined by real growth)	Yes (real growth and expectations may vary)

TABLE 15.3

How Fiscal Policy Matters: Monetarist vs. Keynesian Views

Monetarists and Keynesians have very different views on the impact of fiscal policy. Monetarists assert that changes in government spending (G) and taxes (T) don't alter the velocity of money (V). As a result, fiscal policy alone can't alter total spending. Keynesians reject this view, arguing that V is changeable. They claim that tax cuts and increased government spending increase the velocity of money and so alter total spending.

[2]Milton Friedman and Walter W. Heller, *Monetary vs. Fiscal Policy* (New York: W.W. Norton, 1969), pp. 50–51. Used with permission.

Do Changes in *M* Affect	Monetarist View	Keynesian View
1. Aggregate demand?	Yes (*V* stable)	Maybe (*V* may change)
2. Prices?	Yes (*V* and *Q* stable)	Maybe (*V* and *Q* may change)
3. Real output?	No (rate of unemployment determined by structural forces)	Maybe (output responds to demand)
4. Nominal interest rates?	Yes (but direction unknown)	Maybe (liquidity trap)
5. Real interest rates?	No (depends on real growth)	Maybe (real growth may vary)

TABLE 15.4

How Money Matters: Monetarist vs. Keynesian Views

Because monetarists believe that *V* is stable, they assert that changes in the money supply (*M*) must alter total spending. But all the monetary impact is reflected in prices and nominal interest rates; *real* output and interest rates are unaffected.

Keynesians think that *V* is variable and thus that changes in *M* might *not* alter total spending. If monetary policy does alter aggregate spending, however, Keynesians expect all outcomes to be affected.

assert that aggregate demand will be affected as the velocity of money (*V*) changes. Monetarists say no because they anticipate an unchanged *V*.

If aggregate demand isn't affected by a change in *G* or *T*, then fiscal policy won't affect prices (*P*) or real output (*Q*). Thus monetarists conclude that fiscal policy isn't a viable tool for combating either inflation or unemployment. By contrast, Keynesians believe *V will* change and that output and prices will respond accordingly.

Insofar as interest rates are concerned, monetarists recognize that nominal interest rates will be affected (read Friedman's quote again), but *real* rates won't be. Real interest rates depend on real output and growth, both of which are seen as immune to fiscal policy. Keynesians see less impact on nominal interest rates and more on real interest rates.

What all this boils down to is this: fiscal policy, by itself, will be effective only if it can alter the velocity of money. *How well fiscal policy works depends on how much the velocity of money can be changed by government tax and spending decisions.*

How Monetary Policy Works: Two Views. Table 15.4 offers a similar summary of monetary policy. This time the positions of monetarists and Keynesians are reversed, or nearly so. Monetarists say a change in *M* must alter total spending (*P* × *Q*) because *V* is stable. Keynesians assert that *V* may vary, so they aren't convinced that monetary policy will always work. The heart of the controversy is again the velocity of money. Monetary policy works as long as *V* is stable, or at least predictable. *How well monetary policy works depends on how stable or predictable* **V** *is.*

Once the central role of velocity is understood, everything else falls into place. Monetarists assert that prices but not output will be directly affected by a change in *M* because the right side of the equation of exchange contains only two variables (*P* and *Q*), and one of them (*Q*) is assumed to be unaffected by monetary policy. Keynesians, by contrast, aren't so sure that prices will be affected by *M* or that real output won't be. It all depends on *V* and the responsiveness of *P* and *Q* to changes in aggregate spending.

Finally, monetarists predict that nominal interest rates will respond to changes in *M,* although they're not sure in what direction. It depends on how inflationary expectations adapt to changes in the money supply. Keynesian economists aren't so sure nominal interest rates will change but are sure about the direction if they do.

Is Velocity Stable? Tables 15.3 and 15.4 highlight the velocity of money as a critical determinant of policy impact. The critical question appears to be whether *V* is stable. Why hasn't someone answered this simple question and resolved the debate over fiscal versus monetary policy?

Long-Run Stability. The velocity of money (*V*) turns out, in fact, to be quite stable over long periods of time. Over the past 30 years the velocity of money (M2) has averaged about 1.64, as Figure 15.6 illustrates. Moreover, the range of velocity has been fairly narrow, extending from a low of 1.56 in 1987 to a high of 2.05 in 1997. Monetarists conclude that the historical pattern justifies the assumption of a stable *V.*

Short-Run Instability. Keynesians reply that monetarists are farsighted and so fail to see significant short-run variations in *V.* The difference between a velocity of 1.56 and velocity of 2.05 translates into hundreds of billions of dollars in aggregate demand. Moreover, there's a pattern to short-run variations in *V:* velocity tends to decline in recessions (see Figure 15.6). These are precisely the situations in which fiscal stimulus (increasing *V*) would be appropriate.

Money Supply Targets. The differing views of monetarists and Keynesians clearly lead to different conclusions about which policy lever to pull.

Monetarist Advice. The monetarists' policy advice to the Fed is straightforward. ***Monetarists favor fixed money supply targets.*** They believe that *V* is stable in the long run and

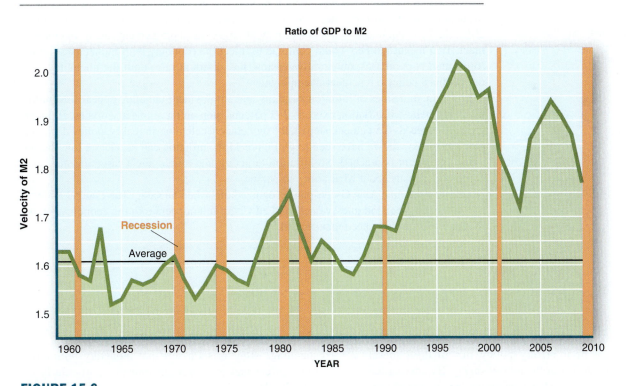

FIGURE 15.6

The Velocity of M2

The velocity of money (the ratio of GDP to M2) averages about 1.64. However, *V* appears to decline in recessions. Keynes urged the use of fiscal stimulus to boost *V.* Monetarists caution that short-run changes in *V* are too unpredictable.

Source: Federal Reserve.

unpredictable in the short run. Hence the safest course of action is to focus on *M*. All the Fed has to do is announce its intention to increase the money supply by some fixed amount (such as 3 percent per year), then use its central banking powers to hit that money growth target.

Interest Rate Targets. Keynesian Advice. *Keynesians reject fixed money supply targets,* favoring more flexibility in control of the money supply. In their view, a fixed money supply target would render monetary policy useless in combating cyclical swings of the economy. Keynesians prefer the risks of occasional policy errors to the straitjacket of a fixed money supply target. *Keynesians advocate targeting interest rates, not the money supply.* Keynesians also advocate liberal use of the fiscal policy lever.

Inflation Targeting. In the past, the Fed has tried both monetarist and Keynesian strategies for managing aggregate demand, depending on the needs of the economy and the convictions of the Fed chairman. The current chair, Janet Yellen, isn't committed to either the monetarist or Keynesian perspective. Instead she tries to walk a thin line between these perspectives. Like her predecessors, Yellen believes that price stability is the Fed's primary goal. The Fed's goal is to keep the inflation rate below the 2–3 percent range. If prices stay below that target, the Fed has typically put monetary policy on autopilot without worrying about constant adjustments of its policy tools.

What market participants like about this **inflation targeting** strategy is that it appears to offer greater predictability about whether and how the Fed will act. Critics point out, though, that *future* inflation, not *past* inflation, is the central policy concern. Because today's price movements may or may not be precursors of future inflation, the decision to pull monetary levers is still a judgment call.

Employment Targeting Further complicating the Fed's task of fighting inflation is a second goal: full employment. It's not enough to keep prices from rising; we also want to create jobs and grow the economy. In the Great Recession of 2008–2009 inflation was a remote worry, but high unemployment was a huge problem. In response, the Fed decided to adopt **employment targeting** as a second component of its policy strategy. In December 2012, the Fed announced that its employment target was a 6.5 percent rate of unemployment. That meant the Fed would continue to inject the economy with monetary stimulus (open market purchases, quantitative easing, low discount rate) until the unemployment rate dropped below 6.5 percent unemployment.

The twin guidelines of inflation targeting and employment targeting appear to simplify monetary policy. If inflation exceeds 2–3 percent, step on the monetary brakes. If unemployment exceeds 6.5 percent, step on the monetary accelerator. In reality, policy decisions aren't that easy. As we have seen (e.g., Figure 11.4), inflation can accelerate long before full employment is reached. So inflation targeting and employment targeting may give conflicting signals about what policy to pursue.

Former Chairman Alan Greenspan recognized this when he said, "The Federal Reserve specializes in precision guesswork." As Fed Chair Yellen peers into the economy tomorrow, she will certainly need that same skill.

---

inflation targeting: The use of an inflation ceiling ("target") to signal the need for monetary policy adjustments.

Employment targeting: The use of an unemployment-rate threshold (6.5 percent) to signal the need for monetary stimulus.

SUMMARY

- The essence of monetary policy lies in the Federal Reserve's control over the money supply. By altering the money supply, the Fed can determine the amount of purchasing power available.   **LO15-2**
- There are sharp disagreements about how monetary policy works. Keynesians argue that monetary policy works indirectly through its effects on interest rates and

spending. Monetarists assert that monetary policy has more direct and more certain impacts, particularly on price levels.   **LO15-4**
- In the Keynesian view, the demand for money is important. This demand reflects desires to hold money (in cash or bank balances) for transactions, precautionary, and speculative purposes. The interaction of money supply

and money demand determines the equilibrium rate of interest.   **LO15-1**

• From a Keynesian perspective, the impact of monetary policy on the economy occurs in three distinct steps: (1) changes in the money supply alter interest rates; (2) changes in interest rates alter spending plans; and (3) the change in desired spending alters (shifts) aggregate demand.   **LO15-2**

• For Keynesian monetary policy to be fully effective, interest rates must be responsive to changes in the money supply, and spending must be responsive to changes in interest rates. Neither condition is assured. In a liquidity trap, people are willing to hold unlimited amounts of money at some low rate of interest. The interest rate won't fall below this level as the money supply increases. Also, investor expectations of sales and profits may override interest rate considerations in investment decisions.   **LO15-3**

• Fed policy has the most direct impact on short-term interest rates, particularly the overnight federal funds rate. Long-term rates are less responsive to open market operations.   **LO15-3**

• The monetarist school emphasizes long-term linkages. Using the equation of exchange ($MV = PQ$) as a base, monetarists assert that the velocity of money (V) is stable, so that changes in M must influence ($P \times Q$). Monetarists

focus on the money supply; Keynesians, on interest rates.   **LO15-4**

• Some monetarists also argue that the level of real output (Q) is set by structural forces, as illustrated by the vertical, long-run aggregate supply curve. Q is therefore insensitive to changes in aggregate spending. If both V and Q are constant, changes in M directly affect P.   **LO15-4**

• Monetary policy attempts to influence total expenditure by changing M and will be fully effective only if V is constant. Fiscal policy attempts to influence total expenditure by changing V and will be fully effective only if M doesn't change in the opposite direction. The controversy over the effectiveness of fiscal versus monetary policy depends on whether the velocity of money (V) is stable or instead is subject to policy influence.   **LO15-4**

• The velocity of money is more stable over long periods of time than over short periods. Keynesians conclude that this makes fiscal policy more powerful in the short run. Monetarists conclude that the unpredictability of short-run velocity makes any short-run policy risky.   **LO15-4**

• Inflation targeting signals monetary restraint when inflation rises above a policy-set ceiling ("target"), currently 2–3 percent.   **LO15-2**

• Employment targeting signals the need for monetary stimulus when the unemployment rate is above 6.5 percent.   **LO15-2**

Key Terms

monetary policy
interest rate
money supply (M1, M2)
demand for money
portfolio decision
transactions demand for money
precautionary demand for money

speculative demand for money
equilibrium rate of interest
federal funds rate
aggregate demand
liquidity trap
equation of exchange
velocity of money (V)

natural rate of unemployment
real interest rate
crowding out
inflation targeting
employment targeting

Questions for Discussion

1. What proportions of your money balance are held for transactions, precautionary, and speculative purposes? Can you think of any other purposes for holding money?   **LO15-1**

2. How would people "adjust their portfolios" in Figure 15.1?   **LO15-1**

3. Why do high interest rates so adversely affect the demand for housing and yet have so little influence on the demand for pizzas?   **LO15-2**

4. If the Federal Reserve banks mailed everyone a brand-new $100 bill, what would happen to prices, output, and

income? Illustrate your answer by using the equation of exchange.   **LO15-2**

5. Can there be any inflation without an increase in the money supply? How?   **LO15-4**

6. When prices started doubling (see News, p. 329), why didn't the Continental Congress print even *more* money so Washington's army could continue to buy supplies? What brings an end to such "inflation financing"?   **LO15-2**

7. Could long-term interest rates rise when short-term rates are falling? What would cause such a pattern?   **LO15-3**

8. Why did the stock market "surge" when the Fed announced it intended to buy $1.2 trillion of bonds (see News, p. 321)? **LO15-2**

9. Why were banks reluctant to use their lending capacity in 2008? (See News, p. 323.) What did they do with their increased reserves? **LO15-3**

10. If mortgage rates fell to 0 percent ("free money"), why might consumers still hesitate to borrow money to buy a home? **LO15-3**

11. What should the Fed do when prices are rising at a 3.5 percent rate and unemployment is at 7 percent? **LO15-2**

 mobile app Visit your mobile app store and download the Schiller: Study Econ app *today!*

LO15-1 1. In Table 15.1, what is the implied price of holding money in a 6-month CD rather than in Treasury bonds? _____

LO15-2 2. Suppose home owners owe $6 trillion in mortgage loans.
    (*a*) If the mortgage interest rate is 5 percent, approximately how much are home owners paying in annual mortgage interest? _____
    (*b*) If the interest rate drops to 4 percent, by how much will annual interest payments decline? _____

LO15-2 3. According to Bernanke's policy guide (p. 321), what is the fiscal policy equivalent of a 0.5 percent cut in long-term interest rates? _____

LO15-2 4. Illustrate the effects on investment of
    (*a*) An interest rate cut (point *A*).
    (*b*) An interest rate cut accompanied by decreased sales expectations (point *B*).

LO15-2 5. How much would the Fed have had to reduce long-term interest rates to get the same stimulus as President Obama's $800 billion fiscal stimulus? _____

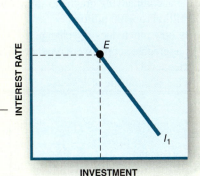

LO15-4 6. Suppose that an economy is characterized by

$$M = \$3 \text{ trillion}$$
$$V = 2.5$$
$$P = 1.0$$

    (*a*) What is the real value of output (*Q*)? _____

Now assume that the Fed increases the money supply by 10 percent and velocity remains unchanged.
    (*b*) If the price level remains constant, by how much will real output increase? _____%
    (*c*) If, instead, real output is fixed at the natural level of unemployment, by how much will prices rise? _____%
    (*d*) By how much would *V* have to fall to offset the increase in *M*? _____

LO15-1 7. If the nominal rate of interest is 6 percent and the real rate of interest is 3 percent, what rate of inflation is anticipated? _____

LO15-2 8. Suppose the Fed decided to purchase $100 billion worth of government securities in the open market. What impact would this action have on the economy? Specifically, answer the following questions:
    (*a*) How will M1 be affected initially? _____
    (*b*) By how much will the banking system's lending capacity increase if the reserve requirement is 20 percent? _____
    (*c*) Must interest rates rise or fall to induce investors to utilize this expanded lending capacity? _____
    (*d*) By how much will aggregate demand increase if investors borrow and spend all the newly available credit? _____
    (*e*) Under what circumstances (A = "recession" or B = "inflation") would the Fed be pursuing such an open market policy? _____
    (*f*) To attain those same objectives, what should the Fed do (A = "increase" or B = "decrease") with the
        (*i*) Discount rate? _____
        (*ii*) Reserve requirement? _____

LO15-2 9. According to Bernanke's rule of thumb (p. 321), how much fiscal restraint would be equivalent to a 1-point increase in long-term interest rates?   _____

LO15-3 10. The following data describe market conditions:

Money supply (in billions)	$100	$200	$300	$400	$ 500	$ 600	$ 700
Interest rate	8.0	7.5	7.0	6.5	6.0	5.5	5.5
Rate of investment (in billions)	$ 12	$ 12	$ 15	$ 16	$16.5	$16.5	$16.5

(a) At what rate of interest does the liquidity trap emerge?   _____
(b) At what rate of interest does investment demand become totally inelastic?   _____

LO15-3 11. Use the accompanying graphs to show what happens in the economy when M increases from $300 billion to $400 billion.
(a) By how much does PQ change if V is constant?   _____
(b) If aggregate supply were fixed (vertical) at the initial output level, what would happen to the price level?   _____
(c) What is the value of V?   _____

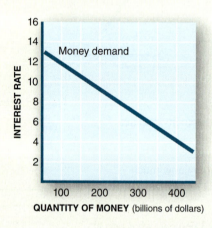
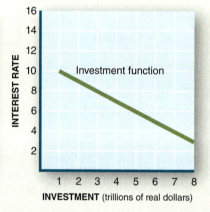
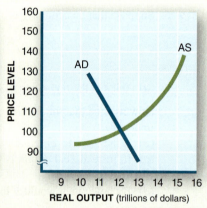

LO15-1 12. Use the data on the end covers of this text to determine for 2007 and 2012
(a) The interest rate on 10-year Treasury bonds.
(b) The U.S. inflation rate.
(c) The real rate of interest.

	2007	2012
(a)	_____	_____
(b)	_____	_____
(c)	_____	_____

Supply-Side Options

Fiscal and monetary policies attempt to alter macro outcomes by managing aggregate demand. Supply-side policies focus instead on possibilities for shifting the aggregate *supply* curve. In the short run, any increase in aggregate supply promotes more output and less inflation. Supply-siders also emphasize how rightward shifts of aggregate supply are critical to long-run economic growth. Chapter 16 focuses on short-run supply-side options; Chapter 17 takes the long-run view.

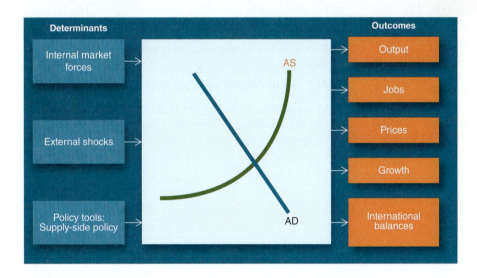

Determinants

- Internal market forces
- External shocks
- Policy tools: Supply-side policy

AS

AD

Outcomes

- Output
- Jobs
- Prices
- Growth
- International balances

16

Supply-Side Policy:
Short-Run Options

After reading this chapter, you should know

LO16-1 Why the short-run AS curve slopes upward.

LO16-2 How an unemployment–inflation trade-off arises.

LO16-3 The tools of supply-side policy.

Fiscal and monetary policies focus on the *demand* side of the macro economy. The basic premise of both approaches is that macro goals can be achieved by shifting the aggregate demand curve to a desirable macro equilibrium. The aggregate demand curve isn't the only game in town, however; there's an aggregate supply curve as well. Why not focus instead on possibilities for shifting the aggregate *supply* curve?

Any policies that alter the willingness or ability to supply goods at various price levels will shift the aggregate supply curve. This chapter identifies some of those policy options and examines how they affect macro outcomes. The focus is on two questions:

• **How does the aggregate supply curve affect macro outcomes?**

• **How can the aggregate supply curve be shifted?**

As we'll see, the aggregate supply curve plays a critical role in determining how difficult it is to achieve the goals of full employment and price stability.

AGGREGATE SUPPLY

The impetus for examining the supply side of the macro economy sprang up in the stagflation of the 1970s. **Stagflation** occurs when both unemployment *and* inflation increase at the same time. From 1973 to 1974, for example, consumer price inflation surged from 8.7 to 12.3 percent. At the same time, the unemployment rate jumped from 4.9 to 5.6 percent. How could this happen? *No shift of the aggregate demand curve can increase inflation and unemployment at the same time.* If aggregate demand increases (shifts right), the price level may rise, but unemployment should decline with increased output. If aggregate demand decreases (shifts left), inflation should subside, but unemployment should increase. In other words, demand-side theories predict that inflation and unemployment move in *opposite* directions in the short run. When this didn't happen, an alternative explanation was sought. The explanation was found on the supply side of the macro economy. Two critical clues were (1) the shape of the **aggregate supply** curve and (2) potential AS shifts.

stagflation: The simultaneous occurrence of substantial unemployment and inflation.

aggregate supply: The total quantity of output producers are willing and able to supply at alternative price levels in a given time period, *ceteris paribus.*

SHAPE OF THE AS CURVE

As we've seen, the basic short-run objective of fiscal and monetary policy is to attain full employment and price stability. The strategy is to shift the aggregate demand curve to a more favorable position. Now the question turns to the *response* of producers to an aggregate demand shift. Will they increase real output? Raise prices? Or some combination of both?

The answer is reflected in the shape of the aggregate supply curve: *The response of producers to an AD shift is expressed in the slope and position of the aggregate supply curve.* Until now we've used a generally upward-sloping AS curve to depict aggregate supply. Now we'll consider a range of different supply responses.

Three Views of AS

Figure 16.1 illustrates three very different supply behaviors.

Keynesian AS. Part (*a*) depicts what we earlier called the "naive" Keynesian view. Recall that Keynes was primarily concerned with the problem of unemployment. He didn't think there was much risk of inflation in the depths of a recession. He expected producers to increase output, not prices, when aggregate demand expanded. This expectation is illustrated by a *horizontal* AS curve. When fiscal or monetary stimulus shifts the AD curve rightward (e.g., AD_1 to AD_2 in Figure 16.1*a*), output (Q) rises but not the price level (P). Only when capacity (Q_*) is reached do prices start rising abruptly (AD_2 to AD_3).

Monetarist AS. The monetarist view of supply behavior is very different. In the most extreme monetarist view, real output remains at its "natural" rate, regardless of fiscal or monetary interventions. Rising prices don't entice producers to increase output because costs are likely to rise just as fast. They instead make output decisions based on more fundamental factors like technology and market size. The monetarist AS curve is *vertical* because output doesn't respond to changing price levels. (This is the long-run AS curve we first encountered in Chapter 8.) With a vertical AS curve, only prices can respond to a shift in aggregate demand. In Figure 16.1*b,* the AS curve is anchored at the natural rate of unemployment Q_N. When aggregate demand increases from AD_4 to AD_5, the price level (P) rises, but output (Q) is unchanged.

Hybrid AS. Figure 16.1*c* blends these Keynesian and monetarist perspectives into a hybrid AS curve. At low rates of output, the curve is nearly horizontal; at high rates of output, the AS curve becomes nearly vertical. In the broad middle of the AS curve, the curve slopes

FIGURE 16.1

Contrasting Views of Aggregate Supply

The effectiveness of fiscal and monetary policy depends on the shape of the AS curve. Some possibilities include these:

(a) Keynesian AS In the simple Keynesian model, the rate of output responds fully and automatically to increases in demand until full employment (Q^*) is reached. If demand increases from AD_1 to AD_2, equilibrium GDP will expand from Q_1 to Q^*, without any inflation. Inflation becomes a problem only if demand increases beyond capacity—to AD_3, for example.

(b) Monetarist AS Monetarists assert that changes in the money supply affect prices but not output. They regard aggregate supply as a fixed quantum, at the long-run, natural rate of unemployment (here noted as Q_N). Accordingly, a shift of demand (from AD_4 to AD_5) can affect only the price level (from P_4 to P_5).

(c) Hybrid AS The consensus view incorporates Keynesian and monetarist perspectives but emphasizes the upward slope that dominates the middle of the AS curve. When demand increases, both price levels and the rate of output increase. Hence the slope and position of the AS curve limit the effectiveness of fiscal and monetary policies.

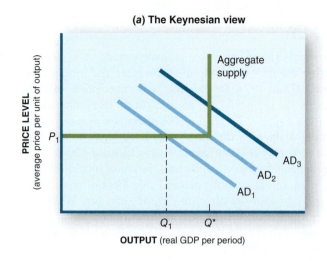

(a) The Keynesian view

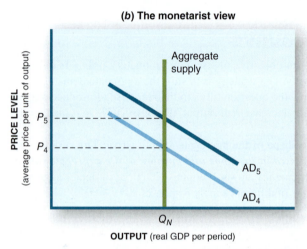

(b) The monetarist view

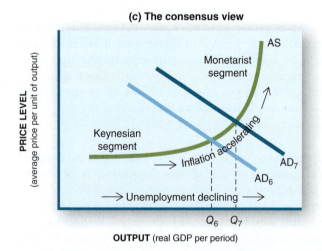

(c) The consensus view

gently upward. In this area, shifts of aggregate demand affect *both* prices and output. The message of this hybrid AS curve is that the outcomes of fiscal and monetary policy depend on how close the economy is to full employment. ***The closer we are to capacity, the greater the risk that fiscal or monetary stimulus will spill over into price inflation.***

The Inflation–Unemployment Trade-Off

Because Figure 16.1c allows for varying output and price responses at different levels of economic activity, that AS curve is regarded as the most realistic for short-run outcomes. However, the upward-sloping section of the AS curve in Figure 16.1c has some disturbing implications. Because both prices and output respond to demand-side shifts, the economy can't reduce both unemployment and inflation at the same time—at least not with fiscal and monetary policies. To see why this is the case, consider the simple geometry of policy stimulus and restraint.

Demand Stimulus. Monetary and fiscal stimulus shift the aggregate demand curve rightward. This demand-side effect is evident in all three graphs in Figure 16.1. However, *all rightward shifts of the aggregate demand curve increase both prices and output if the aggregate supply curve is upward-sloping.* This implies that fiscal and monetary efforts to reduce unemployment will also cause some inflation. How much inflation depends on the slope of the AS curve.

Demand Restraint. Monetary and fiscal restraint shift the aggregate demand curve leftward. *If the aggregate supply curve is upward-sloping, leftward shifts of the aggregate demand curve cause both prices and output to fall.* Therefore, fiscal and monetary efforts to reduce inflation will also increase unemployment. How much unemployment depends again on the slope of the AS curve.

The Phillips Curve. The message of the upward-sloping aggregate supply curve is clear: *Demand-side policies alone can never succeed completely; they'll always cause some unwanted inflation or unemployment.*

Our macro track record provides ample evidence of this dilemma. Consider, for example, our experience with unemployment and inflation during the 1960s, as shown in Figure 16.2. This figure shows a **Phillips curve,** indicating that prices (P) generally started rising before the objective of expanded output (Q) had been completely attained. At a 7 percent rate of unemployment (point H), there would be no inflation. As the unemployment rate fell, however, inflation struck: at 4 percent unemployment (point A), the inflation rate was 4 percent.

The Phillips curve was developed by a New Zealand economist, Alban W. Phillips, to summarize the relationship between unemployment and inflation in England for the years

Phillips curve: A historical (inverse) relationship between the rate of unemployment and the rate of inflation; commonly expresses a trade-off between the two.

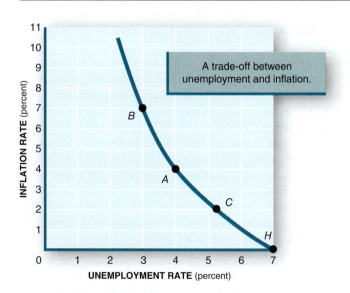

FIGURE 16.2

The Phillips Curve

The Phillips curve illustrates a trade-off between full employment and price stability. In the 1960s it appeared that efforts to reduce unemployment rates below 5.5 percent (point C) led to increasing rates of inflation (points A and B). Inflation threatened to reach unacceptable levels long before everyone was employed.

(a) Increases in aggregate demand cause . . .

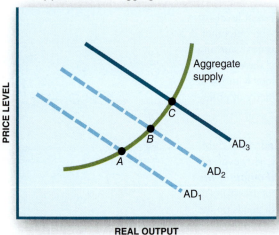

(b) A trade-off between unemployment and inflation.

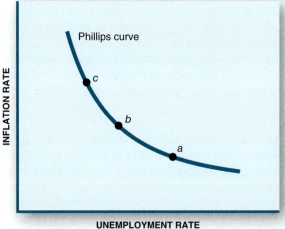

FIGURE 16.3

The Phillips Curve Trade-off

If the aggregate supply curve slopes upward, increases in aggregate demand always cause both prices and output to rise. Thus higher inflation becomes a cost of achieving lower unemployment. In (a), increased demand moves the economy from point A to point B. At B, unemployment is lower, but prices are higher. This trade-off is illustrated on the Phillips curve in (b). Each point on the Phillips curve represents a different AS/AD equilibrium from the graph on the left.

1826–1957.[1] The Phillips curve was raised from the status of an obscure graph to that of a policy issue by the discovery that the same kind of relationship apparently existed in other countries and at other times. Paul Samuelson and Robert Solow of the Massachusetts Institute of Technology were among the first to observe that the Phillips curve was a reasonable description of U.S. economic performance for the years 1900–1960. A seesaw kind of relationship existed between inflation and unemployment: when one went up, the other fell.

The trade-off between unemployment and inflation originates in the upward-sloping AS curve. Figure 16.3a illustrates this point. Suppose the economy is initially at equilibrium A, with fairly stable prices but low output. When aggregate demand expands to AD_2, prices rise along with output, so we end up with higher inflation but less unemployment. This is also shown in Figure 16.3b by the move from point a to point b on the Phillips curve. The move from point a to point b indicates a decline in unemployment (more output) but an increase in inflation (higher price level). If demand is increased further, to AD_3, a still lower unemployment rate is achieved but at the cost of higher inflation (point c).

The Inflationary Flashpoint. The Phillips curve reminds us that there is bound to be a trade-off between unemployment and inflation at some point in economic expansions and contractions. But is there a *specific* point at which the trade-off becomes particularly worrisome? With the Keynesian AS curve (Figure 16.1a) there is *no* trade-off until full employment (Q^*) is reached, then inflation rockets upwards. Hence the output level Q^* represents the **inflationary flashpoint**—the point at which inflationary pressures intensify—on the Keynesian AS curve.

The hybrid AS curve in Figure 16.1a doesn't have such a sharp flashpoint. The slope of the curve seems pretty smooth. In fact, however, inflationary pressures could bubble up as the economy expands. If that were to happen, the AS curve wouldn't be quite so smooth. Instead, at some rate of output, the slope of the AS curve would turn up sharply, as in Figure 16.4. That inflationary flashpoint represents the rate of output at which inflation begins to accelerate significantly. It is a point policymakers want to avoid.

inflationary flashpoint: The rate of output at which inflationary pressures intensify; the point on the AS curve where slope increases sharply.

[1]A. W. Phillips. "The Relationship between Unemployment and the Rate of Change of Money Wage Rates in the United Kingdom, 1826–1957," *Economica* (November 1958). Phillips's paper studied the relationship between unemployment and *wage* changes rather than *price* changes; most later formulations (and public policy) focus on prices.

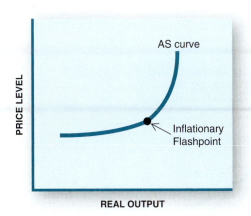

FIGURE 16.4
The Inflationary Flashpoint

As the economy approaches capacity, inflationary pressures intensify. The point at which inflation noticeably accelerates is the "inflationary flashpoint"—a juncture policymakers want to avoid.

SHIFTS OF THE AS CURVE

The unemployment–inflation trade-off implied by the upward-sloping AS curve is not etched in stone. Nor is the inflationary flashpoint unmovable. Many economists argue that the economy can attain lower levels of unemployment *without* higher inflation. This certainly appeared to be the case in the 1990s: unemployment rates fell sharply from 1992 to 2000 and again from 2002 to 2008 without any increase in inflation. How could this have happened? There's no AD shift in any part of Figure 16.3 that would reduce both unemployment *and* inflation.

Rightward AS Shifts: All Good News

Only a rightward shift of the AS curve can reduce unemployment and inflation at the same time. When aggregate supply increases from AS_1 to AS_2 in Figure 16.5, macro equilibrium moves from E_1 to E_2. At E_2 real output is higher, so the unemployment rate must be lower. At E_2 the price level is also lower, indicating reduced inflation. Hence a rightward shift of the AS curve offers the best of two worlds—something aggregate *demand* shifts (Figure 16.1) can't do.

Phillips Curve Shift. As we saw in Figure 16.3, the Phillips curve is a direct by-product of the AS curve. Accordingly, *when the AS curve shifts, the Phillips curve shifts as well.* As Figure 16.6 illustrates, the Phillips curve shifts to the left, the opposite of the AS shift in Figure 16.5. No new information is conveyed here. The Phillips curve simply focuses more directly on the implied change in the unemployment–inflation trade-off. *When the Phillips curve shifts to the left, the unemployment–inflation trade-off eases.*

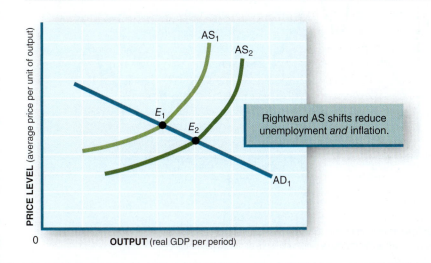

Rightward AS shifts reduce unemployment *and* inflation.

FIGURE 16.5
Shifts of Aggregate Supply

A rightward AS shift (AS_1 to AS_2) reduces both unemployment and inflation. A leftward shift has the opposite effect, creating stagflation.

FIGURE 16.6

A Phillips Curve Shift

If the Phillips curve shifts leftward, the short-run unemployment–inflation trade-off eases. With PC_1, 5 percent unemployment ignites 4 percent inflation (point *a*). With PC_2, 5 percent unemployment causes only 2 percent inflation (point *b*).

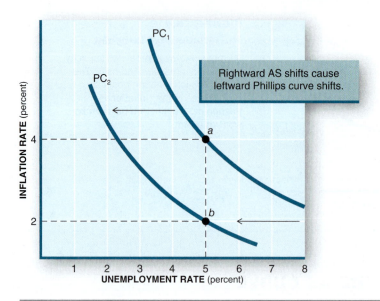

Rightward AS shifts cause leftward Phillips curve shifts.

The Misery Index. To keep track of simultaneous changes in unemployment and inflation, Arthur Okun developed the "misery index"—a simple sum of the inflation and unemployment rates. As the News feature below illustrates, macro misery diminished substantially during the first Reagan administration (1981–1984). President Clinton also benefited from

IN THE NEWS

The Misery Index

Unemployment is a problem, and so is inflation. Being burdened with both problems at the same time is real misery.

The late Arthur Okun proposed measuring the extent of misery by adding together the inflation and unemployment rates. He called the sum of the two rates the "discomfort index." Political pundits quickly renamed it the "misery index."

In essence, the misery index is a measure of stagflation—the simultaneous occurrence of inflation and unemployment. In 1980 the misery index peaked at 19.6 percent as a result of high inflation (12.5 percent) as well as high unemployment (7.1 percent). Stagflation—and the misery it causes—has since receded markedly.

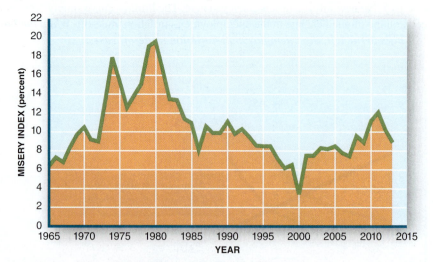

Source: *Economic Report of the President, 2014.*

ANALYSIS: Stagflation refers to the simultaneous occurrence of inflation and unemployment. The "misery index" combines both problems into a single measure of macro performance.

web click

To update the misery index, retrieve data on unemployment and inflation from the U.S. Bureau of Labor Statistics at **www.bls.gov.** Click the "Subject Areas" tab.

a leftward shift of the Phillips curve through 1998 but saw the misery index climb in 1999–2000. President George W. Bush experienced a sharp increase in the misery index during the recession of 2001. The misery index didn't recede until 2004, when strong output growth reduced the unemployment rate. The index jumped again in 2008–2011 when the high jobless rate made everybody miserable.

Leftward AS Shifts: All Bad News

Whereas rightward AS shifts appear to be a dream come true, leftward AS shifts are a real nightmare. Imagine in Figure 16.5 that the AS shift is reversed—that is, from AS_2 to AS_1. What would happen? Output would decrease and prices would rise, exactly the kind of dilemma depicted in the cartoon to the right. In other words, nothing would go in the right direction. This would be rampant stagflation.

A natural disaster can trigger a leftward shift of the AS curve, especially in smaller nations. When a tsunami washed over nations in the Indian Ocean in December 2004, more than 200,000 people were killed. In Sri Lanka, 80 percent of the fishing fleet was destroyed, along with port facilities, railroads, highways, and communications systems. The huge loss of human and physical capital reduced Sri Lanka's production possibilities. This was reflected in a leftward shift of the AS curve. The same kind of devastation hit Japan in 2011, reducing that nation's potential output and intensifying inflationary pressures (see the World View below).

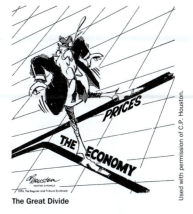

The Great Divide

Analysis: Leftward shifts of the aggregate supply curve push price levels up and output down. The remedy for such stagflation is a rightward shift of aggregate supply.

WORLD VIEW

Japan Sees Quake Damage Bill of Up to $309 Billion, Almost Four Katrinas

Japan's government estimated the damage from this month's record earthquake and tsunami at as much as 25 trillion yen ($309 billion), an amount almost four times the hit imposed by Hurricane Katrina on the U.S.

The destruction will push down gross domestic product by as much as 2.75 trillion yen for the year starting April 1. The figure, about 0.5 percent of the 530 trillion yen economy, reflects a decline in production from supply disruptions and damage to corporate facilities without taking into account the effects of possible power outages.

The figures are the first gauge of the scale of rebuilding Prime Minister Naoto Kan's government will face after the quake killed more than 9,000 people. . .

"The ability to depress economic activity from the supply side is larger than the Great Kobe earthquake and we must bear in mind that these effects could linger for some time," [Bank of Japan board member Ryuzo Miyao] said in a speech in Oita, southern Japan. . . .

—Keiko Ujikrane

Source: *Bloomberg News,* March 23, 2011. Used with permission of Bloomberg L.P. Copyright© 2015. All rights reserved.

ANALYSIS: A natural disaster destroys production facilities, transportation routes, power sources, and people, causing a leftward shift of the AS curve.

In an economy as large as that of the United States, leftward shifts of aggregate supply are less dramatic. But Mother Nature can still push the AS curve around. Hurricanes Katrina and Rita, for example, destroyed vast amounts of production, transportation, and communications infrastructure in August 2005. The resulting delays and cost increases were reflected in a leftward shift of the AS curve and an uptick in the misery index in 2005.

The September 11, 2001, terrorist attacks on the World Trade Center and Pentagon were another form of external shock. The attacks directly destroyed some production capacity (office space, telecommunications links, and transportation links). But they took an even greater toll on the *willingness* to supply goods and services. In the aftermath of the attacks businesses, perceiving new risks to investment and production, held back from making new commitments. Increased security measures also made transporting goods more expensive. All of these responses shifted the AS curve leftward and the Phillips curve rightward, adding to macro misery.

Policy Tools

From the supply side of macro markets, the appropriate response to negative external shocks is clear: shift the AS curve rightward. As the foregoing graphs have demonstrated, *rightward shifts of the aggregate supply curve always generate desirable macro outcomes.* The next question, of course, is how to shift the aggregate supply curve in the desired (rightward) direction. Supply-side economists look for clues among the forces that influence the supply-side response to changes in demand. Among those forces, the following policy options for shifting the AS curve rightward have been emphasized:

- Tax incentives for saving, investment, and work.
- Human capital investment.
- Deregulation.
- Trade liberalization.
- Infrastructure development.

All these policies have the potential to change supply decisions *independently* of any changes in aggregate demand. If they're effective, they'll result in a rightward shift of the AS curve and an *improved* trade-off between unemployment and inflation.

TAX INCENTIVES

web click

Do tax incentives matter? Economists think so. For readings about incentives and taxation, see **www.brookings.edu.** Search for "tax incentives."

The most renowned supply-side policy option for improving the unemployment–inflation trade-off was the "supply-side" tax cuts of the early 1980s. Tax cuts are of course a staple of Keynesian economics. But tax cuts take on a whole new role on the supply side of the economy. *In Keynesian economics, tax cuts are used to increase aggregate demand.* By putting more disposable income in the hands of consumers, Keynesian economists seek to increase expenditure on goods and services. Output is expected to increase in response. From a Keynesian perspective, the form of the tax cut is not important as long as disposable income increases.

The supply side of the economy encourages a different view of taxes. *Taxes not only alter disposable income but also change incentives to work and produce.* High tax rates destroy incentives to work and produce, so they end up reducing total output. Low tax rates, by contrast, allow people to keep more of what they earn and so stimulate greater output. *The direct effects of taxes on the supply of goods are the concern of supply-side economists.* Figure 16.7 shows the difference between demand-side and supply-side perspectives on tax policy.

Marginal Tax Rates

marginal tax rate: The tax rate imposed on the last (marginal) dollar of income.

Supply-side theory places special emphasis on *marginal* tax rates. The **marginal tax rate** is the tax rate imposed on the last (marginal) dollar of income received. In our progressive income tax system, marginal tax rates increase as more income is received. Uncle Sam takes a larger share out of each additional dollar earned. In 2015, the highest marginal tax rate on personal income was 39.6 percent. That top tax rate was far below the 91 percent

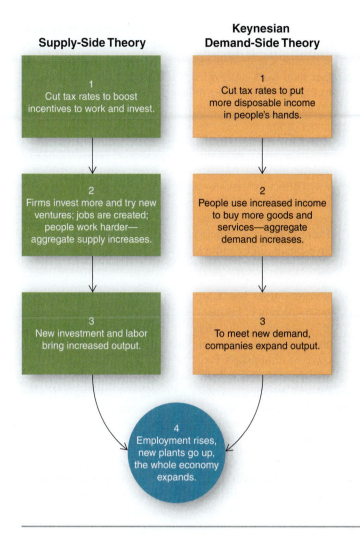

Supply-Side Theory

1
Cut tax rates to boost incentives to work and invest.

2
Firms invest more and try new ventures; jobs are created; people work harder—aggregate supply increases.

3
New investment and labor bring increased output.

Keynesian Demand-Side Theory

1
Cut tax rates to put more disposable income in people's hands.

2
People use increased income to buy more goods and services—aggregate demand increases.

3
To meet new demand, companies expand output.

4
Employment rises, new plants go up, the whole economy expands.

FIGURE 16.7

Two Theories for Getting the Economy Moving

Keynesians and supply-siders both advocate cutting taxes to reduce unemployment. But they have very different views on the kind of tax cuts required and the impact of any cuts enacted.

rate that existed in 1944, but it was also a lot higher than the 12 percent tax rate imposed in 1914 (see Figure 16.8).

In view of the wild history of tax rates, one might wonder whether the rate selected matters. Specifically, does the marginal tax rate affect supply decisions? Will people work and invest as much when the marginal tax rate is 91 percent as when it is only 12 percent? Doesn't seem likely, does it?

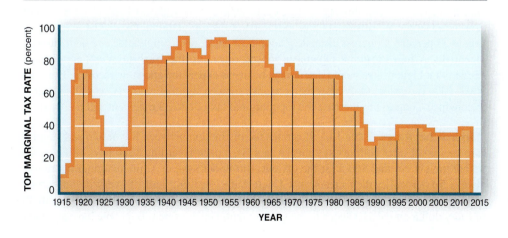

FIGURE 16.8

Changes in Marginal Tax Rates since 1915

The top marginal tax rate on income has varied from a low of 12 percent in 1914 to a high of 91 percent in 1944. Supply-side theory emphasizes how these varying tax rates affect work, investment, and production decisions—that is, aggregate supply.

Labor Supply. The marginal tax rate directly changes the financial incentive to *increase* one's work. ***If the marginal tax rate is high, there's less incentive to work more***—Uncle Sam will get most of the added income. Confronted with high marginal tax rates, workers may choose to stay home rather than work an extra shift. Families may decide that it doesn't pay to send both parents into the labor market. When marginal tax rates are low, by contrast, those extra work activities generate bigger increases in disposable income.

Entrepreneurship. Marginal tax rates affect not only labor supply decisions but also decisions on whether to start or expand a business. Most small businesses are organized as sole proprietorships or partnerships and are subject to *personal,* not *corporate,* tax rates. Hence a decline in personal tax rates will affect the risk–reward balance for potential entrepreneurs. Columbia Business School professors William Gentry and Glenn Huber have demonstrated that progressive marginal tax rates discourage entry into self-employment. Syracuse professor Douglas Holtz-Eakin and Princeton economist Harvey Rosen have shown that the growth rate, investment, and employment of small businesses are also affected by marginal tax rates. As Holtz-Eakin concluded, "Taxes matter."

Investment. Taxes matter for corporations too. Corporate entities account for nearly 90 percent of business output and 84 percent of business assets. Like small proprietorships, corporations, too, are motivated by *after*-tax profits. Hence corporate **investment** decisions will be affected by corporate tax rates. If Uncle Sam imposes a high tax rate on corporate profits, the payoff to investors will be diminished. Potential investors may decide to consume their income or to purchase tax-free bonds rather than invest in plants and equipment. If that happens, total investment will decline and output will suffer. Accordingly, ***if high tax rates discourage investment, aggregate supply will be constrained.***

investment: Expenditures on (production of) new plants, equipment, and structures (capital) in a given time period, plus changes in business inventories.

Tax-Induced Supply Shifts

If tax rates affect supply decisions, then *changes* in tax rates will shift aggregate supply. Specifically, supply-siders conclude that ***a reduction in marginal tax rates will shift the aggregate supply curve to the right.*** The increased supply will come in three forms: more work effort, more entrepreneurship, and more investment. This increased willingness to produce will reduce the rate of unemployment. The additional output will also help reduce inflationary pressures. Thus we end up with less unemployment *and* less inflation.

From a supply-side perspective, the form of the tax cut is critical. For example, **tax rebates** are a one-time windfall to consumers and have no effect on marginal tax rates. As a consequence, disposable income rises, but not the incentives for work or production. Rebates directly affect only the demand side of the economy.

tax rebate: A lump-sum refund of taxes paid.

To stimulate aggregate *supply,* tax *rates* must be reduced, particularly at the margin. These cuts can take the form of reductions in personal income tax rates or reductions in the marginal tax rates imposed on businesses. In either case, the lower tax rates will give people a greater incentive to work, invest, and produce. This was the motivation for the Reagan tax cuts of 1981–1984. Shifting the aggregate supply curve rightward was also the goal of President George W. Bush's 2001 proposal to cut the top marginal tax rate from 39.6 percent to 33 percent. Congress ultimately adopted a package of supply-side and demand-side incentives. When President Obama proposed reversing the Bush tax cuts, economists warned that higher rates would discourage business expansion and slow recovery from the 2008–2009 recession. Only after the economy showed signs of recovery was Obama able to convince Congress to increase the top marginal tax rate to 39.6 percent again (2013).

Marginal Tax Rates. Table 16.1 illustrates the distinction between Keynesian and supply-side tax cuts. Under both tax systems (A and B), a person earning $200 pays $80 in taxes before the tax cut and $60 after the tax cut. But under system A, the marginal tax rate is always 50 percent, which means that Uncle Sam is getting half of every dollar earned above $100. By contrast, system B imposes a marginal tax rate of only 30 percent—$0.30 of every dollar above $100 goes to the government. Under system B, people have a greater

TABLE 16.1

Supply Side: Focus on Marginal
Tax Rates

Initial Alternatives					
Tax System	Initial Tax Schedule	Tax on Income of $200	Tax Rate Average	Tax Rate Marginal	Disposable Income
A	$30 + 50% of income over $100	$80	40%	50%	$120
B	$50 + 30% of income over $100	$80	40%	30%	$120

The same amount of taxes can be raised via two very different systems. Here a person earning $200 pays $80 in taxes under either system (A or B). Thus the *average* tax rate (total tax ÷ total income) is the same in both cases ($80 ÷ $200 = 40%). The *marginal* tax rates are very different, however. System A has a high marginal rate (50%), whereas system B has a low marginal tax rate (30%). System B provides a greater incentive for people to earn over $100.

Alternative Forms of Tax Cut					
Tax System	Revised Tax Schedule	Tax on Income of $200	Tax Rate Average	Tax Rate Marginal	Disposable Income
A	$10 + 50% of income over $100	$60	30%	50%	$140
B	$30 + 30% of income over $100	$60	30%	30%	$140

The average tax rate could be cut to 30 percent under either system. Under both systems, the revised tax would be $60 and disposable income would be increased to $140. Keynesians would be happy with either form of tax cut. But supply-siders would favor system B because the lower marginal tax rate gives people more incentive to earn higher incomes.

incentive to earn *more* than $100. Although both systems raise the same amount of taxes, system B offers greater incentives to work extra hours and produce more output.

Tax Elasticity of Supply

All economists agree that tax rates influence people's decisions to work, invest, and produce. But the policy-relevant question is, *how much* influence do taxes have? Do reductions in the marginal tax rate shift the aggregate supply curve far to the right? Or are the resultant shifts quite small?

The response of labor and capital to a change in tax rates is summarized by the **tax elasticity of supply.** Like other elasticities, this one measures the proportional response of supplies to a change in price (in this case a tax *rate*). Specifically, the tax elasticity of supply is the percentage change in quantity supplied divided by the percentage in tax rates; that is,

$$\text{Tax elasticity of supply} = \frac{\text{\% change in quantity supplied}}{\text{\% change in tax rate}}$$

Normally we expect quantity supplied to go up when tax rates go down. Elasticity (E) is therefore negative, although it's usually expressed in absolute terms (without the minus sign). The (absolute) value of E must be greater than zero since we expect *some* response to a tax cut. That means that *tax cuts—especially cuts in marginal tax rates—will shift the AS curve to the right.* The policy issue boils down to the question of how large E actually is—how far AS will shift.

If the tax elasticity of supply were large enough, a tax cut might not only shift the AS curve but actually *increase* tax revenues. Suppose the tax elasticity were equal to 1.5. In that case a tax cut of 10 percent would cause output supplied to increase by 15 percent (= 1.5 × 10%).

tax elasticity of supply: The percentage change in quantity supplied divided by the percentage change in tax rates.

Such a large increase in the tax base (income) would result in *more* taxes being paid even though the tax *rate* was reduced. One of President Reagan's economic advisers, Arthur Laffer, actually thought such an outcome was possible. He predicted that tax revenues would *increase* after the Reagan supply-side tax cuts were made. In reality, the tax elasticity of supply turned out to be much smaller (around 0.15), and tax revenues fell substantially. The aggregate supply curve *did* shift to the right, but not very far, when marginal tax rates were cut.

The evidently low tax elasticity of supply helped President Clinton convince Congress to *increase* marginal tax rates in 1993. Although opponents objected that higher tax rates would reduce work and investment, the Clinton administration pointed out that any leftward shift of aggregate supply was likely to be small. President George W. Bush reversed that shift with the 2001–2004 marginal tax rate cuts. According to a 2006 study by the Congressional Research Service, those tax rate cuts elicited a 0.20 tax elasticity of supply. In 2012, the Congressional Budget Office said the tax elasticity of supply might be higher still—at 0.27.

Savings Incentives

Supply-side economists emphasize the importance of *long-run* responses to changed tax incentives. On the demand side, an increase in income translates very quickly into increased spending. On the supply side, things don't happen so fast. It takes time to construct new plants and equipment. People are also slow to respond to new work and investment incentives. Hence the full benefits of supply-side tax cuts—or the damage done by tax hikes—won't be immediately visible.

Of particular concern to supply-side economists is the rate of saving in the economy. Demand-side economists emphasize spending and tend to treat **saving** as a leakage problem. Supply-siders, by contrast, emphasize the importance of saving for financing investment and economic growth. At full employment, a greater volume of investment is possible only if the rate of consumption is cut back. In other words, additional investment requires additional saving. Hence *supply-side economists favor tax incentives that encourage saving as well as greater tax incentives for investment.* This kind of perspective contrasts sharply with the Keynesian emphasis on stimulating consumption, as the accompanying cartoon emphasizes.

saving: That part of disposable income not spent on current consumption; disposable income less consumption.

web click

The U.S. Bureau of Economic Analysis maintains data on the personal saving rate of U.S. households. To view this information, visit **www.bea.gov** and search for "Overview of the Economy."

Analysis: In the short run, consumer saving may reduce aggregate demand. However, saving also finances increased investment, which is essential to long-run growth.

Investment Incentives

An alternative lever for shifting aggregate supply is to offer tax incentives for investment. The 1981 tax cuts focused on *personal* income tax rates. By contrast, President George H. Bush advocated cutting capital gains taxes. These are taxes levied on the increase in the value of property, such as land, buildings, and corporate stock, when it's sold. Lower capital gains taxes, Bush argued, would encourage people to start businesses or invest in them.

President Clinton also emphasized the need for investment incentives. His very first proposal for stimulating the economy was a temporary investment tax credit. People who invested in new plants and equipment would receive a tax credit equal to 10 percent of their investment. In effect, Uncle Sam would pay for part of any new investment by collecting less tax. Because the credit was available only to those who made new investments, it was a particularly efficient lever for shifting the aggregate supply curve.

President George W. Bush pulled this supply-side lever more firmly. After securing the huge *personal* tax cuts in 2001, Bush sought *business* tax cuts. In 2002 Congress approved larger capital expensing, which reduced the after-tax cost of new investments. In 2003 tax rates on dividends and capital gains were reduced, making investment still more profitable. During the 2008 campaign, Barack Obama vowed to reverse the Bush "tax cuts for the rich" by *raising* marginal income tax rates as well as capital gains and inheritance taxes. The Taxpayer Relief Act of 2012 pushed both personal and business tax rates up, trimming supply-side incentives.

HUMAN CAPITAL INVESTMENT

A nation's ability to supply goods and services depends on its *human* capital as well as its *physical* capital. If the size of the labor force increased, more output could be produced in any given price level. Similarly, if the *quality* of the workforce were to increase, more output could be supplied at any given price level. In other words, increases in **human capital**—the skills and knowledge of the workforce—add to the nation's potential output.

human capital: The knowledge and skills possessed by the workforce.

Structural Unemployment

A mismatch between the skills of the workforce and the requirements of new jobs is a major cause of the unemployment–inflation trade-off. When aggregate demand increases, employers want to hire more workers. But the available (unemployed) workers may not have the skills employers require. This is the essence of **structural unemployment.** The consequence is that employers can't increase output as fast as they'd like to. Prices, rather than output, increase.

The larger the skills gap between unemployed workers and the requirements of emerging jobs, the worse will be the Phillips curve trade-off. To improve the trade-off, the skills gap must be reduced. This is another supply-side imperative. *Investments in human capital reduce structural unemployment and shift the aggregate supply curve rightward.*

structural unemployment: Unemployment caused by a mismatch between the skills (or location) of job seekers and the requirements (or location) of available jobs.

Worker Training

The tax code is a policy tool for increasing human capital investment as well as physical capital investment. In this case tax credits are made available to employers who offer more worker training. Such credits reduce the employer's after-tax cost of training.

President Clinton proposed even stronger incentives for employer-based training. He wanted to *require* employers to spend at least 1.5 percent of their total payroll costs on training activities. Employers who didn't provide training activities directly would have to pay an equivalent sum into a public training fund. This "play-or-pay" approach would force employers to invest in the human capital of their employees.

Although the "play-or-pay" concept is intriguing, it might actually shift the aggregate supply curve the *wrong* way. The *costs* of employing workers would rise in the short run as employers shelled out more money for training or taxes. Hence the aggregate supply curve would shift *leftward* in the short run, worsening the unemployment–inflation trade-off. Only later might AS shift rightward, and then only to the extent that training actually improved **labor productivity.**

Education Spending

Another way to increase human capital is to expand and improve the efficacy of the education system. President George H. Bush encouraged local school systems to become more competitive. He suggested they experiment with vouchers that would allow students to attend the school of their choice. Schools would then have to offer services that attracted voucher-carrying students. Schools that didn't compete successfully wouldn't have enough funds (vouchers) to continue.

President Clinton advocated a more conventional approach. He urged Congress to allocate more funds to the school system, particularly programs for preschoolers, like Head Start, and for disadvantaged youth. He acknowledged that vouchers might increase school quality but wanted to limit their use to public schools.

President George W. Bush characterized himself as the "education president." He increased federal spending on education and improved tax incentives for college savings accounts and tuition payments. His No Child Left Behind program also increased school accountability for human capital development. President Obama also emphasized educational improvements as a key to long-run growth. None of these educational tools generate a quick AS curve shift. Rather, any improvements in labor productivity are likely to emerge many years later.

Affirmative Action

Lack of skills and experience aren't the only reasons it's sometimes hard to find the "right" workers. The mismatch between employed workers and jobs is often less a matter of skills than of race, gender, or age. In other words, discrimination can create an artificial barrier between job seekers and available job openings.

If discrimination tends to shift the aggregate supply curve leftward, then reducing discriminatory barriers should shift it to the right. Equal opportunity programs are thus a natural extension of a supply-side approach to macro policy. However, critics are also quick to point out the risks inherent in government regulation of hiring decisions. From a supply-side perspective, laws that forbid discrimination are welcome and should be enforced. But aggressive affirmative action programs that require employers to hire specific numbers or types of workers limit productive capabilities and can lead to excessive costs.

Transfer Payments

Welfare programs also discourage workers from taking available jobs. Unemployment and welfare benefits provide a source of income when a person isn't working. Although these **transfer payments** are motivated by humanitarian goals, they also inhibit labor supply. Transfer recipients must give up some or all of their welfare payments when they take a job, which makes working less attractive and therefore reduces the number of available workers. The net result is a leftward shift of the aggregate supply curve.

In 1996 Congress reformed the nation's core welfare program. The supply-side emphasis of that reform was manifest in the very title of the reform legislation: the Personal Responsibility and Work Opportunity Act. Congress set time limits on how long people can draw welfare benefits. The act also required recipients to engage in job-related activities like job search and training while still receiving benefits.

The 1996 reforms had a dramatic effect on recipient behavior. Nationally, more than 5 million adults left welfare between 1996 and 2001. More than half of these ex-welfare recipients entered the labor force, thereby shifting the AS curve rightward.

Recognizing that income transfers reduce aggregate supply doesn't force us to eliminate all welfare programs. Welfare programs are also intended to serve important social needs.

The AS/AD framework reminds us, however, that the structure of such programs will affect aggregate supply. With more than 60 million Americans receiving income transfers, the effect on aggregate supply can be significant.

DEREGULATION

Government intervention affects the shape and position of the aggregate supply curve in other ways. The government intervenes directly in supply decisions by *regulating* employment and output behavior. In general, such regulations limit the flexibility of producers to respond to changes in demand. Government regulation also tends to raise production costs. The higher costs result not only from required changes in the production process but also from the expense of monitoring government regulations and filling out government forms. Thomas Hopkins, a Rochester Institute of Technology economist, estimates that the total costs of regulation exceed $700 billion a year. These added costs of production shift the aggregate supply curve to the left.

Factor Markets

Government intervention in factor markets increases the cost of supplying goods and services in many ways.

Minimum Wages. Minimum wage laws are one of the most familiar forms of factor market regulation. The Fair Labor Standards Act of 1938 required employers to pay workers a minimum of 25 cents per hour. Over time, Congress has increased the coverage of that act and the minimum wage itself repeatedly.

The goal of the minimum wage law is to ensure workers a decent standard of living. But the law has other effects as well. By prohibiting employers from using lower-paid workers, it limits the ability of employers to hire additional workers. Teenagers especially may not have enough skills or experience to merit the federal minimum wage. Employers may have to rely on more expensive workers rather than hire unemployed teenagers.

Here again the issue is not whether minimum wage laws serve any social purposes but how they affect macro outcomes. By shifting the aggregate supply curve leftward, minimum wage laws make it more difficult to achieve full employment with stable prices.

Mandatory Benefits. Government-directed fringe benefits have the same kind of effect on aggregate supply. One of the first bills President Clinton signed into law was the Family and Medical Leave Act, which requires all businesses with 50 or more employees to grant leaves of absence for up to 12 weeks. The employer must continue to pay health benefits during such absences and must also incur the costs of recruiting and training temporary replacements. The General Accounting Office estimated these benefits add nearly $700 million per year to payroll costs. These added payroll costs raise the costs of production, making producers less willing to supply output at any given price level. President Obama's sweeping health care reforms (the Affordable Care Act of 2010) reduced incentives for both labor supply and labor demand. The Congressional Budget Office says the ACA will reduce 2017 employment by 2 million jobs.

Occupational Health and Safety. Government regulation of factor markets extends beyond wages and benefits. The government also sets standards for workplace safety and health. The Occupational Safety and Health Administration (OSHA), for example, issued new rules in November 2000 to reduce ergonomic injuries at work. The rules would have required employers to redesign workplaces (assembly lines, computer workstations) to accommodate individual workers. The rules would have also required employers to pay higher health care costs and grant more injury-related leave. OSHA itself estimated that the new regulations would cost employers $4.5 billion a year. Employers said the ergonomics regulations would cost *far* more than that—up to $125 billion a year. Concern over the implied upward shift of aggregate supply prompted Congress to rescind the new ergonomics rules before they took effect.

Product Markets

The government's regulation of factor markets tends to raise production costs and inhibit supply. The same is true of regulations imposed directly on product markets, as the following examples illustrate.

Transportation Costs. At the federal level, various agencies regulate the output and prices of transportation services. In 2013 the Federal Motor Carrier Safety Administration issued new regulations for the trucking industry's drivers. The new regulations specify how many hours a driver can work in a week, how much time must elapse between weeks, how often and for how long drivers must get off the road for a break, and even what hours of the night they must sleep. Although the regulators say the new rules will "ensure that drivers get the rest they need to be alert, safe, and awake," the industry says the new rules cut productivity and raise costs—that is, shift the AS curve to the left.

Similar problems continue to inflate intrastate trucking costs. All but eight states limit the routes, the loads, and the prices of intrastate trucking companies. These regulations promote inefficient transportation and protect producer profits. The net cost to the economy is at least $8 billion, or about $128 a year for a family of four.

Many cities and counties also limit the number of taxicabs and regulate their prices. Some also prohibit or constrain new ride-sharing services like Uber and Lyft that offer cheaper transportation. The net effect of such regulation is to limit competition and drive up the cost of transportation.

Food and Drug Standards. The Food and Drug Administration (FDA) has a broad mandate to protect consumers from dangerous products. In fulfilling this responsibility, the FDA sets health standards for the content of specific foods. The FDA also sets standards for the testing of new drugs and evaluates the test results.

The goal of FDA regulation is to minimize health risks to consumers. Like all regulation, however, the FDA standards entail real costs. The tests required for new drugs are expensive and time-consuming. Getting a new drug approved for sale takes years of effort and requires multimillion-dollar investments. The net results are that (1) fewer new drugs are brought to market and (2) those that reach the market are more expensive. In other words, the aggregate supply of goods is shifted to the left.

Other examples of government regulation are commonplace. The Environmental Protection Agency (EPA) regulates auto emissions, the discharge of industrial wastes, and water pollution. The U.S. Congress restricts foreign imports and raises their prices. The Federal Trade Commission (FTC) limits firms' freedom to increase their output or advertise their products. The Consumer Product Safety Commission regulates toys, mandating expensive tests for the chemical content of materials and paint used in children's toys. Toy manufacturers complain that the required tests are unnecessary and too expensive, especially for the many small businesses that make, sell, or resell children's toys and clothes.

Reducing Costs

Many—perhaps most—of these regulatory activities are beneficial. In fact, all were originally designed to serve specific public purposes. As a result of such regulation, we get safer drugs, cleaner air, and less deceptive advertising. We must also consider the costs involved, however. All regulatory activities impose direct and indirect costs. These costs must be compared to the benefits received. ***The basic contention of supply-side economists is that regulatory costs are now too high.*** To improve our economic performance, they assert, we must *deregulate* the production process, thereby shifting the aggregate supply curve to the right again. President Obama responded to this criticism in January 2011 with an executive order requiring regulatory agencies to "strike the right balance" between regulatory goals and economic growth. He continued, however, to expand the scope of government regulation.

Regulation makes toys safer but also more expensive.

EASING TRADE BARRIERS

Government regulation of international trade also influences the shape and position of aggregate supply. Trade flows affect both factor and product markets.

Factor Markets

In factor markets, U.S. producers buy raw materials, equipment parts, and components from foreign suppliers. Tariffs (taxes on imported goods) make such inputs more expensive, thereby increasing the cost of U.S. production. Regulations or quotas that make foreign inputs less accessible or more expensive similarly constrain the U.S. aggregate supply curve. The quota on imported sugar, for example, increases the cost of U.S.-produced soda, cookies, and candy. Just that one trade barrier has cost U.S. consumers more than $2 billion in higher prices.

Product Markets

The same kind of trade barriers affect product markets directly. With completely unrestricted ("free") trade, foreign producers would be readily available to supply products to U.S. consumers. By increasing the quantity of output available at any given price level, foreign suppliers help flatten out the aggregate supply curve.

Despite the success of the North American Free Trade Agreement (NAFTA) and the World Trade Organization (WTO) in reducing trade barriers, half of all U.S. imports are still subject to tariffs. Nontariff barriers (regulation, quotas, and so forth) also still constrain aggregate supply. This was evident in the multiyear battle over Mexican trucking. Although NAFTA authorized Mexican trucking companies to compete freely in the United States by 2000, U.S. labor unions (Teamsters) and trucking companies vigorously protested their entry, delaying the implied reduction in transportation costs for more than 10 years.

Immigration

Another global supply-side policy lever is immigration policy. Skill shortages in U.S. labor markets can be overcome with education and training. But even faster relief is available in the vast pool of foreign workers. In 2000 Congress increased the quota for software engineers and other high-tech workers by 70 percent, to 195,000 workers. The intent was to relieve the skill shortage in high-tech industries, and with it the cost pressures that were increasing the slope of the aggregate supply curve. Temporary visas for farm workers also help avert cost-push inflation in the farm sector. By regulating the flow of immigrant workers, Congress has the potential to alter the shape and position of the short-run AS curve.

THE ECONOMY TOMORROW

REBUILDING AMERICA

Another way to reduce the costs of supplying goods and services is to improve the nation's **infrastructure**—that is, the transportation, communications, judicial, and other systems that bind the pieces of the economy into a coherent whole. The interstate highway system, for example, enlarged the market for producers looking for new sales opportunities. Improved air traffic controls and larger airports have also made international markets and factors of production readily accessible. Without interstate highways and international airports, the process of supplying goods and services would be more localized and much more expensive.

It's easy to take infrastructure for granted until you have to make do without it. In recent years, U.S. producers have rushed into China, Russia, and eastern Europe looking for new profit opportunities. What they discovered is that even simple communication is difficult

infrastructure: The transportation, communications, education, judicial, and other institutional systems that facilitate market exchanges.

web click

For the latest assessment of U.S. infrastructure, visit **www.infrastructure-reportcard.org**.

where Internet access and even telephones are often scarce. Outside the major cities business facilities and accommodations are often equally scarce. There are few established clearinghouses for marketing information, and labor markets are fragmented and localized. Getting started sometimes requires doing everything from scratch.

Although the United States has a highly developed infrastructure, it too could be improved. There are roads and bridges to repair, more airports to be built, faster rail systems to construct, and telecommunications networks to install. As we look to the future, we have to wonder whether that infrastructure will satisfy the needs of the economy tomorrow. If it doesn't, it will become increasingly difficult and costly to increase output.

Declining Infrastructure Investment. The United States has more than $2 trillion worth of public, nonmilitary infrastructure, including highways, bridges, sewage systems, buildings, hospitals, and schools. Like private capital (business plants, equipment, and structures), this *public* capital contributes to our production possibilities.

Investment in public infrastructure slowed down in the 1970s and 1980s. The rate of infrastructure investment peaked at around 3.5 percent of GDP in the mid-1960s. It then declined steadily to a low of about 0.5 percent of GDP in the early 1980s. As a result of this decline in spending, the United States has barely been able to *maintain* existing infrastructure, much less *expand* it. In 2013 the American Society of Civil Engineers said 4,095 of the nation's 85,000 dams are in need of repair. They estimate that the nation's infrastructure—everything from highways to sewers—needs a $3.6 trillion upgrade. Studies by Alan Aschauer and others suggest that ***declining infrastructure investment has reduced actual and potential output.*** In other words, crumbling infrastructure has shifted the aggregate supply curve leftward.

Not everyone agrees that the nation's infrastructure is actually crumbling. Accident rates on the roads, on the rails, and in the air have been declining. Moreover, the quality of interstate roads—including the 155,000-mile national highway system—has improved significantly since 1980. But everyone agrees that ***the transportation system isn't keeping up with a growing economy.*** Highway traffic is increasing at 2.5 percent a year, while airline passenger traffic is rising at closer to 4 percent a year. To accommodate this growth, we need more and better transportation systems.

The Cost of Delay. The failure to expand the infrastructure could prove costly. The U.S. Department of Transportation estimates that people now spend nearly 3.5 billion hours a year in traffic delays. If the nation's highways don't improve, those delays will skyrocket to more than 4 billion hours a year a decade from now. That's a lot of labor resources to leave idle. Moreover, cars stuck on congested highways waste a lot of gasoline—nearly 4 billion gallons a year—and spew enormous amounts of carbon dioxide into our atmosphere.

Delays in air travel impose similar costs. The Federal Aviation Administration says air travel delays increase airline operating costs by more than $2 billion a year and idle more than $3 billion worth of passenger time. That time imposes a high opportunity cost in forgone business transactions and shortened vacations. Ultimately, all these costs are reflected in lower productivity, reduced output, higher prices, and greater environmental damage.

The Rebuilding Process. To alleviate these constraints on aggregate supply, Congress has voted to accelerate infrastructure spending. The Transportation Equity Act of 2000 raised federal spending to more than $600 billion in that decade. Among the public investments were the following:

- *Highways:* Highway construction and rehabilitation.
- *Air traffic control:* Modernization of the air traffic control system.
- *Weather service:* Modernization of the weather service (new satellites, a supercomputer).
- *Maglev trains:* Research on magnetically levitated ("maglev") trains that can travel at 300 miles per hour and are environmentally clean.
- *Smart cars and highways:* Research and testing of cars and highways outfitted with radar, monitors, and computers to reduce congestion and accidents.

Other legislation authorized more spending on sewage systems, access to space (for example, the space shuttle), modernization of the postal service, and construction of more hospitals, prisons, and other buildings. To this list President Obama added development of alternative energy sources, expansion of broadband access, an improved electrical grid, and high-speed rail systems. All these infrastructure improvements increase aggregate supply, creating more potential for economic growth without inflation in the economy tomorrow.

SUMMARY

- Fiscal and monetary policies seek to attain full employment and price stability by shifting the aggregate demand curve. Their success depends on microeconomic responses, as reflected in the price and output decisions of market participants. **LO16-1**
- The market's response to shifts in aggregate demand is reflected in the shape and position of the aggregate supply curve. If the AS curve slopes upward, a trade-off between unemployment and inflation exists. The Phillips curve illustrates the trade-off. **LO16-2**
- The inflationary flashpoint is the rate of output where inflation accelerates—where the unemployment–inflation trade-off becomes acute. **LO16-2**
- If the AS curve shifts to the left, the trade-off between unemployment and inflation worsens. Stagflation—a combination of substantial inflation and unemployment—results. This is illustrated by rightward shifts of the Phillips curve. **LO16-2**
- Supply-side policies attempt to alter price and output decisions directly. If successful, they'll shift the aggregate supply curve to the right. A rightward AS shift implies less inflation *and* less unemployment. **LO16-3**
- Marginal tax rates are a major concern of supply-side economists. High tax rates discourage extra work, invest-

- ment, and saving. A reduction in marginal tax rates should shift aggregate supply to the right. **LO16-3**
- The tax elasticity of supply measures the response of quantity supplied to changes in tax rates. Empirical evidence suggests that tax elasticity is modest but still triggers short-run shifts of the aggregate supply curve. **LO16-3**
- Investments in human capital increase productivity and therefore shift aggregate supply also. Workers' training and education enhancement are policy tools. **LO16-3**
- Government regulation often raises the cost of production and limits output. Deregulation is intended to reduce costly restrictions on price and output behavior, thereby shifting the AS curve to the right. **LO16-3**
- Public infrastructure is part of the economy's capital resources. Investments in infrastructure (such as transportation systems) facilitate market exchanges, expand production possibilities, and reduce environmental impacts. **LO16-3**
- Trade barriers shift the AS curve leftward by raising the cost of imported inputs and the price of imported products. Lowering trade barriers increases aggregate supply. **LO16-3**

Key Terms

stagflation	investment	structural unemployment
aggregate supply	tax rebate	labor productivity
Phillips curve	tax elasticity of supply	transfer payments
inflationary flashpoint	saving	infrastructure
marginal tax rate	human capital	

Questions for Discussion

1. Why might prices rise when aggregate demand increases? What factors might influence the extent of price inflation? **LO16-1**
2. How did the 2011 tsunami affect Japan's potential output (World View, p. 349)? **LO16-1**
3. Why did President Obama raise the top marginal tax rate to 39.6 percent if higher tax rates reduce aggregate supply? **LO16-2**
4. Which of the following groups are likely to have the highest tax elasticity of labor supply: (*a*) college students,

(b) single parents, (c) primary earners in two-parent families, and (d) secondary earners in two-parent families? Why are there differences?   **LO16-3**

5. How is the aggregate supply curve affected by (a) minimum wage laws, (b) Social Security payroll taxes, (c) Social Security retirement benefits, and (d) tighter border security? **LO16-3**

6. OSHA predicted that its proposed ergonomics rules (text, pp. 357–358) would have cut repetitive stress injuries by 50 percent. Was Congress correct in repealing those rules?   **LO16-1**

7. Ride-sharing services like Uber and Lyft offer cheaper transportation than traditional taxicabs, which are regulated by local governments. How do these services affect the AS curve? Should they be regulated?   **LO16-3**

8. How does each of the following infrastructure items affect aggregate supply: (a) highways, (b) schools, (c) sewage systems, and (d) courts and prisons?   **LO16-3**

9. How would the volume and timing of capital investments be affected by (a) a permanent cut in the capital gains tax and (b) a temporary 10 percent tax credit?   **LO16-3**

10. How might the inflationary flashpoint affect policy decisions? How would you represent the flashpoint on the Phillips curve?   **LO16-2**

11. Why would anyone object to President Obama's increased infrastructure spending?   **LO16-2**

---

 mobile app Visit your mobile app store and download the Schiller: Study Econ app *today*!

LO16-1 1. On the following graph, draw the (A) Keynesian, (B) monetarist, and (C) hybrid AS curves, all intersecting AD at point E. If AD shifts rightward, which AS curve (A, B, or C) generates
   (a) The biggest increase in output?   _____
   (b) The biggest increase in prices?   _____

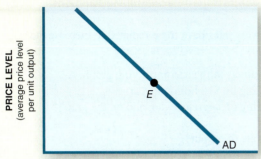

PRICE LEVEL (average price level per unit output)

E

AD

OUTPUT (real GDP per period)

LO16-1 2. Which AS curve (a, b, or c) in Figure 16.1 causes the least unemployment when fiscal or monetary restraint is pursued?   _____

LO16-1 3. The Economy Tomorrow section provides estimates of time spent in traffic delays. If the average worker produces $90 of output per hour, what is the opportunity cost of
   (a) Current traffic delays? $_____
   (b) Estimated delays in 10 years? $_____

LO16-3 4. Suppose taxpayers are required to pay a base tax of $50 plus 30 percent on any income greater than $100, as in the initial tax system B in Table 16.1. Suppose further that the taxing authority wishes to raise by $40 the taxes of people with incomes of $200.
   (a) If marginal tax rates are to remain unchanged, what will the new base tax have to be? $_____
   (b) If the base tax of $50 is to remain unchanged, what will the marginal tax rate have to be?   _____%

LO16-3 5. Suppose households supply 560 billion hours of labor per year and have a tax elasticity of supply of 0.15. If the tax rate is increased by 10 percent, by how many hours will the supply of labor decline?   _____

LO16-3 6. By how much did the disposable income of rich people decrease as a result of the 2012 hike in the top marginal tax rate from 35 to 39.6 percent? Assume they have $2 trillion of gross income in the highest bracket.   _____

LO16-2 7. According to Figure 16.6, what inflation rate would occur if the unemployment rate rose to 6 percent, with
   (a) PC_1?   _____
   (b) PC_2?   _____

LO16-2 8. On the following graph, plot the unemployment and inflation rates for the years 2004–2013 using the data from this book's end covers. Is there any evidence of a Phillips curve trade-off?   _____

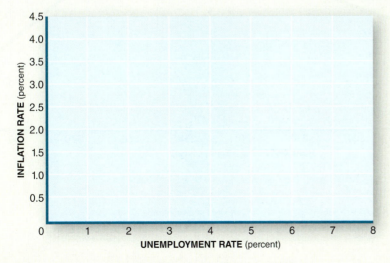

INFLATION RATE (percent)

UNEMPLOYMENT RATE (percent)

LO16-3 9. If the tax elasticity of labor supply is 0.20, by what percentage will the quantity of labor supplied increase in response to
   (*a*) A $500 per person income tax rebate?   _____%
   (*b*) A 4 percent reduction in marginal tax rates?   _____%

LO16-3 10. If the tax elasticity of supply is 0.18, by how much do tax rates have to be reduced to increase the labor supply by 2 percent?   _____

LO16-3 11. Suppose an economy is characterized by the AS/AD curves in the accompanying graph. A decision is then made to increase infrastructure spending by $10 billion a year.
   (*a*) Illustrate the direct impact of the increased spending on aggregate demand on the graph (ignore multiplier effects).
   (*b*) If AS is unaffected, what is the new equilibrium rate of output?   _____
   (*c*) What is the new equilibrium price level?   _____
   (*d*) Now assume that the infrastructure investments increase aggregate supply by $20 billion a year (from the initial equilibrium). Illustrate this effect on the graph.
   (*e*) After both demand and supply adjustments occur, what is the final equilibrium
    (*i*) Rate of output?   _____
    (*ii*) Price level?   _____

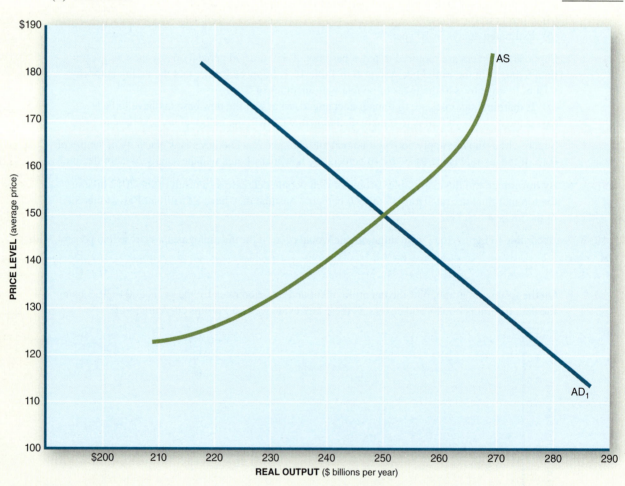

Growth and Productivity:
Long-Run Possibilities

Economic growth is the fundamental determinant of the long-run success of any nation, the basic source of rising living standards, and the key to meeting the needs and desires of the American people.

—*Economic Report of the President, 1992*

Imagine a world with no smartphones, no satellite TV, no social media, and no digital sound. Such a world actually existed—only 40 years ago! At the time, personal computers were still on the drawing board, and laptops weren't even envisioned. Websites were a place where spiders gathered, not locations on the Internet. Home video hadn't been seen, and no one had yet popped any microwave popcorn. Biotechnology hadn't yet produced any blockbuster drugs, and people wore the same pair of athletic shoes for a wide variety of sports.

New products are evidence of economic progress. Over time, we produce not only *more* goods and services but also *new* and *better* goods and services. In the process, we get richer: our material living standards rise.

Rising living standards aren't inevitable, however. According to World Bank estimates, almost 3 *billion* people—nearly half the world's population—continue to live in abject poverty with incomes of less than $2 per day. Worse still, living standards in many of the poorest countries have *fallen* in the last decade.

This chapter takes a longer-term view of economic performance. Chapters 8 to 16 were concerned with the business cycle—that is, *short-run* variations in output and prices. This chapter looks at the prospects for *long-run* growth and considers three questions:

- **How important is economic growth?**
- **How does an economy grow?**
- **Is continued economic growth possible? Is it desirable?**

We develop answers to these questions by first examining the nature of economic growth and then examining its sources and potential limits.

THE NATURE OF GROWTH

Economic growth refers to increases in the output of goods and services. But there are two distinct ways in which output increases, and they have different implications for our economic welfare.

Short-Run Changes in Capacity Utilization

The easiest kind of growth comes from increased use of our productive capabilities. In any given year there's a limit to an economy's potential output. This limit is determined by the quantity of resources available and our technological know-how. We've illustrated these short-run limits with a **production possibilities** curve, as in Figure 17.1a. By using all our available resources and our best expertise, we can produce any combination of goods and services on the production possibilities curve.

We don't always take full advantage of our productive capacity. The economy often produces a mix of output that lies *inside* our production possibilities, like point A in Figure 17.1a. This was our situation in the Great Recession of 2008–2009. When this happens, a major *short-run* goal of macro policy is to achieve full employment—to move us from point A to some point on the production possibilities curve (such as point B). In the process, we produce more output.

Long-Run Change in Capacity

Once we're fully utilizing our productive capacity, further increases in output are attainable only if we *expand* that capacity. To do so we have to *shift* the production possibilities curve outward as in Figure 17.1b. Such shifts imply an increase in *potential* GDP—that is, our productive capacity.

Over time, increases in capacity are critical. Short-run increases in the utilization of existing capacity can generate only modest increases in output. Even high unemployment

production possibilities: The alternative combinations of final goods and services that could be produced in a given time period with all available resources and technology.

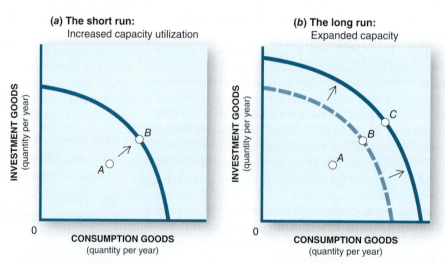

(a) The short run:
Increased capacity utilization

(b) The long run:
Expanded capacity

INVESTMENT GOODS (quantity per year)

CONSUMPTION GOODS (quantity per year)

FIGURE 17.1
Two Types of Growth

Increases in output result from increased use of existing capacity or from increases in that capacity itself. In part *a* the mix of output at point *A* doesn't make full use of production possibilities. We can get additional output by employing more of our available resources or using them more efficiently. This is illustrated by point *B* (or any other point on the curve).

Once we're on the production possibilities curve, we can get more output only by *increasing* our productive capacity. This is illustrated by the outward *shift* of the production possibilities curve in part *b*.

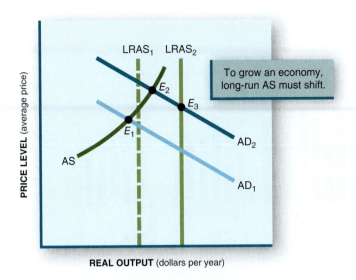

FIGURE 17.2
Shifts of Long-Run Supply

Macro stabilization policies try to shift the aggregate demand curve (e.g., from AD_1 to AD_2) to achieve greater output and employment in the short run.

The vertical long-run AS curve implies that these efforts will have no lasting impact on the natural rate of output, however. To achieve economic growth, the long-run aggregate supply curve must be shifted to the right (e.g., from $LRAS_1$ to $LRAS_2$).

rates, such as 9 percent, leave little room for increased output. *To achieve large and lasting increases in output we must push our production possibilities outward.* For this reason, economists often define **economic growth** in terms of changes in *potential* GDP.

The unique character of economic growth can also be illustrated with aggregate supply and demand curves. Figure 17.2 depicts both a sloped, *short-run* AS curve and a vertical, *long-run* AS curve. In the short run, macro stabilization policies try to shift the AD curve to a more desirable price–output equilibrium. Such demand-side policies are unlikely to change the country's long-run capacity to produce, however. At best they move the macro equilibrium to a more desirable point on the *short-run* AS curve (for example, from E_1 to E_2 in Figure 17.2).

Our productive capacity may increase nevertheless. If it does, the "natural" long-run AS curve will also shift. In this framework, *economic growth implies a rightward shift of the long-run aggregate supply curve.* Should that occur, the economy will be able to produce still more output with less inflationary pressure (e.g., as at E_3 in Figure 17.2).

> **economic growth:** An increase in output (real GDP); an expansion of production possibilities.

Nominal vs. Real GDP

Notice that we refer to *real* GDP, not *nominal* GDP, in our concept of economic growth. Nominal GDP can rise even when the quantity of goods and services falls, as was the case in 1991. The total quantity of goods and services produced in 1991 was less than the quantity produced in 1990. Nevertheless, prices rose enough in 1991 to keep nominal GDP growing.

Real GDP refers to the actual quantity of goods and services produced. Real GDP avoids the distortions of inflation by adjusting for changing prices. By using 2000 prices as a **base year,** we observe that real GDP fell from $7,112 billion in 1990 to only $7,100 billion in 1991 (see the inside cover of this book). Since then real GDP has increased 70 percent—an impressive growth achievement in only 20 years.

> **real GDP:** The value of final output produced in a given period, adjusted for changing prices.

> **base year:** The year used for comparative analysis; the basis for indexing price changes.

MEASURES OF GROWTH

Typically, changes in real GDP are expressed in percentage terms, as a growth *rate*. The **growth rate** is simply the change in real output between two periods divided by total output in the base period. The percentage decline in real output during 1991 was thus $12 billion ÷ $7,112 billion, or less than 0.2 percent. By contrast, real output grew in 1992 by 3.3 percent.

Figure 17.3 illustrates the recent growth experience of the U.S. economy. In the 1960s, real GDP grew by an average of 4.1 percent per year. Economic growth slowed to only 2.8 percent in the 1970s, however, with actual output declines in three years. The steep recession of 1982, as seen in Figure 17.3, reduced GDP growth in the 1980s to an even

> **growth rate:** Percentage change in real output from one period to another.

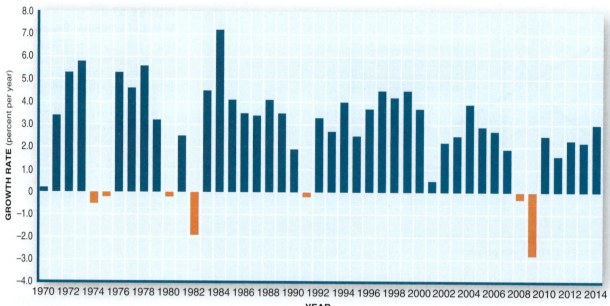

FIGURE 17.3

Recent U.S. Growth Rates

Total output typically increases from one year to another. The focus of policy is on the growth *rate*—that is, how fast real GDP increases from one year to the next. Annual growth rates since 1970 have ranged from a high of 7.2 percent (1984) to a low of *minus* 2.8 percent (2009).

Source: *Economic Report of the President, 2014.*

web click

The U.S. Bureau of Economic Analysis (BEA) maintains quarterly data on GDP growth. Visit **www.bea.gov** and search "Overview of the Economy."

lower rate: 2.5 percent per year. The 1990s started out even worse, with negligible growth in 1990 and a recession in 1991. The economy performed a lot better after that, however. From 1997 to 2000, real GDP grew by more than 4.5 percent a year. That acceleration of the growth rate was so impressive that observers began to talk about a "New Economy," in which faster growth would be the norm (see the News below).

IN THE NEWS

The New Economy

The U.S. economy today displays several exceptional features. The first is its strong rate of productivity growth. . . . A second is its unusually low levels of both inflation and unemployment. . . . A third is the disappearance of federal budget deficits. . . . A fourth is the strength of the U.S. economy's performance relative to other industrial economies. . . . These developments reveal profound changes in economic trends that justify the term "New Economy."

Three interrelated factors lie behind these extraordinary economic gains: technological innovation, organizational changes in business, and public policy. . . . The interactions among these three factors have created a virtuous cycle in which developments in one area reinforce and stimulate developments in another. The result is an economic system in which the whole is greater than the sum of the parts. . . .

This Report defines the New Economy by the extraordinary gains in performance—including rapid productivity growth, rising incomes, low unemployment, and moderate inflation—that have resulted from this combination of virtually reinforcing advances in technologies, business practices, and economic policies.

Source: *Economic Report of the President, 2001*, pp. 22–23.

ANALYSIS: The successes of the late 1990s spawned the hope of continuing rapid gains in productivity and GDP growth—a "new" economy. The recession of 2001, coupled with widespread "dot-com" failures, shed doubt on this concept.

The notion of a fast-growth "New Economy" was badly shaken in 2001. In the first quarter of 2001, GDP fell by 0.2 percent and then by 0.6 percent in the second quarter. In the third quarter (which included the September 11 terrorist attacks), real GDP again declined by 1.3 percent.

The recession of 2008–2009 dealt yet another and more formidable blow to the "New Economy" thesis. At the outset of that recession, people feared that the economy was imploding and might *never* recover. People were praying for *zero* growth (i.e., no more declines in output), not the more remote goals of "fast track" growth in the 3–4 percent range. As it turned out, real GDP declined by 2.8 percent in 2009, the biggest one-year drop since 1938.

The Exponential Process. Although the consequences of *negative* growth (e.g., job layoffs, unemployment, pay cuts, home foreclosures) merit headlines, variations in *positive* growth rates usually elicit yawns. Indeed, the whole subject of economic growth looks rather dull when you discover that "big" gains in economic growth are measured in fractions of a percent. However, this initial impression isn't fair. First, even one year's "low" growth implies lost output. If we had just *maintained* output in 2009 at its 2008 level—that is, "achieved" a *zero* growth rate rather than an outright decline—we would have had $300 billion more worth of goods and services, which works out to about $1,000 worth of goods and services per person. In today's $18 trillion economy, each 1 percent of GDP growth translates into roughly $560 more output per person. Lots of people would like that extra output.

Second, economic growth is a *continuing* process. Gains made in one year accumulate in future years. It's like interest you earn at the bank: if you leave your money in the bank for several years, you begin to earn interest on your interest. Eventually you accumulate a nice little bankroll.

The process of economic growth works the same way. Each little shift of the production possibilities curve broadens the base for future GDP. As shifts accumulate over many years, the economy's productive capacity is greatly expanded. Ultimately we discover that those "little" differences in annual growth rates generate tremendous gains in GDP.

This cumulative process, whereby interest or growth is compounded from one year to the next, is called an "exponential process." At growth rates of 2.5 percent, GDP doubles in 29 years. With 3.5 percent growth, GDP doubles in only 21 years. In a single generation the *difference* between 2.5 percent growth and 3.5 percent growth amounts to more than $11 trillion of output. That *difference* is roughly 60 percent of this year's total output. From this longer-term perspective, the difference between 2.5 percent and 3.5 percent growth begins to look very meaningful.

GDP per Capita: A Measure of Living Standards

The exponential process looks even more meaningful when we translate it into *per capita* terms. We can do so by looking at GDP *per capita* rather than total GDP. **GDP per capita** is simply total output divided by total population. In 2013, the total output of the U.S. economy was $16.8 trillion. Since there were 310 million of us to share that output, GDP per capita was

$$\text{GDP per capita} \atop (2013) = \frac{\$16.8 \text{ trillion of output}}{310 \text{ million people}} = \$54,194$$

This does not mean that every man, woman, and child in the United States received $54,194 worth of goods and services in 2013; it simply indicates how much output was potentially available to the "average" person. GDP per capita is often used as a basic measure of our standard of living.

Growth in GDP per capita is attained only when the growth of output exceeds population growth. In the United States, this condition is usually achieved. Even when *total* GDP growth slowed in the 1970s and 1980s, *per capita* GDP kept rising because the U.S.

GDP per capita: Total GDP divided by total population; average GDP.

TABLE 17.1

The Rule of 72

Small differences in annual growth rates cumulate into large differences in GDP. Shown here are the number of years it would take to double GDP per capita at various net growth rates. *"Net"* growth refers to the GDP growth rate minus the population growth rate.

Doubling times can be approximated by the "rule of 72." Seventy-two divided by the growth rate equals the number of years it takes to double.

Net Growth Rate (%)		Doubling Time (Years)
0.0%	⟶	Never
0.5	⟶	144 years
1.0	⟶	72
1.5	⟶	48
2.0	⟶	36
2.5	⟶	29
3.0	⟶	24
3.5	⟶	21
4.0	⟶	18

web click

To see why the rule of 72 works, visit **www.mathworld.com** and search for "rule of 72."

population was growing by only 1 percent a year. Hence even relatively slow economic growth of 2.5 percent a year was enough to keep raising living standards.

The developing nations of the Third World aren't so fortunate. Many of these countries bear both slower *economic* growth and faster *population* growth. They have a difficult time *maintaining* living standards, much less increasing them. Madagascar, for example, is one of the poorest countries in the world, with GDP per capita of roughly $900. Yet its population continues to grow rapidly (2.8 percent per year), putting constant pressure on living standards. In recent years, Madagascar's GDP grew at a slower rate of only 2.0 percent. As a consequence, GDP per capita *declined* nearly 0.8 percent per year. As we'll see in the chapter titled "Global Poverty" many other poor nations are in similarly dire straits.

By comparison with these countries, the United States has been fortunate. Our GDP per capita has more than doubled since the 1980s, despite several recessions. This means that the average person today has twice as many goods and services as the average person had a generation ago.

What about the future? Will we continue to enjoy substantial gains in living standards? Many Americans harbor great doubts. A 2012 poll revealed that 5 out of 10 adults believe their children's living standards will be no higher than today's. That would happen only if population growth outstrips or equals GDP growth. That seems unlikely. Table 17.1 displays more optimistic scenarios in which GDP continues to grow faster than the population. If GDP *per capita* continues to grow at 2 percent per year—as it did in the 1990s—it will take 36 years to double our standard of living. If GDP per capita grows just half a percent faster, say, by 2.5 percent per year, our standard of living will double in only 29 years. Would you like to have that extra output when you're middle-aged?

GDP per Worker: A Measure of Productivity

The potential increases in living standards depicted in Table 17.1 won't occur automatically. Someone is going to have to produce more output if we want GDP per capita to rise. One reason our living standard rose in the 1980s is that the labor force grew faster than the population. Those in the World War II baby boom had reached maturity and were entering the **labor force** in droves. At the same time, more women took jobs outside the home, a trend that continued into the 1990s (see Figure 6.2). As a consequence, the **employment rate** increased significantly, as Figure 17.4 shows. With the number of workers growing faster than the population, GDP per capita was sure to rise.

The employment rate can't increase forever. At the limit, everyone would be in the labor market, and no further workers could be found. As Figure 17.4 reveals, the employment rate peaked in 2000, then dipped substantially in the 2001 recession and even further in the 2008–2009 recession. As the employment rate declines, increases in per capita income

labor force: All persons over age 16 who are either working for pay or actively seeking paid employment.

employment rate: The percentage of the adult population that is employed.

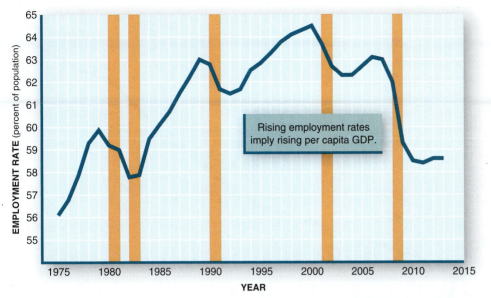

FIGURE 17.4

A Rising Employment Rate

The entry of Baby Boomers (born 1946–1960) into the labor force and increased labor force attachment of women caused the ratio of workers to total population (the employment rate) to rise from 1975 to 2000. This boosted per capita GDP.

Note: Shaded areas indicate recessions.

become more difficult. To offset the decline in the employment rate, we need to increase output per workers.

The most common measure of **productivity** is output per labor-hour, which is simply the ratio of total output to the number of hours worked. As noted earlier, total GDP in 2013 was $16.8 trillion. In that same year 143,929,000 workers were employed. Hence the average worker's productivity was

productivity: Output per unit of input—for example, output per labor-hour.

$$\frac{\text{Labor}}{\text{productivity}} = \frac{\text{Total output}}{\text{Total employment}}$$

$$= \frac{\$16.8 \text{ trillion}}{143,929,000 \text{ workers}}$$

$$= \$116,724$$

This is a *lot* of output per worker! China has many more workers (800 million), but they produce much less output ($12,000) each. So Chinese living standards are far below American standards.

The *increase* in our GDP per capita in recent decades is directly related to the *rising* productivity of the average U.S. worker. The average worker today produces twice as many goods and services as the average worker did in 1980.

The Productivity Turnaround. For economic growth to continue, the productivity of the average U.S. worker must rise still further. Will it? As Figure 17.5 reveals, productivity grew at an average pace of 1.4 percent from 1973 to 1995. Along the way, however, there were many years (e.g., 1978–1984) in which productivity advances slowed to a snail's pace. This productivity slowdown constrained GDP growth.

After 1995 productivity advances accelerated sharply, as shown in Figure 17.5. This productivity jump was so impressive that it raised hopes for a "New Economy" (see the News on page 368), in which technological breakthroughs, better management, and enlightened public policy would keep both productivity and GDP growing at faster rates. Although the economy did stumble into a steep recession in 2008–2009, worker productivity—and thus *potential* output—kept increasing at a fast clip. Recent advances in cloud computing, 3D printing, and robotic manufacturing promise still further gains.

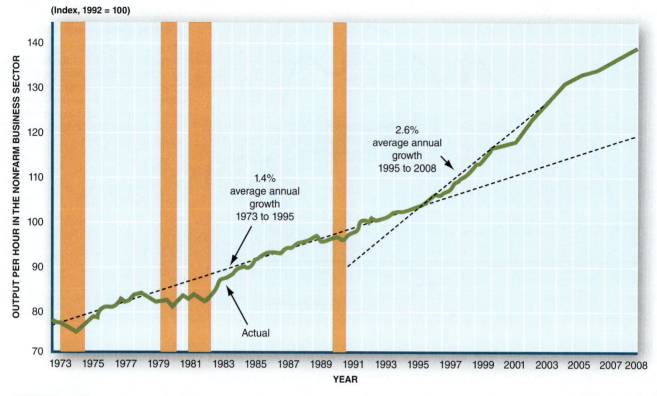

FIGURE 17.5

Productivity Gains

Increasing productivity (output per worker) is the critical factor in raising per capita GDP over time. Productivity advances slowed in 1978–1984 but accelerated sharply in 1995–2008.

Note: Shaded areas indicate recessions.

Source: *U.S. Department of Commerce.*

web click

The U.S. Bureau of Labor Statistics (BLS) maintains quarterly data on labor productivity at **www.bls.gov.** Click the "Subject Areas" tab.

SOURCES OF GROWTH

The arithmetic of economic growth is simple. But what keeps the arithmetic so positive? Future output growth depends on two factors:

$$\begin{array}{c} \text{Growth rate of} \\ \text{total output} \end{array} = \begin{array}{c} \text{Growth rate of} \\ \text{labor force} \end{array} + \begin{array}{c} \text{Growth rate of} \\ \text{productivity} \end{array}$$

Accordingly, how fast GDP increases in the future depends on how fast the labor force grows and how fast productivity advances. Since the long-run growth of the labor force has stabilized at around 1.1 percent, the real uncertainty about future economic growth originates in the unpredictability of productivity advances. Can worker productivity continue to increase at such a fast clip? Forever?

To assess the potential for future productivity gains, we need to examine the sources of productivity improvement. *The sources of productivity gains include*

- *Higher skills:* an increase in labor skills.
- *More capital:* an increase in the ratio of capital to labor.
- *Technological advance:* the development and use of better capital equipment and products.
- *Improved management:* better use of available resources in the production process.

Human Capital Investment

Continuing advances in education and skills training have greatly increased the quality of U.S. labor. In 1950 less than 8 percent of all U.S. workers had completed college. Today

30 percent of the workforce has completed four years of college. There has also been a substantial increase in vocational training, both in the public sector and by private firms.

In the 1970s these improvements in the quality of individual workers were offset by a change in the composition of the labor force. As we observed in Chapter 6, the proportion of teenagers and women in the labor force grew tremendously in the 1960s and 1970s. These Baby Boomers and their mothers contributed to higher output. Because teenagers and women (re)entering the labor market generally have less job experience than adult men, however, *average* productivity fell.

This phenomenon reversed itself in the 1990s as the Baby Boomers reached their prime working years. The increased productivity of the workforce is not a reflection of the aging process itself. Rather, the gains in productivity reflect the greater **human capital** investment associated with more schooling and more on-the-job learning.

human capital: The knowledge and skills possessed by the workforce.

Physical Capital Investment

The knowledge and skills a worker brings to the job don't completely determine his or her productivity. A worker with no tools, no computers, and no machinery won't produce much even if she has a PhD. Similarly, a worker with outmoded equipment won't produce as much as an equally capable worker equipped with the newest machines and the best technology. From this perspective, *a primary determinant of labor productivity is the rate of capital investment.* In other words, improvements in output per *worker* depend in large part on increases in the quantity and quality of *capital* equipment (see the World View below).

WORLD VIEW

High Investment = Fast Growth

Investment in new plants and equipment is essential for economic growth. In general, countries that allocate a larger share of output to investment will grow more rapidly. In recent years, China has had one of the world's fastest GDP growth rates and also one of the highest investment rates.

Country	Gross Investment as Percentage of GDP	Growth Rate of GDP (Average, 2000–2012)
China	51	10.6
India	30	7.7
Vietnam	32	6.6
United States	17	1.7
Greece	10	1.1

Source: *The World Bank*, **www.worldbank.org.**

ANALYSIS: Investment increases production possibilities. Countries that devote a larger share of output to investment tend to grow faster.

U.S. workers are outfitted with an exceptional amount of capital equipment. As we first saw in Chapter 2, U.S. productivity is buttressed by huge investments in equipment and technology. The average U.S. worker is supported by more than $100,000 of capital inputs. To *increase* productivity, however, the quality and quantity of capital available to the average worker must continue to increase. That requires capital spending to increase faster than the labor force. With the labor force growing at 1.1 percent a year, that's not a hard standard to beat. How *much* faster capital investment grows is nevertheless a decisive factor in productivity gains. In the 1990s, investment in information technology (computers, software, and telecommunications equipment) was robust, reaching growth rates as high as 25 percent. In the process, workers got "smarter," communications improved, and productivity jumped. The Council of Economic Advisers credited this boom in information technology investment with nearly one-third of *all* the 1995–1999 GDP growth.

Saving and Investment Rates. The dependence of productivity gains on capital investment puts a new perspective on consumption and saving. In the short run, the primary concern of macroeconomic policy is to balance aggregate demand and aggregate supply. In this context, savings are a form of leakage that requires offsetting injections of investment or government spending. From the longer-run perspective of economic growth, saving and investment take on added importance. *Savings aren't just a form of leakage but a basic source of investment financing.* If we use all our resources to produce consumer, export, and public sector goods, there won't be any investment. In that case, we might not face a short-run stabilization problem—our productive capacity might be fully utilized—but we'd confront a long-run *growth* problem. Indeed, if we consumed our entire output, our productive capacity would actually shrink since we wouldn't even be replacing worn-out plants and equipment. We must have at least enough savings to finance **net investment.**

net investment: Gross investment less depreciation.

Household and Business Saving. Household saving rates in the United States have been notoriously low and falling since the early 1980s. In 2000 and again in 2006, U.S. households actually *dis*saved—spending more on consumption than their disposable incomes. Despite the meager flow of household saving, investment growth actually accelerated in the late 1990s. Virtually all of that investment was financed with *business saving* and *foreign investment.* The retained earnings and depreciation allowances that create business savings generated a huge cash flow for investment in the 1990s. The same cash-rich situation emerged in 2010–2014, setting the stage for another investment surge and faster GDP growth.

Foreign Investment. In addition to this business saving flow, foreign investors continue to pour money into U.S. plants, equipment, software, and financial assets. These two income flows more than compensate for the virtual absence of domestic household saving. Many people worry, though, that foreign investments may get diverted elsewhere and that business saving will drop when profits diminish. If that happens, continued investment growth will be more dependent on a flow of funds from household saving.

Management Training

The accumulation of more and better capital equipment does not itself guarantee higher productivity or faster GDP growth. The human factor is still critical: how well resources are organized and managed will affect the rate of growth. Hence entrepreneurship and the quality of continuing management are also major determinants of economic growth.

It's difficult to characterize differences in management techniques or to measure their effectiveness. However, much attention has been focused in recent years on the alleged shortsightedness of U.S. managers. U.S. firms, it is said, focus too narrowly on short-run profits, neglecting long-term productivity. There is little evidence of such a failure, however. The spreading use of stock options in management ranks ties executives' compensation to multiyear performance. Moreover, productivity trends in the United States not only have accelerated in recent years but also have consistently surpassed productivity gains in other industrial nations (see the World View on the next page). To maintain that advantage, U.S. corporations spend billions of dollars each year on continuing management training. Accordingly, the charge of shortsightedness is better regarded as a precautionary warning than an established fact.

WORLD VIEW

U.S. Workers Compete Well

U.S. workers are the most productive in the world, producing more than $100,000 of output per worker annually. In manufacturing, the U.S. productivity lead continues to widen. Among the 19 industrial nations tracked by the Bureau of Labor Statistics, only two have had faster productivity growth than the United States since 2007.

Annual Growth of Manufactured Output per Hour, 2007–2011

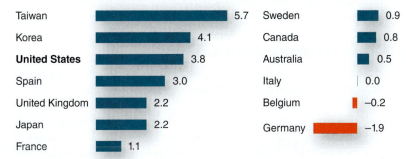

Taiwan	5.7	Sweden	0.9
Korea	4.1	Canada	0.8
United States	3.8	Australia	0.5
Spain	3.0	Italy	0.0
United Kingdom	2.2	Belgium	−0.2
Japan	2.2	Germany	−1.9
France	1.1		

Source: U.S. Bureau of Labor Statistics.

ANALYSIS: U.S. productivity gains are among the fastest of industrial nations. These gains are fueled by research and development and investment spending.

Research and Development

A fourth and vital source of productivity advance is research and development (R&D), a broad concept that includes scientific research, product development, innovations in production techniques, and the development of management improvements. R&D activity may be a specific, identifiable activity such as in a research lab, or it may be part of the process of learning by doing. In either case, the insights developed from R&D generally lead to new products and cheaper ways of producing them. Over time, R&D is credited with the greatest contributions to economic growth. In his study of U.S. growth during the period 1929–1982, Edward Denison concluded that 26 percent of *total* growth was due to "advances in knowledge." Gordon Moore, the cofounder of Intel, doesn't see an end to research-based productivity advance. His "Moore's Law" predicts a *doubling* of computer power every 18 months.

New Growth Theory. The evident contribution of "advances in knowledge" to economic growth has spawned a new perspective called "new growth theory." "Old growth theory," it is said, emphasized the importance of bricks and mortar—that is, saving and investing in new plants and equipment. By contrast, "new" growth theory emphasizes the importance of investing in ideas. Paul Romer, a Stanford economist, asserts that new ideas and the spread of knowledge are the primary engines of growth. Unfortunately, neither Romer nor anyone else is exactly sure how one spawns new ideas or best disseminates knowledge. The only evident policy lever appears to be the support of research and development, a staple of "old" growth theory.

There's an important link between R&D and capital investment. As noted earlier, part of each year's gross investment compensates for the depreciation of existing plants and equipment. However, new machines are rarely identical to the ones they replace. When you get a new computer, you're not just *replacing* an old one; you're *upgrading* your computing capabilities with more memory, faster speed, and a lot of new features. Indeed, the

web click

The National Science Foundation tracks R&D spending. Visit **www.nsf.gov** and click on the "Statistics" tab.

availability of *better* technology is often the motive for such capital investment. The same kind of motivation spurs businesses to upgrade machines and structures. Hence advances in technology and capital investment typically go hand in hand.

POLICY TOOLS

As we've observed, economic growth depends on rightward shifts of the long-run aggregate supply curve (Figure 17.2). It should not surprise you, then, that growth policy makes liberal use of the tools in the supply-side toolbox (Chapter 16). The challenge for growth policy is to select those tools that will give the economy *long*-run increases in productive capacity.

Increasing Human Capital Investment

Since *workers* are the ultimate source of output and productivity growth, the first place to look for growth-accelerating tools is in the area of human capital development.

Education. Governments at all levels already play a tremendous role in human capital development by building, operating, and subsidizing schools. The quantity and quality of continuing investments in America's schools will have a major effect on future productivity. Government policy also plays an *indirect* role in schooling decisions by offering subsidized loans for college and vocational education.

Immigration. Immigration policy is also a determinant of the nation's stock of human capital. At least 1 million immigrants enter the United States every year. Most of the *legal* immigrants are relatives of people already living in the United States as permanent residents (with green cards) or naturalized citizens. In addition to these *family-based* visas, the United States also grants a much smaller number of *employment-based* visas. The H-1B program offers temporary (three-year) visas to highly skilled foreigners who want to work in U.S. firms. By admitting highly skilled workers, the United States gains valuable human capital and relieves some structural unemployment. Only 65,000 H-1B visas are available each year, however—a tiny percent of the U.S. labor force. Temporary visas for agricultural (H-2A) and other less skilled workers (H-2B) are fewer still. To accelerate our productivity and GDP growth, observers urge us to expand these programs.

Increasing Physical Capital Investment

As in the case of human capital, the possibilities for increasing physical capital investment are also many and diverse.

Investment Incentives. The tax code is a mechanism for stimulating investment. Faster depreciation schedules, tax credits for new investments, and lower business tax rates all encourage increased investment in physical capital. The 2002 and 2003 tax cuts were designed for this purpose. President Obama's 2011 stimulus program also provided increased tax incentives (100 percent expensing) for investment in physical capital.

Savings Incentives. In principle, the government can also deepen the savings pool that finances investment. Here again, the tax code offers some policy levers. Tax preferences for individual retirement accounts and other pension savings may increase the marginal propensity to save or at least redirect savings flows to longer-term investments. The Bush 2001 tax package (Chapter 11) included not only a *short-run* fiscal stimulus (e.g., tax rebates) but also enhanced incentives for *long-term* savings (retirement and college savings accounts).

Infrastructure Development. The government also directly affects the level of physical capital through its public works spending. As we observed in Chapter 16, the $2 trillion already invested in bridges, highways, airports, sewer systems, and other infrastructure is an important part of America's capital stock. President Obama's 2009 stimulus program vastly increased spending on roads, bridges, power sources, and educational facilities. Investments of that sort reduce transportation costs, increase market efficiency, reduce environmental impact, and expand potential output.

Fiscal Responsibility. In addition to these many supply-side interventions, the government's *macro* policies also affect the rate of investment and growth. Of particular interest in this regard is the federal government's budget balance. As we've seen, budget deficits may be a useful mechanism for attaining short-run macro stability. Those same deficits, however, may have negative long-run effects. If Uncle Sam borrows more funds from the national savings pool, other borrowers may end up with less. As we saw in Chapter 12, there's no guarantee that federal deficits will result in the **crowding out** of private investment. Let's recognize the risk of such an outcome, however. Hence *fiscal and monetary policies must be evaluated in terms of their impact not only on (short-run) aggregate demand but also on long-run aggregate supply.*

In this regard, the transformation of federal budget deficits to budget surpluses after 1997 facilitated the **crowding in** of private investment. After 1997 more funds were available to private investors and at lower interest rates. This surely contributed to the accelerated growth of capital investment in 1996–2000. Since then, budget balances have swung sharply into the red (see Figure 12.1). Many people feared that the enormous deficits of 2009–2012 would ultimately raise interest rates and crowd out private investment (see the World View below).

crowding out: A reduction in private sector borrowing (and spending) caused by increased government borrowing.

crowding in: An increase in private sector borrowing (and spending) caused by decreased government borrowing.

WORLD VIEW

IMF Warns of Acute Debt Challenges for West

The International Monetary Fund has warned that advanced economies such as the U.K. and U.S. are facing an "acute" challenge in reducing debt loads following the financial crisis, a problem which could in turn hamper economic growth.

John Lipsky, the IMF's first deputy managing director, said that high levels of government debt and fiscal deficits have already led to increased risks for a number of countries.

Mr. Lipsky cautioned that such problems could slow economic growth over the medium term and trigger higher interest rates.

"Maintaining public debt at its post-crisis levels could reduce potential growth in advanced economies by as much as half a percentage point annually compared with pre-crisis performance," he said in a speech in Beijing.

—James Quinn

Source: *The Telegraph*, **www.telegraph.co.uk,** March 22, 2010. © Telegraph Media Group Limited 2010.

ANALYSIS: High levels of national debt may raise interest rates and crowd out investments that promote economic growth.

Maintaining Stable Expectations

The position of the long-run AS curve also depends on a broader assessment of the economic outlook. Expectations are a critical factor in both consumption and investment behavior. People who expect to lose their jobs next year are unlikely to buy a new car or house this year. Likewise, if investors expect interest rates to jump next year, they may be less willing to initiate long-run capital projects.

A sense of political and economic stability is critical to any long-run current trend. Within that context, however, specific perceptions of government policy may also alter investment plans. Investors may look to the Fed for a sense of monetary stability. They may be looking for a greater commitment to long-run price stability than to short-run adjustments of aggregate demand. In the fiscal policy area the same kind of commitment to long-run fiscal discipline rather than to short-run stimulus may be sought. Such possibilities imply that macro policy must be sensitive to long-run expectations.

Institutional Context

Last, but not least, the prospects for economic growth depend on the institutional context of a nation's economy. We first encountered this proposition in Chapter 1. In the World View on page 16, nations were ranked on the basis of an Index of Freedom. Studies have shown how greater economic freedom—secure property rights, open trade, lower taxes, less regulation—typically fosters faster growth. In less regulated economies, there's more scope for entrepreneurship and more opportunity to invest. Recognizing this, nations around the world, from India to China, to Russia, to Latin America, have deregulated industries, privatized state enterprises, and promoted more open trade and investment.

THE ECONOMY TOMORROW

LIMITLESS GROWTH?

Suppose we pulled all the right policy levers and were able to keep the economy on a fast-paced growth track. Could the economy keep growing forever? Wouldn't we use up all available resources and ruin the environment in the process? How much long-term growth is really possible—or even desirable?

The Malthusian Formula for Destruction. The prospect of an eventual limit to economic growth originated in the 18th-century warnings of the Reverend Thomas Malthus. Malthus argued that continued economic growth was impossible because food production couldn't keep pace with population growth. His dire projections earned the economics profession its characterization as the "dismal science."

When Malthus first issued his warnings, in 1798, the population of England (including Wales) was about 9 million. Annual production of barley, oats, and related grains was approximately 162 million bushels, and wheat production was around 50 million bushels, just about enough to feed the English population (a little had to be imported from other countries). Although the relationship between food and population was satisfactory in 1798, Malthus reasoned that starvation was not far off. First of all, he observed that "population, when unchecked, goes on doubling itself every 25 years, or increases in a geometrical ratio."[1] Thus he foresaw the English population increasing to 36 million people by 1850, 144 million by 1900, and more than 1 billion by 1975, unless some social or natural restraints were imposed on population growth.

Limits to Food Production. One natural population check that Malthus foresaw was a scarcity of food. England had only a limited amount of land available for cultivation and was already farming the most fertile tracts. Before long, all available land would be in use, and only improvements in agricultural productivity (output per acre) could increase food supplies. Some productivity increases were possible, Malthus concluded, but "the means of subsistence, under circumstances the most favorable to human industry, could not possibly be made to increase faster than in an arithmetical ratio."[2]

With population increasing at a *geometric* rate and food supplies at an *arithmetic* rate, the eventual outcome is evident. Figure 17.6 illustrates how the difference between a **geometric growth** path and an **arithmetic growth** path ultimately leads to starvation. As Malthus calculated it, per capita wheat output would decline from 5.5 bushels in 1800 to only 1.7 bushels in 1900 (Figure 17.6b). This wasn't enough food to feed the English

geometric growth: An increase in quantity by a constant proportion each year.

arithmetic growth: An increase in quantity by a constant amount each year.

[1]Thomas Malthus, *An Essay on the Principle of Population* (1798; reprint ed., Homewood, IL: Richard D. Irwin, 1963), p. 4.
[2]Ibid., p. 5.

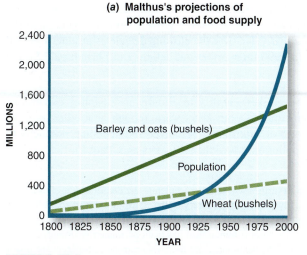

(a) Malthus's projections of population and food supply

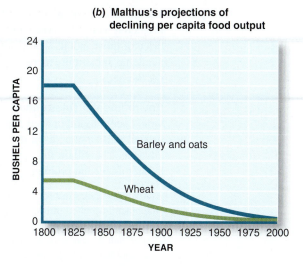

(b) Malthus's projections of declining per capita food output

FIGURE 17.6

The Malthusian Doomsday

By projecting the growth rates of population and food output into the future, Malthus foresaw England's doomsday. At that time, the amount of available food per capita would be too small to sustain

human life. Fortunately, Malthus overestimated population growth and underestimated productivity growth.

Source: Malthus's arithmetic applied to actual data for 1800 (see text).

people. According to Malthus's projections, either England died off about 100 years ago, or it has been maintained at the brink of starvation for more than a century only by recurrent plagues, wars, or the kind of "moral restraint" that's commonly associated with Victorian preachments.

Malthus's logic was impeccable. As long as population increased at a geometric rate while output increased at an arithmetic rate, England's doomsday was as certain as two plus two equals four. Malthus's error was not in his logic but in his empirical assumptions. He didn't know how fast output would increase over time, any more than we know whether people will be wearing electronic wings in the year 2203. He had to make an educated guess about future productivity trends. He based his estimates on his own experiences at the very beginning of the Industrial Revolution. As it turned out (fortunately), he had no knowledge of the innovations that would change the world, and he grossly underestimated the rate at which productivity would increase. *Output, including agricultural products, has increased at a geometric rate, not at the much slower arithmetic rate foreseen by Malthus.* As we observed earlier, U.S. output has grown at a long-term rate of roughly 3 percent a year. This *geometric* growth has doubled output every 25 years or so. That rate of economic growth is more than enough to raise living standards for a population growing by only 1 percent a year.

Resource Constraints. As Yale historian Paul Kennedy has suggested, maybe Malthus's doomsday predictions were just premature, not wrong. Maybe growth will come to a screeching halt when we run out of arable land, water, oil, or some other vital resource.

Malthus focused on arable land as the ultimate resource constraint. Other doomsday prophets have focused on the supply of whale oil, coal, oil, potatoes, and other "essential" resources. All such predictions ignore the role of markets in both promoting more efficient uses of scarce resources and finding substitutes for them. If, for example, the world were really running out of oil, what would happen to oil prices? Oil prices would rise substantially, prompting consumers to use oil more efficiently and prompting producers to develop alternative fuel sources.

If productivity and the availability of substitutes increase fast enough, the price of "scarce" resources might actually fall rather than rise. This possibility prompted a famous "doomsday bet" between University of Maryland business professor Julian Simon and Stanford ecologist Paul Ehrlich. In 1980 Paul Ehrlich identified five metals that he predicted would become so scarce as to slow economic growth. Simon wagered that the price of those metals would actually *decline* over the ensuing decade as productivity and available substitutes increased. In 1990 their prices had fallen, and Ehrlich paid Simon for the bet.

Environmental Destruction. The market's ability to circumvent resource constraints would seem to augur well for our future. Doomsayers warn, though, that other limits to growth will emerge, even in a world of "unlimited" resources and unending productivity advance. The villain this time is pollution. More than 40 years ago, Paul Ehrlich warned about this second problem:

> Attempts to increase food production further will tend to accelerate the deterioration of our environment, which in turn will eventually *reduce* the capacity of the Earth to produce food. It is not clear whether environmental decay has now gone so far as to be essentially irreversible; it is possible that the capacity of the planet to support human life has been permanently impaired. Such technological "successes" as automobiles, pesticides, and inorganic nitrogen fertilizers are major contributors to environmental deterioration.[3]

The "inevitability" of environmental destruction led G. Evelyn Hutchinson to conclude in 1970 that the limits of habitable existence on Earth would be measured "in decades."[4]

It's not difficult for anyone with the basic five senses to comprehend the pollution problem. Pollution is as close these days as the air we breathe. Moreover, we can't fail to observe a distinct tendency for pollution levels to rise along with GDP and population expansion. Scientists are also alarmed by the climate changes that have accompanied population and output growth. If one projects past climate change and pollution trends into the future, things are bound to look pretty ugly.

Although pollution is universally acknowledged to be an important and annoying problem, we can't assume that the *rate* of pollution will continue unabated. On the contrary, the growing awareness of the pollution problem has prompted significant abatement efforts. The Environmental Protection Agency (EPA), for example, is unquestionably a force working for cleaner air and water. Indeed, active policies to curb pollution are as familiar as auto exhaust controls, DDT bans, and tradable CO_2 and SO_2 permits. A computer programmed 10 or 20 years ago to project present pollution levels wouldn't have foreseen these abatement efforts and would thus have overestimated current pollution levels.

This isn't to say that we have in any final way solved the pollution problem or that we're even doing the best job we possibly can. It simply says that geometric increases in pollution aren't inevitable. There's no compelling reason why we have to continue polluting the environment; if we stop, another doomsday can be averted.

The Possibility of Growth. The misplaced focus on doomsday scenarios has a distinct opportunity cost. As Robert Solow summed up the issue,

> My real complaint about the Doomsday school [is that] it diverts attention from the really important things that can actually be done, step by step, to make things better. The end of the world *is* at hand—the earth, if you take the long view, will fall into the sun in a few billion years anyway, unless some other disaster happens first. In the meantime, I think we'd be better off passing a strong sulfur emissions tax, or getting some Highway Trust Fund money allocated to mass transit, or building a humane and decent floor under family incomes, or overriding President Nixon's veto of a strong Water Quality Act, or reforming the tax system, or fending off starvation in Bengal— instead of worrying about the generalized "predicament of mankind."[5]

[3]Paul R. Ehrlich and Anne H. Ehrlich, *Population, Resources, Environment: Issues in Human Ecology,* 2nd ed. (San Francisco: W. H. Freeman, 1972), p. 442.
[4]Evelyn Hutchinson, "The Biosphere," *Scientific American,* September 1970, p. 53; Dennis L. Meadows et al., *The Limits to Growth* (New York: Universe Books, 1972), chapter 4.
[5]Robert M. Solow, "Is the End of the World at Hand?," *Challenge* 16, no. 1 (March/April 1973), p. 50. Copyright © 1973 by M.E. Sharpe, Inc. Used by permission.

Karl Marx expressed these same thoughts nearly a century earlier. Marx chastised "the contemptible Malthus" for turning the attention of the working class away from what he regarded as the immediate problem of capitalist exploitation to some distant and ill-founded anxiety about "natural" disaster.[6]

The Desirability of Growth. Let's concede, then, that continued, perhaps even "limitless," growth is *possible.* Can we also agree that it's *desirable?* Those of us who commute on congested highways, worry about climate change, breathe foul air, and can't find a secluded camping site may raise a loud chorus of nos. But before reaching a conclusion, let's at least determine what it is people don't like about the prospect of continued growth. Is it really economic growth per se that people object to, or instead the specific ways GDP has grown in the past?

First of all, let's distinguish clearly between economic growth and population growth. Congested neighborhoods, dining halls, and highways are the consequence of too many people, not of too many goods and services. Indeed, if we had *more* goods and services—if we had more houses and transit systems—much of the population congestion we now experience might be relieved. Maybe if we had enough resources to meet our existing demands *and* to build a solar-generated "new town" in the middle of Montana, people might move out of the crowded neighborhoods of Chicago and St. Louis. Well, probably not, but at least one thing is certain: with fewer goods and services, more people will have to share any given quantity of output.

This brings us back to the really essential measure of growth: GDP per capita. Are there any serious grounds for desiring *less* GDP per capita, a reduced standard of living? Don't say yes just because you think we already have too many cars on our roads or calories in our bellies. That argument refers to the *mix* of output again and doesn't answer the question of whether we want *any* more goods or services per person. Increasing GDP per capita can take a million forms, including the educational services you're now consuming. The rejection of economic growth per se implies that none of those forms is desirable in the economy tomorrow.

"And so, extrapolating from the best figures available, we see that current trends, unless dramatically reversed, will inevitably lead to a situation in which the sky will fall."

Analysis: Most doomsday predictions fail to recognize the possibilities for behavioral change—or the role of market incentives in encouraging it.

[6]Cited by John Maddox in *The Doomsday Syndrome* (New York: McGraw-Hill, 1972), pp. 40 and 45.

Theory versus Reality

After reading this chapter, you should know

LO18-1 The tools of macro policy.

LO18-2 How macro tools should work.

LO18-3 The constraints on policy effectiveness.

There are no all-powerful, all-knowing superheroes . . . who can rescue . . . the economy all by themselves. You might think that the federal government could revive the economy quickly . . . or that the Fed could fix it. . . . But Washington has far less power over the economy . . . than many people think. We always think there's a person who holds the magic wand. But this society and this economy are far too complex to be susceptible to magic wands.

—Senator Judd Gregg, *Fortune*, November 1, 2010.

Macroeconomic theory is supposed to explain the business cycle and show policymakers how to control it. But something is obviously wrong. Despite our relative prosperity, we haven't consistently achieved the goals of full employment, price stability, and vigorous economic growth. All too often, either unemployment or inflation surges or economic growth slows down. No matter how hard we try to eliminate it, the business cycle seems to persist, as we witnessed again in the last few years.

What accounts for this gap between the promises of economic theory and the reality of economic performance? Are the theories inadequate? Or is sound economic advice being ignored?

Many people blame the economists. They point to the conflicting advice of Keynesians, monetarists, and supply-siders and wonder what theory is supposed to be followed. If economists themselves can't agree, it is asked, why should anyone else listen to them?

Not surprisingly, economists see things a bit differently. First, they point out, the **business cycle** isn't as bad as it used to be. Since World War II, the economy has had many ups and downs, but none as severe as the Great Depression or earlier catastrophes. Second, economists complain that politics often takes precedence over good economic advice. Politicians are reluctant, for example, to raise taxes, cut spending, or slow money growth to control inflation. Their concern is winning the next election, not solving the country's economic problems.

When President Jimmy Carter was in office, he anguished over another problem: the complexity of economic decision making. In the real world, neither theory nor politics can keep up with all our economic goals. As President Carter observed, "We cannot concentrate just on inflation or just on unemployment or just on deficits in the federal budget or our international payments. Nor can we act in isolation from other countries. We must deal with all of these problems simultaneously and on a worldwide basis."

No president learned this lesson faster or more forcefully than George W. Bush. Just as he was putting the final touches on a bipartisan consensus on taxes, spending, and debt reduction, terrorists destroyed the World Trade Center and damaged the Pentagon. In response to those attacks, all major economic policy decisions had to be revised. President Obama also had to revise his economic plans as soon as he took office. An acceleration of the 2008–2009 downturn forced him to abandon promised tax increases on the rich and instead fashion a fiscal stimulus package.

As if the burdens of a continuously changing world weren't enough, the president must also contend with sharply differing economic theories and advice, a slow and frequently hostile Congress, a massive and often unresponsive bureaucracy, and a complete lack of knowledge about the future.

This chapter confronts these and other frustrations of the real world head on. In so doing, we provide answers to the following questions:

- **What's the ideal "package" of macro policies?**
- **How well does our macro performance live up to the promises of that package?**
- **What kinds of obstacles prevent us from doing better?**

The answers to these questions may shed some light on a broader concern that has long troubled students and policymakers alike—namely, "If economists are so smart, why is the economy always in such a mess?"

business cycle: Alternating periods of economic growth and contraction.

POLICY TOOLS

Table 18.1 summarizes the macroeconomic tools available to policymakers. Although this list is brief, we hardly need a reminder at this point of how powerful each instrument can be. Every one of these major policy instruments can significantly change our answers to the basic economic questions of WHAT, HOW, and FOR WHOM to produce.

Fiscal Policy

The basic tools of **fiscal policy** are contained in the federal budget. Tax cuts are supposed to increase aggregate demand by putting more income in the hands of consumers and businesses. Tax increases are intended to curtail spending and reduce inflationary pressures. Table 18.2 summarizes some of the major tax changes of recent years.

The expenditure side of the federal budget is another fiscal policy tool. From a Keynesian perspective, increases in government spending raise aggregate demand and so encourage more production. A slowdown in government spending is supposed to restrain aggregate demand and lessen inflationary pressures.

fiscal policy: The use of government taxes and spending to alter macroeconomic outcomes.

Who Makes Fiscal Policy? As we first observed in Chapter 11, changes in taxes and government spending originate in both economic events and explicit policy decisions. When

Type of Policy	Policy Tools
Fiscal policy	• Tax cuts and increases. • Changes in government spending.
Monetary policy	• Open market operations. • Reserve requirements. • Discount rates.
Supply-side policy	• Tax incentives for investment and saving. • Deregulation. • Human capital investment. • Infrastructure development. • Free trade. • Immigration.

TABLE 18.1

The Policy Tools

Economic policymakers have access to a variety of policy instruments. The challenge is to choose the right tools at the right time.

TABLE 18.2
Fiscal Policy Milestones

Fiscal policy is contained in tax and spending legislation approved by Congress. These are some significant decisions.

web click

The Library of Congress maintains a summary of recent congressional tax legislation at **http://thomas.loc.gov.** Search for "taxes."

1986	Tax Reform Act	Major reduction in tax rates coupled with broadening of tax base.
1990	Budget Enforcement Act	Limits set on discretionary spending; pay-as-you-go financing required.
1993	Clinton "New Direction"	Tax increases and spending cuts to achieve $300 billion deficit reduction.
1994	Contract with America	Republican-led Congress cuts spending, sets seven-year target for balanced budget.
1997	Balanced Budget Act, Taxpayer Relief Act	Package of tax cuts and spending cuts to balance budget by 2002.
2001	Economic Growth and Tax Relief Act	Eight-year, $1.35 trillion in personal tax cuts.
2002	Job Creation and Worker Assistance Act	Business investment tax cuts.
2003	Jobs and Growth Tax Relief Act	Cuts in dividend and capital gains taxes.
2008	Economic Stimulus Act	$168 billion of tax rebates.
2009	American Recovery and Reinvestment Act	$787 billion package of spending and tax cuts.
2010	Continuing Resolution	Extension of tax cuts, unemployment benefits, spending until 2012, plus one-year payroll tax cut.
2011	Deficit Reduction	Package of spending cuts and tax hikes to reduce deficit.
2012	Taxpayer Relief Act	Raised income, estate, gift, and capital gains tax rates on high incomes.

automatic stabilizer: Federal expenditure or revenue item that automatically responds countercyclically to changes in national income, like unemployment benefits and income taxes.

structural deficit: Federal revenues at full employment minus expenditures at full employment under prevailing fiscal policy.

fiscal stimulus: Tax cuts or spending hikes intended to increase (shift) aggregate demand.

fiscal restraint: Tax hikes or spending cuts intended to reduce (shift) aggregate demand.

monetary policy: The use of money and credit controls to influence macroeconomic outcomes.

natural rate of unemployment: The long-term rate of unemployment determined by structural forces in labor and product markets.

the economy slows, tax revenues decline, and government spending increases automatically. Conversely, when real GDP grows, tax revenues automatically rise, and government transfer payments decline. These **automatic stabilizers** are a basic countercyclical feature of the federal budget. They don't represent active fiscal policy. On the contrary, *fiscal policy refers to deliberate changes in tax or spending legislation.* These changes can be made only by the U.S. Congress. Every year the president proposes specific budget and tax changes, negotiates with Congress, then accepts or vetoes specific acts that Congress has passed. The resulting policy decisions represent "discretionary" fiscal policy. Those policy decisions expand or shrink the **structural deficit** and thus give the economy a shot of **fiscal stimulus** or **fiscal restraint.**

Monetary Policy

The policy arsenal in Table 18.1 also contains monetary tools. Tools of **monetary policy** include open market operations, discount rate changes, and reserve requirements.

As we saw in Chapter 15, there are disagreements over how these monetary tools should be used. Keynesians believe that interest rates are the critical policy lever. In their view, the money supply should be expanded or curtailed to achieve whatever interest rate is needed to shift aggregate demand. Monetarists, on the other hand, contend that the money supply itself is the critical policy tool and that it should be expanded at a steady and predictable rate. This policy, they believe, will ensure price stability and a **natural rate of unemployment.**

Who Makes Monetary Policy? Actual monetary policy decisions are made by the Federal Reserve's Board of Governors. Twice a year the Fed provides Congress with a broad overview of the economic outlook and monetary objectives. The Fed's assessment of the economy is updated at meetings of the Federal Open Market Committee (FOMC). The FOMC decides which monetary policy levers to pull.

October 1979	Fed adopts monetarist approach, focusing exclusively on money supply; interest rates soar.
July 1982	Deep into recession, Fed votes to ease monetary restraint.
October 1982	Fed abandons pure monetarist approach and expands money supply rapidly.
May 1983	Fed reverses policy and begins slowing money supply growth.
1985	Fed increases money supply with discount rate cuts and open market purchases.
1987	Fed abandons money supply targets as policy guides; money supply growth decreases; discount rate increases.
1989	Greenspan announces goal of "zero inflation," tightens policy.
1991	Deep in recession, the Fed begins to ease monetary restraint.
1994	Fed slows M2 growth to 1 percent; raises federal funds rate by three percentage points as economy nears full employment.
1995	Greenspan trumpets "soft landing" and eases monetary restraint.
1998	Fed cuts interest rates to cushion United States from Asian crisis.
1999–2000	Fed raises interest rates six times.
2001–2003	Fed cuts interest rates 13 times.
2004–2006	Fed raises fed funds rate 17 times.
2007–2008	Fed cuts interest rates 10 times.
2008–2009	Treasury acquires partial ownership of failing banks; FDIC increases deposit guarantees.
2008–2014	Three rounds of "quantitative easing": Fed buys more than $2 trillion of bonds and securities directly from banks.
November 2014	Quantitative easing ends

TABLE 18.3
Monetary Policy Milestones

Monetary policy is set by the Federal Reserve Board of Governors.

Table 18.3 depicts milestones in recent monetary policy. Of particular interest is the October 1979 decision to adopt a pure monetarist approach. This involved an exclusive focus on the money supply, without regard for interest rates. After interest rates soared and the economy appeared on the brink of a depression, the Fed abandoned the monetarist approach and again began keeping an eye on both interest rates (the Keynesian focus) and the money supply.

Monetarists contend that the Fed never fully embraced their policy. The money supply grew at a very uneven pace in 1980, they argue, not at the steady, predictable rate that they demanded. Nevertheless, the policy shifts of 1979 and 1982 were distinctive and had dramatic effects.

A quick review of Table 18.3 reveals that such monetary policy reversals have been quite frequent. There were U-turns in monetary policy between 1982 and 1983, 1989 and 1991, 1998 and 1999, 2000 and 2001, 2003 and 2004, and again between 2007 and 2008.

In November 2008 the Fed began massive purchases of long-term Treasury bonds and other securities, hoping to bring down long-term interest rates (especially mortgage rates). This first round of "quantitative easing" (QE1) ended in March 2010. When the economic recovery started to look wobbly later that year, the Fed pursued a second round (QE2) of massive ($600 billion) bond purchases from November 2010 to June 2011 and a third round (QE3) from September 2012 to the end of 2014. Monetarists were horrified, fearing that such a huge increase in M would ultimately ignite inflation (P).

Supply-Side Policy

Supply-side theory offers the third major set of policy tools. The focus of **supply-side policy** is to provide incentives to work, invest, and produce. Of particular concern are high tax rates and regulations that reduce supply incentives. Supply-siders argue that marginal tax rates and government regulation must be reduced to get more output without added inflation.

In the 1980s tax rates were reduced dramatically. The maximum marginal tax rate on individuals was cut from 70 to 50 percent in 1981, and then still further, to 28 percent, in

supply-side policy: The use of tax incentives, (de)regulation, and other mechanisms to increase the ability and willingness to produce goods and services.

TABLE 18.4

Supply-Side Milestones

Tax and regulatory decisions affect supply decisions.

Year	Act	Description
1990	Social Security Act amendments	Increased payroll tax to 7.65 percent.
	Americans with Disabilities Act	Required employers to provide greater access for disabled individuals.
	Immigration Act	Increased immigration, especially for highly skilled workers.
	Clean Air Act amendments	Increased pollution controls.
1993	Rebuild America Program	Increased spending on infrastructure and human capital investment.
	Family Leave Act	Required employers to provide unpaid leaves of absence for workers.
	NAFTA	Lowered North American trade barriers.
1994	GATT renewed	Lowered world trade barriers.
1996	Telecommunications Act	Permitted greater competition in cable and telephone industries.
	Personal Responsibility and Work Opportunity Act	Required more welfare recipients to work.
1997	Taxpayer Relief Act	Created tuition tax credits; cut capital gains tax.
1998	Workforce Investment Act	Increased funds for skills training.
2000	Transportation Equity Act	Provided new funding for highways, rails.
2001	Economic Growth and Tax Relief Act	Increased savings incentives; reduced marginal tax rates.
2002	Job Creation and Worker Assistance Act	Provided more tax incentives for investment.
2003	Jobs and Growth Tax Relief Act	Reduced taxes on capital gains and dividends.
2007	Minimum wage hike	Raised from $5.15 to $7.15 in 2009.
2009	American Recovery and Reinvestment Act	Infrastructure and energy development.
2010	Affordable Care and Dodd-Frank Acts	Raised costs and reduced incentives for labor supply, labor demand, and bank lending

1987. The 1980s also witnessed major milestones in the deregulation of airlines, trucking, telephone service, and other industries.

Some of the momentum toward less regulation was reversed during the 1990s (see Table 18.4). New regulatory costs on business were created by the Americans with Disabilities Act, the 1990 amendments to the Clean Air Act, and the Family Leave Act of 1993. All three laws provide important benefits to workers or the environment. At the same time, however, they make supplying goods and services more expensive.

The Obama administration broadened supply-side efforts to include infrastructure development and increased investment in human capital (through education and skill training programs). These activities increase the capacity to produce and so shift the aggregate supply curve rightward. The Obama administration also toughened environmental regulation, however, and introduced new regulations on bank lending (Dodd-Frank) and health care (Affordable Care Act) that shifted the aggregate supply curve leftward.

Who Makes Supply-Side Policy? Because tax rates are a basic tool of supply-side policy, fiscal and supply-side policies are often intertwined. When Congress changes the tax laws, it almost always alters marginal tax rates and thus changes production incentives. Notice, for example, that tax legislation appears in Table 18.4 as well as in Table 18.2. The Taxpayer Relief Act of 1997 not only changed total tax revenues (fiscal policy) but also restructured production and investment incentives (supply-side policy). The 2001–2003 tax cuts also had both demand-side and supply-side provisions.

Supply-side and fiscal policies also interact on the outlay side of the budget. The Transportation Equity Act of 2000, for example, authorized accelerated public works spending (fiscal stimulus) on infrastructure development (increase in supply capacity). The infrastructure and alternative energy development included in President Obama's Recovery and Reinvestment program also affected both aggregate demand and aggregate supply. ***Deciding whether to increase spending is a fiscal policy decision; deciding how to spend available funds may entail supply-side policy.***

Regulatory policy is also fashioned by Congress. The president and executive agencies play a critical role in this supply-side area in the day-to-day decisions on how to interpret and enforce regulatory policies.

IDEALIZED USES

These fiscal, monetary, and supply-side tools are potentially powerful levers for controlling the economy. In principle, they can cure the excesses of the business cycle and promote faster economic growth. To see how, let's review their use in three distinct macroeconomic settings.

Case 1: Recession

When output and employment levels fall far short of the economy's full-employment potential, the mandate for public policy is clear. Aggregate demand must be increased so that producers can sell more goods, hire more workers, and move the economy toward its productive capacity. At such times the most urgent need is to get people back to work and close the **recessionary GDP gap.**

recessionary GDP gap: The amount by which equilibrium GDP falls short of full-employment GDP.

How can the government end a recession? Keynesians emphasize the need to increase aggregate demand by cutting taxes or boosting government spending. The resulting stimulus will set off a **multiplier** reaction. If the initial stimulus and multiplier are large enough, the recessionary GDP gap can be closed, propelling the economy to full employment.

multiplier: The multiple by which an initial change in aggregate spending will alter total expenditure after an infinite number of spending cycles; $1/(1 - \text{MPC})$.

Modern Keynesians acknowledge that monetary policy might also help. Specifically, increases in the money supply may lower interest rates and thus give investment spending a further boost. To give the economy a really powerful stimulus, we might want to pull all these policy levers at the same time. That's what the government did in early 2001—using tax cuts, lower interest rates, and increased spending to jump-start the economy (see the accompanying cartoon). The same one-two punch was used again, on a much more massive scale, in 2008–2010.

Analysis: When the economy is flat on its back, it may need both monetary and fiscal stimulus. Fed Chairman Alan Greenspan and President George W. Bush applied stimulus in 2001. Fed Chairman Ben Bernanke and President Obama did the same in 2008–2010.

velocity of money (V): The number of times per year, on average, that a dollar is used to purchase final goods and services; $PQ \div M$.

Monetarists would proceed differently. First, they see no point in toying with the federal budget. In the pure monetarist model, changes in taxes or government spending may alter the mix of output but not its level. So long as the **velocity of money (V)** is constant, fiscal policy doesn't matter. In this view, the appropriate policy response to a recession is patience. As sales and output slow, interest rates will decline, and new investment will be stimulated.

Supply-siders emphasize the need to improve production incentives. They urge cuts in marginal tax rates on investment and labor. They also look for ways to reduce government regulation. Finally, they urge that any increase in government spending (fiscal stimulus) focus on long-run capacity expansion such as infrastructure development.

Case 2: Inflation

inflationary GDP gap: The amount by which equilibrium GDP exceeds full-employment GDP.

An overheated economy provides as clear a policy mandate as does a sluggish one. In this case, the immediate goal is to restrain aggregate demand until the rate of total expenditure is compatible with the productive capacity of the economy. This entails shifting the aggregate demand curve to the left to close the **inflationary GDP gap.** Keynesians would do this by raising taxes and cutting government spending. Keynesians would also see the desirability of increasing interest rates to curb investment spending.

Monetarists would simply cut the money supply. In their view, the short-run aggregate supply curve is unknown and unstable. The only predictable response is reflected in the vertical, long-run aggregate supply curve. According to this view, changes in the money supply alter prices, not output. Inflation is seen simply as "too much money chasing too few goods." Monetarists would turn off the money spigot. The Fed's job in this situation isn't only to reduce money supply growth but to convince market participants that a more cautious monetary policy will be continued. This was the intent of Chairman Greenspan's 1989 public commitment to zero inflation (Table 18.3).

Supply-siders would point out that inflation implies both "too much money" *and* "not enough goods." They'd look at the supply side of the market for ways to expand productive capacity. In a highly inflationary setting, they'd propose more incentives to save. The additional savings would automatically reduce consumption while creating a larger pool of investable funds. Supply-siders would also cut taxes and regulations that raise production costs and lower import barriers that keep out cheaper foreign goods.

Case 3: Stagflation

stagflation: The simultaneous occurrence of substantial unemployment and inflation.

Although serious inflations and recessions provide clear mandates for economic policy, there's a vast gray area between these extremes. Occasionally the economy suffers from both inflation and unemployment at the same time, a condition called **stagflation.** In 1980, for example, the unemployment rate (7.1 percent) and the inflation rate (12.5 percent) were both too high. With an upward-sloping aggregate supply curve, the easy policy options were foreclosed. If aggregate demand were stimulated to reduce unemployment, the resultant pressure on prices might fuel the existing inflation. And if fiscal and monetary restraints were used to reduce inflationary pressures, unemployment might worsen. In such a situation, there are no simple solutions.

Knowing the causes of stagflation will help achieve the desired balance. If prices are rising before full employment is reached, some degree of structural unemployment is likely. An appropriate policy response might include more vocational training in skill shortage areas as well as a redirection of aggregate demand toward labor surplus sectors.

High tax rates or costly regulations might also contribute to stagflation. If either constraint exists, high prices (inflation) may not be a sufficient incentive for increased output. In this case, reductions in tax rates and regulation might help reduce both unemployment and inflation, which is the basic strategy of supply-side policies.

Stagflation may also arise from a temporary contraction of aggregate supply that both reduces output and drives up prices. In this case, neither structural unemployment nor excessive demand is the culprit. Rather, an "external shock" (such as a natural disaster or a terrorist attack) or an abrupt change in world trade (such as a spike in oil prices) is likely to be the cause of the policy dilemma. Accordingly, none of our familiar policy tools is likely to provide a complete "cure." In most cases, the economy simply has to adjust to a temporary setback.

Fine-Tuning

The apparently inexhaustible potential of public policy to alter the economy's performance has often generated optimistic expectations about the efficacy of fiscal, monetary, and supply-side tools. In the early 1960s such optimism pervaded even the highest levels of government. Those were the days when prices were relatively stable, unemployment rates were falling, the economy was growing rapidly, and preparations were being made for the first trip into space. The potential of economic policy looked great indeed. It was also during the 1960s that a lot of people (mostly economists) spoke of the potential for **fine-tuning,** or altering economic outcomes to fit very exacting specifications. Flexible responses to changing market conditions, it was argued, could ensure fulfillment of our economic goals. The prescription was simple: When unemployment is the problem, simply give the economy a jolt of fiscal or monetary stimulus; when inflation is worrisome, simply tap on the fiscal or monetary brakes. To fulfill our goals for content and distribution, simply pick the right target for stimulus or restraint. With a little attention and experience, the right speed could be found and the economy guided successfully down the road to prosperity. As the economic expansion of the 1990s stretched into the record books, the same kind of economic mastery was claimed. More than a few prominent economists claimed the business cycle was dead.

fine-tuning: Adjustments in economic policy designed to counteract small changes in economic outcomes; continuous responses to changing economic conditions.

Analysis: There are different theories about when and how the government should "fix" the economy. Policymakers must decide which advice to follow in specific situations.

THE ECONOMIC RECORD

The economy's track record doesn't live up to these high expectations. To be sure, the economy has continued to grow, and we've attained an impressive standard of living. We can't lose sight of the fact that our per capita income greatly exceeds the realities and even the expectations in most other countries of the world. Nevertheless, we must also recognize that our economic history is punctuated by periods of recession, high unemployment, inflation, and recurring concern for the distribution of income and mix of output. The Great Recession of 2008–2009 was our latest lesson in humility.

The graphs in Figure 18.1 provide a quick summary of the gap between the theory and reality of economic policy. The Employment Act of 1946 committed the federal government to macro stability. It's evident that we haven't kept that commitment. In the 1970s we rarely came close. Although we approached all three goals in the mid-1980s, our achievements were short-lived. Economic growth ground to a halt in 1989, and the economy slipped into yet another recession in 1990. Although inflation stayed low, unemployment rates jumped.

The economy performed very well again from 1992 until early 2000. After that, however, growth came to an abrupt halt again. With the economy teetering on recession, the unemployment rate started rising in mid-2000. Some of the people who had proclaimed the business cycle to be dead were out of work. Then the economy was hit by the external shock of a terrorist attack that suspended economic activity and shook investor and consumer confidence. It took two years to get unemployment rates back down into the "full-employment" range (4–6 percent). The cycle began to reverse at the end of 2007, leading to the recession of 2008–2009. Unemployment rose to 10 percent and stayed very high for five years.

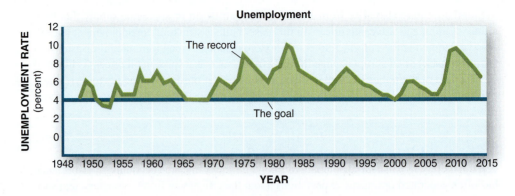

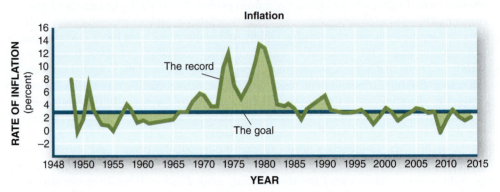

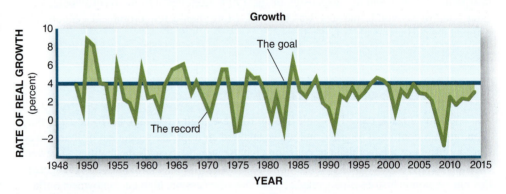

FIGURE 18.1

The Economic Record

The Full Employment and Balanced Growth Act of 1978 established specific goals for unemployment (4 percent), inflation (3 percent), and economic growth (4 percent). We've rarely attained those goals, however, as these graphs illustrate. Measurement, design, and policy implementation problems help explain these shortcomings.

Source: U.S. Bureaus of Labor Statistics and Economic Analysis.

growth recession: A period during which real GDP grows, but at a rate below the long-term trend of 3 percent.

Looking back over the entire postwar (1946–) period, the record includes 12 years of outright recession (actual declines in output) and another 17 years of **growth recession** (growth of less than 3 percent). That adds up to a 43 percent macro failure rate. Moreover, the distribution of income in 2014 looked worse than that of 1946, and more than 40 million people were still officially counted as poor in the later year.

Despite many setbacks, recent economic performance of the United States has been better than that of other Western nations. Other economies haven't grown as fast as the United States nor reduced unemployment as much. But as the World View on the next page shows, some countries did a better job of restraining prices.

WORLD VIEW

Comparative Macro Performance

The performance of the U.S. economy in the 2000s was better than that of most developed economies. Japan had the greatest success in restraining inflation (*minus* 3.5 percent) but suffered from sluggish growth (7.4 percent in an entire decade). The United States grew faster and also experienced less unemployment than most European countries.

Performance, 2000–2010	U.S.	Japan	Germany	United Kingdom	France	Canada
Real growth (10-year increase)	18.0	7.4	8.8	14.9	12.4	20.4
Inflation (10-year change)	26.6	−3.5	17.4	30.0	12.0	22.1
Unemployment (annual average)	6.5	5.2	9.3	6.2	9.8	7.8

Source: International Monetary Fund, *World Economic Outlook, 2011*, **www.imf.org.**

ANALYSIS: Macroeconomic performance varies a lot both over time and across countries. In the 2000s U.S. economic performance was above average on most measures.

WHY THINGS DON'T ALWAYS WORK

There's plenty of blame to go around for the many blemishes on our economic record. Some people blame the president; others blame the Fed or Congress; still others blame China or Mexico. Some forces, however, constrain economic policy even when no one is specifically to blame. In this regard, we can distinguish *four obstacles to policy success:*

- *Goal conflicts.*
- *Measurement problems.*
- *Design problems.*
- *Implementation problems.*

Goal Conflicts

The first factor to take note of is potential conflicts in policy priorities. President Clinton had to confront this problem his first day in office. He had pledged to create new jobs by increasing public infrastructure spending and offering a middle-class tax cut. He had also promised to reduce the deficit, however. This created a clear goal conflict. In the end, President Clinton had to settle for a smaller increase in infrastructure spending and a tax *increase.* President George W. Bush confronted similar problems. In the 2000 presidential campaign he had promised a big increase in federal spending on education. By the time he took office, however, the federal budget surplus was rapidly shrinking, and the goal of preserving the surplus took precedence. The conflict between spending priorities and budget balancing became much more intense when President Bush decided to attack Iraq. We also noted earlier how President Obama had to set aside some campaign promises (e.g., raising taxes on capital gains, estates, and "the rich") when confronted on day 1 with the urgent need to stimulate aggregate demand.

These and other goal conflicts have their roots in the short-run trade-off between unemployment and inflation. With aggressive use of fiscal and monetary stimulus, we can surely increase AD and move the economy toward full employment. But we might set off a multiplier process that pushes the economy past its **inflationary flashpoint.** In view of that risk, should we try to cure inflation, unemployment, or just a bit of both? Answers are likely to vary. Unemployed people put the highest priority on attaining full employment. Labor unions press for faster economic growth. Bankers, creditors, and people on fixed incomes demand an end to inflation.

inflationary flashpoint: The rate of output at which inflationary pressures intensify; point on AS curve where slope increases sharply.

This goal conflict is often institutionalized in the decision-making process. The Fed is traditionally viewed as the guardian of price stability. The president and Congress worry more about people's jobs and government programs, so they are less willing to raise taxes or cut spending.

Distributional goals may also conflict with macro objectives. Anti-inflationary policies may require cutbacks in programs for the poor, the elderly, or needy students. These cutbacks may be politically impossible. Likewise, tight-money policies may be viewed as too great a burden for small businesses, home builders, and auto manufacturers.

Although the policy tools in Table 18.1 are powerful, they can't grant all our wishes. Since we still live in a world of scarce resources, *all policy decisions entail opportunity costs,* which means that we'll always be confronted with trade-offs. The best we can hope for is a set of compromises that yields *optimal* outcomes, not ideal ones.

Measurement Problems

One reason firefighters are pretty successful in putting out fires before entire cities burn down is that fires are highly visible phenomena. But such visibility isn't characteristic of economic problems. An increase in the unemployment rate from 5 to 6 percent, for example, isn't the kind of thing you notice while crossing the street. Unless you work in the unemployment insurance office or lose your own job, the increase in unemployment isn't likely to attract your attention. The same is true of prices; small increases in product prices aren't likely to ring many alarms. Hence both inflation and unemployment may worsen considerably before anyone takes serious notice. Were we as slow and ill-equipped to notice fires, whole neighborhoods would burn before someone rang the alarm.

Measurement problems are a very basic policy constraint. To formulate appropriate economic policy, we must first determine the nature of our problems. To do so, we must measure employment changes, output changes, price changes, and other macro outcomes. The old adage that governments are willing and able to solve only those problems they can measure is relevant here. Indeed, before the Great Depression, a fundamental constraint on public policy was the lack of statistics on what was happening in the economy. One lasting benefit of that experience is that we now try to keep informed on changing economic conditions. The information at hand, however, is always dated and incomplete. *At best, we know what was happening in the economy last month or last week.* The processes of data collection, assembly, and presentation take time, even in this age of high-speed computers. The average recession lasts about 11 months, but official data generally don't even confirm the existence of a recession until 8 months after a downturn starts! As the accompanying News reveals, the 2008–2009 recession ended 15 months before researchers confirmed its demise!

IN THE NEWS

Great Recession Officially Ended Last Year

CAMBRIDGE September 20, 2010—The Business Cycle Dating Committee of the National Bureau of Economic Research met yesterday by conference call. At its meeting, the committee determined that a trough in business activity occurred in the U.S. economy in June 2009. The trough marks the end of the recession that began in December 2007 and the beginning of an expansion. The recession lasted 18 months, which makes it the longest of any recession since World War II. Previously the longest postwar recessions were those of 1973–75 and 1981–82, both of which lasted 16 months. . . .

A recession is a period of falling economic activity spread across the economy, lasting more than a few months, normally visible in real GDP, real income, employment, industrial production, and wholesale-retail sales. The trough marks the end of the declining phase and the start of the rising phase of the business cycle.

Source: National Bureau of Economic Research, September 20, 2010.

ANALYSIS: In the absence of timely information, today's policy decisions are inevitably based on yesterday's perceptions.

Forecasts. In an ideal world, policymakers wouldn't just *respond* to economic problems but would also *anticipate* their occurrence. If an inflationary GDP gap is emerging, for example, we want to take immediate action to keep aggregate spending from increasing. That is, the successful firefighter not only responds to a fire but also looks for hazards that might start one.

Unfortunately, economic policymakers are again at a disadvantage. Their knowledge of future problems is even worse than their knowledge of current problems. *In designing policy, policymakers must depend on economic forecasts*—that is, informed guesses about what the economy will look like in future periods.

Macro Models. Those guesses are often based on complex computer models of how the economy works. These models—referred to as *econometric macro models*—are mathematical summaries of the economy's performance. The models try to identify the key determinants of macro performance and then show what happens to macro outcomes when they change. The apparent precision of such computer models may disguise inherent guesswork, however.

An economist "feeds" the computer two essential inputs. One is a quantitative model of how the economy allegedly works. A Keynesian model, for example, includes equations that show multiplier spending responses to tax cuts. A monetarist model shows that tax cuts raise interest rates, not total spending ("crowding out"), and a supply-side model stipulates labor supply and production responses. The computer can't tell which theory is right; it just predicts what it's programmed to see. In other words, the computer sees the world through the eyes of its economic master.

The second essential input in a computer forecast is the assumed values for critical variables. A Keynesian model, for example, must specify how large a multiplier to expect. All the computer does is carry out the required mathematical routines, once it's told that the multiplier is relevant and what its value is. It can't discern the true multiplier any better than it can pick the right theory.

Given the dependence of computers on the theories and perceptions of their economic masters, it's not surprising that computer forecasts often differ greatly. It's also not surprising that they're often wrong. Even policymakers who are familiar with both economic theory and computer models can make some pretty bad calls. In January 1990 Fed chairman Alan Greenspan assured Congress that the risk of a recession was as low as 20 percent. Although he said he "wouldn't bet the ranch" on such a low probability, he was confident that the odds of a recession were below 50 percent. Five months after his testimony, the 1990–1991 recession began. Greenspan's successor, Ben Bernanke, lost the same bet in 2008 (see the News below).

IN THE NEWS

No Recession, Bernanke Says

WASHINGTON—Federal Reserve Chairman Ben Bernanke said Thursday that the United States will avoid a recession. . . .

In his first public comments since the Fed slashed interest rates in January, the chairman said a softer job market, high energy prices, stock market turmoil, and declining home values likely were weighing on consumers. Their spending accounts for more than two-thirds of all U.S. economic activity.

"My baseline outlook involves a period of sluggish growth, followed by a somewhat stronger pace of growth starting later this year as the effects of (Fed) and fiscal stimulus begin to be felt," Bernanke told committee members. . . .

—Barbara Hagenbaugh

Source: *USA TODAY*, February 15, 2008, p. B1. Reprinted with permission.

ANALYSIS: Policy decisions are based on forecasts of economic performance. Bad forecasts can lead to delayed or wrong policy actions.

Design Problems

Assume for the moment that we somehow are able to get a reliable forecast of where the economy is headed. The outlook, let's suppose, is bad. Now we're in the driver's seat to steer the economy past looming dangers. We need to chart our course—to design an economic plan. What action should we take? Which theory of macro behavior should guide us? How will the marketplace respond to any specific action we take?

Suppose, for example, that we adopt a Keynesian approach to ending a recession. Specifically, we want to use fiscal policy to boost aggregate demand. Should we cut taxes or increase government spending? This was a core decision President Obama confronted as he developed his stimulus program (see the News below). The choice depends in part on the efficacy of either policy tool. Will tax cuts stimulate aggregate demand? In 1998 Japanese households used their tax cut to increase *savings* rather than consumption. In 2001 U.S. households were also slow to spend their tax rebates. When consumers don't respond as anticipated, the intended fiscal stimulus doesn't materialize. Such behavioral responses frustrate even the best-intentioned policy.

IN THE NEWS

Stimulus: Spend or Cut Taxes?

Most Economists Agree That Both Are Needed. The Debate Comes When They Ask How to Split It.

New York (*Fortune*)—As President-elect Barack Obama prepares to take office, the incoming administration and Congress continue to shape a massive stimulus package to help the struggling economy. . . .

While the final breakdown of the package remains to be seen, much of the debate centers on the effectiveness of government spending versus tax cuts as means of reviving the economy. Currently the plan includes roughly $550 billion in spending and $275 billion in tax cuts. . . .

Most economists support the emphasis on spending, saying government expenditure does more to boost gross domestic product, a key indicator of fiscal health.

In other words, spending delivers more bang for the buck because each dollar paid to a worker building a wind turbine, for example, is then spent on groceries or clothing, causing a fiscal ripple effect. Conversely, a worker might save a third of the money he is given in a tax cut, with some of the spending going toward imports, which would also reduce the stimulus to GDP.

According to a January 6 study by Mark Zandi, chief economist at Moody's Economy.com, GDP grows by $1.59 for every dollar spent on infrastructure, while the increase from a corporate tax cut is only $0.30. . . .

Based on Zandi's study, some of the most efficient ways to spend government money are temporarily increasing food stamps (a $1.73 GDP increase per dollar), extending unemployment benefits ($1.63), increasing infrastructure spending ($1.59), and upping direct aid to financially strapped states ($1.38). . . .

Some research shows the positive effect of tax cuts on GDP gets short shrift. Christina Romer, who studied the subject while a professor at the University of California, Berkeley—and whom Obama chose as Chairwoman of his Council of Economic Advisers—says don't underestimate them as an effective means of stimulating the economy.

—Alyssa Abkowitz and Lawrence Delevingne

Source: *Fortune*, January 19, 2009. © 2009 Time Inc. Used under license.

ANALYSIS: Agreement on the *need* for fiscal stimulus doesn't assure consensus on the *content* of fiscal stimulus. What mix of tax cuts, increased government spending, and income transfers should be selected?

Implementation Problems

Measurement and design problems can break the spirit of even the best policymaker (or the policymaker's economic advisers). Yet measurement and design problems are only part of the story. A good idea is of little value unless someone puts it to use. Accordingly, to understand fully why things go wrong, we must also consider the difficulties of *implementing* a well-designed policy.

Congressional Deliberations. Suppose that the president and his Council of Economic Advisers (perhaps in conjunction with the National Economic Council, the secretary of the Treasury, and the director of the Office of Management and Budget) decide that a tax cut is necessary to stimulate demand for goods and services. Can they simply go ahead and cut tax rates? No, because only Congress can legislate tax changes. Once the president decides on the appropriate policy, he must ask Congress for authority to take the required action, which means a delay in implementing policy or possibly no policy at all.

At the very least, the president must convince Congress of the wisdom of his proposed policy. The tax proposal must work its way through separate committees of both the House of Representatives and the Senate, get on the congressional calendar, and be approved in each chamber. If there are important differences in Senate and House versions of the tax cut legislation, they must be compromised in a joint conference. The modified proposal must then be returned to each chamber for approval.

The same kind of process applies to the outlay side of the budget. Once the president has submitted his budget proposals (in January), Congress reviews them, then sets its own spending goals. After that, the budget is broken down into 13 different categories, and a separate appropriations bill is written for each one. These bills spell out in detail how much can be spent and for what purposes. Once Congress passes them, they go to the president for acceptance or veto.

Budget legislation requires Congress to finish these deliberations by October 1 (the beginning of the federal fiscal year), but Congress rarely meets this deadline. In most years, the budget debate continues well into the fiscal year. In some years, the budget debate isn't resolved until the fiscal year is nearly over! The final budget legislation is typically more than 1,000 pages long and so complex that few people understand all its dimensions.

Time Lags. This description of congressional activity isn't an outline for a civics course; rather, it's an important explanation of why economic policy isn't fully effective. ***Even if the right policy is formulated to solve an emerging economic problem, there's no assurance that it will be implemented. And if it's implemented, there's no assurance that it will take effect at the right time.*** One of the most frightening prospects for economic policy is that a policy design intended to serve a specific problem will be implemented much later, when economic conditions have changed. This isn't a remote danger. According to Christina Romer and Paul Romer, the Fed doesn't pull the monetary stimulus lever until a recession is under way, and Congress is even slower in responding to an economic downturn. Indeed, a U.S. Treasury Department study concluded that almost every postwar fiscal stimulus package was enacted well after the end of the recession it was intended to cure!

Figure 18.3 is a schematic view of why macro policies don't always work as intended. There are always delays between the time a problem emerges and the time it's recognized.

FIGURE 18.3

Policy Response: A Series of Time Lags

Even the best-intentioned economic policy can be frustrated by time lags. It takes time for a problem to be recognized, time to formulate a policy response, and still more time to implement that policy. By the time the policy begins to affect the economy, the underlying problem may have changed.

Analysis: Budget cuts are not popular with voters—even when economic conditions warrant fiscal restraint.

There are additional delays between recognition and response design, between design and implementation, and finally between implementation and impact. Not only may mistakes be made at each juncture, but even correct decisions may be overcome by changing economic conditions.

No "Shovel-Ready" Jobs. The lags in implementation were particularly evident in Obama's 2009 fiscal stimulus package. He thought he could kill two birds with one stone by creating short-run jobs with investments in long-term needs like infrastructure and energy development. In his view, there were millions of "shovel-ready" jobs that would fulfill both goals. In fact, though, federal spending doesn't hit the ground that fast. Long delays in federal procurement (bid solicitation, contractor bid preparation, bid review, contract negotiation, environmental impact assessment) create a lag of nearly two years from the time Congress approves funding until a federal shovel actually hits the ground. As a result, most of the stepped-up infrastructure "stimulus" didn't show up until the recession was several years old. Critics said a tax cut would have shifted the AD curve a lot sooner.

Politics vs. Economics. Politics often contributes to delayed and ill-designed policy interventions. Especially noteworthy in this regard is the potential conflict of economic policy with political objectives. The president and Congress are always reluctant to impose fiscal restraint (tax increases or budget cutbacks) in election years, regardless of economic circumstances. As the cartoon above emphasizes, fiscal restraint is never popular.

The tendency of Congress to hold fiscal policy hostage to electoral concerns has created a pattern of short-run stops and starts—a kind of policy-induced business cycle. Indeed, some argue that the business cycle has been replaced with the political cycle: the economy is stimulated in the year of an election and then restrained in the postelection year. The conflict between the urgent need to get reelected and the necessity to manage the economy results in a seesaw kind of instability.

Finally, we must recognize that policy design is obstructed by a certain attention deficit (see the cartoon on the next page). Neither people on the street nor elected public officials focus constantly on economic goals and activities. Even students enrolled in economics courses have a hard time keeping their minds on the economy and its problems. The executive and legislative branches of government, for their part, are likely to focus on economic concerns only when economic problems become serious or voters demand action.

AMERICA'S PROBLEM:

☐ BUDGET DEFICIT   ☐ MEDICARE DEFICIT   ☑ ATTENTION DEFICIT

Mike Thompson; Copley News Service.

Analysis: Economic problems often don't arouse public or policy interest until they become severe.

THE ECONOMY TOMORROW

HANDS ON OR HANDS OFF?

In view of the goal conflicts and the measurement, design, and implementation problems that policymakers confront, it's less surprising that things sometimes go wrong than that things ever work out right. The maze of obstacles through which theory must pass before it becomes policy explains many economic disappointments. On this basis alone, we may conclude that *consistent fine-tuning of the economy isn't compatible with either our design capabilities or our decision-making procedures.* We have exhibited a strong capability to avoid major economic disruptions in the last four decades. We haven't, however, been able to make all the minor adjustments necessary to fulfill our goals completely. As Arthur Burns, former chairman of the Fed's Board of Governors, said,

> There has been much loose talk of "fine tuning" when the state of knowledge permits us to predict only within a fairly broad level the course of economic development and the results of policy actions.[1]

Hands Off. Some critics of economic policy take this argument a few steps further. If fine-tuning isn't really possible, they say, we should abandon discretionary policies altogether and follow fixed rules for fiscal and monetary intervention.

As we saw in Chapter 15, pure monetarism would require the Fed to increase the money supply at a constant rate. Critics of fiscal policy would require the government to maintain balanced budgets, or at least to offset deficits in sluggish years with surpluses in years of high growth. Such rules would prevent policymakers from over- or understimulating the economy. Such rules would also add a dose of certainty to the economic outlook.

Milton Friedman was one of the most persistent advocates of fixed policy rules. With discretionary authority, Friedman argued,

> the wrong decision is likely to be made in a large fraction of cases because the decision makers are examining only a limited area and not taking into account the cumulative consequences of the

[1]*Newsweek,* August 27, 1973, p. 4.

policy as a whole. On the other hand, if a general rule is adopted for a group of cases as a bundle, the existence of that rule has favorable effects on people's attitudes and beliefs and expectations that would not follow even from the discretionary adoption of precisely the same policy on a series of separate occasions.[2]

The case for a hands-off policy stance is based on practical, not theoretical, arguments. *Everyone agrees that flexible, discretionary policies* **could** *result in better economic performance. But Friedman and others argue that the practical requirements of monetary and fiscal management are too demanding and thus prone to failure.* Even former Fed Chairman Alan Greenspan, an advocate of hands-on discretion, later admitted he erred 30 percent of the time. Critics of activist policy say that is too high an error rate.

New Classical Economics. Monetarist critiques of discretionary policy are echoed by a new perspective referred to as new classical economics (NCE). Classical economists saw no need for discretionary macro policy. In their view, the private sector is inherently stable, and government intervention serves no purpose. New classical economics reaches the same conclusion. As Robert Barro, a proponent of NCE, put it, "It is best for the government to provide a stable environment, and then mainly stay out of the way."[3] Barro and other NCE economists based this laissez-faire conclusion on the intriguing notion of **rational expectations.** This notion contends that people make decisions on the basis of all available information, including the *future* effects of *current* government policy.

Suppose, for example, that the Fed decided to increase the money supply to boost output. If people had rational expectations, they'd anticipate that this money supply growth will fuel later inflation. To protect themselves, they'd immediately demand higher prices and wages. As a result, the stimulative monetary policy would fail to boost real output. (Monetarists reach the same conclusion but for different reasons; for monetarists, the countervailing forces are technological and institutional rather than rational expectations.)

Discretionary fiscal policy could be equally ineffective. Suppose Congress accelerated government spending in an effort to boost aggregate demand. Monetarists contend that the accompanying increase in the deficit would push interest rates up and crowd out private investment and consumption. New classical economists again reach the same conclusion via a different route. They contend that people with rational expectations would anticipate that a larger deficit now will necessitate tax increases in later years. To prepare for later tax bills, consumers will reduce spending now, thereby saving more. This "rational" reduction in consumption will offset the increased government expenditure, thus rendering fiscal policy ineffective.

If the new classical economists are right, the only policy that works is one that surprises people—one that consumers and investors don't anticipate. But a policy based on surprises isn't practical. Accordingly, new classical economists conclude that minimal policy intervention is best. This conclusion provides yet another guideline for policy decisions. See Table 18.5 for a roster of competing theories.

Hands On. *Proponents of a hands-on policy strategy acknowledge the possibility of occasional blunders. They emphasize, however, the greater risks of doing nothing when the economy is faltering.* Some proponents of the quick fix even turn the new classical economics argument on its head. Even the wrong policy, they argue, might be better than doing nothing if enough market participants believe that *change* implied *progress.* They cite the jump in consumer confidence that followed the election of Bill Clinton, who had emphasized the need for a *change* in policy but hadn't spelled out the details of that change. The surge in confidence itself stimulated consumer purchases even before President Clinton took office. The same kind of response occurred after the September 11, 2001, terrorist attacks. Consumers were dazed and insecure. There was a serious risk that they would curtail spending if the government didn't *do something.* Details aside, they just wanted reassurance that someone was taking charge of events. Quick responses by the Fed (increasing the money supply), the Congress (authorizing more spending), and President

---

[2]Milton Friedman, *Capitalism and Freedom* (Chicago: University of Chicago Press, 1962), p. 53.
[3]Robert Barro, "Don't Fool with Money, Cut Taxes," *The Wall Street Journal,* November 21, 1991, p. A14.

---

rational expectations:
Hypothesis that people's spending decisions are based on all available information, including the anticipated effects of government intervention.

Keynesians	Keynesians believe that the private sector is inherently unstable and prone to stagnate at low levels of output and employment. They want the government to manage aggregate demand with changes in taxes and government's spending.
Modern ("neo") Keynesians	Post–World War II followers of Keynes worry about inflation as well as recession. They urge budgetary restraint to cool an overheated economy. They also use monetary policy to change interest rates.
Monetarists	The money supply is their only heavy hitter. By changing the money supply, they can raise or lower the price level. Pure monetarists shun active policy, believing that it destabilizes the otherwise stable private sector. Output and employment gravitate to their natural levels.
Supply-siders	Incentives to work, invest, and produce are the key to their plays. Cuts in marginal tax rates and government regulation are used to expand production capacity, thereby increasing output and reducing inflationary pressures.
New classical economists	They say fine-tuning won't work because once the private sector realizes what the government is doing, it will act to offset it. They also question the credibility of quick-fix promises. They favor steady, predictable policies.

TABLE 18.5

Who's on First? Labeling Economists

It's sometimes hard to tell who's on what side in economic debates. Although some economists are proud to wear the colors of monetarists, Keynesians, or other teams, many economists shun such allegiances. Indeed, economists are often accused of playing on one team one day and on another team the next, making it hard to tell which team is at bat. To simplify matters, this guide may be used for quick identification of the players. Closer observation is advised, however, before choosing up teams.

Bush (mobilizing security and military forces) kept consumer confidence from plunging. President Obama argued that a similar situation existed in early 2009. Claiming that the economy would slide into another Depression if Congress didn't act, he said doing *something*—even if not perfect—was better than doing *nothing*.

Just doing *something* isn't the purpose of a hands-on policy, of course. Policy activists believe that we have enough knowledge about how the economy works to pull the right policy levers most of the time. They also point to the historical record. Our economic track record may not be perfect, but the historical record of prices, employment, and growth has improved since active fiscal and monetary policies were adopted: recessions have gotten shorter and economic expansions longer.

Finally, one must contend with the difficulties inherent in enforcing fixed rules. How is the Fed, for example, supposed to maintain a steady rate of growth in the money supply? As we observed in Chapter 13, people move their funds back and forth between different kinds of "money." Also, the demand for money is subject to unpredictable shifts. Maintaining a steady rate of growth in M2 or any other measure of money would require superhuman foresight and responses. As former Fed Chairman Paul Volcker told Congress, it would be "exceedingly dangerous and in fact practically impossible to eliminate substantial elements of discretion in the conduct of Federal Reserve policy."

The same is true of fiscal policy. Government spending and taxes are directly influenced by changes in unemployment, inflation, interest rates, and growth. These automatic stabilizers make it virtually impossible to maintain any fixed rule for budget balancing. Moreover, if we eliminated the automatic stabilizers, we'd risk greater instability.

Modest Expectations. The clamor for fixed policy rules is more a rebuke of past policy than a viable policy alternative. We really have no choice but to pursue discretionary policies. Recognition of measurement, design, and implementation problems is important for an understanding of the way the economy functions. Even though it's impossible to reach all our goals, we can't abandon conscientious attempts to get as close as possible to goal fulfillment. If public policy can create a few more jobs, a better mix of output, a little more growth and price stability, or an improved distribution of income in the economy tomorrow, those initiatives are worthwhile.

SUMMARY

- The government possesses an array of macro policy tools, each of which can significantly alter economic outcomes. **LO18-1**
- To end a recession, we can cut taxes, expand the money supply, or increase government spending. To curb inflation, we can reverse each of these policy tools. To overcome stagflation, we can combine fiscal and monetary levers with improved supply-side incentives.   **LO18-2**
- Although the potential of economic theory seems impressive, the economic record doesn't look as good. Persistent unemployment, recurring economic slowdowns, and nagging inflation suggest that the realities of policymaking are more difficult than theory implies.   **LO18-3**
- To some extent, the failures of economic policy are a reflection of scarce resources and competing goals. Even when consensus exists, however, serious obstacles to effective economic policy remain. These obstacles include
  (a) Measurement problems. Our knowledge of economic performance is always dated and incomplete.

  (b) Design problems. We don't know exactly how the economy will respond to specific policies.
  (c) Implementation problems. It takes time for Congress and the president to agree on an appropriate plan of action. Moreover, political needs may take precedence over economic needs.
  For all these reasons, discretionary policy rarely lives up to its theoretical potential.   **LO18-3**
- Monetarists and new classical economists favor rules rather than discretionary macro policies. They argue that discretionary policies are unlikely to work and risk being wrong. Critics respond that discretionary policies are needed to cope with ever-changing economic circumstances. **LO18-3**

Key Terms

business cycle	monetary policy	inflationary GDP gap
fiscal policy	natural rate of unemployment	stagflation
automatic stabilizer	supply-side policy	fine-tuning
structural deficit	recessionary GDP gap	growth recession
fiscal stimulus	multiplier	inflationary flashpoint
fiscal restraint	velocity of money (V)	rational expectations

Questions for Discussion

1. What policies would Keynesians, monetarists, and supply-siders advocate for (a) restraining inflation and (b) reducing unemployment? **LO18-1**
2. Why did Fed Chairman Bernanke expect there would be no recession in 2008 (see News, p. 397)? Why was he wrong? **LO18-3**
3. If policymakers had instant data on the economy's performance, should they respond immediately? Why or why not? **LO18-3**
4. Suppose it's an election year and aggregate demand is growing so fast that it threatens to accelerate inflation. Why might Congress and the president hesitate to cut government spending or raise taxes, as theory suggests? **LO18-3**
5. Should military spending be subject to macroeconomic constraints? What programs should be expanded or con-

tracted to bring about needed changes in the budget? **LO18-2**
6. Why is the multiplier higher for unemployment benefits than for infrastructure spending (see News, p. 399)? Which occurs faster? **LO18-2**
7. Suppose the government proposes to cut taxes while maintaining the current level of government expenditures. To finance this deficit, it may either (a) sell bonds to the public or (b) print new money (via Federal Reserve cooperation). What are the likely effects of each of these alternatives on each of the following? Would Keynesians, monetarists, and supply-siders give the same answers? **LO18-2**
   (a) Interest rates.
   (b) Consumer spending.
   (c) Business investment.
   (d) Aggregate demand.

8. Suppose the economy is slumping into recession and needs a fiscal policy boost. Voters, however, are opposed to larger federal deficits. What should policymakers do? **LO18-2**

9. What are the pros and cons of tax cuts or increased government spending as stimulative tools (see News, p. 399)? **LO18-3**

10. What is the "magic wand" referred to in this chapter's opening quotation? **LO18-2**

 mobile app Visit your mobile app store and download the Schiller: Study Econ app *today!*

PROBLEMS FOR CHAPTER 18

Name: _____

LO18-3 1. If the Congressional Budget Office makes its average error this year, by how much will it underestimate next year's budget deficit? (See News, p. 399.) (Note: Assume a GDP of $15 trillion.) _____%

LO18-1 2. In 2013 the unemployment rate was 7.4 percent, far above the full-employment threshold (5 percent).
(a) How many jobs were lost, as a result, in a labor force of 155 million? _____
(b) If the average worker produces $116,000 of output, how much output was lost? _____
(c) By how much did GDP per capita decline as a result (310 million people)? _____

LO18-1 3. According to the World View on page 395,
(a) Which country had the greatest macro misery in the 2000s? (Compute the "misery index" from Chapter 16.) _____
(b) Which country had the fastest growth? _____

LO18-1 4. What MPC for tax cuts is assumed in the News on page 399? _____

LO18-2 5. According to the News on page 399, what is the implied value of the multiplier for
(a) Increased unemployment benefits? _____
(b) Infrastructure spending? _____

LO18-3 6. The following table displays Congressional Budget Office forecasts of federal budget balances for the following fiscal year. Compare these forecasts with *actual* surplus and deficits for those same years (see Table 12.3 for data).

Year:	2000	2001	2002	2003	2004	2005	2006	2007	2008	2009
Deficit forecast (in billions of dollars)	+161	+268	+176	−315	−480	−348	−314	−285	−155	−438

(a) In how many years was the CBO too optimistic (underestimating the deficit or overestimating the surplus)? _____
(b) In how many years was the CBO too pessimistic? _____

LO18-2 7. Complete the following chart by summarizing the policy prescriptions of various economic theories:

Policy Approach	Policy Prescription for	
	Recession	Inflation
Fiscal	_____	_____
Classical	_____	_____
Keynesian	_____	_____
Monetarist	_____	_____
Monetary	_____	_____
Keynesian	_____	_____
Monetarist	_____	_____
Supply side	_____	_____

International Economics

Our interactions with the rest of the world have a profound impact on the mix of output (WHAT), the methods of production (HOW), and the distribution of income (FOR WHOM). Trade and global money flows can also affect the stability of the macro economy. Chapters 19 and 20 explore the motives, the nature, and the effects of international trade and finance.

Chapter 21 examines one of the world's most urgent problems—the deprivation that afflicts nearly 3 billion people worldwide. In this last chapter, the dimensions, causes, and potential cures for global poverty are discussed.

International Trade

LEARNING OBJECTIVES

After reading this chapter, you should know

LO19-1 What comparative advantage is.

LO19-2 What the gains from trade are.

LO19-3 How trade barriers affect prices, output, and incomes.

The 2014 World Series between the San Francisco Giants and the Kansas City Royals was played with Japanese gloves, baseballs made in Costa Rica, and Mexican bats. Most of the players were wearing shoes made in Korea or China. And during the regular season, many of the games throughout the major leagues were played on artificial grass made in Taiwan. Baseball, it seems, has become something less than the "all-American" game.

Imported goods have made inroads into other activities as well. All DVDs, smartphones, and video game consoles are imported, as are most televisions, fax machines, personal computers, and iPads. Most of these imported goods could have been produced in the United States. Why did we purchase them from other countries? For that matter, why does the rest of the world buy computers, tractors, chemicals, airplanes, and wheat from us rather than produce such products for themselves? Wouldn't we all be better off relying on ourselves for the goods we consume (and the jobs we need) rather than buying and selling products in international markets? Or is there some advantage to be gained from international trade?

This chapter begins with a survey of international trade patterns—what goods and services we trade, and with whom. Then we address basic issues related to such trade:

- **What benefit, if any, do we get from international trade?**
- **How much harm do imports cause, and to whom?**
- **Should we protect ourselves from "unfair" trade by limiting imports?**

After examining the arguments for and against international trade, we draw some general conclusions about trade policy. As we'll see, international trade tends to increase *average* incomes, although it may diminish the job and income opportunities for specific industries and workers.

U.S. TRADE PATTERNS

The United States is by far the largest player in global product and resource markets. In 2013 we purchased 20 percent of the world's exports and sold 15 percent of the same total.

Imports

In dollar terms, our imports in 2013 exceeded $2.7 trillion. These **imports** included the consumer items mentioned earlier as well as capital equipment, raw materials, and food. Table 19.1 represents the goods and services we purchase from foreign suppliers.

Although imports represent only 16 percent of total GDP, they account for larger shares of specific product markets. Coffee is a familiar example. Since virtually all coffee is imported (except for a tiny amount produced in Hawaii), Americans would have a harder time staying awake without imports. Likewise, there'd be no aluminum if we didn't import bauxite, no chrome bumpers if we didn't import chromium, no tin cans without imported tin, no smartphones, and a lot fewer computers without imported components. We couldn't even play the all-American game of baseball without imports because baseballs are no longer made in the United States.

We import *services* as well as *goods*. If you fly to Europe on Virgin Airways, you're importing transportation services. If you stay in a London hotel, you're importing lodging services. When you go to Barclay's Bank to cash traveler's checks, you're importing foreign financial services. These and other services now account for one-sixth of U.S. imports.

imports: Goods and services purchased from international sources.

Country	Imports from	Exports to
Australia	Beef Alumina Autos	Airplanes Computers Auto parts
Belgium	Jewelry Cars Optical glass	Cigarettes Airplanes Diamonds
Canada	Cars Trucks Paper	Auto parts Cars Computers
China	Computers Clothes Toys	Scrap and trash Electrical generators Oil seeds
Germany	Cars Engines Auto parts	Airplanes Computers Cars
Japan	Cars Computers Telephones	Airplanes Computers Timber
Russia	Oil Platinum Artworks	Corn Wheat Oil seeds
South Korea	Shoes Cars Computers	Airplanes Leather Iron ingots and oxides

Source: U.S. Department of Commerce.

web click

After long-standing trade sanctions, the United States has restored limited trade with Cuba in recent years. For information on trade with Cuba, see **www.cubatrade.org**.

TABLE 19.1

A U.S. Trade Sampler

The United States imports and exports a staggering array of goods and services. Shown here are the top exports and imports with various countries. Notice that we export many of the same goods we import (such as cars and computers). What's the purpose of trading goods we produce ourselves?

Exports

exports: Goods and services sold to foreign buyers.

While we're buying goods (merchandise) and services from the rest of the world, global consumers are buying our **exports.** In 2013 we exported $1.6 trillion of *goods,* including farm products (wheat, corn, soybeans), tobacco, machinery (computers), aircraft, automobiles and auto parts, raw materials (lumber, iron ore), and chemicals (see Table 19.1 for a sample of U.S. merchandise exports). We also exported $687 billion of services (movies, software licenses, tourism, engineering, financial services, etc.).

Although the United States is the world's largest exporter of goods and services, exports represent a relatively modest fraction of our total output. As the World View below illustrates, other nations export much larger proportions of their GDP. Belgium is one of the most export-oriented countries, with tourist services and diamond exports pushing its export ratio to an incredible 86 percent. By contrast, Myanmar (Burma) is basically a closed economy with few exports (other than opium and other drugs traded in the black market).

WORLD VIEW

Export Ratios

Very poor countries often have little to export and thus low export ratios. Saudi Arabia, by contrast, depends heavily on its oil exports. Fast-developing countries in Asia also rely on exports to enlarge their markets and raise incomes. The U.S. export ratio is low by international standards.

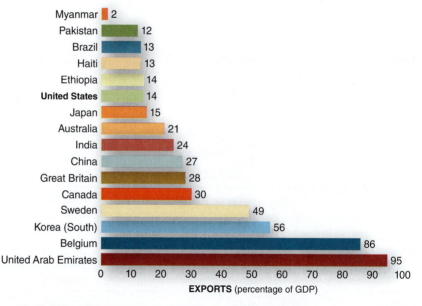

EXPORTS (percentage of GDP)

Country	Exports (% of GDP)
Myanmar	2
Pakistan	12
Brazil	13
Haiti	13
Ethiopia	14
United States	14
Japan	15
Australia	21
India	24
China	27
Great Britain	28
Canada	30
Sweden	49
Korea (South)	56
Belgium	86
United Arab Emirates	95

Source: *The World Bank, WDI2014 Data Set,* **http://data.worldbank.org.**

ANALYSIS: The relatively low U.S. export ratio reflects the vast size of our domestic market and our relative self-sufficiency in food and resources. European nations are smaller and highly interdependent.

web click

Find the most recent data on trade flows at **http://tse.export .gov.** Click "National Trade Data."

The low U.S. export ratio (14 percent) disguises our heavy dependence on exports in specific industries. We export 25 to 50 percent of our rice, corn, and wheat production each year, and still more of our soybeans. Clearly a decision by international consumers to stop eating U.S. agricultural products could devastate a lot of American farmers. Such companies as Boeing (planes), Caterpillar Tractor (construction and farm machinery), Weyerhaeuser (logs, lumber), Dow (chemicals), and Oracle (computer workstations) sell more than one-fourth of their output in foreign markets. McDonald's sells hamburgers to nearly 60 million people a day in 128 countries around the world; to do so, the company exports management and marketing services (as well as frozen food) from the United States. The Walt Disney Company

Product Category	Exports ($ billions)	Imports ($ billions)	Surplus (Deficit) ($ billions)
Merchandise	$1,593	$2,294	$(701)
Services	687	462	225
Total trade	$2,280	$2,756	$(476)

Source: U.S. Department of Commerce.

TABLE 19.2
Trade Balances

Both merchandise (goods) and services are traded between countries. The United States typically has a merchandise deficit and a services surplus. When combined, an overall trade deficit remained in 2013.

produces the most popular TV shows in Russia and Germany, publishes Italy's best-selling weekly magazine, and has the most popular tourist attraction in Japan (Tokyo Disneyland). The 500,000 foreign students attending U.S. universities are purchasing $5 billion of American educational services. All these activities are part of America's service exports.

Trade Balances

Although we export a lot of products, we usually have an imbalance in our trade flows. The trade balance is the difference between the value of exports and imports:

$$\text{Trade balance} = \text{Exports} - \text{Imports}$$

During 2013 we imported much more than we exported and so had a *negative* trade balance. A negative trade balance is called a **trade deficit.**

Although the overall trade balance includes both goods and services, these flows are usually reported separately, with the *merchandise* trade balance distinguished from the *services* trade balance. As Table 19.2 shows, the United States had a merchandise (goods) trade deficit of $701 billion in 2013 and a *services* trade *surplus* of $225 billion, leaving the overall trade balance in the red.

When the United States has a trade deficit with the rest of the world, other countries must have an offsetting **trade surplus.** On a global scale, imports must equal exports because every good exported by one country must be imported by another. Hence *any imbalance in America's trade must be offset by reverse imbalances elsewhere.*

Whatever the overall balance in our trade accounts, bilateral balances vary greatly. Table 19.3 shows, for example, that our 2013 aggregate trade deficit ($476 billion) incorporated huge bilateral trade deficits with China, Germany, and Japan. In the same year, however, we had trade surpluses with Brazil, the Netherlands, Belgium, Australia, and Hong Kong.

trade deficit: The amount by which the value of imports exceeds the value of exports in a given time period.

trade surplus: The amount by which the value of exports exceeds the value of imports in a given time period.

Country	Exports to ($ billions)	Imports from ($ billions)	Trade Balance ($ billions)
Top Deficit Countries			
China	$161	$456	−$295
Germany	75	148	−73
Japan	113	171	−58
Mexico	257	304	−47
Canada	366	369	−3
Top Surplus Countries			
Hong Kong	$53	$13	+$40
Brazil	71	35	+36
The Netherlands	59	29	+30
Australia	45	16	+29
Belgium	37	25	+12

Source: U.S. Department of Commerce, International Trade Administration.

TABLE 19.3
Bilateral Trade Balances

The U.S. trade deficit is the net result of bilateral deficits and surpluses. We had huge trade deficits with China, Germany, and Japan in 2013, for example, but small trade surpluses with Brazil, the Netherlands, Belgium, Australia, and Hong Kong. International trade is *multi*national, with surpluses in some countries being offset by trade deficits elsewhere.

MOTIVATION TO TRADE

Many people wonder why we trade so much, particularly since (1) we import many of the things we also export (like computers, airplanes, clothes), (2) we *could* produce many of the other things we import, and (3) we worry so much about trade imbalances. Why not just import those few things that we can't produce ourselves, and export just enough to balance that trade?

Specialization

Although it might seem strange to be importing goods we could produce ourselves, such trade is entirely rational. Our decision to trade with other countries arises from the same considerations that motivate individuals to specialize in production: satisfying their remaining needs in the marketplace. Why don't you become self-sufficient—growing all your own food, building your own shelter, and recording your own songs? Presumably because you've found that you can enjoy a much higher standard of living (and better music) by working at just one job and then buying other goods in the marketplace. When you do so, you're no longer self-sufficient. Instead you are *specializing* in production, relying on others to produce the array of goods and services you want. When countries trade goods and services, they are doing the same thing—*specializing* in production and then *trading* for other desired goods. Why do they do this? Because **specialization increases total output.**

To see how nations benefit from trade, we'll examine the production possibilities of two countries. We want to demonstrate that two countries that trade can together produce more output than they could in the absence of trade. If they can, **the gain from trade is increased world output and a higher standard of living in all trading countries.** This is the essential message of the *theory of comparative advantage.*

Production and Consumption without Trade

Consider the production and consumption possibilities of just two countries—say, the United States and France. For the sake of illustration, assume that both countries produce only two goods: bread and wine. Let's also set aside worries about the law of diminishing returns and the substitutability of resources, thus transforming the familiar **production possibilities** curve into a straight line, as in Figure 19.1.

The "curves" in Figure 19.1 suggest that the United States is capable of producing much more bread than France. With our greater abundance of labor, land, and other resources, we assume that the United States is capable of producing up to 100 zillion loaves of bread per year. To do so, we'd have to devote all our resources to that purpose. This capability is indicated by point *A* in Figure 19.1*a* and in row *A* of the accompanying production possibilities schedule. France (Figure 19.1*b*), on the other hand, confronts a *maximum* bread production of only 15 zillion loaves per year (point *G*) because it has little available land, less fuel, and fewer potential workers.

The capacities of the two countries for wine production are 50 zillion barrels for us (point *F*) and 60 zillion for France (point *L*), largely reflecting France's greater experience in tending vines. Both countries are also capable of producing alternative *combinations* of bread and wine, as evidenced by their respective production possibilities curves (points *A–F* for the United States and *G–L* for France).

A nation that doesn't trade with other countries is called a **closed economy.** In the absence of contact with the outside world, the production possibilities curve for a closed economy also defines its **consumption possibilities.** Without imports, a country cannot consume more than it produces. Thus the only immediate issue in a closed economy is which mix of output to choose—*what* to produce and consume—out of the domestic choices available.

Assume that Americans choose point *D* on their production possibilities curve, producing and consuming 40 zillion loaves of bread and 30 zillion barrels of wine. The French, on the other hand, prefer the mix of output represented by point *I* on their production possibilities curve. At that point they produce and consume 9 zillion loaves of bread and 24 zillion barrels of wine.

production possibilities: The alternative combinations of final goods and services that could be produced in a given time period with all available resources and technology.

closed economy: A nation that doesn't engage in international trade.

consumption possibilities: The alternative combinations of goods and services that a country could consume in a given time period.

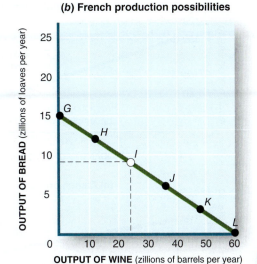

(a) U.S. production possibilities

(b) French production possibilities

In a closed economy, production possibilities and consumption possibilities are identical.

U.S. Production Possibilities		
Bread (Zillions of Loaves)	+	Wine (Zillions of Barrels)
A 100	+	0
B 80	+	10
C 60	+	20
D 40	+	30
E 20	+	40
F 0	+	50

French Production Possibilities		
Bread (Zillions of Loaves)	+	Wine (Zillions of Barrels)
G 15	+	0
H 12	+	12
I 9	+	24
J 6	+	36
K 3	+	48
L 0	+	60

FIGURE 19.1

Consumption Possibilities without Trade

In the absence of trade, a country's consumption possibilities are identical to its production possibilities. The assumed production possibilities of the United States and France are illustrated in the graphs and the corresponding schedules. Before entering into trade, the United States chose to produce and consume at point D, with 40 zillion loaves of bread and 30 zillion barrels of wine. France chose point I on its own production possibilities curve. By trading, each country hopes to increase its consumption beyond these levels.

To assess the potential gain from trade, we must focus the *combined* output of the United States and France. In this case, total world output (points D and I) comes to 49 zillion loaves of bread and 54 zillion barrels of wine. What we want to know is whether world output would increase if France and the United States abandoned their isolation and started trading. Could either country, or both, consume more output by engaging in a little trade?

Production and Consumption with Trade

Because both countries are saddled with limited production possibilities, trying to eke out a little extra wine and bread from this situation might not appear very promising. Such a conclusion is unwarranted, however. Take another look at the production possibilities confronting the United States, as reproduced in Figure 19.2. Suppose the United States were to produce at point C rather than point D. At point C we could produce 60 zillion loaves of

FIGURE 19.2

Consumption Possibilities with Trade

A country can increase its consumption possibilities through international trade. Each country alters its mix of domestic output to produce more of the good it produces best. As it does so, total world output increases, and each country enjoys more consumption. In this case, trade allows U.S. consumption to move from point *D* to point *N*. France moves from point *I* to point *M*.

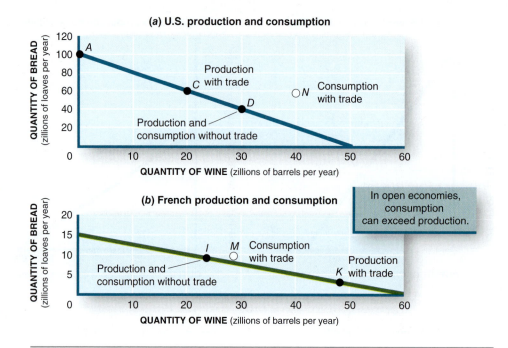

bread and 20 zillion barrels of wine. That combination is clearly *possible* because it lies on the production possibilities curve. We didn't choose that point earlier because we assumed the mix of output at point *D* was preferable. The mix of output at point *C* could be produced, however.

We could also change the mix of output in France. Assume that France moved from point *I* to point *K*, producing 48 zillion barrels of wine and only 3 zillion loaves of bread.

Two observations are now called for. The first is simply that output mixes have changed in each country. The second, and more interesting, is that total world output has *increased*. Notice how this works. When the United States and France were at points *D* and *I*, their *combined* output consisted of

	Bread (Zillions of Loaves)	Wine (Zillions of Barrels)
United States (at point *D*)	40	30
France (at point *I*)	9	24
Total pre-trade output	49	54

After they moved along their respective production possibilities curves to points *C* and *K*, the combined world output became

	Bread (Zillions of Loaves)	Wine (Zillions of Barrels)
United States (at point *C*)	60	20
France (at point *K*)	3	48
Total output with trade	63	68

Total world output has increased by 14 zillion loaves of bread and 14 zillion barrels of wine. *Just by changing the mix of output in each country, we've increased total world output.* This additional output creates the potential for making both countries better off than they were in the absence of trade.

This almost seems like a magic trick, but it isn't. Here's what happened. The United States and France weren't initially producing at points *C* and *K* before because they simply didn't want to *consume* those particular output combinations. Nevertheless, our discovery that points *C* and *K* allow us to produce *more* output suggests that everybody can consume more goods and services if we change the mix of output in each country. This is our first clue as to how specialization and trade can benefit an **open economy**—a nation that engages in international trade.

open economy: A nation that engages in international trade.

Suppose we Americans are the first to discover the potential benefits from trade. Using Figure 19.2 as our guide, we suggest to the French that they move their mix of output from point *I* to point *K*. As an incentive for making such a move, we promise to give them 6 zillion loaves of bread in exchange for 20 zillion barrels of wine. This would leave them at point *M*, with as much bread to consume as they used to have, plus an extra 4 zillion barrels of wine. At point *I* they had 9 zillion loaves of bread and 24 zillion barrels of wine. At point *M* they can have 9 zillion loaves of bread and 28 zillion barrels of wine. Thus by altering their mix of output (from point *I* to point *K*) and then trading (point *K* to point *M*), the French end up with more goods and services than they had in the beginning. Notice in particular that this new consumption possibility (point *M*) lies *outside* France's domestic production possibilities curve.

The French will be quite pleased with the extra output they get from trading. But where does this leave us? Does France's gain imply a loss for us? Or do we gain from trade as well?

Mutual Gains

As it turns out, *both* the United States and France gain by trading. The United States, too, ends up consuming a mix of output that lies outside our production possibilities curve.

Note that at point *C* we *produce* 60 zillion loaves of bread per year and 20 zillion barrels of wine. We then *export* 6 zillion loaves to France. This leaves us with 54 zillion loaves of bread to *consume*.

In return for our exported bread, the French give us 20 zillion barrels of wine. These imports, plus our domestic production, permit us to *consume* 40 zillion barrels of wine. Hence we end up consuming at point *N*, enjoying 54 zillion loaves of bread and 40 zillion barrels of wine. Thus by first changing our mix of output (from point *D* to point *C*), then trading (point *C* to point *N*), we end up with 14 zillion more loaves of bread and 10 zillion more barrels of wine than we started with. International trade has made us better off, too.

Table 19.4 recaps the gains from trade for both countries. Notice that U.S. imports match French exports and vice versa. Also notice how the trade-facilitated consumption in each country exceeds no-trade levels.

	Production and Consumption with Trade						Production and Consumption with No Trade
	Production	**+** **Imports**	**−** **Exports**	**=** **Consumption**			
United States at . . .	Point *C*			Point *N*			Point *D*
Bread	60	+ 0	− 6	= 54		compare	40
Wine	20	+ 20	− 0	= 40			30
France at . . .	Point *K*			Point *M*			Point *I*
Bread	3	+ 6	− 0	= 9		compare	9
Wine	48	+ 0	− 20	= 28			24

TABLE 19.4

Gains from Trade

When nations specialize in production, they can export one good and import another and end up with *more* total goods to consume than they had without trade. In this case, the United States specializes in bread production. Notice how U.S. *consumption* of both goods increases (compare total U.S. consumption of bread and wine at point *N* [with trade] to consumption at point *D* [no trade]).

All these numbers do indeed look like some kind of magic trick, but there's no sleight of hand going on here; the gains from trade are due to specialization in production. When each country goes it alone, it's a prisoner of its own production possibilities curve; it must make production decisions on the basis of its own consumption desires. When international trade is permitted, however, each country can concentrate on the exploitation of its production capabilities. ***Each country produces those goods it makes best and then trades with other countries to acquire the goods it desires to consume.***

The resultant specialization increases total world output. In the process, each country is able to escape the confines of its own production possibilities curve, to reach beyond it for a larger basket of consumption goods. ***When a country engages in international trade, its consumption possibilities always exceed its production possibilities.*** These enhanced consumption possibilities are emphasized by the positions of points *N* and *M* outside the production possibilities curves (Figure 19.2). If it weren't possible for countries to increase their consumption by trading, there'd be no incentive for trading, and thus no trade.

PURSUIT OF COMPARATIVE ADVANTAGE

Although international trade can make everyone better off, it's not so obvious which goods should be traded, or on what terms. In our previous illustration, the United States ended up trading bread for wine in terms that were decidedly favorable to us. Why did we export bread rather than wine, and how did we end up getting such a good deal?

Opportunity Costs

comparative advantage: The ability of a country to produce a specific good at a lower opportunity cost than its trading partners.

opportunity cost: The most desired goods or services that are forgone in order to obtain something else.

The decision to export bread is based on **comparative advantage**—that is, the *relative* cost of producing different goods. Recall that we can produce a maximum of 100 zillion loaves of bread per year or 50 zillion barrels of wine. Thus the domestic **opportunity cost** of producing 100 zillion loaves of bread is the 50 zillion barrels of wine we forsake in order to devote all our resources to bread production. In fact, at every point on the U.S. production possibilities curve (Figure 19.2a), the opportunity cost of a loaf of bread is ½ barrel of wine. We're effectively paying half a barrel of wine to get a loaf of bread.

Although the cost of bread production in the United States might appear outrageous, even higher opportunity costs prevail in France. According to Figure 19.2b, the opportunity cost of producing a loaf of bread in France is a staggering 4 barrels of wine. To produce a loaf of bread, the French must use factors of production that could otherwise be used to produce 4 barrels of wine.

Comparative Advantage. A comparison of the opportunity costs prevailing in each country exposes the nature of comparative advantage. The United States has a comparative advantage in bread production because less wine has to be given up to produce bread in the United States than in France. In other words, the opportunity costs of bread production are lower in the United States than in France. ***Comparative advantage refers to the relative (opportunity) costs of producing particular goods.***

A country should specialize in what it's *relatively* efficient at producing—that is, goods for which it has the lowest opportunity costs. In this case, the United States should produce bread because its opportunity cost (½ barrel of wine) is less than France's (4 barrels of wine). Were you the production manager for the whole world, you'd certainly want each country to exploit its relative abilities, thus maximizing world output. Each country can arrive at that same decision itself by comparing its own opportunity costs to those prevailing elsewhere. ***World output, and thus the potential gains from trade, will be maximized when each country pursues its comparative advantage. To do so, each country***

- ***Exports goods with relatively low opportunity costs.***
- ***Imports goods with relatively high opportunity costs.***

That's the kind of situation depicted in Table 19.4.

Absolute Costs Don't Count

In assessing the nature of comparative advantage, notice that we needn't know anything about the actual costs involved in production. Have you seen any data suggesting how much labor, land, or capital is required to produce a loaf of bread in either France or the United States? For all you and I know, the French may be able to produce both bread and wine with fewer resources than we're using. Such an **absolute advantage** in production might exist because of their much longer experience in cultivating both grapes and wheat or simply because they have more talent.

We can envy such productivity, and even try to emulate it, but it shouldn't alter our production or trade decisions. All we really care about are *opportunity costs*—what *we* have to give up in order to get more of a desired good. If we can get a barrel of wine for less bread in trade than in production, we have a comparative advantage in producing bread. As long as we have a *comparative* advantage in bread production, we should exploit it. It doesn't matter to us whether France could produce either good with fewer resources. For that matter, even if France had an absolute advantage in *both* goods, we'd still have a *comparative* advantage in bread production, as we've already confirmed. The absolute costs of production were omitted from the previous illustration because they were irrelevant.

To clarify the distinction between absolute advantage and comparative advantage, consider this example. When Charlie Osgood joined the Willamette Warriors football team, he was the fastest runner ever to play football in Willamette. He could also throw the ball farther than most people could see. In other words, he had an *absolute advantage* in both throwing and running. Charlie would have made the greatest quarterback or the greatest end ever to play football. *Would have.* The problem was that he could play only one position at a time. Thus the Willamette coach had to play Charlie either as a quarterback or as an end. He reasoned that Charlie could throw only a bit farther than some of the other top quarterbacks but could far outdistance all the other ends. In other words, Charlie had a *comparative advantage* in running and was assigned to play as an end.

TERMS OF TRADE

It definitely pays to pursue one's comparative advantage by specializing in production. It may not yet be clear, however, how we got such a good deal with France. We're clever traders; but beyond that, is there any way to determine the **terms of trade**—the quantity of good A that must be given up in exchange for good B? In our previous illustration, the terms of trade were very favorable to us; we exchanged only 6 zillion loaves of bread for 20 zillion barrels of wine (Table 19.4). The terms of trade were thus 6 loaves = 20 barrels.

Limits to the Terms of Trade

The terms of trade with France were determined by our offer and France's ready acceptance. But why did France accept those terms? France was willing to accept our offer because the terms of trade permitted France to increase its wine consumption without giving up any bread consumption. Our offer of 6 loaves for 20 barrels was an improvement over France's domestic opportunity costs. France's domestic possibilities required it to give up 24 barrels of wine in order to produce 6 loaves of bread (see Figure 19.2*b*). Getting bread via trade was simply cheaper for France than producing bread at home. France ended up with an extra 4 zillion barrels of wine (take another look at the last two columns in Table 19.4).

Our first clue to the terms of trade, then, lies in each country's domestic opportunity costs. *A country won't trade unless the terms of trade are superior to domestic opportunities.* In our example, the opportunity cost of 1 barrel of wine in the United States is 2 loaves of bread. Accordingly, we won't *export* bread unless we get at least 1 barrel of wine in exchange for every 2 loaves of bread we ship overseas.

All countries want to gain from trade. Hence we can predict that *the terms of trade between any two countries will lie somewhere between their respective opportunity costs in production.* That is, a loaf of bread in international trade will be worth at least ½ barrel of

absolute advantage: The ability of a country to produce a specific good with fewer resources (per unit of output) than other countries.

terms of trade: The rate at which goods are exchanged; the amount of good A given up for good B in trade.

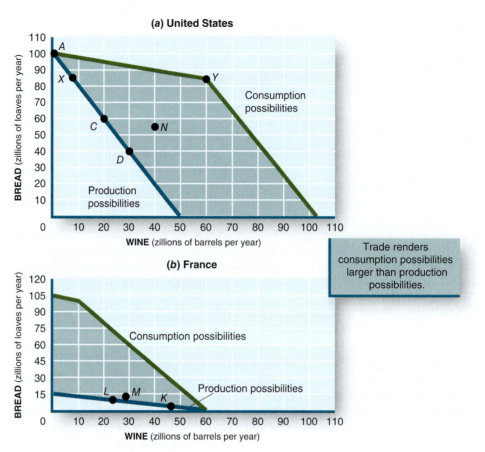

web click

Find out more about trade patterns and policy from the International Trade Commission at **dataweb.usitc.gov.**

Trade renders consumption possibilities larger than production possibilities.

FIGURE 19.3

Searching for the Terms of Trade

Assume the United States can produce 100 zillion loaves of bread per year (point A). If we reduce output to only 85 zillion loaves, we could move to point X. At point X we have 7.5 zillion barrels of wine and 85 zillion loaves of bread.

Trade increases consumption possibilities. If we continued to produce 100 zillion loaves of bread, we could trade 15 zillion loaves to France in exchange for as much as 60 zillion barrels of wine. This would leave us *producing* at point A but *consuming* at point Y. At point Y we have more wine and no less bread than we had at point X. This is our motivation to trade.

A country will end up on its consumption possibilities curve only if it gets *all* the gains from trade. It will remain on its production possibilities curve only if it gets *none* of the gains from trade. The terms of trade determine how the gains from trade are distributed, and thus at what point in the shaded area each country ends up.

Note: The kink in the consumption possibilities curve at point Y occurs because France is unable to produce more than 60 zillion barrels of wine.

---

wine (the U.S. opportunity cost), but no more than 4 barrels (the French opportunity cost). In our example, the terms of trade ended up at 1 loaf = 3.33 barrels (that is, at 6 loaves = 20 barrels). This represented a very large gain for the United States and a small gain for France. Figure 19.3 illustrates this outcome and several other possibilities.

The Role of Markets and Prices

Relatively little trade is subject to such direct negotiations between countries. More often than not, the decision to import or export a particular good is left up to the market decisions of individual consumers and producers.

Individual consumers and producers aren't much impressed by such abstractions as comparative advantage. Market participants tend to focus on prices, always trying to allocate their resources in order to maximize profits or personal satisfaction. Consumers tend to buy the products that deliver the most utility per dollar of expenditure, while producers try to get the most output per dollar of cost. Everybody's looking for a bargain.

So what does this have to do with international trade? Well, suppose that Henri, an enterprising Frenchman, visited the United States before the advent of international trade. He observed that bread was relatively cheap while wine was relatively expensive—the opposite of the price relationship prevailing in France. These price comparisons brought to his mind the opportunity for making a fast euro. All he had to do was bring over some French wine and trade it in the United States for a large quantity of bread. Then he could return to France and exchange the bread for a greater quantity of wine. *Alors!* Were he to do this a few times, he'd amass substantial profits.

Henri's entrepreneurial exploits will not only enrich him but will also move each country toward its comparative advantage. The United States ends up exporting bread to France, and France ends up exporting wine to the United States, exactly as the theory of comparative advantage suggests. The activating agent isn't the Ministry of Trade and its 620 trained economists but simply one enterprising French trader. He's aided and encouraged, of course, by consumers and producers in each country. American consumers are happy to trade their bread for his wines. They thereby end up paying less for wine (in terms of bread) than they'd otherwise have to. In other words, the terms of trade Henri offers are more attractive than the prevailing (domestic) relative prices. On the other side of the Atlantic, Henri's welcome is equally warm. French consumers are able to get a better deal by trading their wine for his imported bread than by trading with the local bakers.

Even some producers are happy. The wheat farmers and bakers in the United States are eager to deal with Henri. He's willing to buy a lot of bread and even to pay a premium price for it. Indeed, bread production has become so profitable in the United States that a lot of people who used to grow and mash grapes are now growing wheat and kneading dough. This alters the mix of U.S. output in the direction of more bread, exactly as suggested in Figure 19.2*a*.

In France the opposite kind of production shift is taking place. French wheat farmers are planting more grape vines so they can take advantage of Henri's generous purchases. Thus Henri is able to lead each country in the direction of its comparative advantage while raking in a substantial profit for himself along the way.

Where the terms of trade and the volume of exports and imports end up depends partly on how good a trader Henri is. It will also depend on the behavior of the thousands of individual consumers and producers who participate in the market exchanges. In other words, trade flows depend on both the supply and the demand for bread and wine in each country. *The terms of trade, like the price of any good, depend on the willingness of market participants to buy or sell at various prices.* All we know for sure is that the terms of trade will end up somewhere between the limits set by each country's opportunity costs.

PROTECTIONIST PRESSURES

Although the potential gains from world trade are impressive, not everyone will be cheering at the Franco–American trade celebration. On the contrary, some people will be upset about the trade routes that Henri has established. They'll not only boycott the celebration but actively seek to discourage us from continuing to trade with France.

Microeconomic Pressures

Consider, for example, the winegrowers in western New York. Do you think they're going to be happy about Henri's entrepreneurship? Americans can now buy wine more cheaply from France than they can from New York. Before long we may hear talk about unfair foreign competition or about the greater nutritional value of American grapes (see the News on the next page). The New York winegrowers may also emphasize the importance of maintaining an adequate grape supply and a strong wine industry at home, just in case of terrorist attacks.

IN THE NEWS

California Grape Growers Protest Mixing Foreign Wine

California wine grape growers are growing increasingly frustrated and angry at each market percentage point gain of foreign wine in the U.S. wine market.

By the end of the year, burgeoning wine imports are expected to account for 30 percent of the U.S. market.

As the overall wine market in the United States grows at a healthy 2 percent to 5 percent annual clip, California grape growers continue to rip out vineyards. More than 100,000 acres in the Central Valley have been destroyed in the past five years. Growers are beyond weary of prices offered at less than production costs. . . .

Rubbing salt into the open economic sore this season includes record bulk, inexpensive wine imports that are being blended with California wines and sold by California wineries as "American" appellation wine. . . .

"California grape growers made a significant investment in wine grape vineyards on the signals from wineries that there was a bright future in California wine." Those same growers are seeing at least some of that bright future being taken by imports.

—Harry Cline

Source: **WesternFarmPress.com**, December 6, 2006. Used with permission of Penton Media, Inc.

ANALYSIS: Although trade increases consumption possibilities, imports typically compete with a domestic industry. The affected industries will try to restrict imports in order to preserve their own jobs and incomes.

Import-Competing Industries. Joining with the growers will be the farmworkers and the other merchants whose livelihood depends on the New York wine industry. If they're clever enough, the growers will also get the governor of the state to join their demonstration. After all, the governor must recognize the needs of his people, and his people definitely don't include the wheat farmers in Kansas who are making a bundle from international trade, much less French vintners. New York consumers are of course benefiting from lower wine prices, but they're unlikely to demonstrate over a few cents a bottle. On the other hand, those few extra pennies translate into millions of dollars for domestic wine producers.

The wheat farmers in France are no happier about international trade than are the wine-growers in the United States. They'd dearly love to sink all those boats bringing cheap wheat from America, thereby protecting their own market position.

If we're to make sense of trade policies, then, we must recognize one central fact of life: Some producers have a vested interest in restricting international trade. In particular, *workers and producers who compete with imported products—who work in import-competing industries—have an economic interest in restricting trade.* This helps explain why GM, Ford, and Chrysler are unhappy about auto imports and why shoe workers in Massachusetts want to end the importation of Italian shoes. It also explains why textile producers in South Carolina think China is behaving irresponsibly when it sells cheap cotton shirts and dresses in the United States.

Export Industries. Although imports typically mean fewer jobs and less income for some domestic industries, exports represent increased jobs and income for other industries. Producers and workers in export industries gain from trade. Thus on a microeconomic level there are identifiable gainers and losers from international trade. *Trade not only alters the mix of output but also redistributes income from import-competing industries to export industries.* This potential redistribution is the source of political and economic friction.

Net Gain. We must be careful to note, however, that the microeconomic gains from trade are greater than the microeconomic losses. It's not simply a question of robbing Peter to enrich Paul. We must remind ourselves that consumers enjoy a higher standard of living as a result of international trade. As we saw earlier, trade increases world efficiency and total output. Accordingly, we end up slicing up a larger pie rather than just reslicing the same old smaller pie.

The gains from trade will mean little to workers who end up with a smaller slice of the (larger) pie. It's important to remember, however, that the gains from trade are large enough to make everybody better off. Whether we actually choose to distribute the gains from trade in this way is a separate question, to which we shall return shortly. Note here, however, that *trade restrictions designed to protect specific microeconomic interests reduce the total gains from trade.* Trade restrictions leave us with a smaller pie to split up.

Additional Pressures

Import-competing industries are the principal obstacle to expanded international trade. Selfish micro interests aren't the only source of trade restrictions, however. Other arguments are also used to restrict trade.

National Security. The national security argument for trade restrictions is twofold. We can't depend on foreign suppliers to provide us with essential defense-related goods, it is said, because that would leave us vulnerable in time of war. The machine tool industry used this argument to protect itself from imports. In 1991 the Pentagon again sided with the toolmakers, citing the need for the United States to "gear up military production quickly in case of war," a contingency that couldn't be assured if weapons manufacturers relied on imported lathes, milling machines, and other tools. After the September 11, 2001, terrorist attacks on the World Trade Center and Pentagon, U.S. farmers convinced Congress to safeguard the nation's food supply with additional subsidies. The steel industry emphasized the importance of not depending on foreign suppliers.

Dumping. Another argument against free trade arises from the practice of **dumping.** Foreign producers "dump" their goods when they sell them in the United States at prices lower than those prevailing in their own country, perhaps even below the costs of production.

dumping: The sale of goods in export markets at prices below domestic prices.

Dumping may be unfair to import-competing producers, but it isn't necessarily unwelcome to the rest of us. As long as foreign producers continue dumping, we're getting foreign products at low prices. How bad can that be? There's a legitimate worry, however. Foreign producers might hold prices down only until domestic producers are driven out of business. Then we might be compelled to pay the foreign producers higher prices for their products. In that case, dumping could consolidate market power and lead to monopoly-type pricing. The fear of dumping, then, is analogous to the fear of predatory pricing.

The potential costs of dumping are serious. It's not always easy to determine when dumping occurs, however. Those who compete with imports have an uncanny ability to associate any and all low prices with predatory dumping. The United States has used dumping *charges* to restrict imports of Chinese shrimp, furniture, lingerie, solar panels, and other products in which China has an evident comparative advantage. The Chinese have retaliated with dozens of their own dumping investigations, including the fiber optic cable case. As the World View on the next page explains, such actions slow imports and protect domestic producers.

Infant Industries. Actual dumping threatens to damage already established domestic industries. Even normal import prices, however, may make it difficult or impossible for a new domestic industry to develop. Infant industries are often burdened with abnormally high start-up costs. These high costs may arise from the need to train a whole workforce and the expenses of establishing new marketing channels. With time to grow, however, an infant industry might experience substantial cost reductions and establish a comparative advantage. When this is the case, trade restrictions might help nurture an industry in its infancy. Trade restrictions are justified, however, only if there's tangible evidence that the industry can develop a comparative advantage reasonably quickly.

U.S. Imposes Tariffs on Steel from Nine Countries Accused of Dumping

The U.S. government on Friday announced substantial punitive tariffs on hundreds of millions of dollars worth of steel products imported from South Korea and eight other countries.

The much-anticipated decision marks one of the largest dumping cases in recent memory and could embolden domestic steel makers to file more claims of unfair pricing against foreign shippers.

Steel from the nine countries will be hit with tariffs of up to 118%, but the lion's share of imported steel products in this case, from South Korea, were levied much smaller duties of 10% to 16%.

In the short term, the decision is expected to curb steel imports and lift prices of certain steel goods that could be felt by American businesses and consumers—and it could help restore a few hundred steel factory jobs that were idled because of pressures from imports. . . .

There's little doubt that the surge of imports has undercut some of the expected benefits for American producers such as United States Steel Corp. As fracking and other techniques to tap natural gas and oil has sharply boosted demand for steel tubes used for drilling and building pipelines, imports of these products from the nine countries topped $1.7 billion last year, more than a jump of 31% from 2010. . . .

Despite an international oversupply, U.S. Steel Corp. and other domestic operators charged substantially more than global competitors for these tubular goods. That's possible, analysts say, because the industry has gone through severe restructuring over the decades and is now not only more lean and productive, but also more concentrated with greater ability to dictate prices.

—Don Lee

Source: "U.S. imposes tariffs on steel from nine countries accused of dumping," *Los Angeles Times,* July 11, 2014. Used with permission.

ANALYSIS: *Dumping* means that a foreign producer is selling exports at prices below cost or below prices in the home market, putting import-competing industries at a competitive disadvantage. *Accusations* of dumping are an effective trade barrier.

Improving the Terms of Trade. A final argument for restricting trade rests on how the gains from trade are distributed. As we observed, the distribution of the gains from trade depends on the terms of trade. If we were to buy fewer imports, foreign producers might lower their prices. If that happened, the terms of trade would move in our favor, and we'd end up with a larger share of the gains from trade.

One way to bring about this sequence of events is to put restrictions on imports, making it more difficult or expensive for Americans to buy foreign products. Such restrictions will reduce the volume of imports, thereby inducing foreign producers to lower their prices. Unfortunately, this strategy can easily backfire. Retaliatory restrictions on imports, each designed to improve the terms of trade, will ultimately eliminate all trade and therewith all the gains people were competing for in the first place.

BARRIERS TO TRADE

The microeconomic losses associated with imports give rise to a constant clamor for trade restrictions. People whose jobs and incomes are threatened by international trade tend to organize quickly and air their grievances. The World View on the next page depicts the efforts of farmers in the Czech Republic to limit imports of Austrian pork. They wanted their government to impose restrictions on imports. More often than not, governments grant the wishes of these well-organized and well-financed special interests.

Embargoes

embargo: A prohibition on exports or imports.

The surefire way to restrict trade is simply to eliminate it. To do so, a country need only impose an embargo on exports or imports, or both. An **embargo** is nothing more than a prohibition against trading particular goods.

WORLD VIEW

Meat Imports "Threaten" Farmers

Around 200 Czech farmers held a protest action March 26 on the Czech–Austrian border crossing in Dolni Dvořiště, South Bohemia, against meat imports. The protest was to draw attention to the situation of Czech pig breeders who claim they are threatened by growing pork imports to Czech retail chains and low purchasing prices.

Representatives of the Agricultural Chamber (AK) said it was a token protest, but didn't rule out further actions.

"We will . . . send an appeal to the Ministry of Agriculture, the Chamber of Deputies, and the Senate, asking them for public support of Czech farmers and Czech food," said Jan Veleba, president of the AK. . . .

Minister of Agriculture Petr Gandalovič said blockades won't resolve the situation and would probably only worsen relations between the Czech Republic and Austria.

Source: *Czech Business Weekly,* April 2, 2007. Used with permission.

ANALYSIS: Import-competing industries cite lots of reasons for restricting trade. Their primary concern, however, is to protect their own jobs and profits.

In 1951 Senator Joseph McCarthy convinced the U.S. Senate to impose an embargo on Soviet mink, fox, and five other furs. He argued that such imports helped finance world communism. Senator McCarthy also represented the state of Wisconsin, where most U.S. minks are raised. The Reagan administration tried to end the fur embargo in 1987 but met with stiff congressional opposition. By then U.S. mink ranchers had developed a $120 million per year industry.

The United States has also maintained an embargo on Cuban goods since 1959, when Fidel Castro took power there. This embargo severely damaged Cuba's sugar industry and deprived American smokers of the famed Havana cigars. It also fostered the development of U.S. sugar beet and tobacco farmers, who now have a vested interest in maintaining the embargo.

Tariffs

A more frequent trade restriction is a **tariff,** a special tax imposed on imported goods. Tariffs, also called *customs duties,* were once the principal source of revenue for governments. In the 18th century, tariffs on tea, glass, wine, lead, and paper were imposed on the American colonies to provide extra revenue for the British government. The tariff on tea led to the Boston Tea Party in 1773 and gave added momentum to the American independence movement. In modern times, tariffs have been used primarily as a means to protect specific industries from import competition. The current U.S. tariff code specifies tariffs on more than 9,000 different products—nearly 50 percent of all U.S. imports. Although the average tariff is less than 5 percent, individual tariffs vary widely. The tariff on cars, for example, is only 2.5 percent, while cotton sweaters confront a 17.8 percent tariff.

The attraction of tariffs to import-competing industries should be obvious. *A tariff on imported goods makes them more expensive to domestic consumers and thus less competitive with domestically produced goods.* Among familiar tariffs in effect in 2014 were 50 cents per gallon on Scotch whisky and 76 cents per gallon on imported champagne. These tariffs made American-produced spirits look relatively cheap and thus contributed to higher sales and profits for domestic distillers and grape growers. In the same manner, imported baby food is taxed at 34.6 percent, maple sugar at 9.4 percent, golf shoes at 8.5 percent, and imported sailboats at 1.5 percent. In 2009 President Obama imposed a 35 percent tariff on imported Chinese tires and a 26 percent tariff on Chinese solar panels in 2014 (see the World View on the next page). In each case, domestic producers in import-competing industries gain. The losers are domestic consumers, who end up paying higher

tariff: A tax (duty) imposed on imported goods.

U.S. Imposes Tariffs on Solar Panels from China

Last year, China sold more than $2 billion worth of solar panels and equipment in the United States, about a third of all sales. Domestic producers say those sales were unfairly facilitated by Chinese government subsidies and deliberate "dumping." Chinese solar panels sell for about 70 cents per watt, compared with 83 cents per watt for panels produced in the United States. The market for panels in 2014 is expected to hit 6,000 megawatts.

On Friday, the Commerce Department sided with domestic producers, concluding that China's solar equipment was being sold at "unfairly low prices." To offset that unfair price advantage, the department imposed tariffs of 26 percent or more on imported Chinese panels. Several U.S. manufacturers said the move would prompt them to expand production capacity in the United States.

Source: U.S. Department of Commerce; news reports, July 25–27, 2014.

ANALYSIS: By raising the price of imported goods, tariffs reduce imports and protect import-compelling industries. But consumers lose.

prices. The tariff on orange juice, for example, raises the price of drinking orange juice by $525 million a year. Tariffs also hurt foreign producers, who lose business, and world efficiency, as trade is reduced.

"Beggar Thy Neighbor." Microeconomic interests aren't the only source of pressure for tariff protection. Imports represent leakage from the domestic circular flow and a potential loss of jobs at home. From this perspective, reducing imports looks like an easy solution to the problem of domestic unemployment. Just get people to "buy American" instead of buying imported products, so the argument goes, and domestic output and employment will surely expand. President Obama used this argument to include "buy American" rules in his 2009 stimulus package.

Congressman Willis Hawley used this same argument in 1930. He assured his colleagues that higher tariffs would "bring about the growth and development in this country that has followed every other tariff bill, bringing as it does a new prosperity in which all people, in all sections, will increase their comforts, their enjoyment, and their happiness."[1] Congress responded by passing the Smoot-Hawley Tariff Act of 1930, which raised tariffs to an average of nearly 60 percent, effectively cutting off most imports.

Tariffs designed to expand domestic employment are more likely to fail than to succeed. If a tariff wall does stem the flow of imports, it effectively transfers the unemployment problem to other countries, a phenomenon often referred to as "beggar thy neighbor." The resultant loss of business in other countries leaves them less able to purchase our exports. The imported unemployment also creates intense political pressures for retaliatory action. That's exactly what happened in the 1930s. Other countries erected trade barriers to compensate for the effects of the Smoot-Hawley tariff. World trade subsequently fell from $60 billion in 1928 to a mere $25 billion in 1938. This trade contraction increased the severity of the Great Depression (see the World View on the next page).

The same kind of macroeconomic threat surfaced in 2009. The "buy American" provisions introduced by the Obama administration angered foreign nations that would lose export sales. When they threatened to retaliate with trade barriers of their own, President Obama had to offer reassurances about America's commitment to "free trade."

[1]*The New York Times*, June 15, 1930, p. 25.

"Beggar-Thy-Neighbor" Policies in the 1930s

President Herbert Hoover signed the Smoot-Hawley Tariff Act on June 17, 1930, despite the pleas from 1,028 economists to veto it. The Act raised the effective tariff on imports by 50 percent between 1929 and 1932. Although designed to limit import competition and boost domestic employment, the Act triggered quick retaliation from America's trading partners:

- Spain passed the Wais tariff in July in reaction to U.S. tariffs on grapes, oranges, cork, and onions.
- Switzerland, objecting to new U.S. tariffs on watches, embroideries, and shoes, boycotted American exports.
- Italy retaliated against tariffs on hats and olive oil with high tariffs on U.S. and French automobiles in June 1930.
- Canada reacted to high duties on many food products, logs, and timber by raising tariffs threefold in August 1932.
- Australia, Cuba, France, Mexico, and New Zealand also joined in the tariff wars.

From 1930 to 1931 U.S. imports dropped 29 percent, but U.S. exports fell even more, 33 percent, and continued their collapse to a modern-day low of $2.4 billion in 1933. World trade contracted by similar proportions, spreading unemployment around the globe.

In 1934 the U.S. Congress passed the Reciprocal Trade Agreements Act to empower the president to reduce tariffs by half the 1930 rates in return for like cuts in foreign duties on U.S. goods. The "beggar-thy-neighbor" policy was dead. Since then, the nations of the world have been reducing tariffs and other trade barriers.

Source: The World Bank, "'Beggar-Thy-Neighbor' Policies in the 1930s," *World Development Report 1987*, p. 139, Box 8.4. Used with permission.

ANALYSIS: Tariffs inflict harm on foreign producers. If foreign countries retaliate with tariffs of their own, world trade will shrink and unemployment will increase in all countries.

web click

The tariff schedule for imported products is available online from the U.S. International Trade Commission. Go to **www.usitc.gov** and click the "Tariff Affairs" tab, and then "Harmonized Tariff Schedule."

Quotas

Tariffs reduce the flow of imports by raising import prices. The same outcome can be attained more directly by imposing import **quotas,** numerical restrictions on the quantity of a particular good that may be imported. The United States limits the quantity of ice cream imported from Jamaica to 950 gallons a year. Only 1.4 million kilograms of Australian cheddar cheese and no more than 7,730 tons of Haitian sugar can be imported. Textile quotas are imposed on every country that wants to ship textiles to the U.S. market. According to the U.S. Department of State, approximately 12 percent of our imports are subject to import quotas.

quota: A limit on the quantity of a good that may be imported in a given time period.

Comparative Effects

Quotas, like all barriers to trade, reduce world efficiency and invite retaliatory action. Moreover, their impact can be even more damaging than tariffs. To see this, we may compare market outcomes in four different contexts: no trade, free trade, tariff-restricted trade, and quota-restricted trade.

No-Trade Equilibrium. Figure 19.4*a* depicts the supply-and-demand relationships that would prevail in an economy that imposed a trade *embargo* on foreign textiles. In this situation, the **equilibrium price** of textiles is completely determined by domestic demand and supply curves. The no-trade equilibrium price is p_1, and the quantity of textiles consumed is q_1.

equilibrium price: The price at which the quantity of a good demanded in a given time period equals the quantity supplied.

FIGURE 19.4

The Impact of Trade Restrictions

In the *absence of trade,* the domestic price and sales of a good will be determined by domestic supply and demand curves (point *A* in part *a*). Once trade is permitted, the market supply curve will be altered by the availability of imports. With *free trade* and unlimited availability of imports at price p_2, a new market equilibrium will be established at world prices (point *B*).

Tariffs raise domestic prices and reduce the quantity sold (point *C*). *Quotas* put an absolute limit on imported sales and thus give domestic producers a great opportunity to raise the market price (point *D*).

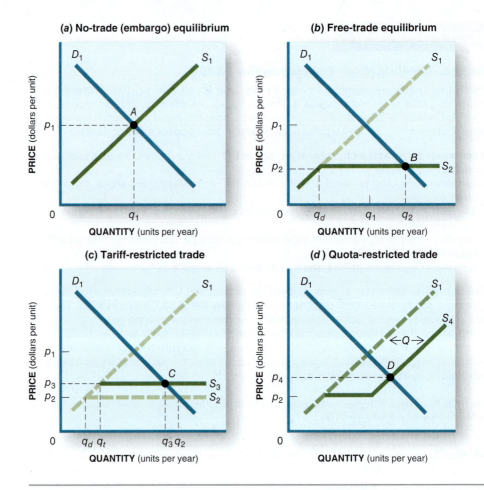

"TELL ME AGAIN HOW THE QUOTAS ON JAPANESE CARS HAVE PROTECTED US"

A 1987 Herblock Cartoon © The Herb Block Foundation.

Analysis: Trade restrictions that protect import-competing industries also raise consumer prices.

* Reprinted by permission of SLL/Sterling Lord Literistic, Inc. Copyright by Herbert Block.

Free-Trade Equilibrium. Suppose now that the embargo is lifted. The immediate effect of this decision will be a rightward shift of the market supply curve, as foreign supplies are added to domestic supplies (Figure 19.4*b*). If an unlimited quantity of textiles can be bought in world markets at a price of p_2, the new supply curve will look like S_2 (infinitely elastic at p_2). The new supply curve (S_2) intersects the old demand curve (D_1) at a new equilibrium price of p_2 and an expanded consumption of q_2. At this new equilibrium, domestic producers are supplying the quantity q_d while foreign producers are supplying the rest ($q_2 - q_d$). Comparing the new equilibrium to the old one, we see that ***free trade results in reduced prices and increased consumption.***

Domestic textile producers are unhappy, of course, with their foreign competition. In the absence of trade, the domestic producers would sell more output (q_1) and get higher prices (p_1). Once trade is opened up, the willingness of foreign producers to sell unlimited quantities of textiles at the price p_2 puts a lid on domestic prices. Domestic producers hate this.

Tariff-Restricted Trade. Figure 19.4*c* illustrates what would happen to prices and sales if the United Textile Producers were successful in persuading the government to impose a tariff. Assume that the tariff raises imported textile prices from p_2 to p_3, making it more difficult for foreign producers to undersell domestic producers. Domestic production expands from q_d to q_t, imports are reduced from $q_2 - q_d$ to $q_3 - q_t$, and the market price of textiles rises. Domestic textile producers are clearly better off. So is the U.S. Treasury, which will collect increased tariff revenues. Unfortunately, domestic consumers are worse off (higher prices), as are foreign producers (reduced sales).

Quota-Restricted Trade. Now consider the impact of a textile *quota*. Suppose we eliminate tariffs but decree that imports can't exceed the quantity Q. Because the quantity of imports can never exceed Q, the supply curve is effectively shifted to the right by that amount. The new curve S_4 (Figure 19.4d) indicates that no imports will occur below the world price p_2 and above that price the quantity Q will be imported. Thus the *domestic* demand curve determines subsequent prices. Foreign producers are precluded from selling greater quantities as prices rise further. This outcome is in marked contrast to that of tariff-restricted trade (Figure 19.4c), which at least permits foreign producers to respond to rising prices. Accordingly, ***quotas are a greater threat to competition than tariffs because quotas preclude additional imports at any price.*** The actual quotas on textile imports raise the prices of shirts, towels, and other textile products by 58 percent. As a result, a $10 shirt ends up costing consumers $15.80. All told, U.S. consumers end up paying an extra $25 billion a year for textile products.

The sugar industry is one of the greatest beneficiaries of quota restrictions. By limiting imports to 15 percent of domestic consumption, sugar quotas keep U.S. prices artificially high (see the News below). This costs consumers nearly $3 billion a year in higher prices. Candy and soda producers lose sales and profits. According to the U.S. Department of Commerce, more than 6,000 jobs have been lost in sugar-using industries (e.g., candy manufacturing) due to high sugar costs. Hershey alone closed plants in Pennsylvania, Colorado, and California and moved candy production to Canada. Foreign sugar producers (mainly in poor nations) also lose sales, profits, and jobs. Who gains? Domestic sugar producers—who, coincidentally, are highly concentrated in key electoral states like Florida.

IN THE NEWS

End the Import Quotas on Sugar

For years, domestic sugar producers have profited from quotas limiting sugar imports, boosting prices to American users.

Such protectionism takes from American consumers for politically powerful sugar producers. And it is an issue now that the difference between American prices (35.02 cents per pound) and world prices (19.67 cents per pound) has reached its highest level in over a decade. . . .

Quotas effectively impose a steep sugar tax on consumers, with the proceeds paid to domestic producers. One result? The makers of Life Savers, Red Hots, Jaw Breakers, and other candies have shifted production elsewhere in response. . . .

America's sugar protectionism has never been anything but a concentrated interest group—sugar producers . . . —using government power to keep out lower-cost foreign producers and rip off American consumers on their behalf. It is a sweet deal for them only because it is such a sour deal for the rest of us.

—Gary M. Galles

Source: Editorial, "End the Import Quotas on Sugar," *St. Petersburg Times*, March 23, 2010. Used with permission via icopyright.

ANALYSIS: Import quotas preclude increased foreign competition when domestic prices rise. Protected domestic producers enjoy higher prices and profits while consumers pay higher prices.

Voluntary Restraint Agreements

A slight variant of quotas has been used in recent years. Rather than impose quotas on imports, the U.S. government asks foreign producers to "voluntarily" limit their exports. These so-called **voluntary restraint agreements** have been negotiated with producers in Japan, South Korea, Taiwan, China, the European Union, and other countries. Korea, for example, agreed to reduce its annual shoe exports to the United States from 44 million pairs to 33 million pairs. Taiwan reduced its shoe exports from 156 million pairs to 122 million pairs per year. In 2005 China agreed to slow its exports of clothing, limiting its sales growth to 8–17 percent a year. For their part, the Japanese agreed to reduce sales of color TV sets in the United States from 2.8 million to 1.75 million per year. In 2006 Mexico agreed to limit its cement exports to the United States to 3 million tons a year.

voluntary restraint agreement (VRA): An agreement to reduce the volume of trade in a specific good; a voluntary quota.

All these voluntary export restraints, as they're often called, represent an informal type of quota. The only difference is that they're negotiated rather than imposed. But these differences are lost on consumers, who end up paying higher prices for these goods. The voluntary limit on Japanese auto exports to the United States alone cost consumers $15.7 billion in only four years.

Nontariff Barriers

Tariffs and quotas are the most visible barriers to trade, but they're only the tip of the iceberg. Indeed, the variety of protectionist measures that have been devised is testimony to the ingenuity of the human mind. At the turn of the century, the Germans were committed to a most-favored-nation policy: a policy of extending equal treatment to all trading partners. The Germans, however, wanted to lower the tariff on cattle imports from Denmark without extending the same break to Switzerland. Such a preferential tariff would have violated the most-favored-nation policy. Accordingly, the Germans created a new and higher tariff on "brown and dappled cows reared at a level of at least 300 meters above sea level and passing at least one month in every summer at an altitude of at least 800 meters." The new tariff was, of course, applied equally to all countries. But Danish cows never climb that high, so they weren't burdened with the new tariff.

With the decline in tariffs over the last 20 years, nontariff barriers have increased. The United States uses product standards, licensing restrictions, restrictive procurement practices, and other nontariff barriers to restrict roughly 15 percent of imports. In 1999–2000 the European Union banned imports of U.S. beef, arguing that the use of hormones on U.S. ranches created a health hazard for European consumers. Although both the U.S. government and the World Trade Organization disputed that claim, the ban was a highly effective nontariff trade barrier. The United States responded by slapping 100 percent tariffs on dozens of European products.

Mexican Trucks. One of the more flagrant examples of nontariff barriers is the use of safety regulations to block Mexican trucking companies from using U.S. roads to deliver goods. The resulting trade barrier forces Mexican trucks to unload their cargoes at the U.S. border, and then reload them into U.S. (Teamster-driven) trucks for shipment to U.S. destinations. The U.S. agreed to lift that restriction in 1995, but didn't. In 2009 President Obama actually solidified the Mexican roadblock, despite the fact that Mexican trucks passed all 22 safety (nontariff) regulations the U.S. Department of Transportation had imposed. In so doing, President Obama secured more jobs for Teamster-union drivers, but raised costs for U.S. shippers and consumers and drove down sales and employment for Mexican trucking companies. Fed up with U.S. protectionism, Mexico retaliated by slapping tariffs on 90 U.S. export products (see the World View below). By early 2011, U.S. exports to Mexico of those products had declined by 81 percent. This prompted President Obama to offer Mexico a new round of negotiations for a "reciprocal, phase-in program" that would ease trade barriers.

WORLD VIEW

Mexico Retaliates for Loss of Truck Program

Mexico announced Monday it will increase tariffs on 90 U.S. industrial and agricultural goods in reprisal for the United States canceling a test program that gave Mexican trucks access to U.S. highways. Mexican Economy Minister Gerardo Ruiz said around $2.4 billion worth of U.S. exports would be affected and that the government would soon publish a list. U.S. labor, highway safety, and consumer groups have opposed the truck access permitted under the North American Free Trade Agreement.

Source: *USA TODAY*, March 17, 2009, p. B1. Reprinted with permission.

ANALYSIS: Nontariff barriers like extraordinary safety requirements on Mexican trucks limit import competition and invite retaliation.

THE ECONOMY TOMORROW

POLICING WORLD TRADE

Proponents of free trade and import-competing industries are in constant conflict. Most of the time the trade policy deck seems stacked in favor of the special interests. Because import-competing firms and workers are highly concentrated, they're quick to mobilize politically. By contrast, the benefits of freer trade are less direct and spread over millions of consumers. As a consequence, the beneficiaries of freer trade are less likely to monitor trade policy—much less lobby actively to change it. Hence the political odds favor the spread of trade barriers.

Multilateral Trade Pacts. Despite these odds, the long-term trend is toward *lowering* trade barriers, thereby increasing global competition. Two forces encourage this trend. ***The principal barrier to protectionist policies is worldwide recognition of the gains from freer trade.*** Since world nations now understand that trade barriers are ultimately self-defeating, they're more willing to rise above the din of protectionist cries and dismantle trade barriers. They diffuse political opposition by creating across-the-board trade pacts that seem to spread the pain (and gain) from freer trade across a broad swath of industries. Such pacts also incorporate multiyear timetables that give affected industries time to adjust.

Trade liberalization has also been encouraged by firms that *export* products or use imported inputs in their own production. Tariffs on imported steel raise product costs for U.S.-based auto producers and construction companies. In 2007 the European Union eliminated a tariff on frozen Chinese strawberries, largely due to complaints from EU yogurt and jam producers who were incurring higher costs.

Global Pacts: GATT and WTO. The granddaddy of the multilateral, multiyear free-trade pacts was the 1947 *General Agreement on Tariffs and Trade (GATT)*. Twenty-three nations pledged to reduce trade barriers and give all GATT nations equal access to their domestic markets.

Since the first GATT pact, seven more "rounds" of negotiations have expanded the scope of GATT; 117 nations signed the 1994 pact. As a result of these GATT pacts, average tariff rates in developed countries have fallen from 40 percent in 1948 to less than 4 percent today.

WTO. The 1994 GATT pact also created the *World Trade Organization (WTO)* to enforce free-trade rules. If a nation feels its exports are being unfairly excluded from another country's market, it can file a complaint with the WTO. This is exactly what the United States did when the EU banned U.S. beef imports. The WTO ruled in favor of the United States. When the EU failed to lift its import ban, the WTO authorized the United States to impose retaliatory tariffs on European exports.

The EU turned the tables on the United States in 2003. It complained to the WTO that U.S. tariffs on imported steel violated trade rules. The WTO agreed and gave the EU permission to impose retaliatory tariffs on $2.2 billion of U.S. exports. That prompted the Bush administration to scale back the tariffs in December 2003.

In effect, the WTO is now the world's trade police force. It is empowered to cite nations that violate trade agreements and even to impose remedial action when violations persist. Why do sovereign nations give the WTO such power? Because they are all convinced that free trade is the surest route to GDP growth.

Regional Pacts. Because worldwide trade pacts are so complex, many nations have also pursued *regional* free-trade agreements.

NAFTA. In December 1992 the United States, Canada, and Mexico signed the *North American Free Trade Agreement (NAFTA),* a 1,000-page document covering more than 9,000 products. The ultimate goal of NAFTA is to eliminate all trade barriers between these three countries. At the time of signing, intraregional tariffs averaged 11 percent in Mexico, 5 percent in Canada, and 4 percent in the United States. NAFTA requires that all tariffs among the three countries be eliminated. The pact also requires the elimination of specific nontariff barriers.

The NAFTA-initiated reduction in trade barriers substantially increased trade flows between Mexico, Canada, and the United States. It also prompted a wave of foreign investment in Mexico, where both cheap labor and NAFTA access were available. Overall, NAFTA accelerated economic growth and reduced inflationary pressures in all three nations. Some industries (like construction and apparel) suffered from the freer trade, but others (like trucking, farming, and finance) reaped huge gains (see the News below).

IN THE NEWS

NAFTA Reallocates Labor: Comparative Advantage at Work

More Jobs in These Industries		but . . .	Fewer Jobs in These Industries	
Agriculture	+10,600		Construction	−12,800
Metal products	+6,100		Medicine	−6,000
Electrical appliances	+5,200		Apparel	−5,900
Business services	+5,000		Lumber	−1,200
Motor vehicles	+5,000		Furniture	−400

Source: Congressional Budget Office.

The lowering of trade barriers between Mexico and the United States is changing the mix of output in both countries. New export opportunities create jobs in some industries while increased imports eliminate jobs in other industries. (Estimated gains and losses are during the first five years of NAFTA.)

ANALYSIS: The specialization encouraged by free trade creates new jobs in export but reduces employment in import-competing industries. In the process, total world output increases.

CAFTA. The success of NAFTA prompted a similar 2005 agreement between the United States and Central American nations. The Central American Free Trade Agreement (CAFTA) aims to standardize trade and investment policies in CAFTA nations, while eliminating tariffs on thousands of products.

As trade barriers continue to fall around the world, the global marketplace is likely to become more open. The resulting increase in competition should spur efficiency and growth in the economy tomorrow.

SUMMARY

- International trade permits each country to specialize in areas of relative efficiency, increasing world output. For each country, the gains from trade are reflected in consumption possibilities that exceed production possibilities. **LO19-2**
- One way to determine where comparative advantage lies is to compare the quantity of good A that must be given up in order to get a given quantity of good B from domestic production. If the same quantity of B can be obtained for less A by engaging in world trade, we have a comparative advantage in the production of good A. Comparative advantage rests on a comparison of relative opportunity costs. **LO19-1**

- The terms of trade—the rate at which goods are exchanged—are subject to the forces of international supply and demand. The terms of trade will lie somewhere between the opportunity costs of the trading partners. The terms of trade determine how the gains from trade are shared. **LO19-2**
- Resistance to trade emanates from workers and firms that must compete with imports. Even though the country as a whole stands to benefit from trade, these individuals and companies may lose jobs and incomes in the process. **LO19-3**
- Trade barriers take many forms. Embargoes are outright prohibitions against import or export of particular goods.

Quotas limit the quantity of a good imported or exported. Tariffs discourage imports by making them more expensive. Other nontariff barriers make trade too costly or time-consuming. **LO19-3**

- The World Trade Organization (WTO) seeks to reduce worldwide trade barriers and enforce trade rules. Regional accords such as the North American Free Trade Agreement (NAFTA) and the Central American Free Trade Agreement (CAFTA) pursue similar objectives among fewer countries. **LO19-3**

Key Terms

imports	consumption possibilities	dumping
exports	open economy	embargo
trade deficit	comparative advantage	tariff
trade surplus	opportunity cost	quota
production possibilities	absolute advantage	equilibrium price
closed economy	terms of trade	voluntary restraint agreement (VRA)

Questions for Discussion

1. Suppose a lawyer can type faster than any secretary. Should the lawyer do her own typing? Can you demonstrate the validity of your answer? **LO19-1**
2. What would be the effects of a law requiring bilateral trade balances? **LO19-2**
3. If a nation exported much of its output but imported little, would it be better or worse off? How about the reverse—that is, exporting little but importing a lot? **LO19-2**
4. How does international trade restrain the price behavior of domestic firms? **LO19-3**
5. Suppose we refused to sell goods to any country that reduced or halted its exports to us. Who would benefit and who would lose from such retaliation? **LO19-2**
6. Domestic producers often base their demands for import protection on the fact that workers in country X are paid substandard wages. Is this a valid argument for protection? **LO19-1**
7. On the basis of the News on page 432, how do U.S. furniture manufacturers feel about NAFTA? How about farmers? **LO19-3**
8. According to the U.S. Department of Commerce, three candy-making jobs are lost for every one job protected by import quotas in the raw sugar industry. How does this happen? **LO19-3**
9. Who gains and who loses from nontariff barriers to Mexican trucks (World View, p. 430)? What made President Obama offer renewed negotiations? **LO19-3**
10. Has the tariff on Chinese solar panels (p. 426) affected you or your family? Who has been affected? **LO19-3**

mobile app Visit your mobile app store and download the Schiller: Study Econ app *today!*

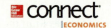
LO19-2 1. Which countries are

    (*a*) the two largest export markets for the United States? (See Table 19.3.)   (1) _____

                                                          (2) _____

    (*b*) The two biggest sources of imports?   (1) _____

                                                           (2) _____

LO19-1 2. Suppose a country can produce a maximum of 12,000 jumbo airliners or 2,000 aircraft carriers.

    (*a*) What is the opportunity cost of an aircraft carrier?   _____

    (*b*) If another country offers to trade eight planes for one aircraft carrier, should the offer be accepted?   _____

    (*c*) What is the implied price of the carrier in trade?   _____

LO19-1 3. If it takes 15 farmworkers to harvest 1 ton of strawberries and 3 farmworkers to harvest 1 ton of wheat, what is the opportunity cost of 5 tons of strawberries?   _____

LO19-2 4. Alpha and Beta, two tiny islands off the east coast of Tricoli, produce pearls and pineapples. The following production possibilities schedules describe their potential output in tons per year:

Alpha			Beta	
Pearls	**Pineapples**		**Pearls**	**Pineapples**
0	30		0	20
2	25		10	16
4	20		20	12
6	15		30	8
8	10		40	4
10	5		45	2
12	0		50	0

    (*a*) Graph the production possibilities confronting each island.

    (*b*) What is the opportunity cost of pineapples on each island (before trade)?   Alpha: _____

                                                          Beta: _____

    (*c*) Which island has a comparative advantage in pearl production?   _____

    (*d*) Graph the consumption possibilities of each island with free trade.

    (*e*) If Beta produced only pearls,

        (*i*) How many could it produce?   _____

        (*ii*) How many pearls would it have to export to get 20 pineapples in return?   _____

        (*iii*) What is the net gain to Beta in this case?   _____

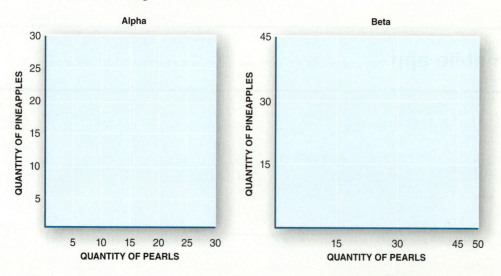

PROBLEMS FOR CHAPTER 19 (cont'd)   Name: _____

LO19-3 5. (*a*) How much more are U.S. consumers paying for the 24 billion pounds of sugar they consume
each year as a result of the quotas on sugar imports? (See News, p. 429.)   _____
(*b*) How much sales revenue are foreign sugar producers losing as a result of those same quotas?   _____

LO19-2 6. (*a*) What was the price difference between U.S. and Chinese solar panels in 2013?   _____
(*b*) How much money did U.S. consumers save as a result of this price difference if they
purchased 2,000 megawatts of Chinese paneling in 2013?   _____
(*c*) By how much did the price of Chinese solar panels rise in 2014 as a result of the new tariff?   _____

LO19-2 7. Suppose the two islands in Problem 4 agree that the terms of trade will be one for one and
exchange 10 pearls for 10 pineapples.
(*a*) If Alpha produced 6 pearls and 15 pineapples while Beta produced 30 pearls and   Alpha: _____
8 pineapples before they decided to trade, how many pearls would each be producing   Beta: _____
after trade? Assume that the two countries specialize according to their comparative advantage.
(*b*) How much would the combined production of pineapples increase for the two islands due to
specialization?   _____
(*c*) How much would the combined production of pearls increase?   _____

LO19-3 8. Suppose the following table reflects the domestic supply and demand for compact discs (CDs):

Price ($)	18	16	14	12	10	8	6	4
Quantity supplied	8	7	6	5	4	3	2	1
Quantity demanded	2	4	6	8	10	12	14	16

(*a*) Graph these market conditions and identify
(*i*) The equilibrium price.   _____
(*ii*) The equilibrium quantity.   _____
(*b*) Now suppose that foreigners enter the market, offering to sell an unlimited supply of CDs for
$6 apiece. Illustrate and identify
(*i*) The new market price.   _____
(*ii*) Domestic consumption.   _____
(*iii*) Domestic production.   _____
(*c*) If a tariff of $2 per CD is imposed, what will be
(*i*) The market price?   _____
(*ii*) Domestic consumption?   _____
(*iii*) Domestic production?   _____
Graph your answers.

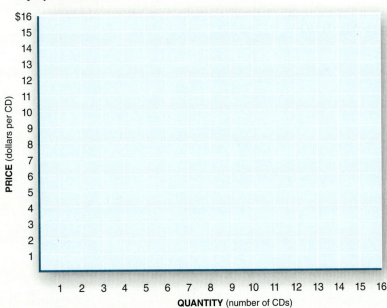

International Finance

After reading this chapter, you should know

LO20-1 The sources of foreign exchange demand and supply.

LO20-2 How exchange rates are established.

LO20-3 How changes in exchange rates affect prices, output, and trade flows.

Textile, furniture, and shrimp producers in the United States want China to increase the value of the yuan. They say China's undervalued currency makes Chinese exports too cheap, undercutting American firms. On the other hand, Walmart thinks a cheap yuan is a good thing because it keeps prices low for the *$16 billion* of toys, tools, linens, and other goods it buys from China each year. Those low import prices help Walmart keep its own prices low and its sales volume high.

This chapter examines how currency values affect trade patterns and ultimately the core questions of WHAT, HOW, and FOR WHOM to produce. We focus on the following questions:

- **What determines the value of one country's money compared to the value of another's?**
- **What causes the international value of currencies to change?**
- **Should governments intervene to limit currency fluctuations?**

EXCHANGE RATES: THE GLOBAL LINK

As we saw in Chapter 19, the United States exports and imports a staggering volume of goods and services. Although we trade with nearly 200 nations around the world, we seldom give much thought to where imports come from and how we acquire them. Most of the time, all we want to know is which products are available and at what price.

Suppose you want to buy an Apple iPad. You don't have to know that iPads are manufactured in China. And you certainly don't have to fly to China to pick it up. All you have to do is drive to the nearest electronics store; or you can just "click and buy" at the Internet's virtual mall.

But you may wonder how the purchase of an imported product was so simple. Chinese companies sell their products in yuan, the currency of China. But you purchase the iPad in dollars. How is this possible?

There's a chain of distribution between your dollar purchase in the United States and the yuan-denominated sale in China. Somewhere along that chain someone has to convert your dollars into yuan. The critical question for everybody concerned is how many yuan we can get for our dollars—that is, what the **exchange rate** is. If we can get eight yuan for every dollar, the exchange rate is 8 yuan = 1 dollar. Alternatively, we could note that the price of a yuan is 12.5 U.S. cents when the exchange rate is 8 to 1. Thus *an exchange rate is the price of one currency in terms of another.*

Which currency is most valuable? It depends on exchange rates.

exchange rate: The price of one country's currency expressed in terms of another's; the domestic price of a foreign currency.

FOREIGN EXCHANGE MARKETS

Most exchange rates are determined in foreign exchange markets. Stop thinking of money as some sort of magical substance, and instead view it as a useful commodity that facilitates market exchanges. From that perspective, an exchange rate—the price of money—is subject to the same influences that determine all market prices: demand and supply.

The Demand for Dollars

When the Japanese Toshiba Corporation bought Westinghouse Electric Co. in 2006, it paid $5.4 billion. When Belgian beer maker InBev bought Anheuser-Busch (Budweiser, etc.) in 2008, it also needed dollars—more than 50 billion of them. When Fiat acquired control of Chrysler in 2011, it also needed U.S. dollars. In all three cases, the objective of the foreign investor was to acquire an American business. To attain their objectives, however, the buyers first had to buy *dollars*. The Japanese, Belgian, and Italian buyers had to exchange their own currency for American dollars.

Canadian tourists also need American dollars. Few American restaurants or hotels accept Canadian currency as payment for goods and services; they want to be paid in U.S. dollars. Accordingly, Canadian tourists must buy American dollars if they want to warm up in Florida.

Some foreign investors also buy U.S. dollars for speculative purposes. When Argentina's peso started losing value in 2012–2013, many Argentinians feared that its value would drop further and preferred to hold U.S. dollars; they *demanded* U.S. dollars. Ukrainians clamored for U.S. dollars when Russia invaded its territory in 2014.

All these motivations give rise to a demand for U.S. dollars. Specifically, *the market demand for U.S. dollars originates in*

- *Foreign demand for American exports* (including tourism).
- *Foreign demand for American investments.*
- *Speculation.*

Governments also create a demand for dollars when they operate embassies, undertake cultural exchanges, or engage in intergovernment financial transactions.

The Supply of Dollars

The *supply* of dollars arises from similar sources. On the supply side, however, it's Americans who initiate most of the exchanges. Suppose you take a trip to Mexico. You'll need to buy Mexican pesos at some point. When you do, you'll be offering to *buy* pesos by offering to *sell* dollars. In other words, **the** demand *for foreign currency represents a* **supply** *of U.S. dollars.**

When Americans buy BMW cars, they also supply U.S. dollars. American consumers pay for their BMWs in dollars. Somewhere down the road, however, those dollars will be exchanged for European euros. At that exchange, dollars are being *supplied* and euros *demanded.*

American corporations demand foreign exchange too. General Motors builds cars in Germany, Coca-Cola produces Coke in China, and Exxon produces and refines oil all over the world. In nearly every such case, the U.S. firm must first build or buy some plants and equipment, using another country's factors of production. This activity requires foreign currency and thus becomes another component of our demand for foreign currency.

We may summarize these market activities by noting that **the supply of dollars originates in**

- *American demand for imports* (including tourism).
- *American investments in foreign countries.*
- *Speculation.*

As on the demand side, government intervention can also contribute to the supply of dollars.

The Value of the Dollar

web click

The Federal Reserve Bank of New York carries out foreign exchange–related activities for the Fed. To learn more, visit **www.newyorkfed.org,** and click the "Markets" tab.

Whether American consumers will choose to buy an imported BMW depends partly on what the car costs. The price tag isn't always apparent in international transactions. Remember that the German BMW producer and workers want to be paid in their own currency, the euro. Hence the *dollar* price of an imported BMW depends on two factors: (1) the German price of a BMW and (2) the *exchange rate* between U.S. dollars and euros. Specifically, the U.S. price of a BMW is

$$\frac{\text{Dollar price}}{\text{of BMW}} = \frac{\text{Euro price}}{\text{of BMW}} \times \frac{\text{Dollar price}}{\text{of euro}}$$

Suppose the BMW company is prepared to sell a German-built BMW for 100,000 euros and that the current exchange rate is 2 euros = $1. At these rates, a BMW will cost you

$$\frac{\text{Dollar price}}{\text{of BMW}} = 100{,}000 \text{ euros} \times \frac{\$1}{2 \text{ euros}}$$
$$= \$50{,}000$$

If you're willing to pay this much for a shiny new German-built BMW, you may do so at current exchange rates.

Now suppose the exchange rate changes from 2 euros = $1 to 1 euro = $1. Now you're getting only 1 euro for your dollar rather than 2 euros. In other words, euros have become more expensive. *A higher dollar price for euros will raise the dollar costs of European goods.* In this case, the dollar price of a euro increases from $0.50 to $1. At this new exchange rate, the BMW plant in Germany is still willing to sell BMWs at 100,000 euros apiece. And German consumers continue to buy BMWs at that price. But this constant euro price now translates into a higher *dollar* price. That same BMW that you previously could buy for $50,000 now costs you $100,000—not because the cost of manufacturing the car in Germany went up, but simply because the exchange rate changed.

As the dollar price of a BMW rises, the number of BMWs sold in the United States will decline. As BMW sales decline, the quantity of euros demanded may decline as well. Thus the quantity of foreign currency demanded declines when the exchange rate rises because foreign goods become more expensive and imports decline. When the dollar price of European currencies actually increased in 1992, BMW decided to start producing cars in South Carolina. A year later Mercedes-Benz decided to produce cars in the United States as

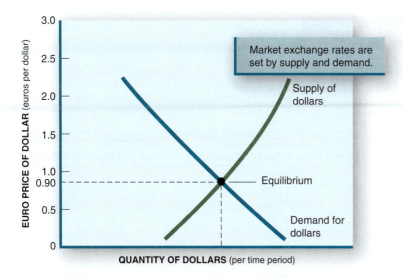

FIGURE 20.1
The Foreign Exchange Market

The foreign exchange market operates like other markets. In this case, the "good" bought and sold is dollars (foreign exchange). The price and quantity of dollars actually exchanged are determined by the intersection of market supply and demand.

well. Sales of American-made BMWs and Mercedes no longer depend on the exchange rate of the U.S. dollar. But the dollar price of German-made Audis, French wine, and Italian shoes does.

The Supply Curve. These market responses suggest that the supply of dollars is upward-sloping. If the value of the dollar rises, Americans will be able to buy more euros. As a result, the dollar price of imported BMWs will decline. American consumers will respond by demanding more imports, thereby supplying a larger quantity of dollars. The supply curve in Figure 20.1 shows how the quantity of dollars supplied rises as the value of the dollar increases.

The Demand Curve. The demand for dollars can be explained in similar terms. Remember that the demand for dollars arises from the foreign demand for U.S. exports and investments. If the exchange rate moves from 2 euros = $1 to 1 euro = $1, the euro price of dollars falls. As dollars become cheaper for Germans, all American exports effectively fall in price. Germans will buy more American products (including trips to Disney World) and therefore demand a greater quantity of dollars. In addition, foreign investors will perceive in a cheaper dollar the opportunity to buy U.S. stocks, businesses, and property at fire-sale prices. Accordingly, they join foreign consumers in demanding more dollars. Not all these behavioral responses will occur overnight, but they're reasonably predictable over a brief period of time.

Equilibrium

Given market demand and supply curves, we can predict the **equilibrium price** of any commodity—that is, the price at which the quantity demanded will equal the quantity supplied. This occurs in Figure 20.1 where the two curves cross. At that equilibrium, the value of the dollar (the exchange rate) is established. In this case, the euro price of the dollar turns out to be 0.90.

The value of the dollar can also be expressed in terms of other currencies. The World View on the next page displays a sampling of dollar exchange rates in August 2014. Notice how many Indonesian rupiah you could buy for $1: a dollar was worth 11,699 rupiah. By contrast, a U.S. dollar was worth only 0.75 euro. The *average* value of the dollar is a weighted mean of the exchange rates between the U.S. dollar and all these currencies. The value of the dollar is "high" when its foreign exchange price is above recent levels, and it is "low" when it is below recent averages.

equilibrium price: The price at which the quantity of a good demanded in a given time period equals the quantity supplied.

Foreign Exchange Rates

The foreign exchange midrange rates here show (a) how many U.S. dollars are needed to buy one unit of foreign currency and (b) how many units of foreign currency are needed to buy one U.S. dollar.

Country	(a) U.S. Dollar per Unit (Dollar Price of Foreign Currency)	(b) Currency per U.S. Dollar (Foreign Price of U.S. Dollar)
Brazil (real)	0.442	2.2627
Britain (pound)	1.668	0.5993
Canada (dollar)	0.918	1.0890
China (yuan)	0.163	6.1494
Indonesia (rupiah)	0.001	11,699.5000
Japan (yen)	0.009	102.3284
Mexico (peso)	0.077	13.0693
Russia (ruble)	0.028	35.9339
Euroland (euro)	1.340	0.7464

Source: August 15, 2014, data from Federal Reserve Board of Governors.

ANALYSIS: The exchange rates between currencies are determined by supply and demand in foreign exchange markets. The rates reported here represent the equilibrium exchange rates on a particular day.

balance of payments: A summary record of a country's international economic transactions in a given period of time.

web click

The latest statistics on the balance of payments are available from the Bureau of Economic Analysis at www.bea.gov.

The Balance of Payments

The equilibrium depicted in Figure 20.1 determines not only the *price* of the dollar but also a specific *quantity* of international transactions. Those transactions include the exports, imports, international investments, and other sources of dollar supply and demand. A summary of all those international money flows is contained in the **balance of payments**—an accounting statement of all international money flows in a given period of time.

Trade Balance. Table 20.1 depicts the U.S. balance of payments for 2013. Notice first how the millions of separate transactions are classified into a few summary measures. The trade

TABLE 20.1

The U.S. Balance of Payments

The balance of payments is a summary statement of a country's international transactions. The major components of that activity are the trade balance (merchandise exports minus merchandise imports), the current account balance (trade, services, and transfers), and the capital account balance. The net total of these balances must equal zero because the quantity of dollars paid must equal the quantity received.

Item	Amount ($ billions)
1. Merchandise exports	$1,593
2. Merchandise imports	(2,294)
3. Service exports	687
4. Service imports	(462)
Trade balance (items 1–4)	−476
5. Income from U.S. overseas investments	780
6. Income outflow for foreign-owned U.S. investments	(580)
7. Net transfers and pensions	(124)
Current account balance (items 1–7)	−400
8. U.S. capital inflow	1,018
9. U.S. capital outflow	−645
Capital account balance (items 8–9)	373
10. Statistical discrepancy	27
Net balance (items 1–10)	0

Source: U.S. Department of Commerce (2013 data).

balance is the difference between exports and imports of goods (merchandise) and services. In 2013 the United States imported more than $2.7 trillion of goods and services but exported only $2.3 trillion. This created a **trade deficit** of $476 billion. That trade deficit represents a net outflow of dollars to the rest of the world.

trade deficit: The amount by which the value of imports exceeds the value of exports in a given time period.

$$\text{Trade balance} = \text{Exports} - \text{Imports}$$

Current Account Balance. The current account balance is a second subtotal in Table 20.1. It includes the trade balance as well as private transfers such as wages sent home by foreign citizens working in the United States. It also includes the income flows from international investments.

$$\frac{\text{Current account}}{\text{balance}} = \frac{\text{Trade}}{\text{balance}} + \frac{\text{Unilateral}}{\text{transfers}} + \frac{\text{Net investment}}{\text{income}}$$

The current account balance is the most comprehensive summary of our trade relations. As indicated in Table 20.1, the United States had a current account deficit of $400 billion in 2013.

Capital Account Balance. The current account deficit is offset by the capital account surplus. The capital account balance takes into consideration assets bought and sold across international borders:

$$\frac{\text{Capital account}}{\text{balance}} = \frac{\text{Foreign purchase}}{\text{of U.S. assets}} - \frac{\text{U.S. purchases}}{\text{of foreign assets}}$$

As Table 20.1 shows, foreign consumers demanded $1,018 billion in 2013 to buy farms and factories as well as U.S. bonds, stocks, and other investments (item 8). This exceeded the flow of U.S. dollars going overseas to purchase foreign assets (item 9).

The net capital inflows were essential in financing the U.S. trade deficit (negative trade balance). As in any market, the number of dollars demanded must equal the number of dollars supplied. Thus *the capital account surplus must equal the current account deficit.* In other words, there can't be any dollars left lying around unaccounted for. Item 10 in Table 20.1 reminds us that our accounting system isn't perfect—we can't identify every transaction. Nevertheless, all the accounts must eventually "balance out":

$$\frac{\text{Net balance}}{\text{of payments}} = \frac{\text{Current account}}{\text{balance}} + \frac{\text{Capital account}}{\text{balance}} = 0$$

That's the character of a market *equilibrium:* the quantity of dollars demanded equals the quantity of dollars supplied.

MARKET DYNAMICS

The interesting thing about markets isn't their character in equilibrium but the fact that prices and quantities are always changing in response to shifts in demand and supply. The U.S. demand for BMWs shifted overnight when Japan introduced a new line of sleek, competitively priced cars (e.g., Lexus). The reduced demand for BMWs shifted the supply of dollars leftward. That supply shift raised the value of the dollar vis-à-vis the euro, as illustrated in Figure 20.2. (It also increased the demand for Japanese yen, causing the yen value of the dollar to *fall.*)

Depreciation and Appreciation

Exchange rate changes have their own terminology. **Depreciation** of a currency occurs when one currency becomes cheaper in terms of another currency. In our earlier discussion of exchange rates, for example, we assumed that the exchange rate between euros and dollars changed from 2 euros = $1 to 1 euro = $1, making the euro price of a dollar cheaper. In this case, the dollar *depreciated* with respect to the euro.

depreciation (currency): A fall in the price of one currency relative to another.

(a) Dollar–euro market

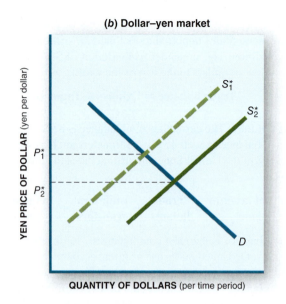

(b) Dollar–yen market

FIGURE 20.2

Shifts in Foreign Exchange Markets

When the Japanese introduced luxury autos into the United States, the American demand for German cars fell. As a consequence, the supply of dollars in the dollar–euro market (part *a*) shifted to the left and the euro value of the dollar rose. At the same time, the

increased American demand for Japanese cars shifted the dollar supply curve in the yen market (part *b*) to the right, reducing the yen price of the dollar.

appreciation: A rise in the price of one currency relative to another.

If the dollar is rising in value (appreciating), the euro must be depreciating.

The other side of depreciation is **appreciation,** an increase in value of one currency as expressed in another country's currency. *Whenever one currency depreciates, another currency must appreciate.* When the exchange rate changed from 2 euros = $1 to 1 euro = $1, not only did the euro price of a dollar fall, but also the dollar price of a euro rose. Hence the euro appreciated as the dollar depreciated. It's like a see-saw relationship (see figure).

Figure 20.3 illustrates actual changes in the exchange rate of the U.S. dollar since 1980. The trade-adjusted value of the U.S. dollar is the (weighted) average of all exchange rates for the dollar. Between 1980 and 1985, the U.S. dollar appreciated more than 80 percent. This appreciation greatly reduced the price of imports and thus increased their quantity. At the same time, the dollar appreciation raised the foreign price of U.S. exports and so reduced their volume. U.S. farmers, aircraft manufacturers, and tourist services suffered huge sales losses. The trade deficit ballooned.

The value of the dollar briefy reversed course after 1985 but started appreciating again, slowing export growth and increasing imports throughout the 1990s. After a long steep appreciation, the dollar started losing value in 2003. Between 2003 and 2011, the U.S. dollar depreciated by 25 percent. This was good for U.S. exporters but bad for U.S. tourists and foreign producers (see the World View on the next page).

Market Forces

Exchange rates change for the same reasons that any market price changes: the underlying supply or demand (or both) has shifted. Among the more important sources of such shifts are

- *Relative income changes.* If incomes are increasing faster in country A than in country B, consumers in A will tend to spend more, thus increasing the demand for B's exports and currency. B's currency will appreciate (and A's will depreciate).
- *Relative price changes.* If domestic prices are rising rapidly in country A, consumers will seek out lower-priced imports. The demand for B's exports and currency will increase. B's currency will appreciate (and A's will depreciate).
- *Changes in product availability.* If country A experiences a disastrous wheat crop failure, it will have to increase its food imports. B's currency will appreciate.

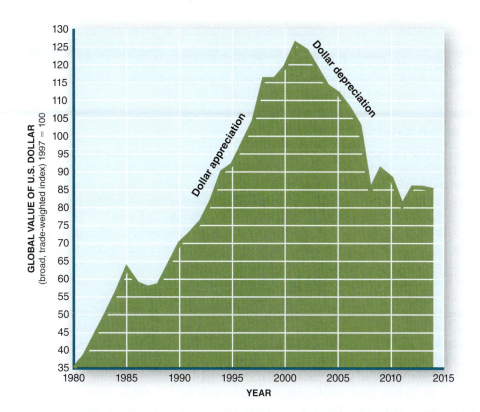

FIGURE 20.3

Changing Values of U.S. Dollar

Since 1973, exchange rates have been flexible. As a result, the value of the U.S. dollar has fluctuated with international differences in inflation, interest rates, and economic growth. U.S. economic stability has given the U.S. dollar increasing value over time.

Source: Federal Reserve Board of Governers.

web click

How much are 100 Japanese yen worth in U.S. dollars? Find out by using the currency converter at **www.xe.com/ucc**.

- *Relative interest rate changes.* If interest rates rise in country A, people in country B will want to move their deposits to A. Demand for A's currency will rise and it will appreciate.
- *Speculation.* If speculators anticipate an increase in the price of A's currency, for the preceding reasons or any other, they'll begin buying it, thus pushing its price up. A's currency will appreciate.

WORLD VIEW

Who Gains, Who Loses from Strong Dollar

The value of the U.S. dollar has been rising since 2010. In the past 4 years, the dollar has risen by nearly 6 percent against the world's major currencies. Should we be cheering? Some of us, perhaps, but not all. Here's who in the United States wins and who loses from a strong dollar:

The winners:
Consumers of imported goods
Producers like Apple that use imported parts and equipment
Retailers like Walmart that sell imported goods
Investors in foreign stocks and production facilities
American tourists

The losers:
U.S. exporters like Boeing, Caterpiller, farmers
Import-competing industries like steel, autos, solar panels
Companies like Disney that attract foreign visitors
Companies with overseas factories and outlets

ANALYSIS: Depreciation of a nation's currency is good for that nation's exporters but bad for that nation's importers (including its tourists).

foreign exchange markets:
Places where foreign currencies are
bought and sold.

All these various changes are taking place every minute of every day, thus keeping **foreign exchange markets** active. On an average day, more than *$4 trillion* of foreign exchange is bought and sold in the market. Significant changes occur in currency values, however, only when several of these forces move in the same direction at the same time. This is what caused the Asian crisis of 1997–1998.

The Asian Crisis of 1997–1998

In July 1997 the Thai government decided the baht was overvalued and let market forces find a new equilibrium. Within days, the dollar price of the baht plunged 25 percent. This sharp decline in the value of the Thai baht simultaneously increased the Thai price of the U.S. dollar. As a consequence, Thais could no longer afford to buy as many American products.

The devaluation of the baht had a domino effect on other Asian currencies. The plunge in the baht shook confidence in the Malaysian ringget, the Indonesian rupiah, and even the Korean won. People wanted to hold "hard" currencies like the U.S. dollar. As people rushed to buy U.S. dollars with their local currencies, the value of those currencies plunged. At one point the Indonesian rupiah had lost 80 percent of its dollar value, making U.S. exports five times more expensive for Indonesians. As a result, Indonesians could no longer afford to buy imported rice, machinery, cars, or pork. Indonesian students attending U.S. colleges could no longer afford to pay tuition. The sudden surge in prices and scarcity of goods led to street demonstrations and a change in government. Similar problems erupted throughout Southeast Asia.

The "Asian contagion" unfortunately wasn't confined to that area of the world. Hog farmers in the United States saw foreign demand for their pork evaporate. Koreans stopped taking vacations in Hawaii. Thai Airways canceled orders for Boeing jets. Japanese consumers bought fewer Washington State apples and California oranges. This loss of export markets slowed economic growth in the United States, Europe, Japan, and other nations.

Ukraine Crisis of 2014

The Russian invasion of Ukraine in early 2014 was a classic case of an external shock. Foreign exchange markets reacted quickly, sending the value of the hryvnia (Ukraine's currency) into a prolonged depreciation. The dollar value of the hryvnia plunged from 12.3 cents to 7.6 cents in a couple of months. That 40 percent depreciation in the value of the hryvnia substantially increased the cost of badly needed food, oil, and weapons imports.

RESISTANCE TO EXCHANGE RATE CHANGES

Given the scope and depth of currency crises, it's easy to understand why people crave *stable* exchange rates. The resistance to exchange rate fluctuations originates in various micro- and macroeconomic interests.

Micro Interests

The microeconomic resistance to changes in the value of the dollar arises from two concerns. First, people who trade or invest in world markets want a solid basis for forecasting future costs, prices, and profits. Forecasts are always uncertain, but they're even less dependable when the value of money is subject to change. An American firm that invests $2 million in a ski factory in Sweden expects not only to make a profit on the production there but also to return that profit to the United States. If the Swedish krona depreciates sharply in the interim, however, the profits amassed in Sweden may dwindle to a mere trickle, or even a loss, when the kronor are exchanged back into dollars. Even the Nobel Prize loses a bit of its luster when the krona depreciates (see the World View on the next page). From this view, the uncertainty associated with fluctuating exchange rates is an unwanted burden.

Even when the direction of an exchange rate move is certain, those who stand to lose from the change are prone to resist. ***A change in the price of a country's money automatically***

Nobel Prize Was Nobler in October

STOCKHOLM—Winners of the four Nobel science awards said yesterday that the honor is more important than the money, so it does not matter much that each award has lost $242,000 in value since October.

"If we had been more intelligent, we would have done some hedging," said Gary S. Becker, 61, a University of Chicago professor and a Nobel economics laureate. Sweden's decision last month to let the krona float caused the prizes' value to drop from $1.2 million each when announced in October to $958,000 when King Carl XVI Gustaf presents them Thursday.

The recipients are Becker; American Rudolph A. Marcus, the chemistry laureate; Frenchman Georges Charpak, the physics laureate; and medicine prize winners Edmond Fischer and Edwin Krebs of the University of Washington in Seattle.

Source: Associated Press, December 8, 1992. Used with permission of The Associated Press. Copyright © 2015. All rights reserved.

ANALYSIS: Currency depreciation reduces the external value of domestic income and assets. The dollar value of the Nobel Prize fell when the Swedish krona depreciated.

alters the price of all its exports and imports. When the Russian ruble and Japanese yen depreciated in 2000–2001, for example, the dollar price of Russian and Japanese steel declined as well. This prompted U.S. steelmakers to accuse Russia and Japan of "dumping" steel. Steel companies and unions appealed to Washington to protect their sales and jobs.

Even in the country whose currency becomes cheaper, there will be opposition to exchange rate movements. When the U.S. dollar appreciates, Americans buy more foreign products. This increased U.S. demand for imports may drive up prices in other countries. In addition, foreign firms may take advantage of the reduced American competition by raising their prices. In either case, some inflation will result. The consumer's insistence that the government "do something" about rising prices may turn into a political force for "correcting" foreign exchange rates.

Macro Interests

Any microeconomic problem that becomes widespread enough can turn into a macroeconomic problem. The huge U.S. trade deficits of the 1980s effectively exported jobs to foreign nations. Although the U.S. economy expanded rapidly in 1983–1985, the unemployment rate stayed high, partly because American consumers were spending more of their income on imports. Yet fear of renewed inflation precluded more stimulative fiscal and monetary policies.

The U.S. trade deficits of the 1980s were offset by huge capital account surpluses. Foreign investors sought to participate in the U.S. economic expansion by buying land, plants, and equipment and by lending money in U.S. financial markets. These capital inflows complicated monetary policy, however, and greatly increased U.S. foreign debt and interest costs.

U.S. a Net Debtor

The inflow of foreign investment also raised anxieties about "selling off" America. As Japanese and other foreign investors increased their purchases of farmland, factories, and real estate (e.g., Rockefeller Center), many Americans worried that foreign investors were taking control of the U.S. economy.

Fueling these fears was the dramatic change in America's international financial position. From 1914 to 1984, the United States had been a net creditor in the world economy. We owned more assets abroad than foreign investors owned in the United States. Our financial position changed in 1985. Continuing trade deficits and offsetting capital inflows transformed the United States into a net debtor in that year. Since then foreigners have owned more U.S. assets than Americans own of foreign assets.

America's debtor status can complicate domestic policy. A sudden flight from U.S. assets could severely weaken the dollar and disrupt the domestic economy. To prevent that from occurring, policymakers must consider the impact of their decisions on foreign investors. This may necessitate difficult policy choices.

There's a silver lining to this cloud, however. The inflow of foreign investment is a reflection of confidence in the U.S. economy. Foreign investors want to share in our growth and profitability. In the process, their investments (like BMW's auto plant) expand America's production possibilities and stimulate still more economic growth.

Foreign investors actually assume substantial risk when they invest in the United States. If the dollar falls, the foreign value of *their* U.S. investments will decline. Hence foreigners who've already invested in the United States have no incentive to start a flight from the dollar. On the contrary, a strong dollar protects the value of their U.S. holdings.

EXCHANGE RATE INTERVENTION

Given the potential opposition to exchange rate movements, governments often feel compelled to intervene in foreign exchange markets. The intervention is usually intended to achieve greater exchange rate stability. But such stability may itself give rise to undesirable micro- and macroeconomic effects.

Fixed Exchange Rates

gold standard: An agreement by countries to fix the price of their currencies in terms of gold; a mechanism for fixing exchange rates.

One way to eliminate fluctuations in exchange rates is to fix a currency's value. The easiest way to do this is for each country to define the worth of its currency in terms of some common standard. Under a **gold standard,** each country declares that its currency is worth so much gold. In so doing, it implicitly defines the worth of its currency in terms of all other currencies that also have a fixed gold value. In 1944 the major trading nations met at Bretton Woods, New Hampshire, and agreed that each currency was worth so much gold. The value of the U.S. dollar was defined as being equal to 0.0294 ounce of gold, while the British pound was defined as being worth 0.0823 ounce of gold. Thus the exchange rate between British pounds and U.S. dollars was effectively fixed at $1 = 0.357 pound, or 1 pound = $2.80 (or $2.80/0.0823 = $1/0.0294).

Balance-of-Payments Problems. It's one thing to proclaim the worth of a country's currency; it's quite another to *maintain* the fixed rate of exchange. As we've observed, foreign exchange rates are subject to continual and often unpredictable changes in supply and demand. Hence two countries that seek to stabilize their exchange rate at some fixed value will have to somehow neutralize such foreign exchange market pressures.

Suppose the exchange rate officially established by the United States and Great Britain is equal to e_1, as illustrated in Figure 20.4. As is apparent, that particular exchange rate is

FIGURE 20.4
Fixed Rates and Market Imbalance

If exchange rates are fixed, they can't adjust to changes in market supply and demand. Suppose the exchange rate is initially fixed at e_1. When the demand for British pounds increases (shifts to the right), an excess demand for pounds emerges. More pounds are demanded (q_D) at the rate e_1 than are supplied (q_S). This causes a balance-of-payments deficit for the United States.

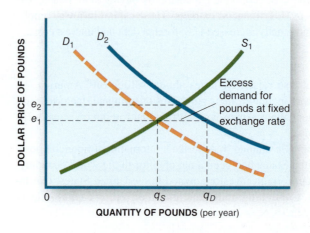

consistent with the then-prevailing demand and supply conditions in the foreign exchange market (as indicated by curves D_1 and S_1).

Now suppose that Americans suddenly acquire a greater taste for British cars and start spending more income on Jaguars, Bentleys, and Mini Coopers. This increased desire for British goods will *shift* the demand for British currency from D_1 to D_2 in Figure 20.4. Were exchange rates allowed to respond to market influences, the dollar price of a British pound would rise, in this case to the rate e_2. But we've assumed that government intervention has *fixed* the exchange rate at e_1. Unfortunately, at e_1, American consumers want to buy more pounds (q_D) than the British are willing to supply (q_S). The difference between the quantity demanded and the quantity supplied in the market at the rate e_1 represents a **market shortage** of British pounds.

The excess demand for pounds implies a **balance-of-payments deficit** for the United States: more dollars are flowing out of the country than into it. The same disequilibrium represents a **balance-of-payments surplus** for Britain because its outward flow of pounds is less than its incoming flow.

Basically, there are only two solutions to balance-of-payments problems brought about by the attempt to fix exchange rates:

- Allow exchange rates to rise to e_2 (Figure 20.4), thereby eliminating the excess demand for pounds.
- Alter market supply or demand so they intersect at the fixed rate e_1.

Since fixed exchange rates were the initial objective of this intervention, only the second alternative is of immediate interest.

The Need for Reserves. One way to alter market conditions would be for someone simply to supply British pounds to American consumers. The U.S. Treasury could have accumulated a reserve of foreign currency in earlier periods. By selling some of those **foreign exchange reserves** now, the Treasury would be *supplying* British pounds, helping to offset excess demand. The rightward shift of the pound supply curve in Figure 20.5 illustrates the sale of accumulated British pounds—and related purchase of U.S. dollars—by the U.S. Treasury.

Although foreign exchange reserves can be used to fix exchange rates, such reserves may not be adequate. Indeed, Figure 20.6 should be testimony enough to the fact that today's deficit isn't always offset by tomorrow's surplus. A principal reason that fixed exchange rates didn't live up to their expectations is that the United States had balance-of-payments deficits for 22 consecutive years. This long-term deficit overwhelmed the government's stock of foreign exchange reserves.

The Role of Gold. Gold reserves are a potential substitute for foreign exchange reserves. As long as each country's money has a value defined in terms of gold, we can use gold to buy British pounds, thereby restocking our foreign exchange reserves. Or we can simply

market shortage: The amount by which the quantity demanded exceeds the quantity supplied at a given price; excess demand.

balance-of-payments deficit: An excess demand for foreign currency at current exchange rates.

balance-of-payments surplus: An excess demand for domestic currency at current exchange rates.

foreign exchange reserves: Holdings of foreign currencies by official government agencies, usually the central bank or treasury.

web click

Gold has traded widely for centuries. To see recent data on gold prices and exchanges, visit **http://finance.yahoo.com**. Search "gold."

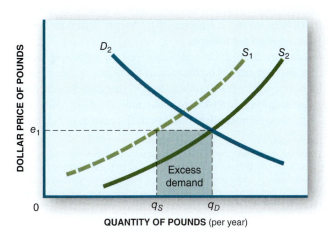

FIGURE 20.5

The Impact of Monetary Intervention

If the U.S. Treasury holds reserves of British pounds, it can use them to buy U.S. dollars in foreign exchange markets. As it does so, the supply of pounds will shift to the right, to S_2, thereby maintaining the desired exchange rate, e_1. The Bank of England could bring about the same result by offering to buy U.S. dollars with pounds (i.e., *supplying* pounds).

FIGURE 20.6

The U.S. Balance of Payments, 1950–1973

The United States had a balance-of-payments deficit for 22 consecutive years. During this period, the foreign exchange reserves of the U.S. Treasury were sharply reduced. Fixed exchange rates were maintained by the willingness of foreign countries to accumulate large reserves of U.S. dollars. However, neither the Treasury's reserves nor the willingness of foreigners to accumulate dollars was unlimited. In 1973 fixed exchange rates were abandoned.

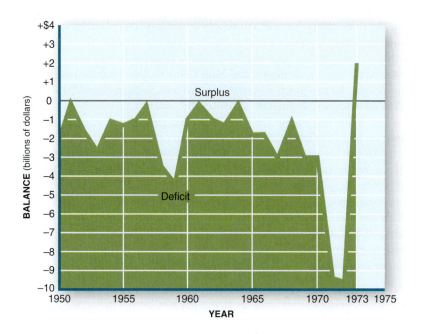

gold reserves: Stocks of gold held by a government to purchase foreign exchange.

use the gold to purchase U.S. dollars in foreign exchange markets. In either case, the exchange value of the dollar will tend to rise. However, we must have **gold reserves** available for this purpose. Unfortunately, the continuing U.S. balance-of-payments deficits recorded in Figure 20.6 exceeded even the hoards of gold buried under Fort Knox. As a consequence, our gold reserves lost their credibility as a guarantor of fixed exchange rates. When it appeared that foreigners would demand more gold than the U.S. government possessed, President Nixon simply ended the link between the U.S. dollar and gold. As of August 15, 1971, the U.S. dollar had no guaranteed value.

Domestic Adjustments. Government can also use fiscal, monetary, and trade policies to achieve a desired exchange rate. With respect to trade policy, *trade protection can be used to prop up fixed exchange rates.* We could eliminate the excess demand for pounds (Figure 20.4), for example, by imposing quotas and tariffs on British goods. Such trade restrictions would reduce British imports to the United States and thus the demand for British pounds. In August 1971 President Nixon imposed an emergency 10 percent surcharge on all imported goods to help reduce the payments deficit that fixed exchange rates had spawned. Such restrictions on international trade, however, violate the principle of comparative advantage and thus reduce total world output. Trade protection also invites retaliatory trade restrictions.

Fiscal policy is another way out of the imbalance. An increase in U.S. income tax rates will reduce disposable income and have a negative effect on the demand for all goods, including imports. A reduction in government spending will have similar effects. In general, *deflationary (or restrictive) policies help correct a balance-of-payments deficit by lowering domestic incomes and thus the demand for imports.*

Monetary policies in a deficit country could follow the same restrictive course. A reduction in the money supply raises interest rates. The balance of payments will benefit in two ways. The resultant slowdown in spending will reduce import demand. In addition, higher interest rates may induce international investors to move more of their funds into the deficit country. Such moves will provide immediate relief to the payments imbalance.[1]

---

[1]Before 1930, not only were foreign exchange rates fixed, but domestic monetary supplies were tied to gold stocks as well. Countries experiencing a balance-of-payments deficit were thus forced to contract their money supply, and countries experiencing a payments surplus were forced to expand their money supply by a set amount. Monetary authorities were powerless to control domestic money supplies except by erecting barriers to trade. The system was abandoned when the world economy collapsed into the Great Depression.

Russia tried this strategy in 1998, tripling key interest rates (to as much as 150 percent). But even that wasn't enough to restore confidence in the ruble, which kept depreciating. Within three months of the monetary policy tightening, the ruble lost half its value.

A surplus country could help solve the balance-of-payments problem. By pursuing expansionary—even inflationary—fiscal and monetary policies, a surplus country could stimulate the demand for imports. Moreover, any inflation at home will reduce the competitiveness of exports, thereby helping to restrain the inflow of foreign demand. Taken together, such efforts would help reverse an international payments imbalance.

Even under the best of circumstances, domestic economic adjustments entail significant costs. In effect, *domestic adjustments to payments imbalances require a deficit country to forsake full employment and a surplus country to forsake price stability*. China has had to grapple with these domestic consequences of fixing the value of its currency. The artificially low value of the yuan promoted Chinese exports and accelerated China's GDP growth. But it also created serious macro problems. To keep the value of the yuan low, the Chinese had to keep buying dollars. By 2011 China had more than $3 trillion of foreign currency reserves (see the accompanying World View). It paid for those dollars with yuan, adding to China's money supply. All that money stoked inflation in China. Ultimately, the Chinese government had to adopt restrictive monetary and fiscal policies to keep inflation in check. The Chinese government also had to be willing to keep accumulating U.S. dollars and other currencies.

There's no easy way out of this impasse. Market imbalances caused by fixed exchange rates can be corrected only with abundant supplies of foreign exchange reserves or deliberate changes in fiscal, monetary, or trade policies. At some point, it may become easier to let a currency adjust to market equilibrium.

WORLD VIEW

The Risks of China's Foreign-Exchange Stockpile

China's foreign-exchange stockpile topped $4 trillion this month, a sum equal to the entire value of China's equity markets. Some see this stockpile of U.S. dollars, euros, yen, and pounds as a testament to China's economic strength. But others warn of substantial risks to the Chinese economy of this foreign-exchange build-up.

The most obvious risk is a decline in the values of the U.S. dollar or U.S. Treasury bonds. About two-thirds of the stockpile consists of U.S. Treasury bonds. When U.S. interest rates start rising—as everyone expects—the market value of Treasury bonds will fall, cutting the value of China's holdings. Inflation poses an even greater risk. China must print more yuan every time exports exceed imports. The Bank of China says the money supply will grow 12-13 percent this year as a result. All that money threatens to accelerate domestic inflation, a problem that has already raised political concerns in China.

Critics say the problem originates in the undervalued yuan. Observers accuse China of intervening in the market to keep the value of the yuan artificially low. This helps drive exports, but adds to China's already gargantuan stockpile of foreign exchange.

Source: News reports, December 2014.

ANALYSIS: When a currency is deliberately undervalued, strong export demand may kindle inflation. The trade surplus that results also increases foreign exchange reserves.

The Euro Fix. The original 12 nations of the European Monetary Union (EMU) fixed their exchange rates in 1999. They went far beyond the kind of exchange rate fix we're discussing here. Members of the EMU *eliminated* their national currencies, making the euro the common currency of Euroland. They don't have to worry about reserve balances or domestic adjustments. However, they do have to reconcile their varied national interests to a single monetary authority, which has proven to be difficult politically in times of economic stress.

Flexible Exchange Rates

Balance-of-payments problems wouldn't arise in the first place if exchange rates were allowed to respond to market forces. Under a system of **flexible exchange rates** (often called floating exchange rates), the exchange rate moves up or down to choke off any excess supply of or demand for foreign exchange. Notice again in Figure 20.4 that the exchange rate move from e_1 to e_2 prevents any excess demand from emerging. *With flexible exchange rates, the quantity of foreign exchange demanded always equals the quantity supplied,* and there's no imbalance. For the same reason, there's no need for foreign exchange reserves.

Although flexible exchange rates eliminate balance-of-payments and foreign exchange reserves problems, they don't solve all of a country's international trade problems. *Exchange rate movements associated with flexible rates alter relative prices and may disrupt import and export flows.* As noted before, depreciation of the dollar raises the price of all imported goods, contributing to domestic cost-push inflation. Also, domestic businesses that sell imported goods or use them as production inputs may suffer sales losses. On the other hand, appreciation of the dollar raises the foreign price of U.S. goods and reduces the sales of American exporters. Hence *someone is always hurt, and others are helped, by exchange rate movements.* The resistance to flexible exchange rates originates in these potential losses. Such resistance creates pressure for official intervention in foreign exchange markets or increased trade barriers.

The United States and its major trading partners abandoned fixed exchange rates in 1973. Although exchange rates are now able to fluctuate freely, it shouldn't be assumed that they necessarily undergo wild gyrations. On the contrary, experience with flexible rates since 1973 suggests that some semblance of stability is possible even when exchange rates are free to change in response to market forces.

Speculation. One force that often helps maintain stability in a flexible exchange rate system is—surprisingly—speculation. Speculators often counteract short-term changes in foreign exchange supply and demand. If a currency temporarily rises above its long-term

"Damn it! How can I relax, knowing that out there, somewhere, somehow, someone's attacking the dollar?"

Analysis: A "weak" dollar reduces the buying power of American tourists.

equilibrium, speculators will move in to sell it. By selling at high prices and later buying at lower prices, speculators hope to make a profit. In the process, they also help stabilize foreign exchange rates.

Speculation isn't always stabilizing, however. Speculators may not correctly gauge the long-term equilibrium. Instead they may move "with the market" and help push exchange rates far out of kilter. This kind of destabilizing speculation sharply lowered the international value of the U.S. dollar in 1987, forcing the Reagan administration to intervene in foreign exchange markets, borrowing foreign currencies to buy U.S. dollars. In 1997 the Clinton administration intervened for the opposite purpose: stemming the rise in the U.S. dollar. The Bush administration was more willing to stay on the sidelines, letting global markets set the exchange rates for the U.S. dollar. The Obama administration was accused of keeping the value of the U.S. dollar deliberately low to boost exports and create more jobs.

These kinds of interventions are intended to *narrow* rather than *eliminate* exchange rate movements. Such limited intervention in foreign exchange markets is often referred to as **managed exchange rates,** or, popularly, "dirty floats."

Although managed exchange rates would seem to be an ideal compromise between fixed rates and flexible rates, they can work only when some acceptable "rules of the game" and mutual trust have been established. As Sherman Maisel, a former governor of the Federal Reserve Board, put it, "Monetary systems are based on credit and faith: If these are lacking, a . . . crisis occurs."[2]

managed exchange rates: A system in which governments intervene in foreign exchange markets to limit but not eliminate exchange rate fluctuations; "dirty floats."

THE ECONOMY TOMORROW

CURRENCY BAILOUTS

The world has witnessed a string of currency crises, including the one in Asia during 1997–1998, the Brazilian crisis of 1999, the Argentine crisis of 2001–2002, the Greek and Portuguese crises of 2010–2012, and recurrent ruble crises in Russia. In every instance, the country in trouble pleads for external help. In most cases, a currency "bailout" is arranged, whereby global monetary authorities lend the troubled nation enough reserves (such as U.S. dollars) to defend its currency. Typically the International Monetary Fund (IMF) heads the rescue party, joined by the central banks of the strongest economies.

The Case for Bailouts. The argument for currency bailouts typically rests on the domino theory. Weakness in one currency can undermine another. This seemed to be the case during the 1997–1998 Asian crisis. After the **devaluation** of the Thai baht, global investors began worrying about currency values in other Asian nations. Choosing to be safe rather than sorry, they moved funds out of Korea, Malaysia, and the Philippines and invested in U.S. and European markets (notice in Figure 20.3 the 1997–1998 appreciation of the U.S. dollar).

The initial baht devaluation also weakened the competitive trade position of these same economies. Thai exports became cheaper, diverting export demand from other Asian nations. To prevent loss of export markets, Thailand's neighbors felt they had to devalue as well. Speculators who foresaw these effects accelerated the domino effect by selling the region's currencies.

When Brazil devalued its currency (the *real*) in January 1999, global investors worried that a "samba effect" might sweep across Latin America. The domino effect could reach across the ocean and damage U.S. and European exports as well. The Greek crisis of 2010 threatened the common currency (euro) of 28 nations. Hence, richer, more stable countries often offer a currency bailout as a form of self-defense.

The Case against Bailouts. Critics of bailouts argue that such interventions are ultimately self-defeating. They say that once a country knows for sure that currency bailouts are in the wings, it doesn't have to pursue the domestic policy adjustments that might stabilize its

devaluation: An abrupt depreciation of a currency whose value was fixed or managed by the government.

[2]Sherman Maisel, *Managing the Dollar* (New York: W. W. Norton, 1973), p. 196.

currency. A nation can avoid politically unpopular options such as high interest rates, tax hikes, or cutbacks in government spending. It can also turn a blind eye to trade barriers, monopoly power, lax lending policies, and other constraints on productive growth. Hence the expectation of readily available bailouts may foster the very conditions that cause currency crises.

Future Bailouts? The decision to bail out a depreciating currency isn't as simple as it appears. To minimize the ill effects of bailouts, the IMF and other institutions typically require the nation in crisis to pledge more prudent monetary, fiscal, and trade policies. Usually there's a lot of debate about what kinds of adjustments will be made—and how soon. As long as the nation in crisis is confident of an eventual bailout, however, it has a lot of bargaining power to resist policy changes. Only after the IMF finally said no to further bailouts in Greece did the Greek parliament pass austerity measures that reduced its fiscal imbalances.

SUMMARY

- Money serves the same purposes in international trade as it does in the domestic economy—namely, to facilitate specialization and market exchanges. The basic challenge of international finance is to create acceptable standards of value from the various currencies maintained by separate countries.   **LO20-1**
- Exchange rates are the mechanism for translating the value of one national currency into the equivalent value of another. An exchange rate of $1 = 2 euros means that one dollar is worth two euros in foreign exchange markets.   **LO20-2**
- Foreign currencies have value because they can be used to acquire goods and resources from other countries. Accordingly, the supply of and demand for foreign currency reflect the demands for imports and exports, for international investment, and for overseas activities of governments.   **LO20-1**
- The balance of payments summarizes a country's international transactions. Its components are the trade balance, the current account balance, and the capital account balance. The current and capital accounts must offset each other.   **LO20-1**
- The equilibrium exchange rate is subject to any and all shifts of supply and demand for foreign exchange. If relative incomes, prices, or interest rates change, the demand for foreign exchange will be affected. A depreciation is a

change in market exchange rates that makes one country's currency cheaper in terms of another currency. An appreciation is the opposite kind of change.   **LO20-2**
- Changes in exchange rates are often resisted. Producers of export goods don't want their currencies to rise in value (appreciate); importers and tourists dislike it when their currencies fall in value (depreciate).   **LO20-3**
- Under a system of fixed exchange rates, changes in the supply and demand for a specific currency can't be expressed in exchange rate movements. Instead such shifts will be reflected in excess demand for or supply of that currency. Such market imbalances are referred to as balance-of-payments deficits or surpluses.   **LO20-2**
- To maintain fixed exchange rates, monetary authorities must enter the market to buy and sell foreign exchange. To do so, deficit countries must have foreign exchange reserves. In the absence of sufficient reserves, a country can maintain fixed exchange rates only if it's willing to alter basic fiscal, monetary, or trade policies.   **LO20-3**
- Flexible exchange rates eliminate balance-of-payments problems and the crises that accompany them. But complete flexibility can lead to disruptive changes. To avoid this contingency, many countries prefer to adopt managed exchange rates—that is, rates determined by the market but subject to government intervention.   **LO20-3**

Key Terms

exchange rate
equilibrium price
balance of payments
trade deficit
depreciation (currency)
appreciation

foreign exchange markets
gold standard
market shortage
balance-of-payments deficit
balance-of-payments surplus
foreign exchange reserves

gold reserves
flexible exchange rates
managed exchange rates
devaluation

Questions for Discussion

1. Why would a decline in the value of the dollar prompt foreign manufacturers such as BMW to build production plants in the United States?   **LO20-3**
2. How do changes in the value of the U.S. dollar affect foreign enrollments at U.S. colleges?   **LO20-3**
3. How would rapid inflation in Canada affect U.S. tourism travel to Canada? Does it make any difference whether the exchange rate between Canadian and U.S. dollars is fixed or flexible?   **LO20-2**
4. Under what conditions would a country welcome a balance-of-payments deficit? When would it *not* want a deficit?   **LO20-3**
5. In what sense do fixed exchange rates permit a country to "export its inflation"?   **LO20-1**
6. Why did the value of the Ukrainian hryvnia depreciate so much when Russia invaded (p. 444)?   **LO20-2**
7. If a nation's currency depreciates, are the reduced export prices that result "unfair"?   **LO20-3**
8. How would each of these events affect the supply or demand for Japanese yen?   **LO20-1**
   (*a*) Stronger U.S. economic growth.
   (*b*) A decline in Japanese interest rates.
   (*c*) Higher inflation in the United States.
   (*d*) A Japanese tsunami.
9. Who in Mexico is helped or hurt by a strong U.S. dollar? Redo the World View on p. 443 for Mexicans.   **LO20-3**
10. Why does the World View on page 449 say the undervalued yuan is "more bane than boom"?   **LO20-3**

mobile app Visit your mobile app store and download the Schiller: Study Econ app *today*!

LO20-2 1. According to the World View on page 440, which nation had
    (a) The cheapest currency? _____
    (b) The most expensive currency? _____

LO20-2 2. If a euro is worth $1.20, what is the euro price of a dollar? _____

LO20-3 3. How many Ukrainian hryvnia (see p. 444) could you buy with one U.S. dollar
    (a) Before the Russian invasion? _____
    (b) After the Russian invasion? _____

LO20-2 4. If a McDonald's Big Mac sells for $4.00, how much will it cost in the currencies of
    (a) Brazil? _____
    (b) Japan? _____
    (c) Indonesia? _____
    (See World View, p. 440.)

LO20-3 5. If a pound of U.S. pork cost 40 baht in Thailand before the Asian crisis (p. 444), how much did it cost after the devaluation? _____

LO20-2 6. If a PlayStation 3 costs 20,000 yen in Japan, how much will it cost in U.S. dollars if the exchange rate is
    (a) 110 yen = $1? _____
    (b) 1 yen = $0.009? _____
    (c) 100 yen = $1? _____

LO20-2 7. Between 1997 and 2000, by how much did the dollar appreciate (Figure 20.3)? _____%

LO20-1 8. If inflation raises U.S. prices by 2 percent and the U.S. dollar appreciates by 5 percent, by how much does the foreign price of U.S. exports change? _____%

LO20-2 9. According to the World View on page 440, what was the peso price of a euro in August 2014? _____

LO20-3 10. For each of the following possible events, indicate whether the global value of the U.S. dollar will A: rise or B: fall.
    (a) American cars become suddenly more popular abroad. _____
    (b) Inflation in the United States accelerates. _____
    (c) The United States falls into a recession. _____
    (d) Interest rates in the United States drop. _____
    (e) The United States experiences rapid increases in productivity. _____
    (f) Anticipating a return to the gold standard, Americans suddenly rush to buy gold from the two big producers, South Africa and the Soviet Union. _____
    (g) War is declared in the Middle East. _____
    (h) The stock markets in the United States collapse. _____

LO20-3 11. The following schedules summarize the supply and demand for trifflings, the national currency of Tricoli:

Triffling price (U.S. dollars per triffling)	0	$4	$8	$12	$16	$20	$24
Quantity demanded (per year)	40	38	36	34	32	30	28
Quantity supplied (per year)	1	11	21	31	41	51	61

Use these schedules for the following:
(a) Graph the supply and demand curves on the next page.
(b) Determine the equilibrium exchange rate. _____
(c) Determine the size of the excess supply or excess demand that would exist if the Tricolian government fixed the exchange rate at $22 = 1 triffling. _____

(d) Which of the following events would help reduce the payments imbalance? Which would not? (A = helps; B = doesn't help)

(i) Domestic inflation. _____

(ii) Foreign inflation. _____

(iii) Slower domestic growth. _____

(iv) Faster domestic growth. _____

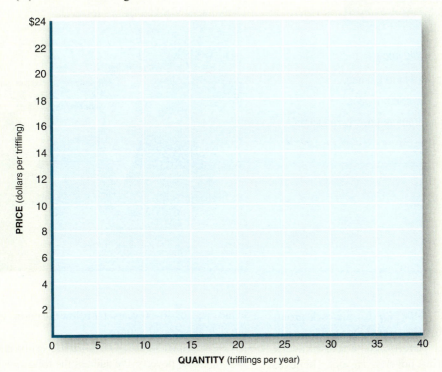

LO20-3 12. As shown in Table 20.1, in 2013 the United States was running a current account deficit. Would the following events increase (I) or decrease (D) the current account deficit?

(a) U.S. companies, the largest investors in Switzerland, see even more promising investment opportunities there. _____

(b) The Netherlands, one of the largest foreign investors in the United States, finds U.S. investment opportunities less attractive. _____

(c) Unemployment rises and recession deepens in the United States. _____

LO20-2 13. The following exchange rates were taken from ExchangeRate.com. On August 15, 2014, by how much did the dollar appreciate or depreciate against the

(a) Argentine peso? _____ %

(b) European euro? _____ %

Currency Rates per 1.00 U.S. Dollar

	August 14	August 15
Argentine peso	8.276652	8.279979
European euro	0.748048	0.747088

Global Poverty

After reading this chapter, you should know

LO21-1 How U.S. and global poverty are defined.

LO21-2 How many people in the world are poor.

LO21-3 What factors impede or promote poverty reduction.

Bono, the lead singer for the rock group U2, has performed concerts around the world to raise awareness of global poverty. He doesn't have a specific agenda for eradicating poverty. He does believe, though, that greater awareness of global poverty will raise assistance levels and spawn more ideas for combating global hunger, disease, and isolation.

The dimensions of global poverty are staggering. According to the World Bank, more than a third of the world's population lacks even the barest of life's necessities. *Billions* of people are persistently malnourished, poorly sheltered, minimally clothed, and at constant risk of debilitating diseases. Life expectancies among the globally poor population still hover in the range of 40–50 years, far below the norm (70–80 years) of the rich, developed nations.

In this chapter we follow Bono's suggestion and take a closer look at global poverty. We address the following issues:

- **What income thresholds define "poverty"?**
- **How many people are poor?**
- **What actions can be taken to reduce global poverty?**

In the process of answering these questions, we get another opportunity to examine what makes economies "tick"—particularly what forces foster faster economic growth for some nations and slower economic growth for others.

AMERICAN POVERTY

Poverty, like beauty, is often in the eye of the beholder. Many Americans feel "poor" if they can't buy a new car, live in a fancy home, or take an exotic vacation. Indeed, the average American asserts that a family needs at least $35,000 a year "just to get by." With that much income, however, few people would go hungry or be forced to live in the streets.

Official Poverty Thresholds

To develop a more objective standard of poverty, the U.S. government assessed how much money a U.S. family needs to purchase a "minimally adequate" diet. Back in 1963 it concluded that $1,000 per year was needed for that purpose alone. Then it asked how much income was needed to purchase other basic necessities like housing, clothes, transportation, and so on. It figured all those *non*food necessities would cost twice as much as the food staples. So it concluded that a budget of $3,000 per year would fund a "minimally adequate" living standard for a U.S. family of four. That standard became the official **U.S. poverty threshold** in 1963.

Inflation Adjustments. Since 1963, prices have risen every year. As a result, the price of the poverty "basket" has risen as well. In 2014, it cost roughly $29,000 to purchase those same basic necessities for a family of four that cost only $3,000 in 1963.

Twenty-nine thousand dollars might sound like a lot of money, especially if you're not paying your own rent or feeding a family. If you break the budget down, however, it doesn't look so generous. Only a third of the budget goes for food. And that portion has to feed four people. So the official U.S. poverty standard provides less than $7 per day for an individual's food. That just about covers a single Big Mac combo at McDonald's. There's no money in the poverty budget for dining out. And the implied rent money is only $800 a month (for the whole family). So the official U.S. poverty standard isn't that generous—certainly not by *American* standards (where the *average* family has an income of nearly $80,000 per year and eats outside their $200,000 home three times a week).

poverty threshold (U.S.): Annual income of less than $29,000 for a family of four (2014, inflation adjusted).

U.S. Poverty Count

The Census Bureau counted more than 40 million Americans as "poor" in 2014 according to the official U.S. thresholds (as adjusted for family size). This was one out of seven U.S. households, for a **poverty rate** of roughly 15 percent. According to the Census Bureau, the official U.S. poverty rate has been in a narrow range of 11–15 percent for the last 40 years.

poverty rate: Percentage of the population counted as poor.

How Poor Is U.S. "Poor"?

Many observers criticize these official U.S. poverty statistics. They say that far fewer Americans meet the government standard of poverty and even fewer are really destitute.

In-Kind Income. A major flaw in the official tally is that the government counts only *cash* income in defining poverty. Since the 1960s, however, the United States has developed an extensive system of **in-kind transfers** that augment cash incomes. Food stamps, for example, can be used just as easily as cash to purchase groceries. Medicaid and Medicare pay doctor and hospital bills, reducing the need for cash income. Government rent subsidies and public housing allow poor families to have more housing than their cash incomes would permit. These in-kind transfers allow "poor" families to enjoy a higher living standard than their cash incomes imply. Adding those transfers to cash incomes would bring the U.S. poverty count down into the 9–11 percent range.

in-kind transfers: Direct transfers of goods and services rather than cash, such as food stamps, Medicaid benefits, and housing subsidies.

Material Possessions. Even those families who remain "poor" after counting in-kind transfers aren't necessarily destitute. More than 40 percent of America's "poor" families own their homes, 70 percent own a car or truck, and 30 percent own at least *two* vehicles. Telephones, color TVs, dishwashers, clothes dryers, air conditioners, and microwave ovens are commonplace in America's poor households.

America's poor families themselves report few acute problems in everyday living. Fewer than 14 percent report missing a rent or mortgage payment, and fewer than 8 percent report a food deficiency. So American poverty isn't synonymous with homelessness, malnutrition, chronic illness, or even social isolation. These problems exist among America's poverty population, but they don't define American poverty.

GLOBAL POVERTY

Poverty in the rest of the world is much different from poverty in America. *American poverty is more about* relative *deprivation than* absolute *deprivation. In the rest of the world, poverty is all about* absolute *deprivation.*

Low Average Incomes

As a starting point for assessing global poverty, consider how *average* incomes in the rest of the world stack up against U.S. levels. By global standards, the United States is unquestionably a very rich nation. As we observed in Chapter 2 (see the World View on page 32), U.S. GDP per capita is five times larger than the world average. More than three-fourths of the world's population lives in what the World Bank calls "low-income" or "lower-middle-income" nations. In those nations the *average* income is under $4,000 a year, less than *one-tenth* of America's per capita GDP. Average incomes are lower yet in Haiti, Nigeria, Ethiopia, and other desperately poor nations. By American standards, virtually all the people in these nations would be poor. By *their* standards, no American would be poor.

World Bank Poverty Thresholds

extreme poverty (world): World Bank income standard of less than $1.25 per day per person (inflation adjusted).

Because national poverty lines are so diverse and culture-bound, the World Bank decided to establish a uniform standard for assessing global poverty. And it set the bar amazingly low. In fact, the World Bank regularly uses two thresholds, namely $1.25 per day for **"extreme"** poverty and a higher $2 per day standard for less "severe" poverty.

The World Bank thresholds are incomprehensibly low by American standards. The $1.25 standard works out to $1,825 per year for a family of four—a mere 6 percent of America's poverty standard. Think about it. How much could you buy for $1.25 a day? A little rice, maybe, and perhaps some milk? Certainly not a Big Mac. Not even a grande coffee at Starbucks. And part of that $1.25 would have to go for rent. Clearly this isn't going to work. Raising the World Bank standard to $2 per day **(severe poverty)** doesn't reach a whole lot further.

severe poverty (world): World Bank income standard of $2 per day per person (inflation adjusted).

The World Bank, of course, wasn't defining "poverty" in the context of American affluence. They were instead trying to define a rock-bottom threshold of absolute poverty—a threshold of physical deprivation that people everywhere would acknowledge as the barest "minimum"—a condition of "unacceptable deprivation."

Global Poverty Counts

On the basis of household surveys in more than 100 nations, *the World Bank classifies more than a* **billion** *people as being in "extreme" poverty (<$1.25/day) and 2.4 billion people as being in "severe" poverty (<$2/day).*

Figure 21.1 shows where concentrations of extreme poverty are the greatest. Concentrations of extreme poverty are alarmingly high in dozens of smaller, less developed nations like Mali, Haiti, and Zambia, where average incomes are also shockingly low. However, the greatest *number* of extremely poor people reside in the world's largest countries. China and India alone contain a third of the world's population and nearly half of the world's extreme poverty.

Table 21.1 reveals that the distribution of severe poverty (<$2/day) is similar. The incidence of this higher poverty threshold is, of course, much greater. Severe poverty afflicts more than 80 percent of the population in dozens of nations and even reaches more than 90 percent of the population in some (e.g., Burundi). By contrast, less than 15 percent of the U.S. population falls below the official *American* poverty threshold, and *virtually no American household has an income below the* **global** *poverty threshold.*

Analysis: Global poverty is defined in terms of absolute deprivation.

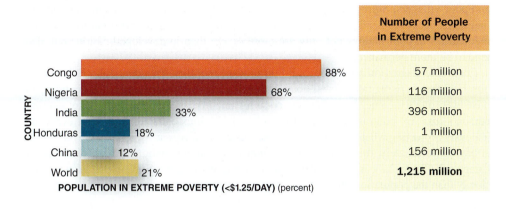

	Number of People in Extreme Poverty
Congo	57 million
Nigeria	116 million
India	396 million
Honduras	1 million
China	156 million
World	**1,215 million**

FIGURE 21.1
Geography of Extreme Poverty

More than a billion people around the world are in "extreme" poverty. In smaller, poor nations, deprivation is commonplace.

Source: *The World Bank, WDR2014 Data Set,* **data.worldbank.org.**

web click

For the latest facts on world poverty, visit **www.globalissues.org** and click on "Poverty Facts and Stats."

Social Indicators

The levels of poverty depicted in Figure 21.1 and Table 21.1 imply levels of physical and social deprivation few Americans can comprehend. Living on less than a dollar or two a day means always being hungry, malnourished, ill-clothed, dirty, and unhealthy. The problems associated with such deprivation begin even before birth. Pregnant women often fail to get enough nutrition or medical attention. In low-income countries only a third of all births are attended by a skilled health practitioner. If something goes awry, both the mother and the baby are at fatal risk. Nearly all of the children in global poverty are in a state of chronic malnutrition. At least 1 out of 10 children in low-income nations will actually die before reaching age 5. In the poorest sectors of the population, infant and child mortality rates are often two to three times higher than that. Children often remain unimmunized to preventable diseases. And AIDS is rampant among both children and adults in the poorest nations. All of these factors contribute to a frighteningly short life expectancy—less than half that in the developed nations.

Fewer than one out of two children from extremely poor households are likely to stay in school past the eighth grade. Women and minority ethnic and religious groups are often wholly excluded from educational opportunities. As a consequence, great stocks of human capital remain undeveloped: in low-income nations only one out of two women and only two out of three men are literate.

web click

For graphic data on wealth and health in specific nations, visit **www.gapminder.org/world.**

Persistent Poverty

Global poverty is not only more desperate than American poverty, but also more permanent. In India a rigid caste system still defines differential opportunities for millions of rich

Country	Living in Severe Poverty (Percent)
Tanzania	95%
Burundi	95
Rwanda	87
Nigeria	83
Bangladesh	80
Ethiopia	78
India	76
China	30
World	**40%**

Source: *The World Bank, WDR2014 Data Set,* **data.worldbank.org.**

TABLE 21.1

Population in Severe Poverty (<$2/day)

More than a third of the world's population has income of less than $2 per person per day. Such poverty is pervasive in low-income nations.

and poor villagers. Studies in Brazil, South Africa, Peru, and Ecuador document barriers that block access to health care, education, and jobs for children of poor families. Hence inequalities in poor nations not only are more severe than in developed nations but also tend to be more permanent.

Economic stagnation also keeps a lid on upward mobility. President John F. Kennedy observed that "a rising tide lifts all boats," referring to the power of a growing economy to raise everyone's income. In a growing economy, one person's income *gain* is not another person's *loss*. By contrast, a stagnant economy intensifies class warfare, with everyone jealously protecting whatever gains they have made. The *haves* strive to keep the *have-nots* at bay. Unfortunately, this is the reality in many low-income nations. As we observed in Chapter 2 (Table 2.1), in some of the poorest nations in the world output grows more slowly than the population, intensifying the competition for resources.

GOALS AND STRATEGIES

Global poverty is so extensive that no policy approach offers a quick solution. Even the World Bank doesn't see an end to global poverty. The United Nations set a much more modest goal back in 2000.

The UN Millennium Goals

The UN established a Millennium Poverty Goal of cutting the incidence of extreme global poverty in half by 2015 (from 30 percent in 1990 to 15 percent in 2015). That goal was pretty much attained. But that didn't significantly decrease the *number* of people in poverty. The world's population keeps growing at upward of 80–100 million people a year. In 2015, there were close to 7.2 billion people on this planet. Fifteen percent of that population would still have left more than a *billion* people in extreme global poverty. In 2014, the World Bank set a new and more ambitious goal of *eliminating* severe poverty by 2030.

Why should we care? After all, America has its own poverty problems and a slew of other domestic concerns. So why should an American—or, for that matter, an affluent Canadian, French, or German citizen—embrace the **UN and World Bank Poverty Goals**? For starters, one might embrace the notion that a poor child in sub-Saharan Africa or Borneo is no less worthy than a poor child elsewhere. And a child's death in Bangladesh is just as tragic as a child's death in Buffalo, New York. In other words, humanitarianism is a starting point for *global* concern for poor people. Then there are pragmatic concerns. Poverty and inequality sow the seeds of social tension both within and across national borders. Poverty in other nations also limits potential markets for international trade. Last but not least, undeveloped human capital anywhere limits human creativity. For all these reasons, the World Bank feels its Poverty Goals should be universally embraced.

UN and World Bank Poverty Goals: Initial UN goal of reducing global rate of extreme poverty to 15 percent by 2015. New World Bank goal of eliminating extreme poverty by 2030.

Policy Strategies

Eliminating severe poverty around the world won't be easy. In principle, ***there are only two general approaches to global poverty reduction:***

- ***Redistribution*** of incomes within and across nations.
- ***Economic growth*** that raises average incomes.

The following sections explore the potential of these strategies for eliminating global poverty.

INCOME REDISTRIBUTION

Many people suggest that the quickest route to eliminating global poverty is simply to *redistribute* incomes and assets, both within and across countries. The potential for redistribution is often exaggerated, however, and its risks underestimated.

Within-Nation Redistribution

Take another look at those nations with the highest concentrations of extreme poverty. Nigeria is near the top of the list in Figure 21.1 and Table 21.1, with an incredible 68 percent of its population in extreme poverty and 83 percent in severe poverty. Yet the other 17 percent of the population lives fairly well, taking more than 45 percent of that nation's income. So what would happen if we somehow forced Nigeria's richest households to share that wealth? Sure, Nigeria's poorest households would be better off. But the gains wouldn't be spectacular: the *average* income in Nigeria is less than $2,800 a year. Haiti, Zambia, and Madagascar also have such low *average* incomes that outright redistribution doesn't hold great hope for income gains by the poor. (See the World View below).

WORLD VIEW

Glaring Inequalities

Inequality tends to diminish as a country develops. In poor nations, the richest tenth of the population typically gets 40 to 50 percent of all income—sometimes even more. In developed countries, the richest tenth gets 20 to 30 percent of total income.

Income Share of Richest Tenth of Population

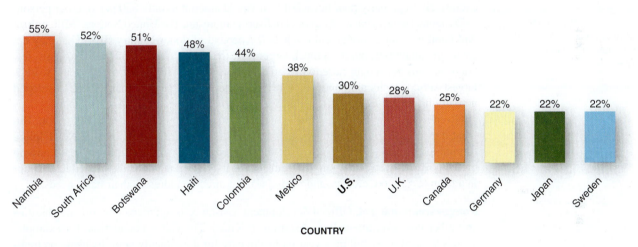

Source: *The World Bank, WDI2014 Data Set,* **data.worldbank.org.**

ANALYSIS: The FOR WHOM question is reflected in the distribution of income. Although the U.S. income distribution is very unequal, inequalities loom even larger in most poor countries.

Economic Risks. Then there's the downside to direct redistribution. How is the income pie going to be resliced? Will the incomes or assets of the rich be confiscated? How will underlying jobs, stocks, land, and businesses be distributed to the poor? How will *total* output (and income) be affected by the redistribution? If savings are confiscated, people will no longer want to save and invest. If large, efficient farms are divided up into small parcels, who will manage them? After Zimbabwe confiscated and fragmented that nation's farms in 2000, its agricultural productivity plummeted and the economy collapsed. Cuba experienced the same kind of economic decline after the government seized and fragmented sugar and tobacco plantations. If the government expropriates factories, mills, farms, or businesses, who will run them? If the *rewards* to saving, investment, entrepreneurship, and management are expropriated, who will undertake these economic activities?

This is not to suggest that *no* redistribution of income or assets is appropriate. More progressive taxes and land reforms can reduce inequalities and poverty. But the potential of direct within-nation redistribution is often exaggerated. Historically, nations have often been forced to reverse land, tax, and property reforms that have slowed economic growth and reduced average incomes.

Expenditure Reallocation. In addition to directly redistributing private income and wealth, governments can also reduce poverty by reallocating direct government expenditures. As we observed in Chapter 1 (Figure 1.3), some poor nations devote a large share of output to the military. If more of those resources were channeled into schools, health services, and infrastructure, the poor would surely benefit. Governments in poor nations also tend to give priority to urban development (where the government and middle class reside), to the neglect of rural development (where the poor reside). Redirecting more resources to rural development and core infrastructure (roads, electricity, and water) would accelerate poverty reduction.

Across-Nation Redistribution

Redistribution *across* national borders could make even bigger dents in global poverty. After all, the United States and other industrialized nations are so rich that they could transfer a lot of income to the globally poor if they chose to.

Foreign Aid. Currently developed nations give poorer nations $120–$140 billion a year in "official development assistance." That's a lot of money. But even if it were distributed exclusively to globally poor households, it would amount to only $50 per year per person.

Developed nations have set a goal of delivering more aid. The United Nations' **Millennium Aid Goal** is to raise foreign aid levels to 0.7 percent of donor-country GDP. That may not sound too ambitious, but it's a much larger flow than at present. As Table 21.2 reveals, few "rich" nations now come close to this goal. Although the United States is by far the world's largest aid donor, its aid equals only 0.19 percent of U.S. total output. For all developed nations, the aid ratio averages around 0.29 percent—just 40 percent of the UN goal.

Given the history of foreign aid, the UN goal is unlikely to be met anytime soon. But what if it were? What if foreign aid *tripled*? Would that cure global poverty? No. Tripling foreign aid would generate only $150 a year for each of the 2.4 billion people now in global poverty. Even that figure is optimistic, as it assumes all aid is distributed to the poor in a form (e.g., food, clothes, and medicine) that directly addresses their basic needs.

Nongovernmental Aid. Official development assistance is augmented by private charities and other nongovernmental organizations (NGOs). The Gates Foundation, for example, spends upward of $1 billion a year on health care for the globally poor, focusing on treatable diseases like malaria, tuberculosis, and HIV infection (see the World View on the next page). Religious organizations operate schools and health clinics in areas of extreme poverty. The International Red Cross brings medical care, shelter, and food in emergencies.

Millennium Aid Goal: United Nations goal of raising foreign aid levels to 0.7 percent of donor-country GDP.

Country	Total Aid ($ billions)	Percentage of Donor Total Income
United States	$ 30	0.19%
United Kingdom	14	0.56
Germany	13	0.38
France	12	0.45
Japan	10	0.17
Canada	6	0.32
Australia	5	0.36
Norway	5	0.93
Italy	3	0.13
24-Nation Total	**$126**	**0.29%**

TABLE 21.2
Foreign Aid

Rich nations give roughly $120–140 billion to poor nations every year. This is a tiny fraction of donor GDP, however.

Source: Organization for Economic Development (2012 data).

WORLD VIEW

The Way We Give

Philanthropy Can Step In Where Market Forces Don't

One day my wife Melinda and I were reading about millions of children dying from diseases in poor countries that were eliminated in this country. . . .

Malaria has been known for a long time. In 1902, in 1907, Nobel Prizes were given for advances in understanding the malaria parasite and how it was transmitted. But here we are a hundred years later and malaria is setting new records, infecting more than 400 million people every year, and killing more than a million people every year. That's a number that's increasing every year, and every day it's more than 2,000 African children. . . .

And this would extend to tuberculosis, yellow fever, AIDS vaccine, acute diarrheal illnesses, respiratory illnesses; you know, millions of children die from these things every year, and yet the advances we have in biology have not been applied because rich countries don't have these diseases. The private sector really isn't involved in developing vaccines and medicines for these diseases because the developing countries can't buy them. . . .

And so if left to themselves, these market forces create a world, which is the situation today, where more than 90 percent of the money spent on health research is spent on those who are the healthiest. An example of that is the billion a year spent on combating baldness. That's great for some people, but perhaps it should get behind malaria in terms of its priority ranking. . . .

So philanthropy can step in where market forces are not there. . . . It can get the people who have the expertise and draw them in. It can use awards, it can use novel arrangements with private companies, it can partner with the universities. . . . And every year the platform of science that we have to do this on gets better.

—Bill Gates

Source: Speech at The Tech Museum, November 15, 2006. © Bill & Melinda Gates Foundation. Used with permission.

ANALYSIS: When markets fail to provide for basic human needs, additional institutions and incentives may be needed.

web click

Go to **www.nptrust.org** and visit the "Charitable Giving Statistics" link for data on philanthropy in the United States.

As with official development assistance, the content of NGO aid can be as important as its level. Relatively low-cost immunizations, for example, can improve health conditions more than an expensive, high-tech health clinic can. Teaching basic literacy to a community of young children can be more effective than equipping a single high school with Internet capabilities. Distributing drought-resistant seeds to farmers can be more effective than donating advanced farm equipment (which may become useless when it needs to be repaired).

ECONOMIC GROWTH

No matter how well designed foreign aid and philanthropy might be, across-nation transfers alone cannot eliminate global poverty. As Bill Gates observed, the entire endowment of the Gates Foundation would meet the health needs of the globally poor for only one year. The World Bank concurs: "Developing nations hold the keys to their prosperity; global action cannot substitute for equitable and efficient domestic policies and institutions."[1] So as important as international assistance is, it will never fully suffice.

Increasing Total Income

The "key" to ending global poverty is, of course, **economic growth.** As we've observed, *redistributing existing incomes doesn't do the job;* total *income has to increase.* This is what economic growth is all about.

economic growth: An increase in output (real GDP); an expansion of production possibilities.

Unique Needs. The generic prescription for economic growth is simple: more resources and better technology. But this growth formula takes on a new meaning in the poorest

[1]World Bank, *World Development Report, 2006* (Washington, DC: World Bank, 2006), p. 206.

nations. Rich nations can focus on research, technology, and the spread of "brain power." Poor nations need the basics—the "bricks and mortar" elements of an economy such as water systems, roads, schools, and legal systems. Bill Gates learned this firsthand in his early philanthropic efforts. In 1996 Microsoft donated a computer for a community center in Soweto, one of the poorest areas in South Africa. When he visited the center in 1997 he discovered the center had no electricity. He quickly realized that growth policy priorities for poor nations are different from those for rich nations.

Growth Potential

The potential of economic growth to reduce poverty in poor nations is impressive. The 40 nations classified as "low-income" by the World Bank have a combined output of only $600 billion. That's about twice the annual sales revenue of Walmart. "Lower-middle-income" nations like China, Brazil, Egypt, and Sri Lanka produce another $5 trillion or so of annual output. Hence every percentage point of economic growth increases total income in these combined nations by nearly $60 billion. According to the World Bank, if these nations could grow their economies by just 3.8 percent a year, that would generate an extra $230 billion of output in the first year and increasing thereafter. That "growth dividend" is twice the amount of foreign aid (Table 21.2).

China has demonstrated just how effective economic growth can be in reducing poverty. Since 1990 China has been the world's fastest-growing economy, with annual GDP growth rates routinely in the 8–10 percent range. This sensational growth has not only raised *average* incomes but has also dramatically reduced the incidence of poverty. In fact, ***the observed success in reducing global poverty from 30 percent in 1990 to 21 percent in 2014 is almost entirely due to the decline in Chinese poverty.*** By contrast, slow economic growth in Africa, Latin America, and South Asia has *increased* their respective poverty populations.

Reducing Population Growth

China not only has enjoyed exceptionally fast GDP growth but also has benefited from relatively slow population growth (now around 0.8 percent a year). This has allowed *aggregate* GDP growth to lift *average* incomes more quickly. In other poor nations, population growth is much faster, making poverty reduction more difficult. As Table 21.3 shows,

TABLE 21.3

Growth Rates in Selected Countries, 2000–2009

The relationship between GDP growth and population growth is very different in rich and poor countries. The populations of rich countries are growing very slowly, and gains in per capita GDP are easily achieved. In the poorest countries, population is still increasing rapidly, making it difficult to raise living standards. Notice how per capita incomes are declining in many poor countries (such as Zimbabwe and Haiti).

	Average Annual Growth Rate (2000–2009) of		
	GDP	Population	Per Capita GDP
High-income countries			
Canada	2.1	1.0	1.1
France	1.5	0.5	1.0
United States	2.0	1.1	0.9
Japan	1.1	0.2	0.9
Low-income countries			
China	10.9	0.8	10.1
India	7.9	1.6	6.3
Ethiopia	7.5	2.8	4.7
Nigeria	6.6	2.4	4.2
Venezuela	4.9	1.7	3.2
Madagascar	3.6	2.9	0.7
Burundi	2.7	2.0	0.7
Haiti	0.7	1.8	−1.1
West Bank/Gaza	−0.9	3.8	−4.7
Zimbabwe	−7.5	0.9	−8.4

Source: *The World Bank, WDR2011 Data Set,* **data.worldbank.org.**

population growth is in the range of 2–3 percent in some of the poorest nations (e.g., Ethiopia, Nigeria, and West Bank/Gaza). *Reducing population growth rates in the poorest nations is one of the critical keys to reducing global poverty.*

Birth control in some form may have to be part of any antipoverty strategy. In the poorest population groups in the poorest nations, contraceptives are virtually nonexistent. Yet within those same nations, contraceptive use is much more common in the richest segments of the population. This suggests that limited access, not cultural norms or religious values, constrains the use of contraceptives. To encourage more birth control, China also used tax incentives and penalties to limit families to one child.

Human Capital Development

Reducing population growth makes poverty reduction easier, but not certain. The next key is to make the existing population more productive—that is, to increase **human capital.**

human capital: The knowledge and skills possessed by the workforce.

Education. In poor nations, the need for human capital development is evident. Only 71 percent of the population in low-income nations completes even elementary school. Even fewer people are *literate*—that is, able to read and write a short, simple statement about everyday life (e.g., "We ate rice for breakfast"). Educational deficiencies are greatest for females, who are often prevented from attending school by cultural, social, or economic concerns (see the accompanying World View). In Chad and Liberia, fewer than one out of six girls completes primary school. Primary school completion rates for girls are in the 25–35 percent range in most of the poor nations of sub-Saharan Africa.

WORLD VIEW

The Female "Inequality Trap"

In many poor nations, women are viewed as such a financial liability that female fetuses are aborted, female infants are killed, and female children are so neglected that they have significantly higher mortality rates. The "burden" females pose results from social norms that restrict the ability of women to earn income, accumulate wealth, or even decide their own marital status. In many of the poorest nations, women

- Have restricted property rights.
- Can't inherit wealth.
- Are prohibited or discouraged from working outside the home.
- Are prohibited or discouraged from going to school.
- Are prevented from voting.
- Are denied the right to divorce.
- Are paid less than men if they do work outside the home.
- Are often expected to bring a financial dowry to the marriage.
- May be beaten if they fail to obey their husbands.

These social practices create an "inequality trap" that keeps returns on female human capital investment low. Without adequate education or training, they can't get productive jobs. Without access to good jobs, they have no incentive to get an education or training. This kind of vicious cycle creates an inequality trap that keeps women and their communities poor.

Source: The World Bank, *World Development Report 2006,* pp. 51–54.

ANALYSIS: Denying women economic rights not only is discriminatory but reduces the amount of human capital available for economic growth.

inequality trap: Institutional barriers that impede human and physical capital investment, particularly by the poorest segments of society.

In Niger and Mali, only one out of five *teenage* girls is literate. This lack of literacy creates an **inequality trap** that restricts the employment opportunities for young women to simple, routine, manual jobs (e.g., carpet weaving and sewing). With so few skills and little education, they are destined to remain poor.

The already low levels of *average* education are compounded by unequal access to schools. Families in extreme poverty typically live in rural areas, with primitive transportation and communication facilities. *Physical* access to school itself is problematic. On top of that, the poorest families often need their children to work, either within the family or in paid employment. In Somalia, only 8 percent of poor young children attend primary schools; in Ethiopia, Yemen, and Mali, about 50 percent attend. These forces often foreclose school attendance for the poorest children.

Health. In poor nations, basic health care is also a critical dimension of human capital development. Immunizations against measles, diphtheria, and tetanus are more the exception than the rule in Somalia, Nigeria, Afghanistan, Congo, the Central African Republic, and many other poor nations. For all low-income nations taken together, the child immunization rate is only 67 percent (versus 96 percent in the United States). Access and education—not money—are the principal barriers to greater immunizations.

Water and sanitation facilities are also in short supply. The World Bank defines "adequate water access" as a protected water source of at least 20 liters per person a day within 1 kilometer of the home dwelling. We're not limited to indoor plumbing with this definition: a public water pipe a half mile from one's home is considered adequate. Yet only three out of four households in low-income nations meet even this minimum threshold of water adequacy (see the World View below). In Afghanistan, Ethiopia, and

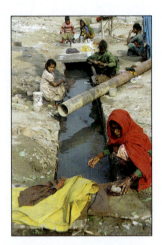

Analysis: Unsafe water is a common problem for the globally poor.

web click

To assess water quality in your area, visit **www.scorecard.org** and click "Clean Water Act."

WORLD VIEW

Dying for a Drink of Clean Water

In the United States and Europe, people take it for granted that when they turn on their taps, clean water will flow out. But for those living in U.S. cities devastated by Hurricane Katrina, as in large parts of the world, obtaining safe water requires a constant struggle.

Water is essential to all aspects of life, yet 99 percent of water on Earth is unsafe or unavailable to drink. About 1.2 billion people lack safe water to consume, and 2.6 billion do not have access to adequate sanitation. There are also stark comparisons: just one flush of a toilet in the West uses more water than most Africans have to perform an entire day's washing, cleaning, cooking, and drinking.

. . . Unsafe water and sanitation are now the single largest cause of illness worldwide, just as they have been a major threat to the health of people affected by Hurricane Katrina. A recent UN report estimated that

- At least 2 million people, most of them children, die annually from waterborne diseases such as diarrhea, cholera, dysentery, typhoid, guinea worm, and hepatitis, as well as such illnesses as malaria and West Nile virus carried by mosquitoes that breed in stagnant water.
- Many of the 10 million child deaths that occurred last year were linked to unsafe water and lack of sanitation. Children can't fight off infections if their bodies are weakened by waterborne diseases.
- Over half of the hospital beds in the developing world are occupied by people suffering from preventable diseases caused by unsafe water and inadequate sanitation.

. . . When poor people are asked what would most improve their lives, water and sanitation are repeatedly one of the highest priorities. We should heed their call.

—Jan Eliasson and Susan Blumenthal

Source: Editorial by Jan Eliasson and Susan Blumenthal printed in *The Washington Post,* Sept. 20, 2005, p. A23. Used with permission.

ANALYSIS: Access to safe water and sanitation is one of the most basic foundations for economic growth. The UN's millennium water goal is to reduce by 2015 half the percentage of people without safe water.

Somalia only one out of four households has even that much water access. Access to sanitation facilities (ranging from pit latrines to flush toilets) is less common still (on average one out of three low-income-nation households). In Ethiopia only 6 percent of the population is so privileged.

When illness strikes, professional health care is hard to find. In the United States, there is one doctor for every 180 people. In Sierra Leone, there is one doctor for every 10,000 people! For low-income nations as a group, there are 2,500 people for every available doctor.

These glaring inadequacies in health conditions breed high rates of illness and death. In the United States, only 8 out of every 1,000 children die before age 5. In Angola, 260 of every 1,000 children die that young. For all low-income nations, the under-5 mortality rate is 13.5 percent (nearly one out of seven). Those children who live are commonly so malnourished (severely underweight and/or short) that they can't develop fully (another inequality trap).

AIDS takes a huge toll as well. Only 0.6 percent of the U.S. adult population has HIV. In Botswana, Lesotho, Swaziland, and Zimbabwe, more than 25 percent of the adult population is HIV-infected. As a result of these problems, life expectancies are inordinately low. In Zambia, only 16 percent of the population lives to age 65. In Botswana, life expectancy at birth is 35 years (versus 78 years in the United States). For low-income nations as a group, life expectancy is a mere 57 years.

Capital Investment

If they are ever going to eradicate poverty and its related social ills, poor nations need sharply increased capital investment in both the public and private sectors. Transportation and communications systems must be expanded and upgraded so markets can function. Capital equipment and upgraded technology must flow into both agricultural and industrial enterprises.

Internal Financing. Acquiring the capital resources needed to boost productivity and accelerate economic growth is not an easy task. Domestically, freeing up scarce resources for capital investment requires cutbacks in domestic consumption. In the 1920s Stalin used near-totalitarian powers to cut domestic consumption in Russia (by limiting output of consumer goods) and raise Russia's **investment rate** to as much as 30 percent of output. This elevated rate of investment accelerated capacity growth, but at a high cost in terms of consumer deprivation.

investment rate: The percentage of total output (GDP) allocated to the production of new plants, equipment, and structures.

Other nations haven't had the power or the desire to make such a sacrifice. China spent two decades trying to raise consumption standards before it gave higher priority to investment. Once it did so, however, economic growth accelerated sharply. Unfortunately, low investment rates continue to plague other poor nations.

Pervasive poverty in poor nations sharply limits the potential for increased savings. Nevertheless, governments can encourage more saving with improved banking facilities, transparent capital markets, and education and saving incentives. And there is mounting evidence that even small dabs of financing can make a big difference. Extending a small loan that enables a poor farmer to buy improved seeds or a plow can have substantial effects on productivity. Financing small equipment or inventory for an entrepreneur can get a new business rolling. Such **microfinance** can be a critical key to escaping poverty (see the World View on the next page).

microfinance: The granting of small ("micro"), unsecured loans to small businesses and entrepreneurs.

Some nations have also used inflation as a tool for shifting resources from consumption to investment. By financing public works projects and private investment with an increased money supply, governments can increase the inflation rate. As prices rise faster than consumer incomes, households are forced to curtail their purchases. This "inflation tax" ultimately backfires, however, when both domestic and foreign market participants lose confidence in the nation's currency. Periodic currency collapses have destabilized many South and Central American economies and governments. Inflation financing also fails to distinguish good investment ideas from bad ones.

WORLD VIEW

Muhammad Yunus: Microloans

Teach a man to fish, and he'll eat for a lifetime. But only if he can afford the fishing rod. More than 30 years ago in Bangladesh, economics Professor Muhammad Yunus recognized that millions of his countrymen were trapped in poverty because they were unable to scrape together the tiny sums they needed to buy productive essentials such as a loom, a plow, an ox, or a rod. So he gave small loans to his poor neighbors, secured by nothing more than their promise to repay.

Microcredit, as it's now known, became a macro success in 2006, reaching two huge milestones. The number of the world's poorest people with outstanding microloans—mostly in amounts of $15 to $150—was projected to reach 100 million. And Yunus, 66, shared the Nobel Peace Prize with the Grameen Bank he founded. The Nobel Committee honored his grassroots strategy as "development from below."

You know an idea's time has come when people start yanking it in directions its originator never imagined. Some, like Citigroup, are making for-profit loans, contrary to Yunus's break-even vision. Others, like Bangladesh's BRAC, are nonprofit but have a more holistic vision than Grameen, offering health care and social services in addition to loans.

Source: "The Best Ideas," *BusinessWeek,* December 18, 2006, pp. 96–106. Used with permission of Bloomberg L.P. Copyright © 2015. All rights reserved.

ANALYSIS: Microloans focus on tiny loans to small businesses and farmers that enable them to increase output and productivity.

External Financing. Given the constraints on internal financing, poor nations have to seek external funding to lift their investment rate. In fact, Columbia University economist Jeffrey Sachs has argued that external financing is not only necessary but, if generous enough, also sufficient for *eliminating* global poverty (see the accompanying World View). As we've observed, however, actual foreign aid flows are far below the "Big Money" threshold that Sachs envisions. Skeptics also question whether more foreign aid would really solve the problem, given the mixed results of previous foreign aid flows. They suggest that more emphasis should be placed on increasing *private* investment flows. Private investment typically entails *direct foreign investment* in new plants, equipment, and technology, or the purchase of ownership stakes in existing enterprises.

WORLD VIEW

Jeffrey Sachs: Big Money, Big Plans

Columbia University economics professor Jeffrey Sachs has seen the ravages of poverty around the world. As director of the UN Millennium Project, he is committed to attaining the UN's goal of reducing global poverty rates by half by 2015. In fact, Professor Sachs thinks we can do even better: the complete *elimination* of extreme poverty by 2025.

How will the world do this? First, rich nations must double their foreign aid flows now, and then double them again in 10 years. Second, poor nations must develop full-scale, comprehensive plans for poverty reduction. This "shock therapy" approach must address all dimensions of the poverty problem simultaneously and quickly, sweeping all inequality traps out of the way.

Critics have called Sachs's vision utopian. They point to the spotty history of foreign aid projects and the failure of many top-down, Big Plan development initiatives. But they still applaud Sachs for mobilizing public opinion and economic resources to fight global poverty.

Source: Jeffrey Sachs, *The End of Poverty,* Penguin, 2006.

ANALYSIS: World poverty can't be eliminated without committing far more resources. Jeffrey Sachs favors an externally financed, comprehensive Big Plan approach.

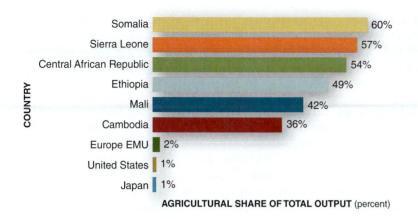

FIGURE 21.2
Agricultural Share of Output

In poor nations, agriculture accounts for a very large share of total output.

Source: *The World Bank, WDR2014 Data Set,* **data.worldbank.org.**

Agricultural Development

When we think about capital investment, we tend to picture new factories, gleaming office buildings, and computerized machinery. In discussing global poverty, however, we have to remind ourselves of how dependent poor nations are on agriculture. As Figure 21.2 illustrates, 60 percent of Somalia's income originates in agriculture. Agricultural shares in the range of 35–55 percent are common in the poorest nations. By contrast, only 1 percent of America's output now comes from farms.

Low Farm Productivity. What keeps poor nations so dependent on agriculture is their incredibly low **productivity.** Subsistence farmers are often forced to plow their own fields by hand with wooden plows. Irrigation systems are primitive and farm machinery is scarce or nonexistent. While high-tech U.S. farms produce nearly $50,000 of output per worker, Ethiopian farms produce a shockingly low $257 of output per worker (see Figure 21.3). Farmers in Sudan produce only 472 kilograms of cereal per hectare, compared with 6,000 kilos per hectare in the United States.

productivity: Output per unit of input—for example, output per labor-hour.

To grow their economies, poor nations have to invest in agricultural development. Farm productivity has to rise beyond subsistence levels so that workers can migrate to other industries and expand production possibilities. One of the catapults to China's growth was an exponential increase in farm productivity that freed up labor for industrial production. (China now produces nearly 5,800 kilos of cereal per hectare.) To achieve greater farm productivity, poor nations need capital investment, technological know-how, and improved infrastructure.

Institutional Reform

Clearly, poor nations need a lot more investment. But more resources alone may not suffice. To attract and keep capital, **a *nation needs an institutional structure that promotes economic growth.***

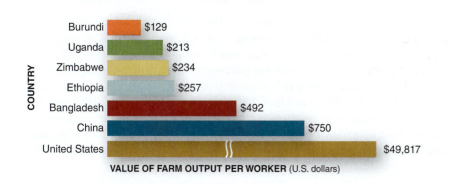

FIGURE 21.3
Low Agricultural Productivity

Farmers in poor nations suffer from low productivity. They are handicapped by low education, inferior technology, primitive infrastructure, and a lack of machinery.

Source: *The World Bank, WDR2014 Data Set,* **data.worldbank.org.**

Analysis: Lack of capital, technology, and markets keeps farm productivity low.

Property Rights. Land, property, and contract rights have to be established before farmers will voluntarily improve their land or invest in agricultural technology. China saw how agricultural productivity jumped when it transformed government-run communal farms into local enterprises and privately managed farms, beginning in 1978. China is using the lessons of that experience to now extend ownership rights to farmers.

Entrepreneurial Incentives. Unleashing the "animal spirits" of the marketplace is also critical. People *do* respond to incentives. If farmers see the potential for profit—and the opportunity to keep that profit—they will pursue productivity gains with more vigor. To encourage that response, governments need to assure the legitimacy of profits and their fair tax treatment. In 1992 the Chinese government acknowledged the role of profits and entrepreneurship in fostering economic advancement. Before then, successful entrepreneurs ran the risk of offending the government with conspicuous consumption that highlighted growing inequalities. The government even punished some entrepreneurs and confiscated their wealth. Once "profits" were legitimized, however, entrepreneurship and foreign investment accelerated, raising China's growth rate significantly.

Cuba stopped short of legitimizing private property and profits. Although Fidel Castro periodically permitted some private enterprises (e.g., family restaurants), he always withdrew that permission when entrepreneurial ventures succeeded. As a consequence, Cuba's economy has stagnated for decades. Venezuela has recently moved further in that direction, expropriating and nationalizing private enterprises (see the accompanying World View), thereby discouraging private investment and entrepreneurship.

WORLD VIEW

Maduro: "Bourgeois Parasites" Thwart Growth

When he won a third presidential term in 2006, Hugo Chávez made his intentions clear. Venezuela, he said, is "heading toward socialism, and no one can prevent it." He embarked on a policy of nationalization, price controls, and a political takeover of Venezuela's central bank. Since then, the Venezuelan economy has stalled; factories, oil fields, and farms have shut down; inflation has soared; and food and energy shortages have become commonplace.

Chávez's successor, Nicolas Maduro, blames the nation's economic woes not on government policy but on the "bourgeois parasites" who have conspired to raise prices, hoard commodities, and strangle the economy. He ordered the nation's largest electronic retailer, Daka, to cut its prices in half and sent the military into its stores to enforce those price cuts. He urged Venezuelans to "leave nothing on the shelves, nothing in the warehouses" and threatened store managers with arrest if they interfered. Critics called the action "government-sanctioned looting." Maduro also levied fines and threatened jail sentences for General Motors executives who he accused of cutting back production and charging "exploitive" prices for new cars. Meanwhile, people have to wait for years to get a new car, while food, water, and energy are now being rationed because of spreading shortages.

Source: News reports, September 2014.

ANALYSIS: By restricting private ownership and market freedom, governments curb the entrepreneurship and investment that may be essential for economic development.

Equity. What disturbed both Castro and Venezuelan President Chávez was the way capitalism intensified income inequalities. Entrepreneurs got rich while the mass of people remained poor. For Castro, the goal of equity was more important than the goal of efficiency. A nation where everyone was equally poor was preferred to a nation of haves and have-nots.

In many of today's poorest nations, policy interests are not so noble. A small elite often holds extraordinary political power and uses that power to protect its privileges. Greed restricts the flow of resources to the poorest segments of the population, leaving them to fend for themselves. These inequalities in power, wealth, and opportunity create inequality traps that restrain human capital development, capital investment, entrepreneurship, and ultimately economic growth.

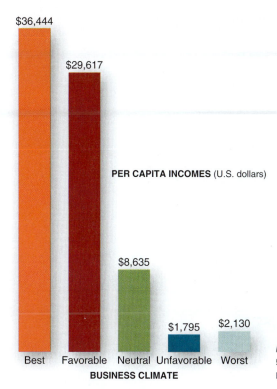

$36,444
$29,617
PER CAPITA INCOMES (U.S. dollars)
$8,635
$1,795 $2,130

Best   Favorable   Neutral   Unfavorable   Worst
BUSINESS CLIMATE

Note: Business climate in 183 nations gauged by 50 measures of government tax, regulatory, and legal policy.

FIGURE 21.4
Business Climates Affect Growth

Nations that offer more secure property rights, less regulation, and lower taxes grow faster and enjoy higher per capita incomes.

Source: Adapted from Heritage Foundation, *2011 Index of Economic Freedom*, p. 7. Washington, DC. Used with permission.

Business Climate. To encourage capital investment and entrepreneurship, governments have to assure a secure and supportive business climate. Investors and business start-ups want to know what the rules of the game are and how they will be enforced. They also want assurances that contracts will be enforced and that debts can be collected. They want their property protected from crime and government corruption. They want minimal interference from government regulation and taxes.

As the annual surveys by the Heritage Foundation document, nations that offer a more receptive business climate grow at a faster pace. Figure 21.4 illustrates this connection. Notice that nations with the most pro-business climate (e.g., Hong Kong, Singapore, Iceland, the United States, and Denmark) enjoy living standards far superior to those in nations with hostile business climates (e.g., North Korea, Cuba, Congo, Sudan, Zimbabwe, and Myanmar). This is no accident; *pro-business climates encourage the capital investment, the entrepreneurship, and the human capital investment that drive economic growth.*

Unfortunately, some of the poorest nations still fail to provide a pro-business environment. Figure 21.5 illustrates how specific dimensions of the business climate differ across fast-growing nations (China) and perpetually poor ones (Cambodia and Kenya). A biannual survey of 26,000 international firms elicits their views of how different government policies restrain their investment decisions. Notice how China offers a more certain policy environment, less corruption, more secure property rights, and less crime. Given these business conditions, where would you invest?

The good news about the business climate is that it doesn't require huge investments to fix. It does require, however, a lot of political capital.

World Trade

When it comes to political capital, poor nations have a complaint of their own. They say that rich nations lock them out of their most important markets—particularly agricultural export markets. Poor nations typically have a **comparative advantage** in the

web click

For another view of national business climates, see the annual Global Competitiveness Report at **www.weforum.org**.

comparative advantage: The ability of a country to produce a specific good at a lower opportunity cost than its trading partners.

FIGURE 21.5

Investment Climate

International investors gravitate toward nations with business-friendly policies. Shown here are the percentages of international firms citing specific elements of the business climate that deter their investment in the named countries.

Source: The World Bank, *World Development Indicators 2006.*
www.worldbank.org.

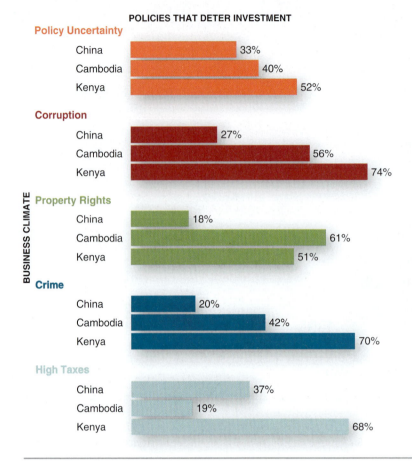

POLICIES THAT DETER INVESTMENT

Policy Uncertainty
- China 33%
- Cambodia 40%
- Kenya 52%

Corruption
- China 27%
- Cambodia 56%
- Kenya 74%

Property Rights
- China 18%
- Cambodia 61%
- Kenya 51%

Crime
- China 20%
- Cambodia 42%
- Kenya 70%

High Taxes
- China 37%
- Cambodia 19%
- Kenya 68%

BUSINESS CLIMATE

---

import quota: A limit on the quantity of a good that may be imported in a given time period.

---

production of agricultural products. Their farm productivity may be low (see Figure 21.3), but their low labor costs keep their farm output competitive. They can't fully exploit that advantage in export markets, however. The United States, the European Union, and Japan heavily subsidize their own farmers. This keeps farm prices low in the rich nations, eliminating the cost advantage of farmers in poor nations. To further protect their own farmers from global competition, rich nations erect trade barriers to stem the inflow of Third World products. The United States, for example, enforces an **import quota** on foreign sugar. This trade barrier has fostered a high-cost, domestic beet sugar industry while denying poor nations the opportunity to sell more sugar and grow their economies faster.

Poor nations need export markets. Export sales generate the hard currency (dollars, euros, and yen) that is needed to purchase capital equipment in global markets. Export sales also allow farmers in poor nations to expand production, exploit economies of scale, and invest in improved technology. Ironically, ***trade barriers in rich nations impede poor nations from pursuing the agricultural development that is a prerequisite for growth.*** The latest round of multilateral trade negotiations dragged on forever because of the resistance of rich nations to opening their agricultural markets. Poor nations plead that "trade, not aid" is their surest path to economic growth.

A 2004 study estimated that 440 million people would be lifted out of severe poverty if all trade barriers were dismantled.[2] China has demonstrated how a vibrant export sector can propel economic growth; South Korea, Taiwan, Malaysia, India, and Costa Rica have also successfully used exports to advance into the higher stages of economic growth. Other poor nations want the same opportunity.

[2]William Cline, *Trade Policy and Global Poverty* (Washington, DC: Institute for International Economics, 2004).

THE ECONOMY TOMORROW

UNLEASHING ENTREPRENEURSHIP

The traditional approach to economic development emphasizes the potential for government policy to reallocate resources and increase capital investment. External financing of capital investment was always at or near the top of the policy agenda (see the World View on page 468). This approach has been criticized for neglecting the power of people and markets.

One of the most influential critics is the Peruvian economist Hernando de Soto. When he returned to his native Peru after years of commercial success in Europe, he was struck by the dichotomy in his country. The "official" economy was mired in bureaucratic red tape and stagnant. Most of the vitality of the Peruvian economy was contained in the unofficial "underground" economy. The underground economy included trade in drugs but was overwhelmingly oriented to meeting the everyday demands of Peruvian consumers and households. The underground economy wasn't hidden from view; it flourished on

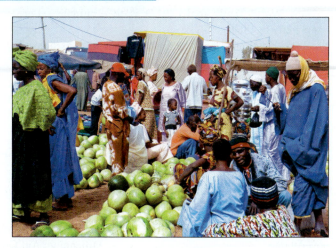

Analysis: Markets exist but struggle in poor nations.

the streets, in outdoor markets, and in transport services. The only thing that forced this thriving economy underground was the failure of the government to recognize it and give it legitimate status. Government restrictions on prices, business activities, finance, and trade—a slew of inequality traps—forced entrepreneurs to operate "underground."

De Soto concluded that countries like Peru could grow more quickly if governments encouraged rather than suppressed these entrepreneurial resources. In his best-selling book *The Other Path,* he urged poor countries to refocus their development policies. This "other path" entails improving the business climate by

- Reducing bureaucratic barriers to free enterprise.
- Spreading private ownership.
- Developing and enforcing legal safeguards for property, income, and wealth.
- Developing infrastructure that facilitates business activity.

Yunus's "microloans" (see the World View on page 468) would also fit comfortably on this other path.

De Soto's book has been translated into several languages and has encouraged market-oriented reforms in Peru, Argentina, Mexico, Russia, Vietnam, and elsewhere. In India the government is drastically reducing both regulation and taxes to pursue De Soto's other path. The basic message of his other path is that poor nations should exploit the one resource that is abundant in even the poorest countries—entrepreneurship.

SUMMARY

- Definitions of "poverty" are culturally based. Poverty in the United States is defined largely in *relative* terms, whereas global poverty is tied more to *absolute* levels of subsistence. **LO21-1**
- About 15 percent of the U.S. population (more than 40 million people) are officially counted as poor. Poor people in America suffer from *relative* deprivation, not *absolute* deprivation, as in global poverty. **LO21-1**

- Global poverty thresholds are about one-tenth of U.S. standards. "Extreme" poverty is defined as less than $1.25 per day per person; "severe" poverty is less than $2 per day (inflation adjusted). **LO21-1**
- One billion people around the world are in extreme poverty; 2.4 billion are in severe poverty. In low-income nations global poverty rates are as high as 70–90 percent. **LO21-2**

- The United Nations' Millennium Poverty Goal was to cut the global poverty rate in half, to 15 percent by 2015. The new World Bank goal (2014) is to eliminate severe poverty by 2030. **LO21-3**
- Redistribution of incomes *within* poor nations doesn't have much potential for reducing poverty, given their low *average* incomes. *Across*-nation redistributions (e.g., foreign aid) can make a small dent, however. **LO21-3**
- Economic growth is the key to global poverty reduction. Many poor nations are held back by undeveloped human capital, primitive infrastructure, and subsistence agriculture. To grow more quickly, they need to meet basic human needs (health and education), increase agricultural productivity, and encourage investment. **LO21-3**
- To move into sustained economic growth, poor nations need capital investment and institutional reforms that promote both equity and entrepreneurship. **LO21-3**
- Poor nations also need "trade, not aid"—that is, access to rich nation markets, particularly in farm products. **LO21-3**

Key Terms

poverty threshold (U.S.)
poverty rate
in-kind transfers
extreme poverty (world)
severe poverty (world)

UN and World Bank Poverty Goals
Millennium Aid Goal
economic growth
human capital
inequality trap

investment rate
microfinance
productivity
comparative advantage
import quota

Questions for Discussion

1. Why should Americans care about extreme poverty in Haiti, Ethiopia, or Bangladesh? **LO21-2**
2. If you had only $14 to spend per day (the U.S. poverty threshold), how would you spend it? What if you had only $2 a day (the World Bank "severe poverty" threshold)? **LO21-1**
3. If a poor nation must choose between building an airport, some schools, or a steel plant, which one should it choose? Why? **LO21-3**
4. How do more children per family either restrain or expand income-earning potential? **LO21-3**
5. Are property rights a prerequisite for economic growth? Explain. **LO21-3**
6. How do unequal rights for women affect economic growth? **LO21-3**
7. How does microfinance alter prospects for economic growth? The distribution of political power? **LO21-3**
8. Can poor nations develop without substantial increases in agricultural productivity? (See Figure 21.2.) How? **LO21-3**
9. Would you invest in Cambodia or Kenya on the basis of the information in Figure 21.5? **LO21-3**
10. Why do economists put so much emphasis on entrepreneurship? How can poor nations encourage it? **LO21-3**
11. How do nations expect nationalization of basic industries to foster economic growth? **LO21-3**
12. If economic growth reduced poverty but widened inequalities, would it still be desirable? **LO21-3**
13. What market failure does Bill Gates (World View, p. 463) cite as the motivation for global philanthropy? **LO21-3**

 mobile app Visit your mobile app store and download the Schiller: Study Econ app *today!*

LO21-1 1. The World Bank's threshold for "extreme" poverty is $1.25 per person per day.
    (a) How much *annual* income does this imply for a family of four? $_____
    (b) What portion of the official U.S. poverty threshold (roughly $29,000 for a family of four) is met by the World Bank's measure?   _____%

LO21-2 2. There are 2.4 billion people in "severe" poverty with less than $2 of income per day.
    (a) What is the maximum *combined* income of this "severely" poor population? $_____
    (b) What percentage of the world's *total* income (roughly $75 trillion) does this represent?   _____%

LO21-2 3. In Namibia,
    (a) What percentage of total output is received by the richest 10 percent of households? (See World View, p. 461.)   _____%
    (b) How much output did this share amount to in 2014, when Namibia's GDP was $14 billion? $_____
    (c) With a total population of 2 million, what was the implied per capita income of
      (i) The richest 10 percent of the population? $_____
      (ii) The remaining 90 percent? $_____

LO21-3 4. (a) How much foreign aid does the United States now provide? (See Table 21.2.) $_____
    (b) How much more is required to satisfy the UN's Millennium Aid Goal if U.S. GDP = $18 trillion? $_____

LO21-3 5. If the industrialized nations were to satisfy the UN's Millennium Aid Goal, how much *more* foreign aid would they give annually? (See Table 21.2.) $_____

LO21-3 6. According to Table 21.3, how many years will it take for per capita GDP to double in
    (a) China?   _____
    (b) Madagascar?   _____
    (c) Zimbabwe?   _____

LO21-3 7. (a) Which low-income nation in Table 21.3 has a GDP growth rate closest to that of the United States?   _____
    (b) How much faster is that nation's population growth?   _____%
    (c) How much lower is its per capita GDP growth?   _____%

LO21-3 8. According to the World View on page 463,
    (a) How much money is spent annually to combat baldness? $_____
    (b) How much medical care would that money buy for each child who dies from malaria each year? $_____

LO21-3 9. Foreign aid to poor nations amounted to $19 per year per person. What percentage did this aid cover of
    (a) The extreme poverty budget?   _____%
    (b) The severe poverty budget?   _____%

PHOTO CREDITS

GLOSSARY

Note: Numbers in parentheses indicate the chapters in which the definitions appear.

absolute advantage: The ability of a country to produce a specific good with fewer resources (per unit of output) than other countries. (19)

AD excess: The amount by which aggregate demand must be reduced to achieve full-employment equilibrium after allowing for price-level changes. (11)

AD shortfall: The amount of additional aggregate demand needed to achieve full employment after allowing for price-level changes. (11)

adjustable-rate mortgage (ARM): A mortgage (home loan) that adjusts the nominal interest rate to changing rates of inflation. (7)

aggregate demand (AD): The total quantity of output (real GDP) demanded at alternative price levels in a given time period, *ceteris paribus.* (8, 9, 10, 11, 13, 15)

aggregate expenditure: The rate of total expenditure desired at alternative levels of income, *ceteris paribus.* (9)

aggregate supply (AS): The total quantity of output (real GDP) producers are willing and able to supply at alternative price levels in a given time period, *ceteris paribus.* (8, 9, 11, 16)

antitrust: Government intervention to alter market structure or prevent abuse of market power. (4)

appreciation: A rise in the price of one currency relative to another. (20)

arithmetic growth: An increase in quantity by a constant amount each year. (17)

asset: Anything having exchange value in the marketplace; wealth. (12)

automatic stabilizer: Federal expenditure or revenue item that automatically responds countercyclically to changes in national income, like unemployment benefits and income taxes. (12, 18)

autonomous consumption: Consumer spending not dependent on current income. (9)

average propensity to consume (APC): Total consumption in a given period divided by total disposable income. (9)

balance of payments: A summary record of a country's international economic transactions in a given period of time. (20)

balance-of-payments deficit: An excess demand for foreign currency at current exchange rates. (20)

balance-of-payments surplus: An excess demand for domestic currency at current exchange rates. (20)

bank reserves: Assets held by a bank to fulfill its deposit obligations. (13)

barter: The direct exchange of one good for another, without the use of money. (13)

base year: The year used for comparative analysis; the basis for indexing price changes. (5, 7, 17)

bond: A certificate acknowledging a debt and the amount of interest to be paid each year until repayment; an IOU. (14)

bracket creep: The movement of taxpayers into higher tax brackets (rates) as nominal incomes grow. (7)

budget deficit: The amount by which government spending exceeds government revenue in a given time period. (12)

budget surplus: An excess of government revenues over government expenditures in a given time period. (12)

business cycle: Alternating periods of economic growth and contraction. (8, 9, 18)

capital: Final goods produced for use in the production of other goods, such as equipment and structures. (1)

capital-intensive: Production processes that use a high ratio of capital to labor inputs. (2)

ceteris paribus: The assumption of nothing else changing. (1, 3)

closed economy: A nation that doesn't engage in international trade. (19)

comparative advantage: The ability of a country to produce a specific good at a lower opportunity cost than its trading partners. (19, 21)

complementary goods: Goods frequently consumed in combination; when the price of good *x* rises, the demand for good *y* falls, *ceteris paribus.* (3)

Consumer Price Index (CPI): A measure (index) of changes in the average price of consumer goods and services. (7)

consumption: Expenditure by consumers on final goods and services. (9)

consumption function: A mathematical relationship indicating the rate of desired consumer spending at various income levels. (9)

consumption possibilities: The alternative combinations of goods and services that a country could consume in a given time period. (19)

core inflation rate: Changes in the CPI, excluding food and energy prices. (7)

cost-of-living adjustment (COLA): Automatic adjustments of nominal income to the rate of inflation. (7)

crowding in: An increase in private sector borrowing (and spending) caused by decreased government borrowing. (12, 17)

crowding out: A reduction in private sector borrowing (and spending) caused by increased government borrowing. (11, 12, 15, 17)

cyclical deficit: That portion of the budget deficit attributable to unemployment or inflation. (12)

cyclical unemployment: Unemployment attributable to a lack of job vacancies—that is, to an inadequate level of aggregate demand. (6, 9, 10)

debt ceiling: An explicit, legislated limit on the amount of outstanding national debt. (12)

debt service: The interest required to be paid each year on outstanding debt. (12)

deficit ceiling: An explicit, legislated limitation on the size of the budget deficit. (12)

deficit spending: The use of borrowed funds to finance government expenditures that exceed tax revenues. (12)

deflation: A decrease in the average level of prices of goods and services. (7)

demand: The willingness and ability to buy specific quantities of a good at alternative prices in a given time period, *ceteris paribus.* (3)

demand curve: A curve describing the quantities of a good a consumer is willing and able to buy at alternative prices in a given time period, *ceteris paribus.* (3)

demand for money: The quantities of money people are willing and able to hold at alternative interest rates, *ceteris paribus.* (15)

demand-pull inflation: An increase in the price level initiated by excessive aggregate demand. (9, 10)

demand schedule: A table showing the quantities of a good a consumer is willing and able to buy at alternative prices in a given time period, *ceteris paribus.* (3)

deposit creation: The creation of transactions deposits by bank lending. (13)

depreciation: The consumption of capital in the production process; the wearing out of plant and equipment. (5)

depreciation (currency): A fall in the price of one currency relative to another. (20)

devaluation: An abrupt depreciation of a currency whose value was fixed or managed by the government. (20)

discount rate: The rate of interest the Federal Reserve charges for lending reserves to private banks. (14)

discounting: Federal Reserve lending of reserves to private banks. (14)

discouraged worker: An individual who isn't actively seeking employment but would look for or accept a job if one were available. (6)

discretionary fiscal spending: Those elements of the federal budget not determined by past legislative or executive commitments. (12)

disposable income (DI): After-tax income of households; personal income less personal taxes. (5, 9, 10, 11)

dissaving: Consumption expenditure in excess of disposable income; a negative saving flow. (9)

dumping: The sale of goods in export markets at prices below domestic prices. (19)

economic growth: An increase in output (real GDP); an expansion of production possibilities. (1, 2, 17, 21)

economics: The study of how best to allocate scarce resources among competing uses. (1)

efficiency: Maximum output of a good from the resources used in production. (1)

embargo: A prohibition on exports or imports. (19)

employment rate: The percentage of the adult population that is employed. (17)

employment targeting: The use of an unemployment-rate threshold (6.5 percent) to signal the need for monetary stimulus. (15)

entrepreneurship: The assembling of resources to produce new or improved products and technologies. (1)

equation of exchange: Money supply (M) times velocity of circulation (V) equals level of aggregate spending ($P \times Q$). (15)

equilibrium (macro): The combination of price level and real output that is compatible with both aggregate demand and aggregate supply. (8, 9, 11)

equilibrium GDP: The value of total output (real GDP) produced at macro equilibrium (AS = AD). (9, 10)

equilibrium price: The price at which the quantity of a good demanded in a given time period equals the quantity supplied. (3, 19, 20)

equilibrium rate of interest: The interest rate at which the quantity of money demanded in a given time period equals the quantity of money supplied. (15)

excess reserves: Bank reserves in excess of required reserves. (13, 14)

exchange rate: The price of one country's currency expressed in terms of another's; the domestic price of a foreign currency. (20)

expenditure equilibrium: The rate of output at which desired spending equals the value of output. (9)

exports: Goods and services sold to foreign buyers. (5, 19)

external debt: U.S. government debt (Treasury bonds) held by foreign households and institutions. (12)

externalities: Costs (or benefits) of a market activity borne by a third party; the difference between the social and private costs (benefits) of a market activity. (2, 4)

extreme poverty (world): World Bank income standard of less than $1.25 per day per person (inflation adjusted). (21)

factor market: Any place where factors of production (e.g., land, labor, capital) are bought and sold. (3)

factors of production: Resource inputs used to produce goods and services, e.g., land, labor, capital, entrepreneurship. (1, 2)

federal funds rate: The interest rate for interbank reserve loans. (14, 15)

fine-tuning: Adjustments in economic policy designed to counteract small changes in economic outcomes; continuous responses to changing economic conditions. (18)

fiscal policy: The use of government taxes and spending to alter macroeconomic outcomes. (8, 11, 12, 18)

fiscal restraint: Tax hikes or spending cuts intended to reduce (shift) aggregate demand. (11, 12, 18)

fiscal stimulus: Tax cuts or spending hikes intended to increase (shift) aggregate demand. (11, 12, 18)

fiscal year (FY): The 12-month period used for accounting purposes; begins October 1 for the federal government. (12)

flexible exchange rates: A system in which exchange rates are permitted to vary with market supply-and-demand conditions; floating exchange rates. (20)

foreign exchange markets: Places where foreign currencies are bought and sold. (20)

foreign exchange reserves: Holdings of foreign currencies by official government agencies, usually the central bank or treasury. (20)

free rider: An individual who reaps direct benefits from someone else's purchase (consumption) of a public good. (4)

frictional unemployment: Brief periods of unemployment experienced by people moving between jobs or into the labor market. (6)

full employment: The lowest rate of unemployment compatible with price stability, variously estimated at between 4 percent and 6 percent unemployment. (6, 10)

full-employment GDP: The value of total market output (real GDP) produced at full employment. (8, 9, 10)

GDP deflator: A price index that refers to all goods and services included in GDP. (7)

GDP per capita: Total GDP divided by total population; average GDP. (5, 17)

geometric growth: An increase in quantity by a constant proportion each year. (17)

gold reserves: Stocks of gold held by a government to purchase foreign exchange. (20)

gold standard: An agreement by countries to fix the price of their currencies in terms of gold; a mechanism for fixing exchange rates. (20)

government failure: Government intervention that fails to improve economic outcomes. (1, 4)

gross business saving: Depreciation allowances and retained earnings. (10)

gross domestic product (GDP): The total market value of all final goods and services produced within a nation's borders in a given time period. (2, 5)

gross investment: Total investment expenditure in a given time period. (5)

growth rate: Percentage change in real output from one period to another. (17)

growth recession: A period during which real GDP grows but at a rate below the long-term trend of 3 percent. (8, 18)

human capital: The knowledge and skills possessed by the workforce. (2, 16, 17, 21)

hyperinflation: Inflation rate in excess of 200 percent, lasting at least one year. (7)

import quota: A limit on the quantity of a good that may be imported in a given time period. (21)

imports: Goods and services purchased from international sources. (5, 19)

income quintile: One-fifth of the population, rank-ordered by income (e.g., top fifth). (2)

income transfers: Payments to individuals for which no current goods or services are exchanged, such as Social Security, welfare, and unemployment benefits. (11, 12)

inequality trap: Institutional barriers that impede human and physical capital investment, particularly by the poorest segments of society. (21)

inflation: An increase in the average level of prices of goods and services. (4, 5, 7, 8)

inflation rate: The annual percentage rate of increase in the average price level. (7)

inflation targeting: The use of an inflation ceiling ("target") to signal the need for monetary-policy adjustments. (15)

inflationary flashpoint: The rate of output at which inflationary pressures intensify; the point on the AS curve where slope increases sharply. (6, 7, 16, 18)

inflationary gap: The amount by which aggregate spending at full employment exceeds full-employment output. (9)

inflationary GDP gap: The amount by which equilibrium GDP exceeds full-employment GDP. (9, 10, 11, 18)

infrastructure: The transportation, communications, education, judicial, and other institutional systems that facilitate market exchanges. (16)

injection: An addition of spending to the circular flow of income. (10)

in-kind transfers: Direct transfers of goods and services rather than cash, such as food stamps, Medicaid benefits, and housing subsidies. (21)

interest rate: The price paid for the use of money. (15)

intermediate goods: Goods or services purchased for use as input in the production of final goods or in services. (5)

internal debt: U.S. government debt (Treasury bonds) held by U.S. households and institutions. (12)

investment: Expenditures on (production of) new plants, equipment, and structures (capital) in a given time period, plus changes in business inventories. (5, 9, 16)

investment rate: The percentage of total output (GDP) allocated to the production of new plants, equipment, and structures. (21)

item weight: The percentage of total expenditure spent on a specific product; used to compute inflation indexes. (7)

labor force: All persons over age 16 who are either working for pay or actively seeking paid employment. (6, 17)

labor force participation rate: The percentage of the working-age population working or seeking employment. (6)

labor productivity: Amount of output produced by a worker in a given period of time; output per hour (or day, etc.). (16)

laissez faire: The doctrine of "leave it alone," of nonintervention by government in the market mechanism. (1, 8)

law of demand: The quantity of a good demanded in a given time period increases as its price falls, *ceteris paribus*. (3, 8)

law of supply: The quantity of a good supplied in a given time period increases as its price increases, *ceteris paribus*. (3)

leakage: Income not spent directly on domestic output but instead diverted from the circular flow—for example, saving, imports, taxes. (10)

liability: An obligation to make future payment; debt. (12)

liquidity trap: The portion of the money demand curve that is horizontal; people are willing to hold unlimited amounts of money at some (low) interest rate. (15)

macroeconomics: The study of aggregate economic behavior, of the economy as a whole. (1, 8)

managed exchange rates: A system in which governments intervene in foreign exchange markets to limit but not eliminate exchange rate fluctuations; "dirty floats." (20)

marginal propensity to consume (MPC): The fraction of each additional (marginal) dollar of disposable income spent on consumption; the change in consumption divided by the change in disposable income. (9, 10, 11)

marginal propensity to save (MPS): The fraction of each additional (marginal) dollar of disposable income not spent on consumption; $1 - MPC$. (9)

marginal tax rate: The tax rate imposed on the last (marginal) dollar of income. (16)

market demand: The total quantities of a good or service people are willing and able to buy at alternative prices in a given time period; the sum of individual demands. (3)

market failure: An imperfection in the market mechanism that prevents optimal outcomes. (1, 4)

market mechanism: The use of market prices and sales to signal desired outputs (or resource allocations). (1, 3, 4)

market power: The ability to alter the market price of a good or service. (4)

market shortage: The amount by which the quantity demanded exceeds the quantity supplied at a given price; excess demand. (3, 20)

market supply: The total quantities of a good that sellers are willing and able to sell at alternative prices in a given time period, *ceteris paribus*. (3)

market surplus: The amount by which the quantity supplied exceeds the quantity demanded at a given price; excess supply. (3)

merit good: A good or service society deems everyone is entitled to some minimal quantity of. (4)

microeconomics: The study of individual behavior in the economy, of the components of the larger economy. (1)

microfinance: The granting of small ("micro"), unsecured loans to small businesses and entrepreneurs. (21)

Millennium Aid Goal: United Nations goal of raising foreign aid levels to 0.7 percent of donor-country GDP. (21)

mixed economy: An economy that uses both market signals and government directives to allocate goods and resources. (1)

monetary policy: The use of money and credit controls to influence macroeconomic outcomes. (8, 14, 15, 18)

money: Anything generally accepted as a medium of exchange. (13)

money illusion: The use of nominal dollars rather than real dollars to gauge changes in one's income or wealth. (7)

money multiplier: The number of deposit (loan) dollars that the banking system can create from $1 of excess reserves; equal to $1 \div$ required reserve ratio. (13, 14)

money supply (M1): Currency held by the public, plus balances in transactions accounts. (13, 14, 15)

money supply (M2): M1 plus balances in most savings accounts and money market funds. (13, 14, 15)

monopoly: A firm that produces the entire market supply of a particular good or service. (2, 4)

multiplier: The multiple by which an initial change in aggregate spending will alter total expenditure after an infinite number of spending cycles; $1/(1 - MPC)$. (10, 11, 18)

national debt: Accumulated debt of the federal government. (12)

national income (NI): Total income earned by current factors of production: GDP less depreciation and indirect business taxes, plus net foreign factor income. (5)

national income accounting: The measurement of aggregate economic activity, particularly national income and its components. (5)

natural monopoly: An industry in which one firm can achieve economies of scale over the entire range of market supply. (4)

natural rate of unemployment: The long-term rate of unemployment determined by structural forces in labor and product markets. (6, 15, 18)

net domestic product (NDP): GDP less depreciation. (5)

net exports: The value of exports minus the value of imports: $(X - M)$. (5)

net investment: Gross investment less depreciation. (5, 17)

nominal GDP: The value of final output produced in a given period, measured in the prices of that period (current prices). (5, 7)

nominal income: The amount of money income received in a given time period, measured in current dollars. (7)

Okun's law: One percent more unemployment is estimated to equal 2 percent less output. (6)

open economy: A nation that engages in international trade. (19)

open market operations: Federal Reserve purchases and sales of government bonds for the purpose of altering bank reserves. (14)

opportunity cost: The most desired goods or services that are forgone in order to obtain something else. (1, 3, 4, 12, 19)

optimal mix of output: The most desirable combination of output attainable with existing resources, technology, and social values. (4, 12)

outsourcing: The relocation of production to foreign countries. (6)

per capita GDP: The dollar value of GDP divided by total population; average GDP. (2)

personal income (PI): Income received by households before payment of personal taxes. (5)

Phillips curve: A historical (inverse) relationship between the rate of unemployment and the rate of inflation; commonly expresses a trade-off between the two. (16)

portfolio decision: The choice of how (where) to hold idle funds. (14, 15)

poverty rate: Percentage of the population counted as poor. (21)

poverty threshold (U.S.): Annual income of less than $29,000 for a family of four (2014, inflation adjusted). (21)

precautionary demand for money: Money held for unexpected market transactions or for emergencies. (15)

price ceiling: An upper limit imposed on the price of a good. (3)

price floor: Lower limit set for the price of a good. (3)

price stability: The absence of significant changes in the average price level; officially defined as a rate of inflation of less than 3 percent. (7)

private good: A good or service whose consumption by one person excludes consumption by others. (4)

product market: Any place where finished goods and services (products) are bought and sold. (3)

production possibilities: The alternative combinations of final goods and services that could be produced in a given period with all available resources and technology. (1, 2, 5, 6, 17, 19)

productivity: Output per unit of input—for example, output per labor-hour. (2, 17, 21)

progressive tax: A tax system in which tax rates rise as incomes rise. (4)

proportional tax: A tax that levies the same rate on every dollar of income. (4)

public choice: Theory of public sector behavior emphasizing rational self-interest of decision makers and voters. (4)

public good: A good or service whose consumption by one person does not exclude consumption by others. (4)

quota: A limit on the quantity of a good that may be imported in a given time period. (19)

rational expectations: Hypothesis that people's spending decisions are based on all available information, including the anticipated effects of government intervention. (18)

real GDP: The value of final output produced in a given period, adjusted for changing prices. (5, 7, 8, 17)

real income: Income in constant dollars; nominal income adjusted for inflation. (7)

real interest rate: The nominal interest rate minus the anticipated inflation rate. (7, 15)

recession: A decline in total output (real GDP) for two or more consecutive quarters. (8)

recessionary gap: The amount by which aggregate spending at full employment falls short of full-employment output. (9)

recessionary GDP gap: The amount by which equilibrium GDP falls short of full-employment GDP. (9, 10, 11, 18)

refinancing: The issuance of new debt in payment of debt issued earlier. (12)

regressive tax: A tax system in which tax rates fall as incomes rise. (4)

relative price: The price of one good in comparison with the price of other goods. (7)

required reserves: The minimum amount of reserves a bank is required to hold; equal to required reserve ratio times transactions deposits. (13, 14)

reserve ratio: The ratio of a bank's reserves to its total transactions deposits. (13)

saving: That part of disposable income not spent on current consumption; disposable income less consumption. (5, 9, 16)

Say's law: Supply creates its own demand. (8)

scarcity: Lack of enough resources to satisfy all desired uses of those resources. (1)

seasonal unemployment: Unemployment due to seasonal changes in employment or labor supply. (6)

severe poverty (world): World Bank income standard of $2 per day per person (inflation adjusted). (21)

shift in demand: A change in the quantity demanded at any (every) price. (3)

speculative demand for money: Money held for speculative purposes, for later financial opportunities. (15)

stagflation: The simultaneous occurrence of substantial unemployment and inflation. (16, 18)

structural deficit: Federal revenues at full employment minus expenditures at full employment under prevailing fiscal policy. (12, 18)

structural unemployment: Unemployment caused by a mismatch between the skills (or location) of job seekers and the requirements (or location) of available jobs. (6, 16)

substitute goods: Goods that substitute for each other; when the price of good x rises, the demand for good y increases, *ceteris paribus*. (3)

supply: The ability and willingness to sell (produce) specific quantities of a good at alternative prices in a given time period, *ceteris paribus*. (3)

supply-side policy: The use of tax incentives, (de)regulation, and other mechanisms to increase the ability and willingness to produce goods and services. (8, 18)

T-accounts: The accounting ledgers used by banks to track assets and liabilities. (13)

tariff: A tax (duty) imposed on imported goods. (19)

tax elasticity of supply: The percentage change in quantity supplied divided by the percentage change in tax rates. (16)

tax rebate: A lump-sum refund of taxes paid. (16)

terms of trade: The rate at which goods are exchanged; the amount of good A given up for good B in trade. (19)

trade deficit: The amount by which the value of imports exceeds the value of exports in a given time period (negative net exports). (19, 20)

trade surplus: The amount by which the value of exports exceeds the value of imports in a given time period (positive net exports). (19)

transactions account: A bank account that permits direct payment to a third party—for example, with a check or debit card. (13)

transactions demand for money: Money held for the purpose of making everyday market purchases. (15)

transfer payments: Payments to individuals for which no current goods or services are exchanged, like Social Security, welfare, and unemployment benefits. (4, 16)

Treasury bonds: Promissory notes (IOUs) issued by the U.S. Treasury. (12)

UN and World Bank Poverty Goals: Initial UN goal of reducing global rate of extreme poverty to 15 percent by 2015. New World Bank goal of eliminating extreme poverty by 2030. (21)

underemployment: People seeking full-time paid employment who work only part-time or are employed at jobs below their capability. (6)

unemployment: The inability of labor force participants to find jobs. (4, 6)

unemployment rate: The proportion of the labor force that is unemployed. (6)

value added: The increase in the market value of a product that takes place at each stage of the production process. (5)

velocity of money (V): The number of times per year, on average, that a dollar is used to purchase final goods and services; $PQ \div M$. (15, 18)

voluntary restraint agreement (VRA): An agreement to reduce the volume of trade in a specific good; a "voluntary" quota. (19)

wealth effect: A change in consumer spending caused by a change in the value of owned assets. (9)

yield: The rate of return on a bond; the annual interest payment divided by the bond's price. (14)

Note: **Bold** page numbers indicate definitions; page numbers followed by *n* indicate material in notes.

NOMINAL GROSS DOMESTIC PRODUCT, Selected Years, 1929–2013 (billions of dollars)

Year	GDP	Personal Consumption Expenditures Total	Gross Private Domestic Investment Total	Net Exports			Government Purchases					Percent Change from Prior Year GDP
				Net	Exports	Imports	Total	Federal			State and Local	
								Total	National Defense	Non-Defense		
1929	103	77	16	0	6	6	8	1	—	—	7	—
1930	90	70	10	0	4	4	9	1	—	—	7	−12.4
1931	75	60	5	0	2	2	9	1	—	—	7	−18.2
1932	58	48	1	0	2	1	8	1	—	—	6	−23.5
1933	55	45	1	0	2	1	7	2	—	—	5	−4.1
1934	65	61	3	0	2	2	9	3	—	—	6	17.1
1935	72	55	6	−2	2	3	10	3	—	—	6	11.1
1936	82	82	8	−2	3	3	12	5	—	—	6	14.4
1937	90	68	12	0	4	4	11	4	—	—	7	9.8
1938	84	64	7	1	3	2	12	5	—	—	7	−6.5
1939	90	67	9	1	3	3	13	5	1	4	8	7.0
1940	100	71	13	1	4	3	13	8	2	3	7	10.2
1941	125	81	18	1	5	4	24	17	13	3	7	25.0
1942	158	88	10	0	4	4	58	52	49	2	7	28.8
1943	192	99	6	−3	4	7	88	61	60	1	7	21.3
1944	211	108	7	−2	4	7	96	89	58	1	7	9.7
1945	213	119	10	−1	6	7	83	75	74	1	7	1.0
1946	211	144	31	7	14	7	29	19	16	2	9	−.8
1947	234	182	36	11	19	8	28	13	10	3	12	10.6
1948	260	173	48	3	13	10	31	16	10	5	14	11.1
1949	259	178	36	5	14	9	38	21	13	7	17	−.4
1980	2,795	1,762	477	−14	278	293	569	245	169	75	324	8.9
1981	3,131	1,944	570	−15	302	317	631	281	197	84	349	12.0
1982	3,259	2,079	516	−20	282	303	684	312	228	84	371	4.1
1983	3,534	2,286	564	−51	277	328	735	344	252	92	391	8.5
1984	3,932	2,498	735	−102	303	405	800	376	283	92	424	11.3
1985	4,213	2,712	736	−114	303	417	878	413	312	101	464	7.1
1986	4,452	2,895	747	−131	320	452	942	438	332	106	503	5.7
1987	4,742	3,105	781	−142	365	507	997	460	351	109	537	6.5
1988	5,108	3,356	821	−106	446	553	1,036	462	355	106	574	7.7
1989	5,489	3,596	872	−80	509	589	1,100	482	363	119	617	7.5
1990	5,803	3,839	846	−78	552	630	1,180	508	374	134	671	5.8
1991	5,995	3,986	803	−27	596	624	1,234	527	383	144	706	3.3
1992	6,337	4,235	848	−33	635	668	1,271	533	376	157	737	5.7
1993	6,657	4,477	932	−65	655	720	1,291	525	362	162	766	5.0
1994	7,072	4,743	1,033	−93	720	814	1,325	519	353	165	806	6.2
1995	7,397	4,975	1,112	−91	812	903	1,369	519	348	170	850	4.6
1996	7,816	5,256	1,209	−96	868	964	1,416	527	354	172	888	5.7
1997	8,304	5,547	1,317	−101	955	1,056	1,468	530	349	181	937	6.2
1998	8,747	5,879	1,438	−159	955	1,115	1,518	530	345	184	987	5.3
1999	9,268	6,282	1,558	−260	991	1,251	1,620	555	360	195	1,065	6.0
2000	9,817	6,739	1,679	−379	1,096	1,475	1,721	578	370	208	1,142	6.5
2001	10,128	7,055	1,646	−367	1,032	1,399	1,825	612	392	220	1,212	3.3
2002	10,469	7,350	1,570	−424	1,005	1,430	1,961	679	437	242	1,281	3.3
2003	10,960	7,703	1,649	−499	1,040	1,540	2,092	756	497	259	1,336	4.9
2004	11,685	8,196	1,889	−615	1,152	1,798	2,217	826	551	275	1,391	6.6
2005	12,422	8,694	2,086	−714	1,312	2,025	2,355	876	588	287	1,480	6.7
2006	13,178	9,207	2,220	−757	1,481	2,238	2,508	932	624	308	1,576	5.8
2007	13,808	9,710	2,130	−708	1,662	2,370	2,675	979	662	317	1,696	4.5
2008	14,291	10,035	2,087	−710	1,849	2,557	2,878	1,080	738	342	1,798	1.7
2009	13,939	9,866	1,547	−392	1,583	518	2,918	1,143	775	368	1,775	−2.0
2010	14,527	10,246	1,795	−517	1,840	562	3,000	1,223	819	404	1,780	3.8
2011	15,518	10,689	2,240	−580	2,106	2,686	3,169	1,304	837	467	1,865	3.7
2012	16,163	11,083	2,479	−568	2,194	2,763	3,169	1,291	818	473	1,878	4.2
2013	16,768	11,484	2,648	−508	2,262	2,770	3,143	1,232	770	462	1,912	3.7

Source: U.S. Department of Commerce.

REAL GROSS DOMESTIC PRODUCT IN CHAIN-WEIGHTED DOLLARS, Selected Decades, 1929–2014 (2009 = 100)

Year	GDP	Personal Consumption Expenditures Total	Gross Private Domestic Investment Total	Exports	Imports	Government Purchases Total	Percent Change from Prior Year GDP
1929	1,057	781	124	41	53	166	—
1930	967	739	84	34	46	183	−8.5
1931	905	716	55	29	40	190	−6.4
1932	788	652	20	22	33	184	−12.9
1933	778	638	27	22	35	178	−1.3
1934	862	683	45	24	35	200	10.8
1935	939	725	79	26	46	206	8.9
1936	1,061	798	99	27	46	239	12.9
1937	1,115	828	122	34	51	229	5.1
1938	1,078	815	84	34	40	247	−3.3
1939	1,164	860	106	36	42	268	8.0
1940	1,266	905	144	40	43	278	8.8
1941	1,490	969	176	41	53	467	17.7
1942	1,772	946	98	27	48	1,054	18.9
1943	2,074	972	61	23	61	1,626	17.0
1944	2,239	1,000	73	25	63	1,826	8.0
1945	2,218	1,061	94	35	67	1,604	−1.0
1946	1,961	1,194	225	75	56	567	−11.6
1947	1,939	1,216	217	85	53	483	−1.1
1948	2,020	1,244	273	67	62	511	4.1
1949	2,009	1,279	211	67	60	566	−0.5
1980	6,450	3,992	881	376	370	1,613	−.2
1981	6,618	4,051	759	381	379	1,628	2.6
1982	6,491	4,108	834	352	375	1,658	−1.9
1983	6,792	4,343	912	343	422	1,723	4.6
1984	7,285	4,572	1,160	370	524	1,783	7.3
1985	7,594	4,812	1,160	383	558	1,904	4.2
1986	7,861	5,014	1,161	412	606	2,008	3.5
1987	8,133	5,184	1,194	457	642	2,067	3.5
1988	8,425	5,401	1,224	531	667	2,095	4.2
1989	8,786	5,558	1,273	593	697	2,155	3.7
1990	8,755	5,673	1,241	645	722	2,224	1.9
1991	8,948	5,686	1,159	688	720	2,251	−.1
1992	9,267	5,897	1,244	735	771	2,262	3.6
1993	9,521	6,101	1,343	759	838	2,242	2.7
1994	9,905	6,338	1,502	827	938	2,246	4.0
1995	10,175	6,528	1,551	912	1,013	2,258	2.7
1996	10,561	6,756	1,687	986	1,101	2,279	3.8
1997	11,035	7,010	1,879	1,104	1,249	2,322	4.5
1998	11,526	7,385	2,058	1,129	1,395	2,371	4.5
1999	12,066	7,776	2,231	1,159	1,536	2,452	4.7
2000	12,560	8,171	2,376	1,258	1,736	2,498	4.1
2001	12,682	8,383	2,231	1,185	1,687	2,592	1.0
2002	12,909	8,599	2,218	1,165	1,749	2,705	1.8
2003	13,271	8,868	2,309	1,185	1,827	2,764	2.8
2004	13,774	9,208	2,511	1,300	2,035	2,808	3.8
2005	14,234	9,532	2,673	1,382	2,164	2,826	3.3
2006	14,614	9,822	2,730	1,507	2,301	2,869	2.7
2007	14,874	10,042	2,644	1,646	2,359	2,914	1.8
2008	14,830	10,007	2,396	1,741	2,299	2,990	−0.3
2009	14,419	9,847	1,898	1,588	1,983	3,089	−2.8
2010	14,784	10,036	2,120	1,777	2,235	3,091	2.5
2011	15,021	10,264	2,230	1,898	2,358	2,997	1.6
2012	15,369	10,450	2,436	1,960	2,413	2,954	2.3
2013	15,710	10,700	2,556	2,020	2,440	2,895	2.2

Source: U.S. Department of Commerce.

Note: Subtotals within Government Purchases based on 1992 prices for years 1929–1989

CONSUMER PRICE INDEX, 1925–2014 (1982–84=100)

Year	Index (all items)	Percent Change
1925	17.5	3.5
1926	17.7	−1.1
1927	17.4	−2.3
1928	17.1	−1.2
1929	17.1	0.6
1930	16.7	−6.4
1931	15.2	−9.3
1932	13.7	−10.3
1933	13.0	0.8
1934	13.4	1.5
1935	13.7	3.0
1936	13.9	1.4
1937	14.4	2.9
1938	14.1	−2.8
1939	13.9	0.0
1940	14.0	0.7
1941	14.7	9.9
1942	16.3	9.0
1943	17.3	3.0
1944	17.6	2.3
1945	18.0	2.2
1946	19.5	18.1
1947	22.3	8.8
1948	24.1	3.0
1949	23.8	−2.1
1950	24.1	5.9
1951	26.0	6.0
1952	26.5	0.8
1953	26.7	0.7
1954	26.9	−0.7
1955	26.8	0.4
1956	27.2	3.0
1957	28.1	2.9
1958	28.9	1.8
1959	29.1	1.7
1960	29.6	1.4
1961	29.9	0.7
1962	30.2	1.3
1963	30.6	1.6
1964	31.0	1.0
1965	31.5	1.9
1966	32.4	3.5
1967	33.4	3.0
1968	34.8	4.7
1969	36.7	6.2
1970	38.8	5.6
1971	40.5	3.3
1972	41.8	3.4
1973	44.4	8.7
1974	49.3	12.3
1975	53.8	6.9
1976	56.9	4.9
1977	60.6	6.7
1978	65.2	9.0
1979	72.6	13.3
1980	82.4	12.5
1981	90.9	8.9
1982	96.5	3.8
1983	99.6	3.8
1984	103.9	3.9
1985	107.6	3.8
1986	109.6	1.1
1987	113.6	4.4
1988	118.3	4.6
1989	124.0	4.6
1990	130.7	6.1
1991	136.2	3.1
1992	140.3	2.9
1993	144.5	2.7
1994	148.2	2.7
1995	152.4	2.5
1996	156.9	3.3
1997	160.5	1.7
1998	163.0	1.6
1999	166.6	2.7
2000	172.2	3.4
2001	177.1	2.8

(continued)

Year	Index (all items)	Percent Change
2002	179.7	1.6
2003	184.0	2.6
2004	188.9	2.7
2005	195.3	3.4
2006	201.6	3.2
2007	207.3	2.8
2008	215.3	3.8
2009	214.5	−0.4
2010	218.1	1.6
2011	224.9	3.2
2012	229.6	2.1
2013	233.0	1.5

Note: Data beginning 1978 are for all urban consumers: earlier data are for urban wage earners and clerical workers.

Source: U.S. Department of Labor. Bureau of Statistics.

CHAIN-WEIGHTED PRICE DEFLATORS FOR GROSS DOMESTIC PRODUCT, 1970–2014 (2009=100)

Year	Index (all items)	Percent Change
1970	22.8	5.3
1971	24.0	5.0
1972	25.0	4.3
1973	26.4	5.5
1974	28.8	9.0
1975	31.4	9.5
1976	33.2	5.7
1977	35.2	6.4
1978	37.7	7.0
1979	40.8	8.3
1980	44.5	9.1
1981	48.7	9.4
1982	51.6	6.1
1983	53.7	3.9
1984	55.6	3.8
1985	57.3	3.0
1986	58.5	2.2
1987	59.9	2.8
1988	62.0	3.4
1989	64.4	3.8
1990	66.8	3.9
1991	69.0	3.5
1992	70.6	2.4
1993	72.3	2.2
1994	73.9	2.1
1995	75.4	2.1
1996	76.8	1.9
1997	78.1	1.8
1998	78.9	1.1
1999	80.1	1.5
2000	81.9	2.2
2001	83.8	2.3
2002	85.0	1.6
2003	86.7	2.2
2004	89.1	2.8
2005	92.0	3.3
2006	94.8	3.3
2007	97.3	2.9
2008	99.2	2.2
2009	100.0	0.9
2010	101.2	1.0
2011	103.3	2.1
2012	105.2	1.8
2013	106.7	1.4

Source: U.S. Department of Commerce, Bureau of Economic Analysis.

INTEREST RATES, 1929–2014 (percent per annum)

Year	Prime Rate Charged by Banks	Discount Rate, Federal Reserve Bank of New York
1929	5.50–6.00	5.16
1933	1.50–4.00	2.56
1939	1.50	1.00
1940	1.50	1.00
1941	1.50	1.00
1942	1.50	1.00
1943	1.50	1.00
1944	1.50	1.00
1945	1.50	1.00
1946	1.50	1.00
1947	1.50–1.75	1.00
1948	1.75–2.00	1.34
1949	2.00	1.50
1950	2.07	1.59
1951	2.56	1.75
1952	3.00	1.75
1953	3.17	1.99
1954	3.05	1.60
1955	3.16	1.89
1956	3.77	2.77
1957	4.20	3.12
1958	3.83	2.15
1959	4.48	3.36
1960	4.82	3.53
1961	4.50	3.00
1962	4.50	3.00
1963	4.50	3.23
1964	4.50	3.55
1965	4.54	4.04
1966	5.63	4.50
1967	5.61	4.19
1968	6.30	5.16
1969	7.96	5.87
1970	7.91	5.95
1971	5.72	4.88
1972	5.25	4.50
1973	8.03	6.44
1974	10.81	7.83
1975	7.86	6.25
1976	6.84	5.50
1977	6.83	5.46
1978	9.06	7.46
1979	12.67	10.28
1980	15.27	11.77
1981	18.87	13.42
1982	14.86	11.02
1983	10.79	8.50
1984	12.04	8.80
1985	9.93	7.69
1986	8.83	6.33
1987	8.21	5.66
1988	9.32	6.20
1989	10.87	6.93
1990	10.01	6.98
1991	8.46	5.45
1992	6.25	3.25
1993	6.00	3.00
1994	7.15	3.60
1995	8.83	5.21
1996	8.27	5.02
1997	8.44	5.00
1998	8.35	4.92
1999	8.00	4.62
2000	9.23	5.73
2001	6.91	3.40
2002	4.67	1.17
2003	4.12	1.15
2004	4.34	2.34
2005	6.19	4.19
2006	7.96	5.96
2007	8.05	5.86
2008	5.09	2.39
2009	3.25	0.50
2010	3.25	0.75
2011	3.25	0.75
2012	3.25	0.75
2013	3.25	0.75
2014	3.25	0.75

Source: Board of Governors of the Federal Reserve System.

POPULATION AND THE LABOR FORCE, 1929–2010

Year	Total Population	Civilian Noninstitutional Population	Armed Forces	Civilian Labor Force	Civilian Unemployment	Civilian		
						Unemployment Rate	Labor-Force Participation Rate	Employment Population Ratio
	Thousands of Persons 14 Years of Age and Over					Percent		
1929	121,767	—	—	49,180	1,550	3.2	—	—
1933	125,579	—	—	51,590	12,830	24.9	—	—
1939	130,880	—	—	55,230	9,480	17.2	—	—
1940	132,122	99,840	—	55,640	8,120	14.6	55.7	47.6
1941	133,402	99,900	—	55,910	5,560	9.9	56.0	50.4
1942	134,860	98,640	—	56,410	2,660	4.7	57.2	54.5
1943	136,739	94,640	—	55,540	1,070	1.9	58.7	57.6
1944	138,397	93,220	—	54,630	670	1.2	58.6	57.9
1945	139,928	94,090	—	53,860	1,040	1.9	57.2	56.1
1946	141,389	103,070	—	57,520	2,270	3.9	55.8	53.6
1947	144,126	106,018	—	60,168	2,356	3.9	56.8	54.5
	Thousands of Persons 16 Years of Age and Over							
1947	144,083	101,827	—	59,350	2,311	3.9	58.3	56.0
1948	146,631	103,068	—	60,621	2,276	3.8	58.8	56.6
1949	149,188	103,994	—	61,286	3,637	5.9	58.9	55.4
1950	152,271	104,995	1,169	62,208	3,288	5.3	59.2	56.1
1951	154,878	104,621	2,143	62,017	2,055	3.3	59.2	57.3
1952	157,553	105,231	2,386	62,138	1,883	3.0	59.0	57.3
1953	160,184	107,056	2,231	63,015	1,834	2.9	58.9	57.1
1954	163,026	108,321	2,142	63,643	3,532	5.5	58.8	55.5
1955	165,931	109,683	2,064	65,023	2,352	4.4	59.3	56.7
1956	168,903	110,954	1,965	66,552	2,750	4.1	60.0	57.5
1957	171,984	112,265	1,948	66,929	2,859	4.3	59.6	57.1
1958	174,882	113,727	1,847	67,639	4,602	6.8	59.5	55.4
1959	177,830	115,329	1,788	68,369	3,740	5.5	59.3	56.0
1960	180,671	117,245	1,861	69,628	3,852	5.5	59.4	56.1
1961	183,691	118,771	1,900	70,459	4,714	6.7	59.3	55.4
1962	186,538	120,153	2,061	70,614	3,911	5.5	58.8	55.5
1963	189,242	122,416	2,006	71,833	4,070	5.7	58.7	55.4
1964	191,889	124,485	2,018	73,091	3,786	5.2	58.7	55.7
1965	194,303	126,513	1,946	74,455	3,366	4.5	58.9	56.2
1966	196,560	128,058	2,122	75,770	2,875	3.8	59.2	56.9
1967	198,712	129,874	2,218	77,347	2,975	3.8	59.6	57.3
1968	200,706	132,028	2,253	78,737	2,817	3.6	59.6	57.5
1969	202,677	134,335	2,238	80,734	2,832	3.5	60.1	58.0
1970	205,052	137,085	2,118	82,771	4,093	4.9	60.4	57.4
1971	207,661	140,216	1,973	84,382	5,016	5.9	60.2	56.6
1972	209,896	144,126	1,813	87,034	4,882	5.6	60.4	57.0
1973	211,909	147,096	1,774	89,429	4,365	4.9	60.8	57.8
1974	213,854	150,120	1,721	91,949	5,156	5.6	61.3	57.8
1975	215,973	153,153	1,678	93,775	7,929	8.5	61.2	56.1
1976	218,035	156,150	1,668	96,158	7,406	7.7	61.6	56.8
1977	220,239	159,033	1,656	99,009	6,991	7.1	62.3	57.9
1978	222,585	161,910	1,631	102,251	6,202	6.1	63.2	59.3
1979	225,055	164,863	1,597	104,962	6,137	5.8	63.7	59.9
1980	227,726	167,745	1,604	106,940	7,637	7.1	63.8	59.2
1981	229,966	170,130	1,645	108,670	8,273	7.6	63.9	59.0
1982	232,188	172,271	1,668	110,204	10,678	9.7	64.0	57.8
1983	234,307	174,215	1,676	111,550	10,717	9.6	64.0	57.9
1984	236,348	176,383	1,697	113,544	8,539	7.5	64.4	59.5
1985	238,466	178,206	1,706	115,461	8,312	7.2	64.8	60.1
1986	240,651	180,587	1,706	117,834	8,237	7.0	65.3	60.7
1987	242,804	182,753	1,737	119,865	7,425	6.2	65.6	61.5
1988	245,021	184,613	1,709	121,669	6,701	5.5	65.9	62.3
1989	247,342	186,393	1,668	123,869	6,528	5.3	66.5	63.0
1990	249,924	188,049	1,637	124,787	6,874	5.5	66.4	62.7
1991	252,688	189,765	1,564	125,303	8,426	6.7	66.0	61.6
1992	255,414	191,576	1,566	126,982	9,384	7.4	66.3	61.4
1993	258,137	193,550	1,705	128,040	8,734	6.8	66.2	61.6
1994	260,660	196,814	1,610	131,056	7,996	6.1	66.6	62.5
1995	263,034	198,584	1,533	132,304	7,404	5.6	66.6	62.9
1996	265,453	200,591	1,479	133,943	7,236	5.4	66.8	63.2
1997	267,901	203,133	1,437	136,297	6,739	4.9	67.1	63.8
1998	270,290	205,220	1,401	137,673	6,210	4.5	67.1	64.1
1999	272,945	207,753	1,411	139,368	5,880	4.2	67.1	64.3
2000	282,434	212,573	1,423	142,583	5,692	4.0	67.1	64.4
2001	285,545	215,092	1,387	143,734	6,801	4.7	66.8	63.7
2002	288,600	217,570	1,416	144,863	8,378	5.8	66.6	62.7
2003	291,049	221,168	1,390	146,510	8,774	6.0	66.2	62.3
2004	293,708	223,357	1,411,287	149,401	8,149	5.5	66.0	62.3
2005	296,639	226,082	1,387,014	149,320	7,591	5.1	66.0	62.7
2006	299,801	228,815	1,414,489	151,428	7,001	4.6	66.2	63.1
2007	302,045	231,867	1,380,401	153,124	7,078	4.6	66.0	63.0
2008	304,906	233,788	1,454,515	154,287	8,924	5.8	66.0	62.2
2009	307,007	235,801	1,443,000	154,142	14,265	9.3	65.4	59.3
2010	309,438	237,830	1,430,895	153,889	14,825	9.6	64.7	58.5

Source: U.S. Department of Labor, Bureau of Labor Statistics.